A HISTORY OF MODERN PSYCHOLOGY

FOURTH EDITION

DUANE P. SCHULTZ

University of South Florida

SYDNEY ELLEN SCHULTZ

Harcourt Brace Jovanovich, Publishers

San Diego   New York   Chicago   Austin

London   Sydney   Tokyo   Toronto

The application of the experimental method to the problem of mind is the great outstanding event in the history of the study of the mind, an event to which no other is comparable.

E. G. BORING

ISBN: 0-15-537465-6

Library of Congress Catalog Card Number: 86-80749

Printed in the United States of America

Photo and Illustration Credits

Figure 2-1, p. 20, The National Museum of American History, Smithsonian Institution; p. 71, Bettmann Archive; p. 144, the Ferdinand Hamburger, Jr. Archives, The Johns Hopkins University; p. 146, Frontispiece, Poffenberger, A.T. (Ed.), (1947). *James McKeen Cattell, Man of Science*. Vol. I, *Psychological Research*. Lancaster, PA: The Science Press; p. 181, Office of Public Information, Columbia University; Figure 9-1, p. 183, After Thorndike, 1898, as reproduced in J.C. Burnham, 1972, "Thorndike's puzzle boxes," *Journal of the History of the Behavioral Sciences*, Brandon, VT: Clinical Psychology Publishing Co.; Figure 9-2, p. 189, Yerkes, R.M., and Margulis, S. (1909) The method of Pavlov in animal psychology. *Psychological Bulletin*, 6: 257–73; p. 212, the Ferdinand Hamburger, Jr. Archives, The Johns Hopkins University; p. 215, Reproduced by Permission, University Archivist, The Bancroft Library, University of California; p. 263, Bettmann Archive; p. 266, Swarthmore College; p. 276, courtesy Yerkes Photo Lab, Emory University; p. 307, © Mary Evans/ Sigmund Freud Copyrights; p. 355, Library of Congress; p. 358, Culver Pictures.

Photos on the following pages are courtesy of the Archives of the History of American Psychology: pp. 45, 78, 80, 133, 158, 160, 177, 196, 220, 230, 235, 237, 265, 281, 304, 324, 333, 344, 361, 367. Photos courtesy of the National Library of Medicine: pp. 23, 30, 35, 47, 50, 60, 76, 87, 111, 116, 129, 142, 185, 245, 291, 297, 326, 339.

Preface

This new edition retains the same overall format, scope, and focus as the previous editions. Three premises continue to underlie and characterize its approach. First, our discussion of the history of psychology concentrates on the last century of development in the field. It does not attempt to cover earlier philosophical thought, except where such thought relates directly to the establishment of psychology as a separate discipline, as is the case with the British empiricists. The book is a history of modern psychology, not of psychology and all the philosophical work that preceded it.

The second premise is defined by one of the most striking and consistent characteristics of the century-old history of modern psychology: the continuous development and decline of different systematic positions or schools of thought. A definite continuity of development can be seen from each of these schools of thought to the one that subsequently replaced it. This developmental pattern is, we believe, the most useful framework within which to understand the history of psychology.

Our discussion demonstrates how each system grew out of or revolted against the existing order, and how each, in turn, inspired a new point of view that opposed and eventually replaced, or at least supplemented, the older system. Outstanding figures in the history of psychology are discussed within the context of the systematic position they helped to formulate, advance, or destroy.

Each systematic position is discussed in terms of three stages of development: (1) historical antecedents or precursors, (2) formal founding and development, and (3) later influence on contemporary psychology. This approach demonstrates the continuity of development from the old to the new—that is, how psychology as we know it today evolved from these earlier positions. The discussion of each school concludes with criticisms and contributions of the position, so that students can see the weaknesses of each system as well as its importance in psychology's development.

The third premise is concerned with the effect of the *Zeitgeist* on each school of thought. The development and decline of each systematic position are discussed in terms of the general intellectual and social climate of the era or region in which it occurred. Using this approach, students should be able to understand that changes in psychological thinking were influenced and augmented by broader changes in our attitudes toward ourselves and the world around us.

Having the opportunity to revise the book has been a stimulating, enjoyable, and rewarding task. Aside from the chance to correct errors and rephrase difficult concepts, a revision allows the time to incorporate the results of new scholarly work in the field and to reflect feedback from the instructors and students who have used the earlier editions. Changes range from the insertion of a clarifying word to the addition of new sections and the rewriting of chapters.

Major changes for the Fourth Edition include a discussion in Chapter 1 of the historic and scientific approaches to truth, showing how the data of history differ from the data of science and how they may be lost, distorted, suppressed, or translated inaccurately. Examples throughout the text illustrate how such events have affected the writing of the history of psychology. Also, the clock is discussed as a seventeenth-century metaphor for the spirit of mechanism and the mechanistic psychology it inspired, and the computer is offered as a metaphor for twentieth-century cognitive psychology. Much supplementary biographical material has been incorporated, and the coverage of early animal psychology has been expanded.

Additional new topics include the impact of nineteenth-century reform in the German universities on the growth of scientific inquiry, the recently amended data of history showing a dissimilarity between the positions of Wundt and Titchener, the popularization of psychology in the United States in the 1920s, the early spread of Gestalt psychology to the United States, and the influence of Darwin on Freud.

Chapter 15 has been rewritten to include a brief history of applied psychology, particularly the psychological testing movement, industrial/organizational psychology, and clinical psychology; an assessment of the impact of humanistic psychology; and a discussion of the role of the cognitive movement in contemporary psychology. The chapter also contains a discussion of the historical reasons why the contributions of women psychologists have not been adequately recognized.

The four original source articles—by Titchener, Carr, Wertheimer, and Watson—have been retained, and a selection from Freud has been added. User reaction to these materials has been favorable. These statements by psychology's important figures are of value to the student because they present a position in the proponent's own words and illustrate what the psychology student of the day was reading.

We are grateful to the many instructors and students who have contacted us over the years with valuable suggestions and comments. The book has also benefited from the rigorous and perceptive evaluation of Robin A. Barr, Ball State University; Ludy T. Benjamin, Jr., Texas A&M University; Donald J. Dickerson, University of Connecticut; Samuel S. Franklin, California State University, Fresno; Kenneth E. Smoot, University of Wisconsin, Eau Claire; and Wayne Viney, Colorado State University. At Harcourt Brace Jovanovich, Karl Yambert (manuscript editor), Robin Risque (art editor), Jamie Fidler (designer), and Tracy White (production editor) have been a pleasure to work with. We appreciate not only their diligence but also their enthusiasm about this project.

D. P. S.
S. E. S.

Contents

Preface   *iii*

1

THE STUDY OF THE HISTORY OF PSYCHOLOGY   1

The Development of Modern Psychology: An Overview   *1*
The Relevance of the Past for the Present   *3*
The Data of History   *6*
The Evolution of Psychology: Conceptions of Scientific History   *9*
The Schools of Thought: Landmarks in the Development of Modern
Psychology   *12*
Suggested Readings   *15*

2

PHILOSOPHICAL INFLUENCES ON PSYCHOLOGY   17

The Spirit of Mechanism   *17*
The Clockwork Universe   *18*
The Beginnings of Modern Science: René Descartes (1596–1650)   *21*
  The Life of Descartes   22
  *The Contributions of Descartes: Mechanism and the Mind–Body
  Problem   24*
British Empiricism and Associationism: Acquiring Knowledge through
Experience   *28*
  John Locke (1632–1704)   29
  George Berkeley (1685–1753)   32
  David Hume (1711–1776)   34
  David Hartley (1705–1757)   35
  James Mill (1773–1836)   36
Contributions of Empiricism to Psychology   *37*
Suggested Readings   *38*

3

PHYSIOLOGICAL INFLUENCES ON PSYCHOLOGY   39

Introduction   *39*
Developments in Early Physiology: An Overview   *40*
The Beginnings of Experimental Psychology   *42*
  Why Germany?   42
Hermann von Helmholtz (1821–1894)   *44*
  The Life of Helmholtz   44
  The Contributions of Helmholtz   45
  Comment   46
Ernst Weber (1795–1878)   *46*
  The Two-Point Threshold   48
  The Just Noticeable Difference   48
Gustav Theodor Fechner (1801–1887)   *49*
  The Life of Fechner   49
  *The Contributions of Fechner: Quantitative Relationship between Mind
  and Body   51*
  Methods of Psychophysics   53
  Comment   54
The Formal Founding of the New Science   *54*
Suggested Readings   *56*

4

THE NEW PSYCHOLOGY   58

A Case of Distorted Data   *58*
Wilhelm Wundt (1832–1920)   *59*
  The Life of Wundt   59
  Wundt's System of Psychology   64
  The Nature of Conscious Experience   64
  The Method of Study: Introspection   65
  The Elements of Experience   66
  Organizing the Elements of Experience: Apperception   67
  The Research Topics of the Leipzig Laboratory   67
  Comment   69
Other Early European Psychologists   *70*
  Hermann Ebbinghaus (1850–1909)   71
  Georg Elias Müller (1850–1934)   74
  Franz Brentano (1838–1917)   75
  Carl Stumpf (1848–1936)   77
  Oswald Külpe (1862–1915) and the Würzburg School   79
  Comment   83
Suggested Readings   *83*

5

STRUCTURALISM   85

Introduction   *85*
Edward Bradford Titchener (1867–1927)   *85*
  The Life of Titchener   85
  The Content of Conscious Experience   89
  The Method of Study: Introspection   90
  The Elements of Consciousness   92
Original Source Material on Structuralism: From *A Text-Book of Psychology* by E. B. Titchener   *94*
The Fate of Structuralism   *102*
  Criticisms of Structuralism   103
  Contributions of Structuralism   105
Suggested Readings   *106*

6

FUNCTIONALISM: ANTECEDENT INFLUENCES   107

Introduction   *107*
Functionalism: An Overview   *108*
The Evolution Revolution: Charles Darwin (1809–1882)   *108*
  The Life of Darwin   110
  The Works of Darwin   112
  The Influence of Darwin on Psychology   114
Individual Differences: Sir Francis Galton (1822–1911)   *115*
  The Life of Galton   115
  The Works of Galton   117
  Comment   122
The Influence of Animal Psychology on Functionalism   *123*
Comment   *125*
Suggested Readings   *126*

7

FUNCTIONALISM: AMERICAN PIONEERS   128

Only in America: Herbert Spencer (1820–1903) and Synthetic Philosophy   *128*
Anticipator of Functional Psychology: William James (1842–1910)   *131*
  The Life of James   132
  The Works of James   136
  Comment   140

Granville Stanley Hall (1844–1924)   *141*
 The Life of Hall   141
 The Works of Hall   145
 Comment   146
James McKeen Cattell (1860–1944)   *146*
 The Life of Cattell   146
 The Works of Cattell   150
 Comment   151
Ganz Amerikanisch   151
Suggested Readings   *153*

8

FUNCTIONALISM: FORMAL DEVELOPMENT   154

The Founding of Functionalism   *154*
The Chicago School   *155*
 John Dewey (1859–1952)   155
 James Rowland Angell (1869–1949)   157
 Harvey A. Carr (1873–1954)   159
Original Source Material on Functionalism: From *Psychology*
by Harvey A. Carr   *162*
Functionalism at Columbia   *167*
 Robert Sessions Woodworth (1869–1962)   167
Criticisms of Functionalism   *170*
Contributions of Functionalism   *171*
Suggested Readings   *172*

9

BEHAVIORISM: ANTECEDENT INFLUENCES   173

Introduction   *173*
The Influence of Animal Psychology on Behaviorism   *175*
 Clever Hans, the Clever Horse   178
Edward Lee Thorndike (1874–1949)   *179*
 The Life of Thorndike   180
 Thorndike's Connectionism   181
 Comment   184
Ivan Petrovitch Pavlov (1849–1936)   *184*
 The Life of Pavlov   184
 Pavlov's Research   187
 Comment   190
Vladimir M. Bekhterev (1857–1927)   *191*
Comment   *192*
The Influence of Functionalism on Behaviorism   *192*
Suggested Readings   *193*

10

BEHAVIORISM: THE BEGINNING   195

John B. Watson (1878–1958)   *195*
Original Source Material on Behaviorism: From *Psychology
as the Behaviorist Views It* by John B. Watson   *201*
The Reaction to Watson's Program   *207*
The Methods of Behaviorism   *208*
The Subject Matter of Behaviorism   *210*
Specific Topics   *211*
  Instinct   211
  Learning   213
  Emotion   213
  Thought   215
Watson's Popular Appeal   *216*
  An Outbreak of Psychology   218
A Final Note   *219*
Criticisms of Watsonian Behaviorism   *219*
Contributions of Watsonian Behaviorism   *222*
Suggested Readings   *223*

11

BEHAVIORISM: AFTER THE FOUNDING   224

Early Behaviorists   *224*
  Edwin B. Holt (1873–1946)   224
  Albert P. Weiss (1879–1931)   225
  Karl Lashley (1890–1958)   226
The Influence of Operationism   *227*
Neobehaviorists   *228*
  Edward Chace Tolman (1886–1959)   229
  Edwin Ray Guthrie (1886–1959)   234
  Clark Leonard Hull (1884–1952)   237
  Burrhus Frederick Skinner (1904–   )   243
The Cognitive Challenge to Behaviorism   *253*
  Socio-Behaviorism: Albert Bandura (1925–   )   254
  Comment   255
Suggested Readings   *255*

12

GESTALT PSYCHOLOGY   257

Introduction   *257*
Antecedent Influences   *259*

The Founding of Gestalt Psychology   261
  Max Wertheimer (1880–1943)   262
  Kurt Koffka (1886–1941)   264
  Wolfgang Köhler (1887–1967)   265
The Nature of the Gestalt Revolt   267
Original Source Material on Gestalt Psychology: From *Gestalt Theory*
by Max Wertheimer   269
Principles of Perceptual Organization   273
Principles of Learning   274
  The Mentality of Apes   275
  Productive Thinking in Humans   277
The Principle of Isomorphism   278
The Spread of Gestalt Psychology   279
  Field Theory: Kurt Lewin (1890–1947)   280
Criticisms of Gestalt Psychology   284
Contributions of Gestalt Psychology   285
Suggested Readings   286

13

PSYCHOANALYSIS: THE BEGINNINGS   288

Introduction   288
Antecedent Influences   289
  Early Theories of the Unconscious   289
  Psychopathology   292
  The Influence of Darwin   294
  Other Sources of Influence   295
The Development of Psychoanalysis: Sigmund Freud
(1856–1939)   296
Psychoanalysis as a Method of Treatment   305
Freud's Method of Research   308
Psychoanalysis as a System of Personality   309
  Instincts   309
  Unconscious and Conscious Aspects of Personality   309
  Anxiety   311
  Stages of Personality Development   311
Original Source Material on Psychoanalysis: From *An Outline of
Psycho-Analysis* by Sigmund Freud   312
Mechanism and Determinism in Freud's System   315
Conflicts Between Psychoanalysis and Psychology   316
Criticisms of Psychoanalysis   317
The Scientific Credibility of Psychoanalysis   319
Contributions of Psychoanalysis   319
Suggested Readings   321

14

PSYCHOANALYSIS: AFTER THE FOUNDING   323

The Dissenters and the Descendants   *323*
Carl Jung (1875–1961)   *325*
  The Life of Jung   *325*
  Jung's System: Analytical Psychology   *327*
  Comment   *331*
Social Psychological Theories in Psychoanalysis: The *Zeitgeist* Strikes
Again   *331*
Alfred Adler (1870–1937)   *332*
  The Life of Adler   *332*
  Adler's System: Individual Psychology   *334*
  Comment   *336*
Karen Horney (1885–1952)   *337*
  The Life of Horney   *337*
  Horney's System   *340*
  Comment   *341*
Criticisms of the Social Psychological Theories   *341*
The Descendants   *342*
  Gordon Allport (1897–1967)   *343*
  Henry Murray (1893–)   *345*
  Erik Erikson (1902–)   *347*
Comment   *349*
Suggested Readings   *349*

15

BEYOND THE SCHOOLS OF THOUGHT: MORE RECENT DEVELOPMENTS   351

Schools of Thought in Psychology   *351*
The Growth of Applied Psychology   *352*
  The Psychological Testing Movement   *353*
  Industrial/Organizational Psychology   *356*
  Clinical Psychology   *359*
Women in the History of Psychology   *360*
Humanistic Psychology: The Third Force   *362*
  Historical Antecedents of Humanistic Psychology   *362*
  The Nature of Humanistic Psychology   *364*
  Humanistic Psychotherapies   *366*
  Abraham Maslow (1908–1970)   *366*
  Carl Rogers (1902–)   *368*
  The Status of Humanistic Psychology   *370*

The Cognitive Movement in Psychology   371
  The Influence of the Zeitgeist   373
  The Role of the Computer   374
  The Nature of Cognitive Psychology   375
  Comment   376
Suggested Readings   377

References   381
Index   395

1

The Study of the History of Psychology

THE DEVELOPMENT OF MODERN PSYCHOLOGY: AN OVERVIEW

Of all the scholarly disciplines in existence today, psychology is among the oldest. Interest in the topic can be traced to the earliest inquiring minds. We have long been fascinated by our own behavior, and speculations about human nature and conduct fill many philosophical and theological volumes. As early as the fourth and fifth centuries B.C., Plato, Aristotle, and other Greek scholars grappled with many of the same problems that concern psychologists today: memory, learning, motivation, perception, dreaming, and irrational behavior. The same kinds of questions now being asked about human nature were asked centuries ago, which shows a vital continuity in subject matter between the present and the past.

It would appear that because psychology had its origins in antiquity, our study must begin there also, but there is another point to consider. Although psychology is one of the older disciplines, it is also one of the newer. This paradox was described succinctly by the nineteenth-century psychologist, Hermann Ebbinghaus, who wrote that "psychology has a long past but only a short history." The intellectual precursors of psychology are ancient indeed, but the modern tradition and form of psychology are only a little more than 100 years old. The centennial of the birth of modern psychology was celebrated in 1979.

The distinction between modern psychology and its antecedents has less to do with the kinds of questions asked about human nature than with the methods used to seek the answers. It is the approach taken and the techniques employed that distinguish the older philosophy from modern psychology and denote the emergence of psychology as a separate discipline.

Until the last quarter of the nineteenth century, philosophers studied human nature through speculation, intuition, and generalization based on their own limited experience. A major transformation occurred when they began to apply the tools and methods of science to questions about human nature, methods that had already proved successful in the biological and physical sciences. Only when researchers came to rely on carefully controlled observation and experimentation as the means for studying the human mind did psychology begin to attain an identity separate from its philosophical antecedents.

The new psychology needed to develop a more precise and objective way of dealing with its subject matter. Thus, much of the history of psychology after its separation from philosophy is an account of the continual refinement of its tools, techniques, and methods of study to achieve increased precision and objectivity in both its questions and its answers.

If we are to understand the complex issues that define and divide psychology today, the proper starting point for the history of the field is the nineteenth century, the time when psychology became an independent discipline with unique methods of inquiry and theoretical rationales. We cannot deny that earlier scholars speculated on problems concerning the nature of the human species. Certainly they did. But their influence on the development of psychology as a separate and primarily experimental science is limited. A contemporary historian of psychology has suggested that "when we examine the topics now filling the literature in professional psychology, we are hard pressed to find one that was not put forth, often in a form still to be improved on, [in] the nineteenth century" (Robinson, 1981, pp. 390–391).

Only in the last 100 years or so have psychologists defined psychology's subject matter and established its foundation, confirming its independence from philosophy. The early philosophers concerned themselves with problems that are still of general interest, but they approached these problems in a manner vastly different from that of today's psychologists. These scholars were not psychologists in the contemporary usage of the term, and we will discuss their ideas only as they relate directly to the establishment of modern psychology.

Psychology became an experimental science at a time when European thought was imbued with positivism, empiricism, and materialism. The idea that the methods of science could be applied to mental phenomena was inherited from both the philosophical thinking and the physiological investigations of the seventeenth to nineteenth centuries, an exciting era that forms the immediate background out of which modern psychology emerged. While the nineteenth-century philosophers were clearing the way for an experimental attack on the functioning of the mind, another group of scholars was independently approaching some of the same problems from a different direction. Nineteenth-century physiologists were making great strides toward understanding the bodily mechanisms that underlie the mental processes. The physiologists' methods of study differed from those of the philosophers, but the eventual union of these disparate disciplines produced a field of study in which, at least in its formative years, an attempt was made to preserve the conflicting traditions and beliefs of both. Fortunately, the new psychology quickly succeeded in attaining an identity and stature of its own.

The first sign of a distinct field of inquiry known as psychology came in the last quarter of the nineteenth century with the adoption of the scientific method as the means for attempting to solve psychology's problems. During that period there were several formal indications that psychology was beginning to flourish. In December 1879, in Leipzig, Germany, Wilhelm Wundt established the world's first psychological laboratory. For many years, controversy existed about whether this event took place in 1879 or 1875. Recent research at the Wilhelm Wundt Archives in Leipzig and at the Dresden State Archives points to 1879 as the correct date (Bringmann, Bringmann, & Ungerer, 1980).

Wundt also established the journal *Philosophische Studien* (*Philosophical Studies*) in 1881, which is considered to be the first journal of psychology to contain experimental reports. In 1888 the University of Pennsylvania appointed James McKeen Cattell professor of psychology, the first such professorship in the world. Before that time psychologists had received appointments in departments of philosophy. With Cattell's appointment, psychology received recognition in academic circles as an independent discipline. In 1887 G. Stanley Hall founded the *American Journal of Psychology*, the first psychology journal to be published in the United States.

Between 1880 and 1895 dramatic and sweeping changes occurred in American psychology. During that time, 26 psychology laboratories and three psychology journals were established. In 1892 the American Psychological Association, the first scientific organization of psychologists, was founded.

William McDougall, a British psychologist, defined psychology in 1908 as the "science of behavior," using this phrase apparently for the first time. Thus, by the early part of the twentieth century American psychology had succeeded in gaining its independence from philosophy, developing laboratories in which to apply the methods of science, forming its own scientific association, and giving itself a formal definition as a science, the science of behavior.

Once the new discipline had been launched, it grew rapidly, particularly in the United States, which assumed and maintains a position of dominance in the psychological world. Today more than half the world's psychologists work in the United States, and a great many psychologists from other countries have received at least a portion of their training at U.S. institutions. The major share of the world's psychological literature is produced in the United States.

Let us consider several objective indicators of the vitality and popularity of psychology. The American Psychological Association, established in 1892 with 26 charter members, had grown to include 1100 psychologists by 1930. By 1986 the membership stood at over 61,000.

This population explosion of psychologists has been paralleled by an information explosion of research reports, theoretical and review articles, books, films, cassettes, and other forms of publication, making it increasingly difficult for psychologists to remain knowledgeable about developments beyond their own specialty areas.

Consider also the number of articles reviewed for *Psychological Abstracts*, the reference journal that summarizes the world's literature in psychology and related fields. In 1961, more than 7000 articles were abstracted. Twenty-five years later, the number had increased to approximately 32,000. To keep abreast of all published works in psychology would require reading nearly 100 publications every day.

Psychology has grown not only in terms of its practitioners, researchers, scholars, and published literature, but also in its impact on our daily lives. Whatever your age, occupation, or interests, your life is influenced in some way by the work of psychologists in education, industry, mental and physical health, criminal justice, and the design of consumer products.

THE RELEVANCE OF THE PAST FOR THE PRESENT

This section might aptly be titled, "Why study the history of psychology?" This is a legitimate type of inquiry when beginning any new course. How will your knowledge of and competence in psychology be enhanced by a study of the history of the field? The methods of today's psychology bear little formal resemblance to those used in the early psychology laboratories and even less to the prescientific philosophical approaches. The development of psychology has been so dynamic that the psychology of only 25 years ago seems outdated. Will knowledge of the history of the field produce a better understanding of contemporary psychology? Taking into account the vast amount of material to be studied in psychology, is it worth the effort to learn what happened 50 or 100 years ago?

Obviously, we believe the answer is yes. One reason for studying the history of psychology relates to the growth and influence of the field. Another reason relates to the divisiveness and fragmentation characteristic of psychology today. There is no single form, approach, or definition of modern psychology on which all psychologists agree, but rather there is an enormous diversity in both professional and scientific specialization and subject matter. For example, psychologists may focus their attention on conscious or unconscious forces, on overt behavior, or on physiological and biochemical processes. There are many areas of contemporary psychology, and they may appear to have little in common other than an interest in human nature and conduct and an approach that attempts, in some way, to be scientific.

The framework that binds these differing areas and approaches is the historical development of the field, the evolution of the discipline of psychology over time. Only by exploring its origins will the diversity of modern psychology become clear; psychology's history explains its present state.

The influence of the past in shaping the present describes a belief and a technique used by many psychologists in their work. Most clinical psychologists attempt to understand the current condition of their patients by exploring the past, by examining the forces that may have caused their patients to behave or think in certain ways. By taking case histories, clinicians reconstruct the evolution of their patients and, in the process, are often able to explain present behavior. Behavioral psychologists also accept the influence of the past in shaping the present. In general, they believe that human behavior is determined by prior conditioning and reinforcing experiences. Thus, the current state of the organism is accounted for in terms of its history.

So it is with the discipline of psychology. The history of psychology may be the only course in the psychology department curriculum that will help you integrate the numerous areas and issues that constitute modern psychology. You should come to recognize the interrelationships among the various facts and theories and to achieve a greater awareness of how all the different (and, in some cases, apparently unrelated) pieces of psychology fit together. You will see that the diverse topics of psychology are inextricably related through the pattern of their historical development. The history of psychology course has been called the "capstone" of the psychology curriculum, referring to the stone that makes a structure complete (Raphelson, 1982). We might also describe the history of psychology as a case history, an exploration of the early events and experiences that may have made psychology what it is today.

Psychologists recognize the value of studying the history of their field. Most psychology departments offer such a course, and many require it for undergraduate and graduate degrees. Most science departments do not give courses in the history of their fields, but psychologists believe that the study of the history of their discipline is a useful addition to the curriculum.

At the professional level there are also signs of a strong interest in the history of psychology. In 1965 a multidisciplinary journal, the *Journal of the History of the Behavioral Sciences*, was begun under the editorship of a psychologist. That same year the Archives of the History of American Psychology was established at the University of Akron, Ohio, to serve the needs of scholars by collecting and preserving source materials in the history of psychology. The Division of the History of Psychology (Division 26) was formed within the American Psychological Association in 1966, and in 1969 the International Society for the History of the Behavioral and Social Sciences (the Cheiron Society) was established. Graduate work in the history of psychology is offered at several universities, and doctoral programs are available at the University of New Hampshire in the United States and Carleton University in Canada. The American Psychological Association now requires course work in the history of psychology for all accredited doctoral programs. The growth in the number of textbooks, monographs, biographies, journal articles, professional meetings, translated works, and sources for archival research reflects the importance that psychologists attribute to the study of the history of psychology.

Why are psychologists so interested in the historical development of their field? Perhaps one reason is that psychology has attracted our attention and interest for centuries. From the beginnings of recorded time people have attempted to understand human behavior and have reached many respectable insights and conclusions—and a number of inaccuracies and myths as well. Because of the complexity of human nature, many of the questions asked centuries ago are still relevant today. There is, then, a continuity of problems and questions, if not of methods, within psychology that is not found in the other sciences. Thus, psychology has a more tangible link with its past, a connection that many psychologists find satisfying and useful to explore.

Scientists must also be concerned with the history of their fields to avoid repeating the past. As we shall see, the history of science contains instances of supposedly new discoveries and insights that had been anticipated years earlier. The new discovery had been made in ignorance of the previous work.

Knowledge of the past might also help to predict the future. Some psychologists reject the idea that history can be used as some sort of crystal ball in which to read the future. Others, however, argue that the past may be the only basis on which we may plan intelligently for the future. One purpose of studying the history of a science is to achieve a better understanding of its present status. Of what functional significance is this understanding if not to provide some preparation for the future?

Another reason for studying the history of psychology is to see the impact of cultural and social forces on the attitudes and goals of the early psychologists. Psychology's methods and theories and, indeed, our selves, are the products of forces and traditions that evolved over time. If we were not aware of these influences, "we shall have cut ourselves off from our very roots. To cut off history is to sever our arterial link with humanity" (May, 1967, p. 55).

Finally, it has been suggested that the study of the history of psychology needs no defense (Michael Wertheimer, 1979). The fascination of the story is sufficient justification, as we shall see in the following chapters. You will find human drama, revolutionary movements, shocking ideas, and tragic defeats for individuals and their beliefs. We hope you will gain some appreciation of the substantial progress that has been made in knowledge and methodology in the comparatively short time since psychology became an independent discipline. There were false starts, errors, and misconceptions, but there is a thread of continuity that has shaped contemporary psychology and that provides us with an explanation for its richness and diversity.

THE DATA OF HISTORY

The data of history—the materials historians use to reconstruct lives, events, and time periods—differ markedly from the data of science. The most important feature of scientific data is that they are created by the scientists themselves. When psychologists want to discover, for example, the conditions under which some persons will help others who are in apparent distress, or the ways in which different reinforcement schedules influence the behavior of laboratory animals, or whether children will imitate the aggressive behavior they observe in others, they construct situations or establish conditions out of which data will be generated. The psychologists conduct a laboratory experiment, observe behavior systematically under controlled conditions in the real world, take a survey, or determine the correlation between two variables. Thus, scientists shape the situations or events they wish to study, and these events can be reconstructed or replicated by other scientists working at other places and in other times. The data can be verified by repeating the observation, by establishing conditions similar to those of the original study.

In contrast, the data of history cannot be reconstructed or replicated. The event or situation of interest occurred at some time in the past, perhaps centuries ago, and historians of the day may not have recorded the details of the event as it unfolded.

> History is an all-or-nothing affair; something happened once, and that is that—you cannot bring past events back into the present to study them and their determinants and effects at leisure, turning them this way and that, as you can examine some scientific statement in the laboratory. (Michael Wertheimer, 1979, p. 1)

The incident itself is thus lost to view. How can historians deal with it? What data can they use to develop an account of it? And how can they possibly tell us what happened? Just because historians cannot replicate a situation and create the pertinent data does not mean that the data do not exist. The data of history are available to us in the form of fragments of past events such as descriptions recorded by participants or witnesses, letters, diaries, memoirs, or official accounts. It is from these data-fragments that historians try to recreate the events and persons of the past.

The historians' approach is similar to that taken by archeologists who, working with fragments of past civilizations—arrowheads, broken pots, human bones—try to describe the characteristics of a civilization. Some archeological excavations yield more complete data, more fragments, than others, allowing for more accurate reconstructions. Similarly, with excavations in history, the amount of data may be so great as to leave little doubt about the accuracy of the reconstruction.

Sometimes, however, historical data are incomplete, that is, they may be lost, suppressed deliberately, translated inaccurately, or distorted by a participant who is motivated by self-interest. The history of psychology contains many examples of such occurrences in the generation of historical truth.

Let us discuss, first, data that have been lost. It has happened that important personal papers were missing for decades or longer before being discovered. In 1984 an extensive collection of the papers of Hermann Ebbinghaus, who was prominent in the study of learning, was found some 75 years after his death. In 1983, 10 large boxes containing the handwritten diaries of Gustav Fechner, the scientist who developed psychophysics, were uncovered. These diaries covered the period 1828–1879, a time of great significance in the early history of psychology, yet for more than 100 years psychologists were unaware of their existence.

The discovery of historical data such as these is not uncommon. It is too early to speculate on how these materials will alter our historical accounts of Ebbinghaus and Fechner or change our assessment of their influence on psychology, but for the past century, historians have written about these scientists and their work without having access to these huge collections of personal papers. New fragments of history now exist and more pieces of the puzzle can be set in place.

Other data may be deliberately hidden from public view, usually for personal reasons. One example involves John B. Watson, the founder of behaviorism. Around 1919, Watson, then at Johns Hopkins University, conducted one of the earliest studies of the physiological changes that occur during human sexual intercourse. Watson undertook this research in a highly personal way, by connecting various scientific measuring instruments to his body and to that of a young woman graduate student and recording the information while they made love.

Watson's wife took issue with his commitment to science and confiscated the data. It was not until 1974 that the research study was even mentioned in print. The equipment was discovered 4 years later, nearly 60 years after the experiments were conducted. No one has yet found the research results themselves.

Sigmund Freud provides another example of suppressed data-fragments. Freud died in 1939, and in the years since his death many of his papers have been released to scholars. A large collection of personal letters and papers is still held by the Library of Congress, however, and at the request of the Freud estate, these will not be made available until well into the twenty-first century. The stated reason for this restriction is the protection of the privacy of some of Freud's patients and their families and perhaps of Freud and his family as well.

Psychologists do not know, of course, how these documents will affect our understanding of Freud and his work: perhaps fundamentally and perhaps not at all. Until the data are open to view, the history of one of psychology's pivotal figures remains incomplete and, possibly, inaccurate.

Another problem with the data of history relates to information that has come to the historian in distorted form. In such cases, the data are available, but they have been changed or biased in some way, through faulty translations or through distortions introduced by a participant in recording his or her own activities.

We may refer to Freud again for examples of the misleading effects of inaccurate translations. Only a minority of American psychologists and students are sufficiently fluent in the German language to read Freud in the original. The majority rely on a translator's view of the most suitable or equivalent words and phrases. The correspondence between the translation and Freud's intended meaning is not always exact. A few instances will make this clear.

Three fundamental concepts in Freud's theory of the structure of personality are the id, the ego, and the superego, terms with which you are familiar. They do not, however, convey Freud's ideas precisely. They are the Latin equivalents of Freud's German words: *ego* for *Ich* (I), *id* for *Es* (it), and *superego* for *Über-Ich* (above-I).

Freud intended to indicate something highly intimate and personal with his use of *Ich* (I) and to distinguish it clearly from *Es* (it), which represents something distinct from or foreign to "I." "The translation of the personal pronouns into their Latin equivalents—the 'ego' and the 'id'—rather than their English ones turned them into cold technical terms, which arouse no personal associations" (Bettelheim, 1982, p. 53). The distinction between "I" or "me," on the one hand, and "it," on the other, is not as forceful in the translation as in the original.

Consider another common Freudian term, "free association." The use of the word "association" implies a conscious link or connection between one idea or thought and another, as though each one acts as a stimulus to elicit the next word in a chain. This is not what Freud believed. His term in German was *Einfall*, which does not mean an association. It means, instead, an intrusion or an invasion, and Freud used the word in the sense of something from the unconscious that is uncontrollably intruding on or breaking into conscious thought.

These differences in meaning are seen by some psychologists to be small and subtle changes, but they are changes nonetheless. The data—in this case, Freud's own words—have not been rendered by historians as carefully as they were written. They have undergone some distortion in the act of translation, and historians who rely on them are dealing with less-than-correct data-fragments.

The data of history are also affected by the actions of the participants in the events. They may, consciously or unconsciously, bias their own accounts to protect themselves or to enhance their public image. For example, B. F. Skinner, the prominent behaviorist, described in his autobiography his rigorous self-discipline while he was a graduate student at Harvard University. The following paragraph has been quoted frequently in biographical material about Skinner.

> I would rise at six, study until breakfast, go to classes, laboratories, and libraries with no more than fifteen minutes unscheduled during the day, study until exactly nine o'clock at night and go to bed. I saw no movies or plays, seldom went to concerts, had scarcely any dates and read nothing but psychology and physiology. (Skinner, 1967, p. 398)

This description seems to be a useful data-fragment in that it provides an insight into Skinner's character. Twelve years after publishing this recollection of his schedule, however, and 51 years after the event itself, Skinner denied that his graduate school days had been as spartan and difficult as he had suggested earlier. Referring to the above-quoted passage, he wrote, "I was recalling a pose rather than the life I actually led" (Skinner, 1979, p. 5).

Although Skinner's school days may be of minor importance in the history of psychology, the two versions in print, both written by the participant, indicate something of the difficulty historians face. Which set of data, which version of this incident, is the more accurate? Which characterization comes closer to reality? Which is biased by the vagaries or the self-serving nature of memory, and how are we to know?

In some cases, it is possible to find corroborating data from other participants or observers. If Skinner's graduate-school regimen were highly significant for historians of psychology, they could try to locate Skinner's classmates or their diaries or letters and compare their memories of Skinner's behavior at Harvard with his own. Thus, some distortions in history can be investigated and corrected by the use of other sources. This has occurred with Freud's descriptions of certain aspects of his life and work. Freud liked to present himself as a martyr to his psychoanalytic cause, a visionary who was constantly opposed, scorned, rejected, and vilified. His first biographer, Ernest Jones, echoed these claims. Data uncovered later indicated that both men were wrong. Far from being ignored, Freud's ideas, by 1906, had begun to exert an immense influence on the younger generation of intellectuals in Vienna. Freud's private practice was thriving, and he could even have been called, in modern terms, something of a celebrity.

For years it was believed that Freud's important book, *The Interpretation of Dreams* (1900), was almost totally disregarded and that, on those rare occasions when it was reviewed, it was severely criticized. In truth, the book received wide recognition in professional journals in philosophy, psychology, psychiatry, and medicine, as well as in popular magazines and newspapers in Vienna, Berlin, and other major European cities (Ellenberger, 1970). Many of these reviews praised the book greatly. Freud himself had distorted the record and these distortions were perpetuated by his biographer. The false impression has now been corrected, but for several decades, until new data-fragments were excavated, our understanding of Freud was inaccurate.

What do these problems with the data of history indicate for our study of the history of psychology? They show primarily that history is not static or stagnant but rather is dynamic, always changing, growing, and being refined as new data are uncovered and inaccuracies are corrected. History can never be considered finished or complete. It is always in progress, a story without an ending. The story told by the historian can only approximate or approach the truth, but it does so more fully with each passing year, with each new find and refinement of the fragments that are the data of history.

THE EVOLUTION OF PSYCHOLOGY: CONCEPTIONS OF SCIENTIFIC HISTORY

Two approaches can be taken to explain how a science such as psychology develops: the *personalistic* or so-called great man theory and the *naturalistic* theory. The personalistic conception of scientific history focuses on the monumental achievements and contributions of certain individuals. According to this view, progress and change are directly attributable to the will and force of unique persons who alone charted and changed the course of history. A Napoleon, a Hitler, and a Darwin were, so this theory goes, the prime movers and shapers of great events. The personalistic theory implies that the events would not have occurred had it not been for the appearance of the great men and women. The theory says, in effect, that the person makes the times.

At first glance, it is obvious that science is indeed the work of extremely creative and intelligent individuals who alone determined its direction. We often define an era by the name of the person whose discoveries or theories marked the period. We talk about physics "after Einstein," psychology "after Watson," and sculpture "after Michelangelo." It is apparent, both in science and in the general culture, that individuals have produced dramatic, and sometimes traumatic, changes that have altered the course of history. We have only to think of Sigmund Freud to realize the truth of that assertion.

Thus, the personalistic theory has merit, but is it sufficient to explain the development of a science or a society? No. The work of scientists and philosophers has too often been ignored or denied at one time, only to achieve full recognition long afterwards. These occurrences imply that the times may determine whether the scholar's ideas will be heeded or ignored, praised or forgotten. The history of science is replete with examples of rejection of new discoveries and insights. Even the greatest minds (perhaps especially the greatest minds) have been constrained by what is called the *Zeitgeist*, the spirit or intellectual climate of the times. Therefore, the acceptance and application of a discovery may be limited by the dominant pattern of thought in a culture, region, or era, but an idea that is too novel to gain acceptance in one period may be readily accepted a generation or a century later. Slow change seems to be the rule for scientific progress.

The notion that the person makes the times is, then, not entirely correct. Perhaps, as the naturalistic theory of history would have it, the times make the person, or at least make possible the recognition of what the person has to say. Unless the *Zeitgeist* is ready for the new idea, its proponent may not be heard, or may be laughed at or even burned at the stake—this, too, depends on the *Zeitgeist*.

The naturalistic theory suggests, for example, that if Darwin had died in his youth, a theory of evolution would still have been advanced in the middle of the nineteenth century. Someone else would have proposed it because the *Zeitgeist* was calling for a new way of looking at the origin of the human species. As we shall see, someone else did propose such a theory; Alfred Russel Wallace's views on evolution were amazingly similar to Darwin's.

The inhibiting or delaying capacity of the *Zeitgeist* operates not only at the level of the culture but also within science itself where its effects may be even more pronounced. There are, as we noted, many cases of scientific discoveries that remained dormant for a long time before being rediscovered and embraced. The concept of the conditioned response, for example, was first suggested by Robert Whytt, a Scottish scientist, in 1763, but no one was interested in it then. It was well over a century later, when researchers in psychology were adopting more objective methods, that Ivan Pavlov elaborated upon these earlier observations and expanded them into the basis of a new system of psychology. The work of the Austrian botanist Gregor Mendel on genetics was little known for 35 years, perhaps because of its publication in an obscure journal. A discovery, then, must await its time. A contemporary psychologist recently remarked that he was amazed at "how frequently discovery is merely rediscovery, perhaps at a more auspicious time" (Atkinson, 1981, p. 125).

Instances of simultaneous discovery also support the naturalistic theory of history. Similar discoveries have been made by individuals working far apart geographically, often in ignorance of one another's work. In 1900, three investigators unknown to one another coincidentally rediscovered Mendel's work.

Current theoretical positions in a scientific field often obstruct or prohibit considera-tion of new points of view. One theory may so dominate a discipline that investigation of a new method of inquiry is stifled. An existing theory can also determine the ways in which phenomena or data are organized and examined, and this may prevent the scientist from considering the data in any other ways. Albert Einstein said, "It is the theory which decides what we can observe" (quoted in Broad & Wade, 1982, p. 138).

The *Zeitgeist* within a science can have this inhibiting effect on methods of investiga-tion, on theoretical formulations, and on the definition of the discipline's proper subject matter. We shall describe in the following chapters the early tendency in scientific psychology to focus on consciousness and the subjective aspects of human nature. Even as the methods of study became more objective and precise, the focus of study continued to be subjective. Not until the end of the second decade of the twentieth century did psychology finally lose its mind. Later it lost consciousness altogether. A half century later, under the impact of a different *Zeitgeist*, psychology began to regain consciousness. Thus, science constantly reacts to the changing intellectual climate of the times.

We can easily understand this situation in terms of an analogy with the evolution of a living species. Both a science and a living species change or evolve in response to the conditions and demands of the environment. What happens to a species over time? Very little, as long as its environment remains largely constant. If the environment were to change, the species would have to adapt to the new conditions or face extinction.

Suppose that an ice age developed or that the climate grew significantly warmer or that a swamp dried out. To survive, the species that lived in the affected areas would have to alter their form. A hairless species would need to grow fur to cope with colder conditions. A short-legged species would need to evolve into a long-legged species if the food once available to it in shallow waters were now only found in deeper waters.

Some species do not adapt to environmental changes, and science knows only their historical remains. Others do change their form somewhat, retaining basic features. In these cases, the newer form of the species is recognizably linked with the older form. Still others are modified so radically that they become new species, and their relation to their predecessors is not readily apparent. However mild or extreme the alteration, the important point is that living species can adapt to environmental demands. The more the environment changes, the more the species must change.

Consider the parallel with the evolution of a science. It, too, exists in the context of an environment to which it must be continually responsive. The environment of a science, its *Zeitgeist*, is not so much physical as it is intellectual and social. Like the physical environment, however, the *Zeitgeist* is subject to change. The intellectual and social climate that characterizes one generation or century may be totally different by the next. Such a situation occurred, to give one example, when the belief in God and the teachings of the Church as the source of human knowledge was replaced by the belief in reason and science.

When these changes take place, the knowledge- and value-systems of a culture must adapt to the new environment. If they do not come to reflect the values of the new *Zeitgeist*, they become extinct. A belief system centered on the worship of the sun has little chance of surviving when the *Zeitgeist* has changed to support the worship of a human figure such as Jesus Christ or the prophet Mohammed.

This evolutionary process marks the entire history of psychology. When the *Zeitgeist* favored speculation, meditation, and intuition as the paths to truth, psychology favored those methods as well. When the spirit of the times dictated an observational and experimental approach to truth, the methods of psychology followed in that direction. When one form of psychology found itself in two different intellectual and social climates, it became two species of psychology; when the initial German form of psychology emigrated to the United States, it was modified to become a uniquely American form, whereas the psychology that remained in Germany evolved at a slower pace.

Our emphasis on the *Zeitgeist* does not negate the importance of the great men and women in the history of science, but it does require us to consider them in a different perspective. A Copernicus or a Marie Curie does not singlehandedly change the course of history through sheer force of genius. He or she does so only because the way has already been cleared. We shall see that this is true for every major figure in the history of psychology.

These great scholars have become *eponyms* (Boring, 1963): their names have been given to systematic positions or laws, and this process fosters the belief that the discovery was the result of one person's sudden insight. The development of the idea, however, has usually been much more gradual. Thus, eponymy may distort history by neglecting the *Zeitgeist* and the contributions made by earlier scholars.

What would the history of a science be like if the names of its leaders were omitted? It seems that a history of science must be eponymous, choosing, as it does, representative individuals to exemplify its development. Without these names, the historian would be forced to select other labels to designate eras, schools of thought, and theories. But an eponymous account of the evolution of psychology need not distort its development as long as we remember that the ideas of its theorists and researchers, as well as the acceptance of their achievements, were affected by the spirit of the times in which they worked.

It is clear that the evolution of psychology must be considered in terms of both the personalistic and the naturalistic theories of history, yet the *Zeitgeist* seems to play the major role. No matter how weighty their contributions seem today, if the significant figures in history and science had held ideas too far out of phase with the climate of the times, their insights would have died in obscurity. Individual creative work is more a prism—diffusing, elaborating, and magnifying the intellectual spirit of the times—than a beacon, although both will shed light on the path ahead.

THE SCHOOLS OF THOUGHT: LANDMARKS IN THE DEVELOPMENT OF MODERN PSYCHOLOGY

We said that psychology evolved as a separate scientific discipline in the last quarter of the nineteenth century. In its initial years, the direction of the new psychology was influenced profoundly by Wilhelm Wundt, who had definite ideas about the form this new science (*his* new science) should take. He determined the subject matter, the method of research, the topics that the researchers should study, and the goals of the new science. He was, of course, affected by the spirit of his times and by the current thinking in philosophy and physiology. Nevertheless, it was Wundt in his role as the agent of the times who drew together the various lines of thought and through the force of his personality and his intensive writing and research fashioned the new psychology. Because he was a compelling promoter of the inevitable, psychology was, for a while, molded in his image.

Before long, the situation changed. Controversy arose among the growing number of psychologists. The *Zeitgeist* was changing and new ideas were being advanced in other sciences and in the general culture. Reflecting these new currents of thought, some psychologists came to disagree with Wundt's version of psychology and proposed their own views. By the turn of the century, several systematic positions or schools of thought coexisted. These were essentially different definitions of the nature of psychology.

The term "school of thought" refers to a group of psychologists who become associated ideologically, and sometimes geographically, with the leader of a movement. Usually, the members of a school work on common problems and share a theoretical or systematic orientation.

The emergence of the different schools of thought and their subsequent decline and replacement by others is one of the more striking characteristics of the history of psychology. B. F. Skinner remarked, "Psychologists want a changing scene. Something new every half-generation" (Skinner, 1983, p. 387). Leona Tyler, a former president of the American Psychological Association, wrote that "Psychology has a way of outgrowing its definitions. The complexity of human life makes this almost inevitable. Whatever aspect of it comes under observation, there are always other aspects that new generations of investigators view as more important" (Tyler, 1981, p. 1).

This stage in the development of a science, when it is still divided into schools of thought, has been called the *preparadigmatic* stage (Kuhn, 1970). The more mature or advanced stage is reached when schools of thought no longer characterize a field, when the majority of the members of a discipline agree on theoretical and methodological rationales. At that time, a common paradigm or model defines the field, and there are no longer competing factions.

In the history of physics we can see paradigms at work. The Galilean–Newtonian concept of mechanism was accepted by physicists for some 300 years, and during that time virtually all work in the field was undertaken within that framework. Paradigms are not inviolate, however. They can and do change, once a majority of the persons in a discipline accepts a new way of ordering or working with the subject matter. In physics, this occurred when the Galilean–Newtonian model was eventually replaced by the Einsteinian model. This replacement of one paradigm by another may be thought of as a "scientific revolution" (Kuhn, 1970).[1]

Psychology has not yet reached the paradigmatic stage. For the more than 100 years of its history, psychology has been seeking, embracing, and rejecting different definitions, but no single system or point of view has succeeded in unifying the various positions. The field remains specialized, with each group adhering to its own theoretical

[1]Kuhn's view of the development of science has been challenged by other theorists (Lakatos, 1978; Laudan, 1977, 1981). Although these newer approaches have provided useful explanations for specific incidents or episodes in the history of psychology and physics, they have yet to be applied to the broader changes that characterize the development of psychology (Gholson & Barker, 1985).

and methodological orientation, approaching the study of human nature with different techniques, and promoting itself with different jargon, journals, and other trappings of a school of thought. This situation has been referred to as psychology's "identity problem" (Kimble, 1984, p. 833).

Each of the early schools of thought in psychology was a movement of protest—some, as we said, were revolutions—against the prevailing systematic position. Each school pointed out what it saw as the shortcomings and failures of the older system and offered new definitions, concepts, and research strategies to correct the perceived weaknesses. When a new school of thought captured the attention of the scientific community, the rejection of a once honored position was the result. These intellectual conflicts between incompatible old and new positions were fought with feverish tenacity on both sides.

Often the leaders of the older school were never wholly converted to the new school of thought. Usually older in years, these psychologists were too deeply committed to their position, intellectually and emotionally, to change. Many of the younger and less committed adherents became supporters of the new position, leaving the others to cling to their traditions, to work in increasing isolation and loneliness.

The physicist Max Planck wrote that "a new scientific truth does not triumph by convincing its opponents and making them see the light, but rather because its opponents eventually die, and a new generation grows up that is familiar with it" (Planck, 1949, p. 33).

Different schools of thought developed over the course of the history of psychology, each one an effective protest against what had gone before. Each new school used its older opponent as a base from which to push and gain momentum. Each position proclaimed loudly what it was not and how it differed from the older theoretical system. As the new system developed and gained adherents and influence, it inspired opposition, and the whole combative process began anew. What was once a pioneering, aggressive revolution became, with success, an established tradition, which then succumbed to the vigorous force of a youthful new movement. Success destroys vigor. A movement feeds on opposition. When the opposition has been defeated, the passion and ardor of the once new movement die.

Although the dominance of at least some of these schools was only temporary, each played a vital part in the development of psychology. The influence of the schools can be seen in contemporary psychology, although the factions in the psychology of today bear little similarity to the earlier systems because new doctrines have again replaced the old. The function of the schools of thought in psychology has been compared to that of the scaffolding used in erecting a tall building (Heidbreder, 1933). Without the scaffolding from which to work, the structure could not be built, yet the scaffolding does not remain; it will be torn down when it is no longer needed. Similarly, the structure of today's psychology has been built within the framework and guidelines—the scaffolding—established by the schools of thought.

We cannot consider any of these schools as complete accounts of scientific fact. They are not finished products in any sense. Rather, they provide the tools, methods, and conceptual schemes that psychology has used to accumulate and organize a body of scientific fact. As we have noted, the psychology of today is not in its final form. New schools have replaced the old but nothing guarantees their permanence in the evolutionary process of building a science. The schools of thought are temporary but necessary stages in the development of psychology.

It is in terms of the historical development of the schools of thought that the exciting advance of psychology can best be understood. Prominent individuals have made outstanding contributions and inspiring pronouncements, but their significance is most notable when considered within the context of the ideas that preceded theirs (on which they often built) and the work that followed.

We first describe the beginnings of experimental psychology (Chapters 2 and 3) and then discuss each of the major psychological schools on three levels: the prescientific development of the position, including the work of early scholars who developed their insights without using the experimental method, the early attempts to attack particular problems using the methods of science, and the formal establishment of each school and its contemporary derivatives.

A continuity of development emerges as we follow each school of thought to the one that subsequently replaced it. This orderly progression provides a framework for understanding the history of psychology. We examine five schools of thought and their interrelationships, showing how each depended on at least one other school or on work in other disciplines to help it define itself.

Structuralism developed from the early work in philosophy and physiology. This initial school of thought was followed by *functionalism, behaviorism,* and *Gestalt psychology,* which either evolved from or revolted against structuralism. On a roughly parallel course in time though not in subject matter, methods, or aims, *psychoanalysis* evolved from philosophical thought on the nature of the unconscious and from psychiatry's attempts to treat the mentally ill. Both psychoanalysis and behaviorism generated a number of subschools. In the 1950s, the humanistic movement developed in reaction to behaviorism and psychoanalysis, while incorporating principles of Gestalt psychology. Around 1960, the cognitive movement successfully challenged behaviorism, and our definition of psychology has once again changed. The major aspect of that change is a return to consciousness and to the study of mental or cognitive processes. Having lost its mind in the behaviorist revolution, psychology has now regained it. Thus, a design is apparent in the cumulative building process that distinguishes the century of the history of psychology, a process that continues today.

SUGGESTED READINGS

History of Science

Barnes, B. (1982). *T. S. Kuhn and social science.* New York: Columbia University Press.

Buss, A. R. (1978). The structure of psychological revolutions. *Journal of the History of the Behavioral Sciences, 14,* 57–64.

Kuhn, T. S. (1970). *The structure of scientific revolutions* (2nd ed.). Chicago: University of Chicago Press.

Simonton, D. K. (1984). *Genius, creativity, and leadership: Historiometric inquiries.* Cambridge, MA: Harvard University Press.

Staats, A. W. (1981). Paradigmatic behaviorism, unified theory, unified theory construction methods, and the Zeitgeist of separatism. *American Psychologist, 36,* 239–256.

History of Psychology

Henle, M. (1976). Why study the history of psychology? *Annals of the New York Academy of Sciences, 270,* 14–20.

Mueller, C. G. (1979). Some origins of psychology as science. *Annual Review of Psychology, 30,* 9–29.

Raphelson, A. C. (1982). The history course as the capstone of the psychology curriculum. *Journal of the History of the Behavioral Sciences, 18,* 279–285.

Sarup, G. (1978). Historical antecedents of psychology: The recurrent issue of old wine in new bottles. *American Psychologist, 33,* 478–485.

Watson, R. I. (1975). The history of psychology as a speciality: A personal view of its first 15 years. *Journal of the History of the Behavioral Sciences, 11,* 5–14.

2

Philosophical Influences on Psychology

THE SPIRIT OF MECHANISM

In the royal gardens of Europe in the seventeenth century there appeared a whimsical form of amusement among the many marvels of a truly exciting age. Water, running through underground pipes, operated mechanical figures that performed a variety of movements, played musical instruments, and even produced wordlike sounds. Hidden pressure plates, activated when people unknowingly stepped on them, sent water flowing through the pipes to the machinery that moved the statues.

These amusements of the aristocracy reflected and reinforced the seventeenth-century fascination with the miracle of the machine. All manner of machines were invented, perfected, and improved for use in science, industry, and entertainment. The mechanical clock—called by one historian "the mother of machines"—is the most important example in terms of its impact on scientific thought. Clockmakers were the first to apply theories from physics and mechanics to the construction of machines (Boorstin, 1983). In addition to clocks, pumps, levers, pulleys, and cranes were developed to serve human needs, and there seemed to be no limit to the kinds of machines that could be devised or the uses to which they could be put.

You may wonder what this has to do with the history of modern psychology. We refer, after all, to a time 200 years before the establishment of psychology as a science, focusing on technology and physics, disciplines seemingly far removed from the study of human nature. The relationship, however, is direct and compelling, because the principles embodied by those mechanical figures and clocks of the seventeenth century influenced the direction and form the new psychology would follow for most of its existence.

We are dealing here with the *Zeitgeist* of the seventeenth to nineteenth centuries, the intellectual soil that nourished the new psychology. The basic idea of the seventeenth century, the philosophy that would nurture the new psychology, was the spirit of *mechanism*, an image of the universe as the great machine.

This idea originated in physics (then known as *natural philosophy*) as a result of the work of Galileo and, later, Newton. The nature of everything that existed in the universe was believed to be nothing more than particles of matter in motion. According to Galileo, matter was composed of discrete corpuscles or atoms that affected each other by direct contact, as billiard balls do.[1]

If the universe consisted of atoms in motion, then every physical effect (the movement of each atom) would follow from a direct cause (the movement of the atom that struck it), and so should be subject to laws of measurement and calculation, and hence prediction. This game of billiards, the physical universe, was orderly, lawful, and predictable, like a clock or any other good machine. The physical universe was designed by God with absolute perfection (in the seventeenth century it was still possible for scientists to attribute cause and perfection to God), and once one knew the laws by which it functioned, it was possible to know how it would behave in the future.

The methods and findings of science were growing apace with technology during this time, and the two meshed effectively. *Observation* and *experimentation* came to be the hallmarks of science, followed closely by *measurement*. Scholars were soon attempting to define or describe every phenomenon by a number, a process vital to the study of the universe as a machine. Thermometers, barometers, slide rules, micrometers, pendulum clocks, and other measuring devices were developed and perfected in this age of the machine and served to reinforce the notion that it was possible to measure all aspects of the mechanical universe.

THE CLOCKWORK UNIVERSE

The perfect metaphor for this new spirit of mechanism was the clock, which has justly been called one of the greatest inventions of all time. Clocks were a technological sensation, not unlike computers today (Landes, 1983). No other machine had such an impact on human thought at all levels of society.

By the seventeenth century, clocks were being produced in large numbers and sizes. Some were small enough to fit on a mantelpiece. Larger ones, housed in the city's towers, could be seen and heard by all the residents. Whereas the mechanical figures in the royal gardens were visible only to the elite, clocks were available to everyone, regardless of his or her station in life. The concept of the mechanical clock "took possession of the minds and spirits of an entire civilization, in a way no other machine had ever done before. . . . Rarely in history has a machine so directly expressed, and in turn affected, the intellectual climate of its time" (Maurice & Mayr, 1980, pp. vii, ix).

Because of the visibility, regularity, and precision of clocks, scholars began to consider them as models for the physical universe. "Might not the universe itself be a vast clock made and set in motion by the Creator Himself?" The seventeenth-century British physicist Robert Boyle was one of many leading scientists—along with the German astronomer Johannes Kepler and René Descartes—who answered this question in the affirmative and who came to look upon the universe as a "great piece of clock work" (Boorstin, 1983, pp. 71, 72). The harmony and order of the universe could now be

---

[1]Newton later improved on the Galilean version of mechanism by postulating that movement was communicated not by physical contact, but by attracting and repelling forces. This idea, although important in physics, did not radically change the concept of mechanism and the way it was used in the new psychology.

explained in terms of the clock's regularity, which is built into the machine by the clockmaker just as the regularity of the universe was thought to be built into it by God.

A German philosopher, Christian Wolff, described the relationship between the clock and the universe in simple terms: "The universe behaves no differently than a clockwork." His student, Johann Cristoph Gottsched, elaborated on this principle (Maurice & Mayr, 1980, p. 290):

> Insofar as the universe is a machine, it has to that extent a resemblance to a clock; and it is in a clock that we can on a small scale make plainer to one's understanding that which takes place in the universe on a large scale. The wheels of the clock represent the parts of the universe; the motions of the hands, the events and changes taking place in the universe. Just as in the clock all positions of the wheels and the hands ensue from the inward arrangement, shape, size, and linkage of all its parts in accordance with the rules of motion, so everything that takes place in the universe also produces its effect.

When seen as a clocklike machine, the universe, once constructed and set in motion, will continue to function efficiently without any outside interference. The use of the clock metaphor also included the idea of *determinism*, the belief that every act is determined by past events. Thus, we can predict the changes that will occur in the clock as well as in the universe because of the regularity and order of the operation of its parts. Gottsched added: "He who has perfect insight into [the clock's] structure can see every future thing from its past and its present state of arrangement" (Maurice & Mayr, 1980, p. 290).

It was not difficult to gain perfect insight into the clock's structure. A person could easily disassemble a clock and see exactly how it operated. Hence, *reductionism* as a method of analysis was propagated as an article of faith in the new science. The workings of machines such as clocks could be understood by analyzing them, by reducing them to their basic components. Similarly, one could understand the physical universe (which, after all, was just another machine) by analyzing it into its simplest parts, its atoms and molecules. This method of analysis would come to characterize every science as it developed, including the new psychology.

If the clock metaphor and scientific analysis could be applied to an explanation of the workings of the physical universe, might they also hold for the study of human nature? If the universe were like a machine—orderly, predictable, observable, and measurable— could not human beings be considered in the same light? Were people—and animals— also a kind of machine?

The intellectual and social aristocracy of the seventeenth century already had the models for such a notion in the mechanical figures that amused them in their royal gardens. The proliferation of clocks provided similar models for everyone. At all levels of society, people had only to look around to see mechanical figures of humans and animals performing marvelous feats with precision and regularity.

Many of these automata can be seen today in the central squares of European cities where mechanical figures march and cavort, play musical instruments, and strike huge bells on the quarter hour. In the Strasbourg Cathedral in France, figures of the Magi bow hourly before a statue of the Virgin Mary while a rooster opens its beak, sticks out its tongue, and flaps its wings as it crows. At the Wells Cathedral in England, pairs of

Figure 2-1   Automaton figure of a monk

knights in armor circle each other in mock combat. As the bell strikes the hour, one knight knocks the other off his horse.

Craftsmen of the period also constructed such figures on a smaller scale. In the Bavarian National Museum in Munich, for example, is a parrot 16 inches tall. On the hour it whistles, moves its bill, flaps its wings, rolls its eyes, and defecates (a steel ball falls from its tail).

In Figure 2-1 you can see the inner workings of a 16-inch figure of a monk, now on display at the National Museum of American History in Washington, D.C. The monk is programmed to move within the space of a two-foot square. The feet appear to kick out from beneath the robe, but the statue is actually moving on wheels. It also beats its chest with its right arm and waves with its left. In addition, the monk turns his head from side to side, nods, opens and shuts his mouth, and rolls his eyes.

This kind of clockwork technology seemed to the philosophers and scientists of the time capable of fulfilling their long-held dream of creating a kind of artificial being. Indeed, many of the early clocks and automata clearly gave that appearance. We might consider them to be the Disneyland figures of their day, and it is easy to understand why people reached the conclusion that humans and animals were simply another form of machine.

Look again at the inner workings of the monk. We can comprehend the functioning of the gears, levers, ratchets, and other devices that account for the figure's movements almost at a glance. As we shall see, Descartes and other philosophers adopted these automata as at least partial models for human beings. Thus, not only was the universe a clockwork machine, so, too, were its people.

Descartes wrote that this idea would not

> appear at all strange to those who are acquainted with the different automata, or moving machines, fabricated by human industry . . . [for] such persons will look upon this body as a machine made by the hands of God, which is incomparably better arranged, and adequate to movements more admirable than in any machine of human invention. (Descartes, 1637/1912, p. 44)

People might be better machines than the ones the clockmakers could build, but they were machines nonetheless.

Thus, clocks paved the way for the idea that humans were mechanical and that the same experimental and quantitative methods that were so successful in exploring the secrets of the physical universe could be applied to the exploration of human nature. In 1748, the French physician Julien de La Mettrie, who later died of an overdose of pheasant and truffles, said, "Let us then conclude boldly that man is a machine." This theme became a driving force of the *Zeitgeist*, not only in philosophy, but in all aspects of life, and it drastically changed our image of ourselves.

And so there emerged during the seventeenth to nineteenth centuries the image of persons as machines and the method by which human nature could be investigated— the *scientific method*. People became machines, the modern world became dominated by the scientific outlook, and all aspects of life became subject to mechanical laws.

THE BEGINNINGS OF MODERN SCIENCE: RENÉ DESCARTES (1596–1650)

We noted that the seventeenth century saw far-ranging developments in science. Until that time philosophers had looked to the past for answers, to the works of Aristotle and other ancient scholars, and to the Bible. The ruling forces of inquiry were dogma and figures of authority.

In the seventeenth century a new force became dominant: *empiricism*, the pursuit of knowledge through the observation of nature. Knowledge handed down from the past became suspect. The golden age of the seventeenth century was illuminated by the discoveries and insights of many scholars who successfully created or reflected the changing atmosphere in which scientific inquiry was flourishing. Although they are important in the history of science, for the most part their work is not directly related to the evolution of psychology.

One scholar, René Descartes, did contribute directly to the history of modern psychology. More than anyone else, he freed inquiry from the rigid theological and traditional dogmas that had controlled it for centuries. "Not since Aristotle had a philosopher constructed a new and influential system of thought that took into account the sum of knowledge, which in two thousand years had grown so significantly" (Herrnstein & Boring, 1965, p. 581). Descartes, who symbolizes the transition from the Renaissance to the modern era of science, applied the idea of clockwork mechanism to the human body. Many believe that he thus inaugurated modern psychology.

The Life of Descartes

Descartes was born in the Touraine region of France in March 1596. His father was a councillor of the parliament of Brittany and from him Descartes inherited enough money to support his life of study and travel. Descartes, unlike others in similar circumstances, did not become a dilettante, a tendency apparently attributable to his genius, curiosity, and hunger for knowledge, his indifference to dogmatic authority, and his desire for evidence and proof.

From 1604 to 1612 he was a student at the Jesuit college at La Flèche, where he was educated in the humanities and mathematics and displayed considerable talent in philosophy, physics, and physiology. Because Descartes's health was frail, the rector, Father Charlet, excused him from morning religious duties and allowed him to lie in bed until noon, a habit he retained all his life. It was during these quiet mornings that he studied his lessons and did his most creative thinking.

After his formal education Descartes sampled the pleasures of Paris for a while and then, finding this life tiresome, went into seclusion to study mathematics. In 1617 he became a gentleman volunteer in the armies of Holland, Bavaria, and Hungary, a strange act for one of such a contemplative nature. He was, at various times in his life, very much a man of the world. He loved to dance and gamble, and he was a good gambler because of his mathematical talents. He was an adventurer and a swordsman who apparently partook of all the human vices and pleasures.

In addition to his theoretical work, Descartes was keenly interested in applying knowledge to practical concerns. He investigated techniques that might keep his hair from turning gray, and he conducted experiments on the use of wheelchairs by handicapped persons.

In November 1619, while serving in the army, Descartes had a series of dreams that would change his life radically. As he told it, he spent the day of November 10 alone in a stove-heated room, thinking about certain mathematical and scientific ideas. He fell asleep and in his dreams was, as he interpreted it, rebuked for his idleness and visited by the Spirit of Truth, which took possession of his mind. This profound experience persuaded him to devote his life to the proposition that mathematics could be applied to all the sciences and thus produce certainty of knowledge. He resolved to undertake no ties of marriage or friendship that might prevent him from pursuing these insights.

His only lasting romantic attachment was a three-year love affair with a Dutch servant

Among the contributions of French nativist philosopher René Descartes (1596–1650) to psychology were the doctrine of innate ideas and the theory of mind–body interaction.

girl, named Helen. In 1635 she gave birth to their child. Descartes adored the little girl and was heartbroken when she died at the age of five. He described the loss as the deepest sorrow of his life.

Although he returned to Paris in 1623 to pursue his favorite study of mathematics, Descartes found Parisian life too distracting. He sold the estates he had inherited and moved to a country house in Holland in 1628. His need for solitude and seclusion was so great during this period that he lived in 13 towns and 24 different houses over the next 20 years, keeping his address secret from all but his most intimate friends, with whom he corresponded voluminously. His only other apparent requirements were proximity to a Roman Catholic church and a university.

Most of Descartes's important works were written during these years in Holland, where freedom of thought was upheld. However, he did encounter some religious persecution. At one time booksellers were forbidden to sell his works and he was brought before the magistrates to answer the charges of the theologians of Utrecht and Leyden that he was an atheist and a profligate, serious charges against a devout Catholic. Descartes "was condemned by Catholics and Protestants alike. Since Roger Bacon, perhaps, no great thinker had been so completely abased and thwarted by theological oppression" (White, 1896/1965, p. 80).

Descartes's growing fame led Queen Christina of Sweden to invite him to instruct her in philosophy. Although reluctant to give up his freedom and solitude, he nonetheless had great respect for royal prerogative and went to Sweden on the warship sent to fetch him in the fall of 1649. The queen, who has been described as resembling a cavalry officer, was not a very good student and she insisted on starting her lessons at 5 every morning in the poorly heated library during an unusually bitter winter. Descartes withstood the early rising and extreme cold for four months before succumbing to pneumonia on February 11, 1650.

An interesting postscript to the death of a man who, as we shall see, devoted much of his life to the study of the interaction of the mind and the body, is the disposition of his own head and body. Sixteen years after Descartes's death, his friends decided that his body should be brought back to France. Unfortunately, the coffin they sent to Sweden was too short to contain the remains. The solution reached by the authorities was to cut off his head and re-inter it in Stockholm until arrangements could be made for its return to Paris.

In the process of preparing the corpse for the journey to France, the French ambassador to Sweden decided that he wanted a souvenir of the great man, and he severed the right forefinger. The body, now minus its head and one finger, was reburied in Paris amid much pomp and splendor. Some time later, an army officer dug up Descartes's skull and kept it as a memento. For 150 years, the skull changed hands from one Swedish collector to another until it finally reached Paris, where it is now on display at Musée de l'Homme.

The Contributions of Descartes:
Mechanism and the Mind–Body Problem

Descartes's most important work for the future development of psychology is his attempt to resolve the mind–body problem, an issue that had been controversial for centuries. Throughout the ages scholars had argued about how the mind or purely mental qualities could be distinguished from the body and all other physical qualities.

The basic and deceptively simple question is this: Are mind and body—the mental world and the material world—distinct essences or natures? Since the time of Plato most scholars had taken a dualistic position; that is, it was held that mind and body were of different natures. However, the acceptance of that position raises another question: What is the nature of the relationship between mind and body? Does one influence the other, or are they independent?

The theory held before Descartes was that there was essentially a one-way effect: the mind could exert an enormous influence on the body, but the body had little effect on the mind. The mind and body were thought to be related to each other in the way a puppeteer and puppet are joined together. In this view, the mind is like the puppeteer, pulling the strings of the body (Lowry, 1982).

Descartes accepted the dualistic position. In his view, mind and body were indeed different, although he deviated from tradition in the definition of the relationship between the two he proposed in his theory of mind–body interaction. It is true, Descartes said, that the mind influences the body, but the body can exert a much greater influence on the mind than previously had been supposed. The relationship is one of mutual interaction. This idea, radical in the seventeenth century, had important implications.

After Descartes proposed this doctrine, scholars no longer believed that the mind (or soul or spirit) was the master of the two entities, the puppeteer functioning almost independently of the body. The body, the material side of human beings, came to be seen as more central, and certain functions previously attributed to the mind were now considered to be functions of the body. For example, in the Middle Ages the mind was held to be responsible not only for thought and reason, but also for reproduction, perception, and locomotion. Descartes argued that the mind had only one function, that of thought. All the other processes were functions of the body.

Descartes was the first to offer an approach to the mind–body problem that focused attention on a strictly physical–*psychological* duality. In so doing, he diverted attention from the abstract concept of the soul to the study of the mind and its mental operations. As a result, methods of inquiry changed from metaphysical analysis to objective observation. Whereas one could only speculate on the existence of the soul, the mind and its processes could be observed.

Mind and body, then, are two separate entities. There is no qualitative similarity between the body or the physical world and the mind. Matter and body are substances with extension in space that operate according to mechanical principles. The mind is unextended, free, and lacking in substance. But the most important point, the idea that was revolutionary, was that mind and body, although distinct, are capable of interacting within the human organism. The mind can influence the body and the body can influence the mind.

Let us take a more detailed look at Descartes's conception of the body. Because the body is composed of physical matter, it must possess those characteristics common to all matter, extension in space and capability of movement. If the body is matter, then the laws of physics and mechanics that account for movement and action in the physical world must also apply to the body. When the body is considered apart from the mind (and it can be so considered because the two are separate entities), the body is like a machine whose operation can be explained by the mechanical laws that govern the movement of objects in space. Following this line of reasoning, Descartes proceeded to account for physiological functioning in physical terms.

Descartes was strongly influenced by the mechanistic spirit of the age as reflected in the mechanical clocks and figures mentioned earlier. While recovering from what biographers have described as a nervous breakdown at the age of 18, he recuperated in a small village near Paris where the only amusement available to him was the recently completed royal gardens. He was fascinated by their mechanical marvels and spent hours walking on the pressure plates that caused the figures to move and dance and speak (Jaynes, 1970).

This experience helped to shape his view of the physical universe, in particular, his view of the human and animal body. He believed that the body operated exactly like a machine. Indeed, he recognized no difference between the hydraulically operated figures and the body, and he explained every aspect of physical functioning (digestion, circulation, sensation, motion) in mechanical terms.

When Descartes described the body, he referred to the figures he had seen in the royal gardens. He compared the body's nerves to the pipes through which the water passed, and the muscles and tendons to engines and springs. The movement of the mechanical models was not caused by voluntary action on their part but by external objects; the involuntary nature of this movement was reflected in Descartes's observation that movements of the body frequently occur without the individual's conscious intention. From this line of thought he arrived at the idea of the *undulatio reflexa*, a movement not supervised or determined by a will to move. Because of this proposal, he is often called the author of the theory of reflex action. This idea of reflex action can also be seen as a precursor of modern stimulus–response psychology, in which an external object (a stimulus) brings about an involuntary response.

Support for his mechanical interpretation of the workings of the human body came from the exciting advances in physiology, of which Descartes was aware. In 1628 William Harvey, an English physician, had discovered the gross facts about the circulation of the blood, and much was being learned about the process of digestion. It was also known that the muscles of the body worked in opposing pairs, and that sensation and movement somehow depended on the nerves. Physiological researchers had made great strides in understanding the human body, although their information was far from complete. The nerves, for instance, were thought to·be hollow tubes through which animal spirits flowed. Our concern, however, is not with the accuracy or comprehensiveness of seventeenth-century knowledge of human physiology, but rather with its consonance with a mechanical interpretation of the body.

Because animals did not possess souls, they were believed to be automata. Thus, the difference between humans and animals so important to the Christian religion was preserved. Also, animals were thought to be devoid of feelings. How could they have feelings if they did not have souls? Descartes dissected live animals, before anesthesia was available, and was described as "amused at their cries and yelps since these were nothing but the hydraulic hisses and vibrations of machines" (Jaynes, 1970, p. 224).

These ideas were part of an overall trend toward the notion that human behavior is predictable. The mechanical body will move and behave in expected ways so long as the inputs are known. Animals, being totally machinelike, belong entirely to the category of physical phenomena. Hence, animals have no immortality, are incapable of thought, and have no freedom of will. Descartes made some minor revisions in his thinking about animals in later years, but he never altered his conviction that animal behavior can be explained in mechanistic terms.

Descartes's writings frequently refer to the clocklike nature of animals. "I know quite well that animals do many things better than we, but that does not astonish me; for precisely that serves to prove that they act naturally and by such spring forces as a clock which indicates what time it is far better than our judgment tells us" (Maurice & Mayr, 1980, p. 5).

The nonmaterial mind, according to Descartes, is capable of thought and consciousness, and, consequently, provides us with knowledge about our external world. The mind has none of the properties of matter. The most important characteristic of the mind is its capacity to think, and this sets it apart from the physical world of matter. This thinking entity is lacking in substance and unextended in space.

Because the mind perceives and wills, it must somehow influence and be influenced by the body. When the mind decides to move from one point to another, for example, this decision is carried out by the body's nerves and muscles. Similarly, when the body is stimulated, for example, by light or heat, the mind recognizes and interprets these sensory data and determines the appropriate response.

Descartes eventually formulated a theory about the interaction of these different entities. First, he needed to find a physical point where the mind and the body engaged in their mutual influence. Several criteria were involved in the search for this place of interaction. Descartes conceived of the soul as unitary, which meant that it must interact with only one part of the body. He also believed that the point of interaction was somewhere within the brain because research had demonstrated that sensations travel to the brain and that movement originates within the brain. Clearly, then, the brain had to be the focal point for the mind's functions. The only structure of the brain that is single and unitary (that is, not divided and duplicated in each hemisphere) is the *pineal body*, or *conarium*, and Descartes considered this the logical choice for a point of interaction.

The manner in which this interaction between mind and body takes place was described in mechanistic terms. Descartes suggested that the movement of the animal spirits in the nerve tubes produces an impression on the conarium, and from this impression the mind produces a sensation. In other words, a quantity of motion (the flow of animal spirits) produces a purely mental quality (a sensation). The reverse also occurs, in that the mind can somehow make an impression on the conarium (in a manner never made clear), which, by inclining to one direction or another, influences the direction of the flow of the animal spirits to the muscles, resulting in a movement. Thus, a mental quality can influence motion, a property of the body.

Descartes did not maintain that the soul was confined or contained in the conarium. The conarium was designated only as the site of the interaction. He believed that the soul was united with all parts of the body and that the entire body becomes the "seat of the soul."

Descartes's *doctrine of ideas* also had a profound influence on the subsequent development of psychology. He proposed that the mind gives rise to two kinds of ideas: *derived* and *innate*. Derived ideas are those produced by the direct application of an external stimulus, such as the sound of a bell or the sight of a tree. Thus, derived ideas are products of the experiences of the senses. Of greater importance is the notion of innate ideas, which are not produced by objects in the external world that impinge on the senses. The label *innate* describes their source. They develop out of the mind or consciousness alone. The potential existence of innate ideas is independent of sense experience, although they may be realized or actualized in the presence of appropriate sense experiences. Some of the innate ideas identified by Descartes are self, God, geometric axioms, perfection, and infinity.

The conception of innate ideas is discussed in later chapters. It eventually culminates in the nativistic theory of perception and the Gestalt school of psychology. We also will see its influence in the spirited opposition it inspired among the early British empiricists and associationists, and among the more modern empiricists such as Helmholtz and Wundt.

The work of Descartes served as a catalyst for many trends that later became prominent in psychology. His most noteworthy systematic contributions are the mechanistic conception of the body, the theory of mind–body interaction, the localization of the mind's functions in the brain, and the doctrine of innate ideas. With Descartes we see the doctrine of mechanism applied to the human body. So pervasive was the mechanistic philosophy, however, that it was only a matter of time before the human mind would also be reduced to nothing more than a machine. It is to that significant event that we now turn.

BRITISH EMPIRICISM AND ASSOCIATIONISM: ACQUIRING KNOWLEDGE THROUGH EXPERIENCE

After Descartes, the development of modern science in general and of psychology in particular was rapid and prolific. By the middle of the nineteenth century, the long period of prescientific psychology had come to an end. During this time European philosophical thought became infused with a new spirit, *positivism*. The term and the conception are the work of Auguste Comte, who was undertaking a systematic survey of all knowledge, an ambitious project indeed. To make the task more manageable, Comte decided to limit his work to facts that were beyond question, those facts that had been determined through the methods of science. Positivism, then, refers to a system based exclusively on facts that are objectively observable and not debatable. Everything of a speculative, inferential, or metaphysical nature is rejected as illusory.

The acceptance of positivism meant that there were now two types of propositions. "One refers to the objects of sense, and it is a scientific statement. The other is nonsense!" (Robinson, 1981, p. 333). Knowledge derived from metaphysics and theology was to be rejected. Only knowledge derived from science was seen to be valid.

Other ideas supporting antimetaphysical positivism were extant in philosophy. Those subscribing to *materialism* believed that all things could be described in physical terms and understood in the light of the physical properties of matter and energy. They thought that consciousness could also be explained in the terms of physics and chemistry. Materialist considerations of mental processes focused on the physical aspect—the anatomical and physiological structure—of the brain.

A third group of philosophers, advocating *empiricism*, were then active. They were concerned with how the mind acquires knowledge, and they argued that all knowledge is derived from sensory experience.

The popular conception of human nature and the world was rapidly changing. Positivism, materialism, and empiricism were to become the philosophical foundations of the new psychology. Discussions of psychological processes were beginning to be conducted within a framework of factual, observational, and quantitative evidence based on sensory experience, and increasing emphasis was being placed on the physiological processes involved in mental functioning.

Of these three philosophical orientations, empiricism played the major role in shaping the early development of the new science of psychology. Empiricism related to the growth of the mind, to how the mind acquires knowledge. According to the empiricist view, the mind grows through the progressive accumulation of sensory experiences. This idea contrasts with the nativistic viewpoint exemplified by Descartes, which states that some ideas are innate. We will now consider some of the major British empiricists: Locke, Berkeley, Hume, Hartley, and Mill.

John Locke (1632–1704)

Locke, the son of an attorney, studied at Westminster and Oxford in England and received his bachelor's degree in 1656 and his master's degree shortly thereafter. He remained at Oxford for several years, tutoring in Greek, rhetoric, and philosophy, then took up the practice of medicine. He had also developed an interest in politics and in 1667 went to London to become secretary to the Earl of Shaftesbury and, in time, the confidant and friend of this controversial statesman. Shaftesbury's influence declined, and in 1681, after participating in a plot against King Charles II, he fled to Holland. Although Locke was not involved in the plot, his relationship with Shaftesbury brought him under suspicion, and he too fled to Holland. In 1689 he was able to return to England, where he became commissioner of appeals and began to write on education, religion, and economics. He was particularly concerned with religious freedom and the right of all people to govern themselves. His writings brought him much fame and power, and he was heralded throughout Europe as a champion of liberalism in government.

Locke's major work of importance to psychology is *An Essay Concerning Human Understanding* (1690) which was the culmination of some 20 years of study and thought. This book, which had appeared in four editions by 1700 and had been translated into French and Latin, marked the formal beginning of British empiricism.

Locke was concerned primarily with cognitive functioning, the ways in which the mind acquires knowledge. In attacking this issue, he denied the existence of Descartes's innate ideas, arguing that humans are not equipped at birth with any knowledge whatever. He admitted that certain concepts (such as the idea of God) may seem to adults to be innate because adults have been taught those ideas since childhood and cannot remember any time when they were unaware of them. Thus, Locke explained the apparent innateness of ideas in terms of learning and habit.

How, then, does the mind acquire knowledge? To Locke, the answer was through experience. All knowledge is empirically derived. In a frequently quoted passage from his *Essay*, Locke noted:

> Let us then suppose the mind to be, as we say, white paper, void of all characters, without any ideas:—How comes it to be furnished? Whence comes it by that vast store which the busy and boundless fancy of man has painted on it with an almost endless variety? Whence has it all the *materials* of reason and knowledge? To this I answer, in one word, from EXPERIENCE. In that all our knowledge is founded; and from that it ultimately derives itself. (Locke, 1690/1959)[2]

[2]Aristotle had a similar notion—that the mind at birth was a *tabula rasa*, a blank slate on which experience would write.

British empiricist John
Locke (1632–1704)
argued that at birth the
mind is a blank slate that
acquires knowledge only
through sense experience.

Locke recognized two different kinds of experiences, one deriving from *sensation* and the other from *reflection*. Some ideas arise from direct sensory input from physical objects in the environment. They are simple sense impressions. In addition to the operation of sensations on the mind, however, the operation of the mind itself in the act of reflecting on these sensations, can give rise to ideas. The mental or cognitive function of reflection as a source of ideas also depends on sensory experience, because the ideas produced by reflection are based on those already experienced through the senses.

In the development of the individual, sensation appears first. It is a necessary precursor to reflection because there must first be a reservoir of sense impressions for the mind to be able to reflect. In reflection, the individual remembers past sensory impressions and combines them in various ways to form abstractions and other higher-level ideas. All ideas, no matter how abstract and complex, arise from these two sources, but the ultimate source remains sense impressions or experience.

Locke also distinguished between *simple* and *complex ideas*. Simple ideas can arise from both sensation and reflection, are received passively by the mind, and are elemental or unanalyzable, that is, they cannot be reduced to simpler ideas. As noted, the mind, through the process of reflection, can actively create new ideas by combining other ideas. These derived ideas are what Locke called complex ideas, and they are formed from simple ideas of both sensation and reflection. Complex ideas are compounded of simple ideas, and hence are capable of being analyzed or resolved into simple ideas.

This notion of a mental combination or compounding of ideas and their analysis marks the beginning of the mental chemistry that characterizes the theory of *association*, in which simple ideas may be linked to form complex ideas. Association is an early name for the process that would come to be called learning. The reduction or analysis of mental life into elements—the simple ideas and the association of these elements to form complex ideas—formed the core of the new scientific psychology. Just as clocks and other machines could be reduced to their component parts and those parts reassembled to form the complex machine, so could human ideas.

In essence, Locke treated the mind as though it behaved in accord with the laws of the physical universe. The basic particles or atoms of the mental world were the simple ideas, which were conceptually analogous to the material atoms in the Galilean–Newtonian mechanistic scheme. "It is possible to see the whole of Locke's psychology as a kind of Newtonian cosmos in miniature" (Lowry, 1982, p. 21). The basic elements of the mind are indivisible. They cannot be broken down into anything simpler and, like their counterparts in the material world, they can join in various ways to form more complex structures. This was a significant step in the direction of considering the mind, like the body, to be a machine.

Another Lockean doctrine of considerable interest to psychology is the notion of *primary* and *secondary qualities* as they apply to simple ideas of sense. Primary qualities exist in the object whether or not we perceive them. For instance, the size and shape of a building are primary qualities, whereas the color of the building is a secondary quality. It is not inherent in the object but is dependent on the experiencing person. Secondary qualities, such as color, odor, sound, and taste, are not in the object but exist in a person's perception of the object. The tickle of a feather is not in the feather itself but in our reaction to the feather. The pain inflicted by a knife is not in the knife itself but in our experience in relation to the knife.

A simple experiment will illustrate this doctrine. Prepare three containers of water—one cold, one lukewarm, and one hot. Place one hand in cold water and the other in hot water, then place both hands in the pan of lukewarm water. One hand will perceive this water as warm and the other will perceive it as cool. The lukewarm water, of course, is one temperature; it is not both warm and cool at the same time. The qualities or experience of heat and cold must exist only in our perception and not in the object (the water).

To repeat, secondary qualities exist only in the act of perception. If we did not bite into a peach, its taste would not exist. Primary qualities, such as the shape of the peach, exist in it whether we perceive them or not.

Locke was not the first to make a distinction between primary and secondary qualities. Galileo had proposed essentially the same point: "I think that if ears, tongues, and noses were removed, shapes and numbers and motions [primary qualities] would remain, but not odors nor tastes nor sounds [secondary qualities]. The latter, I believe, are nothing more than names when separated from living beings" (Boas, 1961, p. 262). The position is necessarily congruent with the spirit of mechanism, and Locke admitted as much when he noted that the distinction resulted from "a little excursion into natural philosophy."

The mechanistic view of the universe held that matter in motion constituted the only objective reality. If matter were all that existed objectively, it would follow that perception of anything else, such as colors, odors, and tastes, would be subjective. Therefore, the primary qualities are all that can exist independently of the perceiver.

In making this distinction, Locke recognized the subjectivity of much of our perception of the world, an idea that enhanced his need to understand the mind and its world of conscious experience. He introduced the secondary qualities in an attempt to explain the lack of precise correspondence between the physical world and our perception of it.

Once scholars accepted the distinction in theory between primary and secondary qualities—that some existed in reality and others existed only in our perception—it was inevitable that someone would ask whether there was, after all, any real difference between primary and secondary qualities. Perhaps all perception is in terms of secondary qualities, that is, subjective and dependent on the observer. The person who did ask and answer this question was George Berkeley.

George Berkeley (1685–1753)

Berkeley was born and educated in Ireland. A deeply religious man, he was ordained a deacon in the Anglican Church at the age of 24. Shortly after, he published two philosophical works that were to exert an influence on psychology: *An Essay towards a New Theory of Vision* (1709) and *A Treatise concerning the Principles of Human Knowledge* (1710).

With these two books, his contribution to psychology ended. He traveled extensively throughout Europe and held a number of posts in Ireland, including a teaching position at Trinity College, Dublin. He became financially independent through a sizable gift of money from a woman he had met once at a dinner party. He traveled in the United States, spending three years at Newport, Rhode Island, and gave his house and library to Yale University when he departed. The last years of his life were spent as Bishop of Cloyne.

Berkeley's fame (or at least his name) lingers in the United States today. In the mid-nineteenth century a clergyman from Yale, the Reverend Henry Durant, established an academy in California. He named it Berkeley in honor of the good bishop, perhaps in recognition of Berkeley's poem ("*On the Prospect of Planting Arts and Learning in America*"), which includes the line: "Westward the course of empire takes its way."

Berkeley agreed with Locke that all knowledge of the external world comes from experience, but he disagreed with Locke's distinction between primary and secondary qualities. Berkeley argued that there are no primary qualities. There are only what Locke called secondary qualities. To Berkeley, all knowledge was a function of the experiencing or perceiving person. The name given to his position some years later was *mentalism*, to denote Berkeley's emphasis on purely mental phenomena.

Berkeley stated that perception is the only reality of which we can be sure. We cannot know with certainty the nature of physical objects in the experiential world. All we can know is how we perceive these objects. Because perception is within ourselves and thus subjective, it does not mirror the external world. A physical object is nothing more than an accumulation of sensations experienced concurrently, so that force of habit renders them associated in the human mind. The experiential world is the summation of our sensations.

There is, then, no material substance of which we can be certain because if we take away the perception, the quality disappears. There can be no color without the perception of color, no shape or motion without the perception of shape or motion. However, Berkeley was not saying that real objects exist in the material world only when they are perceived. His thesis was that because all experience is within ourselves, relative to our own perception, we can never know with certainty the physical nature of objects. We can depend only on our perception of them.

Berkeley recognized, however, that there was a degree of independence, consistency, and stability in the objects in the material world, and he had to find some way to account for this. He did so by invoking God. (He was, after all, a bishop.) God functioned as a kind of permanent perceiver of all the objects in the universe. A tree in the forest could therefore be said to exist and to possess certain characteristics even if no one were there to perceive it, because God would always be perceiving it.

Berkeley applied the theory of association to explain our knowledge of objects in the real world. This knowledge is essentially a construction or composition of simple ideas or mental elements bound by the mortar of association. Complex ideas are formed by the joining of simple ideas received through the various senses, as explained in the following paragraph from Berkeley's *An Essay towards a New Theory of Vision* (1709/1957).

> Sitting in my study I hear a coach drive along the street; I look through the casement and see it; I walk out and enter into it. Thus, common speech would incline one to think, I heard, saw, and touched the same thing, to wit, the coach. It is nevertheless certain the ideas intromitted by each sense are widely different, and distinct from each other; but, having been observed constantly to go together, they are spoken of as one and the same thing.

Thus, the mind constructs complex ideas by fitting together the simple ideas, the basic building blocks of the mind. The mechanical analogy in the use of the words *construct* and *building blocks* is not coincidental.

Berkeley also used association to explain depth perception. He explored the problem of perceiving the third dimension of depth with a retina of only two dimensions. His answer was that we perceive depth as a result of our experience, that is, through the recurring association of visual impressions with the sensations of touch and movement that occur in the ocular adjustments and accommodations made when we look at objects at different distances, or in the bodily movements made in approaching or retreating from the objects that we see. In other words, the continuous sensory experiences of walking toward or reaching for objects, plus the sensations from the eye muscles, become associated to produce the perception of depth. When an object is brought closer to the eyes, the pupils will converge. This convergence diminishes when the object is moved away. Thus, depth perception is not a simple sensory experience, but rather an association of ideas that must be learned.

Here, perhaps for the first time, a purely psychological process was explained in terms of the association of sensations, and thus Berkeley was continuing the growing associationist trend in empiricism. His explanation accurately anticipated the modern view of depth perception in its consideration of the influences of the physiological cues of accommodation and convergence.

David Hume (1711–1776)

Hume, a philosopher and historian, studied law at the University of Edinburgh but did not graduate. He embarked on a career in business but found this not to his liking, so he lived on his small income during three years of self-study in philosophy in France. After returning to England, he published *A Treatise of Human Nature* (1739), his most important work for psychology. Other books followed, and he gained much fame as a writer while working as a tutor, companion, secretary, librarian, and judge advocate in a military expedition. He was well received in Europe and held several posts in government.

Hume supported Locke's notion of the compounding of simple ideas into complex ideas, developing and making more explicit the theory of association. He agreed with Berkeley that the material world did not exist for the individual until it was perceived, and he took this idea a step further. He also abolished mind as a substance and said that it was a secondary quality like matter. The mind is observable only through perception, and it is nothing more than the flow of ideas, sensations, and memories.

Of greater importance to psychology is the distinction Hume drew between two kinds of mental contents: *impressions* and *ideas*. Impressions are the basic elements of mental life and are akin to "sensation" and "perception" in today's terminology. Ideas are the mental experiences we have in the absence of any stimulating object; the modern equivalent is "image."

Hume did not define impressions and ideas in physiological terms or in reference to any external stimulus. He was careful not to assign any ultimate causes to impressions. These mental contents differ not in their source or point of origin but in their relative strength. Impressions are strong and vivid, whereas ideas are but weak copies of impressions. Both of these mental contents may be simple or complex, and a simple idea resembles its simple impression. Complex ideas do not necessarily resemble any simple idea because complex ideas evolve from a combination of several simple ideas in some new pattern.

Complex ideas are compounded from simple ideas by association. Hume proposed two laws of association: *resemblance* or similarity, and *contiguity* in time or place. The more similar and contiguous are two ideas, the more readily they will be associated.

Hume's work fits within the mechanistic framework and continues the development of empiricism and associationism. He argued that just as astronomers had determined the laws and forces by which the planets function, so it is possible to determine the laws of the mental universe. He believed that the laws of the association of ideas were the

David Hartley (1705–1757) formalized the doctrine of associationism, which he used to explain all forms of mental activity.

mental counterpart of the law of gravity in physics, a universal principle of the operation of the mind. Once again we see the notion that complex ideas are constructed mechanically by an amalgamation of simple ideas.

David Hartley (1705–1757)

Hartley, the son of a minister, was preparing for a career in the church, but because of doctrinal difficulties, he turned to medicine instead. He led a quiet and uneventful life, practicing medicine and studying philosophy. In 1749 he published *Observations on*

Man, His Frame, His Duty, and His Expectations, his most important work, often considered the first systematic discourse on association.

Hartley is noteworthy not so much for the originality of his ideas on association but for the clarity and precision with which he organized and systematized previous work. The premises of the doctrine of the association of ideas are not new with Hartley, as we have seen, but he served the significant purpose of bringing together the earlier threads of thought. Therefore, he is often acknowledged as the founder of associationism as a formal doctrine.

Hartley's fundamental law of association is *contiguity*, by which he attempted to explain the processes of memory, reasoning, emotion, and voluntary and involuntary action. Those ideas or sensations that occur together, simultaneously or successively, become associated, so that the occurrence of one results in the occurrence of the other. Thus, repetition as well as contiguity is necessary for the formation of associations.

Hartley agreed with Locke that all ideas and knowledge are derived from sensory experience; there are no associations present at birth. As the child grows and accumulates a variety of sensory experiences, connections and trains of association of increasing complexity are established. In this way, higher systems of thought develop by the time the person reaches adulthood. Higher-order mental life may be analyzed or reduced to the elements or atoms from which it was formed through the mental compounding of associations. Hartley was the first to use the doctrine of association to explain all types of mental activity.

Like others before him, Hartley viewed the mental world in mechanistic terms. In one respect he went beyond the aims of the earlier empiricists and associationists. Not only did he explain psychological processes in mechanical terms, but he also tried to explain their underlying physiological processes within the same framework. It seems a natural thing for him to have attempted because of his training in medicine, which few of his predecessors in philosophy shared.

Newton had stated that impulses in the physical world are vibratory in nature. Hartley used this principle to explain the operation of the brain and nervous system. Vibrations in the nerves (which he believed were solid tubes, not hollow as Descartes had thought) transmitted impulses from one part of the body to another. These vibrations initiate smaller vibrations in the brain, which Hartley considered to be the physiological counterparts of ideas. The importance of this notion for our purposes is not whether the details are correct but the fact that it was yet another attempt to use knowledge of the mechanical universe as a model for the understanding of human nature.

James Mill (1773–1836)

Mill was educated at Edinburgh and served for a short time as a clergyman, but left the Church of Scotland to earn his livelihood as a writer. His books were many and varied, and his most famous literary work is the *History of British India*, which took 11 years to write. His most important contribution to psychology is *Analysis of the Phenomena of the Human Mind* (1829).

Mill applied the doctrine of mechanism to the human mind with a directness and comprehensiveness not shown by his predecessors. His goal was to destroy the idea of subjective, psychic activities and to demonstrate that the mind was nothing more than a machine. Mill believed that other empiricists, in arguing that the mind was similar to a machine in its operations, had not gone far enough. The mind *was* a machine—it functioned in the same mechanical way as a clock—and it was set in operation by external physical forces and run by internal physical forces.

In Mill's view, the mind is a passive entity, acted upon by external stimuli. The person responds to these stimuli automatically and is incapable of acting spontaneously. Obviously, Mill saw no freedom of the will. This point of view persists in the forms of psychology that have derived from the mechanistic tradition, notably Skinnerian behaviorism.

As the title of his major work suggests, Mill believed that the mind should be studied by reducing or analyzing it into elementary components. This is, as we have seen, a tenet of mechanism. To understand complex phenomena in the mental or the physical world—for example, ideas or clocks—it is necessary to break them down into their smallest parts. Mill wrote that "a distinct knowledge of the elements is indispensable to an accurate conception of that which is compounded of them" (1829, Vol. 1, p. 1).

He suggested that sensations and ideas are the only kinds of mental elements that exist. In the familiar empiricist–associationist tradition, all knowledge begins with sensations, from which are derived the higher-level complexes of ideas through the process of association. To Mill, association is a matter of contiguity or concurrence alone and may be either synchronous or successive.

Mill believed that the mind has no creative function because association is a passive process. In other words, sensations that have occurred together in a certain order will be reproduced mechanically as ideas, and these ideas occur in the same order as their corresponding sensations. Association is treated in mechanical terms, and the resulting ideas are merely the accumulation or sum of the individual elements.

CONTRIBUTIONS OF EMPIRICISM TO PSYCHOLOGY

With the development of empiricism, philosophers turned away from the earlier approaches to knowledge. They were still concerned with many of the same problems, but their approach to these problems had become atomistic, mechanistic, and positivistic.

Reconsider the emphases of empiricism: the primary role of the processes of sensation, the analysis of conscious experience into elements, the synthesis of elements to form more complex mental experiences through the mechanism of association, and the focus on conscious processes. The major role empiricism played in shaping the new scientific psychology will soon be evident. We will see that the concerns of the empiricists formed the basic subject matter of psychology.

By the mid-nineteenth century, philosophy had done all it could. The theoretical rationale for a natural science of human nature had been established. What was needed to translate the theory into actuality was an experimental attack on the subject matter. And that was soon to develop under the influence of experimental physiology, which provided the kinds of experimentation that laid the foundation for the new psychology.

SUGGESTED READINGS

Mechanism and the Clockwork Universe

Butterfield, H. (1959). *The origins of modern science: 1300–1800*. New York: Macmillan.

Crombie, A. C. (1964). Early concepts of the senses and the mind. *Scientific American, 210*, 108–116.

Jaynes, J. (1970). The problem of animate motion in the seventeenth century. *Journal of the History of Ideas, 31*, 219–234.

Landes, D. S. (1983). *Revolution in time: Clocks and the making of the modern world*. Cambridge, MA: Harvard University Press.

Lowry, R. (1982). *The evolution of psychological theory: 1650 to the present* (2nd ed.). New York: Aldine.

Matson, F. W. (1964). *The broken image: Man, science and society*. New York: George Braziller.

Sarton, G. (1957). *Six wings: Men of science in the Renaissance*. Bloomington: Indiana University Press.

Descartes and the Mind–Body Problem

Balz, A. (1952). *Descartes and the modern mind*. New Haven, CT: Yale University Press.

Broughton, J., & Mattern, R. (1978). Reinterpreting Descartes on the notion of the union of mind and body. *Journal of the History of Philosophy, 16*, 23–32.

Fearing, R. (1929). René Descartes: A study in the history of the theories of reflex action. *Psychological Review, 36*, 375–388.

Scher, J. M. (Ed.). (1962). *Theories of the mind*. New York: Free Press.

Tibbetts, P. (1973). An historical note on Descartes' psychophysical dualism. *Journal of the History of the Behavioral Sciences, 9*, 162–165.

British Empiricism and Associationism

Bricke, J. (1974). Hume's associationist psychology. *Journal of the History of the Behavioral Sciences, 10*, 397–409.

Drever, J. (1965). The historical background for national trends in psychology: On nonexistence of English Associationism. *Journal of the History of the Behavioral Sciences, 1*, 123–130.

Miller, E. F. (1971). Hume's contribution to behavioral science. *Journal of the History of the Behavioral Sciences, 7*, 154–168.

Misiak, H. (1961). *The philosophical roots of scientific psychology*. New York: Fordham University Press.

Moore-Russell, M. E. (1978). The philosopher and society: John Locke and the English revolution. *Journal of the History of the Behavioral Sciences, 14*, 65–73.

Oberg, B. B. (1976). David Hartley and the association of ideas. *Journal of the History of Ideas, 37*, 441–454.

Rand, B. (1923). The early development of Hartley's doctrine of association. *Psychological Review, 30*, 306–320.

Rasmussen, E. T. (1953). Berkeley and modern psychology. *British Journal for the Philosophy of Science, 4*, 2–12.

Warren, H. C. (1916). Mental association from Plato to Hume. *Psychological Review, 23*, 208–230.

3

Physiological Influences on Psychology

It all started with a difference of five-tenths of a second in the observations made by two astronomers. The year was 1795. The royal astronomer of England, Nicholas Maskelyne, noticed that his assistant's observations of the time it took for a star to pass from one point to another were always slower than his own. Maskelyne admonished the man for making repeated mistakes and warned him to be more careful. The assistant tried, but the differences persisted. In time they increased, and five months later his observations were eight-tenths of a second slower than Maskelyne's. As a result the assistant was fired, and passed into that crowded place known as obscurity.

For the next 20 years the incident was ignored, until the phenomenon was investigated by F. W. Bessel, a German astronomer, who had long been interested in errors of measurement. He suspected that the mistakes made by Maskelyne's assistant were attributable to individual differences, over which one has no control. If this supposition were correct, Bessel reasoned, then such differences in observation would be found among all astronomers. He tested the hypothesis and found it to be correct. Differences were common, even among the most experienced and famous of astronomers.

This finding was important because it pointed to two inexorable conclusions. First, it meant that astronomy would have to take into account the nature of the human observer because personal characteristics could influence the observations reported. Second, if the role of the human observer had to be considered in astronomy, then surely it would also have to be considered in every other science in which human observers were employed.

We described how philosophers such as Locke and Berkeley discussed the subjective nature of perception, arguing that there is not always, or even often, an exact correspondence between the nature of an object and an individual's perception of it. Here we have data from a hard science, astronomy, to demonstrate the same thing.

Scientists now had to focus on the role of the human observer and the nature of the process of observation to account fully for their results. It was this "methodological problem in astronomy that convinced the scientific community that their knowledge of the physical world would not be complete without an understanding of the mental processes through which the scientist was able to make his observations" (Kirsch, 1976, p. 120).

Science was forced to turn to the study of sensing and perceiving—psychological processes—through the study of the sense organs, those physiological mechanisms whereby we receive information about the world. And so the early physiologists began to investigate the process of sensation. Psychology was but a short and inevitable step away.

DEVELOPMENTS IN EARLY PHYSIOLOGY: AN OVERVIEW

The physiological research that directly stimulated and guided the new psychology was a product of the late nineteenth century. As with all endeavors, it had its antecedents, and it is instructive to consider that earlier work in physiology.

Physiology became an experimentally oriented discipline during the 1830s, primarily under the influence of the German physiologist Johannes Müller (1801–1858), who strongly advocated the application of the experimental method to physiology. Müller was a phenomenally productive scientist, publishing, on the average, one scholarly paper every seven weeks. He maintained this pace for 38 years (Boakes, 1984). One of his most influential publications was the *Handbuch der Physiologie des Menschen (Handbook of Physiology of Man)*, which summarized the physiological research of the period and systematized a large body of knowledge. Revisions between 1833 and 1840 cited much new work, indicating how prolific research in experimental physiology had become. The need for such a book was reflected in the rapid translation into English of the first volume in 1838 and the second in 1842.

Müller is also of importance to both physiology and psychology for his theory of the *specific energies of nerves*. He proposed that the arousal or stimulation of a given nerve always gives rise to a characteristic sensation because each sensory nerve has its own specific energy. This idea stimulated a great deal of research that sought to localize functions within the nervous system and to delimit sensory receptor mechanisms on the periphery of the organism.

Several early physiologists made substantial contributions to the study of brain functions. Their work is significant for psychology because of their discoveries of specialized areas of the brain and their development of research methods that became widely used in later physiological psychology.

A pioneer in the investigation of *reflex behavior* was Marshall Hall (1790–1857), who observed that decapitated animals continued to move for some time when subjected to appropriate forms of stimulation. Hall concluded that various levels of behavior depend on different parts of the brain and nervous system. Specifically, he postulated that voluntary movement depends on the cerebrum, reflex movement on the spinal cord, involuntary movement on direct stimulation of the musculature, and respiratory movement on the medulla.

Pierre Flourens (1794–1867) systematically destroyed various parts of the brain and spinal cord and observed the consequences. He concluded that the cerebrum controls the higher mental processes, parts of the midbrain control visual and auditory reflexes, the cerebellum controls coordination, and the medulla governs heartbeat, respiration, and other vital functions.

The findings of Hall and Flourens, although still generally valid, are for our purposes second in importance to their introduction of the method of *extirpation*. This technique essentially consists of investigating the function of a given part of the brain by removing or destroying it and observing the resulting changes in the animal's behavior.

The mid-nineteenth century brought two additional experimental approaches to the study of the brain. The *clinical method* was developed in 1861 by Paul Broca, who performed an autopsy on a man who had been unable to speak intelligibly for many years. The autopsy revealed a lesion in the third frontal convolution of the cerebral cortex. Broca labeled this section of the brain the speech center (since called, appropriately, Broca's area). This method has become a useful supplement to extirpation because it is difficult to secure human subjects who will agree to removal of part of their brains. As a sort of posthumous extirpation, the clinical method provides the opportunity of finding the damaged brain area assumed to be responsible for a behavioral condition that existed before the patient died.

The second new experimental approach to brain study was *electrical stimulation*, introduced by G. Fritsch and E. Hitzig in 1870. As its name suggests, the method involves the exploration of the cerebral cortex with weak electric currents. Fritsch and Hitzig found that stimulating certain cortical areas resulted in motor responses. With the development of more sophisticated and precise electronic equipment, the method of electrical stimulation has become probably the single most productive technique for studying the functions of the brain.

Much was being learned, then, about the structure and functions of the human brain. Considerable research on the structure of the nervous system and the nature of neural activity was also being conducted. As we have noted, there were two earlier theories about how nervous activity was transmitted in the body: the nerve tube theory embraced by Descartes, and Hartley's theory of vibrations.

Toward the end of the eighteenth century, the Italian researcher Luigi Galvani had suggested that the nature of nerve impulses was electrical. His research was continued by his nephew, Giovanni Aldini, "who mixed serious research with showmanship. One of the more gruesome of Aldini's displays, designed to emphasize the effectiveness of electrical stimulation for obtaining spasmodic movements from muscles, involved using the recently severed heads of two criminals" (Boakes, 1984, p. 96). Research proceeded so rapidly and convincingly that by the middle of the nineteenth century the electrical nature of nerve impulses was accepted as fact. It was believed that the nervous system was essentially a conductor of electrical impulses and that the central nervous system functioned much like a switching station, shunting the impulses onto either sensory or motor nerve fibers.

Although this position was a great advance beyond the models of Descartes and Hartley, it was conceptually similar. Both the newer and the older points of view were reflexive in nature. Something from the external world (a stimulus) impinged on a sense organ and excited a nervous impulse that traveled to the appropriate place in the brain or central nervous system. There, in response to the impulse, a new impulse was generated and transmitted via the motor nerves to effect some response by the organism.

The anatomical structure of the nervous system was also being defined during the nineteenth century. It came to be understood that the nerve fibers were actually composed of separate structures called *neurons*, which were somehow joined together at synapses.

Such findings were congruent with a mechanistic and materialistic image of human beings. It was believed that the nervous system, like the mind, was composed of atomistic structures that, when combined, produced a more complex product.

The spirit of mechanism was just as dominant in the physiology of the nineteenth century as it was in the philosophy of that time. Nowhere was this more pronounced than in Germany. In the 1840s a group of scientists, many of them former students of Johannes Müller, formed the Berlin Physical Society. These scientists, all in their twenties, were committed to one proposition: all phenomena, including those that pertained to living matter, could be accounted for in physical terms. What they hoped to do was to relate or connect physiology with physics. A physiology consonant with the spirit of mechanism was their goal.

In a dramatic gesture, four of the young scientists (including Helmholtz, whom we will meet shortly) made a solemn oath—signing it in their own blood, according to legend—stating that the only forces active within the organism are the common physicochemical ones. Materialism, mechanism, empiricism, experimentation, measurement; these forces formed the core of physiology by the mid-nineteenth century.

The developments in early physiology indicate the kinds of research techniques and discoveries that supported a scientific approach to the psychological investigation of the mind. We have suggested how the direction of research in physiology influenced the newly emerging psychology. The major point is that while philosophy was paving the way for an experimental attack on the mind, physiology was experimentally investigating the physiological mechanisms that underlie mental phenomena. The next step was to apply the experimental method to the mind itself.

The British empiricists had argued that sensation is the only source of all our knowledge. The astronomer Bessel had demonstrated the importance of sensation and perception in science itself. Physiologists were defining the structure and function of the senses. It was time to experiment with and to quantify this doorway to the mind, the subjective, mentalistic experience of sensation. Techniques were available to investigate the body; now they were being developed to explore the mind. Experimental psychology was ready to begin.

THE BEGINNINGS OF EXPERIMENTAL PSYCHOLOGY

Four scientists are directly responsible for the initial applications of the experimental method to the subject matter of psychology: Hermann von Helmholtz, Ernst Weber, Gustav Theodor Fechner, Wilhelm Wundt. All four were German, well trained in physiology, and aware of the impressive developments in physiology and in science in the middle of the nineteenth century.

Why Germany?

Scientific thought was developing in most of the countries of Western Europe in the nineteenth century, particularly in England, France, and Germany. No one country had a monopoly on the enthusiasm, conscientiousness, or optimism with which the tools of science were viewed and used. Why, then, did experimental psychology begin in Germany and not in France or England? Were there some unique characteristics that made German science a more fertile breeding ground for the new psychology?

Although generalizations may be suspect and exceptions to the rule frequently found, it can nonetheless be suggested that the times favored Germany as the point of origin for the new psychology. For a century German intellectual history had paved the way for an experimental science of psychology. Experimental physiology was firmly established and was recognized to a degree not yet achieved in France and England. The so-called German temperament was well suited to the careful and minute taxonomic description and classification needed for work in biology, zoology, and physiology. Whereas the deductive and mathematical approach to science was favored in France and England, Germany, with its emphasis on conscientious, thorough, and careful collection of observable facts, had adopted a classificatory or inductive approach.

Because biological and physiological science does not lend itself to grand generalizations from which facts can be deduced, biology was only slowly accepted into the scientific communities of France and England. Germany, however, with its interest and faith in description and categorization, welcomed biology to its family of sciences.

Further, the Germans construed science broadly. Science in France and Britain was limited to physics and chemistry (which could be approached quantitatively), but science in Germany included such areas as phonetics, philology, history, archeology, esthetics, logic, and literary criticism. The French and British were skeptical about applying science to the study of something as complex as the human mind. Not so the Germans, and they plunged ahead, unconstrained by that prejudgment, using the tools of science to explore and measure the mind.

Germany also provided greater opportunities to learn and practice the new scientific techniques. Stated in pragmatic terms, a person could make a living as a research scientist in Germany but not in France or England. The reason for this relates to the wave of reform that swept over German universities, beginning in the early nineteenth century.

A new kind of university, unknown elsewhere in the world, developed in Germany. These institutions were devoted to the principles of academic freedom and to research, and both were available to students and professors alike. Faculty members were free to teach whatever they wished, with no outside interference, and to conduct research on any topic of their choosing. Students were free to take whatever courses they preferred and were not bound by a rigid curriculum.

This style of university provided an ideal environment for the flourishing of scientific inquiry. Professors could not only lecture, but they could also direct students in experimental research in reasonably well-equipped laboratories. In no other country was such an approach to science supported and encouraged.

In contrast, England had only two universities, and they did not facilitate or encourage research. The only way to practice science was on one's own, in the manner of a Darwin or a Galton. As we shall see, that usually required an independent income. The situation in France at the time was similar.

The climate of reform in German universities also involved an increase in their number, and this meant that there were more positions for those interested in science. The chances of becoming a well-paid and respected professor were much higher in Germany, although it was difficult to attain such a position. The promising university scientist was required to produce research judged to be a major contribution by experts in the field, research that went beyond the usual doctoral dissertation. This meant that most of those admitted to a university career were of extremely high caliber. Once these scientists joined the university community, the pressure on them to make ever greater contributions, was keen.

Thus, although the competition was intense and the demands high, the rewards were more than worth the effort. Only the best succeeded in German science of the nineteenth century. The result was a series of breakthroughs in all the sciences, including the new psychology. It is no coincidence that the people who were directly responsible for the emergence of the new scientific psychology were university professors.

HERMANN VON HELMHOLTZ (1821–1894)

Helmholtz, a prolific researcher in physics and physiology, was one of the greatest scientists of the nineteenth century. Psychology ranked third among his areas of scientific contribution, yet, together with the efforts of Fechner and Wundt, his work was instrumental in beginning the new psychology.

The Life of Helmholtz

Born in Potsdam, Germany, where his father taught in the *Gymnasium*,[1] Helmholtz was initially tutored at home because of his delicate health. At the age of 17 he entered a Berlin medical institute where no tuition was charged to those who agreed to serve as surgeons in the army after graduation. Helmholtz served for seven years, during which time he continued his studies in mathematics and physics, published several articles, and presented a paper on the indestructibility of energy in which he mathematically formulated the law of the conservation of energy. After leaving the army, Helmholtz accepted a position as associate professor of physiology at Königsberg. For the next 30 years he held academic appointments in physiology at Bonn and Heidelberg, and in physics at Berlin.

The tremendously energetic Helmholtz published in several different areas. In the course of his work on physiological optics he invented the ophthalmoscope. His three-volume work *Handbuch der Physiologischen Optik (Physiological Optics)* (1856–1866) proved to be so influential and enduring that it was translated into English 60 years later. His research on acoustical problems was published in 1863 in *On the Sensations of Tone*, which summarized his own findings as well as the entire available literature. He also wrote on such diverse subjects as afterimages, color blindness, the Arabian–Persian musical scale, the form of the horopter (a curved surface in the visual field), human eye movements, the formation of glaciers, geometrical axioms, and hay fever. In later years Helmholtz contributed indirectly to the founding of wireless telegraphy and radio. In the fall of 1893, while returning from the Chicago World's Fair and visits to other parts of the United States, Helmholtz suffered a severe fall aboard ship. He never fully recovered his health and died 11 months later.

---

[1]In Europe, a high school–junior college preparatory for the university.

The work of the great physicist–physiologist Hermann von Helmholtz (1821–1894) on nerve conduction, color vision, and audition had a major influence on sensory psychology.

The Contributions of Helmholtz

Of interest to psychology are Helmholtz's investigations of the speed of the neural impulse, vision, and audition. Before Helmholtz's time, it was thought that the neural impulse was instantaneous, or at least that it traveled too fast to be measured. Helmholtz provided the first empirical measurement of the rate of conduction by stimulating a motor nerve and the attached muscle from the leg of a frog, arranged so that the precise moment of stimulation, as well as the resulting movement, could be recorded. Working with different lengths of nerve, he recorded the delay between stimulation of the nerve near the muscle and the muscle's reaction, and did the same for stimulation farther from the muscle. These measurements yielded the time required for conduction, the modest rate of 90 feet per second.

Helmholtz also experimented on the reaction time for sensory nerves of human subjects, studying the complete circuit from stimulation of a sense organ to the resulting motor response. The findings showed such enormous individual differences as well as differences for the same individual from one trial to the next that he abandoned the research.

Helmholtz's demonstrations that the speed of conduction was not instantaneous suggested that thought and movement follow one another at a measurable interval and do not occur simultaneously, as had previously been thought. Helmholtz, however, was interested only in the sheer speed of the nerve impulse and not in its psychological significance. Later, the psychological implications of his research were recognized by others, who went on to make reaction-time experiments a fruitful line of research in the new psychology. Helmholtz's research was one of the first indications that it was possible to experiment on and measure a psychophysiological process.

Helmholtz's work on vision also had a profound influence on psychology. In addition to investigating the external eye muscles and the mechanism by which the internal eye muscles focus the lenses, Helmholtz extended a theory of color vision originally published in 1802 by Thomas Young (now known as the Young–Helmholtz theory of color vision). No less important is Helmholtz's work on the perception of combination tones and individual tones, the nature of harmony and discord, and his resonance theory of hearing. The enduring influence of his theories of vision and audition is attested to by their continued inclusion in modern textbooks of psychology.

Comment

Helmholtz was not a psychologist, nor were psychological problems his main interest, but he contributed a large and important body of knowledge to sensory psychology and helped to strengthen the newly developing experimental approach to the study of psychological problems. He considered psychology to be a separate discipline, allied to metaphysics. The psychology of the senses was an exception, as far as Helmholtz was concerned, because of its association with physiology. He was not concerned with the establishment of psychology as an independent science, yet his influence was of such magnitude that he must be included among the direct contributors to the new science.

ERNST WEBER (1795–1878)

Weber, the son of a theology professor, was born in Wittenberg, Germany. He received his doctorate at the University of Leipzig in 1815, and taught anatomy and physiology there from 1817 until his retirement in 1871. His primary research interest was the physiology of the sense organs, an area in which he made outstanding and lasting contributions.

Previous research on the sense organs had been confined almost exclusively to the higher senses of vision and audition. Weber's work consisted largely of exploring new fields, notably cutaneous and muscular sensations. He is particularly noteworthy for his

The experimental
investigation of threshold
perception by Ernst
Weber (1795–1878) led
to the formulation of the
first quantitative law of
psychology.

brilliant application of the experimental methods of physiology to problems of a psychological nature. His experiments on the sense of touch mark a fundamental shift in the
status of the subject matter of psychology. The ties with philosophy were, if not severed,
at least severely weakened. Weber allied psychology with the natural sciences and
helped to pave the way for the use of experimental investigation in the study of
the mind.

The Two-Point Threshold

One of Weber's two major contributions to the new psychology involved his experimental determination of the accuracy of the two-point discrimination of the skin, that is, the distance between two points that is necessary before subjects report two distinct sensations. Without the use of vision, subjects are asked to report whether they feel one or two points touching the skin. When the two points of stimulation are close together, subjects report a clear sensation of being touched at only one point. As the distance between the two sources of stimulation is increased, using an apparatus resembling a drawing compass, subjects report uncertainty about whether they feel one or two sensations. Finally, a distance is reached where subjects report two distinct points of stimulation. This procedure demonstrates the two-point threshold, the threshold at which the two points of stimulation can be discriminated as such. Weber's research marks the first systematic, experimental demonstration of the concept of threshold, a concept widely used in the new psychology from its beginnings to the present day.

In additional research Weber demonstrated that this two-point threshold varies both in different parts of the body of the same subject, and from one subject to another for the same part of the body. Although his attempt to account for these findings by hypothesizing "sensory circles" (areas in which doubleness is not perceived) has diminished in importance, his experimental method remains significant.

The Just Noticeable Difference

Weber's second major contribution eventually led to the formulation of the first quantitative law of psychology. He wanted to determine the *just noticeable difference*, the smallest difference between weights that could be discriminated. To do so, he had subjects lift two weights, a standard and a comparison weight, and report whether one felt heavier than the other. Small differences between the weights resulted in judgments of sameness; large differences resulted in judgments of disparity between the weights. As the research progressed, Weber found that the just noticeable difference between two weights is a constant ratio, 1:40, of the standard weight. For example, a weight of 41 grams is reported as just noticeably different from a standard weight of 40 grams, an 82-gram weight just noticeably different from a standard weight of 80 grams.

Weber then undertook to investigate the contributions of muscular sensations in the discrimination of weights of differing magnitudes. He found that subjects could discriminate much more accurately when the weights to be judged were lifted by the subjects rather than simply placed in their hands. In lifting the weights, both tactile and muscular sensations occur, whereas when the weight is placed in the hand, only tactile sensations are experienced. Because smaller differences in weight could be discriminated when the weights were lifted (a ratio of 1:40, as already noted) as compared to when the weights were placed in the hand (a ratio of 1:30 being necessary), Weber concluded that the internal muscle sense influenced the ability to discriminate.

From these experiments, Weber found that discrimination seemed to depend not on the absolute difference between two weights, but on the relative difference or the ratio of one to another. The just noticeable difference between two stimuli can then be stated as a fraction that is constant for a given sense modality. Weber conducted experiments involving visual discrimination and found that the fraction was smaller than it was with the muscle sense experiments. From this he suggested that there is a constant fraction for just noticeable differences for each of the senses.

Weber's research showed that there is not a direct correspondence between the physical stimulus and the perception of it. However, like Helmholtz, Weber was concerned with physiological processes, so he did not appreciate the significance of his work for psychology. What his research revealed was a way of investigating the relationship between body and mind, between the stimulus and the resulting sensation. This was indeed a major breakthrough; all that was necessary was for someone to realize its significance.

Weber's research was experimental in the strictest sense of the term. Under well-controlled conditions, he systematically varied the stimuli and recorded the differential effects on the reported experience of the subject. His experiments stimulated a great deal of research and served to focus the attention of subsequent physiologists on the validity and importance of the experiment as a means of studying psychological phenomena. Weber's work on threshold measurement was to be of paramount importance to the new psychology, and his demonstration that sensations can be measured has influenced virtually every aspect of psychology to the present day.

GUSTAV THEODOR FECHNER (1801–1887)

Fechner was a scholar whose remarkably diverse intellectual pursuits ranged over an active career of more than 70 years. Consider the scope of interests of this man, who was a physiologist for 7 years, a physicist for 15, a psychophysicist for 14, an experimental estheticist for 11, a philosopher for 40, and an invalid for 12 years. Of these endeavors, it is the work on psychophysics that brought him his greatest fame, even though he did not wish to be remembered by posterity as a psychophysicist.

The Life of Fechner

Fechner was born in a small village in southeastern Germany where his father was the minister. He began medical studies at the University of Leipzig in 1817 at the age of 16, and remained at Leipzig for the rest of his life.

Even before he graduated from medical school, the humanistic side of Fechner showed signs of rebellion against the prevailing materialism of his scientific training. Under the pen name "Dr. Mises" he wrote satirical essays lampooning medicine and science, a practice that he continued over the next 25 years, suggesting the persistent conflict between these two sides of his personality—a love of science and the metaphysical. His first such essay, "*Proof that the Moon Is Made of Iodine*," attacked the medical fad of using iodine as a panacea. He was troubled by materialism and strove to establish his "day view," that the universe can be regarded from the point of view of consciousness, in opposition to what he called the "night view," which held that the universe, including consciousness, was inert matter.

After completing his medical studies, Fechner began a second career in physics and mathematics at Leipzig, during which time he translated French handbooks of physics and chemistry into German. By 1830 he had translated more than a dozen volumes,

By demonstrating that the amount of sensation depends on the amount of stimulation, Gustav Theodor Fechner (1801–1887) proved that the mental and material worlds could be related quantitatively.

which served to gain him some recognition as a physicist. In 1824 he began lecturing in physics and conducting research of his own. By the late 1830s he had developed an interest in sensation and seriously injured his eyes by looking at the sun through colored glasses while studying afterimages.

In 1833, after many years of hard work, Fechner obtained the prestigious appointment of professor at Leipzig, whereupon he suffered a severe collapse that lasted for several years. He became extremely depressed, had difficulty sleeping, could not digest food (yet felt no hunger and approached a state of starvation), and was unusually sensitive to light. He spent most of his time in a darkened room whose walls were painted black, listening while his mother read to him through a narrow opening in the door.

Fechner's illness was neurotic in nature, a suggestion that is supported by the bizarre way in which he was eventually cured. A friend dreamed that she had made him a meal of spiced raw ham soaked in Rhine wine and lemon juice. The next day she prepared the dish and brought it to Fechner, insisting that he eat it. He did, albeit reluctantly, and began to eat more and more of the meat every day, which caused him to feel somewhat better (Ellenberger, 1970).

Then he had a dream in which the number 77 appeared. This convinced him that he would be completely cured in 77 days. And of course he was. He felt so well that his depression turned to euphoria and delusions of grandeur, and he claimed that God had chosen him to solve all the riddles in the world. Out of that experience he developed the notion of the pleasure principle, which was to influence Sigmund Freud many years later.

In 1844 Fechner was given a small pension from the university and was officially established as an invalid. Yet not one of the next 43 years of his life passed without a serious contribution from him, and his health remained excellent until his death at the age of 86.

The Contributions of Fechner: Quantitative Relationship between Mind and Body

The many hours Fechner spent in meditation and reflection deepened his religious awareness and concern with the problem of the soul. When he turned to philosophy, he directed the full force of his genius toward the question of the relationship between the mind and the body. He decided that the two are identical, that both are aspects of the same fundamental unity. They are related to each other as the inside of a circle is related to the outside. The apparent difference between the two results from the way in which they are viewed. Fechner's fame, however, comes from his psychophysics, not his philosophy, although his attempt to verify his philosophical views empirically is a milestone in the history of psychology.

On the morning of October 22, 1850—an important date in the history of psychology—Fechner had an insight that the law of the connection between mind and body can be found in a statement of quantitative relation between mental sensation and material stimulus. An increase in the intensity of a stimulus, he said, does not produce a one-to-one increase in the intensity of the sensation. Rather, a geometric series characterizes the stimulus, whereas an arithmetic series characterizes the sensation. For instance, adding the sound of one bell to that of an already ringing bell produces a greater increase in sensation than adding one bell to ten others already ringing. The effects of stimulus intensities are not absolute but are relative to the amount of sensation that already exists.

What this simple, yet brilliant, revelation showed was that the amount of sensation (the mental quality) depends on the amount of stimulation (the physical or material quality). To measure the change in sensation, one must measure the change in stimulation. Therefore, it is possible to relate the mental and material worlds quantitatively. Fechner crossed the barrier between body and mind by relating one to the other empirically.

Although the concept was clear, how was it to be translated into actuality? One would have to measure precisely both intensities, the subjective and the objective, the mental sensation and the physical stimulus. To measure the physical intensity, the stimulus, is not difficult, but how does one measure sensation, the conscious experience that subjects report when they respond to a stimulus?

Fechner believed that there were two ways to measure sensations. First, we can determine whether a stimulus is present or absent, sensed or not sensed. Second, we can measure the stimulus intensity at which subjects report that sensation first occurs. What is being measured in the latter case is the *absolute threshold* of sensitivity, that point in stimulus intensity below which no sensation is reported, and above which subjects do experience a sensation.[2]

This measurement, although useful, is limited because only one value of a sensation, its lowest level, is determined. To relate both intensities, we must be able to specify the full range of stimulus values and their resulting sensation values. To accomplish this, Fechner proposed the *differential threshold* of sensitivity, the least amount of change in a stimulus that will give rise to a change in sensation. For example, by how much must a weight be increased in heaviness before subjects will sense the change, before they will report a just noticeable difference in sensation?

To measure how heavy a particular weight feels, how heavy subjects sense it to be, we cannot use the physical measurement of the object's weight. We can, however, use that physical measurement as a basis for measuring the psychological intensity of the sensation. First we measure by how much the weight must be decreased in intensity before subjects are barely able to discriminate the difference. Second, the weight of the object is changed to this lower value and the size of the difference threshold measured again. Because both weight changes are just barely noticeable, Fechner assumed that they were subjectively equal. This process can be repeated until the object is barely felt by the subjects. If every decrement in weight is subjectively equal to every other decrement, the number of times the weight has to be decreased—the number of just noticeable differences—can be used as an objective measure of the subjective magnitude of the sensation. In this way, we are measuring the stimulus values necessary to give rise to a difference between two sensations.

Fechner suggested that for each sense modality there is a certain relative increase in the stimulus that always produces an observable change in the intensity of the sensation. Thus, the sensation (the mind quality) as well as the excitatory stimulus (the body or material quality) can be measured and the relationship between the two stated in the form of an equation: $S = K \log R$, in which S is the magnitude of the sensation, K is a constant, and R is the magnitude of the stimulus. The relationship is logarithmic; one series increases arithmetically and the other geometrically.

Fechner wrote that this notion had not been suggested to him by Weber's work, even though Weber was also at Leipzig and had written about this matter only four years earlier. Fechner did not discover Weber's work until after he had begun the series of experiments designed to test his hypothesis (Heidbreder, 1933). Fechner later realized that the principle to which he gave mathematical form was essentially what Weber's work had demonstrated.

---

[2]This is not the first use of the concept of threshold. Weber, as noted, used it, and earlier in the nineteenth century the German philosopher Herbart also discussed the idea (Chapter 13).

Methods of Psychophysics

The immediate result of Fechner's insight was the development of a program of research on what he later called *psychophysics*. (The word defines itself—psycho–physics, the relationship between the mental and the material world.) In the course of this research, with its classic experiments on lifted weights, visual brightness, and tactile and visual distances, Fechner developed one and systematized two of the three fundamental methods of psychophysics that are still used today: the method of average error, the method of constant stimuli, and the method of limits.

Fechner developed the method of average error (also called the method of adjustment) in cooperation with A. W. Volkmann, a professor of physiology at the University of Halle in Germany. It consists in having subjects adjust a variable stimulus until they perceive it to be equal to a constant standard stimulus. Over a number of trials, the mean value of the differences between the standard stimulus and the subjects' setting of the variable stimulus represents the error of observation. The method assumes that our sense organs are subject to variability, which prevents the obtaining of a true measure. Accordingly, we obtain a large number of approximate measures, the mean of which represents the best single approximation of the true value. The technique is useful for measuring reaction time, visual and auditory discriminations, and the extent of illusions. In an extended form it is fundamental to much current psychological research. Every time we calculate a mean we are, in essence, using the method of average error.

The method of constant stimuli, first called the method of right and wrong cases, was originated by Karl von Vierordt, a physiologist, in 1852, but developed as a tool by Fechner. He used it for his elaborate work with lifted weights, studies that consisted of more than 67,000 comparisons. The technique involves two constant stimuli and the aim is to measure the stimulus difference that is required to produce a given proportion of correct judgments. For example, subjects first lift the standard weight of 100 grams and then lift a comparison weight of, say, 88, 92, 96, 104, or 108 grams. They must judge whether the second weight is heavier, lighter, or equal to the first. The procedure is continued until a certain number of judgments have been made for each comparison. For the heavier weights, subjects almost always report a judgment of "heavier," and the lightest weights almost always are reported as "lighter." From these data, the stimulus difference (standard versus comparison weights) is determined for that point at which subjects correctly report "heavier" 75 percent of the time. A number of variations of the basic procedure render the technique useful for a range of measurement problems in the determination of sensory thresholds and in aptitude measurement.

The third of Fechner's psychophysical methods was originally known as the method of just noticeable differences, and later came to be called the method of limits. The technique has been traced back to 1700, and was formalized by C. Delezenne in 1827. Weber also used the method of just noticeable differences, as we have noted, but it was developed formally by Fechner in connection with his work on vision and temperature sensations. The method involves presenting two stimuli and increasing or diminishing one of them until subjects report that they detect a difference. Fechner recommended starting the variable stimulus at an intensity clearly higher than the standard stimulus at one time, and clearly lower than the standard the next time. Data are obtained from a number of trials, and the just noticeable differences are averaged to determine the differential threshold. A variation, using a single stimulus presented in the ascending and descending approaches, is used to determine the absolute threshold.

Comment

Fechner carried on his research for seven years, publishing part of it for the first time in two short papers in 1858 and 1859. In 1860 the formal and complete exposition of his work appeared in the *Elemente der Psychophysik* (*Elements of Psychophysics*), a text of the exact science "of the functionally dependent relations . . . of the material and the mental, of the physical and psychological worlds" (1860/1966, p. 7). The book is considered one of the outstanding original contributions to the development of the science of psychology.

Fechner failed in his attempt to found a philosophy on exact science, and his research findings have not withstood later criticism. At the time, however, Fechner's statement of the quantitative relationship between stimulus intensity and sensation was considered comparable to Galileo's discovery of the laws of the lever and of falling bodies. Fechner's efforts made it possible to measure the impalpable mind, a truly remarkable breakthrough.

At the beginning of the nineteenth century, the German philosopher Immanuel Kant insisted that psychology could never become a science because it was impossible to experiment on or measure psychological phenomena and processes. Because of Fechner's work, this assertion could no longer be regarded seriously.

It was largely because of Fechner's psychophysical research that Wilhelm Wundt conceived the plan of his experimental psychology. More important, Fechner's methods have proved applicable to a wider range of psychological problems than he ever imagined, and, with only minor modifications, these methods are still used today in psychological research. Fechner gave psychology what every discipline that hopes to be a science must possess—precise, elegant techniques of measurement.

Although Weber's work preceded Fechner's, accolades have been heaped upon Fechner. He seems to have used and built upon Weber's work, but he did much more than extend it. Weber's aims were limited; he was a physiologist working on just noticeable differences, and the larger significance of this work escaped him. Weber has been called an "eventful" man, whereas Fechner was an "event-making" man (Watson, 1978). Fechner sought a mathematical statement of the relationship between the physical and the spiritual worlds. His brilliant and independent insights about measuring sensations and relating them to their stimulus measures were necessary before the implications and consequences of Weber's earlier work could be recognized and applied to make psychology an exact science.

THE FORMAL FOUNDING OF THE NEW SCIENCE

By the mid-nineteenth century, the methods of natural science were being used to investigate purely mental phenomena. Techniques had been developed, apparatus devised, important books written, and widespread interest aroused. British empiricism and the work in astronomy emphasized the importance of the senses, and the German scientists were describing how the senses functioned. The positivistic spirit of the times encouraged the convergence of these two lines of thought. Still lacking, however, was someone to bring them together, in a word, to "found" the new science. This final touch was provided by Wilhelm Wundt.

Wundt is the founder of psychology as a formal academic discipline, the first person in the history of psychology to be designated properly and unreservedly a *psychologist*. As the first experimental psychologist, Wundt founded the first laboratory, edited the first journal, and began experimental psychology as a science. The areas he investigated—including sensation and perception, attention, feeling, reaction, and association—became basic chapters in textbooks that were yet to be written. That so much of the history of psychology following Wundt consists of opposition to his view of psychology does not detract from his achievements and contributions as a founder.

Why have the honors for founding the new psychology fallen to Wundt and not to Fechner? Fechner's *Elements of Psychophysics* was published in 1860, at least 15 years before Wundt is said to have begun psychology. Wundt himself wrote that Fechner's work represented the "first conquest" in experimental psychology (Wundt, 1888, p. 471). Historians agree on Fechner's importance; some even question whether psychology could have begun when it did were it not for Fechner's work. Why, then, does history not credit Fechner with founding psychology? The answer lies in the nature of the process of founding.

Founding is a deliberate, intentional act involving abilities and characteristics that exceed those necessary for brilliant scientific achievement. It requires the integration and consideration of previous work and the publication and promotion of the newly organized material. "When the central ideas are all born, some promoter takes them in hand, organizes them, adding whatever else seems to him essential, publishes and advertises them, insists upon them, and in short 'founds' a school" (Boring, 1950, p. 194).

Founding is thus quite different from originating, although the distinction is not a disparaging one. Originators and founders are both essential to the formation of a science, as indispensable as are the architect and the builder in constructing a house.

With this distinction in mind, we can understand why Fechner is not called the founder of psychology. Stated simply, he was not trying to found a new science. His quest was to understand the nature of the relationship between the mental and material worlds. He sought to demonstrate a unified concept of mind and body that proceeded from mystical speculation but had a scientific basis. Fechner was "more of a forerunner than a founder, as one cannot say that his innovation of psychophysics would have been developed into a discipline of experimental psychology if an institutionally-based movement had not been founded subsequently" (Ben-David & Collins, 1966, p. 455).

Wundt, however, set out deliberately to found a new science. In the preface to the first edition of his *Principles of Physiological Psychology* (1874) he wrote: "The work I here present to the public is an attempt to mark out a new domain of science." Wundt was interested in promoting the idea of psychology as an independent science. Nevertheless, it bears repeating that although Wundt is considered to have founded psychology, he did not originate it. Psychology emerged from a long line of creative efforts.

During the last half of the nineteenth century the *Zeitgeist* was ready for the application of the experimental approach to problems of the mind. Wundt was a vigorous agent and promoter of the inevitable, of what was already developing.

SUGGESTED READINGS

Early Experimental Physiology

Brazier, M. (1959). The historical development of neurophysiology. In J. Field (Ed.), *Handbook of physiology* (vol. 1, pp. 1–58). Baltimore: Williams & Wilkins.

Fearing, F. (1970). *Reflex action: A study in the history of physiological psychology*. Cambridge, MA: MIT Press. (Original work published 1930).

Kirsch, I. (1976). The impetus to scientific psychology: A recurrent pattern. *Journal of the History of the Behavioral Sciences, 12*, 120–129. (On Maskeleyne and Bessel).

Ladd, G. T., & Woodworth, R. S. (1911). *Elements of physiological psychology: A treatise of the activities and nature of the mind, from the physical and experimental points of view* (rev. ed.). New York: Charles Scribner's Sons.

Seashore, E. C. (1908). *Elementary experiments in psychology*. New York: Holt.

Smith, R. (1973). The background of physiological psychology in natural philosophy. *History of Science, 11*, 75–123.

Young, R. M. (1970). *Mind, brain and adaptation in the 19th century*. Oxford, England: Clarendon Press.

Helmholtz

Koenigsberger, L. (1965). *Hermann von Helmholtz*. New York: Dover.

Pastore, N. (1973). Helmholtz's "Popular lectures on vision." *Journal of the History of the Behavioral Sciences, 9*, 190–202.

Stumpf, C. (1895). Hermann von Helmholtz and the new psychology. *Psychological Review, 2*, 1–12.

Turner, R. S. (1977). Hermann von Helmholtz and the empiricist vision. *Journal of the History of the Behavioral Sciences, 13*, 48–58.

Warren, R. M., & Warren, R. P. (1968). *Helmholtz on perception: Its physiology and development*. New York: Wiley.

Weber

Brožek, J. (1980). A pre-Wundtian, pre-Fechnerian root of experimental psychology: A special review. *Journal of the History of the Behavioral Sciences, 16*, 195–198.

Fechner

Boring, E. G. (1928). Did Fechner measure sensation? *Psychological Review, 35*, 443–445.

Boring, E. G. (1961). Fechner: Inadvertent founder of psychophysics. *Psychometrika, 26*, 3–8.

Fechner, G. (1966). *Elements of psychophysics*. New York: Holt, Rinehart & Winston. (Original work published 1860).

Johnson, H. M. (1929). Did Fechner measure "introspectional" sensations? *Psychological Review, 36*, 257–284.

Marshall, M. E. (1969). Gustav Fechner, Dr. Mises, and the comparative anatomy of angels. *Journal of the History of the Behavioral Sciences, 5*, 39–58. (See also the translation of Fechner's "The comparative anatomy of angels. A sketch by Dr. Mises: 1825" in the same volume, pp. 135–151).

Marshall, M. E. (1974). G. T. Fechner: "Premises toward a general theory of organisms" (1823). *Journal of the History of the Behavioral Sciences, 10*, 438–447.

Pliskoff, S. S. (1977). Antecedents to Fechner's Law: The astronomers J. Herschel, W. R. Dawes, and N. R. Pagson. *Journal of the Experimental Analysis of Behavior, 28*, 185–187.

Stevens, S. S. (1961). To honor Fechner and repeal his law. *Science, 133*, 80–86.

Woodward, W. R. (1972). Fechner's panpsychism: A scientific solution to the mind–body problem. *Journal of the History of the Behavioral Sciences, 8*, 367–386.

4

The New Psychology

A CASE OF DISTORTED DATA

Wilhelm Wundt, as the founder of the new science of psychology, is one of the field's most important figures. A knowledge of the approach to psychology that he developed is vital to an understanding of the history of the discipline. Yet more than a century after Wundt founded psychology, new data (or refinements of known data) have led some psychologists to conclude that the accepted view of Wundt's system is wrong. Wundt, who had a "horror of being misunderstood and misrepresented," suffered just that fate (Baldwin, 1980, p. 301).

Many articles published in the late 1970s and early 1980s echo this theme, that the Wundt depicted in psychology's textbooks and classrooms has little in common with the actual person and his views. Our descriptions of Wundtian psychology have often portrayed his positions inaccurately, sometimes ascribing to him beliefs that were the opposite of his own intentions (Blumenthal, 1975, 1979; Leahey, 1981).

How could such a mistake be made with such a prominent person? Wundt wrote many books and articles presenting his views of the nature of psychology. His system was there for all to see, for all who were fluent in German and who were willing to devote the time needed to study Wundt's phenomenal amount of published material.

But why go to all that trouble? Most psychologists did not think it necessary to read Wundt in the original because so many of his most important works were translated into the English language by his student E. B. Titchener, an English psychologist who spent most of his career at Cornell University in New York. Titchener pronounced himself to be Wundt's loyal follower and true interpreter. He proclaimed Wundt "as the source of his psychology and the precursor who validated his credentials" (Anderson, 1980, p. 95).

Therefore, it came to be believed that Titchener's approach to psychology, which he called *structuralism*, was essentially a mirror-image of that of his mentor Wundt. If one knew Titchener's system, then one knew Wundt's as well.

Recent research on Wundt's writings casts doubt on this conclusion. Titchener did not represent Wundt. Evidence suggests that he altered Wundt's positions to make them appear compatible with his own, to lend credibility to his own views by asserting that they were consistent with those of psychology's founder. Titchener apparently elected to translate only those portions of Wundt's publications that supported his own approach to psychology. We do not know whether he made a deliberate decision to do this, but the result—the distorted presentation of Wundt's system of psychology—is the same whether or not Titchener was consciously aware of what he was doing.

Titchener's inaccurate version of Wundt's system influenced contemporary psychologists not only because of the status Titchener achieved within American psychology but also because of the visibility attained by his student, E. G. Boring, who became the premier historian of psychology. Boring wrote that Titchener was a Wundtian "and undertook, with modifications, to continue the Leipzig tradition" (Boring, 1950, p. 410). Although Boring also stated that Titchener's work was "still quite distinct from the [school] of Wundt" (Boring, 1950, p. 419), many psychologists who learned their history from Boring's *A History of Experimental Psychology* (1929, 1950) came to identify Titchener's system with Wundt's.

Thus, generations of students have been offered a portrait of Wundtian psychology that may be more myth than fact, more legend than truth. For 100 years after the event, texts in the history of psychology, including the previous editions of this one, and teachers of the history course, have been compounding and reinforcing the error under the imprimatur of their alleged expertise.

After reviewing Wundt's life, we shall consider his definition of psychology and how it influenced the subsequent development of the field.

WILHELM WUNDT (1832–1920)

The Life of Wundt

Wundt was born and spent his early years in a small town in Germany, a childhood that was marked by intense loneliness. He got poor grades in school and he lived the life of an only child (his older brother was at boarding school). His only friend his own age was a mentally retarded boy who was good natured but could barely speak.

Wundt's father was a clergyman, and though both parents seem to have been jovial and sociable, Wundt's early memories of his father were not pleasant. When Wundt was in his 80s, he could still vividly recall falling down a flight of stairs while trying to follow his father. He also remembered that his father visited his school one day and hit him across the face for not paying attention to the teacher.

Beginning in the second grade, Wundt's education was undertaken by his father's assistant, a young vicar to whom the boy felt a stronger emotional attachment than to his parents. When the vicar was transferred to another town, Wundt became so upset that he was allowed to go to live with the vicar, with whom he remained until the age of 13.

There was a strong tradition of scholarship in the Wundt family, with ancestors of note in virtually every discipline. It has been said that "virtually no family tree in Germany contains as many intellectually active and productive individuals as that of Wundt" (Bringmann, Balance, & Evans, 1975, p. 288). Nonetheless, it appeared for a time that this impressive family tradition would not be continued by young Wundt.

Wilhelm Wundt (1832–1920) founded the experimental science of psychology and established its first laboratory at Leipzig.

He spent much more time daydreaming than studying, and failed in his first year at *Gymnasium*. He did not get along well with his classmates, was frequently slapped by one of his teachers and ridiculed by others, and once ran away from the school. It was not a promising beginning.

Gradually Wundt learned to control his daydreaming and even became more popular. Although he always disliked school, he nevertheless developed his intellectual interests and abilities. By the time he graduated at the age of 19, he was ready for the university.

To earn a living and study science at the same time, Wundt decided to become a physician. His medical studies took him for one year to the University of Tübingen and for the next three and one half years to Heidelberg, where he studied anatomy, physiology, physics, medicine, and chemistry, and was strongly influenced in the latter field by the famous Robert Bunsen. He slowly came to realize that the practice of medicine was not for him, so he shifted to physiology.

After a semester of study in Berlin with the great physiologist Johannes Müller, Wundt returned to Heidelberg to take his doctorate in 1855. He held an appointment as *Dozent* (lecturer) in physiology at Heidelberg from 1857 to 1864. In 1858 he was appointed assistant to Helmholtz, but found the work of drilling new students in their laboratory fundamentals a dreary task, so he resigned after a few years of this routine. In 1864 he was made associate professor and continued at Heidelberg until 1874.

While doing research in physiology at Heidelberg, Wundt's conception of psychology as an independent and experimental science began to emerge. His initial proposal for a new science of psychology appeared in the book entitled *Beiträge zur Theorie der Sinneswahrnehmung* (*Contributions to the Theory of Sensory Perception*), various sections of which were published between 1858 and 1862. In addition to reporting his own original experiments, which he conducted in a crude laboratory in his home, the book contained his views on the methods of the new psychology. Wundt wrote of *experimental psychology* for the first time. Along with Fechner's *Elements* (1860), this work is often considered to mark the literary birth of the new science.

The *Beiträge* was followed in 1863 by another and perhaps more important book, *Vorlesungen über die Menschen- und Thierseele* (*Lectures on the Minds of Men and Animals*). An indication of its importance was its revision almost 30 years later with an English translation and repeated reprintings until after Wundt's death in 1920. It discussed many problems that were to occupy the attention of experimental psychologists for a number of years.

Beginning in 1867, Wundt gave a course on physiological psychology at Heidelberg, the first formal offering of such a course. Out of this work came what is often considered the most important book in the history of psychology, *Grundzüge der physiologischen Psychologie* (*Principles of Physiological Psychology*), published in two parts in 1873 and 1874. Six editions appeared in 37 years, with the last published in 1911. Undoubtedly Wundt's masterpiece, this book firmly established psychology as a laboratory science with its own problems and methods of experimentation. For many years the successive editions of the *Grundzüge* served experimental psychologists as a storehouse of information and a record of the progress of the new psychology. It was in the preface to this book that Wundt stated his goal of attempting "to mark out a new domain of science." That this book uses *physiological psychology* in its title may be misleading. In the mid-nineteenth century, the word "physiological" was used as a synonym for the word "experimental" in German. Thus, Wundt was teaching and writing about experimental psychology, not physiological psychology as we know it today (Blumenthal, 1980).

Wundt began the longest and most important phase of his career in 1875 when he became professor of philosophy at Leipzig, where he worked prodigiously for 45 years. He established his laboratory at Leipzig shortly after his arrival, and in 1881 began the journal *Philosophische Studien* (*Philosophical Studies*), the official organ of the new laboratory and the new science. He had intended to call the journal *Psychological Studies* but changed the name apparently because there already was such a journal, although it dealt with spiritualism, parapsychology, and the occult (Bringmann, Bringmann, & Ungerer, 1980). In 1906, however, Wundt retitled his own journal *Psychological Studies*. With Wundt's handbook, laboratory, and scholarly journal, then, the new psychology was well under way.

Wundt's spreading fame and the laboratory drew a large number of students to Leipzig to work with him. Among these students were many subsequent contributors to psychology, including several Americans, most of whom returned to the United States to begin laboratories of their own. Through these students, the Leipzig laboratory exerted an immense influence on the development of psychology. It served as the model for the many new laboratories that were developed in the latter part of the nineteenth century. The students who flocked to Leipzig, united in point of view and purpose, at least initially, constituted a school of thought in psychology.

Wundt's lectures at Leipzig were very popular and extremely well attended. At one time he had over 600 students in a class. His classroom manner has been described by Titchener as follows:

> Wundt would appear at exactly the correct minute—punctuality was essential—dressed all in black and carrying a small sheaf of lecture notes. He clattered up the side aisle to the platform with an awkward shuffle and a sound as if his soles were made of wood. On the platform was a long desk where demonstrations were performed. He made a few gestures—a forefinger across his forehead, a rearrangement of his chalk—then faced the audience and placed his elbows on the bookrest. His voice was weak at first, then gained in strength and emphasis. As he talked his arms and hands moved up and down, pointing and waving, in some mysterious way illustrative. His head and body were rigid, and only the hands played back and forth. He seldom referred to the few jotted notes. As the clock struck the end of the hour he stopped and, stooping a little, clattered out as he had clattered in. (Miller & Buckhout, 1973, p. 29)

At the first conference with each new group of graduate students, Wundt appeared with a list of research topics. His students recalled the manner in which they received their assignments.

> He had in his hand a memorandum containing a list of subjects for research and taking us in the order in which we stood—there was no question of our being seated—assigned the topics and hours to us. . . . He assigned personally twenty-three subjects of research to as many candidates for the degree. (Baldwin, 1980, pp. 283, 306).

Wundt carefully supervised the research and held absolute power of acceptance or rejection upon completion of the thesis. The spirit of German scientific dogmatism flourished openly at the Leipzig laboratory.

In his personal life Wundt was quiet and unassuming, and his days followed a carefully regulated pattern.[1] In the morning he worked on a book or article, read student theses, and edited his journal. In the afternoon he attended examinations or visited the laboratory. Cattell remarked that Wundt's laboratory visits were limited to 5 or 10 minutes. Apparently, despite his great faith in laboratory research, "he was not himself

---

[1]The diaries of Mrs. Wundt were found in the 1970s, revealing much new material about Wundt's personal life; this is another instance of newly discovered data of history.

a laboratory worker" (1928, p. 545). After this, Wundt would walk while thinking about his afternoon lecture, always given at 4 P.M. In view of this rigorous life of scholarship, it may be surprising to learn that many of his evenings were given over to music, political activities, and, at least in his younger years, matters of student and worker rights. The Wundt family enjoyed a high income, employed servants, and entertained frequently.

A laboratory and a journal established, an immense amount of research under direction, Wundt turned his tremendous energy to philosophy in the years 1880–1891, writing on ethics, logic, and systematic philosophy. He published the second edition of *Principles of Physiological Psychology* in 1880 and the third edition in 1887, all the while contributing articles to the *Studien*.

Another field on which Wundt focused his considerable talent was outlined in the *Beiträge* in 1862—the creation of a cultural psychology. Toward the end of the nineteenth century he returned to this project, which culminated in the 10 volumes of his *Völkerpsychologie (Folk Psychology)* published between 1900 and 1920. Folk or cultural psychology was concerned with the investigation of the various stages of mental development as manifested in language, art, myths, social customs, law, and morals. The implications of this work for psychology are of greater significance than its content; it served to divide the new science of psychology into two parts, the experimental and the social. The simpler mental functions, such as sensation and perception, can and must be studied by laboratory investigation, Wundt believed. But he argued that scientific experimentation is impossible in the study of the higher mental processes because they are so thoroughly conditioned by linguistic habits and other aspects of cultural training.[2] Thus, according to Wundt, the higher thought processes could be studied effectively only by the nonexperimental approaches of sociology, anthropology, and social psychology. This contention that social forces play a major role in the development of the complicated higher mental processes is both true and important. However, Wundt's conclusion—that the higher mental processes cannot be studied experimentally—was refuted not long after he stated it.

Despite the importance of cultural psychology to Wundt, who devoted 10 years to its development and considered it a central part of psychology, it has had little impact on American psychology. A survey covering 90 years of articles published in the *American Journal of Psychology* showed that of all the citations to Wundt's publications, only 3.5 percent were to the *Völkerpsychologie*. In contrast, Wundt's *Principles of Physiological Psychology* accounted for more than 61 percent of the references to his works (Brožek, 1980).

Why was a work of such scope so widely recognized in Germany but virtually ignored in the United States? One possibility is that Titchener, the person who brought his own version of Wundtian psychology to America, dismissed that portion of Wundt's work as unimportant because it was not congruent with Titchener's structural psychology.

Wundt's productivity continued without a break until his death in 1920. Consistent with his systematic lifestyle, he died shortly after completing his psychological reminiscences. Boring (1950) noted that Wundt wrote 53,735 pages between 1853 and 1920, an output of 2.2 pages per day.

---

[2]Wundt's emphasis on language in the *Völkerpsychologie* can be seen as a precursor to contemporary work in psycholinguistics.

Wundt's System of Psychology

Wundt's psychology drew on the experimental methods of the older natural sciences, particularly the techniques used by the physiologists. He adapted these scientific methods of investigation for the new psychology and proceeded to study its subject matter in the same way the physical scientists were studying theirs. Thus, the spirit of the times in physiology and philosophy helped to shape both the methods of investigation and the subject matter of the new psychology.

You may have guessed what the subject matter of Wundt's psychology was: in a word, *consciousness*. In a broad sense, the impact of the nineteenth-century British empiricists and associationists was at least partly reflected in Wundt's system. What Wundt called the "manifold" of conscious experience (Robinson, 1981, p. 346) refers to something that includes many different parts or features, and that reflects Wundt's view of consciousness and his acceptance of the method of analysis or reductionism. Wundt wrote: "The first step in the investigation of a fact must therefore be a description of the individual elements . . . of which it consists" (Diamond, 1980, p. 85).

With that point, however, the similarity between Wundt's approach and that of the empiricists and associationists ends. Wundt did not agree with the British thesis that the elements of consciousness were static entities, the atoms of the mind, passively linked by some mechanical process of association. Wundt believed that consciousness was more active in organizing its own content. Hence, the study of the elements, the content, or the structure of consciousness alone would provide only a beginning of an understanding of psychological processes.

Because of Wundt's focus on the self-organizing capacity of the mind or consciousness, he referred to his system as *voluntarism*, indicating the power of the will to organize the contents of the mind into higher-level thought processes. Wundt emphasized not the elements themselves, as had the British empiricists and associationists, and as Titchener would later do, but rather the process of actively organizing or synthesizing those elements.

It is important to reiterate that although Wundt stressed the power of the mind to synthesize elements into higher-level cognitive processes, he nevertheless recognized that the elements of consciousness were basic; without them, there would be nothing for the mind to organize.

Let us examine in greater detail the parts of Wundt's system.

The Nature of Conscious Experience

According to Wundt, the specific subject that psychologists should study is *immediate experience*, not *mediate experience*. Mediate experience provides us with information or knowledge about something other than the experience itself. This is the usual form in which we use experience to acquire knowledge about our world. When we look at a flower, for example, and say, "The flower is red," this statement implies that our primary interest is in the flower and not in the fact that we are experiencing redness.

The immediate experience of looking at the flower, however, is not in the object itself but rather in the experience of something that is red. Thus, for Wundt, immediate experience is free and unbiased by higher-level interpretations, such as describing the experience of red in terms of the object (the flower).

To give another example, when we describe the experiences we feel when we have a toothache, we are reporting our immediate experience. If we were to say, "I have a toothache," we would be concerned with mediate experience.

To Wundt, it was the basic experiences such as red (the experience of red) that formed the states of consciousness or mental elements that the mind then actively organized or synthesized. Wundt wanted to analyze the mind or consciousness into its elemental components, just as the natural scientists were breaking down their subject matter, the material universe. The work of the chemist Mendeleev, who developed the periodic table of chemical elements, supported Wundt's aim. Indeed, Wundt may have been striving to develop a "periodic table of the mind" (Marx & Hillix, 1979, p. 67).

The Method of Study: Introspection

Because psychology is the science of conscious experience, the method of psychology must involve observation of that experience. No one can observe an experience except the person having it, so the method must involve *introspection*, what Wundt called *internal perception*. The use of introspection was not new with Wundt; even a cursory review can trace its use back to Socrates. What was a major innovation was Wundt's application of precise experimental control over the conditions of introspection. (Some critics worried that continued exposure to self-observation would drive students insane) (Titchener, 1921).

The use of introspection in psychology was derived from physics, in which introspection had been used to study light and sound, and physiology, in which it had been used to study the sense organs. To obtain information about the operations of the sense organs, for example, the investigator would apply a stimulus to a sense organ and ask the subjects to report on the sensation produced; this is similar to Fechner's psychophysical methods.

Wundt set forth explicit rules for the proper use of introspection in his laboratory: (1) observers must be able to determine when the process is to be introduced; (2) they must be in a state of readiness or "strained attention"; (3) it must be possible to repeat the observation several times; and (4) the experimental conditions must be capable of variation in terms of controlled manipulation of stimuli. The last condition invokes the essence of the experimental method—varying the conditions of the stimulus situation and observing the resulting changes in the experiences of the subjects.

Wundt did not usually use the kind of qualitative introspection in which subjects describe in detail their inner experiences. That approach was adopted by his students, notably Titchener and Oswald Külpe, who later developed their own forms of psychology. The type of introspective report Wundt sought in his own laboratory dealt primarily with conscious judgments about the size, intensity, and duration of various physical stimuli, the kinds of judgments made in psychophysical research. Only a small number of studies involved subject reports of a subjective or qualitative nature such as the pleasantness of different stimuli, the intensity of images, or the quality of certain sensations (Danziger, 1980a). The majority of Wundt's studies involved objective measurements that used a variety of sophisticated laboratory equipment. Many of these measurements involved reaction times, which can be recorded quantitatively. Wundt then inferred information about conscious processes and elements from these objective measures (Blumenthal, 1977; Danziger, 1980b).

The Elements of Experience

Having defined psychology's subject matter and method, Wundt then considered its goal. The problem of psychology was threefold: (1) to analyze the conscious processes into their basic elements; (2) to discover how these elements are synthesized or organized; and (3) to determine the laws of connection that govern their organization.

Wundt considered *sensations*—aroused whenever a sense organ is stimulated and the resulting impulse reaches the brain—to be one of the elementary forms of experience. He classified sensations according to modality (vision, hearing, and so on), intensity, and duration. Wundt recognized no fundamental difference between sensations and images because images are also associated with cortical excitation. In keeping with his physiological orientation, he assumed the existence of a direct correspondence between the excitation of the cerebral cortex and the corresponding sensory experience. He regarded the mind and the body as parallel but not interacting systems. The mind did not depend on the body so it could be studied effectively by itself.

Feelings were the other elementary form of experience. Wundt thought that sensations and feelings are simultaneous aspects of immediate experience. Feelings are the subjective complements of sensations, but they do not arise directly from a sense organ. Sensations are accompanied by certain feeling qualities, and when sensations combine to form a more complex state, a feeling quality will result from this combination of sensations.

Wundt developed his controversial *tridimensional theory of feeling* from his own introspective observations. Working with a metronome (which produces audible clicks at regular intervals), Wundt reported that after he experienced a series of clicks, some rhythmic patterns appeared to be more pleasant or more agreeable than others. He concluded that part of the experience of any such pattern is a subjective feeling of pleasure or displeasure. (Note that this subjective feeling is a simultaneous aspect of the sensation of the clicks.) He then suggested that this feeling state can be placed at a point along a continuum ranging from agreeable to disagreeable.

A second kind of feeling was detected while listening to the clicks. Wundt reported a slight tension while waiting for each successive click, followed by relief after the occurrence of the anticipated click. From this he concluded that in addition to a pleasure–displeasure continuum, his feelings seemed to have a tension–relief dimension. Moreover, he reported a mildly excited feeling when the click rate was increased, and a more quiet feeling when the rate was reduced.

Through this laborious procedure of patiently varying the speed of the metronome and meticulously noting his experiences (his sensations and feelings), Wundt arrived at three independent dimensions of feeling: pleasure–displeasure, tension–relaxation, and excitement–depression. Every feeling, he stated, can be located somewhere within this three-dimensional space.

Wundt believed that emotions are complex compounds of these elementary feelings, and that elementary feelings could be effectively described by defining their position on each of the three dimensions. Thus, emotions were reduced to conscious contents of the mind. Wundt's theory of feelings stimulated a great deal of research in the Leipzig and other laboratories, but has not stood the test of time.

Organizing the Elements of Experience: Apperception

Despite his interest in the elements of experience, Wundt recognized that when we look at the real world we see a unity or synthesis of perceptions. For example, we see a tree as a unity; we do not see the many and varied sensations of brightness, hue, or shape that his observers might report in a laboratory. Our visual experience comprehends the tree as a unity and not as each of the numerous elementary sensations and feelings that constitute the tree.

How is this totality of conscious experience compounded or built up from elementary component parts? Wundt postulated the doctrine of apperception to account for our unified conscious experiences. He designated the actual process of organizing the various elements into a unity as the principle of *creative synthesis* or the *law of psychic resultants*. The many elementary experiences are organized into a whole by this process of creative synthesis, which asserts, in essence, that the combination of elements creates new properties. As Wundt stated it, "Every psychic compound has characteristics which are by no means the mere sum of the characteristics of the elements" (1896, p. 375). Something new is created out of the synthesis of the elemental parts of experience. We might say, as the Gestalt psychologists have said since 1912, that the whole is different from the sum of its parts.

This notion of creative synthesis has a counterpart in chemistry. The combination of chemical elements produces resultants that contain properties that were not properties of the original elements. Apperception is, therefore, an active process. The mind is not merely acted upon by the experienced elements; rather, it acts on them in the creative synthesis of the parts to make up the whole. Thus, Wundt did not treat the process of association only in mechanical and passive terms as did James Mill and the other empiricists and associationists.

The Research Topics of the Leipzig Laboratory

Wundt himself determined the problems for experimental psychology during the early years of the Leipzig laboratory. The great man assigned to his students research topics that coincided with his own aims. For a number of years the problems with which the new experimental psychology concerned itself were defined by the work done at the Leipzig laboratory. More important, the extensive research performed there demonstrated that an experimentally based science of psychology was possible.

Because the methods and subject matter of the Leipzig laboratory formed the foundation for the new science, it is necessary to understand the nature of the work during the early years. Wundt believed that his new science should initially be concerned with research problems that had already been investigated and reduced to some kind of empirical and quantitative form. For the most part, he did not occupy himself with new areas of research, but rather with the extension and more formal development of current research problems.

Almost all the work emerging from the laboratory was published in the *Studien*. This journal published very little research that had not been done either at Leipzig or by Wundt's students so soon after leaving Leipzig that it still bore the imprint of the master. More than 100 studies were performed in the first 20 years of the laboratory's existence.

The first series of studies involved the psychological and physiological aspects of vision, hearing, and, to some extent, the so-called minor senses. Typical problems investigated in the area of visual sensation and perception included the psychophysics of color, color contrast, peripheral vision, negative afterimages, visual contrast, color blindness, visual size, and optical illusions. Psychophysical methods were used to investigate auditory sensations. Tactile sensations were studied as well as the time-sense, that is, the perception or estimation of intervals of varying lengths of time.

A topic that claimed a great deal of attention in the laboratory was reaction time, a subject that arose from the work of Bessel on the speed of reaction among astronomers. The speed of a reaction had been a topic of investigation since the end of the eighteenth century and had been studied by Helmholtz and by F. C. Donders, a Dutch physiologist. Wundt believed that he could demonstrate experimentally the three stages that he thought were present in a person's response to a stimulus: perception, apperception, and will.

After a stimulus is presented, subjects first perceive it, then apperceive it, and finally will to react, from which muscular movement results. Wundt hoped to develop a chronometry of the mind by succeeding in measuring the times for the various mental processes such as cognition, discrimination, and will. The promise of the method was not to be realized because in practiced subjects the three stages were not clearly apparent, and the times for the separate processes were not constant from person to person or from study to study.

Studies on reaction time were supplemented by research on attention and feeling. Wundt considered attention to be the most vivid perception of only a small portion of the entire content of consciousness at any one time. The reference is to what is commonly called the focus of attention. Those stimuli in this focus are the most clearly perceived and are quite distinct and separate from the rest of the visual field. A simple example is the words you are now reading relative to the rest of this page and objects in the surrounding environment that are perceived less clearly. In addition to studies on the range and the fluctuation of attention in the Leipzig laboratory, one of Wundt's students, James McKeen Cattell, studied attention span and found that four, five, or six units could be perceived in one short exposure.

Studies of feeling were undertaken in the 1890s to attempt to support the tridimensional theory. Wundt used the method of paired comparisons, which requires the comparison of stimuli in terms of the subjective feeling aroused. Other studies attempted to relate bodily changes, such as pulse rate and breathing, to corresponding feeling states.

Another area of investigation was the analysis of verbal associations, which had been begun by Sir Francis Galton (Chapter 6). Subjects were asked to respond with a single word when presented with the stimulus word. Wundt proceeded to classify the types of word association discovered when single-word stimuli were presented, to determine the nature of all verbal association.

The experimental areas of the psychophysiology of the senses, reaction time, psychophysics, and association constituted more than half of all the work published in the first few years of the *Studien*. Wundt showed some slight concern with child psychology and animal psychology, but apparently undertook no experimentation in these areas, believing that the conditions of study could not be adequately controlled.

Comment

The act of establishing the first psychological laboratory at Leipzig required a great deal of courage. The times required a person well versed in contemporary physiology and in philosophy and capable of combining these disciplines effectively. To accomplish his goal of establishing a new science, Wundt had to reject the nonscientific past and cut the ties between the new scientific psychology and the old mental philosophy.

By postulating that the subject matter of psychology was conscious experience, and that psychology was a science based on experience, Wundt was able to avoid discussions about the nature of the immortal soul and its relationship to the mortal body. He said simply and emphatically that psychology did not deal with this issue. This assertion was a great step forward.

One cannot help but marvel at Wundt's outstanding energy and endurance over a period of more than 60 years. His creation of a scientific experimental psychology commands immense respect and is the source of his greatest influence. He began (as he had announced his intention of doing) a new domain of science, and conducted research in a laboratory he designed exclusively for that purpose. He published the results in his own journal and tried to develop a systematic theory of the human mind. Some of his thoroughly trained students founded additional laboratories and continued experimenting on the problems and with the techniques set forth by the great man. Thus, Wundt provided psychology with all the accouterments of a modern science.

The times were, of course, ready for the Wundtian movement, which was the natural outcome of the development of the physiological sciences, particularly in the German universities. That Wundt was the culmination of this movement and not its originator does not diminish his stature. It did, after all, require a kind of genius, and a firm sense of dedication, courage, and vigor, to bring such a movement to fulfillment. The results of his efforts represent an achievement of such overwhelming importance that Wundt is accorded a position unique among psychologists of the modern period.

Like any great man, Wundt was subject to criticism with regard to many points of his systematic position and his experimental technique of introspection. It is hard to verify research findings obtained by introspection. When introspection by different persons gives different results, how can we decide who is right? Experiments using introspection do not ensure agreement among experimenters because introspective observation is a private affair. As such, disagreements cannot be settled by repeated observations. It was thought, however, that with more training and experience of observers, the method could be improved.

It was difficult to criticize Wundt's total system during his lifetime, primarily because he wrote so much and so fast. By the time a critic had prepared an attack on a particular point, Wundt had changed his argument in a new edition or was writing on a different topic. An opponent would be outwritten and buried under volumes of highly detailed and complex writings. Further, since Wundt's theories were like classificatory schemes, they tended to be somewhat loosely knit and almost impossible to verify. There was no vital center to his program, no point at which a critic might damage him with a single stroke. William James noted that

> He aims at being a sort of Napoleon of the intellectual world. Unfortunately he will never have a Waterloo, for he is a Napoleon without genius and with no central idea which, if defeated, brings down the whole fabric in ruins. . . . Cut him up like a worm, and each fragment crawls; there is no *nœud vital* in his mental medulla oblongata, so that you can't kill him all at once. (H. James, 1920, p. 263)

The Wundtian position has not stood the test of time. It is no longer an active issue in contemporary psychology and has not been for many years. Wundt's achievements are not diminished by that or by the fact that much of the history of psychology after him has consisted of rebellion against some of the limitations he placed on the field. Indeed, that fact enhances his achievements. Forward movement must have something to push against, and Wilhelm Wundt provided a compelling and magnificent beginning to modern experimental psychology. It is no exaggeration to add that "Our modern conceptions of psychology—its problems, its methods, its relation to other sciences, and its limits—all derive in large part from his inquiries" (Bringmann & Tweney, 1980, p. 5).

OTHER EARLY EUROPEAN PSYCHOLOGISTS

Wundt had a monopoly on the new psychology for only a short time. At other laboratories in Germany the science was also beginning to flourish. Although he was obviously the most important organizer and systematizer in the early days of psychology, there were others who began to influence the new science. Although these early non-Wundtian psychologists proposed different points of view, all were engaged in the common enterprise of developing the new psychology. Their endeavors made Germany the undisputed center of the new movement.

There were, however, other developments in England that were to give psychology an entirely new theme and direction. Charles Darwin proposed his theory of evolution and Sir Francis Galton began work on the psychology of individual differences. These forces would influence the development of American psychology even more than the work of Wundt. In addition, early American psychologists, most of whom had studied at Leipzig, returned home and made of the Wundtian psychology something uniquely American in form and temperament. But more of these developments later. The important point for now is that very shortly after its founding, psychology became divided into factions. Although Wundt had founded psychology, his approach shortly became only one of several varieties. Let us turn to a discussion of Wundt's contemporaries in Germany.

Through his studies of learning and memory, Hermann Ebbinghaus (1850–1909) greatly expanded the scope of experimental psychology.

Hermann Ebbinghaus (1850–1909)

Just a few years after Wundt had stated that it was not possible to conduct experiments on the higher mental processes, a then-unknown psychologist who worked alone, isolated from any center of psychology, began successfully to experiment on these processes. Hermann Ebbinghaus became the first psychologist to investigate learning and memory experimentally. In doing so, he not only challenged Wundt but changed radically the way in which association or learning could be dealt with as well.

Before Ebbinghaus, most notably in the work of the British empiricists and associationists, the customary way to study association was to deal with associations that were already formed. The investigator would, in a sense, work backward, attempting to determine how the associations had been formed. Ebbinghaus began at a different starting point—the development of associations. In this way, it was possible to control the conditions under which the associations were formed and thus to make the study of learning considerably more objective.

Accepted as one of the great manifestations of original genius in experimental psychology, Ebbinghaus's investigation of learning and forgetting was the first venture into a truly psychological problem area, one that was not a part of physiology, as was the case with so much of Wundt's research. As a result, experimental psychology was considerably widened in scope.

 Born near Bonn in 1850, Ebbinghaus undertook his university studies first at Bonn in history and philology and then at Halle and Berlin. In the course of his academic training his interests shifted to philosophy, in which he received his degree in 1873, following military service during the Franco–Prussian War. The next seven years were devoted to independent study in Berlin, England, and France, where his interests shifted toward science. About 1876, three years before Wundt established his laboratory, Ebbinghaus bought a secondhand copy of Fechner's *Elemente der Psychophysik* at a bookstall in London (not in Paris, as is generally believed) (Traxel, 1985). This chance encounter influenced him and the new psychology profoundly. Fechner's mathematical approach to psychological phenomena was an exciting disclosure to the young Ebbinghaus, and he resolved to do for the study of memory what Fechner had done for psychophysics, through rigid and systematic measurements. He wanted to apply the experimental method to the higher mental processes and decided, probably as a result of the influence of the British associationists, to make the attempt in the field of memory.

 Consider Ebbinghaus's course of action in light of the problem he chose and his own situation. Learning and memory had never been studied experimentally. Indeed, the eminent Wundt had stated that they could not be. Further, Ebbinghaus had no academic appointment, no university setting in which to conduct his work, no teacher, and no laboratory. Nevertheless, he carried out alone, over a period of five years, a long series of carefully controlled and thorough studies, using himself as the only subject.

 For the basic measure of learning he adapted a technique from the associationists, who were emphasizing the principle of frequency of associations as a condition of recall. He reasoned that the difficulty of learning material could be measured by counting the number of repetitions needed for one perfect reproduction of the material.[3]

 Ebbinghaus used similar, though not identical, lists of syllables as the material to be learned, and repeated the task frequently to be sure of the accuracy of his results. In this way he could cancel out variable errors from trial to trial, and then take an average measure. So systematic was Ebbinghaus in his experimentation that he even regulated his personal habits, keeping them as constant as possible and following a rigid daily pattern, always learning the material at the same time each day.

 For the subject matter of his research—the material to be learned—Ebbinghaus invented the series of meaningless syllables known today as *nonsense syllables,* which revolutionized the study of association or learning. Titchener later commented that the use of nonsense syllables marked the first significant advance in the area of association since Aristotle (Shakow, 1930). Ebbinghaus recognized an inherent difficulty in using prose or poetry. Meanings or associations are already attached to words by those who know the language. These existing associations can facilitate the learning of material and, because they are present at the time of experimentation, they cannot be meaningfully controlled. Ebbinghaus sought material that would be uniformly unassociated,

---

[3]This is an example of the influence of Fechner. As noted in Chapter 3, Fechner measured sensations indirectly by measuring the stimulus intensity necessary to produce a just noticeable difference in sensation. Ebbinghaus approached the problem of measuring memory in a similar way, that is, indirectly, by counting the number of trials or repetitions needed to learn the material.

completely homogeneous, and equally unfamiliar—material with which there could be no past associations. Nonsense syllables, formed of two consonants with a vowel in between, as in *lef, bok*, or *yat*, satisfied these criteria. He put all possible combinations of consonants and vowels on cards, yielding a supply of 2300 syllables from which to draw at random those to be learned.

Ebbinghaus designed a number of experiments to determine the influence of various conditions on learning and retention. One of these studies investigated the difference between his speed in memorizing lists of nonsense syllables and in memorizing meaningful materials. To determine this difference, he memorized stanzas of Byron's *Don Juan*. Each stanza has 80 syllables, and Ebbinghaus found that it required about nine readings to memorize one stanza. He then memorized a list of 80 nonsense syllables and discovered that this task required almost 80 repetitions. He concluded that meaningless material is approximately nine times harder to learn than meaningful material.

He also investigated the effect of the length of the material to be learned on the number of repetitions necessary for a perfect reproduction. He concluded that longer material requires more repetitions and, consequently, more time to learn. He found that the average time per syllable was markedly increased by lengthening the number of syllables to be learned. These results are predictable in a general way: the more we have to learn, the longer it will take us. The significance of Ebbinghaus's work is in the careful control of conditions, the quantitative analysis of the data, and the finding that both total learning time and time per syllable increase with longer lists of syllables.

Ebbinghaus studied a number of other variables thought to influence learning and retention, such as the effect of overlearning (repeating the lists more times than necessary for one perfect reproduction), near and remote associations within lists, repeated learning or review, and the influence of time between learning and recall. His research on the effect of time produced the famous Ebbinghaus curve of forgetting. This curve, as every psychology student knows, demonstrates that material is forgotten very rapidly in the first few hours after learning, and more and more slowly thereafter.

In 1880 Ebbinghaus received an academic appointment at the University of Berlin, where he continued his research on memory, repeating and verifying his earlier studies. He published the results of all his research in the important *Über das Gedächtnis* (*On Memory*) in 1885. "It was epoch-making . . . because it was seen at once to be a breach by experimental psychology in the barrier about the 'higher mental processes.' Ebbinghaus had opened up a new field" (Boring, 1950, p. 388).

This book represents what is perhaps the most brilliant single investigation in the history of experimental psychology. In addition to beginning a whole new field of study, which is still vital today, it provides a striking example of technical skill, perseverance, and ingenuity. It is not possible to find in the history of psychology any other investigator working alone who subjected himself to such a rigid regimen of experimentation. The research was so exacting, thorough, and systematic that it is still cited in contemporary textbooks.

Ebbinghaus did not continue research on memory but instead let others develop the field and extend and refine the methodology. He published relatively little after 1885, and a year later he was promoted to assistant professor at Berlin. He founded a laboratory and a journal (the latter with Arthur König, a physicist), the *Zeitschrift für Psychologie and Physiologie der Sinnesorgane* (*Journal of Psychology and Physiology of the Sense Organs*) in 1890. A new journal was needed in Germany because Wundt's *Studien*, the exclusive organ of the Leipzig laboratory, could not present all the research being conducted at that time. The need for another journal, just nine years after Wundt had begun his, is significant testimony to the phenomenal growth in size and diversity of the new psychology.

Apparently because of his lack of publications, Ebbinghaus was not promoted again at Berlin, and in 1894 he moved to a lesser post in the university hierarchy at Breslau, where he remained until 1905. There, in 1897, he developed a sentence completion test, probably the first successful test of the so-called higher mental capacities, a modified form of which is used in many tests of general intelligence today.

In 1902 Ebbinghaus published a highly successful general textbook, *Die Grundzüge der Psychologie* (*The Principles of Psychology*), dedicated to the memory of Fechner, and in 1908 a more popular text, *Abriss der Psychologie* (*A Summary of Psychology*). Both books appeared in several editions and were revised by others after Ebbinghaus's death. Ebbinghaus left Breslau for Halle in 1905, and died suddenly of pneumonia a few years later, at the age of 59.

Ebbinghaus did not make any theoretical or systematic contributions to psychology; he created no formal system and had no disciples of importance to psychology. He did not found a school, nor did he seem to want to. Yet he is of great importance not only to the study of learning and memory, which he began, but also to experimental psychology as a whole.

One measure of the overall historical worth of a scientist is how well the position and conclusions stand the test of time. By that standard, one might suggest that Ebbinghaus was more important than Wundt. His research brought objectivity, quantification, and experimentation to the study of association or learning, a topic that has become a central one in contemporary psychology. It is because of Ebbinghaus that work on the concept of association changed from mere speculation about its attributes to its investigation with the aid of the scientific method. Many of his conclusions on learning and memory remain valid a century after he published them.

Georg Elias Müller (1850–1934)

A physiologist and philosopher by training, Müller had a strong interest in psychology, which he expressed during a 40-year career at Göttingen. From 1881 until 1921, his well-equipped laboratory rivaled that at Leipzig and attracted many students from Europe and America.

Müller did considerable work on color vision, and extensively criticized and elaborated on Fechner's work in psychophysics. Müller's research contributions were so substantial that Titchener delayed for two years the second volume of his *Experimental Psychology* so that he could incorporate material from Müller's latest book. Müller was one of the first to work in the area begun by Ebbinghaus, the experimental study of learning and memory. His careful research verified and extended many of Ebbinghaus's findings. Ebbinghaus's approach had been strictly objective; he had not recorded introspections about his mental processes while engaged in his learning tasks. Müller believed that these reports tended to make learning appear too mechanical or automatic a process. He thought that the mind was more actively involved in the learning process, and although Müller used the objective methods of Ebbinghaus, he added introspective report. His results indicated that learning did not proceed mechanically, that the subjects were actively involved in consciously organizing and grouping the material, and even in finding meanings in the nonsense syllables.

On the basis of this research, Müller concluded that association by contiguity alone cannot adequately account for learning, because the subjects appeared to be actively seeking relationships among the stimuli to be learned. He suggested that there is a set of mental phenomena, such as readiness, hesitation, and doubt (the so-called conscious attitudes), that actively influence learning. Similar findings soon followed from the work of the Würzburg laboratory, which we discuss later in this chapter.

Müller was the first to propose and to demonstrate in the laboratory the interference theory of forgetting. In his view, forgetting was less a function of memory decay than of new material interfering with the recall of material that had been learned earlier.

One final contribution to the study of learning deserves mention. Along with Friedrich Schumann, Müller developed the memory drum, a revolving drum that makes possible the uniform presentation of material to be learned. By now a familiar piece of laboratory equipment, this apparatus is significant because it increased the precision and objectivity of research on learning.

Franz Brentano (1838–1917)

At about age 16, Brentano began his training for the priesthood, studying at Berlin, Munich, and Tübingen, where he received his degree in philosophy in 1864. He was ordained the same year, and two years later began teaching philosophy at Würzburg, writing and lecturing on Aristotle.

In 1870 the Vatican Council accepted the doctrine of papal infallibility, with which Brentano could not agree. He resigned his professorship (to which he had been appointed as a priest) and left the Church.

Brentano's most famous work, *Psychologie vom empirischen Standpunkte* (*Psychology from an Empirical Standpoint*), was published in 1874, the year in which the second part of the first edition of Wundt's *Principles of Physiological Psychology* was published. Brentano's book was in direct opposition to the Wundtian view, attesting to the dissent apparent in the new psychology. Also in 1874 Brentano was appointed professor of philosophy at the University of Vienna, where he remained for 20 years, during which time his influence grew considerably. He was a popular lecturer, and among his students were several men who achieved their own prominence in the history of psychology— Carl Stumpf, Christian von Ehrenfels, and Sigmund Freud. In 1894 Brentano retired and spent his remaining years in Italy and Switzerland, engaged in study and writing.

Brentano was one of the more important non-Wundtians because of his diverse influences within psychology. (We will see that he is one of the intellectual precursors of Gestalt psychology and of humanistic psychology.) Brentano shared with Wundt the goal of making psychology a science. Whereas Wundt's psychology was experimental, Brentano's was empirical. The primary method of psychology for Brentano was observation, not experimentation, although he did not reject the experimental method. An empirical approach generally is broader in scope in that it obtains its data from observation and individual experience as well as from experimentation.

Brentano opposed Wundt's fundamental idea that psychology should study the con-

Franz Brentano (1838–1917) contended that psychology should be empirical, studying the activity rather than the content of the mind.

tent of conscious experience. He argued that the proper subject matter of psychology is mental activity, for example, the mental act of seeing rather than the mental content (that which is seen).

Thus, Brentano's *act psychology* countered the Wundtian view that the psychic processes involve contents. He argued that the distinction must be drawn between experience as a structure and experience as an activity. The sensory content of red is quite different from the activity of sensing red. Brentano urged that this act of experiencing is the true subject matter for psychology. He stated that a color is not a mental quality but strictly a physical quality. The act of seeing the color, however, is mental. Of course, the act always involves an object, that is, a content is always present because the act of seeing is meaningless unless something is seen.

This new subject matter necessitated a different method of study because acts, unlike sensory contents, are not accessible through the experimental method practiced at Wundt's Leipzig laboratory. The study of mental acts requires observation on a larger scale than that used by Wundt. For this reason, act psychology, as we have noted, is more empirical than experimental in its methodology. This does not imply that Brentano's psychology was a return to speculative philosophy; though not experimental in nature, it did rely on careful observation.

Brentano's position had its loyal adherents, but the Wundtian psychology maintained its prominence in the new psychology. Because Wundt published much more than Brentano, his position was better known. Also, it was easier to study sensations or contents with the new methods of psychophysics than to study the more elusive acts.

Carl Stumpf (1848–1936)

Born into a medical family, Stumpf came into contact with science at an early age but developed a greater interest in music. At the age of 7 he began studying the violin, and by age 10 was composing music. As a student at Würzburg, he was captivated by Brentano and turned his attention to philosophy and science. At Brentano's suggestion he went to Göttingen, where he met both Weber and Fechner and received his doctorate in 1868. He held a number of academic appointments over the following years, during which time he began his work in psychology.

In 1894 Stumpf was awarded an appointment at the University of Berlin, the most prized professorship in German psychology. Wundt, who at that time was the dean of German psychologists, would have seemed the logical choice for the position. It has been suggested that the influential Helmholtz opposed his appointment. The years spent at Berlin were extremely productive, and his original laboratory of three small rooms grew into a large and important institute. Although the laboratory never rivaled Wundt's in scope or intensity of research, Stumpf is often considered to be Wundt's major competitor.

Stumpf's early psychological writings were concerned with space perception, but his most influential work is *Tonpsychologie* (*Psychology of Tone*), which appeared in two volumes in 1883 and 1890. This work, and his other studies of music, earned him a place second only to Helmholtz's in the field of acoustics and were a pioneering effort in the psychological study of music.

The influence of Brentano may explain Stumpf's acceptance of a less rigorous approach to psychology than that considered necessary at Leipzig. Stumpf argued that the primary data of psychology are phenomena. Phenomenology, the kind of introspection he favored, refers to the examination of unbiased experience—experience just as it occurs. He did not agree with Wundt on breaking experience down into elements. To do so, Stumpf argued, is to render the experience artificial and abstract, no longer natural. A student of Stumpf's, Edmund Husserl, later developed the philosophy of

His studies of music and tone led Carl Stumpf (1848–1936) into sharp conflict with Wundt over the proper use of introspection in psychology.

phenomenology. The phenomenological movement in Germany was a precursor of other forms of psychology, notably Gestalt psychology (Chapter 12).

Wundt and Stumpf, in a series of publications, waged a bitter controversy about the introspection of tones. The debate was started by Stumpf on a theoretical level but was personalized by Wundt. Essentially, the issue involved the question of which introspectionist's reports were the more credible. When dealing with tones, should one accept the results of highly trained laboratory observers (Wundt) or of expert musicians (Stumpf)? Stumpf would not accept the results obtained at Wundt's laboratory on this problem.

While continuing to write on music and acoustics, Stumpf established a center for the collection of recordings of primitive music from all over the world, founded the

Berlin Association for Child Psychology, and published a theory of feeling in which he attempted to reduce feeling to sensation. Stumpf was one of a number of German psychologists who maintained their independence from Wundt, and so strove to expand the boundaries of psychology.

Oswald Külpe (1862–1915) and the Würzburg School

Initially a student, disciple, and follower of Wundt, Külpe in the course of his career led a group of students in a movement to break away from what he considered the limitations of the master's work. Although Külpe's movement was not a revolution, it was a declaration of freedom from the narrowness of some of Wundt's views. Külpe worked on a number of problems that Wundt's psychology had disregarded.

At the age of 19 Külpe began his university training at Leipzig. His intention was to study history, but under the influence of Wundt he switched, for a time, to philosophy and to experimental psychology, which, in 1881, was still in its infancy. History maintained a strong attraction for Külpe because after a year with Wundt he resumed its study at Berlin. Two further academic forays into psychology and history followed before he returned to Wundt and Leipzig in 1886 for eight years. After receiving his degree at Leipzig, he stayed on as *Dozent* and assistant to Wundt, carried on research in the laboratory, and wrote a psychology textbook, *Grundriss der Psychologie (Outline of Psychology)*. This text, published in 1893 and dedicated to Wundt, defined psychology as the science of the facts of experience as dependent on the experiencing individual.

In 1894 Külpe became a professor at Würzburg, where two years later he established a laboratory that before long became almost as important as Wundt's Leipzig laboratory. Among the students attracted to Würzburg were several Americans, one of whom, James Rowland Angell, was an important figure in the development of functionalism (Chapter 8). Apparently, Külpe was more concerned with philosophy and esthetics than with psychology during the laboratory's early years. Although his own writings are philosophical in nature, a great deal of research performed under his direction in the laboratory was published. Külpe served not only as the inspiration for his students' research, but also as observer in most of the laborious kinds of introspective experiments practiced at Würzburg.

In the *Grundriss* Külpe did not discuss the higher mental process of thought. At that time, his position was congruent with that of Wundt, in whose shadow he still moved. By the turn of the century, however, Külpe was convinced that the thought processes could be studied experimentally. Memory, another higher mental process, had already been studied experimentally by Hermann Ebbinghaus. If memory could be studied in the laboratory, why not thought? For the first time experimentation was consistently applied to the higher mental processes including memory, thought, and feelings. Posing this question put Külpe into direct opposition to his former mentor, because Wundt had emphasized that the higher mental processes could not be studied experimentally.

A second point of difference between the Würzburg school, as it came to be called, and Wundt's system relates to the method of introspection. Külpe developed a method called *systematic experimental introspection* that involved the performance of a complex task—such as establishing logical connections between concepts—after which subjects were required to render a retrospective report of their experiences during the task. In other words, subjects had to perform some mental process, such as thinking or judging,

Trained at Leipzig, Oswald Külpe (1862–1915) and his Würzburg school extended psychology's subject matter to include higher mental processes.

and then examine how they thought or judged. Wundt had rejected the use of retrospective reports in his laboratory. He wanted to study conscious experience as it occurred, not the memory of what had occurred.

Külpe's method was systematic in that the whole experience was described precisely by fractionating it into time periods. Similar tasks were repeated many times so that the introspective accounts could be corrected, corroborated, and amplified. Introspective reports were often supplemented by questioning to direct the subjects' attention to particular points.

There were other major differences between the introspective approaches of Külpe and Wundt. Wundt, as we noted, did not favor having the subjects describe their inner experiences in detail. Most of his research focused instead on objective, quantitative measurements such as reaction times and the kinds of judgments required in psycho-physical research.

Külpe's systematic experimental introspection emphasized subjective, qualitative, highly detailed reports from subjects on the nature of their own thought processes. Subjects were not just to make simple, straightforward judgments on, say, the intensity of a stimulus. Rather, they were to describe all the complex mental processes they underwent during their exposure to some experimental task. Külpe's approach was geared directly to the investigation of what was going on in a subject's mind during a conscious experience.

Külpe did not reject Wundt's focus on conscious experience, his research tool of introspection, or his fundamental task of analyzing consciousness into its basic content. The Würzburg school did not so much revolt against the master as attempt to expand the conception of psychology's subject matter to include the higher mental processes, and to refine the method of introspection.

What were the results of this attempted expansion and refinement? Wundt's point of view stressed that conscious experience could be reduced to its component sensory or imaginal elements. All experience, Wundt had said, is composed of sensations or images. Külpe's program of direct introspection of thought processes found evidence supporting the opposite point of view—that thinking can occur without any sensory or imaginal content! This finding came to be identified as *imageless thought*, to represent the notion of meanings in thought that do not seem to involve any specific images. Thus, a nonsensory form or aspect of consciousness was identified.

The first important contribution from the Würzburg school was a study by Karl Marbe on the comparative judgment of weights. Marbe found that although sensations and images are indeed present during the task, they seem to play no part in the process of judgment itself. Subjects do not know how the judgments (of lighter or heavier) come into their minds. This finding contradicted the belief about thought that had been held for centuries. It had been supposed that in making a judgment of this kind, subjects retained a mental image of the first object and compared it with the sensory impression of the second object. Marbe's experiment demonstrated that there is no such comparison of image and impression, and that the process of judgment is much more elusive than had been supposed.

These and related experiments conducted at Würzburg demonstrated that although the conscious elements usually considered necessary are not essential for thought, there are apparently other conscious states present that had not been previously suspected. These additional states, such as hesitation, doubt, confidence, searching, or waiting for an answer, were considered to be neither sensations, images, nor feelings, and were initially called "conscious attitudes." In a subsequent work J. Orth suggested that Wundt's feelings of tension–relaxation and excitement–depression could be reduced to these same intangible and obscure conscious attitudes.

The Würzburg group also dealt with association and will. A classic study by Henry Watt demonstrated that in an associative task (for example, asking subjects to find a subordinate or superordinate of a particular word), subjects have little relevant information to report about their conscious process of judgment. This finding provided a further demonstration of conscious experience that could not be reduced to sensations and images. Watt found that his subjects were able to respond correctly without being consciously aware of intending to do so during the time of response. He concluded that the conscious work was done before the task was performed, at the time when the instructions were given and understood. According to Watt, subjects, after receiving these instructions, determined to react in the manner required. When presented with the stimulus word, subjects carried out the instructions without any further conscious effort. Through the instructions, subjects had apparently established an unconscious set, or *determining tendency*, to respond in the way the instructions directed. Once the task had been understood and this determining tendency adopted, the actual task was performed with little, if any, conscious effort. What the Würzburg group suggested is that predispositions outside of consciousness are somehow able to control conscious activities.

A new period in the Würzburg school began in 1907 with the work of Karl Bühler, whose method involved presenting to subjects a question that required some thought before it could be answered. Subjects then gave as complete an account as possible of the steps involved in reaching the answer, with the experimenter interjecting questions about the process. Bühler's importance lies in his careful demonstration of the existence of nonsensory thought processes. This notion had already been uncovered, as we have seen, but it had been only one aspect and not a major focus of the earlier Würzburg work. Bühler stressed the notion of elements of experience that are not sensory in nature. He asserted explicitly that these new types of structural elements, these thought elements, are vital to the process of thought and must be given serious consideration.

Not unexpectedly, Külpe's refinement of Wundt's method of introspection and the attempt to add to the list of elements evoked strong criticism from the more orthodox Wundtians. It came in the form of vigorous and scathing attacks from Wundt. Wundt called the Würzburg form of introspection "mock" experiments and said that their method did not really involve experimentation or introspection.

In a way it is strange that the Wundtians so strongly opposed the Würzburg notion of nonsensory mental life. After all, Külpe was proceeding along paths that Wundt had cleared. Had not Wundt himself thought along not too dissimilar lines? Was not his notion of feelings a recognition of nonsensory elements of conscious experience? It was certainly no accident that Külpe, a product of Wundtian training, had instigated this movement.

The 15 years that Külpe remained at Würzburg were his most influential for the history of psychology. In 1909 he went to Bonn, where he founded a laboratory, and in 1913 he moved to Munich. His interest in philosophical problems, particularly esthetics, came to the fore in his post-Würzburg years. Külpe wrote very little concerning his students' work at Würzburg, and his planned description of the nature of the thought processes was never written.

A major contribution to modern psychology is the Würzburg emphasis on the topic of motivation. The key concept of determining tendency or set has a bearing on motivation as it is treated in today's psychology. Also, the Würzburg demonstration that experience depended not only on conscious elements, but also on unconscious determining tendencies, suggests the role of unconscious determinants of behavior, which forms a major part of Freud's systematic position (Chapter 13).

Comment

We see, then, division and controversy enveloping psychology almost as soon as it was founded. But it must be emphasized that for all their differences, these early psychologists were united in theme and purpose.

Wundt, Ebbinghaus, Brentano, Stumpf, and others had irrevocably changed the study of human nature. Because of their efforts, the new psychology was no longer

> a study of the soul, certainly not an inquiry by rational analysis into its simplicity, substantiality and immortality. It was a study, by observation and experiment, of certain reactions of the human organism not included in the subject matter of any other science. The German psychologists, in spite of their many differences, were to this extent engaged in a common enterprise; and their ability, their industry, and the common direction of their labors all made the developments in the German universities the center of the new movement in psychology. (Heidbreder, 1933, p. 105)[*]

Germany did not remain the center of the new movement for long. A version of Wundt's psychology was soon brought to America by his student, E. B. Titchener.

SUGGESTED READINGS

Wundt

Anderson, R. J. (1975). The untranslated content of Wundt's *Grundzüge der Physiologischen Psychologie*. *Journal of the History of the Behavioral Sciences, 21,* 381–386.

Baldwin, B. T. (1921). In memory of Wilhelm Wundt by his American students. *Psychological Review, 28,* 153–158.

Blumenthal, A. L. (1975). A reappraisal of Wilhelm Wundt. *American Psychologist, 30,* 1081–1088.

Boring, E. G. (1965). On the subjectivity of important historical dates: Leipzig 1879. *Journal of the History of the Behavioral Sciences, 1,* 5–9.

Bringmann, W., Balance, W., & Evans, R. (1975). Wilhelm Wundt 1832–1920: A brief biographical sketch. *Journal of the History of the Behavioral Sciences, 11,* 287–297.

Bringmann, W., & Tweney, R. (Eds.). (1980). *Wundt studies: A centennial collection.* Toronto: C. J. Hogrefe.

Bringmann, W., & Ungerer, G. (1980). The foundation of the Institute for Experimental Psychology at Leipzig University. *Psychological Research, 42,* 5–18.

Cattell, J. McK. (1888). The psychological laboratory at Leipzig. *Mind, 13,* 37–51.

Danziger, K. (1979). The positivist repudiation of Wundt. *Journal of the History of the Behavioral Sciences, 15,* 205–230.

Danziger, K. (1980). Wundt's psychological experiment in the light of his philosophy of science. *Psychological Research, 42,* 109–122.

Haeberlin, H. K. (1916). The theoretical foundations of Wundt's folk-psychology. *Psychological Review, 23,* 279–302.

---

[*]This, and all subsequent quotations credited to Heidbreder, 1933, are from Edna Heidbreder, *Seven Psychologies,* © 1933, renewed 1961. Reprinted by permission of Prentice-Hall, Inc., Englewood Cliffs, New Jersey.

Leahey, T. H. (1979). Something old, something new: Attention in Wundt and modern cognitive psychology. *Journal of the History of the Behavioral Sciences, 15*, 242–252.

Leahey, T. H. (1981). The mistaken mirror: On Wundt's and Titchener's psychologies. *Journal of the History of the Behavioral Sciences, 17*, 273–282.

Mischel, T. (1970). Wundt and the conceptual foundations of psychology. *Philosophical and Phenomenological Research, 31*, 1–26.

Titchener, E. B. (1921). Wilhelm Wundt. *American Journal of Psychology, 32*, 161–178.

Ebbinghaus

Postman, L. (1968). Hermann Ebbinghaus. *American Psychologist, 23*, 149–157.

Shakow, D. (1930). Hermann Ebbinghaus. *American Journal of Psychology, 42*, 505–518.

Müller

Boring, E. G. (1935). Georg Elias Müller, 1850–1934. *American Journal of Psychology, 47*, 344–348.

Boring, E. G. (1941). An operational restatement of G. E. Müller's psychophysical axioms. *Psychological Review, 48*, 457–464.

Brentano

Puglisi, M. (1924). Brentano: A biographical sketch. *American Journal of Psychology, 35*, 414–419.

Rancurello, A. C. (1968). *A study of Franz Brentano: His psychological standpoint and his significance in the history of psychology.* New York: Academic Press.

Sussman, E. J. (1962). Franz Brentano—much alive, though dead. *American Psychologist, 17*, 504–506.

Titchener, E. B. (1921). Brentano and Wundt: Empirical and experimental psychology. *American Journal of Psychology, 32*, 108–120.

Stumpf

Langfeld, H. S. (1937). Carl Stumpf: 1848–1936. *American Journal of Psychology, 49*, 316–320.

Külpe and the Würzburg School

Dallenbach, K. M. (1951). Oswald Külpe: 1862–1915. *American Journal of Psychology, 64*, 3.

Külpe, O. (1973). *Outlines of psychology* (3rd ed.). New York: Arno Press. (Original work published 1909).

Lindenfeld, D. (1978). Oswald Külpe and the Würzburg school. *Journal of the History of the Behavioral Sciences, 14*, 132–141.

Ogden, R. M. (1951). Oswald Külpe and the Würzburg school. *American Journal of Psychology, 64*, 4–19.

5
Structuralism

E. B. Titchener altered Wundt's system dramatically while claiming to be a loyal follower. He offered his own approach, which he called *structuralism*, as representing the form of psychology espoused by Wundt. Yet the two systems were radically different, and the label "structuralism" cannot be applied to Wundt's psychology, only to Titchener's. Structural psychology attained prominence in the United States for some years until it was challenged and overthrown by newer movements. Although Titchener was influential in the history of American psychology, others in the United States, working at the same time—notably William James, G. Stanley Hall, and James McKeen Cattell—were developing their own quite different approach to psychology, as we shall see in Chapter 7.

Although Wundt recognized elements or contents of consciousness, his overriding concern was their organization into higher-level cognitive processes through the principle of apperception. Wundt viewed the mind as having the power to synthesize the elements voluntarily, a position that contrasted with the mechanical and passive notions of association developed by the British empiricists and associationists.

Titchener accepted the empiricist and associationist focus on the elements or contents of the mind and their mechanical linkage through association. This is perhaps not surprising considering that he was born in England and educated at Oxford University. He discarded Wundt's emphasis on apperception and concentrated instead on the elements that form the structure of consciousness. In Titchener's view, the fundamental task of psychology was to discover the nature of these elementary conscious experiences, that is, to analyze consciousness into its separate parts and by so doing discover the structure of consciousness. To accomplish this, Titchener modified Wundt's introspective method so that it resembled Külpe's approach more than Wundt's.

EDWARD BRADFORD TITCHENER (1867–1927)

The Life of Titchener

Titchener spent his most productive years at Cornell University in New York. For Titchener, who is often pictured clad in the academic gown he invariably wore to class, every lecture was a dramatic production. The staging was carefully prepared by assistants under Titchener's watchful eye. The staff and junior faculty, who attended all his lectures, entered through one door to take front-row seats, and the professor came through another that led directly to the lecture platform. Afterward, the lecture was solemnly discussed by the faculty and graduate students.

As Titchener put it, his Oxford gown gave him the right to be dogmatic. Although he spent only two years with Wundt, Titchener resembled his mentor in many respects, including his autocratic nature, his formal lectures, and even his bearded appearance.

Born in Chichester, England, into an old family that had little money, Titchener relied on his considerable intellectual abilities to win scholarships to further his education. He attended Malvern College and then Oxford, where he studied philosophy and the classics for four years and became a research assistant in physiology for the fifth year.

While at Oxford, Titchener became interested in Wundt's new psychology, an interest that was not shared or encouraged by anyone at the university. It was natural, then, that he should journey to Leipzig, the mecca for scientific pilgrims, to study under Wundt for two years, receiving his degree in 1892. There seems no doubt that Wundt made a lifelong impression on the young student, though Titchener apparently saw little of him (Wundt was 35 years older and somewhat aloof). The years at Leipzig determined Titchener's future in psychology and that of his many students. He also had an impact on American psychology, but as we shall see, psychology in America was to follow a course of its own, a course that diverged sharply from Titchener's approach.

After receiving his degree, Titchener wanted to become the pioneer of the new experimental psychology in England. The British, however, were skeptical of a scientific approach to one of their favorite philosophical subjects. Therefore, after a few months as an extension lecturer in biology at Oxford, Titchener went to the United States to teach psychology and direct the laboratory at the new Cornell University. He was then 25 years old, and he remained at Cornell for the rest of his life.

The years 1893–1900 were spent in developing the laboratory, acquiring equipment, conducting research, and writing some 62 articles. As more students were attracted to Cornell, Titchener relinquished the time-consuming task of participating personally in every research study and in later years the research was conducted almost entirely by his students.

It was through direction of his students' research that his systematic position reached fruition. Titchener supervised more than 50 doctoral candidates in psychology in 35 years, and most of their dissertations bear the stamp of his personal thought. He exercised great authority in the selection of the students' research problems, assigning topics that were relevant to the issues with which he was concerned at the time. In this way, Titchener built a unified systematic position, and all graduate students at a given time were expected to work collectively on his ideas. "Titchener thus erected an ivory tower in which he was to sit aloft and direct the course of what he considered to be the only scientific psychology worthy of the name" (Roback, 1952, p. 184).

Titchener's own bibliography includes 216 articles and notes and a number of books. He translated the master, Wundt, and when he had completed the third edition of *Principles of Physiological Psychology*, he found that Wundt had finished another new edition. Titchener then translated this fourth edition, only to learn that the tireless Wundt had published a fifth edition.

Structuralism was established as the first American school of thought in psychology by Edward Bradford Titchener (1867–1927).

Titchener wrote *An Outline of Psychology* in 1896, *Primer of Psychology* in 1898, and the four-volume *Experimental Psychology* in 1901–1905. Külpe is said to have described the last as "the most erudite psychological work in the English language" (Boring, 1950, p. 413). These "manuals," as the volumes of *Experimental Psychology* came to be called, helped to speed the growth of laboratory work in psychology and influenced a genera-tion of American experimental psychologists, including John B. Watson, the founder of behaviorism (Chapter 10). The textbooks enjoyed wide popularity and some were translated into Russian, Italian, German, Spanish, and French.

Titchener engaged in several hobbies that tended to divert time and energy from psychology. He became so proficient in music that he conducted a small ensemble at his home every Sunday evening, and at one time substituted for a music professor at Cornell. His avid interest in coin collecting led him, with typical thoroughness, to learn such difficult languages as Chinese and Arabic to master the characters on the coins. In addition to his knowledge of classical languages, he was conversant in a half-dozen modern languages, including Russian. Throughout his career he maintained a voluminous correspondence with colleagues; the majority of these letters were typewritten by Titchener and contain additional handwritten material.

As he grew older, Titchener withdrew more and more from social and university life. He had become a living legend at Cornell, though a number of faculty members had never met him or even seen him. He did a great deal of his work at home and spent relatively little time at the university. After 1909 he lectured only on Monday evenings of the spring semester of each year. He was well protected in his study at home from intrusions from the outside world. His wife screened all callers and it was understood that no student would telephone him except in an extreme emergency.

Although he did tend to be autocratic, in the mold of the German professor, he was also kind and helpful to students and colleagues, so long as they paid him the deference and respect he felt were his due. Stories are told of how junior faculty members and students washed his car and installed his window screens in the summer, not on command, but out of respect and admiration.

Karl Dallenbach (1967), a former student, quotes Titchener as saying, "A man could not hope to become a psychologist until after he had learned to smoke." Accordingly, most of his students took to cigars, at least in his presence.

> Cora Friedline, one of Titchener's doctoral students, was discussing her research in Titchener's office when his ever-present cigar caught his beard on fire. He was talking at the time and his imposing manner made her reluctant to interrupt. Finally she said, "I beg your pardon, Dr. Titchener, but your whiskers are on fire." By the time he extinguished the flames, the fire had burned through his shirt and his underwear.[1]

Titchener's concern for his students did not end when they left Cornell, nor did his impact on their lives. Dallenbach, upon receiving his Ph.D., intended to go to medical school, but Titchener obtained a teaching position for him at the University of Oregon. Dallenbach thought that Titchener would approve of his going to medical school, "but he did not. I had to go to Oregon, as he did not intend to have his training and work with me wasted" (1967, p. 91).

Titchener's relations with psychologists outside his own group were never very close. Elected to the American Psychological Association by the charter members in 1892, he resigned shortly thereafter because the association would not expel a member he accused of plagiarism. It is said that a friend paid Titchener's dues for a number of years so that his name might be listed.

In 1904 a group of psychologists called the "Titchener experimentalists" was formed and met regularly to compare research notes. Titchener selected both the topics and the guests and generally dominated these meetings. One of his rules for the meetings was

---

[1]From Ludy T. Benjamin, Jr., based on material in the Cora Friedline papers, Archives of the History of American Psychology, University of Akron, Ohio.

that no women were allowed. His student, E. G. Boring, commented that Titchener "wanted oral reports that could be interrupted, dissented from and criticized, in a smoke-filled room with no women present—for in 1904, when the Experimentalists was formed, women were considered too pure to smoke" (Boring, 1967, p. 315).

Stories are told of women students from Bryn Mawr College who tried to attend a meeting. They were told to leave. Others hid under a table throughout a meeting. Boring's fiancée and another woman student hid in the room next door to where a meeting was being held, "with the door ajar to hear what unexpurgated male psychology was like. They came through unscathed" (Boring, 1967, p. 322).

It can be argued that Titchener was not so much practicing sex discrimination deliberately as he was reflecting the patriarchal attitudes of the time. He did not discriminate against women students at Cornell; the first woman to receive a Ph.D. in psychology— and Titchener's first doctoral student—was Margaret Floy Washburn. "He did not quite know what to do with me," she recalled (Washburn, 1961, p. 340). She had chosen Columbia University, but they would not admit a woman graduate student. Titchener accepted her, and she went on to a prominent career that included the presidency of the American Psychological Association. Her professional contributions include a major book on animal psychology, as we shall see in Chapter 9.

Around 1910 Titchener began work on what was intended to be a thorough exposition of his systematic point of view. Unfortunately, it was never completed, though a few sections were published in a journal and reprinted posthumously in a book in 1929. He died of a brain tumor at age 60.

The Content of Conscious Experience

According to Titchener, the subject matter of psychology is conscious experience. All sciences, he noted, share this subject matter—some aspect of the world of human experience—but each deals with a different aspect. The subject matter of psychology is experience as it is dependent on experiencing persons. This kind of experience is vastly different from that studied by other scientists. For example, light and sound may be studied by both a physicist and a psychologist, but the physicist looks at the phenomena from the viewpoint of the physical processes involved, and the psychologist views them in terms of how they are experienced by human observers.

The other sciences, Titchener said, are independent of experiencing persons. The temperature in a room may be 85 degrees whether anyone experiences the level of heat or not. When observers stand in a room and report that they feel uncomfortable, however, this feeling is experienced by and is dependent on the experiencing individuals. This experience alone is the subject matter of psychology.

Titchener cautioned that in the study of experiencing one must not commit what he called the *stimulus error*, that is, confusing the mental process with the object being observed. For instance, observers who see an apple and describe it as an apple, instead of reporting the hues, brightnesses, and spatial characteristics they are experiencing, are committing the stimulus error. The object of observation is not to be described in everyday language, but rather in terms of the conscious content of the experience.

When observers focus on the stimulus object instead of the conscious process, they fail to distinguish what they know about the object (for example, that it is called "apple") from their own immediate experience. The only things observers really know about an object are its color, brightness, and spatial pattern (for example, that the object is red, shiny, and round). When they describe anything other than these characteristics, they are interpreting the object, not observing it, and thus are dealing with mediate experience.

Titchener defined consciousness as the sum total of our experiences as they exist at a given time. Mind is defined as the sum of our experiences accumulated over a lifetime. Thus, mind and consciousness are similar, except that consciousness involves mental processes occurring at the moment instead of the total accumulation of processes.

Titchener argued that psychology must study the generalized human mind, not individual minds, and certainly not individual differences among minds. The purpose of this study is solely that of understanding the mind. Titchener's psychology was a pure science. He argued that psychology has no applied or utilitarian concerns. Psychology was not, he said, in the business of curing "sick minds" or reforming individuals or society. Its only legitimate purpose is to discover the facts or structure of the mind.

He believed that scientists have to remain free of any concern for the practical worth of their work. He opposed child psychology, animal psychology, and any other area of the science that did not fit in with his introspective experimental psychology of the content of consciousness.

The Method of Study: Introspection

Psychology, like all sciences, depends on observation, but it depends on observation of conscious experience, or introspection. Titchener's form of introspection was, however, quite different from Wundt's. Titchener believed that introspection could be performed only by well-trained observers. He realized that everyone learns to describe experience in terms of the stimulus, and that in everyday life this is beneficial and necessary. In the laboratory, however, this habit must be unlearned through intensive training. His intro-spectors were required to relearn how to perceive so as to be able to describe the conscious state and not the stimulus. (The difficulties in specifying precisely what observers learned to do are discussed below in the section "Criticisms of Structuralism.")

Titchener used Külpe's label, *systematic experimental introspection*, to describe his approach. Like Külpe, he used detailed, qualitative, subjective reports of the subjects' mental activities during the act of introspection. He opposed the Wundtian approach with its use of instruments and its focus on objective measurements. In 1912, he publicly criticized the kind of research conducted by Wundt.

> Those who remember the psychological laboratories of twenty years ago can hardly escape an occasional shock of contrast which, for the moment, throws into vivid relief the difference between the old order and the new. The experimenter of the early [eighteen-] nineties trusted, first of all, in his instruments; chronoscope and kymograph and tachistoscope were—it is hardly an exaggeration to say—of more importance than the observer. . . . There were still vast reaches of the mental life which experiment had not touched. (Titchener, 1912a, p. 427)

Those vast reaches of mental life to which Titchener referred were the elementary sensations and images that, in his view, composed the structure of consciousness. These were the core of his psychology, not the synthesis of the elements through apperception but the analysis of complex conscious experience into its component parts. He empha-sized the parts whereas Wundt had emphasized the whole. It was a view Titchener had acquired from James Mill's *Analysis of the Phenomena of the Human Mind* (Danziger, 1980a). Like Mill and the other empiricists and associationists, Titchener's goal was to discover the atoms of the mind.

Titchener was also strongly influenced by the doctrine of mechanism. The influence of the mechanistic spirit is evident in the image developed by structuralists of the human subjects who supplied the data. In the journal articles of the day subjects were sometimes called *reagents*, a term used by scientists to denote substances that, because of their capacity for certain reactions, are used to detect, examine, or measure other substances. A reagent is generally a passive agent, one that is applied to something to elicit certain reactions. The parallel with chemistry is obvious.

Transposing this concept to the human subject in Titchener's laboratory, we see that subjects were considered to be recording instruments, objectively noting the characteristics of the object being observed. Human subjects were nothing more than impartial and detached machines. Titchener wrote of trained observation becoming mechanized or habitual, that is, no longer a conscious process.

If human subjects are considered to be machines, then it is easy to think that all human beings are machines. The point deserves mention because it shows the continuing influence of the Galilean–Newtonian mechanical view of the universe, an influence that did not cease with the demise of structuralism. We shall see as the history of psychology unfolds that this image of human-as-machine characterized much of experimental psychology until the second half of the twentieth century.

Titchener believed that observation in psychology must be not only introspective but also experimental. He diligently observed the rigid rules of scientific experimentation, noting that

> an experiment is an observation that can be repeated, isolated and varied. The more frequently you can *repeat* an observation, the more likely are you to see clearly what is there and to describe accurately what you have seen. The more strictly you can *isolate* an observation, the easier does your task of observation become, and the less danger is there of your being led astray by irrelevant circumstances, or of placing emphasis on the wrong point. The more widely you can *vary* an observation, the more clearly will the uniformity of experience stand out, and the better is your chance of discovering laws. All experimental appliances, all laboratories and instruments, are provided and devised with this one end in view: that the student shall be able to repeat, isolate and vary his observations. (1909, p. 20)

The reagents or subjects in Titchener's laboratory introspected to all manner of stimuli, providing their lengthy and detailed observations of the elements of their experiences. Introspection was a serious endeavor, and the graduate student subjects had to be highly dedicated to pursue what Titchener called the "hard introspective labor." Let us consider three examples of unusual situations in which the subjects were expected to provide introspective data.

Cora Friedline recalled the time when the Cornell laboratory was studying organic sensitivity. The graduate students were made to swallow a stomach tube in the morning and keep it in place throughout the day. Apparently, many of them vomited at first (being unable to stomach the task), before they gradually got used to it. In between their lectures and other activities they would report to the lab where hot water would be poured down the tube, and the subjects would introspect on the sensations they were experiencing. The process would be repeated with iced water.

Introspection sometimes carried over into the students' lives outside the laboratory. Friedline reported that for a time, all the students were required to carry notebooks when they used the toilet to record their sensations and feelings when they urinated or defecated.

Another bit of introspective research provides an example of data lost to history. Married graduate students were asked to make notes of their elementary sensations and feelings during sexual intercourse. In addition, they were to attach various measuring instruments to their bodies to record physiological changes. This research went unpublicized at the time and was revealed by Friedline in 1960.

The sex research did become known around the Cornell University campus, and the psychology laboratory acquired a reputation as a highly immoral place. The housemother in the women's dormitory would not allow her younger students to visit the lab after dark. And to make matters worse, word spread that condoms had been attached to the ends of the stomach tubes the graduate students were swallowing. According to Friedline, the talk in the dormitory was that "the lab was full of condoms. And that it wasn't a safe place for anyone to go."[2]

The more routine research conducted in the laboratory is described by Titchener himself in the original source material reprinted later in this chapter.

The Elements of Consciousness

Titchener's three problems or aims of psychology were (1) to reduce conscious processes to their simplest, most basic components; (2) to determine the laws by which these elements are associated; and (3) to bring the elements into connection with their physiological conditions. Thus, the aims of psychology coincide with those of the natural sciences. After scientists decide which part of the natural world to study, they proceed to discover its elements, to demonstrate how they are compounded into more complex phenomena, and to formulate the laws governing the phenomena. The bulk of Titchener's efforts were devoted to the first aim, discovering the elements of consciousness.

We have noted that one of Titchener's goals for psychology was to reduce consciousness to its component elements. How do we know whether a given conscious process is elemental, that is, cannot be broken down into anything simpler? Titchener's answer is that when the process remains unchanged in the face of rigorous and persistent introspection, it is a true element. In essence, his test of the irreducibility of elements into anything simpler is analogous to the chemist's criterion for establishing chemical elements.

Titchener believed that there are three elementary states of consciousness—sensations, images, and affective states. *Sensations* are the basic elements of perception and occur in the sounds, sights, smells, and other experiences occasioned by physical objects present in the environment. *Images* are the elements of ideas and are found in the process that pictures or reflects experiences not actually present at the moment, such as a memory of a past experience. It is not clear from Titchener's writings whether he

[2] Friedline's recollections were offered on April 11, 1960, at Randolph–Macon Woman's College in Lynchburg, Virginia. We are grateful to Frederick B. Rowe for providing a copy of her remarks.

thought sensations and images belonged to mutually exclusive categories. He emphasized the similarity between the two while arguing that they could be distinguished. *Affections* are the elements of emotion and are found in experiences such as love, hate, or sadness.

In *An Outline of Psychology* (1896) Titchener presented a list of his discovered elements of sensation; it comprises more than 44,000 sensation qualities, the majority of which were visual (32,820) and auditory (11,600). Each element was believed to be conscious and distinct from all others, and each could be blended or combined with others to form perceptions and ideas.

Although basic and irreducible, these elements could still be categorized, just as chemical elements are grouped into various classes. Despite their simplicity, elements have characteristics that enable us to distinguish among them. To the Wundtian attributes of quality and intensity, Titchener added duration and clearness. He considered these four attributes to be basic characteristics of all sensations that are present, to some degree, in all experience.

Quality is the characteristic that clearly distinguishes each element from every other, such as cold or red. *Intensity* refers to the strength or weakness, loudness or brightness, of a sensation. *Duration* refers to the course of a sensation over time, and *clearness* refers to the role of attention in conscious experience. That which is the focus of attention is more dominant than that toward which attention is not directed.

Sensations and images possess all four of these attributes, but affection has only three; it lacks clearness. Titchener thought that it was not possible to focus attention directly on the quality of pleasantness, for example. When we try to do so, the affective quality disappears. Some sensory processes, particularly vision and touch, also possess the attribute of *extensity*, in that they spread out in space.

All conscious processes are reducible to one of these categories. The findings of the Würzburg school did not cause Titchener to modify his position. He recognized that obscure and ill-defined qualities may occur during thought, but he held that these were still sensory or imaginal elements. The subjects in the Würzburg laboratory had, Titchener said, succumbed to the stimulus error because they paid more attention to the object than to their conscious processes.

A good deal of research on affection or feeling was carried out in the Cornell laboratory and resulted in the rejection of Wundt's tridimensional theory. We stated that affection has only three attributes—quality, intensity, and duration. Thus, sensations and affections are processes of the same general type and have these three attributes in common, differing, as noted, in that affection lacks the attribute of clearness. Titchener believed that affection had only one of the dimensions in Wundt's theory, pleasure–displeasure, denying the other two dimensions of tension–relaxation and excitement–depression.

Titchener began to alter his system in major ways toward the end of his life. Although he never formalized these modifications into a new system—he died before being able to do so—the nature of the changes is nevertheless clear from studies of his lectures and correspondence.

His system began to change as early as 1918. Dropping the concept of mental elements from his course, he began to argue that psychology should study not elements, but the dimensional categories or attributes of mental life, which he listed as quality, intensity, protensity (duration), extensity, and attensity (clearness). Later, two years before his death, he wrote to a graduate student that "You must give up thinking in terms of sensations and affections. That was all right ten years ago; but now, as I have told you, it is wholly out of date. . . . You must learn to think in terms of dimensions rather than in terms of systematic constructs like sensation" (Evans, 1972, p. 174). Even the term "structural psychology" fell out of favor with Titchener by the early 1920s, and he began to refer to his new approach as "existential psychology" (Geldard, 1980). Titchener was also having second thoughts about the controlled form of introspection he had been practicing for so long. He came to favor a more open, phenomenological approach.

These are dramatic shifts that, had he lived long enough to implement them, would have radically altered the face if not the fate of structural psychology. As well, they clearly suggest a flexibility and openness that scientists like to think they possess, but which not all demonstrate.

The evidence for these changes was pieced together by Evans (1972) and Henle (1974) from a meticulous examination of Titchener's letters and lectures. The ideas were never incorporated into Titchener's system. They indicate a direction and a goal toward which Titchener was apparently moving, but which his death prevented him from reaching.

ORIGINAL SOURCE MATERIAL ON STRUCTURALISM: FROM *A TEXT-BOOK OF PSYCHOLOGY* BY E. B. TITCHENER

The following material is reprinted from Titchener's popular *A Text-Book of Psychology*, published in 1909.[3] It describes the orthodox structuralist view of the subject matter and methodology of the new science of psychology.

This material supplements our discussion of Titchener and provides an example of the style of exposition that psychology students were studying more than 75 years ago.

> All human knowledge is derived from human experience; there is no other source of knowledge. But human experience, as we have seen, may be considered from different points of view. Suppose that we take two points of view, as far as possible apart, and discover for ourselves what experience looks like in the two cases. First, we will regard experience as altogether independent of any particular person; we will assume that it goes on whether or not anyone is there to have it. Secondly, we will regard experience as altogether dependent upon the particular person; we will assume that it goes on only when someone is there to have it. We shall hardly find standpoints more diverse. What are the differences in experience, as viewed from them?
>
> Take, to begin with, the three things that you first learn about in physics: space, time and mass. Physical space, which is the space of geometry and astronomy and geology, is constant, always and everywhere the same. Its unit is 1 cm., and the cm. has precisely the same value wherever and whenever it is applied. Physical time is similarly constant; and its constant unit is the 1 sec. Physical mass is constant; its unit, the 1 gr., is always and everywhere the same. Here we have experience of space,

[3] Reprinted with permission of Macmillan Publishing Co., Inc., from *A Text-Book of Psychology* by E. B. Titchener (pp. 6–9, 15–25, 36–41). Copyright 1909 by Macmillan Publishing Co., Inc. Revised 1937 by Sophia K. Titchener. (Footnotes omitted.)

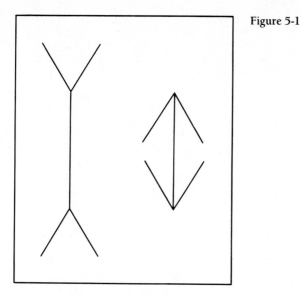

Figure 5-1

time and mass considered as independent of the person who experiences them. Change, then, to the point of view which brings the experiencing person into account. The two vertical lines in Fig. 1 [*Figure 5-1*, this volume] are physically equal; they measure alike in units of 1 cm. To you, who see them, they are not equal. The hour that you spend in the waiting-room of a village station and the hour that you spend in watching an amusing play are physically equal; they measure alike in units of 1 sec. To you, the one hour goes slowly, the other quickly; they are not equal. Take two circular cardboard boxes of different diameter (say, 2 cm. and 8 cm.), and pour sand into them until they both weigh, say, 50 gr. The two masses are physically equal; placed on the pans of a balance, they will hold the beam level. To you, as you lift them in your two hands, or raise them in turn by the same hand, the box of smaller diameter is considerably the heavier. Here we have experience of space, time and mass considered as dependent upon the experiencing person. It is the same experience that we were discussing just now. But our first point of view gives us facts and laws of physics; our second gives us facts and laws of psychology.

Now take three other topics that are discussed in the physical textbooks: heat, sound and light. Heat proper, the physicists tell us, is the energy of molecular motion; that is to say, heat is a form of energy due to a movement of the particles of a body among themselves. Radiant heat belongs, with light, to what is called radiant energy—energy that is propagated by wave-movements of the luminiferous ether with which space is filled. Sound is a form of energy due to the vibratory movements of bodies, and is propagated by wave-movements of some elastic medium, solid, liquid or gaseous. In brief, heat is a dance of molecules; light is a wave-motion of the ether; sound is a wave-motion of the air. The world of physics, in which these types of experience are considered as independent of the experiencing person, is neither warm nor cold, neither dark nor light, neither silent nor noisy. It is only when the experiences are considered as dependent upon some person that we have warmth and cold, blacks and whites and colours and greys, tones and hisses and thuds. And these things are the subject-matter of psychology.

We find, then, a great difference in the aspect of experience, according as it is viewed from the one or the other of our different standpoints. It is the same experience all through; physics and psychology deal with the same stuff, the same material; the sciences are separated simply—and sufficiently—by their point of view. From the standpoint of physics, we get such sciences as physics (in the narrower sense), chemistry, geology, astronomy, meteorology. From the standpoint of psychology we get, in the same way, a special group of sciences. . . .

It must be clearly understood that we are not here attempting to give a strict definition of the subject-matter of psychology. We assume that everybody knows, at first hand, what human experience is, and we then seek to mark off the two aspects of this experience which are dealt with respectively by physics and psychology. Any further definition of the subject-matter of psychology is impossible. Unless one knows, by experience itself, what experience is, one can no more give a meaning to the term "mind" than a stone can give a meaning to the term "matter." . . .

MENTAL PROCESS, CONSCIOUSNESS AND MIND. The most striking fact about the world of human experience is the fact of change. Nothing stands still; everything goes on. The sun will someday lose its heat; the eternal hills are, little by little, breaking up and wearing away. Whatever we observe, and from whatever standpoint we observe it, we find process, occurrence; nowhere is there permanence or stability. Mankind, it is true, has sought to arrest this flux, and to give stability to the world of experience, by assuming two permanent substances, matter and mind: the occurrences of the physical world are then supposed to be manifestations of matter, and the occurrences of the mental world to be manifestations of mind. Such an hypothesis may be of value at a certain stage of human thought; but every hypothesis that does not accord with the facts must, sooner or later, be given up. Physicists are therefore giving up the hypothesis of an unchanging, substantial matter, and psychologists are giving up the hypothesis of an unchanging, substantial mind. Stable objects and substantial things belong, not to the world of science, physical or psychological, but only to the world of common sense.

We have defined mind as the sum-total of human experience considered as dependent upon the experiencing person. We have said, further, that the phrase "experiencing person" means the living body, the organized individual; and we have hinted that, for psychological purposes, the living body may be reduced to the nervous system and its attachments. Mind thus becomes the sum-total of human experience considered as dependent upon a nervous system. And since human experience is always process, occurrence, and the dependent aspect of human experience is its mental aspect, we may say, more shortly, that mind is the sum-total of mental processes. All these words are significant. "Sum-total" implies that we are concerned with the whole world of experience, not with a limited portion of it; "mental" implies that we are concerned with experience under its dependent aspect, as conditioned by a nervous system; and "processes" implies that our subject-matter is a stream, a perpetual flux, and not a collection of unchanging objects.

It is not easy, even with the best will possible, to shift from the common-sense to the scientific view of mind; the change cannot be made all in a moment. We are to regard mind as a stream of processes? But mind is personal, my mind; and my personality continues throughout my life. The experiencing person is only the bodily organism? But, again, experience is personal, the experience of a permanent self. Mind is spatial, just as matter is? But mind is invisible, intangible; it is not here or there, square or round.

These objections cannot be finally met until we have gone some distance into psychology, and can see how the scientific view of mind works out. Even now, however, they will weaken as you look at them. Face that question of personality. Is your life, as a matter of fact, always personal? Do you not, time and again, forget yourself, lose yourself, disregard yourself, neglect yourself, contradict yourself, in a very literal sense? Surely, the mental life is only intermittently personal. And is your personality, when it is realised, unchanging? Are you the same self in childhood and manhood, in your working and in your playing moods, when you are on your best behaviour and when you are freed from restraint? Surely, the self-experience is not only intermittent, but also composed, at different times, of very different factors. As to the other question: mind is, of course, invisible, because sight is mind; and mind is intangible, because touch is mind. Sight-experience and touch-experience are dependent upon the experiencing person. But common sense itself bears witness, against its own belief, to the fact that mind is spatial: we speak, and speak correctly, of an idea in our head, a pain in our foot. And if the idea is the idea of a circle seen in the mind's eye, it is round; and if it is the visual idea of a square, it is square.

Consciousness, as reference to any dictionary will show, is a term that has many meanings. Here it is, perhaps, enough to distinguish two principal uses of the word.

In its first sense, consciousness means the mind's awareness of its own processes. Just as, from the commonsense point of view, mind is that inner self which thinks, remembers, chooses, reasons, directs the movements of the body, so is consciousness the inner knowledge of this thought and government. You are conscious of the correctness of your answer to an examination question, of the awkwardness of your movements, of the purity of your motives. Consciousness is thus something more than mind; it is "the perception of what passes in a man's own mind"; it is "the immediate knowledge which the mind has of its sensations and thoughts."

In its second sense, consciousness is identified with mind, and "conscious" with "mental." So long as mental processes are going on, consciousness is present; as soon as mental processes are in abeyance, unconsciousness sets in. "To say I am conscious of a feeling, is merely to say that I feel it. To have a feeling is to be conscious; and to be conscious is to have a feeling. To be conscious of the prick of the pin, is merely to have the sensation. And though I have these various modes of naming my sensation, by saying, I feel the prick of a pin, I feel the pain of a prick, I have the sensation of a prick, I have the feeling of a prick, I am conscious of the feeling; the thing named in all these various ways is one and the same."

The first of these definitions we must reject. It is not only unnecessary, but it is also misleading, to speak of consciousness as the mind's awareness of itself. The usage is unnecessary, because, as we shall see later, this awareness is a matter of observation of the same general kind as observation of the external world; it is misleading, because it suggests that mind is a personal being, instead of a stream of processes. We shall therefore take mind and consciousness to mean the same thing. But as we have the two different words, and it is convenient to make some distinction between them, we shall speak of mind when we mean the sum-total of mental processes occurring in the life-time of an individual, and we shall speak of consciousness when we mean the sum-total of mental processes occurring *now*, at any given "present" time. Consciousness will thus be a section, a division, of the mind-stream. This distinction is, indeed, already made in common speech: when we say that a man has "lost consciousness," we mean that the lapse is temporary, that the mental life will shortly be resumed; when we say that a man has "lost his mind," we mean—not, it is true, that the mind has altogether disappeared, but certainly that the derangement is permanent and chronic.

While, therefore, the subject-matter of psychology is mind, the direct object of psychological study is always a consciousness. In strictness, we can never observe the same consciousness twice over; the stream of mind flows on, never to return. Practically, we can observe a particular consciousness as often as we wish, since mental processes group themselves in the same way, show the same pattern of arrangement, whenever the organism is placed under the same circumstances. Yesterday's high tide will never recur, and yesterday's consciousnesses will never recur; but we have a science of psychology, as we have a science of oceanography.

THE METHOD OF PSYCHOLOGY. Scientific method may be summed up in the single word "observation"; the only way to work in science is to observe those phenomena which form the subject-matter of science. And observation implies two things: attention to the phenomena, and record of the phenomena; that is, clear and vivid experience, and an account of the experience in words or formulas. In order to secure clear experience and accurate report, science has recourse to experiment. An experiment is an observation that can be repeated, isolated and varied. The more frequently you can *repeat* an observation, the more likely are you to see clearly what is there and to describe accurately what you have seen. The more strictly you can *isolate* an observation, the easier does your task of observation become, and the less danger is there of your being led astray by irrelevant circumstances, or of placing emphasis on the wrong point. The more widely you can *vary* an observation, the more clearly will the uniformity of experience stand out, and the better is your chance of discovering laws. All experimental appliances, all laboratories and instruments, are provided and devised with this one end in view: that the student shall be able to repeat, isolate and vary his observations.—

The method of psychology, then, is observation. To distinguish it from the observation of physical science, which is inspection, a looking-at, psychological observation has been termed introspection, a looking-within. But this difference of name must not blind us to the essential likeness of the methods. Let us take some typical instances.

We may begin with two very simple cases. (1) Suppose that you are shown two paper discs: the one of an uniform violet, the other composed half of red and half of blue. If this second disc is rapidly rotated, the red and blue will mix, as we say, and you will see a certain blue-red, that is, a kind of violet. Your problem is, so to adjust the proportions of red and blue in the second disc that the resulting violet exactly matches the violet of the first disc. You may repeat this set of observations as often as you like; you may isolate the observations by working in a room that is free from other, possibly disturbing colours; you may vary the observations by working to equality of the violets first from a two-colour disc that is distinctly too blue, and secondly from a disc that is distinctly too red. (2) Suppose, again, that the chord c-e-g is struck, and that you are asked to say how many tones it contains. You may repeat this observation; you may isolate it, by working in a quiet room; you may vary it, by having the chord struck at different parts of the scale, in different octaves.

It is clear that, in these instances, there is practically no difference between introspection and inspection. You are using the same method that you would use for counting the swings of a pendulum, or taking readings from a galvanometer scale, in the physical laboratory. There is a difference in subject-matter: the colours and the tones are dependent, not independent experiences: but the method is essentially the same.

Now let us take some cases in which the material of introspection is more complex. (1) Suppose that a word is called out to you, and that you are asked to observe the effect which this stimulus produces upon consciousness: how the word affects you, what ideas it calls up, and so forth. The observation may be repeated; it may be isolated—you may be seated in a dark and silent room, free from disturbances; and it may be varied—different words may be called out, the word may be flashed upon a screen instead of spoken, etc. Here, however, there seems to be a difference between introspection and inspection. The observer who is watching the course of a chemical reaction, or the movements of some microscopical creature, can jot down from moment to moment the different phases of the observed phenomenon. But if you try to report the changes in consciousness, while these changes are in progress, you interfere with consciousness; your translation of the mental experience into words introduces new factors into that experience itself. (2) Suppose, again, that you are observing a feeling or an emotion: a feeling of disappointment or annoyance, an emotion of anger or chagrin. Experimental control is still possible; situations may be arranged, in the psychological laboratory, such that these feelings may be repeated, isolated and varied. But your observation of them interferes, even more seriously than before, with the course of consciousness. Cool consideration of an emotion is fatal to its very existence; your anger disappears, your disappointment evaporates, as you examine it.

To overcome this difficulty of the introspective method, students of psychology are usually recommended to delay their observation until the process to be described has run its course, and then to call it back and describe it from memory. Introspection thus becomes retrospection; introspective examination becomes *post mortem* examination. The rule is, no doubt, a good one for the beginner; and there are cases in which even the experienced psychologist will be wise to follow it. But it is by no means universal. For we must remember *(a)* that the observations in question may be repeated. There is, then, no reason why the observer to whom the word is called out, or in whom the emotion is set up, should not report at once upon the first stage of his experience: upon the immediate effect of the word, upon the beginnings of the emotive process. It is true that this report interrupts the observation. But, after the first stage has been accurately described, further observations may be taken, and the second, third and following stages similarly described; so that presently a complete report upon the whole experience is obtained. There is, in theory, some danger that the stages become artificially separated; consciousness is a flow, a process, and if we divide it up we run the risk of missing certain intermediate links. In practice, however, this danger has proved to be very small; and we may always have recourse to retrospection, and compare our partial results with our memory of the unbroken experience. Moreover, *(b)* the practised observer gets into an introspective habit, has the introspective attitude ingrained in his system; so that it is possible for him, not only to take mental notes while the observation is in progress, without interfering with consciousness, but even to jot down written notes, as the histologist does while his eye is still held to the ocular of the microscope.

In principle, then, introspection is very like inspection. The objects of observation are different; they are objects of dependent, not of independent experience; they are likely to be transient, elusive, slippery. Sometimes they refuse to be observed while they are in passage; they must be preserved in memory, as a delicate tissue is preserved in hardening fluid, before they can be examined. And the standpoint of the observer is different; it is the standpoint of human life and of human interest, not of detachment and aloofness. But, in general, the method of psychology is much the same as the method of physics.

It must not be forgotten that, while the method of the physical and the psychological sciences is substantially the same, the subject-matter of these sciences is as different as it can well be. Ultimately, as we have seen, the subject-matter of all the sciences is the world of human experience; but we have also seen that the aspect of experience treated by physics is radically different from the aspect treated by psychology. The likeness of method may tempt us to slip from the one aspect to the other, as when a text-book of physics contains a chapter on vision and the sense of colour, or a text-book of physiology contains paragraphs on delusions of judgment; but this confusion of subject-matter must inevitably lead to confusion of thought. Since all the sciences are concerned with the one world of human experience, it is natural that scientific method, to whatever aspect of experience it is applied, should be in principle the same. On the other hand, when we have decided to examine some particular aspect of experience, it is necessary that we hold fast to that aspect, and do not shift our point of view as the enquiry proceeds. Hence it is a great advantage that we have the two terms, introspection and inspection, to denote observation taken from the different standpoints of psychology and of physics. The use of the word introspection is a constant reminder that we are working in psychology, that we are observing the dependent aspect of the world of experience.

Observation, as we said above, implies two things: attention to the phenomena, and record of the phenomena. The attention must be held at the highest possible degree of concentration; the record must be photographically accurate. Observation is, therefore, both difficult and fatiguing; and introspection is, on the whole, more difficult and more fatiguing than inspection. To secure reliable results, we must be strictly impartial and unprejudiced, facing the facts as they come, ready to accept them as they are, not trying to fit them to any preconceived theory; and we must work only when our general disposition is favourable, when we are fresh and in good health, at ease in our surroundings, free from outside worry and anxiety. If these rules are not followed, no amount of experimenting will help us. The observer in the psychological laboratory is placed under the best possible external conditions; the room in which he works is fitted up and arranged in such a way that the observation may be repeated, that the process to be observed may stand out clearly upon the background of consciousness, and that the factors in the process may be separately varied. But all this care is of no avail, unless the observer himself comes to the work in an even frame of mind, gives it his full attention, and is able adequately to translate his experience into words. . . .

THE PROBLEM OF PSYCHOLOGY. Science seeks always to answer three questions in regard to its subject-matter, the questions of what, how, and why. What precisely, stripped of all complications and reduced to its lowest terms, is this subject-matter? How, then, does it come to appear as it does; how are its elements combined and arranged? And, finally, why does it appear now in just this particular combination or arrangement? All three questions must be answered, if we are to have a science. . . .

To answer the question "what" is the task of analysis. Physical science, for example, tries by analysis to reduce the world of independent experience to its lowest terms, and so arrives at the various chemical elements. To answer the question "how" is the task of synthesis. Physical science traces the behaviour of the elements in their various combinations, and presently succeeds in formulating the laws of nature. When these two questions have been answered, we have a description of physical phenomena. But science enquires, further, why a given set of phenomena occurs in just this given way, and not otherwise; and it answers the question "why" by laying bare the cause of which the observed phenomena are the effect. There was dew on the ground last night because the surface of the earth was colder than the layer of air above it; dew forms on glass and not on metal because the radiating power of the one is great and of the other is small. When the cause of a physical phenomenon has thus been assigned, the phenomenon is said to be explained.

So far, now, as description is concerned, the problem of psychology closely resembles the problem of physics. The psychologist seeks, first of all, to analyse mental experience into its simplest components. He takes a particular consciousness and works over it again and again, phase by phase and process by process, until his analysis can go no further. He is left with certain mental processes which resist analysis, which are absolutely simple in nature, which cannot be reduced, even in part, to other processes. This work is continued, with other consciousnesses, until he is able to pronounce with some confidence upon the nature and number of the elementary mental processes. Then he proceeds to the task of synthesis. He puts the elements together, under experimental conditions: first, perhaps, two elements of the same kind, then more of that kind, then elementary processes of diverse kinds: and he presently discerns that regularity and uniformity of occurrence which we have seen to be characteristic of all human experience. He thus learns to formulate the laws of connection of the elementary mental processes.[4] If sensations of tone occur together, they blend or fuse; if sensations of colour occur side by side, they enhance one another: and all this takes place in a perfectly regular way, so that we can write out laws of tonal fusion and laws of colour contrast.

If, however, we attempted to work out a merely descriptive psychology, we should find that there was no hope in it of a true science of mind. A descriptive psychology would stand to scientific psychology very much as the old-fashioned natural histories stand to modern text-books of biology, or as the view of the world which a boy gets from his cabinet of physical experiments stands to the trained physicist's view. It would tell us a good deal about mind; it would include a large body of observed facts, which we might classify and, in large measure, bring under general laws. But there would be no unity or coherence in it; it would lack that single guiding principle which biology has, for instance, in the law of evolution, or physics in the law of the conservation of energy. In order to make psychology scientific we must not only describe, we must also explain mind. We must answer the question "why."

But here is a difficulty. It is clear that we cannot regard one mental process as the cause of another mental process, if only for the reason that, with change of our surroundings, entirely new consciousnesses may be set up. When I visit Athens or Rome for the first time, I have experiences which are due, not to past consciousnesses, but to present stimuli. Nor can we, on the other hand, regard nervous processes as the cause of mental processes. The principle of psychophysical parallelism lays it down that the two sets of events, processes in the nervous system and mental processes, run their course side by side, in exact correspondence but without interference: they are, in ultimate fact, two different aspects of the same experience. The one cannot be the cause of the other.

Nevertheless, it is by reference to the body, to the nervous system and the organs attached to it, that we explain mental phenomena. The nervous system does not cause, but it does explain mind. It explains mind as the map of a country explains the fragmentary glimpses of hills and rivers and towns that we catch on our journey through it. In a word, reference to the nervous system introduces into psychology just that unity and coherence which a strictly descriptive psychology cannot achieve.

It is worth while, for the sake of clearness, to dwell on this point in more detail. The physical world, the world of independent experience, just because it is independent of the individual man, is complete and self-contained. All of the processes that make it up are bound together as cause and effect; nowhere is there a gap or break in their connection. Now, among the processes that make up this independent world are the processes of the nervous system. These are linked, as cause and effect, both to one another and also to physical processes, outside the body, which precede and follow them; they have their fixed place in the unbroken chain of physical events; they may themselves be explained, exactly as the occurrence of dew is explained. Mental processes, on the other hand, correspond, not to the whole series of physical events, but only to a small part of them, namely, to certain events within the nervous system. It is natural, then, that mental phenomena should appear scrappy, disconnected, unsystematic. It is also natural that we should seek their explanation in the nervous processes which run parallel to them, and whose causal connection with all the other processes of the independent world ensures the continuity that they so conspicuously lack. Mind lapses every night, and reforms every morning; but the bodily

[4] By using the phrase "connection of the elementary mental processes," Titchener reveals the influence of the empiricists and associationists and their mechanical view of association. In Wundt's view, the elements were synthesized or organized by the active power of the mind, not connected passively and mechanically.

processes go on, in sleep and in waking. An idea drops out of memory, to recur, perhaps quite unexpectedly, many years later; but the bodily processes have been going on without interruption. Reference to the body does not add one iota to the data of psychology, to the sum of introspections. It does furnish us with an explanatory principle for psychology; it does enable us to systematise our introspective data. Indeed, if we refuse to explain mind by body, we must accept the one or the other of two, equally unsatisfactory alternatives: we must either rest content with a simple description of mental experience, or must invent an unconscious mind to give coherence and continuity to the conscious. Both courses have been tried. But, if we take the first, we never arrive at a science of psychology; and if we take the second, we voluntarily leave the sphere of fact for the sphere of fiction.

These are scientific alternatives. Common sense, also, has in its own fashion realised the situation, and has found its own way out. It is precisely because of the incompleteness and disconnectedness of mental experience that common sense constructs a hybrid world, travelling easily from mental to physical and back again, filling up the breaks in the mental by material borrowed from the physical. That way, we may be sure, lies confusion of thought. The truth underlying the confusion is, however, the implicit acknowledgment that the explanatory principle for psychology must be looked for beyond, and not within, the world of dependent experience.—

Physical science, then, explains by assigning a cause; mental science explains by reference to those nervous processes which correspond with the mental processes that are under observation. We may bring these two modes of explanation together, if we define explanation itself as the statement of the proximate circumstances or conditions under which the described phenomenon occurs. Dew is formed under the condition of a difference of temperature between the air and the ground; ideas are formed under the condition of certain processes in the nervous system. Fundamentally, the object and the manner of explanation, in the two cases, are one and the same.

In fine, just as the method of psychology is, on all essential points, the method of the natural sciences, so is the problem of psychology essentially of the same sort as the problem of physics. The psychologist answers the question "what" by analysing mental experience into its elements. He answers the question "how" by formulating the laws of connection of these elements. And he answers the question "why" by explaining mental processes in terms of their parallel processes in the nervous system. His programme need not be carried out in this order: he may get the hint of a law before his analysis is completed, and the discovery of a sense-organ may suggest the occurrence of certain elementary processes before he has found these processes by introspection. The three questions are intimately related, and an answer to any one helps toward the answers to the other two. The measure of our progress in scientific psychology is our ability to return satisfactory answers to all three.

THE FATE OF STRUCTURALISM

People often gain prominence in history because they oppose an older thought or position. The situation may be reversed with Titchener, who "stood out in bold relief because every one near him moved away from him" (Boring, 1950, p. 419). The climate of American and European psychology was changing by the second decade of the twentieth century, but the formal statement of Titchener's system was not, and some came to regard his work as a futile attempt to cling to antiquated principles.

Titchener thought he was establishing the basic pattern for psychology, but his efforts have proved to be only one phase in its history. The era of structuralism collapsed when he died. That it was sustained so long is an effective tribute to the commanding personality of the man himself.

Criticisms of Structuralism

The most severe criticisms of structuralism have been leveled at the method of introspection. These criticisms are much more relevant to Titchener's and Külpe's method of introspection, which dealt with subjective reports of the elements of consciousness, than to Wundt's method of internal perception, which dealt with more objective responses to external stimuli. The method (though in a more broadly defined sense) had been in use for a long time. The attack on introspection was by no means new either. Immanuel Kant had written that an attempt to introspect changes the conscious experience by virtue of introducing an observing element into the content of this conscious experience. The positivist Auguste Comte also attacked the method. Several decades before Titchener began structural psychology, Comte wrote this telling criticism:

> The mind may observe all phenomena but its own. . . . The observing and observed organ are here the same, and its action cannot be pure and natural. In order to observe, your intellect must pause from activity; yet it is this very activity that you want to observe. If you cannot effect that pause, you cannot observe; if you do effect it, there is nothing to observe. The results of such method are in proportion to its absurdity. After two thousand years of psychological pursuit, no one proposition is established to the satisfaction of its followers. (1830/1896, Vol. I, p. 9)

Additional criticisms were leveled against introspection by the Englishman Henry Maudsley in 1867 (Turner, 1967, p. 11).

1. There is little agreement among introspectionists.
2. Where agreement does occur, it can be attributed to the fact that introspectionists must be meticulously trained, and thereby have a bias built into their observations.
3. A body of knowledge based on introspection cannot be inductive; no discovery is possible from those who are trained specifically on what to observe.
4. Due to the extent of the pathology of mind, self-report is hardly to be trusted.
5. Introspective knowledge cannot have the generality we expect of science. It must be restricted to the class of sophisticated, trained adult subjects.
6. Much of behavior (habit and performance) occurs without conscious correlates.

There was, then, substantial criticism of introspection before Titchener sharpened and modified the method to bring it into line with the requirements of experimentalism. The modifications did not reduce the amount of criticism. As the method was made more specific, so were the attacks against it.

One criticism relates to the definition of introspection. Titchener seems to have had a difficult time defining introspection with any degree of rigor, and apparently attempted to do so by relating it to the particular experimental conditions. "The course that an observer follows will vary in detail with the nature of the consciousness observed, with the purpose of the experiment, with the instruction given by the experimenter. Introspection is thus a generic term, and covers an indefinitely large group of specific methodical procedures" (Titchener, 1912b, p. 485). With so much variation, it is difficult to find similarities among the uses of the term.

A point mentioned earlier relates to the question of precisely what the structuralist introspectors were trained to do. Observers learning to introspect had to ignore certain classes of words—the so-called meaning words—that had become an established part of their vocabulary. The phrase, "I see a table," for example, had no scientific meaning to a structuralist; the word "table" is a meaning word, based on previously established and generally agreed-upon knowledge about the specific conglomeration of sensations we have learned to identify and label as "table." The observation, "I see a table," told the structuralist nothing about the observers' conscious experience. The structuralist was interested not in the aggregate of sensations summarized in a meaning word, but in the specific elementary forms of the experience. Observers who said "table" were committing the stimulus error.

If these ordinary words were stricken from the vocabulary, how was the experience to be described? An introspective language or vocabulary would have to be developed. Because Titchener (and Wundt as well) emphasized that the external conditions of the experiment must be carefully controlled so that the conscious experience could be precisely determined, two observers should have the identical experience and their results should corroborate one another. Because of these highly similar experiences under controlled conditions, it seemed possible, theoretically, to develop a working vocabulary devoid of meaning words. It is, after all, because of commonalities of experience in everyday life that we are able to agree on conventional meanings for customary words.

Although the development of such a vocabulary may have been possible in principle, it was never realized. There was frequent disagreement among introspectors, even under the most rigidly controlled conditions of observation. Introspectors at different laboratories obtained different results. Even those at the same laboratory often failed to agree. Titchener nevertheless maintained that agreement would be reached eventually. It is possible that had there been sufficient agreement on introspective findings, structuralism might have lasted longer than it did.

There were other criticisms of the method of introspection. It was charged that introspection was, in reality, retrospection, because some period of time elapsed between the experience itself and the reporting of it. Because, as Ebbinghaus demonstrated, forgetting is most rapid immediately after an experience, it seemed likely that some of the experience was lost. The structuralist answer to this criticism was to specify that the observers work with very short time intervals. The structuralists postulated the existence of a primary mental image that was alleged to maintain the experience for the observer until it could be reported.

Another difficulty is that the act of minutely examining an experience in introspective fashion may radically change that experience. Consider the difficulty in introspecting the conscious state of anger. In the process of rationally attending to and trying to dissect the experience into its elementary components, the anger may subside or disappear. Titchener believed, however, that experienced, well-trained introspectors became unconscious of their observational task with continued practice, as noted in the original source material from Titchener.

The method of the structuralists was not the only target of criticism. The movement was accused of artificiality and sterility because of its attempt to analyze conscious processes into elements. Critics argued that the whole of an experience cannot be recovered by any connecting or associating of the elemental parts. Experience, they argue, does not come to human beings in sensory, imaginal, or affective elements, but rather in unified wholes. Something of the experience must inevitably be lost in what was seen as an artificial breakdown of the conscious experience. We shall see that the Gestalt school (Chapter 12) made effective use of this criticism in launching their new psychology, their revolt against structuralism.

The structuralists' narrow definition of psychology came under attack. Psychology was growing in a number of areas and the structuralists preferred to exclude those areas that were not congruent with their definition and method of psychology. Titchener regarded animal and child psychology as not really psychology at all. His conception of psychology was too circumscribed to contain the new work being carried out by a rapidly increasing number of psychologists. Psychology was moving beyond Titchener, and moving very quickly.

Contributions of Structuralism

There is no denying that structuralism made important contributions to psychology. The subject matter of the structuralists—conscious experience—was sharply defined. Their research methods were certainly in the best tradition of science, involving observation, experimentation, and measurement. Because consciousness was best perceived by the person having the conscious experience, the best method for that subject matter was self-observation.

Although the subject matter and aims of the structuralists are no longer vital issues, introspection—defined as the giving of a verbal report based on experience—continues to be used in many areas of psychology. Researchers in psychophysics, for example, ask a subject whether a second tone sounds louder or softer than the first. Verbal reports are rendered by persons describing their experiences in an unusual experimental environment, such as a sensory deprivation cubicle. Clinical reports from patients and responses on personality tests or attitude scales are introspective in nature. Introspective reports involving cognitive processes such as reasoning can also be obtained from subjects. For example, in developing equipment such as computers, "people's reports about how they do a task or how they use a complex device often are used to evaluate new services or products requiring human interaction" (Egan, 1983, p. 1675). These and other instances involve a verbal report based on experience and are legitimate forms of data collecting. Indeed, "introspective data can be highly reliable and useful, helping not only to predict specific behaviors but to discover fundamental principles of learning and performance" (Lieberman, 1979, p. 332).

Perhaps another contribution of structuralism is its service as a target of criticism. It provided a strong orthodoxy against which newly developing movements could marshal their forces. These newer schools owed their existence in no small measure to their progressive reformulation of the psychology the structuralists began. As we noted earlier, forward movement requires something against which to push. With the help of the structuralist position, psychology advanced far beyond this initial boundary.

SUGGESTED READINGS

Titchener and Structuralism

Angell, F. (1928). Titchener at Leipzig. *Journal of General Psychology, 1*, 195–198.

Bentley, M. (1926). The psychologies called "Structuralism": Historical derivation. In C. Murchison (Ed.), *Psychologies of 1925* (pp. 383–393). Worcester, MA: Clark University Press.

Bentley, M. (1926). The work of the structuralists. In C. Murchison (Ed.), *Psychologies of 1925* (pp. 395–404). Worcester, MA: Clark University Press.

Boring, E. G. (1921). The stimulus-error. *American Journal of Psychology, 32*, 449–471.

Boring, E. G. (1927). Edward Bradford Titchener: 1867–1927. *American Journal of Psychology, 38*, 489–506.

Evans, R. (1972). E. B. Titchener and his lost system. *Journal of the History of the Behavioral Sciences, 8*, 168–180.

Evans, R. (1975). The origins of Titchener's doctrine of meaning. *Journal of the History of the Behavioral Sciences, 11*, 334–341.

Henle, M. (1971). Did Titchener commit the stimulus error? The problem of meaning in structural psychology. *Journal of the History of the Behavioral Sciences, 7*, 279–282.

Henle, M. (1974). E. B. Titchener and the case of the missing element. *Journal of the History of the Behavioral Sciences, 10*, 227–237.

Hindeland, M. J. (1971). Edward Bradford Titchener: A pioneer in perception. *Journal of the History of the Behavioral Sciences, 7*, 23–28.

Leahey, T. H. (1981). The mistaken mirror: On Wundt's and Titchener's psychologies. *Journal of the History of the Behavioral Sciences, 17*, 273–282.

Introspection

Bakan, D. (1954). A consideration of the problem of introspection. *Psychological Bulletin, 51*, 105–118.

Boring, E. G. (1953). A history of introspection. *Psychological Bulletin, 50*, 169–186.

Danziger, K. (1980). The history of introspection reconsidered. *Journal of the History of the Behavioral Sciences, 16*, 241–262.

Dunlap, K. (1912). The case against introspection. *Psychological Review, 19*, 404–413.

McKellar, P. (1962). The method of introspection. In J. Scher (Ed.), *Theories of the mind* (pp. 619–644). New York: Free Press.

Natsoulas, T. (1970). Concerning introspective knowledge. *Psychological Bulletin, 73*, 89–111.

Radford, J. (1974). Reflections on introspection. *American Psychologist, 29*, 245–250.

Washburn, M. F. (1922). Introspection as an objective method. *Psychological Review, 29*, 89–112.

6

Functionalism: Antecedent Influences

Functional psychology, as the name suggests, is concerned with the mind as it functions or is used in the adaptation of the organism to its environment. The movement focused on a practical question: What do mental processes accomplish? Functionalists studied the mind, not from the standpoint of its composition (a structure of elements) but rather as a conglomerate of processes or functions that lead to practical consequences in the real world.

The study of the mind undertaken by Wundt and Titchener revealed nothing of the consequences or accomplishments of mental activity. Nor did it aspire to, of course; such a utilitarian goal was anathema to the pure science approach of Wundt and Titchener.

Functionalism was the first uniquely American system of psychology. It was a deliberate protest against Wundt's psychology and Titchener's structuralism, both of which were viewed as too narrow and restrictive. They could not answer the questions the functionalists wished psychology to answer: What does the mind do? How does it do it?

Functionalism was not a protest against the methods and topics of research at Leipzig and Cornell. The functionalists adopted many of their findings. They did not object to introspection, nor did they argue against the experimental study of consciousness. What they did oppose were the earlier definitions of psychology that ruled out any consideration of the useful and practical functions of the mind, the ongoing activities or operations of consciousness.

Although functionalism was a protest against the current school of thought, its proponents did not intend to become a full-fledged school. The primary reason for this seems to have been personal rather than ideological. None of the proponents of the functionalist position had the ambition to lead a formal movement. In time, functionalism did gain many of the characteristics of a new school of thought, but such was not its aim. The leaders appeared content to challenge the positions of Wundt and Titchener and to broaden the base and scope of the new psychology, which they did with considerable success. They modified the existing orthodoxy without striving to replace it.

As a result, functionalism was never as rigid or formally differentiated a systematic position as structuralism. It cannot, therefore, be described as neatly or precisely as the earlier school. There was not a single functional psychology, as there was a single structural psychology. Several functional psychologies existed, each differing somewhat from the others, but all sharing an interest in the functions of consciousness.

Because of this emphasis on the functioning of an organism in its environment, functionalists became interested in the possible applications of psychology. Thus, applied psychology developed rapidly in the United States.

FUNCTIONALISM: AN OVERVIEW

Functionalism has a long history, ranging from the mid-1850s to the present, at least in modified form. Its historical development, unlike that of structuralism, was influenced by intellectual leaders with various interests and backgrounds. Perhaps it is partly because of this diversified base that functionalism, unlike structuralism, did not stultify and decline.

We will consider the antecedent influences on the functional psychology movement, including the works of Charles Darwin, Sir Francis Galton, and early students of animal behavior. Although these initial sources of influence were British, functionalism formally began and flourished in the United States (Chapter 7). It is important to note the time when the precursors of functionalism were developing their ideas, the period before and during the years in which the new psychology was developing. Darwin's *On the Origin of Species* (1859) was published one year before Fechner's *Elements of Psychophysics* (1860) and 20 years before Wundt established his laboratory at Leipzig. Galton began his work on individual differences in 1869, before Wundt wrote his *Principles of Physiological Psychology* (1874). Animal psychology experiments were conducted in the 1880s, before Titchener had journeyed to Leipzig and come under Wundt's influence. Thus, major work on the functions of consciousness, individual differences, and animal psychology was being done at the time Wundt and Titchener were excluding these areas from the province of psychology. It remained for the new American psychologists, with their different temperament, to bring function, individual differences, and the white rat to positions of prominence in psychology.

American psychology today is functionalist in orientation and attitude. This is evident in the emphasis placed on testing, and on learning, perception, and other functional processes that aid our adaptation and adjustment to our environment.

THE EVOLUTION REVOLUTION: CHARLES DARWIN (1809–1882)

Charles Darwin's *On the Origin of Species by Means of Natural Selection*, published in 1859, is one of the most important books in the history of Western civilization. The theory of evolution presented in this work freed scholars from constraining traditions and superstitions and ushered in the era of maturity and respectability for the life sciences. The theory of evolution was also to have a tremendous impact on contemporary psychology. American psychology today owes its form and substance as much to the influence of evolutionary theory as to any other idea or individual. In addition, evolutionary theory exerted an enormous influence on the work of Sigmund Freud, as we shall see in Chapter 13.

The suggestion that living things change with time, which is the fundamental notion of evolution, did not originate with Darwin. Although intellectual anticipations of this general idea can be traced to the fifth century B.C., not until the late eighteenth century was the theory first investigated systematically. Erasmus Darwin (the 340-pound grandfather of both Charles Darwin and Sir Francis Galton) expressed the belief that all warmblooded animals had evolved from a single living filament, given animation by the Creator. In 1809 Lamarck formulated a behavioral theory of evolution that emphasized the modification of animal bodily form through the organism's efforts to adapt to its environment, modifications that were inherited by succeeding generations. For example, the giraffe developed its long neck over generations by reaching for higher and higher branches to find food. In the mid-1800s Sir Charles Lyell introduced the notion of evolution into geological theory, arguing that the earth had passed through various stages of development in evolving to its present structure.

Why, after so many centuries of acceptance of the biblical account of creation—"every species after its own kind"—were scholars driven to seek an alternative explanation? One reason is that more was being learned about the other species that inhabited the earth. Many new kinds of animal life were being reported by explorers on several continents. It was inevitable that some thinkers should begin to ask: How could Noah have put a pair of all these animals into the ark? There were simply too many species to continue to believe that story.

Explorers and scientists had also discovered fossils and bones of animals that did not match those of existing species. They apparently belonged to creatures that had once roamed the earth and then disappeared. Thus, living forms were no longer believed to be constant, unchanged since creation, but subject to modification. Old species became extinct and new species appeared, some of them alterations of current forms. Perhaps, it was speculated, all of nature is a result of change and is still in the process of evolution.

The impact of continuing change was being observed not only in the intellectual and scientific realm, but also in everyday life. Society was being transformed by the forces of the Industrial Revolution. Values, social relationships, and cultural norms that had remained constant for generations were being torn apart as people migrated from rural areas and small towns to the huge urban manufacturing centers.

Above all, there was the growing influence of science. People were less content to base their knowledge of themselves and their world on what the Bible and ancient authorities had stated to be true. They were ready to put their faith in science.

Change was the *Zeitgeist* of the day. It affected the peasant farmer, whose life now pulsed to the rhythm of the machine instead of the seasons, as much as the scientist, whose time was spent puzzling over a newly found set of bones. The intellectual and social climate rendered the notion of evolution scientifically respectable. There was a great deal of speculating and theorizing, but little in the way of supporting evidence. Then *On the Origin of Species* provided so much well-organized data that evolution could no longer be ignored. The times demanded such a theory, and Charles Darwin became its agent.

The Life of Darwin

As a boy, Darwin gave little indication of becoming the keen, hard-working scientist the world later came to know. Indeed, he showed little indication of becoming anything other than an idler and a gentleman–sportsman. In his early years he showed so little promise that his father, a wealthy physician, worried that young Charles would be a disgrace to the family.

Although he never liked school and, probably as a result, never did well in it, he displayed an early interest in natural history and in collecting coins, shells, and minerals. Sent by his father to Edinburgh to study medicine, Charles found it dull. Aware that the young man was doing poorly, his father decided that Charles should become a clergyman instead.

He spent three years at Cambridge, and described the experience as "entirely wasted" from an academic standpoint. He did, however, have a marvelous time, and later referred to the Cambridge period as the happiest of his life. He collected beetles, went shooting and hunting, and spent a great deal of time drinking, singing, and playing cards with a group of young men he referred to as dissipated and "low-minded."

One of his instructors, the noted botanist John Stevens Henslow, promoted Darwin's appointment as a naturalist aboard *H.M.S. Beagle*, which the British government was preparing for a scientific voyage around the world. This famous excursion, lasting from 1831 to 1836, began in South American waters, proceeded to Tahiti and New Zealand, and returned to England by way of Ascension Island and the Azores. The trip afforded him a unique opportunity to observe a variety of plant and animal life, and Darwin was able to collect an immense amount of data. The voyage altered Darwin's character. No longer the pleasure-loving dilettante, he returned to England a dedicated, committed, serious scientist with but one passion and aim in life—the promulgation of the theory of evolution (F. Darwin, 1892).

In 1839 he married, and three years later he moved to Down, 16 miles from London, so that he could concentrate on his work without the distractions of city life. It was then that he began to be plagued by the physical disturbances, including vomiting, flatulence, and eczema, from which he would suffer for most of his long life. The illnesses were apparently neurotic, brought on by any change in his rigid daily routine. Whenever the outside world intruded, preventing Darwin from working, he would suffer another attack. Illness became a useful device, protecting him from mundane affairs and allowing him the intense solitude and concentration he needed to create his theory. His condition has been described as a "creative malady" (Pickering, 1974).

From the time of his return with the *Beagle*, Darwin was convinced of the validity of the theory of the evolution of species. Why, then, did he wait 22 years before presenting his work to the world? The answer seems to lie in his extremely conservative attitude, a temperamental requisite for a scientist. He knew his theory would have a revolutionary impact, and he wanted to be certain that it was buttressed with sufficient supporting data. So he proceeded with painstaking caution. It was not until 1842 that he felt prepared to write a brief 35-page summary of the development of his theory. Two years later he expanded this into a 200-page essay, but still he was not satisfied. He continued to keep his ideas from the public, sharing them only with Lyell and with Joseph Hooker, a botanist. For 15 more years Darwin pored over the data, checking, elaborating, revis-

The theory of human evolution proposed by Charles Darwin (1809–1882) set the stage for functional psychology, which studied the adaptive role, rather than the content, of consciousness.

ing, to be sure that when he did finally publish, the theory would be unassailable (Richards, 1983).

No one knows how much longer Darwin might have worked over his findings if in June of 1858 he had not received a shattering letter from Alfred Russel Wallace, a young naturalist. Wallace, while staying in the East Indies to recover from an illness, had developed the outline of a theory of evolution that was amazingly similar to Darwin's. His work had taken three days. In his letter to Darwin, Wallace asked the older man's opinion of the theory and for help in getting it published. We can imagine Darwin's feelings after more than two decades of laborious and painstaking work. It must be noted, however, that Wallace's theory did not rest on the wealth of data that Darwin's did.

Darwin possessed another characteristic—personal ambition—not unknown among scientists. Sometime before his explorations on the *Beagle* he had written in his diary that he was "ambitious to take a fair place among scientific men." Later he wrote: "I wish I could set less value on the bauble fame," and, "I rather hate the idea of writing for priority, yet I certainly should be vexed if any one were to publish my doctrines before me" (Merton, 1957, pp. 647–648).

With an enviable sense of fair play, Darwin considered Wallace's letter and decided that "It seems hard on me that I should lose my priority of many years' standing, but I cannot feel at all sure that this alters the justice of the case. . . . It would be dishonourable in me now to publish" (Merton, 1957, p. 648). At this moment of apparent defeat Darwin's mentally retarded son died, throwing him into a greater despair. His friends Lyell and Hooker suggested that he read Wallace's paper and portions of his own forthcoming book at a meeting of the Linnean Society on July 1, 1858. The rest is history.

Every one of the 1250 copies of the first printing of *On the Origin of Species* was sold on the day of publication. The work generated immediate excitement and controversy, and Darwin, though subjected to much abuse and criticism, nevertheless won "the bauble fame."

The Works of Darwin

The Darwinian theory of evolution is so well known that only an overview of the fundamental points is necessary here. Starting with the obvious fact of variation among individual members of a species, Darwin reasoned that this spontaneous variability was inheritable. In nature there is a process of natural selection that results in the survival of those organisms best suited for their environment and the elimination of those not fit. A continuing struggle for survival takes place in nature, Darwin wrote, and those forms that survive are the ones that have made successful adaptations or adjustments to the environmental difficulties to which they have been exposed. Species that cannot adapt do not survive.

Darwin formulated the notion of a struggle for survival after reading *Essay on the Principle of Population*, written by Thomas Malthus in 1789. (Wallace was also influenced by this book.) Malthus had argued that the world's food supply increases arithmetically, while the human population tends to increase geometrically. The inevitable result, which Malthus described as having "a melancholy hue," is that many human beings will live under conditions of near starvation. Only the most forceful and cunning will survive.

Darwin extended this principle to all living organisms and developed the concept of natural selection. Those forms that survive the struggle and reach maturity tend to transmit to their offspring the skills or advantages that enabled them to survive. Further, since variation is another general law of heredity, offspring will show variation among themselves; some will possess the advantageous qualities developed to a higher level than their parents. These qualities tend to survive, so in the course of many generations great changes in form may develop. These changes can be so extensive as to account for the differences among species that exist today.

Natural selection was not the only mechanism of evolution allowed by Darwin. He also believed in the Lamarckian doctrine that changes in form brought about by experience during an animal's lifetime can be passed to subsequent generations.

Although many religionists were receptive to the idea of evolutionary theory, others saw it as a threat because they believed it to be inconsistent with a literal interpretation of the biblical account of creation. A distinguished clergyman called it "an attempt to dethrone God" and "a huge imposture from the beginning." "If the Darwinian theory is true, Genesis is a lie . . . and the revelation of God to man, as we Christians know it, is a delusion and a snare" (White, 1896/1965, p. 93). The controversy raged for many years.

Within a year of the book's publication, a debate took place at Oxford, at a meeting of the British Association for the Advancement of Science, between the biologist Thomas Henry Huxley, who defended Darwin and evolution, and Bishop Wilberforce, defending the Book of Genesis.

> Referring to the ideas of Darwin, [Wilberforce] congratulated himself . . . that he was not descended from a monkey. The reply came from Huxley: "If I had to choose, I would prefer to be a descendant of a humble monkey rather than of a man who employs his knowledge and eloquence in misrepresenting those who are wearing out their lives in the search for truth." (White, 1896/1965, p. 92)

During the debate a man walked about the hall holding a Bible over his head, shouting, "The Book, the Book." He was Robert Fitzroy, captain of the *Beagle* during Darwin's voyage. A religious fundamentalist, Fitzroy blamed himself for his part in the development of the theory of evolution. Five years after the Oxford debate he committed suicide (Gould, 1976, p. 34).

Newly discovered data of history have led to a reevaluation of this famous confrontation. Apparently, the story of the Oxford debate stems from Huxley's own anticlerical attitude and his attempt (perhaps unwitting) to bolster his stature as a scientist. It was less a debate than a series of speeches. Fitzroy merely took his turn at the podium, and Hooker, not Huxley, offered the more effective rebuttal to Wilberforce. Darwin himself remained on good terms with Wilberforce, noting that he found the bishop's remarks "uncommonly clever, not worth anything scientifically, but [he] quizzes me in splendid style" (Gould, 1986, p. 31).

The battle is not yet finished. In 1925, at the famous Scopes "monkey trial" in Dayton, Tennessee, a high school teacher (John T. Scopes) was prosecuted for teaching evolution. Almost half a century later, in 1972, a local clergyman charged that Darwin's theory "breeds corruption, lust, immorality, greed and such acts of criminal depravity as drug addiction, war and atrocious acts of genocide" (*New York Times*, October 1, 1972). A 1985 survey showed that half of a national sample of American adults rejected evolutionary theory (*Washington Post*, June 3, 1986).

Darwin remained aloof from the disputes of his time and wrote other books of interest to psychologists. His second major report on evolution, *The Descent of Man* (1871), marshaled the evidence for human evolution from lower forms of life, emphasizing the similarity between animal and human mental processes and stressing the importance of natural selection as a factor in evolution.

Darwin made an intensive study of emotional expression in humans and animals, and suggested that the changes of gesture and posture that characterize the major emotions could be interpreted in evolutionary terms. In *The Expression of the Emotions in Man and Animals* (1872) he argued that emotional expressions were remnants of movements that at one time had served some practical function.

Beginning in 1840, Darwin kept a diary of his infant son, recording the child's development. He published "A Biographical Sketch of an Infant" in the journal *Mind* in 1877, and the article was one of the early sources for modern child psychology.

The importance of mental factors in the evolution of species was apparent in Darwin's theory, and he frequently cited conscious reactions in humans and animals. Because of this role accorded consciousness in evolutionary theory, psychology was compelled to accept an evolutionary point of view.

The Influence of Darwin on Psychology

Darwin's work in the last part of the nineteenth century was a major force in shaping modern psychology. The theory raised the intriguing possibility of a continuity in mental functioning between animals and humans. The evidence was largely anatomical, but it strongly suggested continuities in the development of behavior and mental processes. If the human mind had evolved from more primitive minds, it would follow that similarities in mentality might exist between animals and humans. The gap between animals and humans posited two centuries earlier by Descartes was thus open to serious question. Scientists turned to the investigation of animal mental functioning, introducing a new subject into the psychological laboratory. Animal psychology, a field with far-reaching implications, was the result.

Darwin's work also brought a change in the subject matter and goal of psychology. The focus of the structuralists was the analysis of conscious content. Darwin influenced some psychologists, particularly Americans, to consider the functions that consciousness might serve. This seemed to many researchers to be a more important task than determining the elements of consciousness. Thus, psychology came to be more concerned with the adaptation of the organism to its environment, and the detailed investigation of mental elements began to lose its appeal.

A third point of influence of Darwin's theory on psychology was the broadening of the methodology the new science could legitimately use. The methods used in Wundt's laboratory were derived primarily from physiology, notably the psychophysical methods of Fechner. Darwin's methods, which produced results applicable to both humans and animals, bore no resemblance to physiologically based techniques.

His data came from a variety of sources, especially geology, paleontology, archeology, demography, observations of wild and domesticated animals, and research on breeding. The information from all these sources provided support for his theory, confirming "the assumption that a wide variety of kinds of evidence could legitimately be applied to the study of fundamental problems about living organisms" (Mackenzie, 1976, p. 334).

Here was tangible and impressive evidence that scientists could study human nature by means of techniques other than experimental introspection. Following Darwin's example, the psychologists who were influenced by evolutionary theory and its emphasis on the functions of consciousness became much more eclectic with regard to the methods of psychology. As a result, the kinds of data psychologists collected were broadened considerably.

A fourth effect of evolution on psychology was seen in the growing focus on individual differences. The fact of variation among members of the same species was obvious to Darwin as a result of his five-year observation of so many species and forms. Evolution could not occur if each generation were identical to its forebears. Hence, variation was an important ingredient of evolutionary theory. While the structuralists continued their search for general laws to encompass all minds, the psychologists influenced by Darwin began to search for ways in which individual minds differed from one another and for techniques to measure those differences. The psychology of the structuralists had little room for the consideration of animal minds and individual differences. It remained for scientists of a functionalist persuasion to pursue these problems. As a result, the nature and form of the new psychology changed.

INDIVIDUAL DIFFERENCES: SIR FRANCIS GALTON (1822–1911)

Galton effectively brought the spirit of evolution to bear on psychology with his work on the problems of mental inheritance and individual differences in human capacity. Before Galton's efforts, the phenomenon of individual differences had not been considered a subject for serious study in psychology; this was a serious omission. Only a few isolated attempts had been made, notably by Weber, Fechner, and Helmholtz, who had reported individual differences in their experiments but had not investigated them systematically. Wundt and Titchener did not consider individual differences to be a part of psychology.

The Life of Galton

Galton possessed an extraordinary intelligence (an estimated IQ of 200) and a wealth of novel ideas. He is perhaps without equal in the history of modern psychology. His creative curiosity and genius attracted him to a variety of problems, the details of which he left to be filled in by others. A few of the areas he investigated are fingerprints (which Scotland Yard adopted for identification purposes), fashions, the geographical distribution of beauty, weight lifting, the future of the race, and the efficacy of prayer. There was little that did not interest this versatile and inventive man.

Galton was born in 1822 near Birmingham, England, the youngest of nine children. His father was a prosperous banker whose wealthy and socially prominent family included important persons in all spheres of influence—Parliament, the clergy, and the military. From an early age Galton was acquainted with influential persons through his family connections.

At the age of 16, at his father's insistence, Galton began the study of medicine as a house pupil at the Birmingham General Hospital. He worked as an apprentice to the hospital physicians, dispensed pills, studied medical books, set broken bones, amputated fingers, pulled teeth, vaccinated children, and found diversion in reading Horace and Homer. It was not a pleasant existence and only the continued pressure from his father kept him there.

Evolution left its first
imprint on psychology in
the work of Sir Francis
Galton (1822–1911) on
mental inheritance and
individual differences.

One incident during this medical apprenticeship reflects his ever-present curiosity. Wanting to learn for himself the effects of the various medicines in the pharmacy, Galton began taking small doses of each, beginning in systematic fashion with those under the letter A. This scientific venture ended at the letter C when he took a dose of croton oil, a powerful purgative.

After a year at the hospital Galton continued his medical education at King's College in London. A year later he changed his plans and enrolled in Trinity College, Cambridge, where, with a bust of Newton opposite his fireplace, he studied mathematics. Although his studies were interrupted by a severe mental breakdown, he did manage to earn his degree, although he graduated without honors, a great disappointment. He returned briefly to the study of medicine until the death of his father released him from this profession, which he had come to dislike intensely.

Travel and exploration claimed Galton's attention. He journeyed to the Sudan in 1845 and to Southwest Africa in 1850. (In 1850 he also invented a teletype printer.) He published accounts of his travels and was awarded a medal from the Royal Geographic Society for his exploration of Southwest Africa, then an unknown land.

In the 1850s he stopped his travels because of marriage and poor health, but he continued to serve on scholarly committees and wrote a guide for explorers (*The Art of Travel*). He also organized expeditions for others, and gave lectures on camp life to soldiers training for duty in the Crimean War.

His spirited restlessness led him next to meteorology and the design of instruments with which to plot weather data. His meteorological findings were summarized in a book that is considered the first attempt to chart weather patterns on an extensive scale.

When his cousin, Charles Darwin, published *On the Origin of Species*, Galton immediately became interested in the new theory. The biological aspect of evolution captivated him at first and he investigated the effects of blood transfusions between rabbits to determine whether acquired characteristics could be inherited. Although the genetic side of evolution did not hold his attention for long, the social implications guided Galton's work and determined his influence on modern psychology.

The Works of Galton

Mental Inheritance

Galton's first important work for psychology was *Hereditary Genius*, published in 1869. His purpose was to demonstrate that individual greatness or genius occurred in families far too often to be explained by environmental influences—hence his thesis that eminent men have eminent sons. For the most part, the biographical studies reported in this book were investigations into the ancestries of influential persons such as scientists and physicians. Galton's data showed that each famous person inherited not only genius but a specific form of genius. A great scientist, for example, was born into a family that had attained eminence in science.

Galton's ultimate aim was to encourage the birth of the more eminent or fit individuals and to discourage the birth of the unfit. To help achieve this end, he founded the science of *eugenics* and argued that the human strain, not unlike livestock, could be improved by artificial selection. He believed that if men and women of considerable talents were selected and mated generation after generation, a highly gifted race would be the result. He proposed that intelligence tests be developed for use in choosing the brightest men and women for selective breeding. He suggested that those who achieved the highest scores be introduced to one another and offered financial inducements for marrying and having a large number of children (Fancher, 1984).[1]

---

[1] It is interesting that Galton, who founded the science of eugenics and believed that only the very intelligent should reproduce, did not have any children. The problem was apparently genetic; neither of Galton's brothers fathered children.

In attempting to verify his eugenic thesis, Galton became involved in problems of measurement and statistics. In *Hereditary Genius* he applied statistical concepts to the problems of heredity and sorted the celebrated men in his sample into classes or categories according to the frequency with which their level of ability occurred in the population. He found that eminent men have a higher probability of fathering eminent sons than do average men. His sample consisted of 977 famous men, each so outstanding as to be one in 4000. On a chance basis this group would be expected to have only one prominent relative; instead it had 332. The probability of eminence in certain families was high, but not high enough for Galton to consider seriously any possible influence of superior environment, education, or opportunity open to the sons of the outstanding families he studied. Eminence, or the lack of it, was a function of heredity, he argued, not of opportunity.

Galton wrote *English Men of Science* (1874), *Natural Inheritance* (1889), and more than 30 papers on problems of inheritance. His interest in heredity grew in scope from the individual and the family to the race as a whole. As he became more concerned with the possibility of improving the race by selective breeding, he made formal his proposal for a science of heredity (eugenics). This was followed by the creation of the journal *Biometrika* in 1901, the establishment of the Eugenics Laboratory at University College, London, in 1904, and the founding of an organization for promoting the idea of racial improvement, all of which are in existence today.

Statistical Methods

We noted Galton's interest in measurement and statistics. Throughout his career he never seemed fully satisfied with a problem unless he had found some means of quantifying the data and analyzing them statistically. He not only applied statistical methods, but he also developed several techniques.

Adolph Quetelet (1796–1874), a Belgian statistician, had been the first to apply statistical methods and the normal probability curve to biological and social data. The normal curve had been discovered and used in work on the distribution of measurements and errors in scientific observation, but the principle of normal distribution had not been applied to human variability until Quetelet demonstrated that anthropometric measurements of unselected samples of persons typically yield a normal curve. He demonstrated that measures of stature of 10,000 subjects approximated the normal curve of distribution, and he used the phrase *l'homme moyen* (the average man) to express the finding that most individuals cluster around the average or center of the distribution, and fewer and fewer are found as one moves from the center toward either extreme.

Galton was impressed by Quetelet's data and assumed that similar results would be obtained for mental characteristics. He found, for instance, that the marks given on university examinations followed the same normal curve distribution as Quetelet's physical measurement data. Because of the simplicity of the normal curve and its consistency over a number of traits, Galton proposed that a range of measurements could be meaningfully defined and summarized by two numbers—the average value of the distribution and the dispersion or range of variation around this average value (essentially, the mean and the standard deviation). Thus, a large set of measurements or values on human traits could be reduced to these two figures.

Galton's work in statistics yielded one of science's most important measures, the *correlation*. The first report of what he called "co-relations" appeared in 1888. Modern techniques for determining the validity and reliability of tests, as well as factor analytic methods, are direct outgrowths of Galton's discovery of correlation, which resulted from his observation that inherited characteristics tend to regress toward the mean. For example, he observed that tall men are, on average, not as tall as their fathers, while the sons of very short men are, on average, taller than their fathers. He devised the graphic means to represent the basic properties of the correlation coefficient and developed a formula for its calculation, though the formula has not remained in use.

Galton applied the correlational method to variations in physical measurements, demonstrating, for example, a correlation between body height and head length. With Galton's encouragement, his student Karl Pearson developed the mathematical formula used today for the precise calculation of the correlation coefficient—the Pearson product–moment coefficient of correlation. The traditional symbol for correlation coefficient, r, is taken from the first letter of the word "regression," in recognition of Galton's discovery of the tendency of inherited human traits to regress toward the average or mean.

Correlation is a fundamental tool in the social and behavioral sciences, as well as in engineering and the natural sciences. Many other statistical techniques have been developed on the basis of Galton's pioneering work.

Mental Tests

With the development of specific mental tests, Galton may properly be called the first practitioner of psychology. It has been said that he originated mental tests, although the term itself came from Cattell, an American disciple of Galton's. Galton began by assuming that intelligence could be measured in terms of a person's level of sensory capacity—the higher the intelligence, the higher the level of sensory discrimination.

He needed to invent the apparatus with which psychological measurements could be made quickly and accurately for large numbers of people. With characteristic ingenuity and enthusiasm, he devised several instruments. To determine the highest frequency of sound that could be heard, he invented a whistle, with which he tested animals as well as people. (He tested animals by walking through the streets of London and the Royal Zoological Gardens with the whistle fixed in the lower end of a hollow walking stick with a rubber bulb at the other end.) The "Galton whistle," in improved form, was a standard piece of psychological laboratory equipment until it was replaced by more sophisticated electronic apparatus in the 1930s.

Galton's other devices included a photometer to measure the precision with which a subject could match two spots of color, a calibrated pendulum to measure reaction time to sounds and lights, a series of weights to be arranged in order of heaviness to measure kinesthetic sensitivity, a bar with a variable distance scale to test estimation of visual extension, and sets of bottles containing different substances to test olfactory discrimination. Most of his tests were prototypes for the standard equipment used in psychological laboratories today.

Armed with his new tests, Galton proceeded to obtain a mass of data. He established the Anthropometric Laboratory in 1884 at the International Health Exhibition, later moved to the South Kensington Museum in London. The laboratory remained active for six years, and data from more than 9000 people were collected. Instruments for the anthropometric and psychometric measurements were arranged on a long table at one end of a narrow room. For a threepence admission fee, a person could pass along the table and be measured by an attendant who then wrote the data on a card. In addition to those noted above, measurements included height, weight, breathing power, strength of pull and squeeze, quickness of blow, hearing, vision, and color sense.

The aim of this large-scale testing program was to determine the range of human capacities. Galton wanted to test the entire population of Great Britain so that the people would know the exact level of their collective mental resources.

A century later a group of American psychologists analyzed Galton's data (Johnson et al., 1985). They found substantial test–retest correlations, indicating the statistical reliability of the data. In addition, the data provided useful information on developmental trends during childhood, adolescence, and maturity within the population tested. Measures such as weight, armspan, breathing power, and strength of squeeze were shown

In his laboratory at South Kensington Museum, Galton used a variety of novel devices to conduct the first large-scale psychological testing.

to be similar to development in these capacities described in the psychological literature today, although the rate of development 100 years ago appears to have been slightly slower. Thus, Galton's data continue to be instructive.

Association

Galton worked on two problems in the area of association: the diversity of associations of ideas and the time required to produce associations. One of his methods for studying the diversity of associations was to walk 450 yards along Pall Mall, the street in London running between Trafalgar Square and St. James Palace, focusing his attention on an object until it suggested one or two associated ideas to him. The first time he did this, he was amazed at the number of associations that developed from the nearly 300 objects he had seen. He found that many of these associations were recollections of past experiences, including incidents long forgotten. Repeating the walk a few days later, he found considerable repetition of the associations that had occurred during the first walk. This greatly diminished his interest in the study of the diversity of associations, and he turned to reaction-time experiments instead, which produced more useful results.

Galton prepared a list of 75 words, writing each on a slip of paper. After a week he viewed them one at a time, using a chronometer to record the time necessary to produce two associations for each word. Many of the associations were single words, but several appeared as images or mental pictures that required a number of words to describe.

His next task was to determine the origin of these associations. He discovered that about 40 percent of them could be traced to events in his childhood and adolescence, an early demonstration of the influence of childhood experiences on the adult personality.

Of greater importance was the introduction of the experimental study of association. Galton's invention of the *word association test* marked the first attempt to subject association to laboratory experimentation. Wundt adapted the technique, limited the response to a single word, and used it at Leipzig. Carl Jung elaborated on it for his own word association studies (Chapter 14).

Mental Imagery

Galton's investigation of mental imagery marks the first extensive use of the psychological questionnaire. Subjects were asked to recall a scene—such as their breakfast table that morning—and to try to elicit images of it. They were instructed to indicate whether the images were dim or clear, bright or dark, colored or not colored, and so on.

To Galton's amazement, his first group of subjects, scientific acquaintances, reported no clear imagery at all. Some were not even sure what Galton was talking about when he questioned them about images. Further investigation, using subjects of more average ability, resulted in reports of clear and distinct images that were often full of detail and color. He found that the imagery of women and children was particularly concrete and detailed. As more people were questioned, it became clear that imagery is more or less normally distributed in the population.

Galton's work began a long line of research on imagery; in general, his results have been supported. As with most of his research, the interest in imagery was rooted in his attempt to demonstrate hereditary similarities. For example, he found that similarity in imagery is greater between siblings than between individuals who are unrelated.

Additional Studies

The areas of research discussed thus far constitute Galton's chief sources of influence on psychology. Because he performed many other studies, we will discuss a few of them to indicate the richness and variety of his talent.

Galton tried to put himself into the state of mind of the insane by imagining that everyone or everything he saw while he was taking a walk was a spy. "By the end of the morning stroll, every horse seemed to be watching him either directly or, just as suspicious, disguising their espionage by elaborately paying no attention" (Watson, 1978, pp. 328–329).

Galton lived at a time when the debate between evolution and fundamentalist theology was acute. With great objectivity, he investigated the problem and concluded that although large numbers of people hold intense religious beliefs, this is not evidence that such beliefs are valid. He discussed the power of prayer to produce results and concluded that it was of no use to physicians in curing patients, or to meteorologists in invoking weather changes, or to clergy in conducting their worldly affairs.

Galton believed that there was little difference between persons who profess a belief in one of the many brands of religion and those who do not, in terms of their dealings with others or in their own emotional lives. He would have liked to give the world a new set of beliefs, structured in terms of science, as a substitute for religious dogma. He thought that the evolutionary development of a finer and nobler race through eugenics should be our goal, rather than a place in heaven.

Galton always seemed to be counting something. He occupied himself at lectures or at the theater by counting the yawns and fidgets of the audience, using the results as a measure of boredom. When he was having his portrait painted, he counted the number of brush strokes—some 20,000. At one time, he decided to try to count by odors instead of numbers. After training himself to forget what the numbers 1, 2, 3, and so on, meant, he assigned number values to odors such as camphor and peppermint. He learned to add and subtract by thinking of odors instead of numbers. Out of this intellectual exercise came a paper entitled "Arithmetic by Smell," which was published in the first issue of the American journal *Psychological Review*.

Comment

Galton spent only 15 years engaged in investigating activities of a psychological nature, yet his efforts during this short period strongly affected the direction psychology would take. He was not truly a psychologist, any more than he was a eugenicist or an anthropologist. He was an extremely gifted individual whose talent and temperament could not be bound by the confines of any one discipline. Consider again the studies that Galton initiated in which psychologists became interested: adaptation, heredity versus environment, comparison of species, child development, the questionnaire method, statistical techniques, individual differences, and mental tests. Galton's work influenced American psychology much more than did Wundt's. "Never again in the history of the science . . . do we meet an investigator so brilliant, so versatile, so wide in his interests and abilities, so little bound by prejudice or preconception [in his approach to science]. Compared with him, all others (with the one exception perhaps of William James) are apt to appear a little ponderous and pedantic, a little blinkered in their outlook" (Flugel & West, 1964, p. 111).

THE INFLUENCE OF ANIMAL PSYCHOLOGY ON FUNCTIONALISM

The evolutionary theory of Charles Darwin provided the impetus for animal psychology. Before Darwin published his theory, there was no reason for scientists to be interested in the animal mind because animals were considered to be soulless or mindless automata, possessing no similarity with humans, a point stressed by Descartes.

On the Origin of Species radically altered this notion. It became clear that there was no sharp break between the human and animal minds. Instead, a continuity between all aspects—mental and physical—of humans and animals was postulated, because we were believed to be derived from animals by the continuous evolutionary process of change and development. "There is no fundamental difference between man and the higher mammals in their mental faculties" (Darwin, 1871, p. 66). If mind could be demonstrated to exist in animals, and if continuity between the animal mind and the human mind could be shown, such evidence would serve as a defense of Darwin's theory against the human–animal dichotomy espoused by Descartes. A quest was begun for evidence of mind or intelligence in animals.

Darwin undertook the defense of his theory in *Expression of the Emotions in Man and Animals* (1872), in which he argued that our emotional behavior results from the inheritance of behavior once useful to animals, but no longer of any use to humans. One of Darwin's famous examples to demonstrate this point is the way our lips curl when we sneer. Darwin held this to be a remnant of the animal baring of the canine teeth in rage. Many such examples were cited to demonstrate a continuity between animals and humans.

In the years that followed the publication of *On the Origin of Species*, the topic of animal intelligence became popular not only among scientists but with the general public as well. In the 1860s and 1870s, letters to scientific and popular magazines reported instances of animal behavior that suggested hitherto unsuspected mental abilities. Thousands of stories circulated about the highly intelligent feats of pet cats and dogs, horses, pigs, snails, birds, and most other creatures.

Even Wilhelm Wundt was affected by the trend. In 1863, before he became the world's first psychologist, he wrote about the intellectual abilities of a wide range of living forms, from polyps to beetles to beavers. He argued that animals that displayed even minimal sensory capacities must also possess powers of judgment and conscious inference. The so-called inferior animals differed from humans not so much in their abilities but in the fact that they had not received as much training and education. Thirty years later Wundt would become much less generous in attributing high intelligence to animals, but, for a time, his voice was added to the many others that suggested that animals might be as intelligent as humans (Richards, 1980).

The person who formalized and systematized the study of animal intelligence was the British physiologist, George John Romanes (1848–1894). As a young man, Romanes had been impressed by Darwin's writings. Some time later, after he and Darwin had become friends, Darwin gave him all of his notes on animal behavior. Darwin chose Romanes to carry on that portion of his work, to apply the theory of evolution to the mind as Darwin had applied it to the body. Romanes became a worthy successor.

In 1883 Romanes published *Animal Intelligence*, generally considered the first book on comparative psychology. Romanes collected data on the behavior of fish, birds, domestic animals, and monkeys. His purpose was to demonstrate the high level of animal intelligence as well as its similarity to human intellectual functioning, thus illustrating a continuity in mental development. His methodology is referred to in somewhat contemptuous terms as the *anecdotal* method—the utilization of observational, often casual, reports about animal behavior. Many of the reports used by Romanes came from uncritical and untrained observers, and, of course, were open to the charges of incorrect observation, careless description, and biased interpretation.

How did Romanes derive his findings on the nature of animal intelligence from anecdotal observations of animal behavior? He worked through a curious and ultimately discarded technique known as *introspection by analogy*. Using this approach, investigators assume that the same mental processes that occur in their own minds also occur in the minds of the animals under observation. The existence of mind and specific mental functions is inferred by observing behavior and then drawing an analogy·from human mental processes to those assumed to be taking place in animals.

Romanes described the process of introspection by analogy in these terms: "starting from what I know subjectively of the operations of my own individual mind, and of the activities which in my own organism these operations seem to prompt, I proceed by analogy to infer from the observable activities displayed by other organisms, the fact that certain mental operations underlie or accompany these activities" (Mackenzie, 1977, pp. 56–57).

Through the use of this technique, Romanes concluded that animals were capable of the same kinds of rationalization, ideation, complex reasoning, and problem-solving ability as humans. Some of Romanes's followers even credited animals with a level of intelligence far superior to that of the average human being.

In a study of cats, which he considered to be more intelligent than any other animal except monkeys and elephants, Romanes wrote about the behavior of the cat that belonged to his coachman. Through an intricate pattern of movements, the cat was able to open a door leading into the stables. Introspecting by analogy, Romanes reached the following conclusion:

> Cats in such cases have a very definite idea as to the mechanical properties of a door; they know that to make it open, even when unlatched, it requires to be *pushed*. . . . First the animal must have observed that the door is opened by the hand grasping the handle and moving the latch. Next she must reason, by "the logic of feelings"— If a hand can do it, why not a paw? . . . the pushing with the hind feet after depressing the latch must be due to adaptive reasoning. (Romanes, 1883, pp. 421–422)

Romanes's work fell far short of modern scientific rigor. He did, however, employ certain criteria for judging the reliability of the reports he used, and he adhered to them strictly. Despite these precautions, the line between fact and subjective interpretation in his data is unclear. Although there are deficiencies in his data and method, Romanes is respected for his pioneer efforts in stimulating the development of comparative psychology and preparing the way for the experimental approach that followed. In many areas of science, reliance on observational data has preceded the development of refined experimental methodology, and it was Romanes who launched the observational stage of comparative psychology.

The weaknesses inherent in the anecdotal method and introspection by analogy were recognized by C. Lloyd Morgan (1852–1936), the person Romanes chose as his successor. Morgan, in addition to being one of the first men ever to ride a bicycle in the city of Bristol, England, was a geologist and zoologist (Jones, 1980). He proposed a *law of parsimony* (often called "Lloyd Morgan's canon"), in an effort to counter the tendency to anthropomorphize and thus attribute too much intelligence to animals. The principle states that an animal's behavior must not be interpreted as the outcome of a higher mental process when it can be explained in terms of lower mental processes. Morgan may have derived his law, which he advanced in 1894, from a law of parsimony published by Wundt just two years earlier. Wundt stated that "complex explanatory principles can be used only when the simpler have proved insufficient" (Richards, 1980, p. 57).

Morgan followed essentially the same methodological approach as Romanes. He observed an animal's behavior and tried to explain that behavior through an introspective examination of his own mental processes. Applying the law of parsimony, however, he refrained from ascribing complex, higher-level mental processes to animals when their behavior could be explained more simply in terms of lower-level processes. He believed, for example, that most animal behavior could be explained as a result of learning or association based on sense experience; learning is a much lower-level "psychical faculty" than rational thought or ideation. With Morgan's canon, introspection by analogy came to be more restricted in use, and finally was superseded by more objective methods.

Morgan was the first to conduct large-scale experimental studies in animal psychology. Although his early experiments were not performed under rigid laboratory conditions, they did involve careful, detailed observations of the behavior of animals in their natural environments, with some artificially induced modifications. These studies did not permit the same degree of control as did laboratory experiments, but they were a great advance over Romanes's anecdotal method.

These early approaches to comparative psychology were British in origin, but leadership in the field rapidly passed to the United States. Reasons for this shift include Romanes's early death and Morgan's change from a career in research to one in administration at the University College of Bristol.

Comparative psychology was an outgrowth of the excitement and controversy engendered by Darwin's notion of continuity. Perhaps comparative psychology would have begun without the theory of evolution, but most likely it would not have had such a sound or early start. We shall continue the story of the development of animal psychology in Chapter 9.

COMMENT

Basic to Darwin's theory of evolution are the notion of function and the assertion that as a species evolves, its physical structure is determined by its requirements for survival. This premise caused biologists to regard each anatomical structure as a functioning element in a total living, adapting system. When psychologists began to consider mental processes in the same manner, they created a new movement—functional psychology. Chapters 7 and 8 consider the development of the new functionalism in the United States.

SUGGESTED READINGS

Darwin and Evolutionary Theory

Angell, J. R. (1909). The influence of Darwin on psychology. *Psychological Review, 16*, 152–169.

Boring, E. G. (1950). The influence of evolutionary theory upon American psychological thought. In S. Persons (Ed.), *Evolutionary thought in America* (pp. 267–298). New Haven, CT: Yale University Press.

Darwin, F. (Ed.). (1958). *The autobiography of Charles Darwin and selected letters.* New York: Dover. (Original work published 1892).

Gruber, H. E. (1974). *Darwin on man: A psychological study of scientific creativity.* New York: Dutton.

Mackenzie, B. (1976). Darwinism and positivism as methodological influences on the development of psychology. *Journal of the History of the Behavioral Sciences, 12*, 330–337.

MacLeod, R. B. (1970). Newtonian and Darwinian conceptions of man, and some alternatives. *Journal of the History of the Behavioral Sciences, 6*, 208–218.

Richards, R. J. (1983). Why Darwin delayed, or interesting problems and models in the history of science. *Journal of the History of the Behavioral Sciences, 19*, 45–53.

Russett, C. E. (1976). *Darwin in America: The intellectual response, 1865–1912.* San Francisco: W. H. Freeman.

Vorzimmer, P. J. (1970). *Charles Darwin, the years of controversy:* The Origin of Species *and its critics, 1859–1882.* Philadelphia: Temple University Press.

Young, R. M. (1973). The role of psychology in the nineteenth-century evolutionary debate. In M. Henle, J. Jaynes, & J. J. Sullivan (Eds.), *Historical conceptions of psychology* (pp. 180–204). New York: Springer.

Galton

Buss, A. R. (1976). Galton and the birth of differential psychology and eugenics: Social, political, and economic forces. *Journal of the History of the Behavioral Sciences, 12*, 47–58.

Buss, A. R. (1976). Galton and sex differences: An historical note. *Journal of the History of the Behavioral Sciences, 12*, 283–285.

Crovitz, H. (1970). *Galton's walk: Methods for the analysis of thinking, intelligence, and creativity.* New York: Harper & Row.

Diamond, S. (1977). Francis Galton and American psychology. *Annals of the New York Academy of Sciences, 291*, 47–55.

Forrest, D. W. (1974). *Francis Galton: The life and work of a Victorian genius.* New York: Taplinger.

Galton, F. (1908). *Memories of my life.* London: Methuen.

Pearson, K. (1914, 1924, 1930). *The life, letters and labors of Francis Galton* (3 vols.). Cambridge, England: Cambridge University Press.

Animal Psychology

Boakes, R. (1984). *From Darwin to behaviourism: Psychology and the minds of animals.* Cambridge, England: Cambridge University Press.

Carr, H. (1927). The interpretation of the animal mind. *Psychological Review, 34*, 87–106.

Lockard, R. B. (1971). Reflections on the fall of comparative psychology: Is there a message for us all? *American Psychologist, 26*, 168–179.

Loeb, J. (1918). *Forced movements, tropisms, and animal conduct.* Philadelphia: J. B. Lippincott.

Morgan, C. L. (1930). *The animal mind.* New York: Longmans, Green.

Richards, R. J. (1977). Lloyd Morgan's theory of instinct: From Darwinism to neo-Darwinism. *Journal of the History of the Behavioral Sciences, 13,* 12–32.

Warden, C. J. (1927). The historical development of comparative psychology. *Psychological Review, 34,* 57–85, 135–168.

Waters, R. H. (1939). Morgan's canon and anthropomorphism. *Psychological Review, 46,* 534–540.

Yerkes, R. M. (1943). Early days of comparative psychology. *Psychological Review, 50,* 74–76.

7

Functionalism: American Pioneers

By the turn of the century, psychology in the United States had assumed a character all its own, distinct from Wundt's psychology and Titchener's structuralism, neither of which was concerned with the purpose or function of consciousness. Why did functional psychology develop and thrive in America rather than in England, where the functional spirit originated? The answer seems to lie in the American temperament; the American *Zeitgeist* was ready for evolutionism and the functionalist attitude that derived from it.

ONLY IN AMERICA: HERBERT SPENCER (1820–1903) AND SYNTHETIC PHILOSOPHY

In 1882 a self-taught 62-year-old British philosopher arrived in the United States, where he was hailed as a national hero. He was met at his ship in New York by Andrew Carnegie, the multimillionaire patriarch of the American steel industry, who praised the Englishman as a messiah (Blumenthal, 1977). In the eyes of many leaders of American science, business, politics, and religion, the man was indeed a savior, and he was wined and dined and lavished with honors and appreciation.

His name was Herbert Spencer, the scholar whom Darwin called "our philosopher." His impact on the American scene was monumental; he was a celebrity of the day. Spencer was highly prolific, producing a large number of books, many of which he dictated while sitting in a rowboat (Boakes, 1984). His works were serialized in popular magazines, his books sold hundreds of thousands of copies, and his system of philosophy was taught in the universities by scholars in almost every discipline. His ideas, read by people at all levels of society, influenced a generation of Americans. Had there been television, Spencer would doubtless have appeared on talk shows and received even greater adulation.

What was the philosophy that brought him so much recognition and acclaim? Briefly stated, it was Darwinism—the notion of evolution and survival of the fittest—carried beyond Darwin.

Herbert Spencer (1820–1903) was acclaimed for his philosophy of social Darwinism: the utopian view that human character and society, without aid or regulation, would naturally evolve toward perfection.

    In the United States, interest in Darwin's theory was intense before Spencer was recognized. The notion of evolution had been accepted more rapidly and fully in America than elsewhere, including England, the country of its birth. Darwin's ideas were discussed and embraced not only in the universities and learned societies, but also in popular magazines and some religious publications.

Spencer pointed out the implications of evolution for human knowledge and experience and argued that the development of all aspects of the universe, including human character and social institutions, is evolutionary, operating in accordance with the principle of survival of the fittest. It was this emphasis on *social Darwinism*, the application of evolution to human nature and human societies, that met with such enthusiasm in the United States. Spencer's utopian view argued that through the survival of the fittest, only the best would survive. Human perfection was inevitable so long as nothing was done to interfere with the natural order of things. He stressed individualism and a laissez-faire economy, and opposed such government attempts to regulate people's lives as subsidized education and housing.

People and organizations were to be left alone to develop themselves and their society in their own way, just as living species were left alone to develop in the world of nature. Any help from the state would interfere with the natural process of evolution. In this view, those individuals or businesses or institutions that could not adapt to the environment were unfit for survival and should be allowed to perish or become extinct, for the betterment of society as a whole. If government continued to support the poor and the weak, they would endure and ultimately weaken the society, in violation of the primary law of nature that states that only the fittest shall survive. Spencer argued that by ensuring that only the strongest survive, human societies can improve themselves and eventually reach a state of human and societal perfection.

This message was highly compatible with America's individualistic creed, and the phrases "survival of the fittest" and "the struggle for existence" became part of the national consciousness. They reflect much of what nineteenth-century American society was all about.

In the closing decades of the nineteenth century the United States was a living example of Spencer's ideas. It was a pioneer nation being settled by hard-working persons who believed in free enterprise, independence from government regulation, and self-sufficiency. And they knew all about the survival of the fittest from their own daily experiences. Land was still freely available to those with the courage, cunning, and ability to take it and wrest a living from it. The principles of natural selection were vividly demonstrated in everyday life, particularly on the Western frontier, where success (and sometimes survival) depended on one's ability to adapt to the demands of an often hostile environment. Those who could not adapt did not survive. The historian Frederick Jackson Turner described nineteenth-century Americans in these terms: "That coarseness and strength combined with acuteness and inquisitiveness; that practical, inventive turn of mind, quick to find expedients; that masterful grasp of material things . . . powerful to effect great ends; that restless, nervous energy; that dominant individualism" (1947, p. 235).

America was oriented toward the practical, the useful, and the functional, and American psychology in its pioneering stages reflected these qualities. Thus, America was more amenable to evolutionism than Germany or even England. American psychology became a functional psychology because evolutionary theory and its derived functional spirit were both in keeping with the basic temperament of the United States.

Spencer's views were thus congruent with the American ethos in general. For more than 20 years his philosophical system influenced every field of learning, including the new psychology.

Spencer had written on the topic of evolution as early as 1850, but these pre-Darwin publications attracted relatively little attention. When Darwin's *On the Origin of Species* was published in 1859, Spencer became associated with the movement, and his own brand of more speculative evolutionism gained strength from Darwin's well-documented position. Their work was complementary; whereas Darwin was cautious about generalizing beyond his detailed data, Spencer was wont to discuss the implications of the theory and to apply evolutionary doctrine universally.

To accomplish this, Spencer developed his *synthetic philosophy*. (The word "synthetic" was used in the sense of "to synthesize" or "to combine," and not to mean something artificial or unnatural.) This all-encompassing system was, as noted, based on the application of evolutionary principles to all human knowledge and experience. Specifically, Spencer argued that the development of all aspects of the universe involves the processes of differentiation followed by integration. Any developing or growing thing is initially homogeneous and simple. Then recognizably distinct parts emerge (*differentiation*), and at a later stage these unique parts are joined or combined in a new, functioning whole (*integration*).

To Spencer, this notion of differentiation followed by integration, in which all things proceed from homogeneity to heterogeneity, was evolutionary. The implication of this view for psychology is that as the nervous system evolves to greater complexity, there is a corresponding increase in the richness and variety of experience to which the organism is exposed, and thus ever higher levels of functioning.

Spencer's system of synthetic philosophy was published in 10 volumes between 1860 and 1897. Two of these volumes constituted *The Principles of Psychology*, published first in 1855, which was used by William James as a textbook for the psychology course he taught at Harvard. In his *Principles* Spencer discussed the notion that the mind exists in its present form because of past and continuing efforts to adapt to various environments. He stressed the adaptive nature of nervous and mental processes, and wrote that increasing complexity of experiences, and hence behavior, is part of the evolutionary process of an organism's need to adapt to its environment in order to survive.

ANTICIPATOR OF FUNCTIONAL PSYCHOLOGY: WILLIAM JAMES (1842–1910)

There is much that is paradoxical about William James and his role and stature in American psychology. On the one hand, he was certainly the leading American precursor of functional psychology. He was also the pioneer of the new scientific psychology in the United States and its senior psychologist, and is still considered by many to be the greatest American psychologist. On the other hand, James at times denied that he was a psychologist or that there was a new psychology. He founded no formal system of psychology and had no disciples.

Although the psychology he embodied was scientific and experimental, James was not an experimentalist in attitude or deed. Psychology—he once called it that "nasty little science"—was not a lifelong passion, as it was for Wundt and Titchener. James worked in psychology for a while and then moved on.

Even when he was actively working in psychology, he remained independent, refusing to be absorbed by any ideology, system, or school. James was neither a follower nor a founder, neither a disciple nor a leader. He was aware of everything that was happening in psychology and was very much a part of it, but he was able to select from among the various positions only those parts that were congenial with his view of psychology, and to reject the rest.

This fascinating man who contributed so greatly to psychology turned his back on it later in life. He said that the field consisted of an "elaboration of the obvious" and allowed it to fumble on without his commanding presence. Still, his place in the history of psychology is both assured and significant.

Although James did not found functional psychology, he wrote and thought most clearly and effectively in the functionalist atmosphere permeating American psychology at that time. In so doing, he influenced the functionalist movement through the inspiration he provided to subsequent generations of psychologists.

The Life of James

William James (and his brother Henry, who became a famous novelist) was born in the Astor House, a New York hotel, into a well-known wealthy family. His father devoted himself with enthusiasm to the education of his five children, alternating between Europe (because of his belief that American schools were too restricted in their outlook) and America (because of an equally strong belief that his children should be educated among their countrymen). James's early formal education, often interrupted by travel, took place in France, England, Switzerland, Germany, Italy, and the United States. (A biography of James contains a chapter on this sporadic education, entitled, appropriately, "Zigzag Voyages.") The father encouraged intellectual independence among his children, whose family ties remained strong throughout their lives.

The stimulating experiences of his youth exposed James to the intellectual and cultural advantages of England and Europe and made him a man of the world. Frequent trips abroad characterized his entire life; his father's method of dealing with illness was to send the ailing family member to Europe rather than to a hospital. Because his health was seldom good, James became a commuter between the United States and Europe.

Although his father seemed to think that none of the children needed to be concerned with learning a vocation or earning a living, he did try to encourage James's early interest in science. At age 15, James received a microscope as a Christmas gift. He already had a "Bunsen burner and vials of mysterious liquids which he mixed, heated, and transfused, staining his fingers and clothes, to his father's annoyance, and sometimes even causing alarming explosions" (Allen, 1967, p. 47). James decided, however, at the age of 18, that he wanted to be an artist. Six months at the studio of William Morris Hunt persuaded him that he lacked promise, and in 1861 he entered the Lawrence Scientific School at Harvard. He soon left his first choice, chemistry, apparently because he disdained the painstaking demands of laboratory work, and enrolled in medical school. He had little enthusiasm for the practice of medicine, however, noting that "there is much humbug therein . . . with the exception of surgery, in which something positive is sometimes accomplished, a doctor does more by the moral effect of his presence on the patient and family, than by anything else. He also extracts money from them" (Allen, 1967, p. 98).

James interrupted his medical studies for a year to assist the zoologist Louis Agassiz on his expedition to Brazil to collect specimens of marine animals in the Amazon. On this trip he sampled another possible career, biology, but found that he could not tolerate

The essence of functionalism—the adaptation of living persons to their environment, especially as assisted by consciousness—is expressed in the writings of William James (1842–1910), often considered the greatest American psychologist.

the precise and orderly collecting and categorizing that this field required. His reaction to chemistry and biology was prophetic of his subsequent distaste for experimentation in psychology.

Although medicine was no more attractive to him after the 1865 expedition than it had been before, James reluctantly resumed his studies because nothing else appealed to him. He interrupted the work again, complaining of depression and physical problems including digestive disorders, insomnia, eye problems, and a weak back.

> It was obvious to everyone that he was suffering from America; Europe was the only cure. In 1867 he went to Dresden and Berlin, where he took baths for his back, read widely in German and other literature, toyed with thoughts of suicide, displayed his loneliness and homesickness by the tremendous volume of his correspondence, and remained just as miserable as he had been at home. (Miller & Buckhout, 1973, pp. 84–85)

He was able to attend lectures on physiology at the University of Berlin and remarked that it was time for "psychology to begin to be a science" (Allen, 1967, p. 140).

James finally obtained his medical degree from Harvard in 1869, but his depression deepened and his will to live was not very strong. In those dark months he began to build a philosophy of life, compelled not so much by intellectual curiosity as by desperation.

After reading a number of essays by the philosopher Charles Renouvier on free will, James became persuaded of its existence and resolved that his first act of free will would be to believe in free will, and to believe that he could cure himself through belief in the efficacy of the will. He apparently succeeded to some extent, because in 1872 he felt well enough to accept a teaching position at Harvard in physiology. After one year he took a year off to travel in Italy, but then returned to teaching.

In 1875–1876 James taught his first course in psychology, called "The Relations between Physiology and Psychology." Harvard thus became the first American university to offer the new experimental psychology. (James had never received formal classroom instruction in psychology; the first psychology lecture he attended was his own.) Also in 1875, James secured $300 from Harvard to purchase laboratory and demonstration equipment for the course.

In 1878 two important events occurred. The first was his marriage, which would produce five children and a certain amount of much needed order in his life. It was James's father who had first met the 27-year-old schoolteacher James was to marry. He returned from a meeting one night and announced that he had just met his son's future wife. Shortly thereafter, James verified his father's prophecy. The second event was the signing of a contract with the publishing house of Henry Holt, which resulted in one of the classic books in psychology. James believed that it would take him two years to write the book; it took 12. He began the work, to the amusement of his friends, on his honeymoon.

In 1880 James was made assistant professor of philosophy. He was promoted to professor of philosophy in 1885, and his title was changed to professor of psychology in 1889. His book was delayed by travels abroad, where he met many European psychologists of the day, including Wundt, who, he wrote, "made a pleasant and personal impression on me, with his agreeable voice and ready, tooth-showing smile." A few years later he wrote that Wundt "isn't a genius, he is a *professor*—a being whose duty is to know everything, and have his own opinion about everything" (Allen, 1967, pp. 251, 304).

The Principles of Psychology finally appeared in two volumes in 1890 and was a tremendous success; it is still considered a major contribution to the field. Almost 80 years after its publication one psychologist wrote: "James' *Principles* is without question the most literate, the most provocative, and at the same time the most intelligible book on psychology that has ever appeared in English or in any other language" (MacLeod,

1969, p. iii). One indication of the book's popularity is that it is often read by people who are not required to do so. In 1892 James published a condensed version.

Not everyone reacted favorably to the book. Wundt and Titchener, whose views James attacked, did not like it. "It is literature," Wundt wrote, "it is beautiful, but it is not psychology" (Bjork, 1983, p. 12).

James's own reaction to the book on its completion was not favorable either. In a letter to his publisher he described the manuscript as "a loathsome, distended, tumefied, bloated, dropsical mass, testifying to nothing but two facts: *1st,* that there is no such thing as a *science* of psychology, and *2nd,* that W.J. is an incapable" (Allen, 1967, pp. 314–315).

With the publication of *The Principles,* James decided that he had said all he wanted to about the science of psychology and no longer wanted to direct the psychological laboratory. He arranged for Hugo Münsterberg, then at the University of Freiburg in Germany, to become director of the Harvard laboratory and to teach courses in psychology, thus freeing James to turn to work in philosophy. Münsterberg had been criticized by Wundt, and this was high praise in James's eyes. Münsterberg, however, never fulfilled James's intention of providing leadership in experimental research for Harvard; he worked in a variety of fields, such as psychotherapy, legal psychology, and industrial psychology, and paid little attention to the laboratory after his first few years there. He helped to popularize psychology, however, and to make it a more applied discipline.

We noted that James was not an experimentalist, although he did begin and equip the laboratory at Harvard. He was never fully convinced of the value of laboratory work in psychology and did not like it personally. "I naturally hate experimental work," he had written to Münsterberg. In 1894 he stated that the United States had too many laboratories, and in *The Principles* he commented that the results of laboratory work were not in proportion to the amount of painstaking effort involved. It is not surprising that James contributed little of importance in the way of experimental work.

We noted earlier that James had no loyal disciples to carry on his point of view, nor did he direct a large number of Ph.D. students, as Titchener did. Several of James's students, however, including Angell, Thorndike, and Woodworth, made noteworthy contributions to the development of psychology. We shall discuss their work in later chapters.

James was also instrumental in facilitating the graduate education of Mary Whiton Calkins, who later became the first woman president of the American Psychological Association. Despite James's high opinion of her abilities, Harvard refused to award the Ph.D. degree to a woman. She had never been allowed to enroll formally at the university, but James had welcomed her into his seminars and had urged the university administration to grant her the degree. Later, she succeeded William James as president of the APA.

James spent the last 20 years of his life refining his philosophical system, and in the 1890s became America's leading philosopher. In 1899 he published *Talks to Teachers,* developed from lectures he had given to teachers, which helped to apply psychology to the classroom learning situation. *The Varieties of Religious Experience* appeared in 1902 and three additional works in philosophy were published in 1907 and 1909.

James's health remained poor and he retired from Harvard in 1907. In 1898, while climbing in the Adirondack Mountains, he became lost for 13 hours and the ordeal aggravated a heart lesion. The condition grew worse and resulted in his death in 1910, two days after his return from a final trip to Europe.

The Works of James

Since James was neither an experimentalist nor a founder (and not even a psychologist for the last several years of his life), how did he come to exert such a profound influence on psychology? Why is he often considered the greatest American psychologist?

Three reasons have been suggested for his overwhelming stature and influence. First, James wrote with a brilliance and clarity rare in science, then as well as now. There is magnetism, spontaneity, and charm throughout his books. The second reason for his influence is negative, in the sense in which all movements are negative. James opposed the analysis of consciousness into elements. The third reason is positive. He offered an alternative way of looking at the mind, an approach congruent with the new American functional approach to psychology. The times were ready for what James had to tell us (Boring, 1950).

The concept of functionalism is explicit in James's psychology, in which he presented what subsequently became the central tenet of American functionalism: the study of living persons as they adapt to their environment, not the discovery of elements of experience. The function of consciousness, James wrote, is to guide us to those ends required for survival. Consciousness is thus depicted as being particularly appropriate to the needs of complex beings in a complex environment; without it, the process of human evolution could not have occurred.

The Principles of Psychology

> The publication of *The Principles* was hailed both at home and abroad as an event of the first magnitude in the psychological world. Not only was it a comprehensive survey of a new field of learning, not only was it a new synthesis of the facts of psychology; it was itself a contribution to psychology. From the first, it was recognized as more than a mere book about psychology. Because of its freshness and power, because of its definite attitudes and stimulating suggestions, it was itself an event in the history of psychology. (Heidbreder, 1933, p. 197)

James's book treats psychology as a natural science, specifically a biological science. This was nothing new in 1890, but in James's hands the science of psychology took a different direction from Wundtian psychology. James was concerned with conscious processes as activities of an organism that produced some change in that organism's life. Mental processes were believed by James to be useful, *functional* activities to living creatures as they attempt to maintain and adapt themselves in the world of nature.

A related attitude is James's emphasis on the nonrational aspect of human nature. We are, he noted, creatures of action and passion as well as of thought and reason. Even when discussing purely intellectual processes, James emphasized the nonrational. For instance, he carefully noted that intellect operates under the physiological influences of the body, that one's beliefs are determined by emotional factors, and that reason and the formation of concepts are affected by various wants and needs. James did not consider the human being a wholly rational creature.

Let us briefly survey this book. The first six chapters of the first volume introduce the reader to the biological foundations that James believed necessary to prepare a base for psychology. He discussed aspects of nervous system activity important to mental functioning. He believed that all of mental life is determined largely by the tendency of the nervous system to undergo modification by each action it makes, so that subsequently the organism will find it easier to perform similar responses. Thus, habit became a vital part of all mental life.

James discussed and criticized all major philosophical conceptions of the relationships between mind and body. He accepted states of consciousness (mind) and brain processes (body) as phenomena in the natural world, and noted a correspondence, term for term, between the succession of conscious states and the succession of brain processes. He believed, however, that psychology as a science could accept whatever mind–body relationships it found, but was under no obligation to explain or account for their existence.

The remainder of the first volume is concerned with the subject matter and methods of investigation for psychology. Here James develops fully his notion of consciousness and its characteristics.

The second volume begins with a treatment of sensation, followed by chapters on perception, belief, reasoning, instinct, and volition. The last two chapters deal with hypnosis and with psychogenesis (the development of the human species and the individual). In the following sections, we discuss several of the major points as expressed in *The Principles*.

Subject Matter for Psychology: A New Look at Consciousness

James stated in the opening sentence of *The Principles* that "psychology is the Science of Mental Life, both of its phenomena and of their conditions." In terms of subject matter, the key words are "phenomena" and "conditions." "Phenomena" indicates that the subject matter is to be found in immediate experience; "conditions" refers to the importance of the body, particularly the brain, in mental life.

According to James, the physical substructures of consciousness form an important part of psychology. He recognized the importance of considering consciousness, the focal point of his interest, in its natural setting—the physical human being. This awareness of biology, of the action of the brain on consciousness, is a unique feature of James's approach to psychology.

James rebelled against what he considered the artificiality and narrowness of the Wundtian position, a revolt that anticipated the more general protest subsequently made by the functionalists (as well as the Gestalt psychologists). Experiences are simply what they are, James said, not groups or amalgamations of elements. The discovery of discrete elements through introspective analysis does not demonstrate that these elements exist independently of the observation. He argued that psychologists may read into an experience what their systematic position in psychology tells them should be there.

A tea-taster can be trained to discriminate individual elements in a flavor that may not be perceived by the untrained individual. The latter, sipping tea, experiences a fusion of the alleged flavor elements, a total blend not capable of analysis. Similarly, James argued, the fact that some people can analyze their conscious experiences does not mean that the resulting discrete elements are present in the consciousness of anyone else exposed to the same experience. James considered the making of such an assumption the "psychologists' fallacy."

Striking at the heart of the Wundtian approach, James declared that individual simple sensations (the elements of the structuralists) do not exist in conscious experience. They exist only as a result of a rather tortuous process of inference or abstraction. In a blunt and characteristically eloquent statement, James wrote: "No one ever had a simple sensation by itself. Consciousness, from our natal day, is of a teeming multiplicity of objects and relations, and what we call simple sensations are results of discriminative attention, pushed often to a very high degree" (1890, p. 224).

In place of the artificial analysis and reduction of conscious experience to alleged elements, James forcefully called for a new positive program for psychology. Mental life is a unity, he argued, a total experience that flows and changes. The basic point of James's conception of consciousness is that it "goes on," it is a stream, and he coined the phrase "stream of consciousness" to express this property. Because consciousness is a continuous flow, any attempt to subdivide it into temporally distinct elements or phases can only distort it.

Another characteristic of consciousness is that it is always changing; one can never have exactly the same state or thought twice. Objects in the environment can occur again and again, but not the identical sensations or thoughts they stimulate. We may think of an object on more than one occasion, but each time we think of it, we do so in a different fashion because of the effect of intervening experiences. Thus, consciousness is cumulative and not recurrent.

The mind is also sensibly continuous, that is, there are no sharp breaks in the stream of consciousness. There may be gaps in time, such as during sleep, but upon awakening, we have no difficulty making connection with the stream of consciousness that was going on before the interruption.

Still another characteristic of the mind is its selectivity. The mind chooses from among the many stimuli to which it is exposed, filtering out some, combining or separating others, selecting or rejecting still others. We can attend to only a small part of our experiential world, and the criterion of selection, according to James, is relevance. The mind selects relevant stimuli so that consciousness may operate in a logical manner and a series of ideas may arrive at a rational end.

Above all, James stressed the purpose of consciousness. He believed that consciousness must have some biological utility or it would not have survived. The purpose or function of consciousness is to enable us to adapt to our environment by enabling us to choose. James distinguished between conscious choice and habit, the latter being involuntary and nonconscious. When the organism faces a new problem and needs a new mode of adjustment, consciousness comes into play. This emphasis on purposiveness clearly reflects the influence of evolutionary theory.

Always interested in increasing his own knowledge of conscious experience, James once tried to expand his consciousness by inhaling nitrous oxide, a gas used as an anesthetic. While under the influence of the gas, he believed that he was experiencing mystical revelations of great cosmic truths that answered some of the riddles of the universe. He could never remember in the morning what those great truths were, but one night he managed to write something down. When he awoke, he rushed to his desk and found that he had written the following.

Hogamous, higamous,
Man is polygamous.

Higamous, hogamous,
Woman is monogamous.

James did not continue with these experiments.

The Methods of Psychology

The discussion of James's subject matter for psychology provides clues to his methods of study. Because psychology deals with a highly personal and immediate consciousness, introspection must be a basic tool. James believed that it is possible to investigate states of consciousness by examining one's own mind through introspection. James considered introspection to be the exercise of a natural gift, consisting in "catching the very life of a moment as it passed, in a fixing and reporting of the fleeting event as it occurred in its natural setting. It was not the introspection of the laboratory, aided by brass instruments; it was the quick and sure arresting of an impression by a sensitive and acute observer" (Heidbreder, 1933, p. 171).

James was aware of the difficulties and limitations of introspection and he accepted it as a less than perfect form of observation. He thought, however, that introspective results could be verified by appropriate checks and through the comparison of the findings of several observers. And though he was not himself a devotee of the experimental method, he did believe in its use as another possible means to psychological knowledge.

To supplement experimental and introspective methods, James urged the use of the comparative method in psychology. By inquiring into the psychological functioning of animals, children, preliterate peoples, and the insane, James believed that the psychologist would discover meaningful and useful variations in mental life.

This discussion of James's methods points up a major difference between structuralism and the newly developing functionalism. The new American movement was not to be restricted to a single technique—introspection. It would apply other methods as well, and this eclecticism broadened the scope of psychology considerably. As noted in Chapter 6, this more diverse methodology was one of Darwin's important legacies.

James emphasized the value for psychology of pragmatism. The basic tenet of the pragmatic point of view is that the validity of an idea, or of any knowledge, must be tested by its consequences. The popular expression of the pragmatic viewpoint is "anything is true if it works." The notion of pragmatism had been advanced in the 1870s by Charles S. Peirce, a philosopher and lifelong friend of James. Peirce's work, however, remained largely ignored until James wrote his *Pragmatism* (1907), which was one of his major contributions as a philosopher.

Emotions

James's most famous theoretical contribution deals with emotions. His theory, published in an article in 1884 and six years later in *The Principles*, contradicted the current thinking about emotions. The experience of emotion had been assumed to precede the physical or bodily expression. The traditional example—we meet a bear, are frightened, and run—exemplifies this notion that the emotion (fright) precedes the bodily expression (running).

James reversed this and stated that the arousal of the physical response precedes the appearance of the emotion. Thus, we see the bear, run, and then are afraid. In essence, the emotion is nothing but the feeling of the bodily changes as they occur. For supporting evidence, James appealed to the introspective observation that if these bodily changes, such as increased heart rate and muscle tension, did not occur, there would be no emotion. As another example of simultaneous discovery, the Danish physiologist Carl Lange published an analogous theory in 1885. The similarity between the two led to the designation "James–Lange theory." James's theory of emotion led to a great deal of controversy and stimulated considerable research.

Habit

The chapter in *The Principles* dealing with habit is in keeping with James's awareness of physiological influences. He considered habit to involve the functioning of the nervous system and postulated that repeated actions serve to increase the plasticity of neural matter. As a result, the action becomes easier to perform on subsequent repetitions and requires less attention on the part of the individual. James also believed that habit had enormous social implications, as noted in this frequently quoted passage.

> Habit is thus the enormous fly-wheel of society, its most precious conservative agent. It alone is what keeps us all within the bounds of ordinance, and saves the children of fortune from the envious uprisings of the poor. It alone prevents the hardest and most repulsive walks of life from being deserted by those brought up to tread therein. It keeps the fisherman and the deck-hand at sea through the winter; it holds the miner in his darkness, and nails the countryman to his log-cabin and his lonely farm through all the months of snow; it protects us from invasion by the natives of the desert and the frozen zone. It dooms us all to fight out the battle of life upon the lines of our nurture or our early choice, and to make the best of a pursuit that disagrees, because there is no other for which we are fitted, and it is too late to begin again. It keeps different social strata from mixing. Already at the age of twenty-five you see the professional mannerism settling down on the young commercial travel-ler, on the young doctor, on the young minister, on the young counsellor-at-law. You see the little lines of cleavage running through the character, the tricks of thought, the prejudices, the ways of the "shop," in a word, from which the man can by-and-by no more escape than his coat-sleeve can suddenly fall into a new set of folds. On the whole, it is best he should not escape. It is well for the world that in most of us, by the age of thirty, the character has set like plaster, and will never soften again. (1890, p. 79)[1]

Comment

Our coverage of James does not attempt to encompass the full scope of his form of psychology. *The Principles* was of major importance and its publication has legitimately been acclaimed as a great event in the history of psychology.

Perhaps it is easier to admire William James than to attempt to analyze his work. His book influenced thousands of students and his position inspired John Dewey and other functional psychologists to shift the new science of psychology away from the structural view. There is no denying that James is one of the most important psychologists the United States has ever produced.

---

[1]From William James, *Psychology (Briefer Course)*. New York: Collier, 1962, pp. 158–159. Reprinted by permission of Alexander R. James, Lit. Exec.

GRANVILLE STANLEY HALL (1844–1924)

Although William James was the first truly great American psychologist, the tremendous growth of psychology in the United States between 1875 and 1900 was not the result of his work alone. Another remarkable figure in the history of American psychology, and a worthy and influential contemporary of James, was Granville Stanley Hall.

Hall's career was one of the most interesting and varied of any psychologist. He worked in bursts of energy and enthusiasm in a number of areas and then moved on, leaving the details to be investigated by others. He was not a founder of functionalism, but his contributions to new fields and activities had a pronounced functional flavor.

American psychology owes Hall a debt because of his outstanding record of "firsts." He received the first American doctorate in psychology, and he was the first American student in the first year of the first psychology laboratory (at Leipzig). He began what is often considered to be the first psychological laboratory in the United States, as well as the first American journal of psychology. He was the first president of Clark University, and the organizer and first president of the American Psychological Association.

The Life of Hall

Hall was born on a farm in Massachusetts and developed at an early age a succession of interests that characterized his later life. Also characteristic was his personal ambition. At the age of 14, "he vowed to leave the farm and 'do and be something in the world.' . . . His most intense adolescent fear was the fear of mediocrity" (Ross, 1972, p. 12). In 1863 he entered Williams College. By the time he graduated, Hall had won a number of honors and had developed an enthusiasm for philosophy and especially evolution, which was to influence his career in psychology.

In 1867 he enrolled in the Union Theological Seminary in New York City, without having a strong commitment to the ministry. His interest in evolution was no advantage in the seminary and he was not noted for his religious orthodoxy. The story has been told that when Hall gave his trial sermon to the faculty and students, the seminary president, whose job it was to criticize such speeches, instead knelt and prayed for Hall's soul.

On the advice of the preacher Henry Ward Beecher, Hall went to Bonn to study philosophy and theology. From there he went to Berlin, where he added studies in physiology and physics. This phase of his education was supplemented by romantic interludes and the frequenting of beer gardens and the theater, all daring experiences for a young man of pious upbringing. He wrote of his amazement and delight at seeing one of his theology professors drinking beer on a Sunday. "The hated Puritan Sunday which all my life before had been a dreaded day of gloom and depression now became one of joy and holiday recreation" (Ross, 1972, p. 35). Hall's European sojourn became a time of liberation.

He returned home in 1871, 27 years old, with no degree and heavily in debt. He completed his divinity studies and preached in a country church for all of 10 weeks. After working as a private tutor for more than a year, Hall secured a teaching job at Antioch College in Ohio. He taught English literature, French and German languages and literature, and philosophy, served as librarian, led the choir, and even preached. In

A man of diverse professional interests, American Psychological Association founder Granville Stanley Hall (1844–1924) made notable contributions to educational psychology, applying a basic belief in evolution to problems of human development.

1874 he read Wundt's *Physiological Psychology*, and his interest in the new psychology was aroused, causing him some uncertainty about his future career. He took a leave of absence from Antioch, settled in Cambridge, Massachusetts, in 1876, and became a tutor in English at Harvard.

In addition to the monotonous and time-consuming work of teaching sophomore English, Hall managed to conduct research at the medical school. In 1878 he presented his dissertation on the muscular perception of space for his doctorate, the first degree in psychology awarded in America. He got to know William James very well. The two were close in age, but far apart in background and temperament.

Immediately after receiving his degree, Hall left for Europe, first to study physiology at Berlin and then to become Wundt's first American student at Leipzig. The anticipation of working with Wundt was apparently greater than the reality. Although he attended Wundt's lectures and dutifully served as a subject in the laboratory, his own research was conducted along more physiological lines. His career demonstrated that he was little influenced by Wundt. When Hall returned to America in 1880 he had no prospect of a job, yet within a span of only 10 years he would become a figure of national renown and a leading American psychologist, second only to William James.

The first step in Hall's rise from obscurity was an invitation from the president of Harvard to give a series of Saturday morning talks on education. These well-received lectures brought Hall much favorable publicity and an invitation to lecture at Johns Hopkins University, which had been established five years earlier as the first graduate school in the United States.

His lectures were successful and he was given a professorship in 1884. During his years at Johns Hopkins, Hall began what is usually considered to be the first American psychology laboratory (in 1883) and taught a number of students who later became prominent psychologists, among them Cattell and Dewey. In 1887 Hall founded the *American Journal of Psychology*, the first journal of psychology in the United States and still an important publication. This journal provided a platform for theoretical and experimental ideas and a sense of solidarity and independence for American psychology. (In a burst of enthusiasm Hall had an excessive number of copies printed of the first issue. It took five years for the journal and Hall to pay back those initial costs.)

In 1888 Hall accepted the invitation to become the first president of the new Clark University. He aspired to make Clark a graduate university along the lines of Hopkins and the German universities, with the primary emphasis on research rather than teaching. Unfortunately, the founder, wealthy merchant Jonas Gilman Clark, had different ideas, and did not provide as much money as Hall had been led to expect. When Clark died in 1900, the endowment was devoted to the founding of an undergraduate college, which had been opposed by Hall but long advocated by Clark.

Hall was professor of psychology as well as university president, and taught in the graduate school for several years. He also found time in 1891 to establish at his own expense another journal, the *Pedagogical Seminary* (now the *Journal of Genetic Psychology*), to serve as an outlet for research in child study and educational psychology.

The American Psychological Association was founded in 1892, largely through Hall's efforts. At his invitation, approximately a dozen psychologists met in his study to plan the organization, and they elected him its first president. By 1900 the organization included 127 members.

Hall's interest in religion persisted. He began the *Journal of Religious Psychology* (1904), which ceased publication after a decade, and in 1917 published a book entitled *Jesus the Christ in the Light of Psychology*. His portrayal of Jesus as "a kind of adolescent superman" (Ross, 1972, p. 418) was not well received by organized religion. In 1915 he founded the *Journal of Applied Psychology*, bringing the number of American psychology journals to 16.

Psychology prospered at Clark under Hall; during his 36 years there, 81 doctorates were awarded in psychology. His students remember the exhausting but exhilarating

Monday evening seminars at Hall's home, during which the doctoral candidates were quizzed by the faculty and the other graduate students. After the meetings, which often lasted as long as four hours, a household servant would bring in a gigantic tub of ice cream (Averill, 1982). At one time it could be claimed that the majority of American psychologists had been associated with Hall either at Clark or at Johns Hopkins, though he was not the primary source of inspiration for them all. Perhaps his personal influence is reflected best in the fact that one-third of his doctoral students eventually went into administration, as he had done.

Hall was one of the first Americans to become interested in psychoanalysis, and was in large part responsible for the attention it received in the United States. To celebrate the twentieth anniversary of Clark University in 1909, he invited Sigmund Freud and Carl Jung to participate in a series of conferences. This was Freud's only visit to the United States, and Hall's invitation was courageous because of the suspicion with which many American psychologists viewed psychoanalysis.

Hall also invited his former teacher, Wundt, who declined because of his advanced age (77). Also, Wundt was scheduled to be the featured speaker at the 500th anniversary of his university.

Hall continued to write after his retirement from Clark University in 1920. He died four years later, a few months after his election for a second term as president of the American Psychological Association.

Granville Stanley Hall's psychology laboratory at Johns Hopkins University is considered the first in the United States.

The Works of Hall

Hall was interested in many areas. However, his intellectual wanderings had a guiding theme—evolutionary theory. His work on a variety of psychological topics was governed by the conviction that the normal growth of the mind involves a series of evolutionary stages. Hall used the theory of evolution as a framework for broad theoretical speculations.

Hall contributed more to educational psychology than to experimental psychology. Only in the early phases of his productive career did he focus on experimental psychology; although he remained favorable toward it, he became impatient with its limitations. Laboratory work in the new psychology proved too narrow for Hall's more general goals and efforts.

Hall is often called a genetic psychologist because of his concern with human and animal development, and with the related problems of adaptation and development. At Clark, Hall's geneticism led him to the psychological study of childhood, and, later, of adolescence. In his child studies he made extensive use of questionnaires, a procedure he had learned in Germany. By 1915 Hall and his students had developed and used 194 questionnaires covering many topics. So extensive was his use of questionnaires that for a time the method came to be associated in America with Hall's name, even though the technique had been used earlier by Galton.

These early studies of children created great public enthusiasm, leading to the so-called child study movement. Although it disappeared in a few years because of poorly executed studies, the movement served to establish the importance of both the empirical study of the child and the concept of psychological development.

Hall's most influential work is the lengthy (about 1300 pages) two-volume *Adolescence: Its Psychology, and Its Relations to Physiology, Anthropology, Sociology, Sex, Crime, Religion, and Education,* published in 1904. This encyclopedia contains the most complete statement of Hall's recapitulation theory of development. He believed that children in their individual development repeat the life history of the race. When children play cowboys and Indians, for example, they are recapitulating the level of preliterate human beings. The book included much material of interest to child psychologists and educators and went through several printings, one 20 years after initial publication.

It also became highly controversial because of what some persons considered its excessive focus on sex. Hall was accused of having prurient interests. In a formal book review, E. L. Thorndike wrote that "the acts and feelings, normal and morbid, resulting from sex are discussed in a way without precedent in English science." Thorndike was even more critical in a letter to a colleague, stating that Hall's book was "chock full of errors, masturbation and Jesus. He is a mad man" (Ross, 1972, p. 385).

In that same year, 1904, Hall began a series of weekly lectures at Clark on sex. This was a scandalous act at the time, even though he did not allow women to attend. He stopped the talks before long, however, because "too many outsiders got in and even listened surreptitiously at the door" (Koelsch, 1970, p. 119).

Many psychologists were uneasy about Hall's enthusiasm for sex. "Is there no turning Hall away from this d----d sexual rut?" James Rowland Angell wrote to Titchener. "I really think it is a bad thing morally and intellectually to harp so much on the sexual string" (Boakes, 1984, p. 163). They need not have worried; the energetic Hall soon moved on to other interests.

As Hall grew older, he became interested in a later stage of development—old age. At the age of 78 he published the two-volume work *Senescence* (1922), the first large-scale geriatric survey of a psychological nature. In the last few years of his life he also wrote two autobiographical books, *Recreations of a Psychologist* (1920) and *The Life and Confessions of a Psychologist* (1923).

Comment

G. Stanley Hall was once introduced to an audience as "the Darwin of the mind." It was a characterization that evidently pleased him and vividly expressed his aspirations and the basic attitude that flavored his work. Throughout his amazing career he remained versatile and agile. His seemingly limitless enthusiasm was bold, diverse, and nontechnical, and it is perhaps this characteristic that made him so stimulating and influential.

In his autobiography he wrote: "All my active conscious life has been made up of a series of fads or crazes, some strong, some weak; some lasting long . . . and others ephemeral" (1923, pp. 367–368). It was a perceptive observation—he was mercurial, aggressive, quixotic, often at odds with his colleagues, but never dull. Hall once noted that Wundt would rather have been commonplace than brilliantly wrong. It has been suggested that Hall would rather have been brilliantly wrong than commonplace.

JAMES McKEEN CATTELL (1860–1944)

The functionalist spirit of American psychology may be best represented in the life and work of Cattell, another contemporary of James. Cattell is generally credited with influencing the movement in American psychology toward a practical, test-oriented approach to the study of mental processes. His psychology was concerned with human abilities rather than conscious content, and in this respect he comes close to being a functionalist, though, like Hall and James, he was never formally associated with the movement. He represented the American functionalist spirit, however, in his emphasis on mental processes in terms of their utility to the organism.

The Life of Cattell

Cattell was born in Easton, Pennsylvania, and received his bachelor's degree in 1880 from Lafayette College, whose president was his father. Following the custom of going to Europe for graduate study, Cattell first went to Göttingen and then to Leipzig and Wundt.

A paper in philosophy won him a fellowship at Johns Hopkins in 1882. At the time, his major interest was philosophy, and during his first semester no psychology courses were even offered. It appears that Cattell became interested in psychology as a result of his personal experimentation with drugs.

He tried a variety of substances ranging from hashish, morphine, and opium to caffeine, tobacco, and chocolate. He found the results to be of both personal and professional interest. Some drugs, notably hashish, cheered him considerably and greatly reduced the depression he had been experiencing. He was also concerned with the effects of the drugs on his mental functioning.

James McKeen Cattell (1860–1944) was not formally a functionalist, but his practical, test-oriented methods reinforced American functional psychology.

"I felt myself making brilliant discoveries in science and philosophy," he confided to his journal, "my only fear being that I could not remember them until morning." A month later he wrote, "Reading has become uninteresting. I keep reading without paying much attention. It takes a long time to write a word. I'm rather confused" (Sokal, 1981a, pp. 51, 52).

Cattell was not so confused, however, that he failed to recognize the psychological importance of drugs, and he observed his own behavior and mental state with increasing fascination. This may be considered his first venture into the study of psychology (Sokal, 1971, p. 632).

During Cattell's second semester at Johns Hopkins University, G. Stanley Hall began to teach psychology, and Cattell (along with John Dewey) enrolled in Hall's laboratory course. Shortly thereafter, Cattell began his research on the time required for different mental activities, work that reinforced his desire to become a psychologist.

Cattell's return to Wundt in 1883 is the subject of some well-known anecdotes in the history of psychology, which provide additional examples of how the data of history can be distorted. Cattell allegedly appeared at the Leipzig laboratory and boldly announced, "Herr Professor, you need an assistant, and I shall be your assistant" (Cattell, 1928, p. 545). He made it clear to Wundt that he would choose his own research project, on the psychology of individual differences, a topic that was hardly central to Wundtian psychology. Wundt is said to have characterized both Cattell and his project as *ganz Amerikanisch* (typically or completely American), a prophetic remark. The interest in individual differences, a natural outcome of an evolutionary point of view, has since been a feature of American and not German psychology.

Cattell supposedly gave Wundt his first typewriter, on which most of Wundt's books were written. For this gift, Cattell was criticized in jest for having "done a serious disservice . . . for it had enabled Wundt to write twice as many books as would otherwise have been possible" (Cattell, 1928, p. 545).

Careful historical research by Sokal (1981) on Cattell's letters and journals indicates that these stories are questionable. Cattell's account of these events, written many years later, is not supported by his own correspondence and journal entries. For example, Sokal points out that Wundt thought highly of Cattell and appointed him as his laboratory assistant in 1886. Also, there is no evidence that Cattell wanted to study individual differences then. Third, Cattell introduced Wundt to the use of the typewriter, but he did not give him one.[2]

Cattell found that he was incapable of Wundtian introspection—fractionating the reaction time into various activities, such as perception or choice—and questioned whether anyone was equal to the task. This attitude did not ingratiate him with Wundt, who did not allow in his laboratory anyone who was unable to benefit from his method. Consequently, Cattell conducted some of his research in his own room.

In spite of their differences, Wundt and Cattell did agree on the value of studying reaction time. Cattell believed it to be useful for the study of the time necessary for various mental operations, and for research on individual differences. Many of the classic reaction-time studies were carried out by Cattell during his three years at Leipzig and he published several articles on reaction time before leaving there.

After obtaining his degree in 1886, Cattell lectured in psychology at Bryn Mawr and at the University of Pennsylvania. He then became a lecturer at Cambridge University in England, where he met Sir Francis Galton. The two men had similar interests and views on individual differences, and Galton, who was then at the zenith of his fame, broadened Cattell's horizons. Cattell admired Galton's versatility and was impressed by his empha-sis on measurement and statistics. As a result, Cattell became one of the first American psychologists to stress quantification, ranking, and ratings. He later developed the order of merit or ranking method, which has been widely used in psychology, and was the first psychologist to teach statistics in his courses and to stress the statistical analysis of experimental results (Diamond, 1977). Wundt did not favor the use of statistical tech-

[2]We are grateful to Michael M. Sokal for providing this information from his research on *An education in psychology: James McKeen Cattell's journal and letters from Germany and England, 1880–1888* (Cambridge, Mass.: MIT Press, 1981).

niques. The influence of Galton on Cattell in this regard is one reason the new American psychology came to resemble Galton's work more than Wundt's.

Cattell was also influenced by Galton's work in eugenics. He argued for sterilization of delinquents and defectives and for giving incentives to the brightest and healthiest people to marry their own kind. He offered his seven children $1000 each if they would marry the sons or daughters of college professors (Sokal, 1971).

In 1888 Cattell was appointed professor of psychology at the University of Pennsylvania. This appointment was significant because, as the first professorship of psychology in the world, it represented formal recognition of psychology's separate status. Earlier academic appointments of psychologists had been in departments of philosophy. Cattell left Pennsylvania in 1891 to become professor of psychology and head of the department at Columbia University, where he remained for 26 years.

Because of his dissatisfaction with Hall's *American Journal of Psychology*, Cattell began *The Psychological Review* in 1894 with J. Mark Baldwin. In 1894 Cattell acquired from Alexander Graham Bell the weekly journal *Science*, which was ceasing publication for lack of funds. Five years later it became the official journal of the American Association for the Advancement of Science. Cattell began in 1906 a series of reference works including *American Men of Science* and *Leaders in Education*. He bought *Popular Science Monthly* in 1900; after selling the name in 1915, he continued to publish it as *Scientific Monthly*. Another weekly, *School and Society*, was established in 1915. The phenomenal organizing and editing work required a great deal of time and, not surprisingly, Cattell's research productivity declined.

During his career at Columbia more doctorates in psychology were awarded there than at any other graduate school in the United States. Cattell stressed the importance of independent work and gave his students considerable freedom to do research on their own. He believed that a professor should be independent of both the university and the students, and to make this point, he lived 40 miles from the campus, opposite the military academy at West Point. He set up a laboratory and editorial office at home and went to the university only certain days each week. Thus, he was able to avoid the frequent distractions common to academic life.

This independence was only one of several factors that strained relations between Cattell and the university administration. He urged increased faculty participation in university affairs, arguing that many decisions should be made by faculty and not by administrators. To this end, he helped to found the American Association of University Professors.

Cattell was not tactful in his dealings with the Columbia University administration. He has been described as "a difficult man to get along with . . . 'ungentlemanly,' 'irretrievably nasty,' and 'lacking in decency'" (Gruber, 1972, p. 300). He did not play by the rules of social conduct, preferring slashing satire to gentlemanly argument in his attacks on the administration. Cattell's days at Columbia were numbered. On three occasions between 1910 and 1917 the trustees considered "retiring" him. The final blow came during World War I, when Cattell wrote letters to Congress protesting the practice of sending conscientious objectors into combat. This was an unpopular position to take, but Cattell, characteristically, remained adamant. He was dismissed from Columbia in 1917 on the grounds that he had been disloyal to his country. He sued the university for libel, and although he was awarded $40,000, he was not reinstated. He isolated himself from his colleagues and wrote caustic pamphlets about the university administration. He made many enemies and remained bitter about the experience for the rest of his life.

Cattell never returned to academic life. He devoted himself with greater zest to his publications and to the American Association for the Advancement of Science and other learned societies. His promotional efforts as a spokesman for psychology to the other sciences elevated psychology to a higher standing in the scientific community.

In 1921 Cattell realized one of his greatest ambitions—the promotion of the application of psychology. He organized the Psychological Corporation, with stock purchased by members of the American Psychological Association, to provide psychological services to industry, the psychological community, and the public. This organization has grown considerably and is today an international enterprise.

Cattell remained active as an editor and a spokesman for psychology until his death in 1944. His extremely rapid rise in American psychology deserves mention. He was a professor at the University of Pennsylvania at 28, chairman of the department at Columbia at 31, president of the American Psychological Association at 35, and, at 40, the first psychologist elected to the National Academy of Sciences.

The Works of Cattell

We have already mentioned Cattell's early work on reaction time and his interest in the study of individual differences. The scope of his work was illustrated in 1914, when a group of his students assembled his numerous short papers. In addition to reaction time and individual differences, his research dealt with reading and perception, association, psychophysics, and the order of merit method. Although the importance of all of these areas cannot be denied, it can be said that Cattell influenced psychology most through his work on individual differences and mental tests. The theme of all his research was the problem of individual differences. By the time he went to Columbia in 1891, his interest in the development and promotion of mental tests had become paramount. (Again we see the influence of Galton.) A few years earlier he had administered a series of tests to students at the University of Pennsylvania, and in a paper published in 1890 had coined the term *mental tests*. "Psychology," Cattell wrote, "cannot attain the certainty and exactness of the physical sciences unless it rests on a foundation of experiment and measurement. A step in this direction could be made by applying a series of mental tests and measurements to a large number of individuals" (1890, p. 373). This is precisely what Cattell was attempting to do. He continued the testing program at Columbia and collected data from several classes of entering students.

It is instructive to consider the kinds of tests Cattell used in trying to measure the range and variability of the human capacity. Different from the later *intelligence* tests, which used more complex tasks of mental ability, Cattell's tests, like Galton's, dealt with elementary bodily or sensory–motor measures. These included dynamometer pressure, rate of movement (how quickly the hand can be moved 50 centimeters), sensation (using the two-point threshold), pressure causing pain (amount of pressure on the forehead necessary to cause pain), just noticeable differences in weight, reaction time for sound, time for naming colors, bisection of a 50-centimeter line, judgment of a 10-second period of time, and the number of letters remembered after one presentation.

By 1901 enough data had been collected to correlate the test scores with the students' academic performance. The correlations proved disappointingly low, as did intercorrelations among individual tests. Since similar results had been obtained in Titchener's laboratory using sensory–motor tests, it seemed that tests of this type were not valid predictors of intellectual ability.

As every student of psychology knows, in 1905 the French psychologist Alfred Binet, together with Victor Henri and Theodore Simon, developed an intelligence test using more complex measures of higher mental abilities. This approach provided what was considered to be an effective measure of intelligence and marked the beginning of the phenomenal growth of intelligence testing.

Despite his failure to measure mental abilities, Cattell's influence on the mental test movement was strong. His student, E. L. Thorndike (Chapter 9), became a leader in the psychology of mental tests, and Columbia was for years the center of the testing movement.

Building on Galton's work, Cattell undertook a series of studies to investigate the nature and origin of scientific ability using the technique he had developed in 1902, the method of order of merit. Stimuli ranked by a number of judges were arranged in a final rank order by calculating the average rating given to each stimulus item. The method was applied to eminent American scientists by having competent persons in each scientific field rank in order a number of their outstanding colleagues. The source book *American Men of Science* emerged from this work.

Comment

Cattell's impact on American psychology was made not through the development of a system of psychology (he had little patience with theory), or through an impressive list of publications. Rather, his influence was exerted most strongly through his work as an organizer, executive, and administrator of psychological science and practice, and as a spokesman for psychology to the scientific community. Cattell became something of an ambassador of psychology, giving lectures, editing journals, and promoting the practical application of psychology.

He also contributed to the development of psychology through his students. During his years at Columbia he trained more graduate students in psychology than anyone else in the United States, and a number—Woodworth and Thorndike were among them— became prominent in the field. Through his work on mental testing, the measurement of individual differences, and the promotion of applied psychology, Cattell energetically reinforced the functionalist movement in American psychology. When Cattell died, E. G. Boring wrote to one of Cattell's children. "In my opinion your father did more than William James even to give American psychology its peculiar slant, to make it different from the German psychology from which it stemmed" (Bjork, 1983, p. 105).

GANZ AMERIKANISCH

Evolutionary doctrine rapidly took hold in America toward the end of the nineteenth century, and American psychology was influenced, indeed guided, much more by Darwin and Galton than by Wundt. This was a curious phenomenon. Wundt had trained virtually all of the first generation of American psychologists in his form of psychology. Yet "very little of Wundt's actual system of psychology ever survived the return passage back across the Atlantic with those young Americans who traveled abroad around the turn of the century" (Blumenthal, 1977, p. 13). When they came back to the United States, these new psychologists set about establishing a kind of psychology that bore little resemblance to what Wundt had taught them. The new science, not unlike a living species, had to adapt itself to its environment.

Wundt's psychology and Titchener's structuralism could not survive in the American *Zeitgeist*. They evolved into functionalism. They were not practical kinds of psychology. They did not deal with the mind in use; they could not be applied to the everyday demands and problems of life. American culture was oriented toward the practical and the pragmatic, and people valued what worked. The country wanted a utilitarian, shirt-sleeves form of psychology, and through the efforts of James, Hall, Cattell, and other American pioneers, it got it.

When the newly trained American psychologists returned from Germany, in typically direct, aggressive, American fashion they transformed the uniquely German species of psychology into a uniquely American one. They began to study not what the mind is but what it does. They took their psychology into the real world, into education, industry, advertising, child development, clinics, and testing centers, and made of it something functional in subject matter and application.

Psychology grew and prospered in America, along with the country. The vibrant and dynamic development of American psychology during the period 1880–1900 is a striking event in science. In 1880 there were no laboratories; by 1895 there were 26. In 1880 there were no journals; by 1895 there were three. In 1880 Americans were going to Germany to study psychology; by 1900 they could study it at many of their own universities. In little more than 20 years after psychology had begun in Europe, American psychologists had assumed leadership of the field. In Cattell's presidential address to the American Psychological Association in 1895, he reported that "the academic growth of psychology in America during the past few years is almost without precedent. . . . Psychology is a required subject in the undergraduate curriculum wherever studies are required, and among university courses psychology now rivals the other leading sciences in the number of students attracted and in the amount of original work accomplished" (Cattell, 1896, p. 134).

The English publication, *Who's Who in Science*, stated in 1913 that the United States was predominant in psychology, having more of the world's leading psychologists—84—than Germany, England, and France combined (Jonçich, 1968, p. 444).

Psychology made its debut before the general public at the Chicago World's Fair in 1893. Hugo Münsterberg and Joseph Jastrow, in a program reminiscent of Galton's Anthropometric Laboratory, set up exhibits of psychological apparatus and a testing laboratory in which, for a fee, people could measure and learn about their capacities. William James called it "Münsterberg's circus." Such popular display would not have found favor with Wundt. He would, no doubt, have characterized this attempt at popularizing psychology as *ganz Amerikanisch*. And so it was, again reflecting the American temperament that transformed Wundtian and structural psychology into functional psychology.

Psychology became firmly established in America, not only in college catalogues, but also in our daily lives. We have all been influenced and affected by its practical application to a degree not thought possible by the American pioneers of functionalism.

SUGGESTED READINGS

Early Psychology in America

Blumenthal, A. L. (1977). Wilhelm Wundt and early American psychology: A clash of two cultures. *Annals of the New York Academy of Sciences, 291*, 13–20.

Canfield, T. M. (1973). The professionalization of American psychology: 1870–1917. *Journal of the History of the Behavioral Sciences, 9*, 66–75.

Hofstadter, R. (1955). *Social Darwinism in American thought* (rev. ed.). New York: George Braziller.

Jastrow, J. (1943). American psychology in the '80s and '90s. *Psychological Review, 50*, 65–67.

Sokal, M. M., Davis, A. B., & Herzbach, U. C. (1976). Laboratory instruments in the history of psychology. *Journal of the History of the Behavioral Sciences, 12*, 59–64.

James

Allen, G. W. (1967). *William James*. New York: Viking.

Allport, G. W. (1943). The productive paradoxes of William James. *Psychological Review, 50*, 95–120.

Allport, G. W. (1966). William James and the behavioral sciences. *Journal of the History of the Behavioral Sciences, 2*, 145–147.

Bjork, D. W. (1983). *The compromised scientist: William James in the development of American psychology*. New York: Columbia University Press.

Boring, E. G. (1942). Human nature vs. sensation: William James and the psychology of the present. *American Journal of Psychology, 55*, 310–327.

Century of the birth of William James. (1943). *Psychological Review, 50*, 81–139. (Articles by Angell, Thorndike, Dewey, and others on the life and thought of James).

Feinstein, H. M. (1984). *Becoming William James*. Ithaca, NY: Cornell University Press.

James, W. (1962). *Psychology: Briefer course*. New York: Collier Books. (Original work published 1892).

Perry, R. B. (1954). *The thought and character of William James: Briefer version*. New York: George Braziller.

Hall

Burnham, W. H. (1925). The man, G. Stanley Hall. *Psychological Review, 32*, 89–102.

Dallenbach, K. M. (1937). The *American Journal of Psychology*: 1887–1937. *American Journal of Psychology, 50*, 489–506.

Dennis, W., & Boring, E. G. (1952). The founding of APA. *American Psychologist, 7*, 95–97.

Hall, G. S. (1923). *The life and confessions of a psychologist*. New York: Appleton.

McCullers, J. C. (1969). G. Stanley Hall's conception of mental development and some indications of its influence on developmental psychology. *American Psychologist, 24*, 1109–1114.

Ross, D. (1972). *Granville Stanley Hall: The psychologist as prophet*. Chicago: University of Chicago Press.

Cattell

Sokal, M. M. (1971). The unpublished autobiography of James McKeen Cattell. *American Psychologist, 26*, 626–635.

Sokal, M. M. (Ed.). (1981). *An education in psychology: James McKeen Cattell's journal and letters from Germany and England, 1880–1888*. Cambridge, MA: MIT Press.

Woodworth, R. S. (1944). J. McKeen Cattell, 1860–1944. *Psychological Review, 51*, 201–209.

8

Functionalism: Formal Development

THE FOUNDING OF FUNCTIONALISM

In Chapters 6 and 7 we discussed the major themes of the functionalist movement and how they evolved from the work of Darwin and Galton. Functionalism is concerned with the operation and processes of conscious phenomena rather than with their structure or content. Its interest is the utility or purpose of mental processes to the living organism in its continuing attempt to adapt to the environment. Mental processes are regarded as activities leading to practical consequences, not as elements in some kind of composition. Functionalism's practical cast inevitably led to an interest in the application of science to the affairs of the world. Thus, applied psychology, disdained by Wundt and Titchener, was accepted and practiced by the functionalists.

These themes of functionalism were developed in the laboratory and in the real world by American psychologists such as Hall, Cattell, and James. They shaped this new movement from the works of Darwin, Galton, and, to some extent, Wundt without feeling the need to formalize it, to make of it a firm doctrine.

Although there was no formal school of functionalism by the end of the nineteenth century, functionalist ideas had permeated American psychology. How did this general attitude or approach, loosely structured around several universities and individuals, take on the characteristics of a formal school of thought?

The scholars associated with the founding of functionalism were not ambitious to start a new school of psychology. They did protest against the strictures of Wundtian psychology and Titchenerian structuralism, but they did not aim to replace them with another "ism" characterized by the rigidity and narrowness formalization usually entails. A graduate student at the University of Chicago, the major center of functionalism, recalled that the psychology department was clearly functionalist in orientation but "without self-consciousness and certainly without promoting functional psychology as a school" (McKinney, 1978, p. 145). The formalization of the movement of protest—the founding of functionalism—was partly imposed on its leaders by E. B. Titchener.

Paradoxically, it was Titchener who may have founded functional psychology when he adopted the word *structural* as opposed to *functional* in a paper published in the *Philosophical Review* in 1898 entitled "The Postulates of a Structural Psychology." In this paper he pointed out the differences between a structural psychology and a functional psychology, and argued that structuralism was the only proper province of psychology. But by viewing functionalism as an opponent, Titchener unwittingly served to bring it into clearer focus. "What Titchener was attacking was in fact nameless until he named it; hence he thrust the movement into high relief and did more than anyone else to get the term *functionalism* into psychological currency" (Harrison, 1963, p. 395).

Of course, not all the credit for founding functionalism can go to Titchener, but those whom history has labeled the founders of the school, to whom we now turn, were reluctant founders at best.

THE CHICAGO SCHOOL

In 1894 John Dewey and James Rowland Angell came to the newly organized University of Chicago. Their combined influence was largely responsible for that university's becoming a leading center of functionalism, but the university itself played a role in the founding of the new school of psychology.

> It is appropriate, surely, that the first distinctively American school of psychology arose at the new university that was itself an expression of so much that is characteristically American. The almost incredible feat of creating a great university outright—of actualizing a plan, of assembling a distinguished faculty, of bringing into being the whole complex organization, body and soul—gave the place an air of great things accomplished and about to be accomplished; and it is not surprising that a school of thought, starting in such circumstances, should thrive and grow. (Heidbreder, 1933, p. 204)

John Dewey (1859–1952)

When functionalism is considered as a distinct school of psychology, rather than as an orientation or attitude, John Dewey is usually credited with sparking its development. An 1896 paper by Dewey is generally cited as a landmark in the formal establishment of functionalism, and Dewey exerted a great influence on this school of thought, though his years of active contribution to psychology were few.

Dewey had an undistinguished early life and showed no great intellectual promise until his junior year at the University of Vermont. After graduation he taught high school for a few years and studied philosophy on his own, publishing several scholarly articles. He went to graduate school at Johns Hopkins and received his doctorate in philosophy in 1884, after which he taught at the University of Michigan and the University of Minnesota. In 1886 he published the first American textbook in the new psychology (called, appropriately, *Psychology*), which was popular until it was eclipsed by James's *Principles*.

In 1894 Dewey was invited to the University of Chicago, where he remained for 10 years, during which time he became a moving force in psychology. He began an experimental or laboratory school, which at the time was a radical innovation in education. It served as the cornerstone for the modern progressive education movement, which made him famous and controversial. He spent the years 1904–1930 at Columbia University, working on the application of psychology to educational and philosophical problems.

Dewey was a brilliant man but not a good teacher. One of his students recalled that Dewey "always wore a little green cap—a beret. . . . He would come [to class], sit down at a desk, and he'd lay the green cap down in front of him, and then he would lecture to the green cap—in a monotone. . . . If there was anything that would put students to sleep, it was that. But if you could pay attention to what that guy had to say, it was well worth it" (May, 1978, p. 655).

Dewey's 1896 paper, "The Reflex Arc Concept in Psychology," published in *Psychological Review*, was the point of departure for the new movement. In this his most important and, unfortunately, last contribution to psychology proper, Dewey attacked the psychological molecularism, elementism, and reductionism of the reflex arc with its distinction between stimulus and response. He argued that the behavior involved in a reflex response cannot be meaningfully reduced to its basic sensory–motor elements any more than consciousness can be meaningfully analyzed into its elementary components.

When this form of artificial analysis and reduction of behavior is undertaken, Dewey believed, behavior loses all meaning and only abstractions in the minds of the psychologists performing the dissection are left. Dewey wrote that behavior should be treated not as an artificial scientific construct, but rather in terms of its significance to the organism in adapting to the environment. He argued that the proper subject matter for psychology is the study of the total organism functioning in its environment.

Dewey was strongly influenced by the theory of evolution and his philosophy was based on the notion of social change. He was against the idea of things remaining static, and was in favor of progress achieved through the struggle of the human intellect with reality. In this struggle for survival, both consciousness and behavior function for the organism, with consciousness bringing about the appropriate behavior that enables the organism to survive and to progress. A function is a total coordination of an organism toward the accomplishment of the goal of survival. Thus, functional psychology is the study of the organism in use.

Dewey's philosophical position brought him more acclaim than his psychological studies. As a social philosopher, he was concerned with human welfare and physical, social, and moral adjustment. He considered psychological processes such as thinking and learning to be vital to our adjustment to life. Thinking, he said, was a tool applied to meet the exigencies of life: We think so that we may live.

The human effort to survive results in knowledge, and knowledge is a weapon in the fight for survival, a tool in the adjustment process. Because life is learning, the problem of learning is an important issue for psychology.

The time Dewey spent in psychology was all too short. In keeping with his functional orientation, he devoted most of his efforts to education. His program for the progressive education movement is spelled out in "Psychology and Social Practice," a lecture given in 1899 on his retirement as president of the American Psychological Association (Dewey, 1900). He remained titular head of the progressive education movement for the rest of his life. More than anyone else, Dewey is responsible for the pragmatic spirit of American education. He believed that teaching should be oriented toward the student rather than toward the subject matter.

Dewey's significance for psychology lies in his influence on psychologists and other scholars and his development of the philosophical framework for functionalism. When he left Chicago, the leadership of functionalism passed to James Rowland Angell.

James Rowland Angell (1869–1949)

Angell molded the functionalist movement into a working school. In the process he made the psychology department at Chicago the most influential of the day, the major training ground for functional psychologists.

Angell was born into an academic family in Vermont. His grandfather had been president of Brown University and his father president of the University of Vermont, and later of the University of Michigan. Angell did his undergraduate work at Michigan, where he studied under Dewey, and then he worked under James for a year at Harvard, receiving his M.A. in 1892. He continued his graduate studies at the University of Halle, in Germany, after learning, to his disappointment, that Wundt could not take on another student that year, but did not obtain his Ph.D. His thesis was accepted subject to revision (rendering it into better German), but to undertake this task he would have had to remain at Halle without remuneration. He chose instead to accept an appointment at the University of Minnesota, where the salary, though low, was better than nothing, particularly for a young man eager to get married. Although he did not earn his Ph.D., he was instrumental in the granting of many doctorates to others, and in the course of his career was awarded 23 honorary degrees.

After a year at Minnesota, Angell went to Chicago, where he remained for 25 years. Following in the family tradition, he became president of Yale University and helped to develop the Institute of Human Relations there. In 1906 he was elected the fifteenth president of the American Psychological Association. After retiring from academic life, he served as an officer of the National Broadcasting Company.

In 1904 Angell published a textbook (*Psychology*) that embodied the functionalist approach to psychology. The book was so successful that it had appeared in four editions by 1908, indicating the appeal of the functionalist position by that time. He maintained that the function of consciousness is to improve the adaptive abilities of the organism, and that psychology must study how the mind aids this adjustment of the organism to its environment. A more important contribution to functional psychology is Angell's presidential address to the American Psychological Association in 1906, published in 1907 in *Psychological Review*. "The Province of Functional Psychology" clearly spells out the functionalist position.

Angell began by noting that

> functional psychology is at the present moment little more than a point of view, a program, an ambition. It gains its vitality primarily perhaps as a protest against the exclusive excellence of another starting point for the study of the mind, and it enjoys for the time being at least the peculiar vigor which commonly attaches to Protestantism of any sort in its early stages before it has become respectable and orthodox. (Angell, 1907, p. 61)

We have seen that a new movement gains its vitality and momentum only with reference to, or in opposition to, the established position. Angell drew the battle lines from the beginning, but concluded his introductory remarks modestly: "I formally renounce any intention to strike out new plans; I am engaged in what is meant as a dispassionate summary of actual conditions."

Functional psychology, he argued, was not at all new but had been a significant part

By articulating
functionalism's utilitarian
aims, James Rowland
Angell (1869–1949)
transformed the
perspective into a school
that flourished under his
leadership at Chicago.

of psychology from the earliest times. It was structural psychology that had set itself
apart from the older and more truly pervasive functional form of psychology.

Angell brought together three conceptions of functionalism that he considered the
major themes of the movement.

1. Functional psychology is the psychology of *mental operations*, in contrast to the
psychology of mental elements (structuralism). Titchenerian elementism was still strong
and Angell promoted functionalism in direct opposition to it. The task of functionalism
is to discover how a mental process operates, what it accomplishes, and under what
conditions it occurs. Angell argued that a mental function, unlike a given moment of
consciousness studied by the structuralists, is not a momentary or perishable thing. It

persists and endures in the same manner as biological functions. A physiological function may operate through different structures, and a mental function may operate through ideas that are different in content.

2. Functionalism is the psychology of the *fundamental utilities of consciousness.* Consciousness, viewed in this utilitarian spirit, serves to mediate between the needs of the organism and the demands of its environment. Functionalism studies mental processes not as isolated and independent events, but as an active, ongoing part of biological activity, and as part of the larger movement of organic evolution. Structures and functions of the organism exist because by adapting the organism to the conditions of its environment they have enabled it to survive. Angell believed that because consciousness has survived, it, too, must perform an essential service for the organism. Functionalism had to discover precisely what this service was, not only for consciousness, but also for more specific mental processes such as judging and willing.

3. Functional psychology is the psychology of *psychophysical relations,* concerned with the total relationship of the organism to the environment. Functionalism encompasses all mind–body functions and leaves open the study of nonconscious or habitual behavior. It assumes a relationship between the mental and the physical, an interplay of the same sort that occurs between forces in the physical world. Functionalism holds that there is no real distinction between the mind and the body. It considers them not as different entities but as belonging to the same order, and assumes an easy transfer from one to the other.

Angell's 1906 presidential address was given at a time when the spirit of functionalism was already an established and influential force. Angell shaped this force into an active, prominent enterprise with a laboratory, a body of research data, a vital and enthusiastic staff of teachers, and a core of graduate students. In guiding functionalism to the status of a formal school, he gave it the focus and stature necessary to make it effective.

Angell insisted, however, that functionalism did not really constitute a school and should not be identified exclusively with the psychology taught at Chicago. He believed that the movement was too broad to be encompassed within the framework of a single school. The school of functionalism flourished despite Angell's protestations, and was definitely associated with the kind of psychology practiced at the University of Chicago.

Harvey A. Carr (1873–1954)

Carr, who majored in mathematics at DePauw University and the University of Colorado, switched to psychology as a result of the friendliness and interest of a professor who was a disciple of Hall. Because there was no laboratory at Colorado, Carr transferred to the University of Chicago, where his first course in experimental psychology was taught by a young assistant professor, Angell, who influenced Carr considerably. In his second year, in which he served as a "handy man" in the laboratory, Carr worked with John B. Watson, who was then an instructor. It was Watson who introduced Carr to animal psychology.

Carr received his Ph.D. in 1905 and after much difficulty obtained jobs first at a high school in Texas and then at a state normal school in Michigan. In 1908 he returned to Chicago to replace Watson, who had left for Johns Hopkins University. Later Carr

Under Harvey A. Carr (1873–1954), Angell's successor at Chicago, functionalism ceased to be a protest against structuralism and assumed final systematic form.

succeeded Angell as chairman of the psychology department and went on to develop and extend Angell's position on functionalism. During Carr's tenure as chairman, from 1919 to 1938, the psychology department awarded 150 doctoral degrees.

The work of Carr represents functionalism when it ceased to be a crusade against structuralism and became a recognized system in its own right. Under Carr, Chicago functionalism reached its peak as a formally defined system. Carr took the position that functional psychology was *the* American psychology. The work being done at Chicago was the psychology of the time, and as such, it did not need a highly developed systematic formulation.

Other approaches to psychology, such as behaviorism, Gestalt psychology, and psychoanalysis, were regarded as needlessly exaggerated developments, operating on more limited aspects of psychology. It was thought that these schools had little to add to the all-encompassing functionalist psychology.

Because Carr's *Psychology* (1925) is an expression of the finished form of functionalism, it is instructive to consider two of its major points. Carr defined the subject matter of psychology as mental activity—processes such as memory, perception, feeling, imagination, judgment, and will. The function of mental activity is to acquire, fixate, retain, organize, and evaluate experiences, and to use these experiences in the determination of action. Carr called the specific form of action in which mental activities appear *adaptive* or *adjustive* behavior.

We see here the familiar emphasis on mental processes rather than on the elements and content of consciousness. And we see also a description of mental activity in terms of what it accomplishes in enabling the organism to adapt or adjust to its environment. It is significant that by 1925 these points were discussed dispassionately as fact, no longer as matters for argument.

In discussing the methods of studying mental activity, Carr recognized the validity of both introspective and objective observation. He noted that the experimental method is the more desirable, but admitted that adequate experimental investigation of the mind is difficult, if not impossible. Carr believed, as Wundt did, that the study of cultural products, such as literature, art, language, and social and political institutions, could provide information on the kinds of mental activities that produced them. He also recognized the value of knowledge of the physiological processes involved in mental activity.

Functionalism did not adhere to any one method of study, as did structuralism. In practice, however, there was a marked emphasis on objectivity in the functionalists' research. A great deal of the research undertaken at Chicago did not use introspection, and in those cases where it was used, it was checked as much as possible by objective controls. It is important to note that animal as well as human studies were carried out at Chicago.

The Chicago school of functionalism started the shift away from the exclusive study of the subjective (mind or consciousness) toward the study of the objective (overt behavior). Functionalism helped to move American psychology to the opposite extreme from structuralism, eventually to the point where it focused only on behavior, dropping the study of the mind altogether. Thus, the functionalists provided a bridge between structuralism and behaviorism.

ORIGINAL SOURCE MATERIAL ON FUNCTIONALISM: FROM *PSYCHOLOGY* BY HARVEY A. CARR

The following discussion is reprinted from the first chapter of Carr's *Psychology* of 1925.[1] It indicates the finished form of functionalism and covers subject matter and methodology, as well as the psychophysical nature of mental activity and the relationship between functional psychology and the other sciences.

[1]Harvey A. Carr, *Psychology* (New York: Longmans, Green, 1925), pp. 1–14.

THE SUBJECT MATTER OF PSYCHOLOGY. Psychology is primarily concerned with the study of mental activity. This term is the generic name for such activities as perception, memory, imagination, reasoning, feeling, judgment, and will. The essential features of these various activities can hardly be characterized by a single term, for the mind does various things from time to time. Stated in comprehensive terms, we may say that mental activity is concerned with the acquisition, fixation, retention, organization, and evaluation of experiences, and their subsequent utilization in the guidance of conduct. The type of conduct that reflects mental activity may be termed adaptive or adjustive behavior. . . . An adaptive act is a response on the part of an organism in reference to its physical or social environment of such a character as to satisfy its motivating conditions. Illustrations of these mental operations may be drawn from the professional education of a physician. At times his mind is mainly engaged in the task of acquisition from lectures, books, and clinics, or from his experiences as a practitioner. At other moments his mind is primarily engaged in the attempt to memorize certain important data. Again, the reflective activities may predominate, and his mind is concerned with the task of analyzing, comparing, classifying, and relating the data in hand to other aspects of his medical knowledge. Finally comes the aspect of adaptive conduct—the use of this knowledge and skill in diagnosis, treatment, or surgical operation.

Every mental act is thus more or less directly concerned with the manipulation of experience as a means of attaining a more effective adjustment to the world. Every mental act can thus be studied from three aspects—its adaptive significance, its dependence upon previous experience, and its potential influence upon the future activity of the organism. For example, perception is a constituent part of a larger act; it is a process of cognizing objects on the basis of what we are doing, or in terms of their relation to some contemplated mode of behavior. Perception also involves the use of past experience, for the significance of any object can be appreciated only in terms of our previous experiences connected with that object. Likewise every experience with an object is likely to exert some effect upon the way in which that object is apprehended on subsequent occasions.

The importance of these various aspects of mental activity is apparent on a moment's reflection. Retention is essential to all learning, mental development, and social progress. The acquisition of an act of skill involves a series of successive trials or practice periods during which the act is gradually perfected and established. Each step of progress is a result of the preceding trials. The effects of each practice period are retained and it is these accumulated effects that render the succeeding attempts more facile. Without retention there could be no mind. If any individual should suddenly lose all his past experiences, he would become almost as helpless as an infant.

Our experiences must be properly organized and systematized in order to be utilized effectively. In popular speech, we often say that an insane person has lost his mind. As a matter of fact these people do have minds. They accumulate, organize, and evaluate their experiences in some sort of fashion, and they react to the world on the basis of these experiences. These people have disordered minds. Their experiences are improperly organized and evaluated. Theoretically, any group of experiences can be organized in various ways. An individual's manner of thinking and the character of his conduct are functions to a large extent of his previous organization. Certain types of organization are conducive to irrational modes of thought and to anti-social forms of behavior. Experiences must not only be organized, but they must be properly organized in order to be utilized effectively in reacting to the world in an intelligent and rational fashion.

The mind is also continuously evaluating the various aspects of experience. The mind not only labels things as good, bad, and indifferent, but it also arranges the good things of life in a crude scale of relative worth. Aesthetic appreciation in the realms of literature, music, and the graphic arts illustrates this function. Ethical values may also be cited. We label social conduct as right and wrong and develop concepts of such virtues as charity, chastity, honesty, sobriety, and punctuality. An individual's system of values constitutes perhaps the most important aspect of his personality. Some students overemphasize the relative value of study and become bookworms and grinds. Some boys attach too great an importance to the value of financial independence, and leave school to seek a job. Some people under-estimate the importance of neatness of dress, correct habits of speech, courtesy, kindliness, and many other traits that make for an effective personality in social relations. Some individuals take their politics, their religion, or their science too seriously, and over-estimate the relative importance of those aspects of life. . . . The mind does evaluate its experiences, and . . . an individual's conduct is to a large extent a function of his ideals and system of values.

All experiences of an individual during life are thus organized into a complex but unitary system of reaction tendencies that determine to a large extent the nature of his subsequent activity. The reactive disposition of an individual, i.e., what he does and what he can and can not do, is a function of his native equipment, of the nature of his previous experiences, and of the way in which these have been organized and evaluated. The term "self" is generally employed to characterize an individual from the standpoint of his reactive disposition. We also speak of an individual's person-ality when we wish to refer to all those traits and characteristics of his self that make or mar his efficiency in dealing with other individuals, while the term "mind" is used when we wish to characterize an individual from the standpoint of his intellectual characteristics and potentialities. . . . Psychology is thus concerned with the study of personality, mind, and the self, but these are conceptual objects that can be studied only indirectly through their manifestations—only insofar as they express them-selves in the reactions of the individual. The various concrete activities involved in an act of adjustment are the observable data and the subject matter of psychology.

THE PSYCHO-PHYSICAL NATURE OF MENTAL ACTIVITY. These various mental operations that are involved in the performance of an adjustive response are usually termed psycho-physical processes. By their physical character, we mean that they are acts of which the individual has some knowledge. For example, an individual not only perceives and reacts to an object, but he is at least aware of the fact and he may have some knowledge of the nature and significance of those acts. Individuals are not accustomed to reason, make decisions and react on the basis of those decisions and be wholly oblivious of the fact. The performance of any mental act on the part of an individual implies some sort of experiential contact with that act. For this reason we shall refer to these mental acts from time to time as experiences or as experiential activities. These acts are not only experienced, but they are also the reactions of a physical organism. They are acts that directly involve such structures as the sense organs, muscles, and nerves. The participation of sense organs and muscles in such activities as perception and voluntary acts is obvious. The nervous system is also concerned in every mental act. While this fact is not one of the obvious sort, yet the truth of the doctrine has been thoroughly established. The integrity of these structures is essential to normal mental activity. An excision or lesion in any part of the brain is usually correlated with some sort of a mental disturbance. All conditions that affect the metabolism of these structures also influence the character of the mental operations. We shall make no attempt to explain the nature of this psycho-physical relationship. We merely note the fact that these mental acts are psycho-physical events and insist that they must be studied as such.

In contrast with our conception, mental acts are often identified with the psychical aspects of these adjustive activities. This doctrine assumes that these psycho-physical activities are composed of two parallel series of processes that belong to different orders of reality. There are the "conscious" or immaterial processes on the one hand, and the organic or material processes on the other. The conscious processes constitute the subject matter of psychology, while the latter belong to the domain of physiology. Mind is thus defined in purely psychical or immaterial terms. Mental acts are regarded as a series of immaterial or psychical events that can occur only in conjunction with a series of physiological processes.

Two objections may be urged against this doctrine. 1. When we speak of the psychical or conscious characteristic of an act, we are dealing with an abstract or conceptual object that has no independent existential reality. This doctrine thus involves the logical fallacy of assuming that these conceptual objects are independent entities. Consciousness is an abstraction that has no more independent existence than the grin of a Cheshire cat. 2. By identifying mental acts with the psychical aspects of these adaptive activities, the exponents of this doctrine are logically confronted with the problem of explaining how these mental processes can exert any effect upon conduct. In other words, this conception necessarily raises the problem of the nature of the psycho-physical relation. We do not deny the validity of this problem, but we do assert that it is a metaphysical or philosophical problem that does not belong to the domain of an empirical or natural science.

According to our conception, psychology can not be differentiated from physiology in terms of the metaphysical character of its subject matter. Both psychology and physiology are concerned with the study of the functional activities of organisms. Psychology is concerned with all those processes that are directly involved in the adjustment of the organism to its environment, while physiology is engaged in the study of the vital activities such as circulation, digestion, and metabolism that are primarily concerned with the maintenance of the structural integrity of the organism. Psychology and physiology are thus concerned with two mutually related and interactive groups of organic processes. . . .

METHODS OF APPROACH. Mental acts can be studied from several avenues of approach. Mental acts can be directly observed, they can be studied indirectly through their creations and products, and finally they can be studied in terms of their relation to the structure of the organism.

Mental acts may be subjectively or objectively observed. Objective observation refers to the apprehension of the mental operations of another individual insofar as these are reflected in his behavior. Subjective observation refers to the apprehension of one's own mental operations. Subjective observation is often termed introspection, and in times past it was regarded as an unique mode of apprehension different in kind from that involved in perceiving an external event. As a matter of fact, the two processes are essentially alike in nature and they can be differentiated only in terms of the objects cognized. Each mode of observation possesses certain advantages and limitations.

1. Introspection gives us a more intimate and comprehensive knowledge of mental events. Some mental events can not be objectively apprehended. For example, we might know from an individual's behavior that he is engaged in thought without being able to tell what he is thinking about. The individual himself not only knows that he is thinking but is keenly aware of the topic under consideration. Neither will objective observation give us any clue as to whether these thoughts are mediated in terms of words or visual imagery. Introspection often reveals the motives and considerations derived from past experience that influence us in any particular act. It would be very difficult to obtain knowledge of this character by the exclusive use of the objective method.

2. Subjective observations are rather difficult. Many mental operations consist of a series of complex and rapidly shifting events that are difficult to analyze and apprehend in a comprehensive manner. Inasmuch as our minds are usually engaged in dealing with objective situations, many people encounter a considerable amount of difficulty in the attempt to break this habit and become introspective.

3. The validity of a subjective observation can not always be tested. Given a report by a subject that he thinks by means of visual imagery, any verification or disproof of this statement is practically impossible inasmuch as this particular mental event can be observed only by that individual. Neither can we decide that the statement is untrue because other people assert that they think in verbal terms, for it is possible that individuals may differ in their manner of thinking. On the other hand, any objective act can be observed by several people and their reports compared.

4. Naturally the use of the subjective method must be confined to subjects of training and ability. Psychology must thus rely upon the objective method in the study of animals, children, primitive peoples, and many cases of insanity.

5. Instruments may be used to record and measure any of the objective manifestations of mind. These records can then be analyzed at leisure. Acts can be detected in this manner that would otherwise escape our notice. For example, photography has been utilized as a means of studying the finer eye movements that are involved in an act of perception. This method has been extensively employed in the study of the perceptual activities involved in reading and in certain visual illusions.

Subsidiary to observation is the method of experimentation. In an experiment, the mental operations are observed under certain prescribed and defined conditions. An experiment is often called a controlled observation. An experiment may be relatively simple or quite complex according to the degree of control that is exercised. As an illustration of a simple type of experiment, we may cite the case of memorizing a list of words for the purpose of analyzing this process and discovering some of the conditions that influence our ability to recall this material on some subsequent occasion. In general, the performance of any mental act for the purpose of studying that act may be termed an experiment. A psychological experiment does not necessarily involve the employment of an elaborate technique and complicated forms of apparatus. The character of the apparatus is a function of the problem. Instruments are employed as a means of controlling the experimental conditions, or as a means of measuring and recording any feature of the experimental situation. The primary value of an experiment depends upon the fact that the observations are made under certain prescribed and specified conditions. An experiment is thus a means of discovering facts and relations that would escape detection during the ordinary course of experience. Furthermore the results of any experiment can be tested by other investigators. The experimental method has its limitations in the field of psychology. Not all aspects of the human mind are subject to control. An individual's mental reactions are to a very large extent a function of his previous experiences. A complete experimental control of a human mind implies a freedom in manipulating its development throughout life in ways that are both impossible and socially undesirable.

The nature of mind may also be studied indirectly through its creations and products—industrial inventions, literature, art, religious customs and beliefs, ethical systems, political institutions, etc. This method might well be termed the social avenue of approach. Naturally this method will not be used when the mental operations themselves can be studied. Consequently the method is mainly utilized in the study of primitive races or of past civilizations. The method in practice is essentially historical or anthropological. Obviously our knowledge of the human mind would be exceedingly limited if we were forced to rely exclusively upon such data. Facts of this character, however, are significant for an understanding of the developmental aspects of mind.

Mental acts can also be studied from the standpoint of anatomy and physiology. The structure of any organ and its functional possibilities are intimately related. The neurologist attempts to conceive of the structural arrangements of the nervous system in terms of their relation to the various activities in which they are involved. A study of the mutual relations between mental acts and the architectural features of the nervous system will obviously clarify the conceptions of both psychology and neurology. We know that the character of mental acts is influenced by the metabolic conditions of the nervous system. Neural defects are frequently correlated with disturbances of perception, memory, recall, and voluntary activity. A considerable portion of our accurate and detailed knowledge of the relation of mental operations to the nervous structures has been gained in this way. Certain parts of the nervous structures are excised in animals and the effect of this loss of nerve tissue upon the subsequent ability of the organism is noted. Many features of mind must be explained in terms of the physiological peculiarities of the nervous system. The fact of retention, certain temperamental peculiarities of mind, and some aspects of the process of forgetting must be explained in this manner.

It is thus apparent that any fact is a psychological datum whenever it can be utilized in comprehending the nature and significance of the mental operations. The same fact may be significant to several sciences such as neurology, psychology, and physiology, and such a fact will constitute a part of the data of each of these branches of knowledge. Psychology like the other sciences utilizes any fact that is significant for its purposes irrespective of how or where or by whom it was obtained. No single avenue of approach can give a complete knowledge of a mental act. The various sources of knowledge supplement each other and psychology is concerned with the task of systematizing and harmonizing the various data in order to form an adequate conception of all that is involved in the operations of mind.

Facts of common observation constitute perhaps the major portion of the factual data upon which the present conceptions of psychology are based. Psychology differs from most of the natural sciences in that it deals to a considerable extent with the obvious facts of everyday life. Mental acts are experienced events, and naturally everyone must acquire a certain amount of knowledge concerning his own mental operations during the course of life. A considerable portion of our time and energy is also devoted to the task of dealing with other minds. Everyone thus acquires a certain amount of psychological knowledge of a practical sort. Psychology as a science differs from the common sense variety in several respects. It observes and analyzes mental operations more carefully and systematically, it employs the experimental method whenever possible, it gathers its factual data from a greater variety of sources, and it attempts to construct a more adequate system of conceptions for comprehending these data. Any such system of conceptions is valuable only insofar as the student utilizes them in comprehending his own mental operations or in understanding the actions of others. To a large extent a student must regard a textbook of psychology merely as a guide to the study of his own mind. . . .

RELATION TO OTHER SCIENCES. So far as its systematic relations are concerned, psychology must be classed with the biological group of sciences which deal with the phenomena of living organisms. Psychology finds its closest kinship with physiology in that both are engaged in studying the reactions of animal organisms. There are no fixed lines of demarcation between the two fields. Psychology is interested in the adaptive reactions of organisms in reference to their environmental conditions insofar as those reactions are dependent upon their previous experiences. Physiologists have evinced but little systematic interest in this topic. They have been concerned for the most part with the study of the vital activities. If physiology be arbitrarily defined as the study of organic functions, psychology must naturally be regarded as a special branch of physiology. However, it is wholly immaterial whether psychology be regarded as subordinate to or coördinate with physiology. As a matter of fact, the two sciences do study different aspects of organic activity.

Psychology gathers materials from a great many fields of human endeavor. Psychology appropriates any facts that are significant for an understanding of mind. A professional psychologist naturally encounters a very limited range of mental phenomena and hence must gather his materials from a great variety of sources. Psychology takes facts from sociology, education, neurology, physiology, biology, and anthropology, and hopes in time to be able to borrow from biochemistry. Most of our factual knowledge concerning the great variety of mental disorders has been contributed by physicians and psychiatrists. Peculiar facts of mind and personality are frequently contributed by the legal profession. The various practices of business and industry contribute many suggestive data. In fact, psychological materials can be gathered from any line of human endeavor.

Psychology in turn is interested in making whatever contributions it can to all allied fields of thought and endeavor such as philosophy, sociology, education, medicine, law, business, and industry. Naturally, any knowledge of human nature will be extremely serviceable to any field of endeavor that is in any way concerned with human thought and action. While psychology has exerted a considerable amount of influence upon certain of these fields, yet this practical program must be regarded as somewhat of an ideal, for psychology has not as yet attained any very adequate or complete knowledge of human nature.

FUNCTIONALISM AT COLUMBIA

We have discussed the work of James McKeen Cattell (Chapter 7) and its functionalist orientation. Two of Cattell's students at Columbia University are also of importance because of the functionalist cast of their work. They are E. L. Thorndike (Chapter 9) and Robert S. Woodworth.

Robert Sessions Woodworth (1869–1962)

Woodworth did not belong formally to the functionalist school in the tradition of Angell and Carr. Indeed, he expressed dislike for the constraints imposed by membership in any school of thought. He wrote in 1930 that the kind of psychology he was developing "does not aspire to be a school. That is the very thing it does not wish to be. Personally, I have always balked on being told, as we have been told at intervals for as long as I can remember, what our marching orders are—what as psychologists we ought to be doing, and what in the divine order of the sciences psychology must be doing" (Woodworth, 1930, p. 327). Although we cannot label Woodworth a functionalist, his work is nevertheless appropriate in a chapter on American functionalism because he did express and reflect a free form of functionalism that still characterizes American psychology. Much of what Woodworth said about psychology is in the functionalist spirit of the Chicago school, but he added an important new ingredient.

Woodworth was active in psychology for more than 70 years as a researcher, beloved teacher, writer, and editor. After receiving his B.A. from Amherst College, he taught high school science for two years, and then mathematics in a small college for two years before beginning his graduate work. He received his M.A. from Harvard, and his Ph.D. from Columbia under Cattell in 1899. He taught physiology in New York City hospitals for three years, and spent a year with the physiologist Sir Charles Scott Sherrington in England. In 1903 he returned to Columbia, where he remained until his first retirement in 1945. In 1958, at the age of 89, he retired from Columbia a second time; he had continued to lecture to large classes after his first retirement.

Woodworth's list of publications is lengthy and his work has influenced several generations of students. His position is put forth in a number of journal articles and in *Dynamic Psychology* (1918) and *Dynamics of Behavior* (1958). In 1911 he revised George Trumbull Ladd's *Physiological Psychology*, and wrote an introductory text, *Psychology*, that first appeared in 1921 and had appeared in five editions by 1947. The book is said to have outsold every other psychology text for 25 years. His *Experimental Psychology*, written in 1938 and revised in 1954 with Harold Schlosberg, became a classic in that area. In 1931 he wrote *Contemporary Schools of Psychology*, which was revised in 1948 and again in 1964 with Mary Sheehan (appearing posthumously). In 1956 Woodworth received the first Gold Medal Award of the American Psychological Foundation and was cited as having made "unequaled contributions to shaping the destiny of scientific psychology," and as an "integrator and organizer of psychological knowledge."

Woodworth maintained that his approach was not really new, but was the one followed by "good" psychologists even in the days before psychology became a science. Psychological knowledge must begin, he wrote, with an investigation of the nature of the stimulus and the response—with objective external events. But when psychology considers *only* the stimulus and the response in attempting to explain behavior, it misses perhaps the most important part, the living organism itself. The stimulus is not the complete cause of a particular response. The organism, with its varying energy levels and its current and past experiences, also acts to determine the response.

Thus, according to Woodworth, psychology must consider the organism as interpolated between the stimulus and response. It follows that the subject matter for psychology must be both consciousness and behavior, a position later taken by humanistic psychologists (Chapter 15). The external stimulus as well as the overt response may be discovered by the objective observation of behavior, but what happens inside the organism can be known only through introspection. Woodworth therefore accepted introspection as a useful method for psychology, but he also made full use of observation and experimentation.

Woodworth introduced into functionalism a dynamic psychology that seemed, in a way, to be a continuation of the teachings of Dewey and James. The word "dynamic" had been used as early as 1884 by Dewey and in 1908 by James. A dynamic psychology—a psychology concerned with change and with the interpretation of the causal factors in change—represented an interest in motivation. Woodworth had said in 1897 that he wanted to develop a "motivology."

The first expression of Woodworth's systematic position is *Dynamic Psychology* (1918), a plea for a functional kind of psychology that included the topic of motivation. Although there are similarities between Woodworth's position and that of the Chicago functionalists, Woodworth stressed more heavily the physiological events underlying

Robert Sessions
Woodworth (1869–1962)
championed an eclectic
approach to psychology,
with a special interest in
motivation.

behavior. His dynamic psychology or motivology is concerned with cause-and-effect
relationships, though his interest was not in the ultimate causes of human conduct, but
rather in more immediate causes. He believed that psychology's goal should be to
determine why people behave as they do, why they feel and act in certain ways, and his
primary concern was the so-called driving forces that activate the human organism.

In discussing causal sequences in behavior, Woodworth distinguished between two
kinds of events—mechanisms and drives. A *mechanism* is concerned with how a task is
performed, such as the mechanical aspects of a physical movement. A *drive* is concerned

with why the task is performed. However, mechanisms and drives are essentially alike in that both are responses of the organism. Mechanisms may become drives and vice versa.

In another example of distorted data of history, Woodworth is usually given credit for being the first to introduce the term "drive" into psychology. Some eight months before Woodworth used the term in print, however, John B. Watson had used it in an article in the *American Journal of Psychology* (Watson & Morgan, 1917) and had given it the same meaning Woodworth later attributed to it (Remley, 1980).

Woodworth's position was essentially eclectic. He did not wish to adhere to a single system, nor did he want to develop a school of his own. His viewpoint was built not from protest but from growth, elaboration, and synthesis. He sought the best features of each system of thought.

CRITICISMS OF FUNCTIONALISM

Attacks on the functionalist movement came quickly and vehemently from the structuralist camp. For the first time, at least in America, the new psychology—so recently independent of philosophy—was divided into warring factions. Some saw this division as an indication that the new field was resisting pressures to become solidified within the confines of a single point of view. Opposition within the field meant vitality and flexibility, receptivity to the exploration of new concepts, goals, and approaches. To others, the division was disturbing because it seemed to indicate a lack of maturity relative to the natural sciences. The older sciences were no longer divided into differing camps or espousing varying approaches.

Cornell and Chicago became the respective headquarters of the structuralist and functionalist enemy camps. Accusations, charges, and countercharges were flung back and forth between the universities with all the righteousness characteristic of those who are convinced that they possess the truth.

One criticism directed against functionalism was that the term itself was not clearly defined. In 1913 C. A. Ruckmick, a student of Titchener's, examined 15 general psychology textbooks to determine how "function" was defined by the various writers. The two most common usages were an activity or process, and a service to other processes or to the whole organism. In the first usage, function is essentially the same as activity; for example, remembering and perceiving are functions. In the second case, function is defined in reference to the utility of some activity to the organism, such as the function of digestion or breathing. Ruckmick suggested that the functionalists sometimes used the word "function" to describe an activity, and sometimes to refer to its utility. He argued that this ambiguity created a tautology—one could speak of the function of an activity, or the function of a function.

It was some years before this charge of inconsistent and ambiguous usage was answered. Carr (1930) argued that the two definitions were not inconsistent because both referred to the same processes. Functionalism was interested in a particular activity both for its own sake (the first definition) and for its relationship to other conditions or activities (the second definition). A similar practice was followed in biology.

Carr's answer to this criticism came 17 years after it was first made. Heidbreder noted that "Functionalism used the concept first and defined it later; and this sequence of events is characteristic of the movement. . . . Functionalism has never been disposed to place definition and systematization in the foreground" (1933, p. 228).

Another criticism, particularly from Titchener, related to the definition of psychology itself. The structuralists charged that functionalism was not psychology at all, because it was not restricted to the subject matter and methodology of structuralism. In Titchener's view, any approach other than the introspective analysis of the mind into elements was not psychology. Of course, it was just this definition of psychology that the functionalists were questioning and trying to replace.

Other critics found fault with the functionalists' interest in activities of a practical or applied nature, a manifestation of the long-standing controversy between pure and applied science. The structuralists did not look favorably on applied psychology. The functionalists, however, were unconcerned with maintaining psychology as a pure science and never apologized for their practical interests. Carr suggested that rigorous scientific procedures can be adhered to in both pure and applied psychology, and equally valid research can be performed in an industrial setting and in a university laboratory. In the final analysis, Carr noted, it is the method and not the subject matter that determines how scientific a field of inquiry is. The controversy between pure and applied science does not exist in such an extreme form in contemporary American psychology, and this may be seen as a contribution of functionalism, not as a fault.

Functionalists were also criticized for their eclecticism. Unlike the more dogmatic structuralists, they consistently made use of any theoretical or methodological approach that seemed appropriate to the solution of the problem at hand. Many see virtue in this more flexible approach to psychology, particularly because it coexisted with a tough-minded insistence on proper scientific control and methodology.

CONTRIBUTIONS OF FUNCTIONALISM

As an attitude or general viewpoint, functionalism became part of the mainstream of American psychology. Its early and vigorous opposition to structuralism was of immense value to the development of psychology in the United States. The long-range consequences of the shift in emphasis from structure to function were also significant. One result was that the rapidly increasing research on animal behavior became an important part of psychology. It was not a part of structural psychology, though Wundt did favor the interpretation of animal consciousness through the technique of introspection by analogy. Indeed, he once wrote about abstract reasoning in spiders (Mackenzie, 1977).

The functionalists' broadly defined psychology also incorporated studies of children, the mentally retarded, and the insane. In addition, it allowed psychologists to supplement the method of introspection with other ways of securing data, such as physiological research, mental tests, questionnaires, and objective descriptions of behavior. All these methods, which were anathema to the structuralists, became respectable sources of information for psychology.

By the time of Wundt's death in 1920, and Titchener's death in 1927, their approaches to psychology had been overshadowed in the United States by the broader, more practical approach of the functionalists. The functionalist victory was complete by 1930, and in the United States today psychology is, to some extent, functional in its orientation, though functionalism as a separate school of thought no longer exists. Because of its success, there is no longer any need for it to retain the characteristics of a school.

SUGGESTED READINGS

Functionalism

Carr, H. A. (1930). Functionalism. In C. Murchison (Ed.), *Psychologies of 1930* (pp. 59–78). Worcester, MA: Clark University Press.

Harrison, R. (1963). Functionalism and its historical significance. *Genetic Psychology Monographs, 68*, 387–423.

Heidbreder, E. (1969). Functionalism. In D. L. Krantz (Ed.), *Schools of psychology* (pp. 35–50). New York: Appleton-Century-Crofts.

James, W. (1904). The Chicago school. *Psychological Bulletin, 1*, 1–5.

McKinney, F. (1978). Functionalism at Chicago—Memories of a graduate student: 1929–1931. *Journal of the History of the Behavioral Sciences, 14*, 142–148.

Raphelson, A. C. (1973). The pre-Chicago association of the early functionalists. *Journal of the History of the Behavioral Sciences, 9*, 115–122.

Dewey

Boring, E. G. (1953). John Dewey: 1859–1952. *American Journal of Psychology, 66*, 145–147.

Crissman, P. (1942). The psychology of John Dewey. *Psychological Review, 49*, 441–462.

Dewey, J. (1896). The reflex arc concept in psychology. *Psychological Review, 3*, 357–370.

Angell

Angell, J. R. (1907). The province of functional psychology. *Psychological Review, 14*, 61–91.

Angell, J. R. (1913). Behavior as a category of psychology. *Psychological Review, 20*, 255–270.

Carr

Carr, H. (1917). The nature of mental process. *Psychological Review, 24*, 181–187.

Whitely, P. L. (1976). A new name for an old idea? A student of Harvey Carr reflects. *Journal of the History of the Behavioral Sciences, 12*, 260–274.

Woodworth

Poffenberger, A. T. (1962). Robert Sessions Woodworth: 1869–1962. *American Journal of Psychology, 75*, 677–692.

Thorne, F. C. (1976). Reflections on the golden age of Columbia psychology. *Journal of the History of the Behavioral Sciences, 12*, 159–165.

Woodworth, R. S. (1939). *Psychological issues: Selected papers of Robert S. Woodworth.* New York: Columbia University Press.

9
Behaviorism: Antecedent Influences

By the second decade of the twentieth century, fewer than 40 years after Wundt formally launched psychology, the science had undergone drastic revisions. No longer did all psychologists agree on the value of introspection, on the existence of elements of the mind, or on the necessity of psychology's remaining "pure." The functionalists were rewriting the rules of psychology, experimenting with and applying psychology in ways that could not be admitted into Leipzig or Cornell.

The movement from Wundtian psychology and from structuralism to functionalism was less revolutionary than evolutionary. The functionalists did not set out to destroy the establishment of Wundt and Titchener. Instead, they modified it, adding a bit here, changing there, so that slowly, over a number of years, a new psychology emerged. It was more a chipping away from within than a deliberate attack from without.

The leaders of the functionalist movement did not even feel the need to solidify or formalize their position into a school. After all, it was, as they saw it, not a break with the past but a building upon it.

The change from structuralism to functionalism was, therefore, not all that noticeable at the time it was taking place. There is no particular day or year that we can point to as the start of functionalism, a time when psychology seemed to change overnight. Indeed, it is difficult, as we have noted, to point to a particular individual as the founder of functionalism. This was the situation in the second decade of the twentieth century in the United States. Functionalism was maturing and structuralism still held a strong but no longer exclusive position.

In 1913 a revolution against both of these positions erupted. This was truly a revolt, an open break, a total war against the establishment, intent on shattering both points of view. Nothing about this event was gradual or smooth. It was sudden, traumatic, and dramatic, no modification of the past, no compromise, but a complete change.

The new movement was called *behaviorism* and its leader was the 35-year-old psychologist John Broadus Watson. Just 10 years earlier Watson had received his Ph.D. under Angell at the University of Chicago, the center of one of the two movements Watson was out to smash.

Watson inaugurated his revolution with an article in the *Psychological Review*. The manifesto he wrote was a broad, slashing attack on the existing systems of psychology. The old order, he stated, was a failure and would have to give way to behaviorism if psychology were to advance. In time these older schools of thought were largely abandoned and behaviorism became the most important and controversial American system of psychology. Moreover, it assumed a prominent role in the cultural and social life of the times, a status that earlier positions had not achieved.

The basic tenets of Watson's behaviorism were simple, direct, and bold. He called for an objective psychology, a *science of behavior* dealing only with observable behavioral acts that could be objectively described in terms such as *stimulus* and *response*. He wanted to apply to human beings the experimental procedures and principles of animal psychology, a field in which he had been active.

Watson's interests shed light on what he wanted to discard. To be an objective science, behavioristic psychology had to reject all mentalistic concepts and terms. Such words as "image," "mind," and "consciousness," carryovers from mentalist philosophy, were meaningless for a science of behavior. Watson was particularly vehement in his rejection of the concept of consciousness. He said that consciousness "has never been seen, touched, smelled, tasted, or moved. It is a plain assumption just as unprovable as the old concept of soul" (Watson & McDougall, 1929, p. 14). The technique of introspection, which assumed the existence of conscious processes, was, therefore, irrelevant.

These basic points were forcefully propounded by the founder of behaviorism. Of course, as we have seen, founding is different from originating. The tenets of the behaviorist revolution that was soon to overtake psychology were not original with Watson. They had been developing in psychology and biology for several years.

It is no criticism of Watson to note that he, like all founders, promoted, organized, and integrated ideas and schemas already in existence. From this amalgamation he constructed his new system of psychology. The point is worth reiterating. "Creations absolutely *de novo* are very rare, if they occur at all; most novelties are only novel combinations of old elements, and the degree of novelty is thus a matter of interpretation" (Sarton, 1936, p. 36).

This chapter examines behaviorism's antecedent influences, the "old elements" Watson so effectively brought together to form his new psychology. At least three major trends affected his work: the philosophical tradition of objectivism and mechanism, animal psychology, and functionalism. Animal psychology and functionalism exerted the most direct and obvious impact. The philosophical traditions of objectivism and mechanism had been developing for quite some time and they favored and reinforced the growth of both functionalism and animal psychology.

Watson's insistence on the need for increased objectivity in psychology was not unusual by 1913. The movement has a long history, beginning perhaps with Descartes, whose attempts at mechanistic explanations of the body were among the first steps in the direction of greater objectivity.

More important in the history of objectivism is Auguste Comte (1798–1857), founder of the movement called *positivism*, which emphasized positive knowledge—facts—the truth of which is not debatable (see Chapter 2). According to Comte, the only valid knowledge is that which is social in nature and objectively observable. These criteria rule out introspection, which depends on a private consciousness that cannot be objectively observed. Comte vigorously protested against mentalism and subjective methodology.

By the beginning of the twentieth century objectivism, mechanism, and materialism had grown strong. Their influence was so pervasive that they led inexorably to a new kind of psychology, one without "consciousness" or "mind" or "soul," one that focused on only what could be seen and heard and touched. The science of behavior, viewing the human being as a machine, was the inescapable result.

We now turn to a discussion of the influence of animal psychology and functionalism on the founding of behaviorism, as both movements were infused by the mechanistic, materialistic, and positivistic climate of the times.

THE INFLUENCE OF ANIMAL PSYCHOLOGY ON BEHAVIORISM

Watson stated succinctly the relationship between animal psychology and behaviorism: "Behaviorism is a direct outgrowth of studies in animal behavior during the first decade of the twentieth century" (1929, p. 327). Clearly, then, the most important single antecedent of the development of Watson's program was animal psychology, which grew out of evolutionary theory. It led to attempts to demonstrate the existence of mind in lower organisms and the continuity between human and animal minds.

We have discussed the work of two pioneer animal psychologists, George John Romanes and C. Lloyd Morgan (Chapter 6). With Morgan's law of parsimony and greater reliance on experimental instead of anecdotal techniques, the new field of animal psychology was becoming more objective. Consciousness was still its concern, however, and information about an animal's level of consciousness was inferred from observations of its behavior. Thus, while the methodology was becoming more objective, the subject matter was not.

The French psychologist, Alfred Binet, published *The Psychic Life of Micro-Organisms* (1889), in which he proposed that protozoa have the ability to perceive and discriminate between objects and to display behavior that is purposive in nature. As late as 1908, Francis Darwin (Charles Darwin's son) discussed the role of consciousness in plants (Boakes, 1984).

In the early years of animal psychology in the United States, we find, not surprisingly, a continuing interest in animal consciousness. The founders of animal, or comparative, psychology, Romanes and Morgan, exerted a strong influence on the field for some time.

A significant step toward greater objectivity in animal psychology was taken by Jacques Loeb (1859–1924), a German physiologist and zoologist who worked mainly in the United States. Reacting against the anthropomorphic tradition of Romanes and the method of introspection by analogy, Loeb developed a new theory of animal behavior. His approach was based on the concept of *tropism* or forced movement. In this view, an animal's response is a direct function of or reaction to a stimulus. The behavior is said to be forced by the stimulus, and thus it does not require any explanation in terms of consciousness. Loeb's theory was influential for a time in the biological sciences. It represented a great change from the earlier work of Romanes and Morgan, and was the most mechanistic and objective animal psychology to have developed.

However, Loeb had not completely thrown off the past. He did not reject consciousness, particularly in animals high on the evolutionary scale (such as humans). Loeb argued that consciousness among animals was revealed by *associative memory*, that is, by their learning to react in a desired way to certain stimuli or signs. For example, when an animal responds to the calling of its name, or when it reacts to a certain sound by going repeatedly to the place where it is fed, this is evidence of associative memory. Even in this otherwise highly mechanistic system, the mind or consciousness (specifically, the association of ideas) was still being invoked.

Watson took several courses with Loeb at the University of Chicago and expressed the desire to do research under his tutelage. This indicates Watson's sympathy with, or at least a curiosity about, Loeb's mechanistic views. Angell and another faculty member, the neurologist H. H. Donaldson, talked Watson out of this desire, arguing that Loeb was "unsafe," a word open to interpretation, but perhaps indicating objection to Loeb's uncompromising objectivism.

By the beginning of the twentieth century the study of animal behavior within a biological framework had become widespread in the United States. At the same time experimental animal psychology, notably the work of Thorndike, was developing rapidly. Robert Yerkes began animal studies in 1900 and his work, using a wide range of animals, greatly strengthened the position and influence of comparative psychology. Also in 1900 the rat maze was introduced by W. S. Small, and the white rat and maze became a standard method of studying learning. Yet the problem of consciousness persisted in animal psychology, even with the white rat in the maze. In interpreting the rat's behavior, Small wrote in mentalistic terms:

> It is also clear, I think, that what properly may be called ideas, find slight place in the associative process. Crass images—visual, olfactory, motor—organic conditions, and instinctive activities are assuredly the main elements. That these elements may bleach out and attenuate into ideas is not impossible. Analogy with human experience would indeed point to that conclusion. (Mackenzie, 1977, p. 85)

Although this comment of Small's is more restricted than Romanes's brand of anthropomorphizing, it nevertheless represents a concern with mental processes, even with mental elements. Watson, in the early years of his career, came under the same influence. His doctoral dissertation, completed in 1903, was entitled "Animal Education: The Psychical Development of the White Rat." As late as 1907 Watson was discussing the conscious experience of sensation in his rats.

In general, however, the field of animal psychology was becoming increasingly objective in its methods and even in its subject matter. The kinds of conscious experiences being invoked were growing narrower and in a short time would disappear altogether.

Laboratories of comparative psychology were being established and many universities offered courses in the subject. Margaret Floy Washburn, Titchener's first doctoral student, wrote a major textbook in comparative psychology, *The Animal Mind* (1908), which went through three subsequent editions, and taught animal psychology at Cornell. Note the title of Washburn's book: *The Animal Mind*. The imputation of consciousness to animals was still a strong tendency in psychology, as was the method of introspecting the animal mind by analogy with the human mind. Washburn noted that "we are obliged to acknowledge that *all psychic interpretation of animal behavior must be*

Margaret Floy Washburn
(1871–1939) was
Titchener's first doctoral
student and wrote a major
textbook in comparative
psychology.

on the analogy of human experience. . . . We must be anthropomorphic in the notions we form of what takes place in the mind of an animal" (Washburn, 1908, p. 88).

In 1911 the *Journal of Animal Behavior* (later the *Journal of Comparative Psychology*) was begun. In 1909 Pavlov's work, which greatly supported an objective psychology and Watson's behaviorism in particular, became known in the United States through an article written by Yerkes and a Russian student, S. Morgulis. The article was published in the *Psychological Review*; the journal's editor at the time was John B. Watson. Because their influence was so important in the development of behaviorism, we shall consider the works of Thorndike and Pavlov. But first, let us tell the tale of the most famous horse in the history of psychology.

Clever Hans, the Clever Horse

In the early 1900s virtually every literate person in the Western world had read about Hans the Wonder Horse, surely the most intelligent four-legged creature who ever lived. The horse was a celebrity throughout Europe and America. Plays and songs were written about him, as were books and magazine articles, and advertisers used the horse's name to sell their products. Hans was a sensation.

The horse could add and subtract, use fractions and decimals, read, spell, tell time, discriminate among colors, identify objects, and give demonstrations of phenomenal memory. Hans replied to the questions put to him by tapping his hoof a specified number of times or by nodding his head toward the correct object or chart.

> "How many of the gentlemen present are wearing straw hats?" the horse was asked.
> Clever Hans tapped the answer with his right foot, being careful to omit the number of straw hats worn by the ladies.
> "What is the lady holding in her hand?"
> The horse tapped out "Schirm," meaning parasol, indicating each of the letters by means of a special chart. He was invariably successful at distinguishing between canes and parasols and also between straw and felt hats.
> More important, Hans could think for himself. When asked a completely novel question, such as how many corners in a circle, he shook his head from side to side to say there were none. (Fernald, 1984, p. 19)

No wonder people were dazzled and amazed. No wonder Hans's owner, Wilhelm von Osten, a retired mathematics teacher in Berlin, Germany, was pleased with what he had accomplished. He had spent several years teaching Hans what he considered to be the fundamentals of human intelligence. The motivation for his painstaking efforts was purely scientific. His goal was to prove that Darwin was correct in suggesting that humans and animals have similar mental processes and abilities.

Von Osten believed that the only reason horses and other animals appeared to be less intelligent than they really were was that they had not been given sufficient education. He was convinced that with the right kind of drill and training, the horse could show that it was an intelligent being.

We should note that von Osten did not profit financially from Hans's performances. He never charged admission fees for the demonstrations he put on frequently in the courtyard of his apartment building, and he never benefitted from the resulting publicity.

A government committee was established to investigate the Clever Hans phenomenon to determine if any deception or trickery was involved. The committee included a circus manager, a veterinarian, horse trainers, a nobleman, the director of the Berlin Zoo, and Carl Stumpf (see Chapter 4), who was the director of the Psychological Institute at the University of Berlin.

In September 1904, after a lengthy investigation, the committee concluded that Hans was not receiving any intentional signs or cues from his owner. No fraud, no deceit. But Stumpf was not completely satisfied. He was curious about how the horse was able to respond correctly to so many different kinds of questions, and he assigned the problem to one of his graduate students, Oskar Pfungst, who approached the task in the careful manner of an experimental psychologist (Rosenthal, 1965).

One of Pfungst's first experiments followed a demonstration that Hans could answer questions correctly even when von Osten was not present. Pfungst formed two groups of questioners, one composed of persons who knew the answers to the questions they put to Hans and the second composed of persons who did not know the answers. This led to a crucial finding, namely, that Hans could only answer questions when the questioners knew the correct answers. Obviously, Hans was receiving information from the person who was questioning him, even when that person was a stranger.

After a series of well-controlled experiments, Pfungst concluded that Hans had been unintentionally conditioned to begin tapping his hoof whenever he perceived an ever-so-slight downward movement of von Osten's head. When the correct number of taps had been reached, von Osten would move his head slightly upward. Pfungst demonstrated that virtually everyone, even persons who had never been around a horse before, made the same barely perceptible head movements when speaking to a horse.

Thus, it was shown that Hans did not have a storehouse of knowledge. He had simply been conditioned to start tapping his hoof, or to incline his head toward an object, whenever his questioner made a certain kind of movement. Further, the horse had been conditioned to stop tapping in response to another kind of movement. During the training period von Osten had reinforced Hans with pieces of carrot or lumps of sugar every time the horse made a correct response. As the training continued, von Osten no longer reinforced Hans's behavior for every correct reply, but instead rewarded him on a partial or intermittent basis. B. F. Skinner would later demonstrate the effectiveness of partial reinforcement in the conditioning process (Chapter 11).

The case of Clever Hans demonstrates the value—indeed, the necessity—of an experimental approach to the study of animal behavior. It made psychologists all the more skeptical of claims of high intelligence in animals. It was clear, however, that animals were capable of learning. They could be conditioned to change their behavior. Therefore, the study of learning seemed much more profitable than the continued speculation about what might be going on in an animal's mind or about their level of alleged intelligence.

Pfungst's report on his experiments with Clever Hans was reviewed by John B. Watson in an American journal and influenced Watson's rapidly growing inclination to deal only with behavior and not with consciousness (Watson, 1908).

EDWARD LEE THORNDIKE (1874–1949)

Thorndike, who was never able to learn how to drive a car, is one of the most important researchers in the development of animal psychology. He worked out an objective and mechanistic theory of learning that focused on overt behavior. He believed that psychology must study behavior, not mental elements or conscious experience in any form. Thus, he reinforced the trend toward greater objectivity that had been begun by the functionalists, and interpreted learning not in terms of subjective ideas, but rather in terms of concrete connections between stimuli and responses. However, as we shall see, there was still some reference to consciousness and mental processes in his system.

The work of Thorndike and Pavlov is another example of simultaneous independent discovery. Thorndike's *law of effect* was developed in 1898 and Pavlov's similar *law of*

reinforcement in 1902, though it was many years before the resemblance between the two was recognized.

Thorndike was one of the first American psychologists to receive all of his education in the United States. It is significant that this was possible just two decades after psychology was founded.

The Life of Thorndike

Thorndike's interest in psychology was awakened (as it was for many others) when he read William James's *Principles* while an undergraduate at Wesleyan University. He later studied under James at Harvard, where he began his investigation of animal learning, apparently inspired by a series of lectures given by Morgan. Thorndike's initial research was with chicks, which he trained to run through mazes improvised by placing books on end. The story is told of Thorndike's difficulties in finding room for his chicks. His landlady took a dim view of his raising them in his bedroom, so he turned to James for help. James was unsuccessful in finding space in either the laboratory or the museum, so he took Thorndike and chicks into the basement of his home, apparently to the delight of the James children.

For personal reasons Thorndike did not complete his education at Harvard. Believing that a certain young lady did not return his affections, he applied to Cattell at Columbia to get away from the Boston area. It was not what he really wanted to do; rather, it was "a move born of youthful despair and deeply felt frustration" (Jonçich, 1968, p. 103). He later married the woman in question.

Offered a fellowship by Cattell, Thorndike went to New York, taking his two best-trained chicks with him. He continued his animal research at Columbia, working with cats and dogs and using puzzle boxes of his own design. He was awarded his doctorate in 1898. His thesis, "Animal Intelligence: An Experimental Study of the Associative Processes in Animals," was subsequently published, along with other research on associative learning in chicks, fish, and monkeys.

Thorndike was intensely ambitious and highly competitive. At the time of his graduation he wrote to his fiancée: "I've decided to get to the top of the psychology heap in five years, teach ten more and then quit" (Boakes, 1984, p. 72).

Thorndike became an instructor in psychology at Teachers College, Columbia, in 1899, and remained there for the rest of his career. At Cattell's suggestion, he applied his animal research techniques to children and young people, and thereafter worked more with human subjects. The rest of his career was spent largely in the areas of human learning, education, and mental testing, and he is considered a leader in the mental testing movement. He also wrote several highly successful textbooks, and he did get to the top of the heap. In 1912 he was elected president of the American Psychological Association. He became quite wealthy, the first psychologist to do so as a result of his work in the field, particularly from royalties from his mental tests and his textbooks. By 1924 he was enjoying an income of nearly $70,000 a year, a tremendous sum at that time (Boakes, 1984).

Thorndike's 50 years at Columbia are among the most productive ever recorded. His bibliography includes 507 items, many of which are lengthy books and monographs. He retired in 1939, but continued to work actively until his death 10 years later.

Edward Lee Thorndike (1874–1949) pioneered the field of learning with connectionism, his theoretical attempt to explain how the organism associates stimuli with responses.

Thorndike's Connectionism

Thorndike created *connectionism*, an experimental approach to associationism that included several important departures from traditional views. He wrote that if he were to analyze the human mind he would

> find connections of varying strength between (a) situations, elements of situations, and compounds of situations and (b) responses, readinesses to respond, facilitations, inhibitions, and directions of responses. If all these could be completely inventoried, telling what the man would think and do and what would satisfy and annoy him, in every conceivable situation, it seems to me that nothing would be left out. . . . Learning is connecting. The mind is man's connection-system. (Thorndike, 1931, p. 122)

This associationist position was a direct descendant of the older philosophical associationism, with one significant difference. Instead of talking about associations or connections between ideas, Thorndike talked about connections between situations and responses. He incorporated a more objective frame of reference into his psychological theory.

His study of learning also differed from classical associationism in that the subjects were animals rather than humans. This method had become acceptable as a result of the Darwinian notion of continuity of species.

Although Thorndike focused on connections between situations and responses and argued that learning does not involve conscious reflection, he nevertheless was concerned with mental or subjective processes. In the quotation above (and in the one below) he spoke about "satisfaction," "annoyance," and "discomfort." These terms are more mentalistic than behavioristic. In other writings he also used mentalistic terms when discussing the behavior of his experimental animals.

Thorndike was still under the influence of the framework established by Romanes and Morgan. "For Thorndike, as for Morgan, detailed analysis of an animal's mental operations on the basis of objective inference was followed by descriptions of the animal's private experience on the basis of subjective inference" (Mackenzie, 1977, p. 70).

It must be noted, however, that like Loeb, Thorndike was not granting high levels of consciousness and intelligence to animals as freely and as wildly as Romanes had. We can see a steady diminution of the role of consciousness in animal psychology from its beginnings to the time of Thorndike, and a greater focus on the use of the experimental method to study more objective behavior.

Therefore, in spite of the mentalistic tinge to Thorndike's work, we must not lose sight of the mechanistic nature of his approach. He argued that to study behavior, it must be broken down or reduced to its simplest elements: stimulus–response units. He shared with the structuralists an analytic and atomistic point of view. The stimulus–response units are the elements of behavior (not of consciousness), the building blocks from which more complex behaviors are compounded.

Thorndike's conclusions were derived through the use of a research apparatus of his own design, the puzzle box (Figure 9-1). An animal placed in the box was required to learn to operate a latch in order to escape. Thorndike's extensive research with cats involved placing a cat that had been deprived of food in the slatted puzzle box. Food was placed outside the box as a reward for escaping. The door of the box was fastened by several latches. The cat had to pull on a lever or a chain, and sometimes engage in several such acts in succession, to open the door.

At first, the cat displayed random, rather chaotic behaviors as it poked and sniffed and clawed in every direction to get to the food. Eventually the cat hit upon the correct behavior and the door opened. During the first trial the correct behavior occurred by accident. On subsequent trials the random behaviors were displayed less frequently until learning was complete and the cat would display the correct behavior as soon as it was placed in the box.

Thorndike used quantitative measures of learning. One technique was to record the number of wrong behaviors, behaviors that did not lead to escaping from the box. Over a series of trials, these became less frequent. Another technique was to record the time that had elapsed from the moment the cat was placed in the box until it succeeded in escaping. As learning took place, this time period decreased.

Thorndike wrote of the "stamping in" or "stamping out" of a response tendency by its favorable or unfavorable results. Unsuccessful response tendencies (those that do nothing to get the cat out of the box) are stamped out over a number of trials. Response tendencies that lead to success are stamped in after a number of trials. This kind of learning has been called "trial and error learning," though Thorndike preferred to call it "trial and accidental success" (Jonçich, 1968, p. 266).

The stamping in or out of a response tendency was formalized in 1905 as Thorndike's *law of effect*.

> Any act which in a given situation produces satisfaction becomes associated with that situation, so that when the situation recurs the act is more likely than before to recur also. Conversely, any act which in a given situation produces discomfort becomes disassociated from that situation, so that when the situation recurs the act is less likely than before to recur. (Thorndike, 1905, p. 203)

A companion law is the *law of exercise* or the *law of use or disuse*, which stated that any response made in a particular situation becomes associated with the situation. The more the response is used in the situation, the more strongly it becomes associated with it. Conversely, prolonged disuse of the response tends to weaken the association. In other words, repetition of any response in the situation tends to strengthen that response. Thorndike's later research convinced him that repetition of a response is relatively ineffective compared to the reward consequences of the response.

In the early 1930s Thorndike reexamined the law of effect in an extensive program of research using human subjects. The results revealed that rewarding a response did

Figure 9-1 Thorndike's puzzle box.

indeed strengthen that response, but punishment of a response did not produce a comparable negative effect. He therefore revised the law of effect to place greater emphasis on reward than on punishment.

Comment

Thorndike's pioneer investigations into the fields of human and animal learning are among the greatest in the history of psychology. His theory of association or learning heralded the rapid rise of learning theory to its later prominent position in American psychology. Although new learning theories and models have appeared since Thorndike's work, the significance of his contributions remains secure. His influence declined with the advent of more sophisticated learning systems, but his work remains a cornerstone of associationism, and the objective spirit in which he conducted his research is an important antecedent of behaviorism.

Pavlov paid tribute to Thorndike's work in the following manner:

> Some years after the beginning of the work with our new method I learned that somewhat similar experiments had been performed in America, and indeed not by physiologists but by psychologists. Thereupon I studied in more detail the American publications, and now I must acknowledge that the honour of having made the first steps along this path belongs to E. L. Thorndike. By two or three years his experiments preceded ours and his book [*Animal Intelligence*] must be considered a classic, both for its bold outlook on an immense task and for the accuracy of its results. (Pavlov, 1928; cited by Jonçich, 1968, pp. 415–416)

IVAN PETROVITCH PAVLOV (1849–1936)

The influence of Ivan Pavlov is felt keenly in many areas of contemporary psychology. His work in the area of association or learning helped to cause associationism to shift from its traditional application to subjective ideas, to completely objective and quantifiable glandular secretions and muscular movements. As a result, Pavlov's work provided John B. Watson with a new way of investigating behavior and a means of attempting to control and modify it.

The Life of Pavlov

Pavlov was born in a provincial town in central Russia, the eldest of 11 children of a village priest. His position in such a large family brought him responsibility and hard work at an early age, characteristics he retained all his life. He was unable to attend school until the age of 11 because of an accident involving a severe blow to the head four years earlier.

His father had tutored him at home, and in 1860 he entered the local theological seminary, intending to prepare for the priesthood. Later, after reading Darwin, he changed his mind, and in 1870 he walked several hundred miles to attend the University of St. Petersburg, where he specialized in animal physiology. With this university training, Pavlov joined the emerging third class in Russian society—the intelligentsia:

> too well-educated and too intelligent for the peasantry from which he came, but too common and too poor for the aristocracy into which he could never rise. These

Awarded the Nobel Prize for his work on digestion, Ivan Petrovitch Pavlov (1849–1936) advanced the cause of objectivity in psychology through his precise research on the physiology of the conditioned reflex.

social conditions often produced an especially dedicated intellectual, one whose entire life was centered on the intellectual pursuits that justified his existence. And so it was with Pavlov, whose almost fanatic devotion to pure science and to experimental research was supported by the energy and simplicity of a Russian peasant. (Miller, 1962, p. 177)

Pavlov obtained his degree in 1875 and began medical training, not to practice medicine, but in the hope of pursuing a career in physiological research. He studied in

Germany for two years, and returned to St. Petersburg for several hard years as a laboratory research assistant.

Pavlov's dedication to research was of paramount importance. His single-mindedness was not distracted by practical issues such as salary, clothing, or living conditions. Luckily, his wife, Sara, whom he married in 1881, devoted her life to protecting him from mundane matters. They made a pact early in their marriage, agreeing that she would allow nothing to distract him from his work. He promised never to drink or play cards and to socialize only on Saturday and Sunday evenings. Throughout his life Pavlov adhered to a rigorous schedule, working seven days a week from September to May and spending summers in the country.

Characteristic of his indifference to everyday affairs is the story that she often had to remind him when it was time to collect his salary. She once said of him that "he shouldn't be trusted to buy a suit of clothes by himself." Nothing mattered to him except his research. When he was 73 and riding the streetcar to his laboratory, he jumped off before it stopped and broke his leg. "He was impetuous—he wouldn't wait for it to stop. A woman standing near him saw it and said, 'My, here is a man of genius, but he doesn't know how to get off a streetcar without breaking his leg'" (Gantt, 1979, p. 28).

Pavlov lived in poverty until 1890 when, at the age of 41, he finally obtained the post of professor of pharmacology at the Military Medical Academy in St. Petersburg. For a time after his marriage he had slept on a cot in his laboratory while his wife lived with a relative because they could not afford an apartment. In 1883, when Pavlov was preparing his doctoral thesis, their first child was born. Frail and sickly, the infant would not live, said the doctor, unless both mother and child could rest in the country. After a great struggle they were able to borrow enough money for the journey to the home of a relative, but it was too late and the child died. Six years later they were still so destitute that his wife and second son again had to board with relatives. A group of Pavlov's students, knowing of his financial problems, gave him money on the pretext of covering the expenses of lectures they had asked him to give. Pavlov spent the money on laboratory animals and kept none for himself. So strong were his dedication and commitment to his work that he was not particularly bothered by financial hardships. He said that they never caused him "any undue worry."

Pavlov was given to explosive emotional tirades, often directed at his research assistants. The anecdote is told that during the Bolshevik Revolution (1917) Pavlov bitterly chastised one of his assistants for being 10 minutes late for an experiment; pitched battles in the streets were not to interfere with research. "What the hell difference does the revolution make," he would shout, "when you've got work to do in the laboratory" (Gantt, 1979, p. 28). Usually these outbursts were quickly forgotten. His students knew exactly what was expected of them; Pavlov never hesitated to tell them. He was honest and direct, if not always considerate, in his dealings with other people.

Pavlov was known as an excellent teacher who was capable of enthralling an audience of students or peers. Merciless in an argument, he was nevertheless willing to admit he had been in error, although this was a rare occurrence. He was popular with his students, and he was one of the few professors who not only allowed but also encouraged students to interrupt his lectures to ask questions. He was also one of the few who allowed women and Jewish students to work in his laboratory. He had a good sense of humor and could enjoy a joke that was played on him. When he received an honorary degree from Cambridge University, some students lowered a stuffed toy dog into his lap by a rope from the balcony. Pavlov kept the dog next to his desk in his apartment (*New York Times*, September 23, 1984).

His relations with the Soviet regime were complicated and difficult; he was openly critical of the revolution and the Soviet government. He wrote dangerously strong, angry letters of protest to Stalin and boycotted Russian scientific meetings to demonstrate his disapproval of the government. Not until 1933 did he finally accept the government and acknowledge that it had achieved some success in uniting the Russian people. For the last three years of his life he lived in peace with the authorities of whom he had been so critical for 16 years. Despite his attitude, Pavlov received generous government support for his research throughout his career and was largely free of government pressure.

The following passage from Pavlov's autobiography sums up his attitude toward his life:

> Looking back on my life I would describe it as being happy and successful. I have received all that can be demanded of life: the complete realization of the principles with which I began life. I dreamed of finding happiness in intellectual work, in science—and I found it. I wanted to have a kind person as a companion in life and I found this companion in my wife . . . who patiently endured all the hardships of our existence before my professorship, always encouraged my scientific aspirations and who devoted herself to our family just as I devoted myself to the laboratory. I have renounced practicality in life with its cunning and not always irreproachable ways, and I see no reason for regretting this; on the contrary, precisely in this I find now certain consolation. (1955, p. 46)

Pavlov remained a scientist almost to the last moment of his life. He had always observed himself whenever he was ill, and the day of his death was no exception. He called in a neuropathologist and described his symptoms. Although he was extremely weak from pneumonia, he said, "My brain is not working well, obsessive feelings and involuntary movements appear; mortification may be setting in." For a while they discussed the meaning of the symptoms until Pavlov fell asleep. When he awakened, he raised himself up and began to search for his clothes, showing the same impatient energy he had demonstrated all his life.

"It is time to get up!" he said. "Help me, I must dress!" And with that, he fell back on the bed and died (Gantt, 1941, p. 35).

Pavlov's Research

During his distinguished and productive career Pavlov worked on three research problems. The first concerned the function of the nerves of the heart and the second the primary digestive glands. His brilliant research on digestion won him worldwide recognition and, in 1904, the Nobel Prize. His third research area, for which he occupies a vital place in the history of psychology, was the study of the higher nervous centers in the brain. He pursued this work with characteristic energetic determination and devotion from 1902 until his death in 1936. In his attack on this problem he made use of conditioning, his greatest scientific achievement. It is instructive to consider how Pavlov developed this technique, which changed the direction of his own career and profoundly influenced the development of psychology.

The notion of conditioned reflexes originated (as so many scientific breakthroughs) in an accidental discovery. In his work on digestive glands, Pavlov used the method of surgical exposure of the subjects (dogs) to permit the collection of the digestive secretions outside the body where they could be observed, measured, and recorded. The surgical operations necessary to divert the secretions of a particular gland through a tube to the outside of the body, without damaging the nerves and blood supply, were difficult. Pavlov displayed considerable ingenuity and technical skill in performing these operations.

One aspect of his work dealt with the function of saliva, which would be involuntarily secreted whenever food was placed in the dog's mouth. Pavlov observed that sometimes saliva would be secreted before the food was given to the animal. An anticipatory saliva flow would occur. The dogs salivated when they saw the food or the man who regularly fed them, and even when they heard his footsteps. The reflex of secretion, with its unlearned response of salivation, had somehow become attached or conditioned to stimuli that had previously been associated with feeding. These "psychic" reflexes (as Pavlov originally called them) were aroused in the animal by stimuli other than the original one (food), and Pavlov realized that this happened because these other stimuli (such as the sight and sounds of the attendant) had so often been associated with the ingestion of food. The associationists called this phenomenon "association by frequency of occurrence."

After a long period of doubting whether he should follow up this observation because of its psychical nature, Pavlov decided in 1902 to investigate these psychic reflexes. He soon became absorbed in the new research.

Pavlov (like Thorndike, Loeb, and others before him), in accordance with the prevailing *Zeitgeist* in animal psychology, initially focused on the mentalistic experiences of his laboratory animals; this can be seen in his original term for conditioned reflexes—psychic reflexes. In his early research he wrote about his animals' desires, judgment, and will, interpreting animal psychic events in subjective, human terms. After a time, however, Pavlov decided to drop all mentalistic references in favor of a straightforward, objective approach. Pavlov described it as follows:

> At first in our psychical experiments with the psychical glands . . . we conscientiously endeavored to explain our results by imagining the subjective state of the animal. But nothing came of this except sterile controversy and individual views that could not be reconciled. And so we could do nothing but conduct the research on a purely objective basis. (Cuny, 1965, p. 65)

Pavlov's research became a model of objectivity and precision. His first experiments were simple. He showed a dog a piece of bread in his hand before giving it to the dog to eat. In time, salivation began as soon as the dog saw the bread. The dog's response of salivating when the bread was placed in its mouth is a natural reflexive response of the digestive system; no learning is necessary for it to occur. Accordingly, Pavlov called this an innate or *unconditioned* reflex. Salivation at the sight of food, however, is not a reflexive response but one that must be learned. This response Pavlov called a *conditional* reflex (having dropped the mentalistic term "psychic reflex"), because it was conditional upon the formation of an association between the sight of food and the subsequent eating of it.

Pavlov soon discovered that any stimulus could produce the conditioned salivary response so long as it was capable of attracting the animal's attention without arousing fear or anger. He used such stimuli as a bell, buzzer, light, and the tick of a metronome.

His typical thoroughness and precision are evidenced by the elaborate and sophisticated technique he used to collect the saliva. A rubber tube was connected to an opening created in the dog's cheek through which saliva flowed. When each drop of saliva fell onto a platform that rested on a sensitive spring, the movement of the platform activated a marker on a revolving drum (Figure 9-2). This arrangement, which made possible the recording of the precise number of drops as well as the exact moment at which each fell, is but one example of Pavlov's painstaking efforts to standardize experimental conditions, use rigid controls, and eliminate sources of error.

He was so concerned about preventing intrusions from the environment that he designed special cubicles for his research. The experimental animal was placed in a harness in one cubicle while the experimenter occupied the other. The experimenter could then operate the various conditioning stimuli, collect the saliva, and present the food without being seen by the animal.

These precautions did not completely satisfy Pavlov. He believed that extraneous stimuli could still reach the animals. He designed a three-story research building, later known as the Tower of Silence, in which the windows were covered with extra-thick sheets of glass, the rooms had double steel doors that sealed hermetically when closed, and the steel girders that supported the floors were embedded in sand. A deep moat filled with straw encircled the building. Vibration, noise, temperature extremes, odors, and even drafts had been eliminated. Nothing could influence the experimental animals except the conditioning stimuli to which they were exposed.

A typical conditioning experiment runs as follows. The conditioned stimulus—a light, let us say—is turned on. Immediately, the unconditioned stimulus—the food—

Figure 9-2 Pavlov's apparatus for studying classical conditioning.

is presented. After a number of pairings of the light and the food, the animal salivates at the sight of the light. The animal has become conditioned to respond to the conditioned stimulus. An association or bond has been formed between the light and the food. Learning or conditioning will not occur unless the light is followed by the food a number of times. Thus, reinforcement (being fed) is necessary for learning to take place.

In addition to studying the formation of conditioned responses, Pavlov and his associates investigated other phenomena—reinforcement, extinction, spontaneous recovery, generalization, discrimination, and higher-order conditioning (all well-known words in the language of psychology today). Some 200 collaborators came to work with Pavlov, and the experimental program extended over a longer period of time and involved more people than any research effort since Wundt's. As noted, the conditioning situation itself was simple, but it generated many specific questions that required years of patient and thorough experimentation to answer.

Pavlov presented a preliminary report on his findings in 1923, after 20 years of research. In 1927 he published a more systematic account of his work. This long interval between the beginning of his research and the reports of his findings testifies not only to the enormous scope of the problem, but also to Pavlov's scientific integrity. He wanted to be certain of the accuracy and validity of his findings before making them widely known.

Comment

With Pavlov's work, more precise and objective measures and terminology were introduced into the study of association or learning. Also, Pavlov demonstrated that higher mental processes could be effectively studied in physiological terms with the use of animal subjects and without any reference to consciousness. He greatly influenced psychology's shift toward objectivity in subject matter and methodology. The effects of this trend are seen more strikingly in the development of behaviorism, in which the conditioned reflex plays a central part. This concept provided the science of psychology with a basic element or atom of behavior, a workable, concrete unit to which highly complex human behavior could be reduced and experimented upon under laboratory conditions. As we shall see, Watson seized upon this unit of behavior and made it the core of his program. Pavlov was highly pleased with Watson's work. He believed that the growth of behaviorism in the United States represented a confirmation of his ideas and his methodology (Windholz, 1983).

It is ironic that Pavlov's greatest influence has been in psychology, a field toward which he was not altogether favorable for some time. He was familiar with both structural and functional psychology and agreed with William James that psychology had not yet reached the status of a science. Consequently, he excluded it from his own work. He fined workers in his laboratory who used psychological rather than physiological terminology. Woodworth noted that in his lectures Pavlov frequently made such remarks as the following:

> In conclusion we must count it an uncontested fact that the physiology of the highest part of the nervous system of higher animals cannot be successfully studied, unless we utterly renounce the untenable pretensions of psychology. (1948, p. 60)

Toward the end of his life, however, Pavlov changed his attitude and even called himself an experimental psychologist. Pavlov's initially negative view did not, of course, prevent psychologists from making effective use of his work. At first, they used the conditioned response to measure sensory discrimination in animals; it is still used for that purpose today. During the 1920s it began to be used, primarily in America, as the foundation for learning theories. Since then, it has generated considerable research and theory as well as controversy.

Pavlov's immense contributions to science are widely recognized and respected, but the social and philosophical implications of his research and the resulting conception of human nature have been criticized. Many find the idea of conditioning people to respond to various stimuli offensive to their vision of human beings as far removed from animals and possessing free will.

VLADIMIR M. BEKHTEREV (1857–1927)

Another important figure in the movement of animal psychology and associationism from subjective ideas toward objectively observed overt behavior is Vladimir Bekhterev. Although less well known than Pavlov, this Russian physiologist, neurologist, and psychiatrist was a pioneer in a number of research areas. He was a contemporary and rival of Pavlov in the opening years of the twentieth century, and independently of Pavlov became interested in conditioning.

Bekhterev received his degree from the Military Medical Academy in St. Petersburg in 1881. He studied in Leipzig with Wundt, and in Berlin and Paris, and returned to Russia to take the chair of mental diseases at the University of Kazan. In 1893 he accepted the chair of mental and nervous diseases at the Military Medical Academy, where he also organized a mental hospital. In 1907 he founded the Psychoneurological Institute and began a program of neurological research.

Whereas Pavlov's conditioning research had been conducted almost exclusively on glandular secretions, Bekhterev was interested in the motor conditioning response, a concern that extended the Pavlovian conditioning principle to striped muscles. His basic discovery was the *associated* reflex as revealed through the study of motor responses. He found that reflexive movements, such as withdrawing a finger from an electric shock, could be elicited not only by the unconditioned stimulus (the electric shock), but also by stimuli that had become associated with the original response-eliciting stimulus. For example, the sounding of a buzzer at the time of the shock soon elicited withdrawal of the finger by itself.

The associationists had explained such connections in terms of the operation of some sort of mental process. Bekhterev, however, considered the reactions to be totally reflexive. He believed that higher-level behaviors of greater complexity could be explained in the same way—as a compounding of the low-level motor reflexes. Thought processes were of the same character in that they depended on inner activities of the speech musculature. Bekhterev argued for a completely objective approach to psychological phenomena and against the use of mentalistic terms and concepts. His stand was expressed in *Objective Psychology*, published in 1907 and translated into German and French in 1913, at which time it was read by Watson. A third edition was published in English in 1932 (*General Principles of Human Reflexology*).

COMMENT

From the beginnings of animal psychology in the work of Romanes and Morgan, we can see a steady and rapid movement toward greater objectivity in both subject matter and methodology. The early work in the field invoked the concepts of consciousness and mental processes and used research methods that were equally subjective. By the early years of the twentieth century, however, animal psychology was completely objective in subject matter and methodology. Glandular secretions, conditioned reflexes, responses, acts, behavior—such terms left no doubt that animal psychology had finally discarded its subjective past.

Animal psychology was shortly to serve as a model for behaviorism, whose leader much preferred animal to human subjects for psychological research. John B. Watson used the findings and methods of the animal psychologists as a foundation for the development of a science of behavior that was applicable to both humans and animals.

THE INFLUENCE OF FUNCTIONALISM ON BEHAVIORISM

Another direct antecedent of behaviorism was functionalism. Although not totally objective, functional psychology in Watson's day did represent greater objectivity than its predecessors. Cattell and other functionalists, who were emphasizing behavior and more objective methodology, had expressed dissatisfaction with introspection. The various areas of applied interest to the functionalists had little use for consciousness and introspection, and essentially constituted an objective functional psychology. Thus, the functional psychologists had moved away from the pure psychology of conscious experience of Wundt and Titchener before Watson came on the scene. In their writings and lectures some functional psychologists were quite specific in arguing for an objective psychology, a psychology that would focus on behavior instead of consciousness.

Cattell, speaking at the 1904 World's Fair in St. Louis, Missouri, commented:

> I am not convinced that psychology should be limited to the study of consciousness as such. . . . The rather wide-spread notion that there is no psychology apart from introspection is refuted by the brute argument of accomplished fact. It seems to me that most of the research work that has been done by me or in my laboratory is nearly as independent of introspection as work in physics or in zoology. . . . I see no reason why the application of systematized knowledge to the control of human nature may not in the course of the present century accomplish results commensurate with the nineteenth century applications of physical science to the material world. (1904, pp. 179–180, 186)

Watson heard this address and the similarity between his later position and Cattell's statement is so striking that it has been suggested that Cattell could be called the "grandfather of Watson's behaviorism" (Burnham, 1968, p. 149).

In the decade before Watson formally founded behaviorism, the *Zeitgeist* favored and reinforced the idea of a totally objective psychology, and the overall movement of American psychology was in a behavioristic direction. Robert Woodworth noted that American psychologists were "slowly coming down with behaviorism . . . as more and more of them, from 1904 on, expressed a preference for defining psychology as the science of behavior rather than as an attempt to describe consciousness" (Woodworth, 1943, p. 28).

In 1911 Walter Pillsbury, who had studied with Titchener, defined psychology in his textbook, *Essentials of Psychology*, as the "science of human behavior." He argued that it was possible to treat human beings as objectively as any other aspect of the physical universe. Also in 1911, Max Meyer published *The Fundamental Laws of Human Behavior*. In 1912 William McDougall published *Psychology: The Study of Behavior*, and Knight Dunlap, a psychologist at Johns Hopkins University, where Watson was teaching, proposed that introspection be banned from psychology.

Angell, perhaps the most forward-looking of the functionalists, predicted that American psychology was ready to move toward greater objectivity. In 1910 he commented that it seemed possible that the term "consciousness" would disappear from psychology, much as had the term "soul." In 1913, shortly before Watson's manifesto appeared, Angell elaborated on this point, suggesting that it would be profitable if the "possible existence" of consciousness were forgotten and animal and human behavior were described objectively instead. Thus, the notion that psychology should be the science of behavior was gaining in popularity. Watson's greatness was not in being the first to propose the idea but in seeing, perhaps more clearly than anyone else, what the times were calling for. He responded vigorously and articulately as the agent of a revolution whose inevitability and success were already ensured.

SUGGESTED READINGS

Antecedents of Behaviorism

Burnham, J. C. (1968). On the origins of behaviorism. *Journal of the History of the Behavioral Sciences, 4*, 143–151.

Diserens, C. M. (1925). Psychological objectivism. *Psychological Review, 32*, 121–152.

Fernald, D. (1984). *The Hans legacy: A story of science.* Hillsdale, NJ: Lawrence Erlbaum.

Mackenzie, B. D. (1977). *Behaviourism and the limits of scientific method.* Atlantic Highlands, NJ: Humanities Press.

Warden, C. J., & Warner, L. H. (1927). The development of animal psychology in the U. S. during the past three decades. *Psychological Review, 34*, 196–205.

Thorndike

Bitterman, M. E. (1969). Thorndike and the problem of animal intelligence. *American Psychologist, 24*, 444–453.

Burnham, J. C. (1972). Thorndike's puzzle boxes. *Journal of the History of the Behavioral Sciences, 8*, 159–167.

Jonçich, G. (1968). *The sane positivist: A biography of Edward L. Thorndike.* Middletown, CT: Wesleyan University Press.

Postman, L. (1947). The history and present status of the Law of Effect. *Psychological Bulletin, 44,* 489–563.

Thorndike, E. L. (1949). *Selected writings from a connectionist's psychology.* New York: Appleton-Century-Crofts.

Pavlov

Cuny, H. (1965). *Ivan Pavlov: The man and his theories.* New York: Paul S. Eriksson.

Liddell, H. S. (1936). Pavlov's contribution to psychology. *Psychological Bulletin, 33,* 583–590.

Lowry, R. (1970). The reflex model in psychology: Origins and evaluation. *Journal of the History of the Behavioral Sciences, 6,* 64–69.

Pavlov, I. P. (1957). *Experimental psychology and other essays.* New York: Philosophical Library. (Includes Pavlov's autobiography).

Razran, G. (1965). Russian physiologists' psychology and American experimental psychology: A historical and a systematic collation and a look into the future. *Psychological Bulletin, 63,* 42–64.

10

Behaviorism: The Beginning

refer to 174-5

JOHN B. WATSON (1878–1958)

We discussed several antecedents of the behaviorist movement that influenced John B. Watson in his attempt to construct a new school of thought for psychology. Watson recognized that founding was not the same as originating, and he described his efforts as a "crystallization" of current trends in psychology. Like Wilhelm Wundt, psychology's first promoter–founder, Watson set out deliberately to found a new school. This intent clearly sets him apart from others whom history now labels precursors of behaviorism.

Watson was born on a farm near Greenville, South Carolina, where his early education was conducted in a one-room schoolhouse. His mother was intensely religious; his father was just the opposite. The elder Watson drank heavily, was prone to violence, and had several love affairs. When Watson was 13, his father ran off with another woman, never to return. Watson described himself as lazy and insubordinate, and he never earned more than passing grades. His teachers remember him as indolent, argumentative, and not easily controlled. He grew up in what could be called a state of delinquency. Watson got into fights and was arrested twice, once for shooting firearms within the city limits. It was not a promising beginning.

Nevertheless, he entered Furman University in Greenville at the age of 16 with a firm plan for his future—he was going to become a minister. Many years earlier he had promised his mother that he would follow the life of a clergyman. At Baptist-affiliated Furman, Watson studied philosophy, mathematics, Latin, and Greek, and was expected to graduate in 1899 and enter Princeton Theological Seminary the following fall.

A curious thing happened during Watson's senior year. One of his professors warned the students (perhaps jokingly, but that is not known for sure) that anyone who handed in a paper backward would fail the course. Watson took the professor up on the challenge, turned in his paper backward, and failed. The stunt prevented him from graduating, which meant that he could not attend the seminary as planned.

He stayed at Furman for another year and received an M.A. in 1900, but during that year his mother died, freeing him from the promise to undertake religious training. It is interesting to speculate whether Watson's deliberate failure to graduate on time was an attempt to escape the life of a minister to which he was committed.

Instead of Princeton Theological Seminary, Watson went to the University of Chicago to pursue graduate work in philosophy under John Dewey. He reported that he found Dewey "incomprehensible." ("I never knew what he was talking about then, and unfortunately for me, I still don't know" [J. B. Watson, 1936, p. 274].) His enthusiasm for philosophy quickly diminished, though he did continue with it as a minor.

Watson became attracted to psychology under the influence of James Rowland Angell, and he took a second minor in neurology. He also studied biology and physiology with Jacques Loeb. He worked at several jobs—he was at various times a waiter in a fraternity house, a rat caretaker, and an assistant janitor, a job in which, among other duties, he

Although his academic career was brief, John B. Watson (1878–1958), the founder of behaviorism, was influential in conceiving an objective psychology free of mentalism and as scientific as physics.

dusted Angell's desk. Toward the end of his graduate studies he suffered a breakdown, experiencing acute attacks of anxiety and an inability to sleep without a light on.

In 1903 Watson received his Ph.D., married a wealthy young student of his (a member of the prominent Ickes family), and accepted a position as an instructor at the University of Chicago, where he remained until 1908. He conducted much research there and demonstrated early his preference for animal subjects. In his autobiographical sketch he wrote:

> I never wanted to use human subjects. I hated to serve as a subject. I didn't like the stuffy, artificial instructions given to subjects. I always was uncomfortable and acted unnaturally. With animals I was at home. I felt that, in studying them, I was keeping close to biology with my feet on the ground. More and more the thought presented itself: Can't I find out by watching their behavior everything that the other students are finding out by using O's [observers]? (J. B. Watson, 1936, p. 276)

Watson's colleagues in graduate school and some of his professors reported that he was not a good introspector. Whatever special talent or temperament was needed for introspection, Watson did not have it. This may have provided some of the impetus that drove him toward a completely objective behavioral psychology. After all, if one were not good at practicing the primary technique in one's field, prospects would appear to be dim, unless one can develop another approach. Another possible reason for Watson's espousal of a purely objective psychology was the relative isolation of animal psychology and its subordination to mainstream human psychology. Behavior, of course, could be studied in animals as well as in humans. If psychology were a science that studied only behavior, then the professional interests of animal psychologists would be advanced (Leys, 1984).

In 1908, when Watson had become eligible for an assistant professorship at Chicago, he was offered a full professorship at Johns Hopkins University in Baltimore. He was reluctant to leave Chicago, but the opportunity to direct the laboratory, the higher position, and the substantial salary increase offered by Hopkins left him little choice. He remained at Hopkins until 1920, and those 12 years were to be his most productive for psychology.

The person who offered Watson the job at Johns Hopkins, J. Mark Baldwin (who, with Cattell, had started the *Psychological Review*), was also instrumental in furthering Watson's career. A year after Watson arrived at Hopkins, Baldwin was forced to resign because of his involvement in a sex scandal. He had been caught in a police raid on a Baltimore brothel.

Baldwin's explanation for his presence in the house of ill repute was not accepted by the university's president. "I foolishly yielded," Baldwin said, "to a suggestion, made after a dinner, to visit [the house] and see what was done there. I did not know before going that immoral women were harbored there" (Evans & Scott, 1978, p. 713). Baldwin became an outcast from American psychology and spent the remainder of his life in Europe. Eleven years later history would repeat itself when the same Hopkins president would ask for the resignation of Baldwin's successor, Watson, because of his involvement in a sex scandal.

At the time, Watson benefitted from Baldwin's resignation. Watson became chairman of the psychology department and replaced Baldwin as editor of the *Psychological Review*, one of the more influential journals in the field. At the age of 31, Watson became a pivotal figure in American psychology. He had surely been in the right place at the right time.

At Hopkins, Watson was extremely popular with the students. The year after his arrival the students dedicated their yearbook to him, and in 1919 the senior class voted him the handsomest professor, certainly a unique accolade in the history of psychology.

Watson said that he began thinking about a more objective approach to psychology around 1903. His thoughts on the subject were expressed publicly for the first time in 1908, in a lecture at Yale University. In 1912, at the invitation of Cattell, he spoke again on the subject in a series of lectures at Columbia University. The following year Watson's famous position paper was published in the *Psychological Review* (Watson, 1913) and behaviorism was officially launched.

Watson's first book, *Behavior: An Introduction to Comparative Psychology*, appeared in 1914. In it he argued for the acceptance of animal psychology and stressed the advantages of animals as subjects in psychological research. Watsonian behaviorism appealed to many younger psychologists and students who believed that Watson was cleansing the muddled atmosphere of psychology by casting off long-standing mysteries and uncertainties carried over from philosophy. Mary Cover Jones, a graduate student during those years, wrote 55 years later that she could still remember the excitement that greeted the publication of one of Watson's books. "It shook the foundations of traditional European-bred psychology, and we welcomed it. . . . It pointed the way from armchair psychology to action and reform and was therefore hailed as a panacea" (1974, p. 582).

Older psychologists were not universally captivated by Watson's program. Indeed, most psychologists rejected his revolutionary approach. We shall examine the reaction among psychologists and among the public later in this chapter.

Only two years after the publication of his *Psychological Review* paper, Watson was elected president of the American Psychological Association at the age of 37. This may not represent an endorsement of his position so much as a recognition of his visibility within the field and his personal connection with many prominent, established psychologists (Samelson, 1981).

Watson's professional activities were interrupted by a tour in the Army Aviation Service as a major during World War I. After the war, in 1918, he began his research on children, one of the earliest attempts at experimental work on human infants.

His second book, *Psychology from the Standpoint of a Behaviorist*, appeared in 1919, and presented a more complete statement of his position. He argued that the methods and principles he had earlier recommended for animal psychology were equally applicable and legitimate for the study of humans.

Around this time, Watson studied the physiological changes that occurred during intercourse by attaching electrodes to the bodies of the man and woman who served as subjects and recording various measurements while they engaged in sexual intercourse. The consequences of this investigation have been described in Chapter 1.

After several casual love affairs, Watson fell deeply in love with his graduate assistant, Rosalie Rayner. She was half his age and the daughter of a wealthy and influential Baltimore family that had donated a considerable sum of money to the university. Watson had written her a number of torrid letters, 15 of which were found by his wife.

Excerpts were printed in the *Baltimore Sun* during the widely publicized divorce proceedings that followed.

"Every cell I have is yours, individually and collectively," Watson had written. "My total reactions are positive and toward you. So likewise each and every heart reaction. I can't be more yours than I am, even if a surgical operation made us one" (Pauly, 1979, p. 40).

Thus ended Watson's promising academic career. He was forced to resign from Hopkins. Shortly thereafter he married Rosalie Rayner but never returned to a full-time university position.

Many academic colleagues, including his mentor, Angell, publicly criticized Watson on personal grounds during this difficult time and, understandably, he became embittered toward them. It is strange, considering his radically different personal temperament and theoretical position, that E. B. Titchener was of great help to Watson during this crisis. "You have done more for me than all the rest of my colleagues put together," Watson wrote to Titchener in 1922 (Larson & Sullivan, 1965, p. 346).

Unemployed and ordered to pay two-thirds of his former salary in alimony and child support, Watson began a second professional career, in the field of advertising. "I shall go into commercial work wholeheartedly and burn all bridges," he wrote (Buckley, 1982, p. 211). He joined the J. Walter Thompson agency in 1921, worked in every department, and made house-to-house surveys, sold coffee, and clerked in Macy's department store to learn about the business world. With characteristic enterprise and success, Watson became a vice president within three years. In 1936 he joined another advertising agency where he remained as vice president until his retirement in 1945.

Watson exerted a major impact on advertising in the United States through his application of behaviorist principles, an effect that is easily seen and heard in today's commercials and ads. Watson believed that people were machinelike. Therefore, their buying behavior could be predicted and controlled just like the behavior of other machines. To control the consumer, "it is only necessary to confront him with either fundamental or conditional emotional stimuli. . . . tell him something that will tie up with fear, something that will stir up a mild rage, that will call out an affectionate or love response, or strike at a deep psychological or habit need" (Buckley, 1982, p. 212).

Watson proposed that consumer behavior be studied scientifically, under laboratory conditions, with careful attention given to surveys. He emphasized that advertising messages should focus on style rather than substance and should convey the impression of new designs and images. The purpose, he said, "is to keep everyone reasonably dissatisfied with what he has in order to keep the factory busy in making new things" (Buckley, 1982, p. 215).

He pioneered the use of celebrity endorsements of products; the manipulation of human motives, emotions, and needs; and the appeal to basic fears to sell products from automobiles to underarm deodorants. In the process, Watson reached a position of prominence and wealth and claimed to be very happy.

After 1920 Watson's contact with academic psychology became less direct. Instead, he spent a great deal of time presenting his case for behaviorism to the general public. He lectured, gave radio talks, and wrote articles for such popular magazines as *Harper's, Cosmopolitan, McCall's, Collier's,* and *The Nation.* The fact that editors of these publications urged him to write for them attests to the great public interest in behaviorism. His second wife wrote an article for *Parent's Magazine* entitled "I Am the Mother of a Behaviorist's Sons."

In his articles Watson embarked on a crusade to sell the message of behaviorism to a wide audience. He wrote in a clear, readable style and he was paid well for his efforts. In his autobiography Watson pointed out that as long as he could no longer publish in the professional journals, he saw no reason why he should not go public and, in the language of his new field of advertising, sell his wares (Watson, 1936). These magazine articles have been described as "interesting, forceful, and assertive, but they are also propagandistic, sometimes simplistic, and occasionally unscholarly" (Herrnstein, 1973, p. 111).

Watson lectured at the New School for Social Research in New York for a while, and out of these lectures came his semipopular book, *Behaviorism* (1925), which described a program for the improvement of society. This book attracted considerable attention, both favorable and unfavorable, from the public.

In 1928 Watson published a work on child care (*Psychological Care of the Infant and Child*), in which he presented a regulatory as opposed to a permissive system of child rearing, in keeping with his strong environmentalist position. The book was full of stern, puritanical advice—the behaviorist way to bring up children. Watson suggested to parents that they should

> never hug and kiss them, never let them sit on your lap. If you must, kiss them once on the forehead when they say good night. Shake hands with them in the morning. Give them a pat on the head if they have made an extraordinarily good job of a difficult task. Try it out. In a week's time you will find how easy it is to be perfectly objective with your child and at the same time kindly. You will be utterly ashamed at the mawkish, sentimental way you have been handling it. (Watson, 1928, pp. 81–82)

The book transformed American child-rearing practices and had a more widespread public impact than anything else he wrote. A generation of children was raised in line with Watson's prescriptions. Watson's behaviorist way of bringing up children, which called for an absence of demonstrable affection, apparently reflected his own personality. Speaking at a 1981 APA symposium on Watson's work, his son recalled that, unfortunately, Watson as a father was unable to show affection. Skinner reported that Watson "later publicly regretted" the book (1959, p. 198). In 1930 Watson revised *Behaviorism*— his last professional activity in psychology.

Watson possessed an attractive combination of personal characteristics and abilities. He was intelligent and articulate, and his handsome appearance and legendary charm would probably have made him a charismatic figure in today's media-oriented culture. He was much in the public eye, a celebrity, throughout most of his life, and he courted and relished the publicity.

In 1935 Rosalie Watson died of a tropical fever contracted on a trip to the West Indies. "In a way the light seemed to go out of Watson's life at this time. He ceased to be a man-about-town and more and more spent time on his estate with his two boys" (Larson, 1979, p. 5).

In 1957, a year before he died, the American Psychological Association honored Watson with a citation, lauding his work as "one of the vital determinants of the form and substance of modern psychology . . . the point of departure for continuing lines of fruitful research." Although his health was poor, and he was unable to receive the award in person, he was said to be pleased by this official professional recognition.

It is tragic that Watson was forced to leave the academic world at the age of 42. From around 1920 on, he made no major contributions to psychology, and by 1930 he had abandoned the science of psychology for his business career.

ORIGINAL SOURCE MATERIAL ON BEHAVIORISM: FROM *PSYCHOLOGY AS THE BEHAVIORIST VIEWS IT* BY JOHN B. WATSON

There is probably no better starting point for a discussion of Watson's behaviorism than the article that began the movement—"Psychology as the Behaviorist Views It"—from the *Psychological Review* of 1913.[1]

> Psychology as the behaviorist views it is a purely objective experimental branch of natural science. Its theoretical goal is the prediction and control of behavior. Introspection forms no essential part of its methods, nor is the scientific value of its data dependent upon the readiness with which they lend themselves to interpretation in terms of consciousness. The behaviorist, in his efforts to get a unitary scheme of animal response, recognizes no dividing line between man and brute. The behavior of man, with all of its refinement and complexity, forms only a part of the behaviorist's total scheme of investigation.
>
> It has been maintained by its followers generally that psychology is a study of the science of the phenomena of consciousness. It has taken as its problem, on the one hand, the analysis of complex mental states (or processes) into simple elementary constituents, and on the other the construction of complex states when the elementary constituents are given. The world of the physical objects (stimuli, including here anything which may excite activity in a receptor), which forms the total phenomena of the natural scientist, is looked upon merely as means to an end. That end is the production of mental states that may be "inspected" or "observed." The psychological object of observation in the case of an emotion, for example, is the mental state itself. The problem in emotion is the determination of the number and kind of elementary constituents present, their loci, intensity, order of appearance, etc. It is agreed that introspection is the method *par excellence* by means of which mental states may be manipulated for purposes of psychology. On this assumption, behavior data (including under this term everything which goes under the name of comparative psychology) have no value *per se*. They possess significance only in so far as they may throw light upon conscious states. Such data must have at least an analogical or indirect reference to belong to the realm of psychology. . . .
>
> I do not wish unduly to criticize psychology. It has failed signally, I believe, during the fifty-odd years of its existence as an experimental discipline to make its place in the world as an undisputed natural science. Psychology, as it is generally thought of, has something esoteric in its methods. If you fail to reproduce my findings, it is not due to some fault in your apparatus or in the control of your stimulus, but it is due to the fact that your introspection is untrained. The attack is made upon the observer and not upon the experimental setting. In physics and in chemistry the attack is made upon the experimental conditions. The apparatus was not sensitive enough,

[1]From J. B. Watson, "Psychology as the behaviorist views it." *Psychological Review*, 1913, **20**, 158–177. Copyright 1913 by the American Psychological Association. Reprinted by permission.

impure chemicals were used, etc. In these sciences a better technique will give reproducible results. Psychology is otherwise. If you can't observe 3–9 states of clearness in attention, your introspection is poor. If, on the other hand, a feeling seems reasonably clear to you, your introspection is again faulty. You see seeing too much. Feelings are never clear.

The time seems to have come when psychology must discard all reference to consciousness; when it need no longer delude itself into thinking that it is making mental states the object of observation. We have become so enmeshed in speculative questions concerning the elements of mind, the nature of conscious content (for example, imageless thought, attitudes, . . . etc.) that I, as an experimental student, feel that something is wrong with our premises and the types of problems which develop from them. There is no longer any guarantee that we all mean the same thing when we use the terms now current in psychology. Take the case of sensation. A sensation is defined in terms of its attributes. One psychologist will state with readiness that the attributes of a visual sensation are *quality, extension, duration,* and *intensity.* Another will add *clearness.* Still another that of *order.* I doubt if any one psychologist can draw up a set of statements describing what he means by sensation which will be agreed to by three other psychologists of different training. Turn for a moment to the question of the number of isolable sensations. Is there an extremely large number of color sensations—or only four, red, green, yellow and blue? Again, yellow, while psychologically simple, can be obtained by superimposing red and green spectral rays upon the same diffusing surface! If, on the other hand, we say that every just noticeable difference in the spectrum is a simple sensation, and that every just noticeable increase in the white value of a given color gives simple sensations, we are forced to admit that the number is so large and the conditions for obtaining them so complex that the concept of sensation is unusable, either for the purpose of analysis or that of synthesis. Titchener, who has fought the most valiant fight in this country for a psychology based upon introspection, feels that these differences of opinion as to the number of sensations and their attributes; as to whether there are relations (in the sense of elements) and on the many others which seem to be fundamental in every attempt at analysis, are perfectly natural in the present undeveloped state of psychology. While it is admitted that every growing science is full of unanswered questions, surely only those who are wedded to the system as we now have it, who have fought and suffered for it, can confidently believe that there will ever be any greater uniformity than there is now in the answers we have to such questions. I firmly believe that two hundred years from now, unless the introspective method is discarded, psychology will still be divided on the question as to whether auditory sensations have the quality of "extension," whether intensity is an attribute which can be applied to color, whether there is a difference in "texture" between image and sensation and upon many hundreds of others of like character.

The condition in regard to other mental processes is just as chaotic. Can image type be experimentally tested and verified? Are recondite thought processes dependent mechanically upon imagery at all? Are psychologists agreed upon what feeling is? One states that feelings are attitudes. Another finds them to be groups of organic sensations possessing a certain solidarity. Still another and larger group finds them to be new elements correlative with and ranking equally with sensations.

My psychological quarrel is not with the systematic and structural psychologist alone. The last fifteen years have seen the growth of what is called functional psychology. This type of psychology decries the use of elements in the static sense of the structuralists. It throws emphasis upon the biological significance of conscious processes instead of upon the analysis of conscious states into introspectively isolable elements. I have done my best to understand the difference between functional psychology and structural psychology. Instead of clarity, confusion grows upon me. The terms sensation, perception, affection, emotion, volition are used as much by the functionalist as by the structuralist. The addition of the word "process" ("mental act as a whole," and like terms are frequently met) after each serves in some way to remove the corpse of "content" and to leave "function" in its stead. Surely if these concepts are elusive when looked at from a content standpoint, they are still more deceptive when viewed from the angle of function, and especially so when function is obtained by the introspection method. It is rather interesting that no functional psychologist has carefully distinguished between "perception" (and this is true of the other psychological terms as well) as employed by the systematist, and "perceptual process" as used in functional psychology. It seems illogical and hardly fair to criticize the psychology which the systematist gives us, and then to utilize his terms without carefully showing the changes in meaning which are to be attached to them. I was greatly surprised some time ago when I opened Pillsbury's book and saw psychology defined as the "science of behavior." A still more recent text states that psychology is the "science of mental behavior." When I saw these promising statements I thought, now surely we will have texts based upon different lines. After a few pages the science of behavior is dropped and one finds the conventional treatment of sensation, perception, imagery, etc., along with certain shifts in emphasis and additional facts which serve to give the author's personal imprint.

I believe we can write a psychology, define it as Pillsbury, and never go back upon our definition: never use the terms consciousness, mental states, mind, content, introspectively verifiable, imagery, and the like. . . . It can be done in terms of stimulus and response, in terms of habit formation, habit integrations and the like. Furthermore, I believe that it is really worth while to make this attempt now.

The psychology which I should attempt to build up would take as a starting point, first, the observable fact that organisms, man and animal alike, do adjust themselves to their environment by means of hereditary and habit equipments. These adjustments may be very adequate or they may be so inadequate that the organism barely maintains its existence; secondly, that certain stimuli lead the organisms to make the responses. In a system of psychology completely worked out, given the response the stimuli can be predicted; given the stimuli the response can be predicted. Such a set of statements is crass and raw in the extreme, as all such generalizations must be. Yet they are hardly more raw and less realizable than the ones which appear in the psychology texts of the day. I possibly might illustrate my point better by choosing an everyday problem which anyone is likely to meet in the course of his work. Some time ago I was called upon to make a study of certain species of birds. Until I went to Tortugas I had never seen these birds alive. When I reached there I found the animals doing certain things: some of the acts seemed to work peculiarly well in such an environment, while others seemed to be unsuited to their type of life. I first studied the responses of the group as a whole and later those of individuals. In order to understand more thoroughly the relation between what was habit and what was hereditary in these responses, I took the young birds and reared them. In this way I was able to study the order of appearance of hereditary adjustments and their complexity, and later the beginnings of habit formation. My efforts in determining the stimuli which called forth such adjustments were crude indeed. Consequently my attempts to control behavior and to produce responses at will did not meet with much success. Their food and water, sex and other social relations, light and temperature conditions were all beyond control in a field study. I did find it possible to control their reactions in a measure by using the nest and egg (or young) as stimuli. It is not necessary in this paper to develop further how such a study should be carried out and how work of this kind must be supplemented by carefully controlled laboratory experiments. Had I been called upon to examine the natives of some of the Australian tribes, I should have gone about my task in the same way. I should have found the problem more difficult: the types of responses called forth by physical stimuli would have been more varied, and the number of effective stimuli larger. I should have had to determine the social setting of their lives in a far more careful way. These savages would be more influenced by the responses of each other than was the case with the birds. Furthermore, habits would have been more complex and the influences of past habits upon the present responses would have appeared more clearly. Finally, if I had been called upon to work out the psychology of the educated European, my problem would have required several lifetimes. But in the one I have at my disposal I should have followed the same general line of attack. In the main, my desire in all such work is to gain an accurate knowledge of adjustments and the stimuli calling them forth. My final reason for this is to learn general and particular methods by which I may control behavior. My goal is not "the description and explanation of states of consciousness as such," nor that of obtaining such proficiency in mental gymnastics that I can immediately lay hold of a state of consciousness and say, "this, as a whole, consists of gray sensation number 350, of such and such extent, occurring in conjunction with the sensation of cold of a certain intensity; one of pressure of a certain intensity and extent," and so on *ad infinitum*. If psychology would follow the plan I suggest, the educator, the physician, the jurist and the business man could utilize our data in a practical way, as soon as we are able, experimentally, to obtain them. Those who have occasion to apply psychological principles practically would find no need to complain as they do at the present time. Ask any physician or jurist today whether scientific psychology plays a practical part in his daily routine and you will hear him deny that the psychology of the laboratories finds a place in his scheme of work. I think the criticism is extremely just. One of the earliest conditions which made me dissatisfied with psychology was the feeling that there was no realm of application for the principles which were being worked out in content terms.

What gives me hope that the behaviorist's position is a defensible one is the fact that those branches of psychology which have already partially withdrawn from the parent, experimental psychology, and which are consequently less dependent upon introspection are today in a most flourishing condition. Experimental pedagogy, the psychology of drugs, the psychology of advertising, legal psychology, the psychology of tests, and psychopathology are all vigorous growths. These are sometimes wrongly called "practical" or "applied" psychology. Surely there was never a worse misnomer. In the future there may grow up vocational bureaus which really apply psychology. At present these fields are truly scientific and are in search of broad generalizations which will lead to the control of human behavior. For example, we find out by experimentation whether a series of stanzas may be acquired more readily if the whole is learned at once, or whether it is more advantageous to learn each stanza separately and then pass to the succeeding. We do not attempt to apply our findings. The application of this principle is purely voluntary on the part of the teacher. In the psychology of drugs we may show the effect upon behavior of certain doses of caffeine. We may reach the conclusion that caffeine has a good effect upon the speed and accuracy of work. But these are general principles. We leave it to the individual as to whether the results of our tests shall be applied or not. Again, in legal testimony, we test the effects of recency upon the reliability of a witness's report. We test the accuracy of the report with respect to moving objects, stationary objects, color, etc. It depends upon the judicial machinery of the country to decide whether these facts are ever to be applied. For a "pure" psychologist to say that he is not interested in the questions raised in these divisions of the science because they relate indirectly to the application of psychology shows, in the first place, that he fails to understand the scientific aim in such problems, and secondly, that he is not interested in a psychology which concerns itself with human life. The only fault I have to find with these disciplines is that much of their material is stated in terms of introspection, whereas a statement in terms of objective results would be far more valuable. There is no reason why appeal should ever be made to consciousness in any of them. Or why introspective data should ever be sought during the experimentation, or published in the results. In experimental pedagogy especially one can see the desirability of keeping all of the results on a purely objective plane. If this is done, work there on the human being will be comparable directly with the work upon animals. For example, at Hopkins, Mr. Ulrich has obtained certain results upon the distribution of effort in learning—using rats as subjects. He is prepared to give comparative results upon the effect of having an animal work at the problem once per day, three times per day, and five times per day. Whether it is advisable to have the animal learn only one problem at a time or to learn three abreast. We need to have similar experiments made upon man, but we care as little about his "conscious processes" during the conduct of the experiment as we care about such processes in the rats.

I am more interested at the present moment in trying to show the necessity for maintaining uniformity in experimental procedure and in the method of stating results in both human and animal work, than in developing any ideas I may have upon the changes which are certain to come in the scope of human psychology. Let us consider for a moment the subject of the range of stimuli to which animals respond. I shall speak first of the work upon vision in animals. We put our animal in a situation where he will respond (or learn to respond) to one of two monochromatic lights. We feed him at the one (positive) and punish him at the other (negative). In a short time the animal learns to go to the light at which he is fed. At this point questions arise which I may phrase in two ways: I may choose the psychological way and say "does the animal see these two lights as I do, i.e., as two distinct colors, or does he see them as two grays differing in brightness, as does the totally color blind?" Phrased by the behaviorist, it would read as follows: "Is my animal responding upon the basis of the difference in intensity between the two stimuli, or upon the difference in wave-lengths?" He nowhere thinks of the animal's response in terms of his own experiences of colors and grays. He wishes to establish the fact whether wave-length is a factor in that animal's adjustment. If so, what wave-lengths are effective and what differences in wave-length must be maintained in the different regions to afford bases for differential responses? If wave-length is not a factor in adjustment he wishes to know what difference in intensity will serve as a basis for response, and whether that same difference will suffice throughout the spectrum. Furthermore, he wishes to test whether the animal can respond to wave-lengths which do not affect the human eye. He is as much interested in comparing the rat's spectrum with that of the chick as in comparing it with man's. The point of view when the various sets of comparisons are made does not change in the slightest.

However we phrase the question to ourselves, we take our animal after the association has been formed and then introduce certain control experiments which enable us to return answers to the questions just raised. But there is just as keen a desire on our part to test man under the same conditions, and to state the results in both cases in common terms.

The man and the animal should be placed as nearly as possible under the same experimental conditions. Instead of feeding or punishing the human subject, we should ask him to respond by setting a second apparatus until standard and control offered no basis for a differential response. Do I lay myself open to the charge here that I am using introspection? My reply is not at all; that while I might very well feed my human subject for a right choice and punish him for a wrong one and thus produce the response if the subject could give it, there is no need of going to extremes even on the platform I suggest. But be it understood that I am merely using this second method as an abridged behavior method. We can go just as far and reach just as dependable results by the longer method as by the abridged. In many cases the direct and typically human method cannot be safely used. Suppose, for example, that I doubt the accuracy of the setting of the control instrument, in the above experiment, as I am very likely to do if I suspect a defect in vision? It is hopeless for me to get his introspective report. He will say: "There is no difference in sensation, both are reds, identical in quality." But suppose I confront him with the standard and the control and so arrange conditions that he is punished if he responds to the "control" but not with the standard. I interchange the positions of the standard and the control at will and force him to attempt to differentiate the one from the other. If he can learn to make the adjustment even after a large number of trials it is evident that the two stimuli do afford the basis for a differential response. Such a method may sound nonsensical, but I firmly believe we will have to resort increasingly to just such a method where we have reason to distrust the language method.

There is hardly a problem in human vision which is not also a problem in animal vision: I mention the limits of the spectrum, threshold values, absolute and relative, flicker, Talbot's law, Weber's law, field of vision, the Purkinje phenomenon, etc. Every one is capable of being worked out by behavior methods. Many of them are being worked out at the present time.

I feel that all the work upon the senses can be consistently carried forward along the lines I have suggested here for vision. Our results will, in the end, give an excellent picture of what each organ stands for in the way of function. The anatomist and the physiologist may take our data and show, on the one hand, the structures which are responsible for these responses, and, on the other, the physico-chemical relations which are necessarily involved (physiological chemistry of nerve and muscle) in these and other reactions.

The situation in regard to the study of memory is hardly different. Nearly all of the memory methods in actual use in the laboratory today yield the type of results I am arguing for. A certain series of nonsense syllables or other material is presented to the human subject. What should receive the emphasis are the rapidity of the habit formation, the errors, peculiarities in the form of the curve, the persistence of the habit so formed, the relation of such habits to those formed when more complex material is used, etc. Now such results are taken down with the subject's introspection. The experiments are made for the purpose of discussing the mental machinery involved in learning, in recall, recollection and forgetting, and not for the purpose of seeking the human being's way of shaping his responses to meet the problems in the terribly complex environment into which he is thrown, nor for that of showing the similarities and differences between man's methods and those of other animals.

The situation is somewhat different when we come to a study of the more complex forms of behavior, such as imagination, judgment, reasoning, and conception. At present the only statements we have of them are in content terms. Our minds have been so warped by the fifty-odd years which have been devoted to the study of states of consciousness that we can envisage these problems only in one way. We should meet the situation squarely and say that we are not able to carry forward investigations along all of these lines by the behavior methods which are in use at the present time. In extenuation I should like to call attention to the paragraph above where I made the point that the introspective method itself has reached a *cul-de-sac* with respect to them. The topics have become so threadbare from much handling that they may well be put away for a time. As our methods become better developed it will be possible to undertake investigations of more and more complex forms of behavior. Problems which are now laid aside will again become imperative, but they can be viewed as they arise from a new angle and in more concrete settings.

Will there be left over in psychology a world of pure psychics, to use Yerkes' term? I confess I do not know. The plans which I most favor for psychology lead practically to the ignoring of consciousness in the sense that that term is used by psychologists today. I have virtually denied that this realm of psychics is open to experimental investigation. I don't wish to go further into the problem at present because it leads inevitably over into metaphysics. If you will grant the behaviorist the right to use consciousness in the same way that other natural scientists employ it—that is, without making consciousness a special object of observation—you have granted all that my thesis requires.

In concluding, I suppose I must confess to a deep bias on these questions. I have devoted nearly twelve years to experimentation on animals. It is natural that such a one should drift into a theoretical position which is in harmony with his experimental work. Possibly I have put up a straw man and have been fighting that. There may be no absolute lack of harmony between the position outlined here and that of functional psychology. I am inclined to think, however, that the two positions cannot be easily harmonized. Certainly the position I advocate is weak enough at present and can be attacked from many standpoints. Yet when all this is admitted I still feel that the considerations which I have urged should have a wide influence upon the type of psychology which is to be developed in the future. What we need to do is to start work upon psychology, making *behavior*, not *consciousness*, the objective point of our attack. Certainly there are enough problems in the control of behavior to keep us all working many lifetimes without ever allowing us time to think of consciousness *an sich*. Once launched in the undertaking, we will find ourselves in a short time as far divorced from an introspective psychology as the psychology of the present time is divorced from faculty psychology.

THE REACTION TO WATSON'S PROGRAM

 Watson's vigorous attack on the old psychology and his call for a new approach was a stirring appeal. Consider the major points. Psychology was to be the science of behavior, not the introspective study of consciousness—a purely objective experimental branch of natural science. Both human and animal behavior would be investigated. The new psychology would discard all mentalistic concepts and use only behavior concepts such as stimulus and response. The goal of psychology would be the prediction and control of behavior.

As we have discussed, these points did not originate with Watson. Objective experimental methods had been used for some time, and functional concepts had been influential, indeed dominant, in America. Research on animal learning had begun to yield data applicable to human learning, and objective tests had been developed and used with some success to predict and control behavior. Even Watson's definition of psychology as the science of behavior had been anticipated.

Thus, Watson's basic issues were not new. What was unique and provocative about his program was what he proposed to eliminate from psychology—the mind and consciousness, mentalistic concepts, speculation about what might be occurring in the brain, and the use of introspection. The ideas were "a breath of fresh air, clearing away the musty accumulation of the centuries" (R. I. Watson, 1978, p. 461).

We noted earlier, however, that Watson's revolution did not succeed immediately. The first published response to Watson's 1913 article was by Mary Whiton Calkins, who disagreed with his rejection of introspection. She reflected the opinion of many psychologists who thought that certain kinds of psychological processes could be studied only by introspection. The argument persisted for several years into the 1920s, and the rhetoric often became heated. Margaret Floy Washburn went so far as to call Watson an "enemy" of psychology (Samelson, 1981).

We are not suggesting that there was a sudden outpouring of attacks on Watson's views. At first, behaviorism received relatively little attention in the professional journals. Support was growing quietly, however, primarily among younger psychologists. By the 1920s, most universities were offering courses in behaviorism, and the word "behaviorist" was appearing in the titles of journal articles. An opponent of behaviorism, William McDougall, was sufficiently worried about these developments to issue a warning about the "flourishing" of behaviorism (Samelson, 1980a).

Behaviorism did succeed, of course, but it did so slowly. The revolution Watson called for was a long time in coming. When it finally arrived, his was not the only form of behaviorism available.

THE METHODS OF BEHAVIORISM

We have seen that when scientific psychology began, it was eager to ally itself with the older, well-established natural science of physics. The new psychology consistently tried to adapt the methods of the natural sciences to its own needs. In no previous form of psychology, however, was this appeal to physics as strong as it was in Watsonian behaviorism. The distinction made by Wundt between mediate and immediate experience—the first yielding the data of physics and the second the data of psychology—was abolished at one stroke.

Under Watson, the data of physics and of psychology were one and the same, that is,

> bodies in motion. Applying this precept to psychology dictated a restriction of concern to publicly observable behaviours. Thus, that behaviour alone is the proper subject matter for psychology was indicated by the example of successful sciences as well as by the example of what was defined as an unsuccessful one, Wundtian introspective psychology. (Mackenzie, 1977, p. 14)

Hence, Watson argued that psychology must restrict itself to the data of the natural sciences, to what can be observed—behavior. Therefore, only the most truly objective methods of investigation were admissible in the behaviorist's laboratory. Watson stated explicitly the methods to be used in research: (1) observation, with and without the use of instruments, (2) testing methods, (3) the verbal report method, and (4) the conditioned reflex method.

The method of *observation*, self-explanatory and fundamental, is a necessary basis for the other methods. Objective *testing methods* were already in use, but Watson proposed that test results be treated as samples of behavior, not as measures of mental qualities. To Watson, a test did not measure intelligence or personality. Rather, it measured the responses the subject made to the stimulus situation of the test and nothing more.

The *verbal report* method is unique to Watson's system and deserves extra comment, indeed perhaps justification. Because Watson was so violently opposed to introspection, his use of verbal reporting in the laboratory has been regarded by some as a questionable compromise whereby he let introspection in the back door after having vigorously thrown it out the front. His system is particularly sensitive to this criticism.

Let us consider why Watson opposed introspection. In addition to the suggestion that he was not good at it, there is the fact that introspection could not be used for animal research unless one accepted Romanes's technique of introspection by analogy, which a behaviorist could not do. Also, Watson distrusted the accuracy of introspection. If highly trained introspectionists could not agree on what they had observed, Watson asked, how was psychology to progress? More fundamental was the argument that a behaviorist could not tolerate in the laboratory anything that could not be objectively observed. Watson wanted to deal only with tangibles, and he disagreed with the introspectionists' pretensions of reporting on occurrences within an organism that could not be verified by observation.

In spite of his opposition to introspection, Watson could not ignore the work in psychophysics, which had made use of introspection. He suggested, therefore, that because speech reactions are objectively observable, they are as meaningful to the behaviorist as any other type of motor reaction.

> Now what can we observe? We can observe *behavior—what the organism does or says.* And let us point out at once: that *saying* is doing—that is, *behaving.* Speaking overtly or to ourselves (thinking) is just as objective a type of behavior as baseball. (J. B. Watson, 1930, p. 6)[2]

The use of the verbal report method in behaviorism was a concession widely debated by Watson's critics, who contended that Watson was proposing merely semantic changes, not a genuine alteration of research procedures. We note that Watson (1914) considered verbal report to be an "inexact" method and not a satisfactory substitute for more objective methods of observation. He wanted to limit its use to those situations in which it was capable of verification, for example, in observing differences in tones. Unverifiable verbal reports, such as imageless thoughts or comments about feeling states, were ruled out. However, he never indicated precisely how he would restrict the use of verbal report.

The most important research method of the behaviorists—the *conditioned reflex method*—was not adopted until 1915, two years after behaviorism's formal beginning. Conditioning methods were being used before the advent of behaviorism, but their adoption by American psychologists had been limited. Watson was largely responsible for their subsequent widespread application in American psychological research. In later writings he acknowledged his debt to Pavlov and Bekhterev for the conditioning method.

Watson wrote of conditioning in terms of "stimulus substitution." A response, he said, is conditioned when it becomes attached or connected to a stimulus other than the one that originally aroused it. (The salivating of Pavlov's dogs to the sound of a bell instead of to the sight of food is a conditioned response.)

Watson seized upon this approach because it provided an objective method of analyzing behavior, that is, of reducing behavior to its elementary units: the *stimulus–response* (S–R) bonds. All behavior, he argued, could be reduced to these elements, providing a method for laboratory investigation of complex human behavior.

---

[2] This and all subsequent quotations credited to J. B. Watson, 1930, are from *Behaviorism* by John B. Watson, reprinted by permission of W. W. Norton & Company, Inc. Copyright 1924, 1925, 1930 by W. W. Norton & Company, Inc. Copyright renewed 1952, 1953, 1958, by John B. Watson.

Thus, Watson continued in the atomistic and mechanistic tradition established by the British empiricists and used by the structuralists. Psychologists must study human behavior in the same way physical scientists study the universe, by breaking it down into the component elements or atoms.

This exclusive focus on the use of objective methods and the elimination of introspection meant a change in the nature and role of the human subject in the psychological laboratory. In Wundt's approach and Titchener's structuralist system, subjects (reagents) were both observer and observed, that is, they observed their own conscious experience. As such, their role was much more important than that of the experimenter. In behaviorism subjects assumed a less important role. They no longer observed but instead were observed by the experimenter. The true observer (the experimenter) set up the conditions of the experiment and then observed how the subjects responded to these conditions. Thus, human subjects were demoted in status; they no longer observed but merely behaved. And almost anyone can behave—children, the mentally ill, animals. This viewpoint reinforced psychology's image or model of the human being as "a stimulus–response machine: you put a stimulus in one of the slots, and out comes a packet of reactions" (Burt, 1962, p. 232).

Initially, Watson's arguments for the use of only objective methods (the so-called methodological behaviorism) seemed to be a major advance. Retrospective analysis, however, suggests that the behaviorists contributed little because objective methodology had characterized psychology since its beginnings as a science. Studies in psychophysics, memory, and conditioning had applied objective methods. Therefore, the behaviorists' contributions consisted more of extending and refining existing methods than of developing new ones.

THE SUBJECT MATTER OF BEHAVIORISM

Watson's conceptual behaviorism (the spirit or basic notion of behaviorism) has proved to be of greater importance for psychology than his methodological behaviorism. The primary subject matter or data must always be items of behavior: muscular movements or glandular secretions. Watson wrote that these responses constitute evidence of the organism's ability to react in discriminating fashion to its environment. Psychology, as the science of behavior, must deal only with acts that can be described objectively in terms such as stimulus and response, habit formation, and habit integration. All human and animal behavior can be reported in this way without resorting to mentalistic concepts and terminology. Through the objective study of behavior, behaviorist psychology can fulfill its aim of predicting the response given the stimulus, and predicting the antecedent stimulus given the response. Human and animal behavior can be effectively understood, predicted, and controlled by reducing behavior to the level of stimulus and response.

Despite the goal of reducing behavior to stimulus–response units, Watson argued that behaviorism deals with the overall behavior of the whole organism. Although a response can be something as simple as a knee jerk or other reflex, it can also be much more complex; in this case the term "act" is applied. Watson considered response acts to include such things as taking food, writing a book, playing baseball, or building a house. Thus, an act involves the organism's response through movement in space—

talking, reaching, walking, and the like. Watson seems to have thought of response in terms of accomplishing some result in the environment rather than as an assemblage of muscular elements—that is, in more molar than molecular terms. Nevertheless, these behavioral acts, no matter how complex, can be reduced to lower-level motor or glandular responses.

Responses are classified in two ways: learned or unlearned, and explicit or implicit. Watson considered it important for behaviorism to distinguish between innate responses and those that are learned, and to discover for the latter the laws of learning.

Explicit responses are overt and therefore directly observable. Implicit responses, such as visceral movements, glandular secretions, and nerve impulses, take place inside the organism. Although such movements are not overt, they are nonetheless items of behavior. In introducing this notion of implicit behavior, Watson modified his initial requirement that the subject matter of psychology be *actually* observable and said instead that everything must be *potentially* observable. The movements or responses occurring within the organism are theoretically observable through the use of instrumentation.

The exciting stimuli, like the responses with which the behaviorist deals, may be complex. A stimulus may be something relatively simple, such as light waves striking the retina, but it can also be a physical object in the environment, or a larger situation (a constellation of specific stimuli). Just as the constellation of responses involved in an act can be reduced to particular responses, so the *stimulus situation* can be resolved into its specific component stimuli.

Thus, behaviorism deals with the behavior of the whole organism in relation to its environment. Specific laws of behavior can be worked out through the analysis of the total stimulus and response complexes into their more elemental stimulus and response segments. This analysis was not to be as detailed as that performed by the physiologist in determining the structure and organization of the central nervous system. Because of the inaccessibility of the "mystery box" (Watson's term for the brain), Watson had little interest in cortical functioning. Behavior, he believed, concerned the total organism and could not be restricted to the nervous system alone. He focused on larger units of behavior—the whole response of the organism to a given situation.

In both subject matter and methodology the new psychology of John B. Watson was an attempt to construct a science that was free of mentalistic notions and subjective methods, a science as objective as physics.

SPECIFIC TOPICS

We consider here Watson's treatment of some of the traditional topics in psychology: instinct, learning, emotion, and thought. Like all systematic theorists, Watson developed his psychology in accordance with his fundamental theses. All areas of behavior were to be treated in objective, stimulus–response terms.

Instinct

Initially, Watson accepted the role of instincts in behavior. In his first book, *Behavior: An Introduction to Comparative Psychology* (1914), he described in detail 11 instincts, including one dealing with random behaviors. Earlier, he had studied the instinctive behaviors of terns in the Dry Tortugas Islands off the Florida Keys with Karl Lashley, a student at Johns Hopkins University. Harlow reported that Lashley later told him that the expedition to the Dry Tortugas was cut short when he and Watson ran out of cigarettes and whiskey. "Had Watson and Lashley only taken more cigarettes and whiskey to the Dry Tortugas, the history of psychology might have been very different" (Harlow, 1969, p. 26).

By 1925, however, Watson had changed his position and ruled out the concept of instinct. All those aspects of human behavior that seem instinctive, he argued, are in reality socially conditioned responses. With the view that learning is the key to understanding the development of human behavior, Watson became an extreme environmen-

Instinct =socially conditioned responses

Watson tests the grasping reflex of an infant.

talist. He went beyond the denial of instincts and refused to admit that there were inherited capacities, temperaments, or talents of any kind. Those things that seemed inherited, he wrote,

> depend on training that goes on mainly in the cradle. The behaviorist would *not* say: "He inherits his father's capacity or talent for being a fine swordsman." He would say: "This child certainly has his father's slender build of body, the same type of eyes. . . ." And he would go on to say: "—and his father is very fond of him. He put a tiny sword into his hand when he was a year of age, and in all their walks he talks sword play, attack and defense, the code of duelling and the like." A certain type of structure, plus early training—*slanting*—accounts for adult performance. (J. B. Watson, 1930, p. 94)

This emphasis on the overwhelming influence of the environment, with its corollary that one can train children to be whatever one wants them to be, was one reason for Watson's large public following.

Learning

According to Watson, there are no instincts or inherited capacities. The adult is a product of childhood conditioning. Therefore, learning plays a major role in behaviorism. Watson's views on learning progressed to incorporate conditioning. In his 1913 article there is no mention of conditioning, and *Behavior* (1914) gives but slight emphasis to Pavlov's conditioning experiments. Indeed, Watson expressed doubt that the method could be used with primates.

In his 1915 presidential address to the American Psychological Association, however, Watson suggested that the conditioned reflex method should displace introspection. From that time, conditioning became an important research method for the behaviorists. It is surprising that, in spite of his enthusiasm for classical conditioning, Watson failed to recognize the importance of Pavlov's law of reinforcement and its similarity to Thorndike's law of effect. Watson never developed a satisfactory theory of learning, and conceptually seemed to belong with the antiquated pre-Thorndikian associationists. Thus, although he accepted conditioning principles and used them in his research, he continued to cling to a law of exercise and to emphasize frequency and recency as primary factors in learning.

Emotion

Emotions, to Watson, were simply bodily responses to specific stimuli. The stimulus (the presence of danger, for instance) produces internal body changes and the appropriate learned overt responses. This notion implies no conscious perception of the emotion or mass of sensations from the internal organs. Each emotion involves its particular pattern of changes in the general body mechanism, particularly in the visceral and glandular systems. Although Watson recognized that all emotional responses involve overt bodily movements, the internal responses predominate in his conception. Emotion, then, is a form of implicit behavior in which the hidden visceral responses are evident, at least to some extent, as physical changes in, for example, pulse rate, breathing, or blushing.

Watson's theory of emotion is less complex than that of William James, discussed in Chapter 7. In James's theory, the bodily changes immediately follow the perception of the exciting stimulus, and the feeling of these bodily changes is the emotion. Watson was critical of this position and wrote that "James gave to the psychology of the emotions a setback from which it has only recently begun to recover" (1930, p. 140). Discarding the conscious process of perception of the situation and the feeling state, he claimed that emotions can be understood in terms of the objective stimulus situation, the overt bodily response, and the internal visceral changes.

A famous study is the investigation of the stimuli that produce emotional responses in infants. Watson described what he believed to be the three fundamental emotions—fear, rage, and love. Fear is produced by loud sounds and sudden loss of support, rage by the hampering of body movement, and love by the stroking of the skin and by rocking and patting. Watson also found characteristic reaction patterns to these stimuli. He believed that fear, rage, and love are the only unlearned emotional responses. The remaining human emotional responses are built up from these three emotions through the process of conditioning. The basic emotional responses may become attached, through conditioning, to environmental stimuli that were not originally capable of eliciting them.

Watson experimentally demonstrated this theory in his study of an 11-month-old infant, Albert, who was conditioned to fear a white rat, something he had not feared before the conditioning trials (Watson & Rayner, 1920). The fear was established by making a loud noise (striking a steel bar with a hammer) behind Albert's head whenever the rat was presented to him. In a short time the mere sight of the rat produced signs of fear and discomfort in the child. Watson demonstrated that this conditioned fear could be generalized to similar stimuli, such as a rabbit, a white fur coat, and a set of Santa Claus whiskers. Watson believed that adult fears, aversions, and anxieties are likewise conditioned in early childhood.

The Albert study has never been successfully replicated. Watson described his research as a "preliminary exposition," a pilot study, and psychologists have since noted serious flaws in the methodology. Nevertheless, the results of the Albert study have come to be accepted as scientific evidence. They are cited in virtually every introductory psychology textbook (usually incorrectly) and are rarely questioned (Harris, 1979; Samelson, 1980b).

Although Albert may have been conditioned to fear the objects mentioned, he was no longer available as a subject for Watson to attempt to remove or eliminate those fears. Not long after this experiment Watson left academics and so did not pursue the problem. Some time later, when he was working in the advertising business, he gave a talk to a New York City audience on his research with young Albert. Among the listeners was Mary Cover Jones, a former student of Washburn's at Vassar. Watson's remarks sparked her interest, and she wondered whether the conditioning technique could be used to remove children's fears, a sort of "unconditioning" or "reconditioning" approach (Logan, 1980). She got her former Vassar classmate, Rosalie Rayner Watson, to introduce her to Watson, and then undertook a study that has become another classic in the history of psychology (Jones, 1924).

The subject was another child, Peter, who already showed a fear of rabbits; his fear had not been conditioned in the laboratory. While the child was eating, the rabbit was

Mary Cover Jones anticipated modern behavior therapy with her experiments on reconditioning techniques.

brought into the room, but kept at a distance great enough so as not to elicit the fear response. The rabbit was brought progressively closer, always while the child was eating. Eventually the child could handle the rabbit without fear. Generalized fear responses to similar objects could also be eliminated by this procedure, which may be seen as the first example of behavior therapy, performed almost 50 years before the technique became popular.

Watson's behaviorist approach to the emotions and his interest in the physiological changes that accompany emotional behavior stimulated research on emotional development in children and on the reaction patterns for the specific emotions.

Thought

Until the advent of behaviorism, the traditional view of the thought processes was the "centralist" theory of thinking, which held that thought processes occur in the brain "so faintly that no neural impulse passes out over the motor nerve to the muscle, hence no response takes place in the muscles and glands" (J. B. Watson, 1930, p. 239). According to this thesis, thought processes, because they occur in the absence of muscular movements, are not accessible to observation and experimentation. Thought is regarded as intangible, something exclusively mental with no physical referents. The concept of image used by the structuralists is an example of this viewpoint.

Watson's *peripheral theory of thinking*, perhaps his most widely known theory, takes issue with the older notion and attempts to reduce thinking to nothing more than implicit motor behavior. Watson argued that thinking, like all other aspects of human functioning, must be sensorimotor behavior of some sort. He reasoned that the behavior of thinking is implicit speech movements. Verbal thinking is reduced to subvocal talking that involves muscular habits learned in overt speech. These muscular habits become inaudible as the child grows up.

> The child talks incessantly when alone. At three he even plans the day *aloud*, as my own ear placed outside the key hole of the nursery door has very often confirmed. Soon society in the form of nurse and parents steps in. "Don't talk aloud—daddy and mother are not always talking to themselves." Soon the overt speech dies down to whispered speech and a good lip reader can still read what the child thinks of the world and of himself. Some individuals never even make this concession to society. When alone they talk aloud to themselves. A still larger number never go beyond even the whispering stage when alone. Watch people reading on the street car; peep through the key hole sometime when individuals not too highly socialized are just sitting and thinking. But the great majority of people pass on to the third stage under the influence of social pressure constantly exerted. "Quit whispering to yourself," and "Can't you even read without moving your lips?" and the like are constant mandates. Soon the process is forced to take place behind the lips. Behind these walls you can call the biggest bully the worst name you can think of without even smiling. (J. B. Watson, 1930, pp. 240–241)

After we learn to talk (by conditioning), thought becomes simply talking silently to ourselves. Watson suggested that the focal points for much of this implicit behavior are the muscles of the larynx and the tongue. Watson's term for thinking was "laryngeal habits"; initially, the larynx was considered to be the organ of thought. In addition to these laryngeal habits, language or thought is mediated by gestures, frowns, and shrugs, which symbolize more overt reactions to situations.

One obvious source of corroboration for Watson's hypothesis is that most of us are aware that we often talk to ourselves while thinking. This is inadmissible evidence, however, because it is purely introspective, and Watson could hardly use introspection to support a tenet of behaviorism. Behaviorism required objective evidence of these implicit speech movements, so attempts were made to record movement in the tongue and larynx during thought. Such measurements revealed slight movements some of the time that the subjects were thinking. Similarly, measurements taken from the hands and fingers of deaf-mutes revealed movement some of the time during thought. In spite of the inability to secure more supportive results in these studies, Watson was convinced that implicit speech movements existed and that their demonstration awaited only the development of more sophisticated instrumentation.

WATSON'S POPULAR APPEAL

Watson's bold pronouncements won him a large following among the lay public. Why this public acclaim? Surely people were not fascinated because some psychologists practiced introspection and others refuted its use, or because some psychologists pretended to be conscious while others joyously proclaimed that psychology had finally lost its mind, or because there was dispute about whether thinking took place in the head or in the neck. These issues aroused comment among psychologists, but hardly concerned others.

What did stir the public was Watson's call for a world based on scientifically shaped and controlled behavior, free from myths, customs, and conventions. This idea offered hope to people who had become disenchanted with the older guiding creeds. In fervor and faith, behaviorism had many of the aspects of a religion, and large numbers of people flocked to this new cult. "Some behaviorists even read a chapter from Watson's latest book before going to bed each night!" (Sokal, 1981b, p. 61). One of the many articles and books about behaviorism of that time was entitled *The Religion Called Behaviorism* (Berman, 1927), written by an endocrinologist. A young man of 23 read the book and wrote a review of it for a popular literary magazine. That young man, B. F. Skinner, later wrote that "They did not publish [my review] but in writing it I was more or less defining myself for the first time as a behaviorist" (1976, p. 299).

Some of the ferment generated by Watson's ideas can be appreciated from newspaper reviews of *Behaviorism*. *The New York Times* said dramatically, "it marks an epoch in the intellectual history of man" (August 2, 1925); the *New York Herald Tribune* commented, "perhaps this is the most important book ever written. One stands for an instant blinded with a great hope" (June 21, 1925).

The hope stemmed in part from Watson's environmentalist position, as reflected in the following passage:

> Give me a dozen healthy infants, well-formed, and my own specified world to bring them up in and I'll guarantee to take any one at random and train him to become any type of specialist I might select—doctor, lawyer, artist, merchant-chief and, yes, even beggarman and thief, regardless of his talents, penchants, tendencies, abilities, vocations, and race of his ancestors. (1930, p. 104)

Watson's conditioning experiments, such as the study of Albert, persuaded him that emotional disturbances in adults cannot be traced to sex alone, as Freud held. Watson argued that adult problems can be traced instead to conditioned and transferred responses established in infancy and adolescence. If such disturbances were a function of faulty conditioning in childhood, a proper program of childhood conditioning should prevent their emergence. Watson believed that this sort of practical control of infant behavior (and hence of adult behavior) was not only possible but absolutely necessary. He developed a plan for social improvement, a program of experimental ethics, based on the principles of behaviorism.

No one gave him a dozen healthy infants so that he might test his claim, and he admitted that in making it he was going beyond the facts. He noted, however, that those who believed in the predominance of heredity over environment had been arguing their case for thousands of years and still had no real supporting evidence.

The following paragraph from the end of *Behaviorism* reveals some of the fervor with which Watson described his program for living under the banner of behaviorism, and may help to explain why it became a new faith to so many people.

> Behaviorism ought to be a science that prepares men and women for understanding the principles of their own behavior. It ought to make men and women eager to rearrange their own lives, and especially eager to prepare themselves to bring up their own children in a healthy way. I wish I could picture for you what a rich and

wonderful individual we should make of every healthy child if only we could let it shape itself properly and then provide for it a universe in which it could exercise that organization—a universe unshackled by legendary folk-lore of happenings thousands of years ago; unhampered by disgraceful political history; free of foolish customs and conventions which have no significance in themselves, yet which hem the individual in like taut steel bands. I am not asking here for revolution; I am not asking people to go out to some God-forsaken place, form a colony, go naked and live a communal life, nor am I asking for a change to a diet of roots and herbs. I am not asking for "free love." I am trying to dangle a stimulus in front of you, a verbal stimulus which, if acted upon, will gradually change this universe. For the universe will change if you bring up your children, not in the freedom of the libertine, but in behavioristic freedom—a freedom which we cannot even picture in words, so little do we know of it. Will not these children in turn, with their better ways of living and thinking, replace us as society and in turn bring up their children in a still more scientific way, until the world finally becomes a place fit for human habitation? (1930, pp. 303–304)

Watson's program of experimental ethics to replace the older speculative ethics based on religion remained only a hope; it was never carried out. He outlined his plan in brief terms and left it as a framework for future research. As we shall see in Chapter 11, a later behaviorist, B. F. Skinner, formulated a more detailed program for a scientifically shaped utopia that seems to be in the spirit of the one Watson espoused.

An Outbreak of Psychology

Psychology had become a popular subject among the general public during the functionalist reign in the first decade of the twentieth century. Under Watson's influence, however, given his charisma, charm, persuasiveness, and message of hope, Americans were almost overcome with what the humorist Stephen Leacock called an "outbreak" of psychology. A large portion of the American public was convinced by the 1920s that the only path to happiness, health, and prosperity was through psychology (Benjamin, 1986).

Psychological advice columns appeared in newspapers throughout the country. Psychologist Joseph Jastrow's column, "Keeping Mentally Fit," was syndicated in more than 150 daily papers. One Albert Wiggam, who was not a psychologist, produced a column called "Exploring Your Mind." Much of the public agreed with his views.

Men and women never needed psychology so much as they need it today. Young men and women need it in order to measure their own mental traits and capacities with a view to choosing their careers early and wisely . . . businessmen need it to help them select employees; parents and educators need it as an aid in rearing and educating children; all need it in order to secure the highest effectiveness and happiness. You cannot achieve these things in the fullest measure without the new knowledge of your own mind and personality that the psychologists have given us. (Wiggam, 1928, cited in Benjamin, 1986)

Leacock noted that psychology used to be confined to college campuses, where it had no connection with reality and did no visible harm to those who studied it. Now, he wrote in 1924, it appeared that psychology could be used everywhere.

For almost every juncture of life we now call in the services of an expert psychologist as naturally as we send for an emergency plumber. In all our great cities there are

already, or soon will be, signs that read "Psychologist—Open Day and Night."
(Leacock, 1924, cited in Benjamin, 1986)

Psychology was truly epidemic in the United States, and Watson may have done more
than any other individual to help it spread.

A FINAL NOTE

Although Watson's productive career in psychology lasted less than 20 years, he profoundly influenced the course of psychology and his impact compels us to include him
among psychology's leaders. Watson was an effective agent of the *Zeitgeist*, and the times
were changing not only in psychology but in general scientific attitudes as well. The
nineteenth century had witnessed magnificent advances in every branch of science. The
twentieth century promised even more marvels. It was thought that science, if given
enough time, was capable of finding answers to every problem. It was an era in which
idealism was rapidly yielding to a spirit of tough-minded realism. Watson's behaviorist
crusade helped American psychology in its transition from a focus on consciousness
and subjectivism to materialism and objectivism in the study of behavior.

Although Watson's program did not realize its ambitious goals, the behavioristic
orientation in general remained a strong and active force in modern psychology for
decades, and Watson is widely recognized for his founding role. The centennial of his
birth was celebrated in April 1979, the same year as the centennial of the birth of
psychology as a science. A symposium at Watson's alma mater, Furman University,
whose psychology laboratory is named after him, drew psychologists and others from
all over the country. The speakers included B. F. Skinner, whose talk was entitled "What
J. B. Watson Meant to Me."[3]

CRITICISMS OF WATSONIAN BEHAVIORISM

Any systematic program that so blatantly attacks the existing order—indeed, suggests
discarding the earlier version of the truth—and proposes radical and sweeping revisions
is bound to receive criticism. We know that American psychology was already moving
toward greater objectivity when Watsonian behaviorism was formally founded, but not
all psychologists were pleased at the extreme form of objectivity Watson proposed.
Many, including some who supported the objectivity movement, believed that Watson's
system omitted important components of psychology, such as sensory and perceptual
processes.

One of Watson's outstanding opponents was William McDougall (1871–1938), an
English psychologist who came to the United States in 1920. McDougall is recognized
for his instinct theory of behavior. He is also known for the impetus his book, *Introduc-*

[3] Apparently, Watson is remembered less favorably by the residents of his home town, many of whom
"regarded him as an upstart and an atheist who had turned his back on his Southern heritage and Baptist
upbringing" (*Greenville South Carolina News*, April 5, 1979). We are grateful to Cedric A. Larson for this
information.

tion to Social Psychology, gave to the area of social psychology. This book, published in 1908, appeared in 14 editions by 1921. McDougall was an ardent supporter of a number of unpopular causes, including freedom of the will, Nordic superiority, and psychic research.

McDougall's instinct theory states that all human action results from innate tendencies to thought and action. It was well received initially by social scientists, but rapidly lost ground when behaviorism came to the fore. By 1925 Watson had rejected the notion of instincts, and on this issue the two men locked horns.

They met to debate their differences on February 5, 1924, at the Psychology Club in Washington, D.C. Washington was only a small city at that time—some described it as a sleepy Southern town—and the fact that it had a psychology club not affiliated with a university attests to the widespread popularity of psychology. One thousand people attended the debate. Only a few were psychologists because there were only 464 mem-

In a debate with John B. Watson, William McDougall (1871–1938) argued that psychology must study not only behavior but also consciousness.

bers of the American Psychological Association nationwide. Thus, the size of the crowd also reflects the popularity of Watson's behaviorism. The judges of the debate, however, voted in McDougall's favor. Much of the argument was published by Watson and McDougall in 1929 in *The Battle of Behaviorism*.

McDougall began the debate on a falsely optimistic note: "I have an initial advantage over Dr. Watson, an advantage which I feel to be so great as to be unfair; namely, all persons of common-sense will of necessity be on my side from the outset" (Watson & McDougall, 1929, p. 40).

McDougall agreed with Watson that the data of behavior are necessary to the science of psychology, but he argued forcefully that the data of consciousness are equally indispensable. He (and other critics as well) emphasized that psychology must use both kinds of data, a position taken in more recent times by humanistic psychologists.

Without the use of introspection, McDougall asked, how can psychology determine the meaning of a subject's response or the accuracy of speech behavior (verbal report)? How can we know anything of the world of daydreams and fantasies, or understand and appreciate esthetic experiences?

In an eloquent challenge to Watson, McDougall asked how a strict behaviorist would account for the experience of enjoying a concert. McDougall said:

> I come into this hall and see a man on this platform scraping the guts of a cat with hairs from the tail of a horse; and, sitting silently in attitudes of rapt attention, are a thousand persons, who presently break into wild applause. How will the Behaviorist explain these strange incidents? How explain the fact that the vibrations emitted by the cat-gut stimulate all the thousands into absolute silence and quiescence; and the further fact that the cessation of the stimulus seems to be a stimulus to the most frantic activity? Common sense and psychology agree in accepting the explanation that the audience heard the music with keen pleasure, and vented their gratitude and admiration for the artist in shouts and handclappings. But the Behaviorist knows nothing of pleasure and pain, of admiration and gratitude. He has relegated all such "metaphysical entities" to the dust heap, and must seek some other explanation. Let us leave him seeking it. The search will keep him harmlessly occupied for some centuries to come. (Watson & McDougall, 1929, pp. 62–63)[4]

McDougall also questioned Watson's assumption that human behavior is fully determined, that everything we do is the direct result of past experience and can be predicted once the past events are known. Such a psychology leaves no room for free will or freedom of choice.

The issue of whether behavior is predetermined did not, of course, begin with Watson and McDougall. The opposition between advocates of determinism and those of free will is long-standing. Science accepts a determined natural world, whereas some theologies and philosophies accept freedom of the will. Watson belongs in the determinist camp. If all behavior can be interpreted in physical terms, all acts of behavior must be physically predetermined. Watson thus believed that we are not personally responsible for our actions, and this belief has had important social consequences, particularly for the treatment of criminals. According to Watson, such persons should not be punished for their actions, they should be reconditioned.

---

[4]From J. B. Watson and W. McDougall, *The Battle of Behaviorism* (New York: Norton, 1929). Reprinted by permission.

McDougall and others argued that if the determinist position were true—that we have no free will and cannot be held responsible for our actions—then there would be no human striving, exertion, or desire to improve ourselves and our society. No one, he argued, would make any effort to prevent war, alleviate injustice, or achieve other personal or social ideals.

The free will–determinist controversy may never be resolved. A point worth noting is that many determinists, including Watson and B. F. Skinner, have made determined efforts to bring about improvements in the individual and in society.

Mention has already been made of the criticism directed at Watson's admission of verbal report as a method of research. Critics argued that its use was discriminatory, that Watson used it only when it could be verified and rejected it when it could not. But of course that was Watson's point and the point of the entire behaviorist movement: to use only verifiable data.

The attacks on Watsonian behaviorism were many and diverse and were later voiced, in modified form, against the varieties of behaviorism that derived from Watson's work.

The Watson–McDougall debates were held 11 years after behaviorism formally began. McDougall predicted that in a few years Watson's position would disappear without a trace. A few years later, in a postscript to the published version of the debate, McDougall wrote that his forecast had been "too optimistic; it was founded upon a too generous estimate of the intelligence of the American public. . . . Dr. Watson continues, as a prophet of much honor in his own country, to issue his pronouncements" (Watson & McDougall, 1929, pp. 86, 87).

CONTRIBUTIONS OF WATSONIAN BEHAVIORISM

Watson's primary contribution was his advocacy of a completely objective science of behavior. He exerted an enormous influence in rendering psychology more objective in both methods and terminology.

However, although his positions on specific topics have stimulated a great deal of research, Watson's original formulations are no longer useful. Watsonian behaviorism as a separate school has been replaced by newer forms of psychological objectivism that built upon it. Boring said in 1929 that behaviorism was already past its prime as a movement. Because movements depend on protest for their existence and strength, it is an effective tribute to Watsonian behaviorism that only 16 years after its inception, it no longer needed to protest. Watsonian behaviorism had certainly overcome the structuralist position. A graduate student at the University of Wisconsin in 1926, studying under Clark Hull, reported that few of his fellow students had ever heard of Wundt and Titchener (Gengerelli, 1976, p. 10). Objective methodology and terminology have largely become the American psychology, and Watsonian behaviorism died, as have other successful movements, by being incorporated into the main body of thought, where it provided a strong conceptual base for modern psychology.

To some degree, the acceptance of Watsonian behaviorism was a function of the abilities and force of Watson himself. He was a charming and attractive man who expressed his ideas with great enthusiasm, optimism, self-confidence, and clarity. He was a bold and appealing revolutionary who scorned tradition and rejected the current version of psychology. These personal qualities, interacting with the spirit of the times that he reflected so ably, define J. B. Watson as one of psychology's great figures.

SUGGESTED READINGS

Watson

Bergmann, G. (1956). The contributions of John B. Watson. *Psychological Review, 63*, 265–276.

Buckley, K. W. (1982). The selling of a psychologist: John Broadus Watson and the application of behavioral techniques to advertising. *Journal of the History of the Behavioral Sciences, 18*, 207–221.

Creelan, P. G. (1974). Watsonian behaviorism and the Calvinist conscience. *Journal of the History of the Behavioral Sciences, 10*, 95–118.

Jones, M. C. (1974). Albert, Peter, and John B. Watson. *American Psychologist, 29*, 581–583.

Watson, J. B. (1930). *Behaviorism* (rev. ed.). New York: W. W. Norton.

Watson, J. B. (1936). Autobiography. In C. Murchison (Ed.), *A history of psychology in autobiography* (vol. 3, pp. 271–281). Worcester, MA: Clark University Press.

Woodworth, R. S. (1959). John Broadus Watson: 1878–1958. *American Journal of Psychology, 72*, 301–310.

Behaviorism

Bakan, D. (1966). Behaviorism and American urbanization. *Journal of the History of the Behavioral Sciences, 2*, 5–28.

Bode, B. H. (1914). Psychology as a science of behavior. *Psychological Review, 21*, 46–61.

Calkins, M. W. (1921). The truly psychological behaviorism. *Psychological Review, 28*, 1–18.

DeLaguna, G. A. (1919). Emotion and perception from the behaviorist standpoint. *Psychological Review, 26*, 409–427.

Harrell, W., & Harrison, R. (1938). The rise and fall of behaviorism. *Journal of General Psychology, 18*, 367–421.

Harris, B. (1979). Whatever happened to little Albert? *American Psychologist, 34*, 151–160.

Mackenzie, B. D. (1972). Behaviorism and positivism. *Journal of the History of the Behavioral Sciences, 8*, 222–231.

O'Donnell, J. M. (1985). *The origins of behaviorism: American psychology, 1870–1920*. New York: New York University Press.

Samelson, F. (1981). Struggle for scientific authority: The reception of Watson's behaviorism, 1913–1920. *Journal of the History of the Behavioral Sciences, 17*, 399–425.

Watson, J. B., & McDougall, W. (1929). *The battle of behaviorism: An exposition and exposure*. New York: W. W. Norton.

11

Behaviorism: After the Founding

EARLY BEHAVIORISTS

By the 1920s behaviorism seemed to capture the attention and imagination of many American psychologists. However, not everyone in this new generation of behaviorists adopted Watsonian ideas. Some developed their own approaches and were more receptive to divergent views than Watson had been. Although Watson was the founder of behaviorism and its most effective leader for a time, other psychologists who embraced the same general point of view attempted to move in somewhat different directions. We will mention several of these psychologists and then consider the work of more recent psychologists who might appropriately be called *neobehaviorists*.

Edwin B. Holt (1873–1946)

Holt received his Ph.D. at Harvard in 1901 and spent his academic career there and at Princeton. His main influence was in terms of the philosophical framework he provided for behaviorism. His somewhat unorthodox view of behaviorism probably originated in his training as both an experimentalist and a philosopher. Holt did not agree with Watson's complete rejection of consciousness and mental phenomena. He suggested that consciousness be related to epistemological realism, according to which objects exist as perceived even when we are not perceiving them.

Holt believed that consciousness was simply a label given to the process of sensorimotor adjustment to physical objects. To be conscious of an object involved the relation of the sensorimotor aspects of the organism to that object, such as the oculomotor movements necessary to focus clearly on something. Physical objects in the environment have qualities similar to those within consciousness. There were, therefore, physical referents for what Holt called conscious experiencing.

Holt agreed with Watson on the relative unimportance of heredity in shaping human behavior. He believed that our behavior patterns are developed in two ways. The primary way is through learning, which occurs in response to inner or outer motivation. Outer motivation, according to Holt, refers to external forms of stimulation; inner motivation refers to internal needs or drives, such as hunger and thirst. The latter conception anticipated the development of Clark Hull's learning theory, with its emphasis on internal drive reduction as a necessary condition for learning. The second way in which behavior patterns are acquired is through the preservation in adulthood of childhood patterns of behavior.

Holt did not believe that psychology should attempt to reduce behavior to elemental units, whether stimulus–response connections or some other formulation. He wanted to deal with responses on a molar level, as wholes accomplishing some end. He was concerned with behavior on a larger scale, behavior that had both unity and purpose, concepts that Watson could not allow in his behaviorist system.

Holt's unique form of behaviorism enabled him to draw on a variety of sources and to take an interest in problems outside the mainstream of American behaviorism. In one of his books, *The Freudian Wish and Its Place in Ethics* (1915), he attempted to synthesize the major features of behaviorism and psychoanalysis. Perhaps his greatest contribution is his role as a stimulus for a later behaviorist, E. C. Tolman.

Albert P. Weiss (1879–1931)

Weiss was born in Germany and came to the United States when he was very young. He received his Ph.D. in 1916 from the University of Missouri and pursued his career as a behaviorist, primarily studying child development, at Ohio State University. His book, *A Theoretical Basis of Human Behavior* (1925), outlines his program of unabashed behaviorism. He believed that psychology must operate as a natural science. All reference to conscious and mental phenomena had to be eliminated, along with the subjective method of introspection. Anything not accessible to a natural science approach had no place in psychology.

Weiss's behaviorism stressed an extreme form of reductionism that urged psychology to deal only with those elements of matter treated by physics. Thus, all behavior was seen as capable of analysis and reduction to physical–chemical entities. Weiss believed that psychology was actually a branch of physics and as such should not claim a nonphysical entity (consciousness) as its subject matter. We see in Weiss's system an emphasis on biological components of behavior, which are, in turn, reducible to physical elements. If this were his complete system, we might reasonably label him a physiologist and not a psychologist, but there was more. Humans are not only biological, but social as well. Weiss argued that we are a product of both forces, and he coined the term *biosocial* to denote this.

Human organisms are solely biological entities only during infancy, according to Weiss. As we mature and develop, our behavior is shaped and modified by social forces encountered in interaction with other people. The importance of biological forces does not diminish, however. Behavior can be reduced to physical–chemical units whether the individual is alone or is influenced by others. Weiss suggested that psychology must study both physiological and social processes, and that its primary task was to understand how the infant develops into a social adult. He outlined a program of research on child development and learning, but he died before it could be implemented.

Karl Lashley (1890–1958)

Lashley was a student of Watson's at Johns Hopkins University, where he received his Ph.D. in 1915. His productive career as a physiological psychologist took him to the universities of Minnesota and Chicago, to Harvard, and finally to the Yerkes Laboratory of Primate Biology. An ardent supporter of behaviorism, Lashley vigorously championed increased objectivism in psychology and opposed the study of consciousness through introspection.

His thorough research produced some results that differed from Watson's position on certain points. Specifically, he believed that stimulus–response (S–R) connections developed through conditioning were not the most effective approach to the analysis of behavior. However, his adherence to the basic tenets of behaviorist psychology never wavered; only his attitude toward some of Watson's secondary points changed.

Lashley is perhaps best known for his work involving the effect of brain extirpation on the learning abilities of rats. The results of this research were surprising, and disturbing, because they contradicted accepted views of localization of function within the cortex. Earlier investigators had demonstrated specific sensory and motor areas within the cortex. Lashley's research showed that even though destruction of large cortical areas resulted in slower learning, it seemed not to matter which specific cortical area was destroyed. Animals were able to learn just as well with one part of the cortex as with another. This perplexing finding seemed to indicate that other cortical centers were capable of taking over the functions performed by the destroyed centers, and Lashley concluded that the brain must function as a whole.

Lashley summarized his research findings in *Brain Mechanisms and Intelligence* (1929), in which he plotted errors in learning against the amount of cortical tissue destroyed and the difficulty of the learning task. His results led him to postulate two famous principles: mass action and equipotentiality.

The law of *mass action* states that the efficiency of learning is a function of the total mass of the cortex left intact. In other words, the more cortical tissue available, the better the learning.

Learning depends on the amount of cortex left functioning rather than on the integrity of a particular part. Lashley's principle of *equipotentiality* states that one part of the cortex is essentially equal to another in terms of its contribution to tasks such as maze learning. There are, however, some exceptions to this principle. Visual perception of a shape or pattern, for example, requires that a certain part of the cortex be intact, though within that specific cortical area the subparts are, to a large degree, equal in potential.

Lashley had expected to find in his research specific pathways and connections between sensory and motor apparatus, with definite points of localization in the cortex. Such findings would have supported the primacy of the reflex arc as an elemental unit of behavior. His results, however, challenged the Watsonian notion of a simple point-to-point connection in reflexes, according to which the brain serves merely to switch incoming sensory nerve impulses into outgoing motor impulses. Lashley's results suggested that the brain plays a more active role in learning and challenged Watson's assumption that behavior is compounded bit by bit through conditioned reflexes.

Although Lashley's work discredited a basic point of Watson's system, it did not weaken the behaviorists' fundamental contention that only completely objective methods should be used. Indeed, his research demonstrates the value of objective methods in psychological research.

THE INFLUENCE OF OPERATIONISM

The increasingly dominant behaviorist movement in American psychology was further strengthened by the development of the principle known as *operationism*. Actually, the relationship between this principle and behaviorism was somewhat circular. On the one hand, behaviorism was fortified by operationism. On the other, the increasingly objective framework of behaviorist psychology prepared the way for the acceptance of operationism.

Operationism is an attitude or general principle, not a formal school in the sense in which we have been using the term. Its purpose is to render the language and terminology of science more objective and precise and to rid science of those problems that are not actually observable or physically demonstrable (the so-called pseudo-problems). Briefly, operationism holds that the validity of a given scientific finding or theoretical construct is dependent on the validity of the operations used in arriving at that finding.

The operationist viewpoint was championed by the Harvard physicist Percy W. Bridgman in *The Logic of Modern Physics* (1927), which captured the attention of many psychologists. Bridgman proposed that physical concepts be defined in more precise and rigid terms and that all concepts lacking physical referents be promptly discarded.

> The new attitude toward a concept is entirely different. We may illustrate by considering the concept of length: what do we mean by the length of an object? We evidently know what we mean by length if we can tell what the length of any and every object is, and for the physicist nothing more is required. To find the length of an object, we have to perform certain physical operations. The concept of length is therefore fixed when the operations by which length is measured are fixed: that is, the concept of length involves as much as and nothing more than a set of operations; *the concept is synonymous with the corresponding set of operations.* (Bridgman, 1927, p. 5)

Thus, a physical concept is the same as the set of operations or procedures by which it is determined. Many psychologists quickly found this principle to be of use in the science of psychology, and some applied it eagerly. But as promptly as it was accepted by some psychologists, it provoked opposition from others.

Bridgman's concern with pseudo-problems—the questions that defy answer by any known objective test—is noteworthy. Notions or propositions that cannot be put to experimental test are meaningless for science. An example of a pseudo-problem is the issue of the existence and nature of the soul. What is this thing "soul?" Can it be observed in the laboratory? Can it be measured and manipulated under controlled conditions to determine its effects on behavior? If something cannot be so observed, measured, and manipulated, it has no use, no meaning, and no relevance for science. It follows that the concept of an individual and private consciousness is a pseudo-problem for psychology.

Neither its existence nor its characteristics can be determined or even investigated through objective methods. Therefore, according to the operationist viewpoint, consciousness has no place in a scientific psychology.

It can be argued that operationism was not much more than a formal statement of principles already in use in psychology when the meanings of words and concepts were defined in terms of their physical referents. There is little in operationism that cannot be found in the works of the British empiricists (Turner, 1967). We have noted the long-term trend in American psychology toward an increasing objectification of methods and subject matter, so it can be said that operationism—as an attitude and a framework within which to conduct research and formulate theories—had already been accepted by a number of American psychologists for some years before the publication of Bridgman's 1927 book. Since the time of Wundt, however, physics had been the paragon of scientific respectability for the newer psychology, and when physics favored operationism as a formal doctrine, psychology followed suit. Indeed, psychology accepted and used operationism to a much greater degree than physics did.

As noted, operationism did not win universal recognition in psychology. Controversy raged about the relative utility or futility of limiting psychology's subject matter to that which has empirical reference. "The reduction of concepts to their operations turned out to be dull business. No one wants to trouble with it when there is no special need" (Boring, 1950, p. 658). Others took the position that operationism was no longer the orthodoxy it was in the 1920s and 1930s. Even Bridgman had second thoughts about the use psychology made of the concept. Writing 27 years after proposing the operationist viewpoint, he said, "I feel that I have created a Frankenstein which has certainly gotten away from me. I abhor the word *operationalism* or *operationism*. . . . The thing I have envisaged is too simple to be so dignified by so pretentious a name" (Bridgman, 1954, p. 224).

This appears to be another case in which the disciples became more fanatical than their leader. Nevertheless, the important point about operationism for our purpose is that the generation of behaviorists that came of age in the late 1920s and 1930s characteristically included operationism in their approach to psychology.

NEOBEHAVIORISTS

The second stage in the evolution of behaviorism has been called *neobehaviorism*. Lasting for some 30 years, from about 1930 to about 1960, this period of relative stability had as its most prominent representatives Edward Tolman, Edwin Guthrie, Clark Hull, and B. F. Skinner. During this time large numbers of American experimental psychologists agreed on several points, despite their differing theoretical and methodological approaches to psychology. The first of these was a common data base derived from animal learning. Through conditioning and discrimination learning experiments, the neobehaviorists collected enormous numbers of facts, and, in general, they agreed on what the important facts or data were for psychology.

The second characteristic of the neobehaviorists involved the explanatory systems designed to account for their data. In Watsonian behaviorism there were many facts and findings but little in the way of useful explanatory and predictive principles or theories comparable to those in the physical sciences. Instead, hypotheses seemed only loosely related to data (Koch, 1964).

In the neobehaviorist stage of development the explanatory systems were of several varieties, providing the psychologists of the day with different theoretical options. Hull offered a hypothetico–deductive approach, Skinner a radical empiricism demonstrating functional relations between variables, and Tolman the concept of intervening variables. The important point here is not so much the differences among the neobehaviorists as their shared concern with establishing some way to explain the behavior being observed.

Other aspects of the neobehaviorist position include the acceptance of operationism and positivism, and the beliefs that the core of psychology is the study of learning, that association of a mechanical sort is the key concept of learning, and that all behavior, no matter how complex, can be described in terms of the laws of conditioning.

We shall discuss the work of the four leading neobehaviorists (Tolman, Guthrie, Hull, and Skinner), and then note the third stage in behaviorism's evolution, *neo-neobehaviorism*, which is described more fully in Chapter 15.

Edward Chace Tolman (1886–1959)

One of the early adherents of behaviorism, Tolman originally studied engineering at the Massachusetts Institute of Technology. He changed to psychology and studied under Holt at Harvard, where he received his Ph.D. in 1915. In the summer of 1912 he worked with one of the Gestalt psychologists, Kurt Koffka, in Germany. In his last year of graduate work, while being trained in the Titchener tradition, Tolman became acquainted with Watsonian behaviorism. As a graduate student, he had already questioned the scientific usefulness of introspection, and he wrote in his *Autobiography* (1952) that Watson's behaviorism came as a "tremendous stimulus and relief."

After receiving his degree Tolman became an instructor at Northwestern University, and in 1918 went to the University of California at Berkeley. It was at Berkeley, where he taught comparative psychology and conducted research on learning with rats, that he definitely became a behaviorist, though of a different sort than Watson.

Tolman's career at Berkeley was interrupted twice. During World War II he served in the Office of Strategic Services (1944–1945), and from 1950 to 1953 he was a leader in the spirited and commendable faculty opposition to the California state loyalty oath. During this latter period he taught at Harvard and at the University of Chicago.

Tolman's Purposive Behaviorism

The definitive statement of Tolman's position is presented in his first and most important book, *Purposive Behavior in Animals and Men* (1932). His system may appear at first glance to be a curious blend of two contradictory terms: *purpose* and *behavior*. Attributing purpose to an organism seems to imply consciousness. Surely such a mentalistic concept can have no place in a behaviorist system.

Tolman made it clear, however, both in this book and in his careful research that he was very much the behaviorist in subject matter and methodology, and that he was not urging psychology to return to consciousness. He vigorously rejected introspection of the structuralist sort. Like Watson, he had no interest in assumed internal experiences that were not accessible to objective observation. Any reference to conscious processes in Tolman's system was phrased in terms of cautious inference from observed behavior.

It is equally clear that Tolman was not a Watsonian behaviorist, for the two men differed in at least two important respects. First, Tolman was not interested in studying behavior at the molecular level—in terms of stimulus–response connections. Unlike Watson, he was not concerned with elemental units of behavior, the activities of the nerves, muscles, and glands. His focus was molar behavior—the total response actions of the whole organism. In this respect, his system combines behaviorist and Gestalt concepts (see Chapter 12).

The second and more important difference between Watson and Tolman, and the major tenet of Tolman's system, is the notion of purposive behavior. Purposiveness in behavior, Tolman said, can be defined in objective behavioral terms without appeal to

Employing some Gestalt concepts, Edward Chace Tolman (1886–1959) invoked purposive behaviorism to give empirical form to the unobservable processes prompting an organism's goal-directed behavior.

introspection or to how the organism might "feel" about an experience. It seemed obvious to him that all behavior is goal directed: the cat tries to get out of the puzzle box, the rat learns a difficult maze, the human studies music. Behavior, he said, "reeks of purpose." All behavior is oriented toward the achievement of some goal object, learning the means to an end. The rat persistently goes through a maze, making fewer errors, getting to the goal faster each time. In other words, the rat is learning, and the fact of learning, in a rat or a human, is highly objective behavioral evidence of purpose. Note that Tolman is dealing with the response of the organism, and that his measures are in terms of the response behavior changing as a function of learning; these are objective data.

Watsonian behaviorists were quick to criticize the attribution of purpose to behavior because, they argued, did this not rest on the assumption of consciousness in the organism? Tolman's answer was that it made no difference to him whether the animal was conscious or not. The conscious experience—if any—associated with purposing did not in any way influence the behavioral responses of the organism. Tolman was concerned only with the overt response behavior.

If there were a conscious awareness of the goal, Tolman said, this would be a private matter within each organism and not available to the objective tools of science. Anything that is internal and cannot be observed from outside the organism is not within the realm of science. Woodworth described Tolman's argument in the following fashion:

> If I try to describe to you my sensation of the color red, I find it cannot be done. I can point to a red object, I can say that red is somewhat like orange or purple, and very different from green and blue, quite a gay, stimulating color, very nice for a tie but a little too gay for a professor's overcoat—I can put red in many such relations but I cannot describe the sensation itself. I should have the same difficulty in trying to describe my feelings of pleasantness. Now what is essentially private cannot be made the subject matter of science. . . . Only to the extent that private experience can be *reported*, made public, can it have any place in science. (Woodworth, 1948, p. 106)

Intervening Variables

Tolman's unique and, in the long run, most useful contribution to psychology may be the concept of the *intervening variable*. As a behaviorist, Tolman believed that the initiating causes of behavior and the final resulting behavior must be capable of objective observation and operational definition. He suggested that the initiating causes of behavior consist of five independent variables: the environmental stimuli (S), physiological drive (P), heredity (H), previous training (T), and age (A). With animal subjects the experimenter can control these variables, but with humans there is obviously less control. Behavior, then, is a function of these independent variables:

$$B = f_x (S, P, H, T, A)$$

Between these observable independent variables and the final response measure (the observable dependent or behavior variable), Tolman postulated a set of inferred and unobserved factors, the intervening variables, which are the actual determinants of behavior. They are the internal processes that connect the antecedent stimulus situation with the observed response. The statement S–R must now read S–O–R. The intervening variable is what is going on within O (the organism) that brings about a given response to a given stimulus.

Because this intervening variable cannot be objectively observed, it is of no use to science unless it can be clearly related to both the experimental (independent) variable and the behavior (dependent) variable. The classic example is the intervening variable of hunger, which cannot be seen in a person or laboratory animal. Hunger can, however, be precisely and objectively related to an objective experimental variable—the length of time since the organism last had food. It can also be related to an objective response variable such as the amount of food eaten or how rapidly it is consumed. Thus, this unobservable inferred variable can be given precise empirical referents and is therefore amenable to quantification and experimental manipulation.

Tolman introduced the concept of intervening variable so that psychology would have a way to make precise and objective statements about inner states and processes that cannot be observed. In other words, intervening variables were a way of rendering these states useful to psychology. By specifying the independent and dependent variables (observable events), Tolman was, in effect, able to provide operational definitions of unobservable inner states. Before he chose the term *intervening variable*, he called his new approach "operational behaviorism."

Tolman originally proposed two kinds of intervening variables: demand variables and cognitive variables. The demand variables are essentially motives and include sex, hunger, and the demand for safety in the face of danger. The cognitive or "know-how" variables are abilities and include perception of objects, motor skills, and the like.

In 1951 Tolman revised his intervening variables and established three categories: (1) *need systems*—which are the physiological deprivation or drive situation at a given moment in time; (2) *belief–value motives*—which represent the intensity of preference for certain goal objects and the relative strength of these objects in satisfying needs; and (3) *behavior spaces*—within which the behavior of the individual takes place. In the behavior space, some objects are attractive to the individual (have a positive valence), whereas others are repellent (have a negative valence).

Tolman's concept of the intervening variable has been useful to psychology, though it has not gone uncriticized. Intervening variables appear to be of value in developing an acceptable theory of behavior so long as they are empirically related to both experimental and behavior variables. Doing this comprehensively and completely, however, turned out to be such a monumental task that Tolman later came "to repudiate the hope of ever making a complete definition of any intervening variables and declared that, if they were not to be abandoned altogether, then at best all they could be considered was 'an aid to thinking'" (Mackenzie, 1977, p. 146).

Theory of Learning

Tolman's research on learning has proved stimulating to subsequent researchers and provides considerable support for his position. He believed that all animal and human behavior (with the exception of tropisms and simple reflexes) is capable of modification through experience. Thus, learning plays a major role in his system. He rejected Thorndike's law of effect, saying that reward or reinforcement has little, if any, role in learning. In its place he proposed a cognitive theory of learning in which the continued performance of a task builds up *sign Gestalts*, which are learned relationships between cues in the environment and the organism's expectations. The animal, Tolman said, gets to know some of its environment.

Let us follow Tolman's system as we watch a hungry rat placed in a maze. The animal moves about in the maze, sometimes in correct alleys and sometimes in blind alleys. Eventually, it discovers the food. In subsequent trials in the maze, Tolman argued, purpose and direction are given to the rat's behavior by the goal. At each choice point expectations are established. The rat comes to expect that certain cues associated with the choice point will lead on to food. When the rat's expectancy is confirmed (when it gets food), the sign Gestalt of cue expectancy associated with that choice point is strengthened. Over all the choice points in the maze there is established a pattern of sign Gestalts, which Tolman called a *cognitive map*. This pattern is what the animal learns—a cognitive map of the maze, not a set of motor habits. In a sense, then, the rat establishes a comprehensive knowledge of the maze or of any familiar environment. Something like a field map is developed in its brain, enabling it to go from one spot in the environment to another without being restricted to a fixed series of bodily movements.

More than 30 years of research was conducted in Tolman's laboratory, and it is important to consider the nature of the research that supports his theory of learning.

One classic experiment investigated the basic question whether the rat in the maze learns a set of motor responses or a cognitive map of the maze. A cross-shaped maze was used. One set of rats always found food at the same place, even though (using different starting points) the rats had sometimes to turn to the right and other times to the left to reach the food. Thus, the motor responses differed, but the location of the food remained the same.

The second group of rats always made the same response regardless of the starting point, but the food was found in different places. For example, starting from one end of the cross, the rats would find food only by turning to the right at the choice point; when starting from the other end of the cross, they also found food only by turning to the right.

The results showed that the "place learners" (the first group) performed significantly better than the "response learners." Tolman concluded that the same thing occurs with persons who are familiar with their town or neighborhood. They can go from one point to another by a number of different routes because of the cognitive map that they have developed of the area.

Another experiment involved *latent learning*—learning that cannot be observed at the time it is taking place. A hungry rat was placed in a maze and allowed to wander about freely. There was no food to be found. Was the rat learning anything in the absence of reinforcement? After a number of no-reinforcement trials, the rat found food. Its improvement thereafter in running the maze was extremely rapid, indicating that some learning had taken place during the period of no reinforcement. Its performance quickly equaled that of a control group, which had been reinforced with food on every trial.

Comment

Tolman's work had a great influence on psychology, particularly in the area of learning, and its impact is recognized today in the cognitive movement (see Chapter 15). Tolman has been criticized for his failure to develop a fully integrated theoretical system, and many psychologists believe that he never adequately related behavior to the more covert functioning, such as cognitive states. A more obvious point of attack relates to Tolman's language, which many find subjective and mentalistic.

On the positive side, Tolman initiated many important research topics in learning and introduced the concept of the intervening variable to psychology. Because intervening variables are a way of operationally defining unobservable states such as hunger, they have made these states scientifically respectable to some behaviorists. Intervening variables have become a necessary format for dealing with hypothetical constructs and have been widely used by other neobehaviorists, namely, Guthrie and Hull. For a time they were used by Skinner.

Another significant contribution is Tolman's support for the rat as an appropriate subject for psychological study. An essay written in 1945 clearly and delightfully states his position on this issue:

> What . . . can we now say as to the contributions of us rodent psychologists to human behavior? What is it that we rat runners still have to contribute to the understanding of the deeds and the misdeeds, the absurdities and the tragedies of our friend, and our enemy—*homo sapiens*? The answer is that, whereas man's successes, persistences, and socially unacceptable divagations . . . are all ultimately shaped and materialized by specific cultures, it is still true that most of the formal underlying laws of intelligence, motivation, and instability can still be studied in rats as well as, and more easily than, in men.

> And, as a final peroration, let it be noted that rats live in cages; they do not go on binges the night before one has planned an experiment; they do not kill each other off in wars; they do not invent engines of destruction, and, if they did, they would not be so inept about controlling such engines; they do not go in for either class conflicts or race conflicts; they avoid politics, economics, and papers on psychology. They are marvelous, pure, and delightful. And, as soon as I possibly can, I am going to climb back again out on that good old phylogenetic limb and sit there, this time right side up and unashamed, wiggling my whiskers at all the silly, yet at the same time far too complicated, specimens of *homo sapiens*, whom I shall see strutting and fighting and messing things up, down there on the ground below me. (Tolman, 1945, p. 166)[1]

Edwin Ray Guthrie (1886–1959)

Guthrie received his Ph.D. in 1912 from the University of Pennsylvania, and began his academic career in 1914 at the University of Washington, where he remained until his retirement in 1956. While in graduate school, he became an ardent convert to a behaviorist approach to psychology, an approach from which he never wavered. He believed that science must deal only with objectively observable conditions and events. So extreme an empiricist was Guthrie that he opposed the practice of attempting to relate behavioral events to what he considered the invisible brain and nervous system. Although his basic orientation is definitely behavioristic, he cannot be described as a Watsonian behaviorist.

Guthrie's most important influence on psychology is his formulation of an extremely simple learning theory, set forth in *The Psychology of Learning* (1935). Variously described

---

[1] From E. C. Tolman, A stimulus–expectancy need–cathexis psychology. *Science*, 1945, *101*, 160–166. Reprinted by permission of the American Association for the Advancement of Science.

Edwin Ray Guthrie (1886–1959) proposed a simple learning theory, maintaining that behavior is learned during a single pairing of stimulus and response.

as the most persistent advocate of conditioning and the most radical of all those who dealt with association, Guthrie remained for several decades a forceful proponent of a theory of learning based on one principle—*contiguity*. To account for the strengthening of learned responses, he rejected Thorndike's laws of effect and frequency as well as Pavlovian reinforcement. He relied instead on what he called "simultaneous conditioning," which he considered the most general law for psychology.

To Guthrie, all learning depends on the contiguity of stimulus and response. When a stimulus just once elicits a response, then the S–R association is established. It is, in essence, a *one-trial learning* situation, which is Guthrie's most famous principle. Repetition and reinforcement form no essential part of his system. His only formal law of learning states: "A combination of stimuli which has accompanied a movement will on its recurrence tend to be followed by that movement" (Guthrie, 1935, p. 26). Note that there is no mention of internal drive states, repetitions of the stimulus–response pairings, or any form of reinforcement. One pairing of the stimulus and the resulting movement serves to establish the association; thus, the behavior is learned.

Note also that the law refers to movements, which Guthrie carefully distinguished from acts. He defined a movement as a pattern of motor and glandular responses or actions. An act, on the other hand, is a movement or series of movements that brings about results. Although an act is a movement, a movement is not an act. An act is on a larger scale. For example, hitting a nail with a hammer is an act composed of a number of separate movements. Guthrie believed that in measuring learning, the performance of the complete act is usually taken as the criterion of learning, whereas it is the movements that are actually conditioned as responses.

He considered this focus on movements to be a distinguishing feature of his theory. He argued that Thorndike, for instance, was concerned with the total act, with the acquisition of a skill (such as a cat escaping from a puzzle box) that is a function of a number of individual muscular movements. These individual movements are developed or acquired in single trials, but learning of the total act calls for repeated practice. The movements, or individual parts of the learned act, are the raw data in Guthrie's system. Because they are smaller, these movements are more difficult to observe in a learning situation, which, Guthrie explained, is why they are often overlooked.

Just as the response of the organism is composed of a number of separate components, so too is the stimulation to which the organism is exposed. Because the stimulus and response are made up of many parts, it is necessary to have a large number of pairings of the total stimulus and response situations to achieve any consistency in the behavior under study. Therefore, practice is necessary to bring about improvement of the constellation of movements (the act), but each component movement is learned after a single pairing with the stimulus.

Comment

Guthrie seemed to prefer writing and anecdotal observation to experimentation. He believed in the importance of theory for the development of psychology, and commented that theories, not facts, endure. His several books contain evidence of an anecdotal nature and comparatively little experimental evidence. There is some empirical support for his theory, mainly his own research involving stereotypy in the behavior of the cat in a puzzle box. Compared to some other theoretical positions in neobehaviorist psychology, however, there is relatively little empirical support. Much of the appeal of Guthrie's system rests upon its simplicity and its consistency over the years. It is easy to understand when compared with more complex learning theories, particularly Hull's.

The inherent simplicity of Guthrie's system draws praise from some psychologists, but it provides a point of criticism for others. It has been suggested that Guthrie maintained this simplicity by failing to deal explicitly with major problems in learning that might defy explanation within his framework. "It is undoubtedly true that many reviews of Guthrie in the literature have mistaken incompleteness for simplicity" (Mueller & Schoenfeld, 1954, p. 368). Such critics suggest that additional constructs and assumptions are necessary to encompass the major problem areas of learning.

Nevertheless, Guthrie was able to maintain his theoretical position and stature as a leading learning theorist. His contributions received formal recognition in 1958 when the American Psychological Foundation presented him with their Gold Medal Award. Statistical models of learning have grown largely out of the Guthrian scheme.

Clark Leonard Hull (1884–1952)

First and foremost a behaviorist, Hull has achieved a highly respected position in contemporary psychology. Perhaps no previous psychologist was so consistently and keenly devoted to the problems inherent in scientific method. He had a prodigious command of mathematics and formal logic and applied them to psychological theory in a way no one had done before.

The Life of Hull

For most of his childhood and young adult life, Hull was plagued by poor health. Illnesses struck him frequently, and poor eyesight affected him all his life. At the age of

The radical behaviorism of Clark Leonard Hull (1884–1952) saw all behavior as quantifiable and conditioned by the reinforcement an organism derives from reducing its biological needs.

24 he contracted polio, which left him disabled in one leg, forced to wear a heavy iron brace of his own design. His family had little income and he was forced to interrupt his education several times to take teaching jobs to earn money. Hull's greatest asset, however, was a driving motivation and aspiration to greatness, and he persevered in the face of many obstacles.

In 1918 he received his Ph.D. from the University of Wisconsin, where he had studied mining engineering before switching to psychology. He remained a member of the faculty at Wisconsin for 10 years.

Hull's early research presaged his lifelong emphasis on objective methods and functional laws. He investigated concept formation and the effects of tobacco on behavioral efficiency, and surveyed the literature on tests and measurements, publishing an important early text in that area in 1928. He worked on the development of practical methods of statistical analysis, and invented a machine for calculating correlations.

Hull devoted 10 years to the study of hypnosis and suggestibility, publishing 32 papers and a book, *Hypnosis and Suggestibility* (1933), that summarized the research. In 1929 he became a research professor at Yale, where he developed his final major research interest: a theory of behavior based on Pavlov's laws of conditioning. He had first read Pavlov in 1927 and become greatly interested in the problem of conditioned reflexes and learning.

In the 1930s Hull wrote articles on conditioning, arguing that complex higher-order behaviors could be explained in terms of the basic principles of conditioning. In 1940 he published, with five colleagues, *Mathematico–Deductive Theory of Rote Learning: A Study in Scientific Methodology*. Although the book was considered a notable achievement in the development of scientific psychology, it was difficult to understand and so was read by very few people.

Hull's next major publication, *Principles of Behavior* (1943), was considerably easier to read. In it he outlined, in great detail and with characteristic precision, a theoretical framework so comprehensive as to include all behavior. With the publication of this book, Hull's system assumed a position of importance in the area of learning in the United States. It stimulated a great deal of research, and Hull soon became the most frequently cited psychologist in the field. He revised the system in a number of journal articles, and the final statement appeared in *A Behavior System* (1952). Hull had been ill for a number of years, and he died before reading the galley proofs of this book.

Hull's System: The Frame of Reference

Hull believed that human behavior involves a continuing interaction between the organism and the environment. The objective stimuli provided by the environment and the objective behavioral responses provided by the organism are, of course, observable facts. This interaction takes place, however, within a larger context that cannot be totally defined in observable stimulus–response terms.

This broader context, or *frame of reference*, is the biological adaptation of the organism to its unique environment. The survival of the organism is aided by this biological adaptation. When survival is in jeopardy, the organism is in a state of need. Thus, to Hull, need involves a situation in which the biological requirements for survival are not being met. When in a state of need, the organism behaves in a manner designed to reduce that need. Its behavior serves to reinstate the optimal biological conditions necessary for survival.

Hull's concern with biological survival grew out of his interest in evolutionary theory. It is also consistent with the functionalist emphasis on adaptation to the environment.

Hull was committed to an objective behaviorist psychology. There was no place in his system for consciousness, purpose, or any other mentalistic notion. The system was an uncompromising radical behaviorism in which Hull attempted to reduce every concept to physical terms. Although his methodological behaviorism was perhaps more rigid than Watson's, he did allow for the notion of intervening variables. However, these variables were closely and concretely tied to objective stimulus and response conditions, which could be quantified and measured with precision.

Hull's system and his image of human nature were couched in mechanistic terms. He regarded human behavior as automatic and cyclical, capable of reduction to the terminology of physics, and warned against the intrusion of "anthropomorphic subjectivism," that is, giving subjective interpretations of the behavior being observed. The observation and interpretation of behavior must be uncompromisingly objective. One way of attaining this, Hull initially suggested, was to think in terms of the behavior of animals. Even this had its dangers, however.

> [It] all too often breaks down when the theorist begins thinking what he would do if he were a rat, a cat, or a chimpanzee; when that happens, all his knowledge of his own behavior, born of years of self-observation, at once begins to function in place of the objectively stated general rules or principles which are the proper substance of science. (Hull, 1943, p. 27)

There must be a more rigid safeguard against subjectivism, and Hull found it in an attitude that considers "the behaving organism as a completely self-maintaining robot, constructed of materials as unlike ourselves as may be" (Hull, 1943, p. 27).

Thus, behaviorists should view their subject matter as robotlike. The spirit of mechanism represented by the mechanical figures of seventeenth-century European gardens and clocks was faithfully followed and strengthened in Hull's work. One advantage of this robot approach, according to Hull, is that it precludes explaining behavior by attributing it to causes other than strictly mechanical ones. There is little difference between psychology and physics, to Hull. Any such difference is only in degree, not in kind.

Methodology

Our discussion of Hull's mechanistic, reductionist, and objective behaviorism provides a clear view of what his methods of study must be. Obviously, they are characterized by as much objectivity as possible.

In addition, Hull's approach to psychology is distinguished by quantification. The laws of behavior must be stated or expressed in the precise language of mathematics, and quantification became a second cornerstone on which Hull erected his behaviorism.

Psychologists, he wrote, must not only develop a thorough understanding of mathematics, they must *think* mathematics. In *Principles of Behavior*, Hull wrote how a mathematically defined psychology would proceed.

> Progress . . . will consist in the laborious writing, one by one, of hundreds of equations; in the experimental determination, one by one, of hundreds of the empirical constants contained in the equations; in the devising of practically usable units in which to measure the quantities expressed by the equations; in the objective

definition of hundreds of symbols appearing in the equations; in the rigorous deduction, one by one, of thousands of theorems and corollaries from the primary
definitions and equations; in the meticulous performance of thousands of critical
quantitative experiments. (Hull, 1943, pp. 400–401)

This statement provides a good indication of the rigor—and patience—required of a
follower of the Hullian system.

Hull described four specific methods that could be useful to science. Three of these
were already in use: (1) simple observation, (2) systematic controlled observation, and
(3) experimental testing of hypotheses. In addition, Hull argued for strict adherence to
the *hypothetico–deductive method*, which utilizes rigorous deduction from a set of formulations that are determined *a priori*. The method involves establishing postulates
from which experimentally testable conclusions can be deduced. These conclusions are
then submitted to experimental test. Failure results in revision and verification allows
for their incorporation into the body of science. Hull believed that if psychology were
to become an objective science on the order of other natural sciences (in accordance
with the behaviorist program), the only appropriate approach would be the hypothetico–deductive one.

Drives

Hull considered bodily need arising from a deviation from optimal biological conditions
to be the basis of motivation. However, rather than introducing the concept of biological
need directly into his system, he postulated the intervening variable of *drive*, a term that
had already come into use in psychology. Drive was posited as a stimulus (S_D), arising
from a state of tissue need, that arouses or activates behavior. The strength of the drive
can be empirically determined by the length of deprivation, or the intensity, strength,
and energy expenditure of the resulting behavior. Hull considered the duration of
deprivation to be a rather imperfect index, and he placed greater emphasis on behavior
strength.

It is important to note that Hull considered drive to be nonspecific. In other words,
any kind of deprivation—food, water, or sex, for example—contributed in the same
way (though perhaps in differing degree) to the drive. This nonspecificity means that
drive does not direct behavior, but functions solely to energize it. The steering or guiding
of behavior is accomplished by environmental stimuli. Also, according to Hull, drive
reduction is the sole basis for reinforcement.

Hull's system postulates two major kinds of drive: primary and secondary. *Primary*
drives are associated with biological need states and are directly and intimately involved
with the organism's survival. These drives, which arise from a state of tissue need,
include the needs for food, water, air, temperature regulation, defecation, urination,
sleep, activity, sexual intercourse, and relief from pain. These are basic, innate processes
of the organism and are vital to its survival.

Hull recognized that humans and animals are motivated by forces other than primary
drives. Accordingly, he postulated the *secondary, or learned, drives*, which refer to
situations or stimuli in the environment that are associated with the reduction of primary
drives, and which may, as a result, become drives themselves. This means that previously
neutral stimuli may assume drive characteristics because they are capable of eliciting
responses that are similar to those aroused by the original need state or primary drive.

A simple example involves being burned by touching a stove. The painful burn (tissue damage) produces a primary drive (relief from pain). Other stimuli associated with this primary drive, such as the sight of the stove, may lead to the withdrawing of the hand when this visual stimulus is perceived. Thus, the sight of the stove may become the stimulus for the learned drive of fear. These secondary drives or motivating forces develop on the basis of the primary drives. Because of this focus on learned drives, learning obviously plays a key role in Hull's system.

Learning

Hull's system is primarily concerned with motivation. This may surprise those who first heard of Hull in discussions of learning. Certainly he focused great attention on problems of learning, but only as "an instrumentality that permitted an organism to extend the range and variety of its efforts to satisfy its needs" (Cofer & Appley, 1964, p. 469). In the course of developing his system, Hull became less concerned with learning and more concerned with other factors capable of influencing behavior, although he is most frequently studied in terms of his theory of learning.

A major part of Hull's theory is his attempt to integrate, or at least reconcile, Thorndike's law of effect with Pavlovian conditioning. He believed that learning could not be adequately explained by the principles of recency and frequency. His learning theory focuses mainly on the principle of reinforcement, which is essentially Thorndike's effect principle.

Hull's law of primary reinforcement states that when a stimulus–response relationship is followed by a reduction in need, the probability is increased that on subsequent occasions the same stimulus will evoke the same response. Note that reward or reinforcement is defined not in terms of Thorndike's notion of satisfaction, but rather in terms of reduction of a primary need. Thus, primary reinforcement, referring to the reduction of a primary drive, is the cornerstone of Hull's system of learning.

Just as his system contains secondary drives, it also deals with secondary reinforcement. If the intensity of the stimulus is reduced as the result of a secondary or learned drive, it will act as a secondary reinforcement.

> It follows that any stimulus consistently associated with a reinforcement situation will through that association acquire the power of evoking the conditioned inhibition, i.e., reduction in stimulus intensity, and so of itself producing the resulting reinforcement. Since this indirect power of reinforcement is acquired through learning, it is called *secondary reinforcement*. (Hull, 1951, pp. 27–28)

Hull believed that the stimulus–response connection is strengthened by the number of reinforcements that have taken place. He called the strength of the S–R connection *habit strength*, which refers to the persistence of the conditioning and is a function of reinforcement.

Learning cannot take place in the absence of reinforcement that is necessary to bring about a reduction of the drive. Because of this emphasis on reinforcement, Hull's system is called a *need-reduction* theory, as opposed to Guthrie's contiguity theory and Tolman's cognitive theory.

Hull's system is presented in terms of specific and detailed postulates and corollaries expressed in verbal and mathematical form. In its last presentation (Hull, 1952), there are 18 postulates and 12 corollaries. Although the system was based on conditioning principles, Hull believed that his fundamental position could be expanded to include complex processes such as problem solving, social behavior, and forms of learning other than conditioning. He lived to see only a portion of this ambition realized.

Comment

This brief review of Hull's system cannot fully encompass the scope of his work. Our purpose in dealing with later systems is to point out how they derive from earlier ways of thinking. There has been a continuity of development in psychology, and our descriptions of derivations of past systems are intended to provide an appreciation of the relevance of the past for the present.

Hull's system achieved such prominence that it generated a great deal of criticism. A few general points are noted. As a leading exponent of neobehaviorism, Hull is subject to the same attacks aimed at Watson and others who followed in the behaviorist tradition. Those who oppose a behaviorist approach to psychology on methodological and theoretical grounds will, of course, include Hull in the enemy camp.

Hull's system is faulted for its lack of generalizability. It has been asserted that in his attempt to define his variables so precisely in quantitative terms, he functioned at times on a narrow, miniature-system basis. In other words, his approach was extremely particularistic in that he often formulated postulates from results obtained in a single experimental situation. Opponents argue that generalization to all behavior on the basis of such specific experimental demonstrations is questionable.

> Surely a set of laws of mammalian behavior ought not reflect in the constants of its basic postulates such specialized information as the most favorable interval for human eyelid conditioning (Postulate 2) . . . the weight in grams of food needed to condition a rat (Postulate 7) . . . or the amplitude in millimeters of galvanometer deflection in human conditioning (Postulate 15). (Hilgard, 1956, p. 181)

Although precise quantification is necessary and commendable in a natural science approach to psychology, Hull's extreme approach does tend to reduce the range of applicability of the findings.

Thus, Hull's adherence to a mathematical and formal system of theory building is open to both praise and criticism. Hull may have become a victim of his enthusiasm for mathematics, quantifying his propositions so thoroughly and minutely that incomplete or inaccurate formulations are relatively easy to spot. Gaps and inconsistencies in a theory expressed in ordinary verbal terms can be easily filled in with appropriate illustrative examples. Critics have found such gaps in Hull's system and argue that at least some of Hull's formulations are not so tightly constructed as was originally thought.

Damaging though these points are, Hull's influence on contemporary psychology cannot be minimized. We have already mentioned the great amount of research occasioned by his work, perhaps more than by any other theory; this alone constitutes a major contribution to psychology. He provided an objective terminology that was well accepted and represented a new approach to psychological data rather than a simple relabeling of older concepts. It is also a tribute to the greatness of the man to note a few of the more contemporary psychologists who were his disciples and followers: John Dollard, Carl Hovland, Neal Miller, Robert Sears, Hobart Mowrer, and Kenneth Spence. Few psychologists have had such a pronounced and extensive effect on the professional motivation of so many other psychologists. Further, Hull defended, extended, and expounded the objective behaviorist approach as had never been done before. Although psychologists question parts or all of Hull's theory, there is general respect and admiration for the rigorous methods used to develop it. "It is not often in any field that a true theoretical genius comes along; of the very few to whom psychology can lay claim, Hull must surely rank among the foremost" (Lowry, 1982, p. 211).

Burrhus Frederick Skinner (1904–   )

B. F. Skinner has become the most important and influential individual in psychology today. His areas of interest over his long career, and their implications for modern society, are diverse. The magazine *Psychology Today* called him "very much the man of today. . . . When history makes its judgment, he may well be known as the major contributor to psychology in this century" (September 1967).

For many years Skinner has been America's leading behaviorist, with a large, loyal, and enthusiastic band of followers. He has developed a program for behavioral control of societies, invented an automatic crib for the care of infants, and more than anyone else is responsible for the large-scale use of both teaching machines and techniques of behavior modification. In addition, he wrote a novel (*Walden Two*) which continues to be popular 40 years after publication, and in 1971 his book, *Beyond Freedom and Dignity*, became a best-seller nationwide. He has published many professional articles and books and has been compared to Sir Francis Galton in the diversity and scope of his interests.

The Life of Skinner

Skinner was born and raised in a small town in northeastern Pennsylvania where he lived until he went away to college. By his own report, his childhood environment was warm and stable (Skinner, 1976). He attended the same high school from which his parents had graduated. There were only seven others in his graduating class.

He liked school and was always the first to arrive every morning. As a child and adolescent, he was interested in building things: sleds, wagons, rafts, merry-go-rounds, slingshots, model airplanes, and a steam cannon with which he shot potato and carrot plugs over the roofs of his neighbors' houses. He even spent years trying to develop a perpetual motion machine.

He was also interested in the behavior of animals. He read a great deal about animals and kept an assortment of pets: turtles, snakes, lizards, toads, and chipmunks. At a county fair he once observed a flock of performing pigeons. Years later Skinner would train pigeons to perform a variety of amusing and amazing feats, from playing Ping-Pong to guiding a missile to its target.

Skinner's system of psychology is, in many ways, a reflection of his own early life experiences. He views life as a product of past reinforcements, and his own life has been just as predetermined, lawful, and orderly as his system dictates that all human lives will be. He believes that all aspects of his own life can be traced to environmental sources alone (Skinner, 1983).

On the advice of a family friend, Skinner enrolled in Hamilton College where, he wrote,

> I never fitted into student life . . . I joined a fraternity without knowing what it was all about. I was not good at sports and suffered acutely as my shins were cracked in

ice hockey or better players bounced basketballs off my cranium. . . . In a paper I wrote at the end of my freshman year, I complained that the college was pushing me around with unnecessary requirements (one of them daily chapel) and that almost no intellectual interest was shown by most of the students. By my senior year I was in open revolt. (Skinner, 1967, p. 392)

As part of his revolt, Skinner participated in hoaxes that disrupted the college community and indulged in verbal attacks on the faculty and administration. His disobedience continued up to graduation day when, at commencement ceremonies, the college president warned Skinner and his friends that if they did not settle down they would not graduate.

Skinner did graduate with a degree in English, a Phi Beta Kappa key, and a desire to become a writer. As a child he had written poems and stories, and in 1925, at a summer writing school, the poet Robert Frost had commented favorably on his work.

For two years after his graduation Skinner worked at writing, then decided that he had "nothing important to say." After reading about the works of Watson and Pavlov, he turned from a literary investigation of human behavior to a scientific one. He enrolled as a graduate student in psychology at Harvard, never having taken a psychology course before, and in 1931 received his Ph.D. His dissertation topic provides an early glimpse of the position to which he has consistently adhered throughout his career. His major proposition was that a reflex is the correlation between a stimulus and a response, and nothing more.

Following several years of postdoctoral fellowships, Skinner taught at the University of Minnesota (1936–1945) and Indiana University (1945–1947). In 1947 he returned to Harvard, where he has remained. His 1938 book, *The Behavior of Organisms*, describes the basic points of his system. *Science and Human Behavior* (1953) was written as a textbook for his behaviorist psychology.

Skinner's System: General Approach

In a number of important respects Skinner's position represents a renewal of Watsonian behaviorism. "Watson's spirit is indestructible. Cleaned and purified, it breathes through the writings of B. F. Skinner" (MacLeod, 1959, p. 34).

Although Hull was also a behaviorist, there are marked differences between Hull's and Skinner's approaches to psychology. Whereas Hull stressed the importance of theory, Skinner advocates a strictly empirical system with no theoretical framework within which to conduct research. Where Hull's work consisted of postulating theory on an *a priori* basis, then checking the deduced conclusions against experimental evidence, Skinner avoids theory and practices a stringent brand of positivism. Skinner begins with empirical data and proceeds carefully and slowly toward tentative generalizations. Hull represents the deductive method; Skinner represents the inductive method.

Skinner's point of view is summarized in this way:

I never attacked a problem by constructing a Hypothesis. I never deduced Theorems or submitted them to Experimental check. So far as I can see I had no preconceived Model of Behavior—certainly not a physiological or mentalistic one, and I believe not a conceptual one. (Skinner, 1956, p. 227)

Skinner's position is an exclusively descriptive kind of behaviorism devoted to the study of responses. As such, it is atheoretical in nature. His concern is with describing behavior rather than explaining it. He deals only with observable behavior and believes that the task of scientific inquiry is to establish functional relations between the antecedent experimenter-controlled stimulus conditions and the organism's subsequent response.

In *Science and Human Behavior* (1953), Skinner wrote about the mechanical figures in the royal gardens of seventeenth-century Europe and the mechanical image of humans

All behavior is operant and subject to reinforcement contingencies, according to leading behaviorist B. F. Skinner (1904–   ), who has applied his laboratory data to problems of childrearing and education and proposed large-scale programs for behavior control.

they portrayed. Under the heading "Man a Machine," he described how his view is compatible with that earlier mechanical image. The human organism, Skinner said flatly, is a machine. And, like any other machine, a human being behaves in lawful and predictable ways in response to external forces (stimuli) that impinge on it.

Thus, Skinner is not at all concerned with theorizing or speculating about what might be going on inside the organism. His program includes no reference to presumed internal entities, whether described as intervening variables or physiological processes. Whatever might occur between the stimulus and the response does not represent objective data for a Skinnerian behaviorist. This purely descriptive behaviorism has been called, with good reason, the "empty-organism" approach. There is nothing inside the organism that is useful or necessary for explaining behavior. We are operated by forces in the environment, the external world, not by forces within ourselves.

It is important to note that although his system is atheoretical, Skinner is not totally opposed to theorizing. Rather, he is against premature theorizing in the absence of adequate supporting data. In an interview in 1968 Skinner said that he looks forward "to an overall theory of human behavior which will bring together a lot of facts and express them in a general way. That kind of theory I would be very much interested in prompting" (Evans, 1968, p. 88).

In contrast to many contemporary psychologists, Skinner does not believe in the use of large numbers of subjects and statistical comparisons between mean responses of groups. Instead, he has focused on the intense and thorough investigation of a single subject:

> A prediction of what the *average* individual will do is often of little or no value in dealing with a particular individual. . . . A science is helpful in dealing with the individual only insofar as its laws refer to individuals. A science of behavior which concerns only the behavior of groups is not likely to be of help in our understanding of the particular case. (Skinner, 1953, p. 19)

Skinner believes that truly valid replicable results can be obtained without the use of statistical analysis so long as sufficient data are collected from a single subject under well-controlled experimental conditions. He argues that the use of a large group of subjects forces the experimenter to attend to average behavior. As a result, individual response behavior and individual differences in behavior do not appear as part of the data of the experiment. In 1958 the Skinnerians established their *Journal for the Experimental Analysis of Behavior* because of the unwritten requirements of the current journals concerning subject sample size and statistical analysis.

Operant Conditioning

All psychology students are aware of the Skinner box[2] and of Skinner's emphasis on operant as opposed to respondent behavior. In the Pavlovian conditioning situation, a known stimulus is paired with a response under conditions of reinforcement. The behavioral response is elicited by a specific observable stimulus and is called, by Skinner, a respondent behavior.

---

[2]Skinner deplores the term "Skinner box" as a label for his operant conditioning apparatus. "I do not like being an eponym," he wrote. "I have asked my friends not to use the expression 'Skinner box'" (Skinner, 1983, p. 411). The term has become so popular, however, that it is listed in recent editions of *Webster's Dictionary* and is accepted usage in psychology.

Operant behavior, on the other hand, occurs without any observable external stimulus. The organism's response is seemingly spontaneous in that it is not related to any known observable stimulus. This is not to say that there is definitely no stimulus eliciting the response, but rather that no stimulus is detected when the response occurs. As far as the experimenters are concerned, there is no stimulus because they have not applied any and cannot see any.

Another difference between the two kinds of behavior is that operant behavior operates on the organism's environment and respondent behavior does not. The harnessed dog in Pavlov's laboratory can do nothing but respond when the experimenter presents the stimulus. The dog cannot act on its own to secure the stimulus. The operant behavior of the rat in the Skinner box, however, is instrumental in securing the stimulus (food). When the rat presses the bar, it receives food, and it does not get any food until it does press the bar.

Skinner believes that operant behavior is much more representative of the real-life human learning situation. Because behavior is mostly of the operant variety, the most effective approach to a science of behavior, according to Skinner, is to study the conditioning and extinguishing of operant behaviors.

Skinner's classic experimental demonstration involved bar pressing in a Skinner box constructed to eliminate extraneous stimuli. In this experiment a rat that had been deprived of food was placed in the box and allowed to explore. In the course of this general exploratory behavior the rat sooner or later accidentally depressed a lever activating a food magazine that released a food pellet into a tray. After a few reinforcements, conditioning was usually rapid. Note that the rat's behavior operated on the environment (pressed the lever) and was instrumental in securing food. The dependent variable in this kind of experiment is simple and direct: the rate of the response. A cumulative recorder attached to the Skinner box keeps a moment-by-moment record of the rate of bar pressing.

From this basic experiment Skinner derived his *law of acquisition, which states that the strength of an operant is increased when that operant is followed by presentation of a reinforcing stimulus.* Although practice is important in the establishment of high rates of bar pressing, the key variable is *reinforcement*. Practice by itself will not increase the rate; all it does is provide the opportunity for additional reinforcement to occur.

Skinner's law of acquisition differs from the positions of Thorndike and Hull on learning. Skinner does not speak in terms of pleasure–pain consequences of reinforcement, as did Thorndike. In opposition to Hull, Skinner makes no attempt to interpret reinforcement in terms of drive reduction. Whereas the systems of Thorndike and Hull are explanatory, Skinner's is descriptive. Skinner does not view drive as a stimulus or a physiological state. He considers drive as simply a set of operations that influence response behavior in a certain way. He defines drive objectively in terms of number of hours of deprivation.

Skinner and his followers have conducted a great deal of research on various problems in learning. Their topics include the role of punishment in the acquisition of responses, the effect of different schedules of reinforcement, the extinction of operant response, secondary reinforcement, and generalization.

Skinner has also worked with other animals and with human subjects, using the same basic approach as the Skinner box. With pigeons, the operant behavior involves pecking at a spot, with food as a reinforcement. The operant behavior for human subjects involves problem solving, reinforced by verbal approval or by knowledge of having given the correct answer.

Schedules of Reinforcement

To many psychologists, Skinner's most notable research is that devoted to the determination of the effects of different schedules of reinforcement. The initial research on bar pressing in the Skinner box demonstrated the necessary role of reinforcement in operant behavior. In that situation the rat's behavior was reinforced for every bar press; that is, it received food every time it made the correct response.

However, as Skinner points out, reinforcement in the real world is not always so consistent or continuous, yet learning occurs and behaviors continue even when reinforced only intermittently. There are many examples.

> We do not always find good ice or snow when we go skating or skiing. . . . We do not always get a good meal in a particular restaurant because cooks are not always predictable. We do not always get an answer when we telephone a friend because the friend is not always at home. . . . The reinforcement characteristic of industry and education are almost always intermittent because it is not feasible to control behavior by reinforcing every response. (Skinner, 1953, p. 99)

Even though you may study consistently, you may not get an A on every examination or term paper. On the job, you do not receive praise or a pay increase every day. In a football pool or at a slot machine you do not win every time. How is behavior affected by such intermittent reinforcement? Is one schedule of reinforcement optimal in terms of influencing behavior? Skinner and his colleagues devoted years of research to these questions.

The impetus for this research came not from intellectual curiosity but from expediency, and it demonstrates that science sometimes operates in a manner that is quite different from the idealized picture presented in some textbooks. One Saturday afternoon Skinner found that his supply of food pellets was running low. At that time (the 1930s) food pellets could not be purchased from a laboratory supply company. They had to be made by the experimenter, through a time-consuming and laborious process. So rather than spend the weekend making more pellets, Skinner asked himself what would happen if he reinforced his rats only once a minute regardless of how many responses they were making. That way, of course, many fewer food pellets would be needed. Skinner went on to conduct a lengthy series of experiments.

One set of studies compared the response rates of animals reinforced for every response versus those reinforced only after a certain time interval. The latter is known as _fixed-interval reinforcement._ A reinforcement could be given, for instance, once per minute or once every four minutes. The point is that the animal's response will be reinforced only after the passage of a fixed interval of time. A job in which a salary is paid once a week or once a month provides reinforcement on a fixed-interval schedule. Workers in such systems are paid not for the number of items they produce (the number of responses made), but for the number of days or weeks that elapse.

The research has shown that the shorter the interval between reinforcements, the more rapidly the animal will respond. Conversely, as the interval between reinforcements gets longer, the rate of responding falls off.

The frequency of reinforcement also affects the extinguishing of a response. Behaviors are extinguished more quickly when they have been reinforced continuously and the reinforcement is then stopped than when they have been reinforced intermittently. Some pigeons have responded as many as 10,000 times in the absence of reinforcement when they had been conditioned on a schedule of intermittent reinforcement.

Skinner also investigated a *fixed-ratio reinforcement* schedule. In this case, reinforcement is presented not after a certain time interval, but after a predetermined number of responses. The animal's behavior determines how often it will be reinforced. It must respond, for example, 10 times or 20 times after the last reinforcement to get another.

Not surprisingly, animals on a fixed-ratio schedule respond much faster than those on a fixed-interval schedule. Responding faster on fixed-interval reinforcement will not make any difference. The animal may press the bar 5 times or 50 times and it will still be reinforced only when the predetermined time interval has passed.

The higher rate of responding on the fixed-ratio schedule has been found to hold for rats and pigeons as well as humans. A fixed-ratio schedule of payment is used in industry and business in situations where a worker's pay depends on the number of units produced, or a sales commission on the number of items sold. This reinforcement schedule is effective as long as the ratio is not set too high (that is, an impossible amount of work required for each unit of pay or reinforcement) and the reinforcement is worth the effort.

Other reinforcement schedules include variable ratios, variable intervals, and mixed schedules. The research is discussed in *Schedules of Reinforcement* (1957) by C. B. Ferster and Skinner, and *Contingencies of Reinforcement* (Skinner, 1969).

Verbal Behavior

Skinner has long had an interest in verbal behavior, the only area in which he admits that there is any difference between rat and human. The sounds the human organism makes in speech, Skinner argues, are responses that can be reinforced (by other speech sounds or gestures) in the same way a rat's bar-pressing behavior can be reinforced by food. For the infant, the sounds that will be reinforced depend on the culture in which it is being raised, but the mechanics of verbal behavior apply independently of culture.

Verbal behavior, Skinner said, requires two people in interaction—one speaking and one listening. The speaker makes a response, that is, utters a sound. The listener, by his or her behavior in reinforcing, not reinforcing, or punishing the speaker for what has been said, can control the speaker's subsequent behavior. For example, if every time the speaker used a certain word or phrase, the listener smiled or said, "That's nice," the listener would increase the probability that the speaker would use that word or phrase again. If the listener responded by frowning, making hostile gestures, or commenting unfavorably on certain words, he or she would increase the likelihood that the speaker would avoid using those words in the future.

We can see this process in the behavior of parents when their children are learning to speak. Unacceptable words, incorrect usage, or poor pronunciation elicit different reactions from correct usage and pronunciation. In this way the child is taught the proper use of speech, at least as its parents understand it.

These simple examples do not fully encompass the complexity of Skinner's work in this field. The point to be remembered is that, to Skinner, speech is behavior and is subject to contingencies of reinforcement and prediction and control. His work in this area is summarized in *Verbal Behavior* (1957).

The Machines of Skinner's Behaviorism

We have discussed the Skinner box and its use in operant conditioning, but that was not the only machine Skinner developed. The Skinner box brought him prominence in psychology, but it was another invention that first gained him notice (or at least notoriety) among the general public. In 1945, in an article in the *Ladies Home Journal*, Skinner described his aircrib—a device to mechanize the care of an infant.

When Skinner and his wife decided they wanted a second child, she protested that caring for a baby through the first two years required too much attention and menial labor, so Skinner invented a way of relieving parents of that task. The aircribs were made available commercially but never became a big success. The aircrib

> is a large, air-conditioned, temperature controlled, germ free, soundproof compartment in which a baby can sleep and play without blankets or clothing other than a diaper. It allows complete freedom of movement, and relative safety from the usual colds and heat rashes. (Rice, 1968, p. 98)

Skinner and his wife raised the child in an aircrib. Except for a broken leg the child suffered in a skiing accident while out of the box, she apparently bore no ill effects and learned to beat Skinner at chess.

Skinner's best-known apparatus is the teaching machine, invented by psychologist Sidney Pressey in the 1920s. Unfortunately for Pressey, the machine was far ahead of its time, and no one expressed any interest in it (Hobbs, 1980). "I had not known of Pressey's work," Skinner reported. "Obviously, he had been a generation ahead of me in saying that machines would help both the teacher and the student" (Skinner, 1983, p. 70). Skinner popularized the machine after a visit to his daughter's fourth-grade class, when he decided that something had to be done to improve the teaching process. Whether his innovation was an improvement is controversial, but there is no denying that teaching machines and programmed instruction have been put to use in a great many ways, from the teaching of elementary mathematics skills to more complex job training. Skinner summarized his contributions to this field in *The Technology of Teaching* (1968).

Walden Two—A Behaviorist Society

More than any other behaviorist, Skinner has mapped out a program of behavioral control in which he attempts to transpose the findings from his laboratory to society at large. What he has tried to develop is a "technology of behavior." Whereas Watson talked in general terms about a foundation for saner living through the principles of conditioning, Skinner has outlined in detail the operation of such a society.

In 1948 he published a novel, *Walden Two*, which describes a 1000-member rural community in which every aspect of life is controlled by positive reinforcement. The book was both hailed and reviled in reviews, and never sold more than a few thousand copies a year until the early 1960s when, for some reason, sales increased sharply. The book continues to be popular and is required reading in many college courses. It had sold more than two million copies in English by 1982.

A national Walden Two conference was held in 1966 and small Walden Two communities have been reported in several parts of the United States. One such community, Twin Oaks (Louisa, Virginia 23093), publishes a newsletter for those interested in how the experiment is working.[3]

The long line of thought from Galileo and Newton through the British empiricists to Watson reaches its culmination in Skinner's designed society and his basic assumption about the nature of the human being as a machine.

> If we are to use the methods of science in the field of human affairs, we must assume that behavior is lawful and determined. . . . that what a man does is the result of specifiable conditions and that once these conditions have been discovered, we can anticipate and to some extent determine his actions. (Skinner, 1953, p. 6)

The mechanistic, analytic, and deterministic approach of natural science, reinforced by Skinner's conditioning experiments, has persuaded the behaviorists that human behavior can be controlled, guided, modified, and shaped by the proper use of positive reinforcement.

In the free will–determinism controversy it is easy to see on which side of the fence the Skinnerians sit. Skinner repeatedly makes the point that

> the issue of personal freedom must not be allowed to interfere with a scientific analysis of human behavior. . . . We cannot expect to profit from applying the methods of science to human behavior if for some extraneous reason we refuse to admit that our subject matter can be controlled. (Skinner, 1953, p. 322)

This position is discussed in *Beyond Freedom and Dignity* (1971), a book that generated a great deal of publicity, brought about Skinner's appearance on several television talk shows, and became a best-seller. As with *Walden Two*, the work was praised by some and derided by others. The fact that it was read by so many people certainly demonstrates public curiosity about the Skinnerian position.

Behavior Modification

Skinner's program for society based on positive reinforcement exists only in fictional terms (so far), but the control or modification of behavior at the level of individuals and small groups is widespread. Behavior modification through positive reinforcement has become immensely popular and has been used with great success in mental hospitals, factories, prisons, and schools to change abnormal or undesirable behaviors to more desirable ones. In essence, the technique of behavior modification works with people in the same way the Skinner box works to change the behavior of rats, through reinforcing the desired behavior and not reinforcing undesired behavior.

Consider the child who throws temper tantrums to get its own way. By giving in to the child, the parents are reinforcing the undesirable temper tantrums. In behavior modification such behavior would never be reinforced. Instead, more desirable and pleasant behaviors would be reinforced. After a time the child's behavior will be modified because the temper tantrums no longer work to bring attention and rewards, whereas more pleasant behaviors do.

[3] See K. Kinkade, *A Walden Two Experiment: The First Five Years of Twin Oaks Community* (New York: Morrow, 1973). Foreword by B. F. Skinner. Also C. Cordes, "Easing toward perfection at Twin Oaks" (*APA Monitor*, November 1984).

Operant conditioning has been applied in the business world where behavior-modification programs have successfully reduced absenteeism and abuse of sick-leave time and have improved job performance and safety. Also, behavior-modification techniques have been used to teach job skills to disadvantaged workers, often succeeding where more traditional training has failed.

These principles have also been applied to groups of mental patients. By rewarding these people with tokens (which can be exchanged for possessions or privileges) when they behave in the desired ways, and by not reinforcing negative or disruptive behavior, positive changes in behavior are induced. Note that unlike traditional clinical techniques, there is no concern with what might be going on in the minds of the patients, no more than there is for what might be going on inside the rats in the Skinner box. The focus is exclusively on overt behavior and positive reinforcement.

Note also that punishment is not used. The subjects are not punished for failing to behave in desirable ways. Instead, they are reinforced only when their behavior changes in positive ways. Skinner's research has demonstrated, as Thorndike's did earlier, that positive reinforcement is much more effective than punishment in getting people or animals to alter their behavior. (Skinner wrote that as a child he was never physically punished by his father and only once by his mother. She washed out his mouth with soap and water for saying a "naughty" word. He did not say whether the punishment was effective in changing his behavior.)

Comment

However one might view Skinner's intentions—as a savior or enslaver of human beings—there is no denying the extent of his influence on contemporary psychology. Skinner has received much criticism, however, both from inside and outside the psychological establishment. His attitude toward his critics is to ignore them. Discussing a particularly scathing review of one of his books, he said, "I read a bit of it and saw that he missed the point, so I never read the rest. I never answer any of my critics. I generally don't even read them. There are better things to do with my time than clear up their misunderstanding" (Rice, 1968, p. 90).

Perhaps the most frequent criticism is directed at Skinner's extreme brand of positivism and its accompanying opposition to theory. Opponents argue that it is impossible to eliminate all theorizing, as Skinner would have it. Because the details of an experiment must be planned in advance of the actual situation, this in itself is evidence of theorizing, however simple. It has been noted that Skinner's acceptance of the basic principles of conditioning as the framework for his research constitutes some degree of theorizing. Further, Skinner has made confident assertions about economic, social, political, and religious affairs that apparently are derived from his system. This willingness to extrapolate beyond the data, particularly in regard to proposals about complex human problems, is inconsistent with an antitheory stand. Certainly, critics argue, Skinner has gone beyond the observable data in presenting blueprints for the redesign of society; this seems contrary to the principles of his system.

The narrow range of behavior studied in Skinnerian laboratories (bar pressing and key pecking, for example) has also been attacked. Critics argue that numerous aspects or examples of behavior have been largely ignored.

Whether the criticism or the praise will prevail in the long run, it can be said that Skinner is the incontestable leader and champion of behaviorist psychology. Most of his critics would be forced to agree that the American psychology of the day was molded more by his work than by the work of any other psychologist.

The American Psychological Association recognized the magnitude of Skinner's contribution when in 1958 it granted him the Distinguished Scientific Contribution Award, with the following citation:

> An imaginative and creative scientist, characterized by great objectivity in scientific matters and by warmth and enthusiasm in personal contacts. Choosing simple operant behavior as subject matter, he has challenged alternative analyses of behavior, insisting that description take precedence over hypotheses. By careful control of experimental conditions, he has produced data which are relatively free from fortuitous variation. Despite his antitheoretical position, he is considered an important systematist and has developed a self-consistent description of behavior which has greatly increased our ability to predict and control the behavior of organisms from rat to man. Few American psychologists have had so profound an impact on the development of psychology and on promising younger psychologists.

In 1968 Skinner was awarded the National Medal of Science, the highest accolade given by the United States government for distinguished contributions to science. In 1971 the American Psychological Foundation presented him with its gold medal. That same year, he appeared on the cover of *Time*.

There is no question that Skinner's radical behaviorism achieved a strong position in psychology. The Skinnerian *Journal of the Experimental Analysis of Behavior* continues to flourish, as does the Division for the Experimental Analysis of Behavior (Division 25) of the American Psychological Association. Behavior modification has gained much popularity and its results provide additional support for Skinner's approach. By any standard of public acclaim, Skinnerian behaviorism has overshadowed all other varieties of behaviorism (Herrnstein, 1977).

THE COGNITIVE CHALLENGE TO BEHAVIORISM

Behaviorism, like the other systematic positions, has a long history, as we have seen in these three chapters. Watson gave voice to the changing climate of the times in American psychology, revolted against its mentalistic background, and formally established an objective science of behavior. This vigorous Watsonian revolt marked the beginning of the positivist era in American psychology. There followed enthusiastic formulations of different kinds of behaviorism. Fifty years after the publication of Watson's article, which formally began behaviorism, Skinner celebrated the anniversary with an article entitled "Behaviorism at Fifty" (Skinner, 1963), in which he noted that the tremendous progress in experimental psychology in America was due primarily to the influence of behaviorism.

For all its popularity and influence, behaviorism has come under attack from large numbers of psychologists, including many who consider themselves to be behaviorists. These critics have questioned behaviorism's total denial of mental or cognitive processes. This movement, the so-called cognitive revolution, marks the third stage—the *neo-neobehavioristic* stage—in the development of behaviorism.

Since about 1960 there has been a gradual movement of psychology "away from the restrictive shackles of behaviorism toward a more flexible emphasis on cognitive processes" (Bruner, 1982, p. 42). Today, consciousness has returned to psychology in full measure. As you might expect, Skinner has decried this trend, noting that "mentalism returned in a flood. . . . It became fashionable to insert the word 'cognitive' wherever possible" (Skinner, 1983, p. 194).

We discuss the cognitive movement, its origins, and its impact on contemporary psychology in Chapter 15. For now, let us offer one example of how the return to consciousness changed the nature of behaviorism, namely, the work of Albert Bandura, a neo-neobehaviorist.

Socio-Behaviorism: Albert Bandura (1925–   )

Beginning in the early 1960s, Bandura developed a version of behaviorism, called *social learning theory,* that takes a socio-behaviorist approach (Bandura, 1977). It is a less extreme form of behaviorism than Skinner's, and it reflects and reinforces the impact of the cognitive revolution. It must be remembered, however, that Bandura's approach remains behavioristic. Its research focuses on the observation of the behavior of human subjects in interaction, it does not use introspection, and it stresses the role of reinforcement in acquiring and modifying behaviors.

In addition to being behavioral, Bandura's system is also cognitive. It considers the influence on external reinforcement schedules of such thought processes as beliefs, expectations, and instructions. In Bandura's view, behavioral responses are not automatically triggered by external stimuli in the manner of a robot or a machine. Instead, reactions to stimuli are self-activated. When an external reinforcement changes behavior, it does so because the individual is consciously aware of what is being reinforced and anticipates the same reinforcement for behaving in the same way again.

Although Bandura agrees with Skinner that our behavior can change as a result of reinforcement, he also believes—and has empirically demonstrated—that virtually all kinds of behavior can be learned in the absence of directly experienced reinforcement. Rather than always having to experience reinforcement ourselves, we can learn through vicarious reinforcement, by observing the behavior of other people and the consequences of those behaviors.

The ability to learn by example and by vicarious reinforcement assumes the capacity to anticipate and appreciate consequences that we have only observed in others and not yet experienced ourselves. Thus, we can regulate and guide our behavior by visualizing or imagining as yet unexperienced consequences of that behavior and by making a conscious decision to behave or not behave in the same way.

Bandura also discusses the concept of *self-efficacy,* our sense of self-worth and self-esteem, our feeling of adequacy and efficiency in dealing with life (Bandura, 1982). This internal state can influence our behavior in many ways.

We can see how powerful cognitive processes are in Bandura's approach and how it differs from Skinner's. For example, in Bandura's view, it is not the actual schedule of reinforcement that is so effective in changing behavior, as Skinner argues, but rather what the person thinks that schedule is.

Rather than learning by experiencing reinforcement directly, we learn through *modeling,* observing other people and modeling our behavior after theirs. In Skinner's view, whoever controls the reinforcers controls behavior. In Bandura's view, whoever controls the models in a society controls behavior.

Bandura's cognitive–behavioral approach is popular with psychologists and has generated a great deal of supportive research. It has also led to an approach to behavior therapy in which subjects watch models who display desired behaviors.

The recognition of Bandura's contribution to contemporary psychology is indicated by his election to the presidency of the American Psychological Association in 1974 and by his Distinguished Scientific Contribution Award from the APA in 1980.

Comment

Influential though the cognitive movement has been in modifying behaviorism, the general behaviorist approach has not been destroyed by this newer force. Bandura and others who subscribe to the cognitive viewpoint are still behaviorists. Behavior remains their theoretical focus and the subject of their research.

Behaviorism is still prominent in American psychology today, although it is a different form of behaviorism than was promoted during the first half-century of its existence. The species has evolved, but it is still recognizably similar to its earlier form.

Behaviorism has been broadened and strengthened by this infusion of the recognition of consciousness. That behaviorism has been able to adapt to such a dramatic change in its environment attests to its basic vitality and validity. Not all behaviorists have accepted or embraced the cognitive revolution, and it is too early to judge its final impact. It is not yet history; it is very much history in the making.

SUGGESTED READINGS

Early Behaviorists

Beach, F. A., Hebb, D. O., Morgan, C. T., & Nissen, H. W. (Eds.) (1960). *The neuropsychology of Lashley.* New York: McGraw-Hill.

Carmichael, L. (1959). Karl Spencer Lashley, experimental psychologist. *Science, 129,* 1409–1412.

Erickson, R. W. (1950). An examination of the system of Professor K. S. Lashley. *Journal of General Psychology, 42,* 243–260.

Gundlach, R. (1927). Some difficulties with Weiss's behavioristic postulates. *American Journal of Psychology, 38,* 469–475.

Holt, E. B. (1973). *The concept of consciousness.* New York: Arno Press. (Original work published 1914).

Lashley, K. S. (1923). The behavioristic interpretation of consciousness. *Psychological Review, 30,* 237–272, 329–353.

Weiss, A. P. (1917). Relation between structural and behavioral psychology. *Psychological Review, 24,* 301–317.

Weiss, A. P. (1917). Relation between functional and behavioral psychology. *Psychological Review, 24,* 353–368.

Williams, K. A. (1931). Five behaviorisms. *American Journal of Psychology, 43,* 337–360.

Operationism

Bergmann, G. (1954). Sense and nonsense in operationism. *Scientific Monthly, 79,* 210–214.

Bergmann, G., & Spence, K. W. (1941). Operationism and theory in psychology. *Psychological Review, 48,* 1–12.

Bridgman, P. W. (1954). Remarks on the present state of operationism. *Scientific Monthly, 79,* 209–210.

Stevens, S. S. (1935). The operational basis of psychology. *American Journal of Psychology, 47,* 323–330.

Neobehaviorists

Erickson, R. W. (1948). An examination of Edward C. Tolman's system of psychology. *Journal of General Psychology, 39,* 73–90.

Evans, R. (1968). *B. F. Skinner: The man and his ideas.* New York: Dutton.

Guthrie, E. R. (1950). The status of systematic psychology. *American Psychologist, 5,* 97–101.

Guthrie, E. R. (1952). *The psychology of learning* (rev. ed.). New York: Harper & Row.

Guthrie, E. R. (1959). Association by contiguity. In S. Koch (Ed.), *Psychology: A study of a science* (vol. 2, pp. 158–195). New York: McGraw-Hill.

Guttman, N. (1977). On Skinner and Hull: A reminiscence and projection. *American Psychologist, 32,* 321–328.

Hull, C. L. (1937). Mind, mechanism and adaptive behavior. *Psychological Review, 44,* 1–32.

Pepper, S. C. (1934). The conceptual framework of Tolman's purposive behaviorism. *Psychological Review, 41,* 108–133.

Skinner, B. F. (1953). *Science and human behavior.* New York: Macmillan.

Skinner, B. F. (1959). A case history in scientific method. In S. Koch (Ed.), *Psychology: A study of a science* (vol. 2, pp. 359–379). New York: McGraw-Hill.

Skinner, B. F. (1963). Behaviorism at fifty. *Science, 140,* 951–958.

Skinner, B. F. (1974). *About behaviorism.* New York: Alfred A. Knopf.

Spence, K. W. (1948). The postulates and methods of behaviorism. *Psychological Review, 55,* 67–78.

Tolman, E. C. (1922). A new formula for behaviorism. *Psychological Review, 29,* 44–53.

Tolman, E. C. (1932). *Purposive behavior in animals and men.* New York: Appleton-Century-Crofts.

Tolman, E. C. (1959). Principles of purposive behavior. In S. Koch (Ed.), *Psychology: A study of a science* (vol. 2, pp. 92–157). New York: McGraw-Hill.

Socio-Behaviorism

Bandura, A. (1974). Behavior theory and the models of man. *American Psychologist, 29,* 859–869.

Bandura, A. (1977). *Social learning theory.* Englewood Cliffs, NJ: Prentice-Hall.

Woodward, W. R. (1982). The "discovery" of social behaviorism and social learning theory, 1870–1980. *American Psychologist, 37,* 396–410.

12

Gestalt Psychology

We have traced the development of psychology from the initial ideas of Wilhelm Wundt and their elaboration by E. B. Titchener, through the growth of the functionalist school, to the spread of the behaviorism of John B. Watson and B. F. Skinner, which arose in opposition to the earlier movements.

While all these movements were forming in the United States, the Gestalt revolution was taking hold in Germany.[1] It was yet an additional protest against Wundtian psychology, further testimony to the importance of that initial approach as an inspiration for opposing points of view and as an effective base from which to launch new systems of psychology.

In its attack on the Wundtian establishment, the Gestalt revolution focused primarily on one aspect of Wundt's work, his atomism or elementism. The Gestalt psychologists seized upon the fact that Wundt had recognized the fundamental status of sensory elements, and they made that the target of their opposition. "We had been shocked," wrote Wolfgang Köhler, a founder of Gestalt psychology, "by the thesis that all psychological facts . . . consist of unrelated inert atoms and that almost the only factors which combine these atoms and thus introduce action are associations" (Köhler, 1959, p. 728).

To understand the nature of the Gestalt revolution, we must return to around 1912, the year described as a "time of troubles" for the old approach to psychology, the time when behaviorism was beginning its violent attack against Wundt, Titchener, and the newer functionalism. The animal research of Thorndike and Pavlov had been on the rise for a decade. Thorndike's first full statement of his position was made in 1911–1913, and the significance for psychology of Pavlov's conditioned reflex was soon to be acknowledged. Another fresh approach, psychoanalysis, was also more than a decade old.

---

[1]Gestalt psychology should not be confused with Frederick (Fritz) Perls's Gestalt psychotherapy, which was popular in the 1960s, although many people mistakenly make such a connection. There is no conceptual relationship between these two approaches other than their common use of the word *Gestalt*. Perls wrote that he was not a Gestalt psychologist and that he had never read any of the Gestalt psychologists' books (Henle, 1978a; Wertheimer, 1979).

The Gestalt psychologists' attack on atomism in Germany was simultaneous with, although independent of, the American behaviorist movement. Both movements started by opposing the same thing, but later they came to oppose each other. There were sharp differences between the Gestalt psychologists and the behaviorists. Gestalt psychology accepted the value of consciousness but criticized the attempt to analyze it into elements. Behaviorism refused even to acknowledge the existence of consciousness for psychology.

Gestalt psychologists referred to the Wundtian approach (as they understood it) as "brick-and-mortar psychology," implying that the elements (the bricks) were held together by the mortar of the process of association. They argued that when one looks out a window one immediately sees the trees and the sky, not the alleged sensory elements such as brightnesses and hues that constitute the perception of the trees and the sky. They accused the Wundtians of claiming that our perception of objects consists of the accumulation of elements into groups or bundles. The Gestalt psychologists maintained that when sensory elements are combined, something new is formed. Put together a number of musical notes and something new, a melody, emerges from their combination, something that did not exist in any of the individual notes. Stated succinctly: the whole is different from the sum of its parts, a point recognized by Wundt in his doctrine of apperception.

Miller (1962)[2] described an imaginary visit to a psychological laboratory in Germany around 1912, which points out the difference between the Gestalt and the Wundtian approaches to perception.

As you walk into the laboratory, the psychologist asks you what you see on the table:

"A book."

"Yes, of course, it is a book," he agrees, "but what do you *really* see?"

"What do you mean, 'What do I *really* see'?" you ask, puzzled. "I told you that I see a book. It is a small book with a red cover."

The psychologist is persistent. "What is your perception *really*?" he insists. "Describe it to me as precisely as you can."

"You mean it isn't a book? What is this, some kind of trick?"

There is a hint of impatience. "Yes, it is a book. There is no trickery involved. I just want you to describe to me *exactly* what you can see, no more and no less."

You are growing very suspicious now. "Well," you say, "from this angle the cover of the book looks like a dark red parallelogram."

"Yes," he says, pleased. "Yes, you see a patch of dark red in the shape of a parallelogram. What else?"

"There is a grayish white edge below it and another thin line of the same dark red below that. Under it I see the table—" He winces. "Around it I see a somewhat mottled brown with wavering streaks of lighter brown running roughly parallel to one another."

"Fine, fine." He thanks you for your cooperation.

As you stand there looking at the book on the table you are a little embarrassed that this persistent fellow was able to drive you to such an analysis. He made you so

[2] From pp. 103–105 in *Psychology* by George A. Miller. Copyright 1962 by George A. Miller. Reprinted by permission of Harper & Row, Publishers, Inc.

cautious that you were not sure any longer what you really saw and what you only thought you saw. You were, in fact, as suspicious as the New England farmer who would admit only that, "It looks like a cow on this side." In your caution you began talking about what you saw in terms of sensations, where just a moment earlier you were quite certain that you perceived a book on a table.

Your reverie is interrupted suddenly by the appearance of a psychologist who looks vaguely like Wilhelm Wundt. "Thank you, for helping to confirm once more my theory of perception. You have proved," he says, "that the book you see is nothing but a compound of elementary sensations. When you were trying to be precise and say accurately what it was you really saw, you had to speak in terms of color patches, not objects. It is the color sensations that are primary, and every visual object is reducible to them. Your perception of the book is constructed from sensations just as a molecule is constructed from atoms."

This little speech is apparently a signal for battle to begin. "Nonsense!" shouts a voice from the opposite end of the hall. "Nonsense! Any fool knows that the *book* is the primary, immediate, direct, compelling, perceptual fact!" The psychologist who charges down upon you now bears a faint resemblance to William James, but he seems to have a German accent, and his face is so flushed with anger that you cannot be sure. "This reduction of a perception into sensations that you keep talking about is nothing but an intellectual game. An object is not just a bundle of sensations. Any man who goes about seeing patches of dark redness where he ought to see books is sick!"

As the fight begins to gather momentum you close the door softly and slip away. You have what you came for, an illustration that there are two different attitudes, two different ways to talk about the information that our senses provide.

The Gestalt psychologists believed there was more to perception than meets the eye, so to speak, that our perception somehow goes beyond the basic physical data (the sensory elements) provided to the sense organs. As with other movements, the ideas of the Gestalt protest have their historical antecedents. After we examine these early influences, we shall discuss the three major figures in the formal founding of the Gestalt movement and the basic principles of the Gestalt school.

ANTECEDENT INFLUENCES

The basis of the Gestalt position, its focus on the unity of perception, can be found in the work of the German philosopher Immanuel Kant (1724–1804). This eminent man, who never ventured more than 60 miles from his place of birth, dominated philosophical thinking for more than a generation. Although his contribution to psychology is less extensive than his contribution to philosophy, it is important nonetheless.

Kant influenced psychology through his emphasis on the unity of a perceptual act. He argued that when we perceive what we call objects, we encounter mental states that might seem to be composed of bits and pieces; these are the sensory elements of which the British empiricists and associationists spoke. These elements are meaningfully organized in *a priori* fashion and not through the mechanical process of association. The mind, in the process of perceiving, forms or creates a unitary experience. According to Kant, perception is not a passive impression and combination of sensory elements, as the empiricists and associationists claimed, but an active organization of these elements into a coherent experience. Thus, the raw material of perception is given form and organization by the mind. This position is contrary to the heart of associationism. To Kant, some of the forms that the mind imposes on experience are innate—such as space, time, and causality—in that they do not derive from experience but exist in the mind as intuitively knowable.

Franz Brentano anticipated the formal Gestalt movement through his insistence that psychology study the process or act of experiencing rather than the content of experience (elementary sensations). He considered Wundtian introspection to be artificial and favored a less rigid and more direct observation of experience as it occurs, much like the later Gestalt method.

Ernst Mach (1838–1916), a physicist, exerted more direct influence on the Gestalt revolution. In his book, *The Analysis of Sensations* (1885), Mach wrote about sensations of space-form and time-form. He considered spatial patterns such as geometric figures and temporal patterns such as melodies to be sensations. These space-form and time-form sensations were independent of their elements. For example, a circle might be white or black, large or small, and lose nothing of its elemental quality of circularity.

Mach argued that our visual or aural perception of an object does not change, even though we may change our spatial orientation with regard to the object. A table remains a table in our perception whether we look at it from the side or from the top or from an angle. Similarly, a series of sounds such as in a melody remains the same in our perception even when the tempo is altered.

Mach's work was expanded by Christian von Ehrenfels (1859–1932), who may be the most important forebear of Gestalt psychology. Von Ehrenfels suggested that there are qualities of experience that cannot be explained in terms of combinations of the traditional kinds of sensations. He called these qualities *Gestalt qualitäten*, or form qualities, perceptions based on something beyond the individual sensations. A melody, for example, is a form quality because it sounds the same even when transposed to different keys. The melody is independent of the particular sensations of which it is composed. To von Ehrenfels, and the Austrian school of *Gestalt qualität* founded at Graz, form itself was an element (although not a sensation), a new element created by the action of the mind operating on the sensory elements. Thus, the mind creates form out of elementary sensations.

Although Mach and von Ehrenfels thought along the lines that came to be known as Gestalt psychology, they deviated little from the older elementist position. Rather than oppose the notion of elementism, as the Gestalt psychologists later did, they simply added a new element, that of form. Although they criticized the same position as the Gestalt psychologists, they offered a quite different solution. Still, von Ehrenfels became influential in the Gestalt movement. The primary founder of Gestalt psychology, Max Wertheimer, studied under von Ehrenfels. In Wertheimer's article reprinted later in this chapter he noted that "the most important impulse" for the movement came from von Ehrenfels.

William James, by opposing psychological elementism, served as a precursor of Gestalt psychology. James regarded elements of consciousness as artificial abstractions and noted that we see objects, not bundles of sensations.

Another early influence is the phenomenological movement in German philosophy and psychology. Methodologically, phenomenology refers to a free and unbiased description of immediate experience exactly as it occurs. It is uncorrected observation in which an experience is not analyzed into elements or otherwise artificially abstracted. It involves the almost naïve experience of common sense rather than experience as reported by a trained introspector with a special systematic orientation.

The phenomenological tradition in psychology is assumed to have begun with Goethe, and its active use can be traced to a number of scholars in psychology and other disciplines. A group of phenomenological psychologists was at G. E. Müller's laboratory at Göttingen in the years 1909–1915. There, Erich R. Jaensch, David Katz, and Edgar Rubin conducted extensive phenomenological research that anticipated the formal Gestalt school, which was later to use the phenomenological approach.

Not to be neglected among antecedent influences of Gestalt psychology is the *Zeitgeist*, particularly with regard to physics. In the closing decades of the nineteenth century, physics was becoming less atomistic as it came to recognize and accept the notion of fields of force. The classic example of this new direction in physics is magnetism, a property or quality that seemed difficult to define or understand in traditional Galilean–Newtonian terms. For example, when iron filings are shaken onto a sheet of paper that is resting on top of a magnet, the filings become arranged in a characteristic pattern. The filings do not touch the magnet, yet they are obviously affected by the field of force around the magnet. At the time, light and electricity were considered to operate similarly. These fields of force were thought to possess both spatial extension and configuration or pattern. They were, in other words, believed to be new structural entities, not summations of effects of individual elements or particles.

Thus, the notion of atomism, which had been so influential in the establishment of the new science of psychology, was under serious attack in physics. Physicists were beginning to think in terms of organic wholes, a concept congruent with Gestalt psychology. The changes offered to psychology by the Gestalt psychologists paralleled the changes in the physics of the day. Psychology was again emulating the older, well-established natural sciences.

The impact on psychology of this changing emphasis in physics came about in a personal way. Wolfgang Köhler had a strong background in physics and had studied for a time under Max Planck, one of the great physicists of the twentieth century. Köhler wrote that it was because of Planck's influence that he began to sense a connection between field physics and the Gestalt emphasis on wholes. He saw in physics an increasing reluctance to continue to deal with elements and a focus instead on larger systems or fields. He wrote that "Gestalt psychology has since become a kind of application of field physics to essential parts of psychology" (Köhler, 1969, p. 77).

The founder of behaviorism, John B. Watson, by contrast, apparently had no training in the new physics and so could continue to develop a reductionist approach to psychology, focusing on elements of behavior, a view compatible with the principles of the older atomistic physics.

THE FOUNDING OF GESTALT PSYCHOLOGY

The formal movement known as Gestalt psychology grew out of a research study conducted in 1910 by the German psychologist Max Wertheimer. While riding on a train during his vacation, Wertheimer had an idea for an experiment on the seeing of motion when no actual motion had taken place. Promptly forgetting his vacation, he left the train at Frankfurt, purchased a toy stroboscope,[3] and verified his insight in a preliminary way in his hotel room. He later carried out more formal research at the University of Frankfurt, which provided a tachistoscope for his use. In Frankfurt were two other young German psychologists, Kurt Koffka and Wolfgang Köhler, who, some years earlier, had been students at the University of Berlin. Although each had been working productively in psychology, they shortly embarked on a joint crusade.

Wertheimer's research problem, on which Koffka and Köhler served as subjects, involved the perception of apparent movement, that is, the perception of motion when no actual physical movement has occurred. Wertheimer referred to it as "the impression of movement" (Seaman, 1984, p. 3). Using the tachistoscope, Wertheimer projected light through two slits, one vertical and the other 20 or 30 degrees from the vertical. If light were shown through one slit and then the other, with a relatively long interval in between (over 200 milliseconds), the subjects saw what appeared to be two successive lights, first a light at one slit and then a light at the other. When the interval between the lights was short, the subjects saw what appeared to be two lights, each on continuously. With an optimal interval (about 60 milliseconds) between the lights, the subjects saw a single line of light appear to move from one slit to the other and back again.

These findings may seem straightforward. The phenomenon had been known for years and may even be considered a matter of common sense. According to the prevailing psychological position, the Wundtian viewpoint, all conscious experience could be analyzed into its sensory elements. Yet how could this perception of apparent movement be explained in terms of a summation of individual sensory elements? Could one stationary stimulus be added to another to produce a sensation of movement? It could not, and this was precisely the point of Wertheimer's brilliantly simple demonstration: it defied explanation by the Wundtian system.

Wertheimer believed that the phenomenon verified in his laboratory was, in its own way, as elementary as a sensation, yet it obviously differed from a sensation or even a succession of sensations. He gave the occurrence a name befitting its unique status: the *phi phenomenon*. We may ask how Wertheimer explained the phi phenomenon when the traditional psychology of the day could not. His answer was as simple and ingenious as the verifying experiment itself: apparent movement did not need explaining. It existed as perceived and could not be reduced to anything simpler.

According to Wundt, introspection of the stimulus would produce two successive lines and nothing else, but no matter how rigorously one might introspect the two exposures, the experience of a single line in motion persisted. Any further attempt at analysis was a failure. The whole (the movement) was different from the sum of its parts (the two stationary lines). The traditional associationist–atomistic psychology, dominant for so many years, had been challenged, and it was a challenge it could not meet. Wertheimer's results were published in 1912 in an article, "Experimental Studies of the Perception of Movement," that is considered to mark the beginning of the new school.

Max Wertheimer (1880–1943)

Born in Prague, Max Wertheimer attended the local *Gymnasium* until the age of 18 and studied law for 2½ years at the university. He shifted to philosophy, attending the

---

[3] The stroboscope, invented about 80 years earlier by J. Plateau, was a forerunner of the motion picture camera. It is an instrument that rapidly projects a series of different pictures on the eye, producing apparent motion.

From his study of the perception of apparent motion, Max Wertheimer (1880–1943) started the formal movement of Gestalt psychology.

lectures of von Ehrenfels, and later studied philosophy and psychology at Berlin. He obtained his degree in 1904 at Würzburg under Oswald Külpe, at the height of the imageless–thought controversy. Between 1904 and 1912, Wertheimer spent his time at Prague, Vienna, and Berlin before settling in Frankfurt. He lectured at Frankfurt for four years and in 1929 was granted a professorship. During World War I, he conducted research of military value on listening devices for submarines and harbor fortifications.

Wertheimer was the oldest of the three original Gestalt psychologists and the intellectual leader of the movement. (Koffka and Köhler served to promote Wertheimer's prominent position, but each was influential in his own right.) Wertheimer produced important papers on creative thinking and on perceptual grouping.

In 1921 Wertheimer, Koffka, and Köhler, assisted by Kurt Goldstein and Hans Gruhle, founded the journal *Psychologische Forschung* (*Psychological Research*), which became the official organ of the Gestalt school. Twenty-two volumes were published before it was suspended in 1938 under the Hitler regime.

Wertheimer was among the first group of refugee scholars from Germany to arrive in New York in 1933. In 1934 he became associated with the New School for Social Research, where he remained until his death in 1943. His years in the United States were busy, but he became increasingly exhausted by the burdens of adapting to a new language and culture. His research was conducted rather informally and was communicated personally to his friends and at meetings of psychologists.

During his last years in New York Wertheimer made a strong impression on a young American psychologist, Abraham Maslow. Maslow was so in awe of Wertheimer that he began to study the man's personal qualities and characteristics. It was from these initial observations of Wertheimer (and of Ruth Benedict, an anthropologist) that Maslow developed his concept of self-actualization (see Chapter 15).

Kurt Koffka (1886–1941)

Koffka was probably the most productive of these three Gestalt psychologists. He received his education at Berlin, his place of birth, and during his youth developed an interest in science and philosophy that was strengthened at Edinburgh in 1903–1904. After returning to Berlin he studied psychology with Carl Stumpf, receiving his degree in 1909. He took a number of research positions and in 1910 began his long and fruitful association with Wertheimer and Köhler in Frankfurt. In 1911 he went to the University of Giessen, and remained there until 1924. At Giessen he conducted a good deal of research and during World War I worked with brain-damaged and aphasic patients at the psychiatric clinic.

After the war, when American psychology was becoming vaguely aware of the school developing in Germany, Koffka was persuaded to write an article on the new movement for the *Psychological Bulletin*. This article, "Perception: An Introduction to Gestalt-Theorie" (Koffka, 1922), presented the basic concepts of Gestalt psychology and the results and implications of much research.

Although the article was important as the first formal exposition of the Gestalt revolution to many American psychologists, it may have done a disservice to the spread of Gestalt psychology. The title, with "perception" its first word, started a misunderstanding that lingers today, namely, the idea that Gestalt psychology deals exclusively with perception and therefore has no relevance for other areas of psychology.

In reality Gestalt psychology was "primarily concerned with thinking, with philosophical questions, and with learning; the main reason why the early Gestalt psychologists concentrated their systematic publications on perception was because of the *Zeitgeist*: Wundt's psychology, against which the Gestaltists rebelled, had obtained most of its support from studies of sensation and perception, so the Gestalt psychologists chose perception as the arena in order to attack Wundt in his own stronghold" (Michael Wertheimer, 1979, p. 134).

In 1921 Koffka published *The Growth of the Mind*, a book on developmental child psychology that became a great success in Germany and the United States. He was a visiting professor at Cornell University and at the University of Wisconsin in 1924, and in 1927 was appointed professor at Smith College, where he remained until his death in 1941. In 1932 Koffka accompanied an expedition to study the people of Central Asia. While recovering from a recurrent fever contracted on this expedition, he began work

Kurt Koffka (1886–1941) is often considered the most productive of the early Gestalt psychologists.

on his *Principles of Gestalt Psychology*, which was published in 1935. It was a difficult book to read and did not become the definitive treatment of Gestalt psychology he intended it to be.

Wolfgang Köhler (1887–1967)

Köhler, the youngest of the three, was the spokesman for the Gestalt movement. His books, written with great care and precision, became the definitive works on certain aspects of Gestalt psychology. Köhler's considerable training in physics under the emi-

nent Max Planck persuaded him that psychology must ally itself with physics. Born in
Reval (now Tallinn) in Estonia, Köhler was five years old when his family moved to
northern Germany. His university education was at Tübingen, Bonn, and Berlin, and he
received his degree from Stumpf in 1909. He went on to Frankfurt, arriving just before
Wertheimer and his stroboscope.

In 1913, at the invitation of the Prussian Academy of Science, Köhler went to Tenerife
in the Canary Islands to study chimpanzees. Six months after his arrival World War I
began and he was unable to leave. For the next seven years he studied learning in
chimpanzees and produced the classic volume *Mentality of Apes* (1917). The book
appeared in a second edition in 1924, and was translated into English and French.

Wolfgang Köhler (1887–
1967) was originally
trained in physics and
became one of the most
prominent spokesmen for
the Gestalt movement.

In 1920 Köhler returned to Germany and two years later succeeded Stumpf at Berlin, where he remained until 1935. The apparent reason for his appointment to this coveted position was the publication of *Static and Stationary Physical Gestalts* (1920), which won critical acclaim for its high level of scholarship.

In 1925–1926 Köhler lectured at Harvard and at Clark University, where he also taught the graduate students how to tango (Geldard, 1980). In 1929 he published, in English, *Gestalt Psychology*, the most comprehensive argument for the Gestalt movement. In 1935 he left Germany because of his continual conflicts with the Nazi regime. He had written a courageous anti-Nazi letter to a Berlin newspaper, "the last anti-Nazi article to be published openly in Germany under the Nazi regime" (Henle, 1978b, p. 940). Köhler, who was not Jewish, was incensed by Hitler's dismissal of all Jewish professors from German universities, and he spoke openly in his classes against the government. A gang of Nazis invaded his classroom. On the evening his letter appeared in the newspaper, he and a few friends sat quietly at home playing chamber music, waiting for the Gestapo to arrest him. The dreaded knock on the door never came.

Köhler emigrated to the United States where he taught at Swarthmore College. His later books include *The Place of Value in a World of Facts* (1938), *Dynamics in Psychology* (1940), and *Figural After-Effects* (1944), the last with Hans Wallach. In 1956 he received the Distinguished Scientific Contribution Award from the American Psychological Association and in 1959 was elected its president.

THE NATURE OF THE GESTALT REVOLT

The Gestalt principles were in direct opposition to much of the academic tradition of psychology in Germany. Behaviorism was less an immediate revolution against Wundt and structuralism because functionalism had already brought about some changes in American psychology. No such tempering paved the way for the Gestalt revolt in Germany. The pronouncements of the Gestaltists were nothing short of heresy to the German tradition.

The initiators of the Gestalt movement realized that they were taking on a powerful and rigid tradition, that they were striking at the foundation of psychology as it was then defined. Like most revolutionaries, the leaders of the Gestalt school demanded a complete revision of the old order, almost like "intellectual missionaries, spreading a new gospel" (Sokal, 1984, p. 1257). Köhler wrote:

> We were excited by what we found, and even more by the prospect of finding further revealing facts. Moreover, it was not only the stimulating newness of our enterprise which inspired us. There was also a great wave of relief—as though we were escaping from a prison. The prison was psychology as taught at the universities when we still were students. (Köhler, 1959, p. 285)

After the study of apparent movement, the Gestalt psychologists were quick to seize on other perceptual phenomena to support their position. The experience of perceptual constancies afforded ample corroboration. When we stand directly in front of a window, for example, a rectangular image is projected onto the retina, but when we stand off to one side and look at the window, the retinal image becomes a trapezoid, although the window is still perceived as rectangular. Our perception of the window remains unchanged even though the sensory datum (the image projected on the retina) has changed.

The same thing occurs with brightness and size constancy; the actual sensory elements can change radically, yet our perception does not. There are many similar examples in everyday experience. In these cases, as with apparent movement, the perceptual experience has a quality of wholeness that is not found in any of the parts. There can exist, then, a difference between the character of the actual perception and the character of the sensory stimulation. The perception cannot be explained as a collection of sensory elements or as the mere sum of the parts.

> The perception itself shows a character of totality, a form, a *Gestalt*, which in the very attempt at analysis is destroyed; and this experience, as directly given, sets the problem for psychology. It is this experience that presents the raw data which psychology must explain, and which it must never be content to explain away. To begin with elements is to begin at the wrong end; for elements are products of reflection and abstraction, remotely derived from the immediate experience they are invoked to explain. *Gestalt* psychology attempts to get back to naïve perception, to immediate experience "undebauched by learning"; and it insists that it finds there not assemblages of elements, but unified wholes; not masses of sensations, but trees, clouds, and sky. And this assertion it invites any one to verify simply by opening his eyes and looking at the world about him in his ordinary everyday way. (Heidbreder, 1933, p. 331)

The word "Gestalt" has caused some difficulty because it does not clearly indicate, as does "functionalism" or "behaviorism," what the movement stands for. Also, it has no exact counterpart in English. Several equivalents are in common use, such as form, shape, and configuration, and today "Gestalt" has become part of the English language.

In his book, *Gestalt Psychology* (1929), Köhler noted that the word was used in two ways in the German language. One usage denoted shape or form as a property of objects. In this sense, "Gestalt" refers to general properties that could be expressed in such terms as "angular" or "symmetrical." It describes characteristics such as triangularity (in geometrical figures) or temporal sequences (in a melody). The second usage denoted a concrete entity that has as one of its attributes a specific shape or form. In this sense, the word may refer, let us say, to triangles, rather than to the notion of triangularity. Thus, the word can be used for reference to objects rather than to the characteristic forms of these objects. In this sense, "Gestalt" refers to any segregated whole. Also, the term is not restricted to the visual field or even to the total sensory field and may be applied beyond the limits of sensory experience.

> According to the most general functional definition of the term, the processes of learning, of recall, of striving, of emotional attitude, of thinking, acting, and so forth, may have to be included. . . . "Gestalt" in the meaning of shape is no longer the center of the Gestalt Psychologist's attention. (Köhler, 1947, pp. 178–179)

It is in this larger sense of the word, in terms of *Gestalts*, that the Gestalt psychologists wanted to deal with the whole province of psychology, as we shall see in the article by Wertheimer.

ORIGINAL SOURCE MATERIAL ON GESTALT PSYCHOLOGY: FROM *GESTALT THEORY* BY MAX WERTHEIMER

The following material is from a lecture given by Max Wertheimer to the Kant Society in Berlin on December 17, 1924.[4] In a talk that ranges from psychology and mathematics to philosophy and the social sciences, Wertheimer points out the differences between a Gestalt or whole approach and an approach that involves the reduction of the subject matter to elements. He illustrates the basic conflict between these divergent views of the world, as represented by the Gestalt psychologists and by the elementists.

What is Gestalt theory and what does it intend? . . .

The fundamental "formula" of Gestalt theory might be expressed in this way: There are wholes, the behaviour of which is not determined by that of their individual elements, but where the part-processes are themselves determined by the intrinsic nature of the whole. It is the hope of Gestalt theory to determine the nature of such wholes.

With a formula such as this, one might close, for Gestalt theory is neither more nor less than this. It is not interested in puzzling out philosophic questions which such a formula might suggest. Gestalt theory has to do with concrete research; it is not only an *outcome* but a *device*: not only a theory *about* results but a means toward further discoveries. This is not merely the proposal of one or more problems but an attempt to *see* what is really taking place in science. This problem cannot be solved by listing possibilities for systematization, classification, and arrangement. If it is to be attacked at all, we must be guided by the spirit of the new method and by the concrete nature of the things themselves which we are studying, and set ourselves to penetrate to that which is really given by nature.

There is another difficulty that may be illustrated by the following example. Suppose a mathematician shows you a proposition and you begin to "classify" it. This proposition, you say, is of such and such type, belongs in this or that historical category, and so on. Is that how the mathematician works?

"Why, you haven't grasped the thing at all," the mathematician will exclaim. "See here, this formula is not an independent, closed fact that can be dealt with for itself alone. You must see its dynamic *functional* relationship to the whole from which it was lifted or you will never understand it."

What holds for the mathematical formula applies also to the "formula" of Gestalt theory. The attempt of Gestalt theory to disclose the functional meaning of its own formula is no less strict than is the mathematician's. The attempt to explain Gestalt theory in a short essay is the more difficult because of the terms which are used: part, whole, intrinsic determination. All of them have in the past been the topic of endless discussions where each disputant has understood them differently. And even worse has been the cataloguing attitude adopted toward them. What they *lacked* has been actual research. Like many another "philosophic" problem they have been withheld from contact with reality and scientific work.

About all I can hope for in so short a discussion is to suggest a few of the problems which at present occupy the attention of Gestalt theory and something of the way they are being attacked.

[4]From M. Wertheimer, "Gestalt Theory." In W. D. Ellis (Ed.), *A Source Book of Gestalt Psychology*. (London: Routledge & Kegan Paul, 1938; New York: Humanities Press, Inc., 1967), pp. 1–11. (Footnotes omitted.)

To repeat: the *problem* has not merely to do with scientific work—it is a fundamental problem of our times. Gestalt theory is not something suddenly and unexpectedly dropped upon us from above; it is, rather, a palpable convergence of problems ranging throughout the sciences and the various philosophic standpoints of modern times.

Let us take, for example, an event in the history of psychology. One turned from a living experience to science and asked what it had to say about this experience, and one found an assortment of elements, sensations, images, feelings, acts of will and laws governing these elements—and was told, "Take your choice, reconstruct from them the experience you had." Such procedure led to difficulties in concrete psychological research and to the emergence of problems which defied solution by the traditional analytic methods. Historically the most important impulse came from v. Ehrenfels who raised the following problem. Psychology had said that experience is a compound of elements: we hear a melody and then, upon hearing it again, memory enables us to recognize it. But what is it that enables us to recognize the melody when it is played in a new key? The sum of the elements is different, yet the melody is the same; indeed, one is often not even aware that a transposition has been made.

When in retrospect we consider the prevailing situation we are struck by two aspects of v. Ehrenfels's thesis; on the one hand one is surprised at the essentially summative character of his theory, on the other one admires his courage in propounding and defending his proposition. Strictly interpreted v. Ehrenfels's position was this: I play a familiar melody of six tones and employ six *new* tones, yet you recognize the melody despite the change. There must be a something *more* than the sum of six tones, viz. a seventh something, which is the form-quality, the *Gestaltqualität*, of the original six. It is this *seventh* factor or element which enabled you to recognize the melody despite its transposition.

However strange this view may seem, it shares with many another subsequently abandoned hypothesis the honour of having clearly seen and emphasized a fundamental problem.

But other explanations were also proposed. One maintained that in addition to the six tones there were intervals—relations—and that *these* were what remained constant. In other words we are asked to assume not only elements but "relations-between-elements" as additional components of the total complex. But this view failed to account for the phenomenon because in some cases the relation *too* may be altered without destroying the original melody.

Another type of explanation, also designed to bolster the elementaristic hypothesis, was that *to* this total of six or more tones there come certain "higher processes" which operate upon the given material to *"produce"* unity.

This was the situation until Gestalt theory raised the radical question: Is it really true that when I hear a melody I have a *sum* of individual tones (pieces) which constitute the primary foundation of my experience? Is not perhaps the reverse of this true? What I really have, what I hear of each individual note, what I experience at each place in the melody is a *part* which is itself determined by the character of the whole. What is given me by the melody does not arise (through the agency of any auxiliary factor) as a *secondary* process from the sum of the pieces as such. Instead, what takes place in each single part already depends upon what the whole is. The flesh and blood of a tone depends from the start upon its role in the melody. . . . It belongs to the flesh and blood of the things given in experience (*Gegebenheiten*), how, in what role, in what function they are in their whole.

Let us leave the melody example and turn to another field. Take the case of threshold phenomena. It has long been held that a certain stimulus necessarily produces a certain sensation. Thus, when two stimuli are sufficiently different, the sensations also will be different. Psychology is filled with careful inquiries regarding threshold phenomena. To account for the difficulties constantly being encountered it was assumed that these phenomena must be influenced by higher mental functions, judgments, illusions, attention, etc. And this continued until the radical question was raised: Is it really true that a specific stimulus *always* gives rise to the same sensation? Perhaps the prevailing whole-conditions will themselves determine the effect of stimulation? This kind of formulation leads to experimentation, and experiments show, for example, that when I see two colours the sensations I have are determined by the whole-conditions of the entire stimulus situation. Thus, also, the same local *physical* stimulus pattern can give rise to either a unitary and homogeneous figure, or to an articulated figure with different parts, all depending upon the whole-conditions which may favour either unity or articulation. Obviously the task, then, is to investigate these "whole-conditions" and discover what influences they exert upon experience. . . .

Our next point is that my field comprises also my Ego. There is not from the beginning an Ego over-against others, but the genesis of an Ego offers one of the most fascinating problems, the solution of which seems to lie in Gestalt principles. However, once constituted, the Ego is a functional part of the total field. Proceeding as before we may therefore ask: What happens to the Ego as a part of the field? Is the resulting behaviour the piecewise sort of thing associationism, experience theory, and the like, would have us believe? Experimental results contradict this interpretation and again we often find that the laws of whole-processes operative in such a field tend toward a meaningful behaviour of its parts.

This field is not a summation of sense data and no description of it which considers such separate pieces to be *primary* will be correct. If it were, then for children, primitive peoples and animals experience would be nothing but piece-sensations. The next most developed creatures would have, in addition to independent sensations, something higher, and so on. But this whole picture is the opposite of what actual inquiry has disclosed. We have learned to recognize the "sensations" of our textbooks as products of a late culture utterly different from the experiences of more primitive stages. Who experiences the sensation of a specific red in that sense? What the man of the streets, children, or primitive men normally reach to is something coloured but at the same time exciting, gay, strong, or affecting—*not* "sensations."

The programme to treat the organism as a part in a larger field necessitates the reformulation of the problem as to the relation between organism and environment. The stimulus–sensation connection must be replaced by a connection between alteration in the field conditions, the vital situation, and the total reaction of the organism by a change in its attitude, striving, and feeling.

There is, however, another step to be considered. A man is not only a part of his field, he is also one among other men. When a group of people work together it rarely occurs, and then only under very special conditions, that they constitute a mere sum of independent Egos. Instead the common enterprise often becomes their mutual concern and each works *as* a meaningfully functioning part of the whole. Consider a group of South Sea Islanders engaged in some community occupation, or a group of children playing together. Only under very special circumstances does an "I" stand out alone. Then the balance which obtained during harmonious and systematic occupation may be upset and give way to a surrogate (under certain conditions, pathological) *new* balance. . . .

The fundamental question can be very simply stated: Are the parts of a given whole determined by the inner structure of that whole, or are the events such that, as independent, piecemeal, fortuitous and blind the total activity is a sum of the part-activities? Human beings can, of course, *devise* a kind of physics of their own—e.g., a sequence of machines—exemplifying the latter half of our question, but this does not signify that *all natural* phenomena are of this type. Here is a place where Gestalt theory is least easily understood and this because of the great number of prejudices about nature which have accumulated during the centuries. Nature is thought of as something essentially blind in its laws, where whatever takes place in the whole is purely a sum of individual occurrences. This view was the natural result of the struggle which physics has always had to purge itself of teleology. Today it can be seen that we are obliged to traverse other routes than those suggested by this kind of purposivism.

Let us proceed another step and ask: How does all this stand with regard to the problem of body and mind? What does my knowledge of another's mental experiences amount to and how do I obtain it? There are, of course, old and established dogmas on these points: The mental and physical are wholly heterogeneous: there obtains between them an absolute dichotomy. (From this point of departure philosophers have drawn an array of metaphysical deductions so as to attribute all the good qualities to mind while reserving for nature the odious.) As regards the second question, my discerning mental phenomena in others is traditionally explained as inference by analogy. Strictly interpreted the principle here is that something mental is meaninglessly coupled with something physical. I observe the physical and infer the mental from it more or less according to the following scheme: I see someone press a button on the wall and infer that he wants the light to go on. There *may be* couplings of this sort. However, many scientists have been disturbed by this dualism and have tried to save themselves by recourse to very curious hypotheses. Indeed, the ordinary person would violently refuse to believe that when he sees his companion startled, frightened, or angry he is seeing only certain physical occurrences which themselves have nothing to do (in their inner nature) with the mental, being only superficially coupled with it: you have frequently seen this and this combined . . . etc. There have been many attempts to surmount this problem. One speaks, for example, of *intuition* and says there can be no other possibility, for I *see* my companion's fear. It is not true, argue the intuitionists, that I see only the bare bodily activities meaninglessly coupled with other and invisible activities. However inadmissible it may otherwise be, an intuition theory does have at least this in its favour, it shows a suspicion that the traditional procedure might be successfully reversed. But the word intuition is at best only a *naming* of that which we must strive to lay hold of.

This and other hypotheses, apprehended as they now are, will not advance scientific pursuit, for science demands fruitful penetration, not mere cataloguing and systematization. But the question is, How does the matter really stand? Looking more closely we find a third assumption, namely that a process such as fear is a matter of consciousness. Is this true? Suppose you see a person who is kindly or benevolent. Does anyone suppose that this person is feeling mawkish? No one could possibly believe that. The characteristic feature of such behaviour has very little to do with consciousness. It has been one of the easiest contrivances of philosophy to identify a man's real behaviour and the direction of his mind with his consciousness. Parenthetically, in the opinion of many people the distinction between idealism and materialism implies that between the noble and the ignoble. Yet does one really mean by this to contrast consciousness with the blithesome budding of trees? Indeed, what is there so repugnant about the materialistic and mechanical? What is so attractive about the idealistic? Does it come from the *material* qualities of the connected pieces? Broadly speaking most psychological theories and textbooks, despite their continued emphasis upon consciousness, are far more "materialistic," arid, and spiritless than a living tree—which probably has no consciousness at all. The point is not what the material pieces are, but what *kind* of whole it is. Proceeding in terms of specific problems one soon realizes how many bodily activities there are which give no hint of a separation between body and mind. Imagine a dance, a dance full of grace and joy. What is the situation in such a dance? Do we have a summation of *physical* limb movements and a *psychical* consciousness? No. Obviously this answer does not solve the problem; we have to start anew—and it seems to me that a proper and fruitful point of attack has been discovered. One finds many processes which, in their dynamical form, are identical regardless of variations in the material character of their elements. When a man is timid, afraid or energetic, happy or sad, it can often be shown that the course of his physical processes is Gestalt-identical with the course pursued by the mental processes.

Again I can only indicate the direction of thought. I have touched on the question of body and mind merely to show that the problem we are discussing also has its philosophic aspects. . . .

This brings us to the close of an attempt to present a view of the problem as illustrated by its specific appearances in various fields. In concluding I may suggest a certain unification of these illustrations somewhat as follows. I consider the situation from the point of view of a theory of aggregates and say: How should a world be where science, concepts, inquiry, investigation, and comprehension of inner unities were impossible? The answer is obvious. This world would be a manifold of disparate pieces. Secondly, what kind of world would there have to be in which a piecewise science would apply? The answer is again quite simple, for here one needs only a system of recurrent couplings that are blind and piecewise in character, whereupon everything is available for a pursuit of the traditional piecewise methods of logic, mathematics, and science generally in so far as these presuppose this kind of world. But there is a third kind of aggregate which has been but cursorily investigated. These are the aggregates in which a manifold is not compounded from adjacently situated pieces but rather such that a term at its place in that aggregate is determined by the whole-laws of the aggregate itself.

Pictorially: suppose the world were a vast plateau upon which were many musicians. I walk about listening and watching the players. First suppose that the world is a meaningless plurality. Everyone does as he will, each for himself. What happens together when I hear ten players might be the basis for my guessing as to what they all are doing, but this is merely a matter of chance and probability much as in the kinetics of gas molecules.—A second possibility would be that each time one musician played *c*, another played *f* so and so many seconds later. I work out a theory of blind couplings but the playing as a whole remains meaningless. This is what many people think physics does, but the real work of physics belies this.—The third possibility is, say, a Beethoven symphony where it would be possible for one to select one part of the whole and work from that towards an idea of the structural principle motivating and determining the whole. Here the fundamental laws are not those of fortuitous pieces, but concern the very character of the event.

PRINCIPLES OF PERCEPTUAL ORGANIZATION

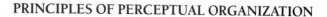

Wertheimer's *principles of perceptual organization* were presented in a paper in 1923. Wertheimer took the position that we perceive objects in the same immediate and unified manner in which we perceive apparent motion, that is, as unified wholes, not as clusters of individual sensations. The principles of organization, which are described in most introductory psychology textbooks, are essentially rules or laws by which our perceptual world is organized.

A basic premise of the principles of perceptual organization is that in perception, organization occurs instantly whenever we see or hear different shapes or patterns. Parts of the perceptual field become connected, and these groups of parts unite to form structures that are distinct from the background. Perceptual organization is spontaneous and inevitable whenever we look around our environment. We do not have to learn to so organize, as the associationists claimed, although higher-level perception, such as labeling an object by name, does depend more on learning.

According to Gestalt theory, the primary brain process in visual perception is not a collection of small, separate activities. The visual area of the brain does not respond in terms of separate elements of visual input, connecting these elements by some mechanical process of association. Rather, the brain is a dynamic system in which all the elements that are active at a given time interact. Elements that are similar or close together tend to combine. Elements that are dissimilar or far apart do not tend to combine.

Several of the principles of organization are listed here and illustrated in Figure 12-1.

1. *Proximity:* Parts that are close together in time or space tend to be perceived together. In Figure 12-1(a) you see the circles in three double columns rather than as one large collection.
2. *Similarity:* Similar parts tend to be seen together as forming a group (Figure 12-1(b)). In Figure 12-1(b), the circles and the dots each appear to belong together and you tend to perceive rows of circles and rows of dots instead of columns.
3. *Closure:* There is a tendency in our perception to complete incomplete figures, to fill in gaps. In Figure 12-1(c) you perceive three squares even though the figures are incomplete.
4. *Prägnanz:* There is a tendency to see a figure as being as good as possible under the stimulus conditions. A good Gestalt is symmetrical, simple, and stable and cannot be made simpler or more orderly. The squares in Figure 12-1(c) are good Gestalts because they are clearly perceived as complete and organized.

These organizing principles do not depend on our higher mental processes or on past experience. They are present in the stimuli themselves. Wertheimer called them peripheral factors but also recognized that central factors (factors within the organism) can influence perception. For example, the characteristics of familiarity and attitude (higher mental processes) can influence perception. In general, however, the Gestalt psychologists tended to concentrate more on the direct and primitive peripheral factors of perceptual organization than on the effect of learning or experience.

PRINCIPLES OF LEARNING

Perception was an early focus of the Gestalt psychologists, and they took the position that learning plays only a small role in the perceptual processes. It is not correct, however, to conclude that the topic of learning, considered independently of perception, received no attention from the Gestalt psychologists. Some of the most significant experiments in the history of psychology are those devised by Köhler to study problem solving in apes.

From its beginning, Gestalt psychology opposed Thorndike's trial-and-error learning, and later, Watson's stimulus–response (S–R) learning. Gestalt psychologists believed that their consistent criticism of associationist and stimulus–response theories of learn-

Figure 12-1
Examples of perceptual organization.

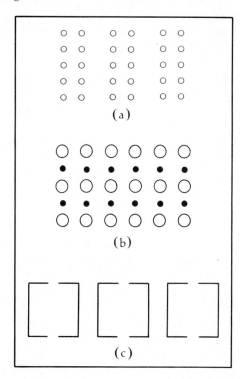

ing constituted a significant contribution to the development of psychology. The Gestalt view of learning is expressed in Köhler's research on the mentality of apes and Wertheimer's work on productive thinking in humans.

The Mentality of Apes

We mentioned Köhler's confinement on the island of Tenerife during World War I, during which time he investigated the intelligence of chimpanzees as shown in their ability to solve problems (Köhler, 1917). These studies were conducted in and around the animals' cages and involved simple props, such as the bars of the cages themselves (to block access), bananas, sticks for drawing the bananas into the cages, and boxes for climbing on. Congruent with the Gestalt view of perception, Köhler interpreted the results of his animal studies in terms of the whole situation and the relations between the various stimuli found therein. He considered problem solving a matter of restructuring the perceptual field.

In one study a banana was placed outside the cage, and a string attached to the banana led into the cage. The apes pulled the banana into the cage with little hesitation. Köhler concluded that in this situation the problem as a whole was easily grasped by the animal. However, if several strings led from the cage in the general direction of the banana, the ape would not recognize at first which string to pull. To Köhler, this indicated that the problem could not be envisioned clearly all at once.

A more explicit example involved placing a banana outside the cage just beyond the ape's reach. If a stick were placed near the bars of the cage (facing the banana), the stick and the banana would be seen as parts of the same situation and the ape would use the stick to pull the banana into the cage. If the stick were placed at the back of the cage, the two objects would be less readily perceived as parts of the same situation. In this case, a restructuring of the perceptual field would be necessary to solve the problem.

Another experiment involved positioning a banana outside the cage, beyond reach, and placing two hollow bamboo sticks inside the cage. Each stick by itself was too short to reach the banana. To reach the banana, the animal would have to push the two sticks together (inserting the end of one into the end of the other) to produce a stick of sufficient length to reach the banana. Thus, the animal had to perceive a new relationship between the sticks to solve the problem.

Sultan, Köhler's brightest ape, failed when initially confronted with this situation. He first tried to get the banana with one stick. Next, he pushed a stick out as far as he could, then pushed it farther with a second stick until the first one touched the banana. Sultan

A chimpanzee uses sticks of different lengths to reach a piece of fruit.

did not succeed during a one-hour trial. Immediately after this trial, while playing with the sticks, Sultan solved the problem, as reported by his keeper.

> Sultan first of all squats indifferently on the box, which has been left standing a little back from the railings; then he gets up, picks up the two sticks, sits down again on the box and plays carelessly with them. While doing this, it happens that he finds himself holding one rod in either hand in such a way that they lie in a straight line; he pushes the thinner one a little way into the opening of the thicker, jumps up and is already on the run toward the railings, to which he has up to now half turned his back, and begins to draw a banana towards him with the double stick. I call the master: meanwhile, one of the animal's rods has fallen out of the other, as he has pushed one of them only a little way into the other; whereupon he connects them again. (Köhler, 1927, p. 127)

In later trials Sultan solved the problem without any difficulty, even when some of the sticks provided would not fit together. Köhler reported that Sultan did not even attempt to join the unsuitable sticks.

Studies such as these were interpreted by Köhler as evidence of *insight*—the apparently spontaneous apprehension of relationships.

> The solutions of such problems, when they came, appeared to come suddenly, as though a new "configuration," embracing the whole complicated means to the desired end, had suddenly sprung up in the animal's consciousness; it was exactly as though the appropriate action followed on a "flash of insight," and, as in the case of all insightful behavior, the insight remained a permanent possession, enabling its possessor to act at once appropriately on a subsequent occasion. (Flugel & West, 1964, p. 206)

This viewpoint differed dramatically from the trial-and-error learning described by Thorndike and others. Köhler was a vocal critic of Thorndike's work, arguing that Thorndike's experimental arrangements were artificial and allowed only for random behavior on the part of the animal. Köhler suggested that the cats in Thorndike's puzzle box could not survey the entire release mechanism (all the elements pertaining to the whole), and thus could only engage in trial-and-error behavior. Similarly, an animal in a maze could not see the overall pattern or design but only each alley as it came to it and so could do nothing but blindly try each path. In the Gestalt view, the organism must be able to see the relationship among the various parts of the problem before insight can occur.

These studies of insight were used to support the Gestalt molar conception of behavior, as opposed to the molecular view of the associationists and behaviorists, and the Gestalt notion that learning involves a reorganization on restructuring of the psychological environment.

Productive Thinking in Humans

Wertheimer's book, *Productive Thinking* (1945), published posthumously, applied the Gestalt principles of learning to creative thinking in humans. He suggested that such thinking be done in terms of wholes. Not only should the learner regard the situation as a whole, but the teacher must also present the situation as a whole. This approach differs from Thorndike's trial-and-error learning in which the solution is, in a sense, hidden, and the learner is required to make errors before chancing upon the correct path.

The case material in Wertheimer's book ranged from children solving geometric problems to the thought processes of the physicist Albert Einstein that led to his theory of relativity (Wertheimer and Einstein had been friends). At all ages and levels of problem difficulty Wertheimer found evidence to support the idea that the whole problem must dominate the parts. He believed that the detailed aspects of a problem should be considered only in relation to the structure of the total situation and that problem solving should proceed from the whole problem downward to the parts, not the reverse.

Wertheimer believed that if a teacher arranged problems so that elements of classroom exercises were organized into meaningful wholes, then insight would occur. He also demonstrated that once the principle of a problem's solution had been grasped, it could readily be transferred to other situations.

Wertheimer attacked the traditional educational practices of mechanical drills and rote learning, which derived from the associationist theory of learning. Repetition is rarely productive, he argued, and he cited as evidence the student's inability to solve a variation of a problem when the solution had been learned by rote rather than by insight. He did agree, however, that material such as names and dates should be learned by rote through association strengthened by repetition. He conceded that repetition was useful to a point but that its habitual use could produce mechanical performance rather than truly creative or productive thinking.

THE PRINCIPLE OF ISOMORPHISM

Having established that perceptions are organized wholes, the Gestalt psychologists turned to the problem of the cortical mechanisms involved in perception. They attempted to develop a theory of the underlying neurological correlates of perceived *Gestalts*. The Gestalt view of the cerebral cortex as a dynamic system, in which the elements active at a given time interact, contrasts with the machine-like conception of the nervous system, which compares neural activity to a telephone switchboard that mechanically links sensory inputs by the principles of association. In the latter view, the brain functions passively and is not capable of actively organizing or modifying the sensory elements received. Also, this view of the brain implies a direct correspondence between the perception and its neurological counterpart.

In his original research on apparent movement Wertheimer suggested that cortical activity is a configural whole process. Because apparent and actual motion are experienced identically, the cortical processes for actual and apparent motion must be similar. On the assumption that these two kinds of movement are identical, there must then be corresponding brain processes. To account for the phi phenomenon, there must be a correspondence between the psychological or conscious experience and the underlying brain experience. This point of view has been called *isomorphism*. A perception may be likened to a map in that it is identical (*iso*) in form or shape (*morphic*) to that which it represents without being a literal copy of the terrain. It does, however, serve as a reliable guide to the perceived real world.

The position was extended by Köhler in *Static and Stationary Physical Gestalts* (1920). He considered that cortical processes behave in a manner similar to fields of force and suggested that, like the behavior of an electromagnetic field of force around a magnet, fields of neuronal activity may be established by electromechanical processes in the brain in response to sensory impulses. He conducted an extensive research program to investigate various aspects of isomorphism and cortical brain fields. To Köhler, isomorphism was but one phase of an ambitious undertaking to demonstrate that physics, chemistry, biology, and psychology all involve *Gestalts*.

THE SPREAD OF GESTALT PSYCHOLOGY

By the mid-1920s the Gestalt movement was a united, cohesive, and forceful school in Germany. It was centered at the Psychological Institute of the University of Berlin, where it attracted large numbers of students from many countries. The Gestalt journal *Psychologische Forschung* was very active, and Gestalt researchers were investigating various psychological problems.

After the Nazis rose to power in Germany in 1933, their rampant anti-intellectualism and repression forced the leaders of Gestalt psychology to leave the country. The movement was reduced to a minor position in the German academic system of the day, and the center of Gestalt psychology shifted to the United States. The work of the Gestalt psychologists had preceded them so that they and their movement were already well known in America by the time they all arrived. Indeed, "the diffusion of Gestalt psychology from Germany to the United States began long before Hitler came to power. . . . By 1930 Gestalt psychology was firmly established in the United States as a psychological school" (Sokal, 1984, p. 1262).

This diffusion was carried out through personal contacts as well as articles and books. In the early years of the twentieth century, even before Gestalt psychology had formally begun, soon-to-be influential American psychologists were studying under future leaders of the Gestalt school (Henle, 1984). Herbert Langfeld of Princeton University had met Koffka in Berlin in the first decade of the century and had sent one of his students, Tolman, to Germany where Tolman served as a subject in Koffka's early Gestalt research. Robert Ogden of Cornell had also met Koffka. Gordon Allport of Harvard spent a year in Germany where he was much impressed by the quality of the experimental research coming from the Gestalt school.

In the early 1920s books by Koffka and Köhler had been translated into English and were widely reviewed in American psychology journals. At the same time, Koffka and Köhler visited the United States to speak about their movement to psychologists and graduate students at universities and conferences. Koffka delivered 30 lectures on Gestalt psychology over a period of three years, and Köhler was one of the keynote speakers at the ninth International Congress of Psychology held at Yale University in 1929. (The other keynote speaker was Ivan Pavlov.)

Although Gestalt psychology was attracting considerable attention in the United States, and some American psychologists were finding it a useful antidote to what they saw as the extremes of behaviorism, it did not meet with overwhelming enthusiasm from all quarters. Its progress as a school of thought was comparatively slow for several reasons. Behaviorism was then at the peak of its popularity in American psychology. Another problem was the language barrier, which delayed the full and accurate dissemination of the tenets of the Gestalt school. And, as noted, many American psychologists believed (incorrectly) that Gestalt psychology dealt only with perception. Also, Wertheimer, Koffka, and Köhler taught at American colleges that lacked graduate programs, so it was difficult for them to attract disciples.

The most important reason, however, for the relatively slow acceptance of Gestalt psychology in the United States was that American psychology had already advanced far beyond the ideas of Wundt and Titchener. Behaviorism was already the second phase of American opposition. Hence, American psychology was much further removed from elementism than was European psychology at that time. As far as American psychologists were concerned, the Gestalt psychologists had come to America protesting something that was already a dead issue. This was dangerous for the Gestalt school. We have seen that revolutionary movements need something to oppose, something to push against, if they are to survive.

When the Gestalt psychologists became aware of the trends within American psychology, they readily perceived a new target, behaviorism, with its reductionistic and atomistic tendencies. The Gestalt psychologists argued that behaviorism also dealt with artificial abstractions. It made little difference whether analysis was in terms of introspective reduction to mental elements or objective reduction to conditioned reflexes. The result was the same: a molecular instead of a molar approach. The Gestalt psychologists also took issue with the behaviorists' denial of the validity of introspection and their elimination of consciousness.

In time, the principles of Gestalt psychology were absorbed by child psychology, applied psychology, psychiatry, education, anthropology, and sociology. In addition, some clinical psychologists began to combine the Gestalt approach with psychoanalysis. The general tendency in American psychology has been to consider the teachings of Gestalt psychology as interesting and potentially useful additions to other systems, but not as the basis of an all-encompassing system. American psychologists have attempted to demonstrate that both elemental and organized responses occur, and that both are useful ways of explaining psychological processes.

For many psychologists, the Gestalt view remains vital and it continues to promote substantial research. Although it no longer boasts the combative spirit of a revolution, many of its adherents are elaborating and refining its basic points. Gestalt psychology has not been totally accepted into the mainstream of American psychology but rather exists as a minority movement (Henle, 1977). Although Gestalt psychology retains some of its separateness, it has exerted a visible influence on many areas of psychology, including perception, thinking, learning, personality, social psychology, and motivation.

Field Theory: Kurt Lewin (1890–1947)

The trend in nineteenth-century science was to think in terms of field relationships and to move away from an atomistic and elementistic framework. As we have seen, Gestalt psychology reflected this trend. Field theory arose within psychology as an analogy to the concept of fields of force in physics.

In psychology the term *field theory* has come to refer almost exclusively to the work of Kurt Lewin.[5] Lewin's position in relation to Gestalt psychology is not clear-cut.

---

[5] Tolman's system (Chapter 11) is often considered a field theory. We noted his attempt to combine parts of behaviorism and Gestalt psychology.

The field theory of Kurt Lewin (1890–1947) has had significant influence on group dynamics, sensitivity training, and social psychology.

Although he is sometimes classified as a member of the Gestalt school, he is equally regarded as the developer of a separate but related system. He began work independently but was later associated with Köhler and Wertheimer at the center of the Gestalt movement in Berlin. In his research he went well beyond the framework of the orthodox Gestalt position.

Lewin's work is Gestalt in orientation, but it centers on needs, personality, and social factors, whereas the Gestalt psychologists emphasized perception and learning. The Gestalt psychologists proposed physiological constructs to attempt to explain behavior, but Lewin considered psychology to be more of a social science. It is simpler to consider Lewin's system as an elaboration or outgrowth of the Gestalt movement for two reasons: (1) he was closely associated with the Gestalt psychologists in Berlin for a time, and (2) his position fits the Gestalt system more readily than any other system.

Lewin was born in Mogilno, Germany, undertook his university education at Freiburg, Munich, and Berlin, and received his Ph.D. in psychology from Berlin in 1914. He also studied mathematics and physics. After a period of military service, for which he was awarded the Iron Cross, he returned to the University of Berlin, where he became such a productive and creative member of the Gestalt group that he was considered a colleague of the three senior Gestalt psychologists. He conducted research on association and motivation and began to develop his field theory, which he presented to American psychologists at the 1929 International Congress of Psychology at Yale.

He was already well known in the United States when, in 1932, he spent six months as visiting professor at Stanford. The following year he decided to leave Germany permanently because of the Nazi menace. He spent two years at Cornell and in 1935 went to the University of Iowa to conduct research on the social psychology of the child. As a result of these efforts in social psychology, Lewin was invited to develop and head the new Research Center for Group Dynamics at the Massachusetts Institute of Technology in 1944. Although he died shortly after, his program was so effective that the research center remains active, located now at the University of Michigan. Throughout his 30 years of professional activity Lewin devoted himself to the broadly defined area of human motivation. His research emphasized the study of human behavior in its total physical and social context (Lewin, 1936, 1939).

Field theory in physics led Lewin to consider that a person's psychological activities occur within a kind of psychological field, or *life space*. The life space encompasses all the past, present, and future events that may possibly influence a person. From a psychological standpoint, each of these aspects of life can determine behavior in any single situation. Thus, the life space consists of the individual's needs interacting with the psychological environment.

The life space may show varying degrees of differentiation as a function of the amount and kind of experience the person has accumulated. Because an infant lacks experiences, he or she has few differentiated regions in the life space. A highly educated, sophisticated adult will show a complex and well-differentiated life space as a function of his or her past experiences.

Lewin wanted to use a mathematical model to represent his theoretical conception of psychological processes. Because he was interested in the single case, statistics were not useful for his purpose. He chose a form of geometry, called topology, to map the life space to show at any given moment all of a person's possible goals and all the paths to those goals. Topology treats transformations in space by representing spatial relationships in nonquantitative fashion. It is a conception of space that deals with the order of relationships, but not with their direction or distance. It can show connections among regions within the life space and their spatial relationships to one another. To represent direction, Lewin developed a new form of qualitative geometry called *hodological space*, in which he used vectors to represent directions of movement toward a goal. To complete the schematic representation of his system, Lewin used the notion of *valences* to refer to the positive or negative value of objects within the life space. Objects that are attractive to the individual or that satisfy needs have positive valence; objects that are threatening have negative valence.

Lewin postulated a state of equilibrium between the person and the environment. When this equilibrium is disturbed, a tension (Lewin's concept of motivation or need) arises that leads to locomotion in the attempt to restore the equilibrium. Lewin believed that human behavior involves the continual appearance of tension, locomotion, and relief. This sequence is akin to need–activity–relief. Whenever a need is felt, a state of tension exists, and the organism acts to release the tension by restoring the equilibrium.

Lewin's "blackboard psychology" included complex diagrams to represent all manner of psychological phenomena. In field theory all forms of behavior can be represented schematically. A simple bit of behavior as it would be represented in Lewin's system is shown in Figure 12-2, which illustrates a situation in which a child wants to go to the movies but is forbidden to do so by his or her parents. The ellipse represents the life space and C represents the child. The arrow is a vector indicating that C is motivated to go to the movie, which, as indicated, has a positive valence, or value, for the child. The vertical line is a barrier (the parents) to the goal and has a negative valence. (This is a simplified example and is not typical of the highly complex psychological phenomena that Lewin was able to represent through his topological and hodological space.)

Lewin's theoretical system generated a great deal of research. One series of studies involved the assumption of a *tension-system*. Tension means, as we noted, motivation or need, and Lewin believed that when a goal is reached, the tension is discharged. The first experimental attempt to test this tension-system proposition was performed, under Lewin's supervision, by Bluma Zeigarnik in 1927. Subjects were given a series of tasks and allowed to complete some of them but were interrupted before they could complete others. Lewin predicted that (1) a tension-system develops in a subject when he or she is given a task to perform, (2) when the task is completed, the tension is dissipated, (3) when the task is not completed, the persistence of the tension results in a greater likelihood that the task will be recalled. Zeigarnik's results confirmed the predictions. The subjects recalled the uncompleted tasks more easily than they recalled the completed tasks. Much subsequent research has been performed on what has come to be known as the *Zeigarnik effect*.

In the early years of his career Lewin was chiefly concerned with theoretical problems and issues. By the late 1930s, however, he became interested in social psychology, and his pioneering efforts in this field alone are sufficient to justify his position in the history of psychology. Some prominent social psychologists associated with Lewin, either as students or as colleagues at the Research Center for Group Dynamics, are Dorwin

Figure 12-2 Example of a life space.

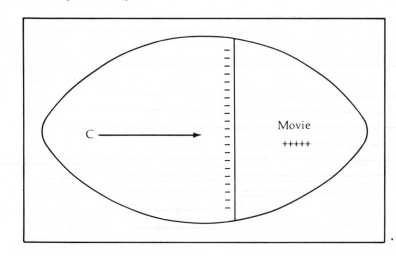

Cartwright, Leon Festinger, J. P. French, Harold H. Kelley, Rensis Likert, Stanley Schachter, and Alvin Zander.

The outstanding feature of Lewin's social psychology is *group dynamics*, the application of concepts dealing with the individual and group behavior. Just as the individual and his or her environment form a psychological field, the group and its environment form a social field. Social behaviors occur in and result from simultaneously existing social entities, such as subgroups, members, barriers, and channels of communication. Thus, group behavior is a function of the total field situation at any given time.

Lewin conducted social psychological research on behavior in various social climates. A classic experiment in social psychology involves democratic and authoritarian leadership and its effects on the productiveness and behavior of groups of boys (Lewin, Lippitt, & White, 1939). Studies such as this one opened up important new areas of social research and contributed to the rapid growth of social psychology.

Lewin emphasized the importance of what he called "social action" research, the study of relevant social problems with a view to introducing change. He concerned himself with racial conflicts and conducted community studies on the effects of integrated housing on prejudice, on equalizing opportunity for employment, and on the development and prevention of prejudice in children. His interest was the realities of everyday life, and his social action research transformed problems such as prejudice into controlled experiments, applying the rigor of the experimental approach without the artificiality and sterility of the academic laboratory.

Lewin was instrumental in developing what is known as *sensitivity training*. The T-groups (training groups) set up in his National Training Laboratories were the beginning of a movement later characterized by encounter groups. Sensitivity training was applied to many situations from industry to education to reduce intergroup conflict and to develop individual potential.

Lewin's experimental programs and research findings are more acceptable to psychologists than are his theoretical views. His influence in social and child psychology, and, to some degree, in experimental psychology, is considerable. Many of his concepts and experimental techniques are widely used in the areas of personality and motivation. His interests are being actively extended and elaborated upon in psychology today.

CRITICISMS OF GESTALT PSYCHOLOGY

Criticisms of the Gestalt position appeared promptly. They included the major charge that the Gestalt psychologists were trying to solve problems simply by changing them into postulates. The organization of conscious perception was not treated as a problem that required solving but as a phenomenon that existed in its own right. Critics argued that this was tantamount to solving a problem by denying its existence. Similarly, it was argued that the Gestalt psychologists never explained the laws of their system. "None of the important phenomena with which Gestalt theory confronted the classical theorists were actually explained by Gestalt theory itself" (Hochberg, 1979, p. 116).

Many tough-minded psychologists have asserted that the Gestalt position is vague, charging that basic concepts and terms are not defined with sufficient rigor to be scientifically meaningful. The Gestalt psychologists countered these charges by insisting that in a young science attempts at explanation and definition must necessarily be incomplete but that being incomplete is not the same as being vague.

It was also claimed that the tenets of Gestalt psychology were not really new, which, of course, is true. The Gestalt movement, like the others we have discussed, had its anticipators, but this point has no bearing on the relative merits of the Gestalt position.

Some critics allege that Gestalt psychology is too occupied with theory at the expense of experimental research and empirical supporting data. The Gestalt school has indeed been theoretically oriented, but since the time of its founders it has also emphasized experimentation. It has been both directly and indirectly responsible for a considerable amount of research.

Related to this point is the suggestion that the experimental work of the Gestalt psychologists is inferior to that of S–R theorists because it lacks adequate controls. Further, the Gestalt psychologists' unquantified data are not amenable to statistical analysis. The Gestalt psychologists take the position that qualitative results take precedence in the investigation of a problem area, so much of their research has deliberately been less quantitative than psychologists of other viewpoints consider necessary. Much Gestalt research is exploratory, investigating problems within a different framework.

Köhler's notion of insight has not gone unchallenged. Replications of Köhler's two-stick experiment by other researchers have provided little support for the role of insight. These later studies suggest that the chimpanzees' solution of the problem does not occur suddenly and that it may depend on prior experience or learning (Windholz & Lamal, 1985).

A final criticism relates to what some psychologists consider to be poorly supported and poorly defined physiological assumptions. The Gestalt psychologists admit that their theorizing in this area is tentative, but they add that their speculations are a useful adjunct to their system. Gestalt psychology has inspired much research, and the validity of the results is not lessened by the speculative framework within which the research was conducted.

CONTRIBUTIONS OF GESTALT PSYCHOLOGY

The Gestalt movement has left an indelible imprint on psychology. Like other movements that challenged traditional views, it had a refreshing and stimulating effect on psychology as a whole. The Gestalt point of view has influenced the areas of perception and learning, as is evident in contemporary psychology textbooks. Recent work deriving from the Gestalt school strongly suggests that the movement still has contributions to make.

Unlike its chief temporal competitor, behaviorism, Gestalt psychology retains much of its separate identity in that its major tenets have not been fully absorbed into the mainstream of psychological thought. It continues to foster interest in conscious experience as a legitimate problem for at least part of psychology. This focus on conscious experience is not of the Wundt–Titchener variety but centers on a modern version of phenomenology. Contemporary adherents of the Gestalt position are convinced that conscious experience does occur and must be studied. They recognize, however, that it cannot be investigated with the same precision and objectivity as overt behavior. Contemporary proponents of a phenomenological psychology are numerous in Europe and the point of view seems to be gaining support in the United States. Although phenomenology is not yet widely accepted in America, psychologists are becoming more familiar with it, and its influence can be seen in the humanistic psychology movement (see Chapter 15).

Finally, the pointed and consistent criticisms of current systems offered by Gestalt psychology have been influential by demanding a thorough reexamination of opposing positions.

SUGGESTED READINGS

Wertheimer

Asch, S. E. (1946). Max Wertheimer's contribution to modern psychology. *Social Research, 13,* 81–102.

Köhler, W. (1944). Max Wertheimer, 1880–1943. *Psychological Review, 51,* 143–146.

O'Neil, W. M., & Landauer, A. A. (1966). The phi-phenomenon: Turning point or rallying point. *Journal of the History of the Behavioral Sciences, 2,* 335–340.

Wertheimer, M. (1959). *Productive thinking* (enl. ed.). New York: Harper & Row. (Original work published 1945).

Koffka

Gibson, J. J. (1971). The legacies of Koffka's principles. *Journal of the History of the Behavioral Sciences, 7,* 3–9.

Harrower, M. (1971). A note on the Koffka papers. *Journal of the History of the Behavioral Sciences, 7,* 141–153.

Koffka, K. (1922). Perception: An introduction to the Gestalt-theorie. *Psychological Bulletin, 19,* 531–585.

Köhler, W. (1942). Kurt Koffka. *Psychological Review, 49,* 97–101.

Köhler

Crannell, C. W. (1970). Wolfgang Köhler. *Journal of the History of the Behavioral Sciences, 6,* 267–268.

Henle, M. (1978). One man against the Nazis—Wolfgang Köhler. *American Psychologist, 33,* 939–944.

Henle, M. (Ed.). (1971). *The selected papers of Wolfgang Köhler.* New York: Liveright.

Köhler, W. (1956). *The mentality of apes* (rev. ed.). London: Routledge & Kegan Paul.

Prentice, W. (1959). The systematic psychology of Wolfgang Köhler. In S. Koch (Ed.), *Psychology: A study of a science* (vol. 1, pp. 427–455). New York: McGraw-Hill.

Lewin

Eng, E. (1978). Looking back on Kurt Lewin: From field theory to action research. *Journal of the History of the Behavioral Sciences, 14,* 228–232.

Frank, J. D. (1978). Kurt Lewin in retrospect—a psychiatrist's view. *Journal of the History of the Behavioral Sciences, 14,* 223–227.

Heider, F. (1959). On Lewin's methods and theory. *Journal of Social Issues*, suppl. no. 13.

Marrow, A. (1969). *The practical theorist: The life and work of Kurt Lewin*. New York: Basic Books.

Gestalt Psychology

Calkins, M. W. (1926). Critical comments on the "Gestalt-theorie." *Psychological Review, 33*, 135–158.

Ellis, W. D. (1967). *A source book of Gestalt psychology*. New York: Humanities Press.

Freeman, F. S. (1977). The beginnings of Gestalt psychology in the United States. *Journal of the History of the Behavioral Sciences, 13*, 352–353.

Heider, F. (1970). Gestalt theory: Early history and reminiscences. *Journal of the History of the Behavioral Sciences, 6*, 131–139.

Helson, H. (1933). The fundamental propositions of Gestalt psychology. *Psychological Review, 40*, 13–32.

Helson, H. (1969). Why did their precursors fail and the Gestalt psychologists succeed? Reflections on theories and theorists. *American Psychologist, 24*, 1006–1011.

Henle, M. (1977). The influence of Gestalt psychology in America. *Annals of the New York Academy of Sciences, 291*, 3–12.

Henle, M. (1984). Robert M. Ogden and Gestalt psychology in America. *Journal of the History of the Behavioral Sciences, 20*, 9–19.

Henle, M. (Ed.). (1961). *Documents of Gestalt psychology*. Berkeley: University of California Press.

Hochberg, J. (1957). Effects of the Gestalt revolution: The Cornell symposium on perception. *Psychological Review, 64*, 73–84.

Katz, D. (1950). *Gestalt psychology: Its nature and significance*. New York: Ronald Press.

Köhler, W. (1959). Gestalt psychology today. *American Psychologist, 14*, 727–734.

Köhler, W. (1969). Gestalt psychology. In D. Krantz (Ed.), *Schools of psychology* (pp. 69–85). New York: Appleton-Century-Crofts.

Seaman, J. D. (1984). On phi-phenomena. *Journal of the History of the Behavioral Sciences, 20*, 3–8.

Sokal, M. (1984). The Gestalt psychologists in behaviorist America. *American Historical Review, 89*, 1240–1263.

Von Ehrenfels, C. (1937). On Gestalt-qualities. *Psychological Review, 44*, 521–524.

Wheeler, R. H. (1935). Gestalt psychology in the light of history. *Psychological Bulletin, 32*, 548.

13

Psychoanalysis: The Beginnings

INTRODUCTION

The term "psychoanalysis" and the name Sigmund Freud are familiar to most literate people. Although other prominent figures in the history of psychology—Fechner, Wundt, and Titchener, for example—are little known outside professional psychology, Freud enjoys phenomenal popularity, although his system may be known to the lay public only superficially and inaccurately. It is often a source of disappointment to teachers of psychology to find that so many beginning students believe that Freud is psychology, and that psychology deals only with the treatment of the emotionally disturbed.

Chronologically, psychoanalysis overlaps to a considerable degree the other schools of psychology with which we have dealt. Consider the situation in 1895, the year in which Freud published his first book, marking the formal beginning of his new movement. In that year Wundt was 63 years old. Titchener, just 28, had been at Cornell only two years and was just beginning to develop his system of structuralism. The spirit of functionalism was beginning to grow in the United States, but it had not yet been formalized into a school. Neither behaviorism nor Gestalt psychology had begun; Watson was then 17 and Wertheimer 15.

Yet by the time of Freud's death in 1939, the entire psychological outlook had changed. Wundtian psychology, structuralism, and functionalism were history, Gestalt psychology was being vigorously transplanted to the United States, and behaviorism had become the dominant American form of psychology. Not only had Freud achieved prominence, but his position had already become splintered into subschools and derivative movements.

The relationship between psychoanalysis and the other schools of psychology we have discussed was only temporal in nature. There was no substantive link, either through assent or dissent, between Freud and the other founders in psychology. The other schools owed their impetus and form to Wundt, either evolving from his work, as was the case with structuralism and functionalism, or revolting against it, as with behaviorism and Gestalt psychology. In contrast, psychoanalysis was not directly related to these evolutionary and revolutionary movements because psychoanalysis did not originate within academic psychology. Freud's study of personality and its disturbances was far removed from the psychology of the university laboratory.

Regardless of their fundamental disagreements, the other systems shared an academic heritage. All of these schools formed their basic concepts and approaches in a milieu of laboratories, libraries, and lecture halls. Their traditional concerns were topics such as perception, sensation, and learning. They were, or strove to be, pure science. Psychoanalysis was neither a product of academe nor a pure science. Further, it was not, and still is not, a school of psychology directly comparable to the others.

Psychoanalysis has not been concerned with traditional areas of psychology primarily because its goal is to provide therapy for emotionally disturbed persons. In aim, subject matter, and method, psychoanalysis diverged from the mainstream of psychological thought from the beginning. Its subject matter is abnormal behavior, which had been relatively neglected by the other schools, and its method is clinical observation instead of controlled laboratory experimentation. Also, psychoanalysis deals with the unconscious, a topic virtually ignored by the other schools of thought in psychology.

Despite its radically different nature, psychoanalysis has exerted an undeniable influence on contemporary psychology. Other areas—the social sciences, literature, language, religion, philosophy, ethics, and the arts—have also felt its impact. We shall see, however, that its acceptance by academic psychology has been, for the most part, less than enthusiastic.

Having pointed out how psychoanalysis differs so strongly from the other schools of thought in psychology, we must also note that it shares similar background characteristics with functionalism and behaviorism. For example, psychoanalysis, functionalism, and behaviorism were influenced by the spirit of mechanism, by the work of Gustav Fechner, and by the revolutionary ideas of Charles Darwin. We now discuss these and other influences on Freud.

ANTECEDENT INFLUENCES

Despite the claims of some of his followers, Freud's insights were not without anticipators. The psychoanalytic movement had definite intellectual and cultural antecedents. Two major sources of influence led to the formal founding of psychoanalysis. One was the early philosophical speculation on the nature of unconscious psychological phenomena, and the other was the earlier work in psychopathology.

Early Theories of the Unconscious

We have noted that most of the early history of scientific psychology was concerned with consciousness. The experimental psychologists of the late nineteenth century were convinced that the only proper field of study was the content of consciousness, and thus the main focus of work in these early years of psychology was the analysis of conscious experience. There was little consideration of unconscious determinants of behavior. Similarly, the empirical philosophers provided for the new psychology a background oriented toward conscious experience. However, not everyone who pioneered the new psychology or its antecedent philosophy agreed with this exclusive focus on conscious mental experience. Some did believe in the importance of nonconscious processes. Although the influence of the unconscious can be traced to Plato, more recent thought on the topic followed Descartes after the seventeenth century.

In the early eighteenth century the German mathematician and philosopher Gottfried Wilhelm Leibnitz (1646–1716) developed his theory of *monadology.* Monads, which Leibnitz considered the individual elements of all reality, were not physical atoms. They were not even material in the usual sense of the word. Each monad was an unextended psychic entity. Leibnitz insisted that although each monad was mental in nature, it had some of the properties of physical matter. When enough of them were collected into an aggregate, they created an extension.

Monads were centers of activity and energy. In general terms, they could be likened to perception and are similar to consciousness. Leibnitz believed that mental events (the activity of monads) had differing degrees of clearness or consciousness, which could range from the completely unconscious to the most clear or definitely conscious. Thus, there were lesser degrees of consciousness, called *petites perceptions.* The conscious actualization of these was called *apperception.*

For example, the sound of waves breaking on the shore is an apperception. This apperception is composed of all the falling drops of water. The individual drop of water, like the monad, is the *petite perception* and is not consciously perceived by itself. When sufficient numbers of them congregate, however, they summate to produce an apperception.

A century later, Johann Friedrich Herbart (1776–1841) developed the Leibnitzian notion of the unconscious into the concept of threshold or limen of consciousness. Those ideas below the limen are unconscious. When an idea rises to a conscious level of awareness, it is apperceived, in Leibnitz's terms, but Herbart went beyond this. For an idea to rise into consciousness, it must be compatible and congruent with the ideas already in consciousness. Incongruous ideas cannot exist in consciousness at the same time, and ideas that are irrelevant are forced out of consciousness to become what Herbart called *inhibited ideas.* Inhibited ideas existed below the threshold of consciousness and were akin to Leibnitz's *petites perceptions.* According to Herbart, there is a conflict among ideas in which they actively struggle for realization in consciousness. Herbart's work showed the influence of the mechanistic spirit. His goal was to develop what he called a "mathematics of the mind," and he went so far as to propose equations and formulas to account for the mechanics of ideas as they entered into or were pushed out of conscious awareness.

Fechner also contributed to the development of theories about the unconscious. He used the notion of limen or threshold, but his suggestion that the mind is analogous to an iceberg, in that a considerable portion of it is hidden below the surface where it is influenced by unobservable forces, had a greater influence on Freud.

It is interesting that Fechner, to whom experimental psychology owes so much, was also a precursor of psychoanalysis. Freud quoted from Fechner's *Elements of Psychophysics* in several of his books and derived some major concepts from his work, including the pleasure principle, the notion of psychic or mental energy, the topographical concept of mind, and the importance of the destructive instinct. Freud's biographer noted that "Fechner was the only psychologist from whom Freud ever borrowed any idea" (Jones, 1957, p. 268).

The theory of monadology proposed by Gottfried Wilhelm Leibnitz (1646–1716) was an early attempt to explain unconscious processes.

The notion of the unconscious was very much part of the *Zeitgeist* of the 1880s in Europe, the time when Freud was beginning his clinical practice. Not only was the idea of interest to professionals, but it was also considered by the lay public to be a fashionable topic of conversation. A book entitled *Philosophy of the Unconscious* (von Hartmann, 1869) was so popular that it appeared in nine editions between 1869 and 1882, and in the decade 1870–1880 at least a half dozen other books were published in Germany that contained the word "unconscious" in their titles.

Freud, therefore, was not the first to discover or even to discuss seriously the unconscious. Although some early thinkers had merely mentioned the unconscious, others had attributed great importance to it. No one before Freud, however, had realized the significance of unconscious motivation or found a way to study it. Freud thought that in exploring the unconscious he would be able to explain what had previously been considered inexplicable. He believed that unconscious feelings and thoughts directly or indirectly influence behavior.

Psychopathology

We have observed that a new movement always requires something to revolt against, something to push away from in order to gain momentum. Because psychoanalysis did not develop within academic psychology, the existing order that it opposed was not Wundtian psychology or any other school of psychological thought. To discover what Freud opposed, we must consider the prevailing thought in the area in which he worked: the understanding and treatment of mental disorders.

The history of the treatment of the mentally ill is itself both fascinating and depressing and presents a striking picture of inhumanity. In the Middle Ages the disturbed individual received almost no understanding and very little treatment. The mind was alleged to be a free agent, responsible for its own condition. The treatment for mentally disturbed persons consisted primarily of blame and punishment, because the causes of emotional disturbance were believed to be wickedness, witchcraft, and possession by demons.

Conditions did not improve during the Renaissance. Boring (1950) recounts events and attitudes characteristic of that period.

> The great changes in the social structure at the time of the Renaissance created a general feeling of uncertainty and insecurity. . . . Insecure men, uncertain of the future, frustrated by change, stand ready to exorcise the threat of evil by an uncritical distribution of blame and punishment. Then, as now, they were ready to go witch hunting because they were afraid, and in the fifteenth century the Church did it for them. In 1489 *Jacob Sprenger* and *Heinrich Kraemer*, two Dominican brothers, taking advantage of the recent invention of the printing press, published the *Malleus maleficarum*, a title which perhaps can best be translated as the *Witch Hammer*, since the book was designed to be a tool for hammering at the witches. The *Malleus maleficarum* is a cruel encyclopedia on witchcraft, the detection of witches and the procedures for examining them by torture and for sentencing them. . . . It identified witchcraft with heresy and for us it identifies witchcraft with the mental disorders, many of whose symptoms it describes with care. For three hundred years in nineteen editions this malevolent compendium remained the authority and guide of the Inquisition as it sought out heresy and demoniacal possession among the people. (pp. 694–695)

The Inquisition continued through the eighteenth century, but in the nineteenth century a more humane and rational attitude toward the mentally ill took hold. In Europe and America the chains were struck—literally—from the insane as a decline in the influence of religious superstition paved the way for the scientific investigation of the causes of mental illness.

The treatments offered were primitive at best and sometimes caused more suffering than the disturbances they were supposed to cure. Consider some of the techniques developed by Benjamin Rush (1745–1813), the first psychiatrist to practice in the United States. He believed that some bizarre behaviors were caused by either too much or too little blood. His remedy was to pump blood into or drain blood out of the patient. He developed a rotating chair that spun the unfortunate person at a high speed, a procedure that often led to a loss of consciousness.

In an early form of shock treatment, Rush dunked patients in a tub of water, keeping them submerged for some time. Also, he may be credited with the invention of the first tranquilizing technique. Patients were strapped in a so-called tranquilizing chair and pressure was applied to their heads by large wooden blocks. This procedure may not have been very relaxing. Several patients suffered broken bones attempting to escape the viselike grip on their skulls.

Although these techniques sound cruel to us today, we must remember that Rush was trying to help the mentally ill instead of dumping them in custodial institutions where their needs were ignored. Rush recognized that his patients were sick, and he established the first hospital in the United States solely for the treatment of emotional disturbance.

During the nineteenth century there were two main schools of thought in psychiatry, the somatic and the psychic. The *somatic* school held that abnormalities of behavior had physical causes: lesions in the brain and nervous system, overstimulation or under-stimulation of the nerves, or nerves that were too tight or too lax (Drinka, 1984). The *psychic* school believed in mental or psychological causes of emotional illness. On the whole, nineteenth-century psychiatry was dominated by the somatic school. Psycho-analysis developed as one aspect of a revolt against this somatic orientation. As work with the mentally ill continued, some scientists became convinced that emotional stress was of greater importance than brain lesions or other possible physical causes in the etiology of abnormal behavior.

Hypnosis played an important role in fostering interest in the psychic causes of abnor-mal behavior. In the latter part of the eighteenth century, hypnosis was brought to the attention of the medical world by Franz Anton Mesmer. For a century *mesmerism* was almost universally rejected by the medical profession, which regarded it as quackery. In England, James Braid (1795–1860) called the phenomena characteristic of the hypnotic state "neurypnology," from which the term hypnosis was later derived. His careful work and disdain for exaggerated claims earned some scientific respectability for hypnosis.

Hypnosis achieved greater prominence with the work of Jean Martin Charcot (1825–1893), who was a physician and the head of a neurological clinic at Salpêtrière, the Parisian hospital for insane women. Charcot treated hysterical patients by means of hypnosis with some degree of success. More important, he described the symptoms of both hysteria and hypnosis in medical terms, making the latter phenomenon more readily acceptable to medicine and to the French Academy of Science (which had rejected mesmerism three times). Approval by the Academy was vital because it made it acceptable for neurologists to begin to investigate the psychological aspects of mental illness.

Charcot's work remained primarily neurological, emphasizing physical disturbances, paralysis, and the like. Hysteria continued to be ascribed to somatic causes until Charcot's pupil and successor, Pierre Janet (1859–1947), accepted Charcot's invitation in 1889 to become director of the psychological laboratory at Salpêtrière. Janet rejected the opinion that hysteria was a physiological disturbance and saw it instead as a mental disorder. Accordingly, he emphasized mental phenomena, particularly impairments of memory, fixed ideas, and the influence of unconscious forces, and preferred hypnosis as a method of treatment. Thus, in the early years of Freud's career, the published literature on hypnosis and on the psychological causes of mental illness, was growing rapidly. The work of Janet, in particular, anticipated many of Freud's ideas.

We have mentioned only briefly the important work of Charcot and Janet in the treatment of the mentally disturbed. The relevant point here is the change in beliefs about the cause of mental illness from the somatic to the psychic or mental. More and more people were beginning to think in terms of curing emotional disturbances through the mind instead of through the body, and the term *psychotherapy* was widely accepted before Freud started to publish his ideas.

The Influence of Darwin

In 1979, Frank J. Sulloway, a distinguished historian of science, published *Freud: Biologist of the Mind*, in which he argued that Freud had been greatly influenced by the work of Charles Darwin. Sulloway drew upon new data of history, or, more precisely, he examined data that had existed for years but which no one else had viewed in the same way.

Sulloway examined the books in Freud's personal library and found copies of Darwin's works. Freud had read them all, had made copious notes in their margins, and was known to have praised them highly. Freud acknowledged that Darwin's work, along with an essay by Goethe on nature, had influenced his choice of medicine as a profession. In addition, many similarities with Darwin's work can be detected in Freud's writings. Sulloway concluded that Darwin "probably did more than any other individual to pave the way for Sigmund Freud and the psychoanalytic revolution" (Sulloway, 1979, p. 238).

Darwin discussed a number of ideas that Freud later made central issues in psychoanalysis, including unconscious mental processes and conflicts, the significance of dreams, the hidden symbolism of bizarre symptoms of behavior, and the importance of sexual excitation. Overall, Darwin focused (as Freud did later) on nonrational aspects of thought and behavior.

Darwin also influenced Freud's thinking on childhood development. We noted in Chapter 6 that Darwin gave his notes and unpublished materials to Romanes, who later wrote two books on mental evolution in man and animals based on Darwin's material. Sulloway found copies of both books in Freud's library, again with Freud's handwritten comments in the margins. Romanes elaborated upon Darwin's notion of the continuity in emotional behavior between childhood and adulthood and, more importantly, on the suggestion that the sex drive appears in infants as early as seven weeks after birth. Both of these themes were to become central to Freudian psychoanalysis.

Darwin insisted that people were driven by biological forces, particularly those of love and hunger, which he believed were the foundation of all behavior. Less than a decade later, Richard von Krafft-Ebing, the noted German psychiatrist, wrote, in agreement with Darwin, that self-preservation and sexual gratification were the only two instincts in human physiology. Thus, respected scientists following Darwin's lead were increasingly recognizing the role of sex as a basic human motivation.

There are other points of similarity between Darwin and Freud. Freud's emphasis on internal conflict is conceptually identical to Darwin's theme of the struggle for existence.

Freud wrote that "The individual perishes from his internal conflicts, the species [per-ishes] in its struggle with the external world to which it is no longer adapted" (Freud, 1938/1941, p. 299). In both cases there is a struggle to the death, be it psychological or physiological.

Certainly we must count Darwin among the precursors to Freud, who drew up-on many aspects of evolutionary theory to develop his own revolutionary theory of psychoanalysis.

Other Sources of Influence

Several other influences on Freud deserve mention. The intellectual climate of the eighteenth and nineteenth centuries included the motivational doctrine of *hedonism*, which states, in essence, that we strive to gain pleasure and to avoid pain. Associated primarily with Jeremy Bentham and his notion of utilitarianism, hedonism was also supported by some of the British associationists. One of Freud's concepts, the pleasure principle, was strongly supported by hedonism.

During Freud's university training he came in contact with the mechanistic school of thought, as represented by the physiologists Carl Ludwig, Emil du Bois-Reymond, Ernst Brücke, and Hermann von Helmholtz. These students of the great Johannes Müller had united to take the position that no forces are to be found in living things that do not exist in inanimate objects. They argued that there are no forces active within the organ-ism other than the common physical and chemical ones. Freud was a student of Brücke's, and this mechanistic orientation influenced him in the formulation of his notion of the deterministic nature of human behavior, a concept he called "psychic determinism."

Another aspect of the *Zeitgeist* that influenced and reinforced Freud's work was the sexual climate in Vienna in the late nineteenth century. It has often been alleged that because society in Freud's day was repressive and puritanical, he was far ahead of his time in discussing sexual matters so frankly and openly. Although such inhibitions may have characterized the upper-middle-class neurotic women who were Freud's patients (as well as Freud himself), it certainly did not characterize the culture as a whole. Turn-of-the-century Vienna was a sexually permissive and open society. Further, this wide-spread sensuality was not accompanied by feelings of guilt or by repression. In addition, recent research suggests that even Victorian England and Puritan America may not have been characterized by the excessive prudery and inhibitions usually associated with those cultures (Gay, 1983).

Interest in sexual matters was visible in everyday Viennese life and in the scientific literature. In the years before Freud advanced his sex-based theory, a large number of studies had been published on sexual pathologies, infantile sexuality, and the suppres-sion of sexual impulses and its effects on mental and physical health. A colleague of Freud's in Vienna, the neurologist Moritz Benedikt, was achieving dramatic results in curing hysterics by getting them to talk about problems with their sex lives. The French psychologist, Alfred Binet, published work on sexual perversions in the late 1880s and early 1890s. Even the word "libido," which was to assume such importance in psycho-analysis, was already in use and had the same meaning Freud later gave it. With regard to the sexual component of Freud's work, then, much had been anticipated in one form or another. Because both public and professional interest in sex was so strong, Freud's ideas received a great deal of attention.

The concept of *catharsis* was also popular before Freud published any of his work. In 1880, a year before Freud received his M.D., an uncle of his future wife wrote a book on Aristotle's concept of catharsis. There ensued "a craze for the topic of catharsis. . . . For a time catharsis was one of the most discussed subjects among scholars and one of the topics of conversation in sophisticated Viennese salons" (Ellenberger, 1972, p. 272). By 1890 there were more than 140 publications in German on the topic (Sulloway, 1979).

Thus, there were many, diverse sources of influence on Freud's thinking. No small part of Freud's genius was the ability to draw on these various ideas to develop his system, a characteristic possessed by all the founders we have discussed.

THE DEVELOPMENT OF PSYCHOANALYSIS: SIGMUND FREUD (1856–1939)

The psychoanalytic movement is a highly personal school centered primarily on Freud and secondarily on his disciples. The system Freud developed is intimately related to his own life and is, to a large degree, autobiographical; consequently, the story of his life is vital to an understanding of his system.

Freud was born on May 6, 1856, in Freiberg, Moravia (now Pribor, Czechoslovakia). His father was a relatively unsuccessful Jewish wool merchant who, when his business failed in Moravia, moved his family first to Leipzig and then (when Freud was 4 years old) to Vienna. Freud remained in Vienna for nearly 80 years.

Freud's father was 20 years older than his mother and was somewhat strict and authoritarian. As a young boy, Freud apparently felt both fear and love toward him. His mother was protective and loving, and he felt a passionate attachment to her. This fear of the father and sexual attraction to the mother is, of course, what Freud later called the *Oedipus complex*, and it seems to have been derived from his boyhood experiences and recollections.

One of eight children, Freud early demonstrated great intellectual ability, which his family did everything possible to encourage. His was the only room in the house to have an oil lamp, providing better light for study; other family members used candles. The other children, toward whom he displayed much rivalry and resentment, were not allowed to study music, lest their practicing disturb the young scholar.

Freud entered *Gymnasium* a year earlier than normal and was a brilliant student, graduating with distinction at the age of 17. He was undecided about his career; his interests included civilization, human culture, human relationships, and even military history. Darwin's theory of evolution awakened in him an interest in a scientific approach to an understanding of life, and with some hesitation Freud decided on medicine. He had no real desire to be a practicing physician, but selected medicine in the hope that it would lead to a career in scientific research.

Freud began his studies at the University of Vienna in 1873. Because of his interests in several fields not directly connected with medical training, he spent eight years completing his studies. At first he concentrated on biology and dissected more than 400

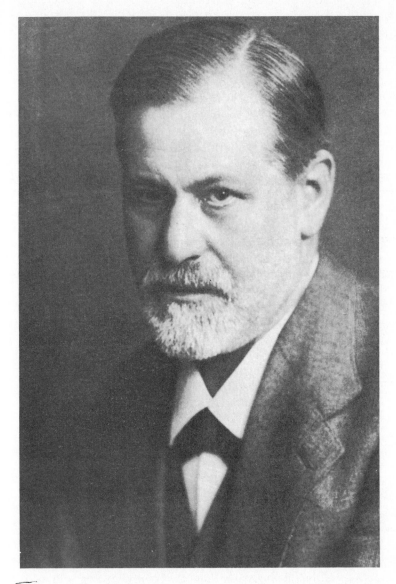

The psychoanalytic movement began with Sigmund Freud (1856–1939) and grew to become one of the most important forces of the time. His work has had a profound influence on the development of modern psychology and on many aspects of western culture.

male eels in search of the precise structure of the testes. His results were not conclusive, but it is noteworthy that his first attempt at research concerned sex.

He moved on to physiology and work on the spinal cord of the fish. Apparently he enjoyed physiology because he worked for six years over a microscope in Brücke's physiological institute.

During his medical training Freud began experimenting with the drug cocaine. He used it himself, made it available to his fiancée, his sisters, and his friends, and was responsible for introducing cocaine into medical practice. He was enthusiastic about the substance and found that it cured his depression and helped his almost chronic indiges-

tion. He was convinced that he had discovered a wonder drug that would cure everything from sciatica to seasickness and win for him the fame and recognition he sought
so eagerly.

But this was not to be. One of Freud's medical colleagues, after hearing his casual
conversation about cocaine, found that the drug could be used to anesthetize the human
eye, thus making eye surgery possible for the first time. Although the colleague became
famous, Freud was criticized severely for advocating the use of cocaine for purposes
other than eye surgery. For many years it was believed that Freud never used cocaine
after finishing medical school. New data of history, in the form of Freud's own letters,
which were long kept from public view, reveal that he used the drug for at least 10 years
more, well into middle age (Masson, 1985).

Freud wanted to remain in scientific work within a university setting, but Brücke
discouraged this inclination because of Freud's financial circumstances. He was too poor
to support himself during the many years he would have to wait to secure one of the
few available professorships. Freud reluctantly agreed that it would be too long a time
before he could earn a living in the Austrian university system, so he decided to take his
medical examinations and enter private practice as a physician. This meant that he had
to undertake work in clinics and hospitals, because he had neglected the clinical aspect
of his medical education to pursue his research in physiology. During his hospital
training he specialized as much as possible in the anatomy and organic diseases of the
nervous system, particularly paralysis, aphasia, brain injuries in children, and speech
pathology.

Freud received his M.D. in 1881 and the following year established a practice as a
clinical neurologist. It was a difficult step; although he had become well known for his
research in neurology, he was not greatly attracted to private practice in the field. The
most compelling reason for beginning a practice was his engagement in 1882 to Martha
Bernays, who was as poor as he. Their marriage was postponed several times for financial
reasons but finally, after a frustrating four-year engagement, they were married. During
the first few months of marriage Freud had to borrow money and even pawn their
watches. The situation eventually improved, but he never forgot those early years of
poverty.

Freud's long working hours prevented his spending a great deal of time with his wife
and children (of whom there were eventually six). He also vacationed alone or with his
sister-in-law, because his wife could not maintain the pace of hiking and sightseeing he
set for himself.

During these years a friendship of utmost importance to Freud developed with Josef
Breuer (1842–1925), a physician who had gained renown for his study of respiration and the discovery of the functioning of the semicircular canals. A successful and
sophisticated general practitioner, Breuer gave the impoverished young Freud advice and friendship, and even loaned him money. They frequently discussed some
of Breuer's patients, including Anna O.,[1] whose case is pivotal in the development of
psychoanalysis.

---

[1] Anna O.'s real name was Bertha Pappenheim, and she later became a social worker in West Germany. See
L. Freeman, *The Story of Anna O.* (New York: Walker, 1972).

An intelligent and attractive 21-year-old woman, Anna showed a wide range of severe hysterical symptoms including paralysis, memory losses, mental deterioration, nausea, and disturbances of vision and speech (Hollender, 1980). Breuer began treating her by using hypnosis. He found that while she was under hypnosis, she would remember specific experiences that seemed to have given rise to certain symptoms, and talking about the experiences while in a hypnotic state seemed to relieve the symptoms.

For example, Anna went through a period when she could not drink water, despite feelings of thirst. Under hypnosis, she related that she had had a similar aversion to water in childhood, and she recalled seeing a dog she disliked drinking from a glass. After relating this incident to Breuer, she found that she could drink water again with no difficulty and the symptom never recurred.

Breuer saw Anna every day for more than a year. During their meetings Anna would recount the disturbing incidents of the day, after which she often experienced some relief from her symptoms. She referred to her talks with Breuer as "chimney sweeping" and the "talking cure."

As the treatment continued, Breuer realized (and described to Freud) that the incidents Anna recalled under hypnosis involved some thought or experience that was repulsive to her. When she was able to relive these experiences under hypnosis, her symptoms either became less severe or disappeared altogether.

Breuer's wife grew jealous of the close emotional relationship that arose between Anna and Breuer. Anna exhibited what was later called a "positive transference" to Breuer, that is, she transferred her feelings for her father to Breuer. Later in the development of psychoanalysis transference was considered a necessary part of the therapeutic process. Breuer, however, saw the situation as a threat and stopped Anna's treatment. A few hours after he told Anna that he could not continue to see her, she experienced the symptoms of hysterical childbirth. Breuer terminated this event through hypnosis and, according to legend, left with his wife the next day for a second honeymoon in Venice, at which time his wife became pregnant.

This tale seems to have been a myth perpetuated by several generations of psychoanalysts and historians and provides another example of the distortions that can occur in the data of history. In this case, the myth persisted for almost 100 years before being corrected by new findings. Breuer and his wife may have gone to Venice for a second honeymoon, but the dates of birth of their children reveal that none could have been conceived at that time (Ellenberger, 1972).

Indeed, much of the story of Anna O. seems to be more fiction than fact, particularly with regard to her cure by Breuer's cathartic treatments. Research by Ellenberger has disclosed that "the famed 'prototype of a cathartic cure' was neither a cure nor a catharsis" (1972, p. 279), and that Anna O. was institutionalized for a period of time after Breuer stopped treating her. A year after he had stopped seeing her, Breuer expressed the hope that she might die so as to end her suffering. She never spoke of her experiences with Breuer and held a negative attitude toward psychoanalysis for the rest of her life (Sulloway, 1979).

Breuer's treatment of Anna O. is, however, important in the development of psychoanalysis because it did introduce Freud to the "talking cure" that figures so prominently in his work.

In 1885 a small postgraduate grant enabled Freud to spend 4½ months studying in France under Charcot. A significant incident took place during this stay in Paris. At a reception one evening, Freud heard Charcot assert that a certain patient's difficulties had a sexual basis. "But in this sort of case it's always a question of the genitals—always, always, always" (Freud, 1914). To Freud, this assessment was an illuminating and exciting insight. Thereafter, he was alert to the suggestion of sexual problems in his patients.

He also had an opportunity to observe Charcot's use of hypnosis in the treatment of hysterics. The French physician had shown that the traditional view of hysteria as an exclusively female malady (the word is derived from the Greek *hystera*, meaning womb) was incorrect; he had demonstrated the existence of hysterical symptoms in some of his male patients.

A year after his return from Paris, Freud was once again reminded of the possible sexual basis of a patient's disturbance. A noted gynecologist asked Freud if he would take the case of a woman who suffered strong anxiety attacks that were relieved only when she knew where her doctor was at every moment. The physician told Freud that the woman's anxieties were caused by her impotent husband; the woman was still a virgin after 18 years of marriage. "The sole prescription for such a malady," the doctor told Freud, "is familiar enough to us, but we cannot order it. It runs: ℞ *Penis normalis dosim repetatur!*" (Freud, 1914).

Freud had adopted Breuer's methods of hypnosis and catharsis in dealing with his patients. He gradually became less satisfied with hypnosis. Although it was apparently successful in removing symptoms, it did not seem able to effect a complete cure. Many patients returned with a different set of symptoms. Furthermore, some neurotic patients could not be easily or deeply hypnotized.

These and other problems induced Freud to abandon the hypnotic portion of the treatment, but he retained catharsis. Gradually he developed what has been called the most important step in the evolution of the psychoanalytic method: the technique of *free association*, which, as we noted in Chapter 1, Freud called "intrusion" or "invasion" in German, not "association." In this procedure the patient lies on a couch and is encouraged to talk openly and spontaneously, giving complete expression to every idea, no matter how embarrassing, unimportant, or foolish it may seem. The aim of Freud's developing method of psychoanalysis was to bring into conscious awareness repressed memories or thoughts, presumably the source of the patient's abnormal behavior.

Freud believed that there was nothing random about the material uncovered during free association, and that it was not subject to a patient's conscious choice. The information revealed by patients during free association was predetermined, that is, forced or intruded upon them by the nature of their conflict.

Through the technique of free association, Freud found that his patients' memories invariably went far back into their childhood experiences, and that many of these repressed memories concerned sexual matters. Already alert to the possible role of sexual factors in the etiology of his patients' illnesses, and certainly aware of the current literature on sexual pathology, Freud became more attuned to the occurrence of sexual material in the narratives of his patients.

In 1895 Breuer and Freud published *Studies on Hysteria*, often considered the formal starting point of psychoanalysis. The book contained a joint paper that had been published previously; five case histories, including that of Anna O.; a theoretical paper by Breuer; and a chapter by Freud on psychotherapy. Although the book received some negative reviews, it also received positive ones in scientific and literary journals, not only in Austria but in other countries as well. It was a definite, if modest, beginning of the recognition Freud wanted. Breuer had been reluctant to publish the book, and this decision may mark the beginning of the end of his personal relationship with Freud. The split was apparently caused by Freud's contention that sex was the sole cause of neurosis. Breuer agreed that sex could be important in neurosis, but he was not convinced that it was the only cause. He suggested that Freud did not have sufficient evidence to support his conclusion.

Freud disagreed. He was convinced that he was correct and that there was no need to accumulate additional data to support his position. Perhaps Freud was reluctant to wait for more documentation because the delay might allow someone else to publish the idea and thus claim priority. Freud's ambition for success and fame may have taken precedence over scientific caution about rushing into print with insufficient evidence.

Freud's attitude disturbed Breuer, and around 1898 the break between them was complete. Freud became embittered toward the man who had done so much for him, telling a friend that the mere sight of Breuer made him want to emigrate to another country (Sulloway, 1979).

By the mid-1890s Freud was more convinced than ever that sex played the determining role in neurosis. He observed that most of his patients reported traumatic sexual experiences in their childhoods, often involving members of their own families. He came to believe that neurosis was not possible in a person who led a normal sex life.

In a paper presented to the Society of Psychiatry and Neurology in Vienna in 1896, Freud reported that his patients had revealed experiences resembling seduction in childhood, with the seducer usually being an older relative, most often the father. Today such experiences are labeled "child abuse." These seduction traumas, Freud believed, caused the adult neurotic behavior. He further reported that his patients were hesitant when describing the seduction experience in detail and that the entire situation seemed somewhat unreal. Patients recounted the events in a manner suggesting that they were not fully remembered; it was as though they had never happened. The paper was received with skepticism, and the president of the Society, Krafft-Ebing, commented that "It sounds like a scientific fairy tale" (Jones, 1953, p. 263).

About a year after the presentation of this paper, Freud experienced a sudden revelation: in most cases, the childhood seduction experiences his patients had described had never actually occurred. This realization marks a turning point in the history of psychoanalysis. At first, the awareness that his patients were reporting fantasies was a blow to Freud, whose theory of hysteria was based on the reality of these childhood sexual traumas. On reflection, however, he concluded that his patients' fantasies were quite real to them. Also, because their fantasies centered on sexual matters, sex remained the root of their problems. Thus, Freud's basic thesis of sex as a causative factor in neurosis was intact.

In 1984 controversy erupted when Jeffrey Masson, a psychoanalyst who had briefly been director of the Freud Archives, charged that Freud had been lying about the reality of the childhood sexual experiences. Masson claimed that the sexual abuses reported by Freud's patients had, in most cases, actually occurred and that Freud had labeled them "fantasies" to make his system more palatable to colleagues and to the public (Masson, 1984).

Most reputable scholars denounced Masson's claims, arguing that he did not present convincing evidence (Malcolm, 1984). The dispute received nationwide newspaper and magazine publicity. In an interview published in the Washington *Post*, Freud scholars Paul Roazen and Peter Gay described Masson's proposal as "a hoax," "a grave slander," and "a severe distortion of the history of psychoanalysis" (February 19, 1984). Freud never abandoned his belief that the childhood sexual abuses had sometimes taken place. What he denied was his earlier view that they had always taken place.

The incident testifies to the strength of the interest in Sigmund Freud nearly 50 years after his death, and it also demonstrates how the data of history are subject to different interpretations.

It is interesting that Freud, who so strongly stressed the role of sex in our emotional lives, held a negative personal attitude toward sex. He consistently wrote of the dangers of sexuality, even for people who were not neurotic, and argued that we should strive to rise above that "common animal need." The sex act, he wrote, is degrading; it contaminates both the mind and the body. In 1897, when he was 41 years old, he reported that he had personally given up sex altogether, writing to a friend that "sexual excitation is of no more use to a person like me" (Freud, 1954, p. 227). Freud had occasionally been impotent and had sometimes abstained from sex for periods of time because of his abhorrence of condoms and coitus interruptus, the then standard methods of birth control.

Also in 1897 Freud began the monumental task of self-analysis. He had experienced a number of neurotic difficulties for several years. He diagnosed his condition as anxiety neurosis, which he said was caused by the accumulation of sexual tension. This was a time of intense inner turmoil for Freud, yet it was also one of the most creative periods of his life. He undertook self-analysis as a means toward better understanding of himself and his patients, and the method he used was *dream analysis*.

In the course of his work Freud had discovered that a patient's dreams could be a rich source of significant emotional material. Dreams often contained valuable clues to the underlying causes of a disturbance. Because of his positivist belief that everything had a cause, he thought that events in a dream could not be completely without meaning; they must result from something in the person's unconscious. (This notion that dream images are symbolic is not unique to Freud; it is actually an ancient theory.)

Realizing that he could not analyze himself by the technique of free association (it being difficult to assume the roles of patient and therapist at the same time), Freud decided to investigate his dreams. Upon waking each morning, he recorded his dream material of the night before and then free-associated to this material. His self-analysis continued for about two years, culminating in the publication of *The Interpretation of Dreams* (1900), a book that is now considered his major work. In it he outlined for the first time the nature of the Oedipus complex, drawing largely on his own childhood experiences. The work was not universally praised, but it nevertheless achieved far-ranging recognition and much favorable comment. Professional journals in fields as diverse as philosophy and neuropsychiatry reviewed it, as did popular magazines and newspapers in Vienna, Berlin, and other major European cities. In Zurich a young man by the name of Carl Jung read the book and quickly became a convert to the new psychoanalysis, at least for a time.

The Interpretation of Dreams was eventually so successful that it appeared in eight editions during Freud's lifetime. He incorporated dream analysis into the body of techniques used in psychoanalysis, and for the remainder of his life devoted the last half-hour of each day to self-analysis.

In the productive years after 1900 Freud developed and expanded his new ideas. In 1901 he published *The Psychopathology of Everyday Life*, which contained the description of the now famous Freudian slip. He suggested that in the everyday behavior of the normal person as well as in neurotic symptoms unconscious ideas are struggling for expression and thus are capable of modifying thought and action. What might seem to be casual slips of the tongue or forgetting, Freud suggested, are actually reflections of real, though unacknowledged, motives.

His next book, *Three Essays on the Theory of Sexuality*, appeared in 1905 (Freud, 1905b). Three years earlier some students had urged him to conduct a weekly discussion group so that they might learn about his psychoanalysis, as he had then begun to call his work. These early disciples, including Alfred Adler and Carl Jung, later achieved fame through their opposition to Freud (see Chapter 14), who tolerated no dissent from his emphasis on the role of sexuality. Anyone who did not accept this tenet was promptly excommunicated, and this happened to several of his major disciples. Later Freud wrote: "psycho-analysis is my creation; for ten years I was the only person who concerned himself with it . . . No one can know better than I do what psycho-analysis is" (Freud, 1914).

During the first decade of the twentieth century Freud's personal and professional positions improved. His practice increased and a growing number of people took his pronouncements seriously. In 1909 he received the first sign of international recognition when he and Carl Jung were invited by G. Stanley Hall to speak at the twentieth anniversary celebration of Clark University in Massachusetts. He was awarded an honorary doctorate in psychology (Jung was awarded a degree in education and social hygiene). It was a deeply moving experience for Freud, and he met many prominent psychologists of the day, including William James, James McKeen Cattell, and E. B. Titchener. The five lectures that he gave at Clark were published the following year in the *American Journal of Psychology*, and were later translated into several languages (Freud, 1909/1910).

Freud was well received and honored on this visit to the United States, yet he left with an unfavorable impression of America, which he harbored for many years. He complained of the quality of American cooking, the scarcity of bathrooms, difficulties with the language, and the informality in manners, which seemed shockingly free to a cultured European. He was offended by a guide at Niagara Falls who referred to him as "the old fellow."

He never returned to America, and commented to his biographer, Ernest Jones, that "America is a mistake; a gigantic mistake, it is true, but none the less a mistake" (Jones, 1955, p. 60). In the interest of fairness, it should be noted that Freud also disliked Vienna, the city in which he lived for so many years.

During the first two decades of the twentieth century, the official psychoanalytic family was torn by discord, dissent, and defections. The break with Adler came in 1911, and with Jung, whom Freud had considered his spiritual son and the heir to psychoanalysis, in 1914. By World War I, three rival groups existed, but Freud managed to keep the name "psychoanalysis" for his group. The war years impeded his intellectual

Freud, surrounded by members of the American psychological community, at Clark University in 1909. The lectures he gave here were later published in the *American Journal of Psychology. First row, left to right:* Franz Boas, E. B. Titchener, William James, William Stern, Leo Burgerstein, G. Stanley Hall, Sigmund Freud, Carl G. Jung, Adolf Meyer, H. S. Jennings. *Second row:* C. E. Seashore, Joseph Jastrow, J. McK. Cattell, E. F. Buchner, E. Katzenellenbogen, Ernest Jones, A. A. Brill, Wm. H. Burnham, A. F. Chamberlain. *Third row:* Albert Schinz, J. A. Magni, B. T. Baldwin, F. Lyman Wells, G. M. Forbes, E. A. Kirkpatrick, Sandor Ferenczi, E. C. Sanford, J. P. Porter, Sakyo Kanda, Hikoso Kakise. *Fourth row:* G. E. Dawson, S. P. Hayes, E. B. Holt, C. S. Berry, G. M. Whipple, Frank Drew, J. W. A. Young, L. N. Wilson, K. J. Karlson, H. H. Goddard, H. I. Klopp, S. C. Fuller.

advancement and reduced the number of his patients and hence his income. With a wife, six children, and a sister-in-law to support, Freud had to be continually concerned with financial matters.

He reached the pinnacle of his fame in the period from 1919 to 1939, the year of his death. He continued to work hard and saw patients for several hours each day, but was able to take three months' vacation every summer. During the 1920s psychoanalysis developed as a theoretical system for the understanding of all human motivation and personality, rather than solely as a method of treatment for the disturbed. (This conceptual system is discussed later in this chapter.)

In 1923 it was discovered that Freud suffered from cancer of the mouth. The last 16 years of his life were marked by almost continuous pain. He underwent 33 operations, and portions of his palate and upper jaw were removed. He also underwent X-ray and radium treatments and had a vasectomy, which some physicians believed could reverse the growth of the cancer (Romm, 1984). The prosthetic device that his surgery made necessary hampered his speech, and it became increasingly difficult to understand him.[2]

[2] The writer Anthony Burgess described a visit to Freud's home in Vienna, which is now a museum (New York *Times*, October 7, 1984). There you can purchase a vivid reminder of Freud's last, grim years: "You can buy a phonograph record in which [Freud] speaks from the dead in precise English tortured by the clicks of his prosthesis."

Although Freud continued to see patients and disciples, he shunned other personal contact. He had typically smoked 20 cigars a day, and he continued to smoke after his illness was diagnosed.

When Hitler came to power in 1933, the official Nazi position on psychoanalysis was made clear when Freud's books were publicly burned in May 1933 at a rally in Berlin. As the volumes were flung onto the fire, a Nazi speaker shouted, "Against the soul-destroying overestimation of the sex life—and on behalf of the nobility of the human soul—I offer to the flames the writings of one Sigmund Freud!" (Schur, 1972, p. 446). Freud commented, "What progress we are making. In the Middle Ages they would have burnt me; nowadays they are content with burning my books" (Jones, 1957, p. 182). By 1934 the more farsighted Jewish psychoanalysts had left Germany. The vigorous Nazi campaign to eradicate psychoanalysis in Germany was so effective that knowledge of Freud, once so widespread, was almost completely obliterated. A student at the German Institute for Psychological Research and Psychotherapy, established by the Nazis in Berlin, recalled that "Freud's name was never mentioned, and his books were kept in a locked bookcase" (New York *Times*, July 3, 1984).

Against the advice of his friends, Freud insisted on remaining in Vienna. In March 1938 Germany invaded Austria, and on March 15 his home was overrun by a gang of Nazis. A week later his daughter, Anna, was arrested and detained for a day. Freud was finally convinced that he should flee, but he was not permitted to go until his unsold books had been brought back from Switzerland to be burned. Partly because of the intervention of the American ambassador to France, the Nazis agreed to let Freud go to England. Four of Freud's sisters were later killed in Nazi concentration camps.

A wry note attended Freud's departure from Vienna. To secure an exit visa, he had to sign a document attesting to his "respectful and considerate" treatment by the Gestapo, and noting that he had no reason to complain. He signed the form and asked if he might add, "I can heartily recommend the Gestapo to anyone" (Jones, 1957, p. 226).

Although Freud was received well in England, he was unable to enjoy the last year of his life because his health was failing rapidly. He remained mentally alert, however, and worked almost to the very end. Years before, when he selected Max Schur to be his personal physician, Freud made him promise that he would not let him suffer unnecessarily. On September 21, 1939, he reminded Schur of their earlier talk. "You promised me then not to forsake me when my time comes. Now it's nothing but torture and makes no sense any more" (Schur, 1972, p. 529). The doctor gave Freud two centigrams of morphine and repeated the dose 12 hours later. Freud went into a coma, his years of suffering finally at an end, and died on September 23, 1939.

PSYCHOANALYSIS AS A METHOD OF TREATMENT

Freud found that the method of free association did not always operate so freely. Sooner or later his patients reached a point in their narratives where they were unable or unwilling to continue. Freud believed that these *resistances* indicated that the patients had called up memories or ideas that were too horrible, shameful, or repulsive to be faced. He thought the resistance was a form of protection from emotional pain, and the presence of the pain itself was an indication that the analysis was getting close to the source of the difficulty.

Thus, resistance indicated that treatment was proceeding in the right direction and must continue to probe in that area. Freud placed great emphasis on helping patients to overcome their resistances. He insisted that they face the hidden experiences, no matter how disturbing, and see them in the light of reality. In the course of a complete analysis it was expected that resistance would be encountered and overcome a number of times.

Freud's notion of resistance led to the formulation of the fundamental psychoanalytic principle of *repression*, which involved the ejecting of painful ideas or memories from conscious awareness. Freud regarded repression as the only adequate explanation for the occurrence of resistance. Unpleasant ideas are pushed out of consciousness and forcefully kept out. The therapist must help patients bring this repressed material back into conscious awareness so that they can face it and learn to live with it. It has been suggested that Freud developed the concepts of resistance and repression from the philosopher Arthur Schopenhauer. In 1938 Freud noted that he had arrived at these ideas without having read Schopenhauer, to whom, however, he did yield precedence.

Freud recognized that effective work with neurotic patients depends on the development of a personal, intimate relationship between patient and therapist. We noted earlier how the *transference* that Anna O. developed toward Breuer so disturbed him that he felt compelled to end the treatment. Freud viewed the transference of a patient's emotional attitudes from parent to therapist as vital and necessary. The therapist had to wean the patient from childish dependence and help him or her to assume a more adult role in life.

Freud's recognition of the importance of dream material has already been mentioned. He believed that dreams represent a disguised satisfaction of repressed desires and wishes, and therefore the dream story is much more meaningful and complex than it might otherwise seem.[3]

Dreams have both a manifest and a latent content. The *manifest* content is the actual story told in recalling the events that occurred in the dream. The true significance of the dream, however, lies in the *latent* content, which is its hidden or symbolic meaning. To interpret this hidden meaning, the therapist must proceed from manifest to latent content, that is, interpret the symbolic meaning of the events that are related in the manifest content.

This is a complex task. Freud believed that the forbidden desires in the latent dream content are expressed in symbolic form in the manifest content. Although many symbols that appear in dreams are relevant only to experiences of the particular dreamer, others are common to all persons, and hence always have the same meaning. According to Freud, these universal symbols include gardens, balconies, and doors to signify the female body, and church spires, candles, and serpents to signify the male genitals. Dreams of falling represent giving in to erotic wishes, and dreams of flying represent a desire for sexual achievement. Freud warned that despite the universality of these common symbols, interpretation of a patient's dreams requires knowledge of the patient's specific conflicts.

---

[3]On Wednesday evening, July 24, 1895, at a table in the northeast corner of the terrace of the Bellevue Restaurant in Vienna, Freud realized that the essence of a dream is wish fulfillment. In accordance with the notion that genius often flatters itself by dating its own inspirations, Freud quipped that a tablet should be erected at that spot noting that "Here the secret of dreams was revealed to Dr. Sigm. Freud on July 24, 1895" (Jones, 1953, p. 354).

Freud in his Vienna study in 1937 surrounded by his collection of Greek, Roman, and Egyptian antiquities.

Freud also wrote that not all dreams are caused by emotional conflicts. Some dreams arise from such mundane stimuli as the temperature of the room, contact with one's partner, or overeating before bedtime. Therefore, not all dreams contain hidden, symbolic material.

Freud believed that a long and intensive course of therapy was required to effect a cure. With his own patients, he found that no fewer than five sessions a week, for months or even years, were necessary. With such extensive care, an analyst could handle only a few patients in the course of a year.

Freud also had definite ideas about the training of analysts. He thought that each should be analyzed and should work for at least two years under supervision before treating patients. He also believed that the practice of psychoanalysis should be a profession independent from medicine.

Despite the widespread use of psychoanalysis as a method of treatment, Freud had little interest in its potential therapeutic value. He was not primarily concerned with curing people but rather with understanding the dynamics that underlie human behavior. He saw himself more as a scientist than a therapist and considered his techniques of free association and dream analysis to be research tools for the collection of data. That these techniques also had therapeutic use was, to Freud, secondary to their scientific value.

Perhaps because of his relative lack of interest in the therapeutic application of psychoanalysis, Freud has been described as impersonal and brisk in dealing with patients. He placed his chair at the head of the psychoanalytic couch because he could not bear to be stared at by patients. He noted that he had become a therapist with reluctance and felt indifferent toward his patients. "I lack that passion for helping," he wrote to a friend (Jones, 1955, p. 446). Freud's passion was his research and the data on which he based his theory of personality.

FREUD'S METHOD OF RESEARCH

Freud's system differed greatly in content and methodology from traditional experimental psychology. It is difficult to reconcile some of Freud's theories with his scientific training, especially his years of physiological research. Despite his background, Freud did not use experimental research methods. Although he was familiar with experimental psychology, he did not collect data from controlled experiments or analyze his results quantitatively. The data he collected and the ways in which he interpreted them were at variance with the methods of experimental psychology. They had to be different because of the subject matter Freud chose to study.

Freud derived his theories from his observations of the narratives and behavior of his patients who were undergoing analysis, primarily through the free-association and dream-analysis techniques. Because psychoanalysis was such a lengthy process, Freud accumulated a mass of such data, which he tested for internal consistency. Assumptions and interpretations derived from the data were then carefully examined to make sure they were well grounded. We discuss some criticisms of Freud's research methods later in this chapter.

Freud found no inherent obstacles to making relevant and meaningful observations from this material.

> When I set myself the task of bringing to light what human beings keep hidden within them, not by the compelling power of hypnosis, but by observing what they say and what they show, I thought the task was a harder one than it really is. He that has eyes to see and ears to hear may convince himself that no mortal can keep a secret. If the lips are silent, he chatters with his finger-tips; betrayal oozes out of him at every pore. And thus the task of making conscious the most hidden recesses of the mind is one which it is quite possible to accomplish. (Freud, 1901/1905a, pp. 77–78)

Freud's theories were formulated, revised, and extended in terms of the evidence as he alone interpreted it. Thus, his own critical abilities were the predominant, indeed the only, guide in his theory building. He ignored criticism from others, particularly from those who were not sympathetic to psychoanalysis, and even the wide-ranging comments from close friends and colleagues throughout his life had little influence on his thinking. Only rarely did he bother to reply to critics. Psychoanalysis was his system, and his alone.

PSYCHOANALYSIS AS A SYSTEM OF PERSONALITY

Freud's theoretical system did not cover the topics that were usually included in psychology textbooks of the day. He explored areas that traditional psychology tended to ignore. His theoretical formulations dealt with unconscious motivating forces, the conflicts among these forces, and the effects of these conflicts on human behavior.

Instincts

Instincts are the propelling or locomotive factors in the dynamics of personality, the biological forces of the individual that release mental energy. Although the word "instinct" has come to be the accepted usage in English, it does not convey the meaning Freud intended. Freud did not use the German word *Instinkt* when referring to humans, only when referring to the innate drives of animals (Bettelheim, 1982). Freud's term in German, *Trieb*, is best translated as driving force or impulse. The Freudian instincts are not inherited predispositions (the usual meaning of "instinct"), but rather refer to sources of stimulation within the body. Their aim is to remove or reduce the stimulation through some activity such as sex, eating, or drinking.

Freud did not attempt to delimit the number of instincts, but he classified them in two categories: the life instincts and the death instinct. The *life instincts* (eros), including hunger, sex, and thirst, are concerned with self-preservation and survival of the species. These are the creative forces that sustain life itself, and the form of energy through which they are manifested is called *libido*. The *death instinct* (thanatos) is a destructive force. It can be directed inward as in suicide or masochism, or outward as in aggression and hatred. Freud believed that we are irresistibly drawn toward death, that "the goal of all life is death" (1920, p. 160).

Freud gradually acknowledged that aggression and hostility as well as sex are important forces in personality. As he grew older, he became convinced that aggression was as powerful as sex in motivating human behavior. He even became aware of an aggressive tendency within himself. Colleagues described him as a good hater, and some of his writings, as well as the sharpness and finality of his breaks with dissenters, suggest a high level of aggressiveness.

Freud's concept of aggression has been much better accepted than his suggestion of a death instinct. One psychoanalyst wrote that the idea of the death instinct could "now securely be relegated to the dust bin of history" (Becker, 1973, p. 99).

Unconscious and Conscious Aspects of Personality

In his early work Freud expressed the belief that psychic life consists of two parts—the conscious and the unconscious. The *conscious* part, like the visible portion of an iceberg, is small and insignificant, presenting but a superficial aspect of total personality. The vast and powerful *unconscious* contains the instincts that are the driving power behind all human behavior. Freud also postulated the existence of the *preconscious*, or foreconscious. Unlike the material in the unconscious, that in the preconscious has not been actively repressed and can be easily summoned into conscious awareness. For example, if your mind strayed from the words on this page and you began thinking about something you did last night, you would be summoning material from the preconscious to your conscious awareness.

Freud later revised this simple conscious–unconscious distinction and introduced the id, ego, and superego constructs of the mental apparatus. The *id,* corresponding somewhat to Freud's previous notion of the unconscious, is the most primitive and least accessible part of the personality. The powerful forces of the id include sexual and aggressive instincts: "We call it a chaos, a cauldron full of seething excitations." Freud further noted that "the id of course knows no judgments of value: no good and evil, no morality" (Freud, 1933, p. 74). The id seeks immediate satisfaction without regard for the circumstances of objective reality, and thus operates according to what Freud called the *pleasure principle,* which is concerned with the reduction of tension. We noted in Chapter 1 that Freud's term for the id was *es,* meaning "it."

Our basic psychic energy, or libido, is contained in the id and is expressed through tension reduction. Increases in libidinal energy result in increased tension that we attempt to reduce to a more tolerable level. To satisfy our needs and maintain a comfortable tension level, we must interact with the real world. For example, the person who is hungry must make appropriate movements in the environment to find food, thus discharging the tension induced by hunger. An effective and appropriate liaison between the demands of the id and the circumstances of reality must be effected. The *ego,* which serves as a mediating agent between the id and the external world, develops to facilitate this interaction. The ego represents what we mean by reason or rationality, in contrast to the blind, insistent passions of the id. Freud called the ego *ich,* which, in English, means "I."

The id craves blindly, unaware of reality; the ego is aware of reality, perceives and manipulates it, and regulates the id with reference to it. The ego operates in accordance with what Freud called the *reality principle,* holding in abeyance the pleasure-seeking demands of the id until an appropriate object has been found with which to satisfy the need and reduce or discharge the tension. The ego does not exist independently of the id; indeed, it derives its power from the id. It serves to help and not to hinder the id, and is constantly striving to bring about id satisfaction. Freud compared the relationship of the ego and the id to a rider on a horse. The horse supplies the energy that is directed along the path the rider wants to travel. However, the power of the horse must be constantly guided or checked, or the horse may throw the rider to the ground. Similarly, the id must be constantly guided and checked, or it will overthrow the rational ego.

The third part of Freud's structure of personality, the *superego,* develops early in childhood, when rules of conduct taught by parents through a system of rewards and punishments are assimilated. Behaviors that are wrong (that bring punishment) become part of the child's *conscience,* which is one part of the superego. Behaviors that are right (that are rewarded) become part of the child's *ego-ideal,* the other part of the superego. Thus, childhood behavior is initially governed by parental control, but once the superego has formed a pattern for conduct, behavior is determined by self-control. The behavior-guiding rewards and punishments are then administered by the individual. Freud's term for superego was a word he coined himself, *über-ich,* meaning, literally, "above I."

The superego represents "every moral restriction, the advocate of a striving towards perfection—it is, in short, as much as we have been able to grasp psychologically of what is described as the higher side of human life" (Freud, 1933, p. 67). Obviously, the superego is in conflict with the id. Unlike the ego, the superego does not merely attempt to postpone id satisfaction; it tries to inhibit it completely.

The ego is in a difficult position, pressured on three sides by insistent and opposing forces. It must try to delay the relentless urgings of the id, perceive and manipulate reality to relieve the tensions of the id impulses, and deal with the superego's striving for perfection. Whenever the ego is too sorely pressed, the inevitable result is the development of *anxiety*.

Anxiety

Anxiety functions as a warning that the ego is being threatened. Freud described three kinds of anxiety. *Objective anxiety* is occasioned by fear of actual dangers in the real world; neurotic anxiety and moral anxiety derive from objective anxiety.

Neurotic anxiety arises from recognition of the potential danger inherent in instinctual gratification. It is fear not of the instincts but of the punishment likely to follow indiscriminate id-dominated behavior. In other words, neurotic anxiety is a fear of being punished for expressing impulsive desires. *Moral anxiety* arises out of a fear of the conscience. When a person performs or thinks of performing some act that is contrary to the conscience's set of moral values, he or she may experience guilt or shame. Moral anxiety, then, is a function of how well developed one's conscience is. The less virtuous individual is less likely to develop moral anxiety.

Anxiety is a tension-inducing force in human behavior, motivating the individual to reduce this state of tension. Freud believed that the ego develops a number of protective defenses against anxiety, the *defense mechanisms*, which are unconscious denials or distortions of reality. In the mechanism of *identification*, a person identifies with (for example, takes on the manner, dress, or speech of) someone who seems admirable and less vulnerable to the danger giving rise to the anxiety. Another defense mechanism, *repression*, is the barring from conscious awareness of an anxiety-provoking impulse or thought. *Sublimation* involves substituting a socially acceptable goal for one that cannot be directly satisfied. For example, sexual energy may be diverted or sublimated into artistically creative behaviors. In *projection*, the source of anxiety is attributed to someone else, for example, by saying "He hates me" instead of "I hate him." In *reaction formation*, a person conceals a disturbing impulse by converting it into its opposite, for instance, by replacing hate with love. With the mechanism of *fixation*, a person's development becomes arrested at an early stage because the next stage is too fraught with anxiety. The defense mechanism of *regression* involves behavior that indicates a reversion to an earlier developmental stage, one at which there was greater security and the current source of anxiety was not operative. Freud believed that anxiety with which an individual cannot adequately cope becomes traumatic, reducing the person to a state of infantile helplessness.

Stages of Personality Development

Freud was convinced that the neurotic disturbances manifested by his patients had originated in childhood experiences. Consequently he became one of the first theorists to assign a central role to the development of the child. He believed that the adult personality pattern was established early in life and was almost completely formed by the age of five.

In the psychoanalytic theory of development, the child passes through a series of *psychosexual stages*. During these stages the child is considered autoerotic, that is, he or she derives sensual or erotic pleasure by stimulating the various erogenous zones of the body or by being stimulated by parents or caregivers in their handling of the child. Each stage tends to be localized in a specific erogenous zone.

The *oral stage* lasts from birth into the second year of life. During this stage, stimulation of the mouth, such as sucking, biting, and swallowing, is the primary source of erotic satisfaction. Inadequate satisfaction (too much or too little) at this stage may produce an oral personality, whereby the person becomes preoccupied with mouth habits, such as smoking, kissing, and eating. Freud believed that a wide range of adult behaviors, from excessive optimism to sarcasm and cynicism, were attributable to incidents that occurred during the oral stage of development.

In the *anal stage* sexual gratification shifts from the mouth to the anus and the child derives pleasure from the anal zone. During this stage, which coincides with the period of toilet training, the child may expel or withhold feces, in•either case defying the parents. Conflict during this period can result in an anal-expulsive adult, who is dirty, wasteful, and extravagant, or an anal-retentive adult, who is excessively neat, clean, and compulsive.

During the *phallic stage*, which occurs at around the fourth year, erotic gratification shifts to the genital region. There is much fondling and exhibiting of the genitals and sexual fantasizing. Freud posited the development at this stage of the *Oedipus complex* (named for the Greek legend in which Oedipus unknowingly killed his father and married his mother). The child becomes sexually attracted to the parent of the opposite sex and fearful of the parent of the same sex, who is now perceived as a rival. Ordinarily, the child overcomes this complex by identifying with the parent of the same sex and substituting affection for sexual longing for the parent of the opposite sex. However, the attitudes toward the opposite sex that develop during this stage persist and influence adult relations with members of the opposite sex. One of the results of identifying with the parent of the same sex is the development of the superego. In taking on the mannerisms and attitudes of that parent, the child also adopts the parent's superego standards.

Children who are able to outlast the many struggles of these early stages enter a period of *latency*, which lasts from about the fifth to the twelfth year. At the start of adolescence with the onset of puberty, the *genital stage* begins. Heterosexual behavior is evident and various activities by which the individual prepares for marriage and family are undertaken.

ORIGINAL SOURCE MATERIAL ON PSYCHOANALYSIS: FROM *AN OUTLINE OF PSYCHO-ANALYSIS* BY SIGMUND FREUD[4]

The following material deals with the development of sexual life in infants and children. It was written approximately 30 years after Freud first proposed the psychosexual stages of personality and thus represents his later thinking on sexual development.

[4] From Sigmund Freud, *An Outline of Psycho-Analysis*. In J. Strachey (Ed. and Trans.), *The standard edition of the complete psychological works of Sigmund Freud* (1940, Vol. 23, pp. 141–207). London:

According to the prevailing view human sexual life consists essentially in an endeavour to bring one's own genitals into contact with those of someone of the opposite sex. With this are associated, as accessory phenomena and introductory acts, kissing this extraneous body, looking at it and touching it. This endeavour is supposed to make its appearance at puberty—that is, at the age of sexual maturity—and to serve the purposes of reproduction. Nevertheless, certain facts have always been known which do not fit into the narrow framework of this view. (1) It is a remarkable fact that there are people who are only attracted by individuals of their own sex and by their genitals. (2) It is equally remarkable that there are people whose desires behave exactly like sexual ones but who at the same time entirely disregard the sexual organs or their normal use; people of this kind are known as 'perverts'. (3) And lastly it is a striking thing that some children (who are on that account regarded as degenerate) take a very early interest in their genitals and show signs of excitation in them.

It may well be believed that psycho-analysis provoked astonishment and denials when, partly on the basis of these three neglected facts, it contradicted all the popular opinions on sexuality. Its principal findings are as follows:

(*a*) Sexual life does not begin only at puberty, but starts with plain manifestations soon after birth.

(*b*) It is necessary to distinguish sharply between the concepts of 'sexual' and 'genital'. The former is the wider concept and includes many activities that have nothing to do with the genitals.

(*c*) Sexual life includes the function of obtaining pleasure from zones of the body—a function which is subsequently brought into the service of reproduction. The two functions often fail to coincide completely.

The chief interest is naturally focused on the first of these assertions, the most unexpected of all. It has been found that in early childhood there are signs of bodily activity to which only an ancient prejudice could deny the name of sexual and which are linked to psychical phenomena that we come across later in adult erotic life—such as fixation to particular objects, jealousy, and so on. It is further found, however, that these phenomena which emerge in early childhood form part of an ordered course of development, that they pass through a regular process of increase, reaching a climax towards the end of the fifth year, after which there follows a lull. During this lull progress is at a standstill and much is unlearnt and there is much recession. After the end of this period of latency, as it is called, sexual life advances once more with puberty; we might say that it has a second efflorescence. And here we come upon the fact that the onset of sexual life is *diphasic*, that it occurs in two waves—something that is unknown except in man and evidently has an important bearing on hominization. It is not a matter of indifference that the events of this early period, except for a few residues, fall a victim to *infantile amnesia*. Our views on the aetiology of the neuroses and our technique of analytic therapy are derived from these conceptions; and our tracing of the developmental processes in this early period has also provided evidence for yet other conclusions.

The first organ to emerge as an erotogenic zone and to make libidinal demands on the mind is, from the time of birth onwards, the mouth. To begin with, all psychical activity is concentrated on providing satisfaction for the needs of that zone. Primarily, of course, this satisfaction serves the purpose of self-preservation by means of nourishment; but physiology should not be confused with psychology. The baby's obstinate persistence in sucking gives evidence at an early stage of a need for satisfaction which, though it originates from and is instigated by the taking of nourishment,

Hogarth Press. (Chapter III: The Development of the Sexual Function; 2 footnotes omitted.)
(Original work published 1938.)

nevertheless strives to obtain pleasure independently of nourishment and for that reason may and should be termed *sexual*.

During this oral phase sadistic impulses already occur sporadically along with the appearance of the teeth. Their extent is far greater in the second phase, which we describe as the sadistic-anal one, because satisfaction is then sought in aggression and in the excretory function. Our justification for including aggressive urges under the libido is based on the view that sadism is an instinctual fusion of purely libidinal and purely destructive urges, a fusion which thenceforward persists uninterruptedly.*

The third phase is that known as the phallic one, which is, as it were, a forerunner of the final form taken by sexual life and already much resembles it. It is to be noted that it is not the genitals of both sexes that play a part at this stage, but only the male ones (the phallus). The female genitals long remain unknown: in children's attempts to understand the sexual processes they pay homage to the venerable cloacal theory—a theory which has a genetic justification.†

With the phallic phase and in the course of it the sexuality of early childhood reaches its height and approaches its dissolution. Thereafter boys and girls have different histories. Both have begun to put their intellectual activity at the service of sexual researchers; both start off from the premiss of the universal presence of the penis. But now the paths of the sexes diverge. The boy enters the Oedipus phase; he begins to manipulate his penis and simultaneously has phantasies of carrying out some sort of activity with it in relation to his mother, till, owing to the combined effect of a threat of castration and the sight of the absence of a penis in females, he experiences the greatest trauma of his life and this introduces the period of latency with all its consequences. The girl, after vainly attempting to do the same as the boy, comes to recognize her lack of a penis or rather the inferiority of her clitoris, with permanent effects on the development of her character; as a result of this first disappointment in rivalry, she often begins by turning away altogether from sexual life.

It would be a mistake to suppose that these three phases succeed one another in a clear-cut fashion. One may appear in addition to another; they may overlap one another, may be present alongside of one another. In the early phases the different component instincts set about their pursuit of pleasure independently of one another; in the phallic phase there are the beginnings of an organization which subordinates the other urges to the primacy of the genitals and signifies the start of a co-ordination of the general urge towards pleasure into the sexual function. The complete organization is only achieved at puberty, in a fourth, genital phase. A state of things is then established in which (1) some earlier libidinal cathexes are retained, (2) others are taken into the sexual function as preparatory, auxiliary acts, the satisfaction of which produces what is known as fore-pleasure, and (3) other urges are excluded from the organization, and are either suppressed altogether (repressed) or are employed in the ego in another way, forming character-traits or undergoing sublimation with a displacement of their aims.

This process is not always performed faultlessly. Inhibitions in its development manifest themselves as the many sorts of disturbance in sexual life. When this is so,

---

*The question arises whether the satisfaction of purely destructive instinctual impulses can be felt as pleasure, whether pure destructiveness without any libidinal admixture occurs. Satisfaction of the death instinct remaining in the ego seems not to produce feelings of pleasure, though masochism represents a fusion which is entirely analogous to sadism.

†The occurrence of early vaginal excitations is often asserted. But it is most probable that what is in question are excitations in the clitoris—that is, in an organ analogous to the penis. This does not invalidate our right to describe the phase as phallic.

we find fixations of the libido to conditions in earlier phases, whose urge, which is independent of the normal sexual aim, is described as *perversion*. One such developmental inhibition, for instance, is homosexuality when it is manifest. Analysis shows that in every case a homosexual object-tie was present and in most cases persisted in a *latent* condition. The situation is complicated by the fact that as a rule the processes necessary for bringing about a normal outcome are not completely present or absent, but *partially* present, so that the final result remains dependent on these *quantitative* relations. In these circumstances the genital organization is, it is true, attained, but it lacks those portions of the libido which have not advanced with the rest and have remained fixated to pregenital objects and aims. This weakening shows itself in a tendency, if there is an absence of genital satisfaction or if there are difficulties in the real external world, for the libido to hark back to its earlier pregenital cathexes (*regression*).

During the study of the sexual functions we have been able to gain a first, preliminary conviction, or rather a suspicion, of two discoveries which will later be found to be important over the whole of our field. Firstly, the normal and abnormal manifestations observed by us (that is, the phenomenology of the subject) need to be described from the point of view of their dynamics and economics (in our case, from the point of view of the quantitative distribution of the libido). And secondly, the aetiology of the disorders which we study is to be looked for in the individual's developmental history—that is to say, in his early life.

MECHANISM AND DETERMINISM IN FREUD'S SYSTEM

During Freud's university training he was influenced by the mechanistic school of thought in German physiology. At first glance, the notion of mechanism, which pervades so much of academic psychology, would seem to be irrelevant to Freud's work on the hidden motives of behavior. The structuralists, and then the behaviorists, considered humans to be machine-like in their processes and functions. First the human mind and then human behavior were reduced to their most elemental components, analyzed, and studied in positivist and materialist terms. Thus, it is surprising to many readers of Freud to learn that he too was influenced by the mechanistic tradition. No less than experimental psychologists, Freud believed that all mental events, even mistakes and dreams, were determined. No bit of behavior or thought can occur by chance or by free will. There is always a cause for each act; there is always a conscious or unconscious motive.

But there is more to this general mechanistic spirit than determinism. In Chapter 3 we discussed the solemn pledge taken by Brücke, Ludwig, du Bois-Reymond, and Helmholtz: "No other forces than the common physical–chemical ones are active within the organism." Freud, early in his career, subscribed to this physicalism, the notion that all phenomena of life could be reduced to the principles of physics.

In 1895 Freud worked on his "Project for a Scientific Psychology," in which he attempted to show that psychology must have a physical basis and that purely mental phenomena exhibit many of the same patterns and characteristics as the neurophysiological processes on which they are based. Psychology, in Freud's view, must be a natural science whose aim is "to represent psychical processes as quantitatively determined states of specifiable material particles" (Freud, 1895, p. 359). His project was never completed, but we can discern throughout his later writings the physicalist principles with which he grappled, along with terminology from mechanics, electricity, and hydraulics. Although he modified his original intention to model his psychology after physics, finding that his subject matter was not amenable to physical and chemical techniques, he remained true to the abiding positivist philosophy (particularly determinism) that nurtured academic psychology.

Although Freud was influenced by this model, he was not constrained by it. When and where he saw that it would not fit, he modified or discarded it. In the end he demonstrated how restrictive the mechanistic conception of human beings was. Freud used this framework where appropriate, but he was also a critic of mechanism when the doctrine was not appropriate.

Freud's "Project for a Scientific Psychology" provides another example of data lost to history for a period of time. The work was not found until 1950, 55 years after he wrote it and 11 years after he died. Until then, no one knew that Freud had even considered such an idea, much less worked on it (Sulloway, 1979).

CONFLICTS BETWEEN PSYCHOANALYSIS AND PSYCHOLOGY

Psychoanalysis developed outside the mainstream of academic psychology. The fact that both the system and its originator were outsiders complicated and delayed their acceptance. Indeed, this was even a barrier to serious consideration of psychoanalysis for a time.

A number of factors operated to keep psychoanalysis and academic psychology apart (Jahoda, 1963; Shakow, 1969). The first involves the absence of a sense of continuity in Freud's work relative to advances in psychology. There were no parallels, no overlapping efforts, because Freud's work had no precedent in the development of psychology. Psychologists could not find a meaningful way of connecting Freud's efforts with their own or with those of their predecessors.

Wundt, for example, was never moved to admit the unconscious into psychology because it did not relate to his efforts to investigate the nature of consciousness. In talking about Wundt's work, Freud said, "We cannot help thinking that the old psychology has been killed by my . . . doctrine; but the old psychology is quite unaware of the fact, and goes on teaching as usual" (Wittels, 1924, p. 130).

A second point of difference is that Freud and most of his disciples were trained in medicine, not in psychology; they were M.D.s, not Ph.D.s. Not only did this mean that they spoke and thought in different terms, but it also reinforced the notion of psychoanalysts as outsiders. A major source of resistance to any new discovery or theory in science is a difference in professional specialization between the innovator and the discipline to which he or she offers the new work (Barber, 1961).

This difference in training highlights a third reason for opposition. Psychology, in its early attempts to become or remain a pure science, was method centered. Psychoanalysis was problem centered. The application of psychoanalysis—attempting to help neurotic persons—was at variance with psychology's aim of finding laws of human behavior through the methods of natural science.

These different goals and subject matter necessitated different methods. Freud's concern was more global than that of psychology, the total human personality as opposed to specific functions such as perception and learning. Psychology, trying to be a natural science, had adopted the experimental method in which each variable, each minute aspect of behavior, was isolated for study. Psychoanalysis dealt with the total human being—not for a short period in the laboratory, but over a long period of time—and used data covering all aspects of the person's past and present experiences.

Academic psychologists, steeped in the rigor of science, seeking precision and operational definitions of concepts, distrusted and disliked the Freudian concepts that could not be quantified or related precisely to concrete empirical variables. Terms such as "ego," "id," and "repression" were anathema to psychologists who sought to work only with specific stimulus–response terms.

There were, then, several reasons for the antipathy shown by psychologists toward psychoanalysis. In spite of these differences, however, the barriers between the two disciplines, at first so rigid and absolute, have been breached here and there.

CRITICISMS OF PSYCHOANALYSIS

The amount of criticism directed against Freud and his theories, much of which has come from outside of psychology, is enormous, but we shall restrict our discussion to criticisms from psychologists. Some of these points were noted in the preceding section.

Particularly vulnerable to attack by experimental psychologists are Freud's methods of collecting data. He drew his insights and conclusions from his patients' responses while they were undergoing analysis. Consider some of the deficiencies of such an approach in the light of the experimental method of systematically collecting objective data under controlled conditions of observation.

First, the conditions under which Freud collected his data are unsystematic and uncontrolled. He did not make a verbatim transcript of each patient's words but worked from notes made several hours after seeing a patient. Some of the original data (the patient's words) must surely have been lost in the interim as a result of the vagaries of recall and the well-documented possibility of distortion and omission. The data consisted only of what Freud remembered.

Also, it is possible that in the course of recollection Freud reinterpreted the data. His reconstruction of the data may not accurately reflect the raw data. In drawing his inferences, he may have been guided by his desire to find material that supported his hypotheses. In other words, he may have remembered and recorded only what he wanted to hear. Of course, we must also consider the possibility that Freud's notes were accurate, but it is impossible to know this with any degree of certainty because the original data have not survived.

There is a more basic criticism of the raw data. Even if a complete, verbatim record had been kept, it would not always have been possible to determine the validity of what the patients reported. Freud made few attempts to verify his patients' stories. Critics argue that he should have tried to check the accuracy of the patients' reports, for example, by questioning relatives and friends about the events described. Thus, the first step in Freud's theory building—data collection—may be characterized as incomplete, imperfect, and inaccurate.

As for the next step—drawing inferences and generalizations from the data—no one knows exactly how this was done because Freud never explained the process. This is, of course, another major point of criticism. In addition, because Freud's data were not amenable to quantification, it is impossible to determine the reliability or statistical significance of his findings.

These are serious charges from the standpoint of scientific methodology and theory building. The reader of Freud must, in a sense, accept on faith the validity of his operations and conclusions. Freud wrote that his work was "based on an incalculable number of observations and experiences, and only someone who has repeated those observations on himself and on others is in a position to arrive at a judgement of his own upon it" (Freud, 1938/1940, p. 144). But, of course, Freud's observations cannot be repeated because it is not known exactly what he did in collecting data and translating observations into generalizations and hypotheses. The language of science is precise and orderly, leaving no room for ambiguities, distortions, and vagaries. It seems that Freud did not speak that language and it is difficult to translate from one to the other.

Another point of criticism concerns the difficulty of deriving empirically testable propositions from many of Freud's hypotheses. How, for instance, would we test the notion of a death wish? It may be used to explain behavior such as suicide, after the fact, but how can we use it empirically to predict behavior?

Adherents of operationism argue that Freud's concepts are not operationally defined. In his discussion of operationism, Bridgman addressed the issue of pseudo-problems, questions that defy answer by any known experimental test (see Chapter 11). Because many of Freud's concepts cannot be experimentally tested, some critics suggest that they are pseudo-problems, meaningless, indeed useless, for science. This objection has been questioned, however, and some of Freud's ideas have been submitted to scientific test, as we shall see in the following section.

In addition to points of methodology, Freud's theories and assumptions about human behavior have been criticized. Even supporters of Freud agree that he often contradicted himself and that his definitions of some key concepts are ambiguous. There is confusion in the definitions of such concepts as id, ego, and superego, making it difficult to know precisely what they are. In his later writings Freud himself noted the difficulties and ambiguities in defining these and other ideas.

Many psychologists have challenged what they see as Freud's degrading views on women. Targets of criticism include Freud's ideas that women have poorly developed superegos and feel inferior about their bodies because they lack penises. The analyst Karen Horney left Freud's circle because of these views on feminine psychology (see Chapter 14).

In Chapters 14 and 15 we examine the work of other theorists who broke with Freud and offered additional criticisms, which they attempted to deal with as they modified Freud's position. They argued that Freud placed too much emphasis on biological forces, particularly sex, as the primary shapers of personality. They believed that personality was influenced more by social forces. Others challenged Freud's extreme determinism, which denies free will, and his exclusive emphasis on past behavior to the exclusion of hopes, goals, and dreams as influences on personality. Some attacked Freud for developing a theory of human personality based only on observations of neurotics, ignoring the characteristics of emotionally healthy persons. All of these points were used to construct competing views of personality, which quickly led to divisiveness in the psychoanalytic camp and to the formation of derivative schools of Freudian psychoanalysis.

THE SCIENTIFIC CREDIBILITY OF PSYCHOANALYSIS

We have discussed how psychoanalysis is weak from the standpoint of scientific methodology and theory building and noted that many of Freud's concepts cannot be submitted to experimental test. Some of his ideas have been tested scientifically, however, provided that the term "science" is broadened to include techniques other than the experimental method. In an analysis of some 2000 studies from psychiatry, psychology, anthropology, and other disciplines, Fisher and Greenberg (1977) evaluated the scientific credibility of some of Freud's formulations. Case histories, the major research method in the psychoanalytic literature, were not used, for some of the reasons listed in the previous section. Fisher and Greenberg accepted only those data that had been "secured through procedures that are repeatable and involve techniques that make it possible to check on the objectivity of the reporting observer" (1977, p. 15).

Although some large-scale Freudian concepts continue to resist attempts at scientific validation—there are no conclusions in the Fisher–Greenberg book about the id, ego, superego, death wish, libido, or anxiety—other concepts were amenable to testing. Those that appear to be supported by the published literature include aspects of the oral and anal personality types; causative factors of homosexuality; the notion that dreams serve as an outlet for tension; and parts of the Oedipus complex in boys (rivalry with the father, sexual fantasy about the mother, and castration anxiety).

Freudian concepts not supported by research include the notion that dreams represent a disguised satisfaction of repressed wishes and desires; aspects of the Oedipus complex in boys (the idea that the child resolves the complex, identifies with the father, and accepts the father's superego standards out of fear of the father); and certain theories about women (that women have an inferior concept of their bodies, have a less severe set of superego standards than men, and find it more difficult to achieve an identity).

Fisher and Greenberg concluded that those of Freud's concepts that were amenable to validation fared well. More important is the demonstration that at least some of Freud's ideas can be reduced to propositions that are scientifically testable. It must be remembered, however, that major portions of Freudian psychoanalysis defy testing by the methods of science.

CONTRIBUTIONS OF PSYCHOANALYSIS

We have described the important and damaging criticisms of psychoanalysis offered primarily by experimentally oriented psychologists. We must ask why, then, psychoanalysis has not only survived but also prospered. All theories of behavior can be criticized for lacking in scientific validity to some degree. Psychologists in search of a theory must choose on the basis of criteria other than formal scientific rigidity and precision. Those who select psychoanalysis do not do so in the absence of any evidence, however. Psychoanalysis does offer evidence, but it is not of the variety traditionally accepted by science.

That psychoanalytic evidence is not strictly scientific does not necessarily mean that the theory is incorrect or misleading. Belief in psychoanalysis, however, must be based on the intuitive grounds of an appearance of plausibility in Freud's system.

> Any one who accepts or rejects the psychoanalytic theories does so by means of the same kind of reasoning that gives him the thousand and one judgments he is forced to make in everyday life on the basis of insufficient or inadequate evidence—the kind of judgments, in fact, that he is forced to live by, but which have no standing in science. Such estimates, growing out of a multitude of impressions and interpretations, guesses and insights, often result in unshakable convictions, convictions which may be right or wrong but which, from the standpoint of science, cannot be recognized as either proved or disproved. (Heidbreder, 1933, pp. 403–404)

Freud's influence on psychiatry and clinical psychology has been profound, and his theories are of considerable significance in American academic psychology. Certain Freudian concepts have gained wide acceptance and have been assimilated into the mainstream of contemporary psychology. These include the role of unconscious motivation, the importance of childhood experiences in shaping adult behavior, and the operation of the defense mechanisms. Interest in these areas has generated much research. In recent years, academic psychologists have shown increasing interest in the unconscious, and research is providing support for the existence of unconscious influences on behavior. This interest in the unconscious is not of the Freudian variety, but the recognition of the unconscious within psychology is nonetheless a legacy of Freud's work.

Freud's impact on the general culture has, of course, been enormous. This was felt immediately after his visit to Clark University. Newspapers in the United States carried many articles about Freud, and by 1920 more than 200 books had been published in the United States on Freudian analysis. Articles on psychoanalysis were written not only for medical journals, but also for such popular magazines as *Ladies' Home Journal, The Nation*, and *The New Republic*. In 1935, MGM, a major motion picture studio, offered Freud $100,000 to collaborate on a movie above love. He refused (Green & Rieber, 1980). Thus, Freud's acceptance by the lay public came much earlier and with greater force than his acceptance by academic psychology.

The twentieth century has seen a gradual loosening of sexual restraint in behavior as well as in art, literature, and entertainment. The culture seems to have adopted the view that it is harmful to inhibit or repress sexual satisfaction. It is ironic that Freud's message with regard to sex has been subject to such misinterpretation. He was not arguing for a weakening of sexual codes of conduct or for greater sexual freedom. His consistent position was that inhibition of sex was necessary for the survival of civilization. Despite his intention, the greater sexual freedom of the twentieth century is partly a result of Freud's work. His emphasis on sex helped to popularize his views. Even in scientific writing, sex has a sensational appeal.

Despite criticism of his lack of scientific rigor and methodology, Freud's psychoanalysis has become an important force in modern psychology. Boring, in the 1929 edition of his *History of Experimental Psychology*, expressed regret that psychology had no truly great exponent of the stature of a Darwin or a Helmholtz. Only 21 years later, in the second edition of his text, Boring revised his opinion. Reflecting the development of psychology during those two decades, Boring spoke of Freud with admiration. "Now he is seen as the greatest originator of all, the agent of the *Zeitgeist* who accomplished the invasion of psychology by the principle of the unconscious process" (Boring, 1950, p. 743).

Despite Freud's recognized genius and the acceptance, or at least consideration, of parts of his system, psychoanalysis retains a separate identity today, and has not been absorbed as a whole by the mainstream of psychological thought. However, no matter what one's evaluation of psychoanalysis and whatever the eventual status of the system, there is no denying that Freud possessed the attributes of greatness.

> He was a pioneer in a field of thought, in a new technique for the understanding of human nature. He was also an originator, even though he picked his conceptions out of the stream of the culture—an originator who remained true to his fundamental intent for fifty years of hard work, while he altered and brought to maturity the system of ideas that was his contribution to knowledge. . . . It is not likely that the history of psychology can be written in the next three centuries without mention of Freud's name and still claim to be a general history of psychology. And there you have the best criterion of greatness: posthumous fame. (Boring, 1950, pp. 706–707)

SUGGESTED READINGS

Psychopathology

Bromberg, W. (1975). *From shaman to psychotherapist: A history of the treatment of mental illness* (4th ed.). Chicago: Henry Regnery.

Cardno, J. A. (1968). The aetiology of insanity: Some early American views. *Journal of the History of the Behavioral Sciences, 4,* 99–108.

Carlson, E. T., & Simpson, M. M. (1964). The definition of mental illness: Benjamin Rush (1745–1813). *American Journal of Psychiatry, 121,* 209–214.

Deutsch, A. (1949). *The mentally ill in America: A history of their care and treatment from colonial times* (2nd ed.). New York: Columbia University Press.

Diethelm, O. (1970). The medical teaching of demonology in the 17th and 18th centuries. *Journal of the History of the Behavioral Sciences, 6,* 3–15.

Drinka, G. F. (1984). *The birth of neurosis: Myth, malady, and the Victorians.* New York: Simon and Schuster.

Shor, R. E., & Orne, M. T. (Eds.). (1965). *The nature of hypnosis: Selected basic writings.* New York: Holt, Rinehart & Winston.

Winters, B. (1950). Franz Anton Mesmer: An inquiry into the antecedents of hypnotism. *Journal of General Psychology, 43,* 63–75.

Freud

Brome, V. (1968). *Freud and his early circle.* New York: William Morrow.

Decker, H. S. (1978). *Freud in Germany: Revolution and reaction in science, 1893–1907.* New York: International Universities Press.

Fancher, R. E. (1971). The neurological origin of Freud's dream theory. *Journal of the History of the Behavioral Sciences, 7,* 59–74.

Freud, E., Freud, L., & Grubrich-Simitis, I. (Eds.). (1985). *Sigmund Freud: His life in pictures and words.* New York: W. W. Norton.

Hale, N. (1971). *Freud and the Americans: The beginnings of psychoanalysis in the United States, 1876–1917.* New York: Oxford University Press.

Jahoda, M. (1977). *Freud and the dilemmas of psychology.* New York: Basic Books.

McCarthy, T. (1981). Freud and the problem of sexuality. *Journal of the History of the Behavioral Sciences, 17,* 332–339.

Roazen, P. (1974). *Freud and his followers.* New York: Alfred A. Knopf.

Romm, S. (1984). *The unwelcome intruder: Freud's struggle with cancer.* New York: Praeger.

Schur, M. (1972). *Freud: Living and dying.* New York: International Universities Press.

Sulloway, F. J. (1979). *Freud: Biologist of the mind.* New York: Basic Books.

Psychoanalysis

Bruner, J. S. (1956). Freud and the image of man. *American Psychologist, 11,* 463–466.

Cocks, G. (1986). *Psychotherapy in the Third Reich.* New York: Oxford University Press.

Ellenberger, H. F. (1970). *The discovery of the unconscious: The history and evolution of dynamic psychiatry.* New York: Basic Books.

Ellenberger, H. F. (1972). The story of "Anna O": A critical review with new data. *Journal of the History of the Behavioral Sciences, 8,* 267–279.

Evans, R., & Koelsch, W. (1985). Psychoanalysis arrives in America: The 1909 psychology conference at Clark University. *American Psychologist, 40,* 942–948.

Fisher, S., & Greenberg, R. P. (1977). *The scientific credibility of Freud's theories and therapy.* New York: Basic Books.

Hale, N. (1978). From Berggasse XIX to Central Park West: The Americanization of psychoanalysis, 1919–1940. *Journal of the History of the Behavioral Sciences, 14,* 299–315.

Heidbreder, E. (1940). Freud and psychology. *Psychological Review, 47,* 185–195.

Hilgard, E. R. (1957). Freud and experimental psychology. *Behavioral Science, 2,* 74–79.

Jahoda, M. (1963). Some notes on the influence of psychoanalytic ideas on American psychology. *Human Relations, 16,* 111–129.

McGrath, W. J. (1986). *Freud's discovery of psychoanalysis: The politics of hysteria.* Ithaca, NY: Cornell University Press.

Powell, R. C. (1979). The "subliminal" versus the "subconscious" in the American acceptance of psychoanalysis, 1906–1910. *Journal of the History of the Behavioral Sciences, 15,* 155–165.

Shakow, D., & Rapaport, D. (1964). *The influence of Freud on American psychology.* New York: International Universities Press.

Skinner, B. F. (1954). Critique of psychoanalytic concepts and theories. *Scientific Monthly, 79,* 300–305.

14

Psychoanalysis: After the Founding

THE DISSENTERS AND THE DESCENDANTS

As was the case with Wundt and experimental psychology, Freud did not long enjoy a monopoly on his new psychoanalysis. Barely twenty years after he founded the move- ment, it splintered into competing factions led by analysts who disagreed with Freud on one or more basic issues. During Freud's lifetime, they developed their own approaches that, while not completely disavowing Freud's psychoanalytic orientation, tried to cor- rect what they saw as serious deficiencies and inadequacies in his formulations.

Freud did not react well to these dissenters. The analysts who espoused the new positions "left the movement not at all with the tacit agreement to differ but rather in an aura of heavy disapproval and the sort of invective that was once heaped upon the heads of heretics" (Brown, 1963, p. 37). No matter how close they might have been to Freud, both personally and professionally, when they abandoned his teachings he cast them out and never spoke to them again.

We shall discuss three of the most prominent dissenters: Carl Jung, Alfred Adler, and Karen Horney. All were, at one time, orthodox Freudians before they left the master's circle to promote their own views. We will also deal with the descendants of the Freudian position, those who developed their approaches after Freud's death. These were not dissenters from Freud, having never been orthodox Freudians. Rather, they derived their ideas from those of Freud, either elaborating on or opposing his work.

Before proceeding to the dissenters and the descendants, however, we should note that not all who came after Freud in the psychoanalytic tradition were ready and willing to change, abandon, or overthrow his system. There is a large group of neo-Freudian analysts who adhere to the central tenets and premises of Freudian thought but who have, over the years, modified and extended certain aspects of his system.

The major change these Freudian loyalists have introduced into psychoanalysis is an expanded emphasis on the ego (Hartmann, 1964). Rather than being the servant of the id, the ego now has an amplified role. The ego is seen as being more independent of the id, possessing its own energy not derived from the id and having its own functions separate from the id. Another change proposed by the neo-Freudians is the deemphasis

Anna Freud (1895–1982),
daughter of Sigmund
Freud, applied psycho-
analytic therapy to
children.

of biological forces as influences on personality in favor of social and psychological forces. Also, there has been a greater interest in the analysis of children, as reflected in the studies by Anna Freud.[1]

These neo-Freudian loyalists still identify themselves as Freudians, a label that cannot be applied to the dissenters and the descendants.

[1]Anna Freud (1895–1982), the youngest of the six children of Sigmund and Martha Freud, became a teacher and a lay analyst. She relinquished her personal life to become her father's alter ego and to pursue her own work. She developed an approach to psychoanalytic therapy with children that took into account the child's relative immaturity and level of verbal skills. (Freud had analyzed children only if they were able to describe their sexual fantasies.) Her innovations included the use of play materials and the observation of the child in the home environment. Anna Freud's work was reported in annual volumes of *The Psychoanalytic Study of the Child*, published since 1945. She also wrote about the expanded role of the ego, independent of the id (A. Freud, 1936), the revision of orthodox psychoanalysis noted above. She established a child therapy center in England, the Hampstead Clinic, which has trained many American child psychologists (Fine, 1985).

CARL JUNG (1875–1961)

Jung was once regarded by Freud as heir apparent to the psychoanalytic movement. Freud had referred to him as "my successor and crown prince" (McGuire, 1974, p. 218). When his friendship with Freud disintegrated in 1914, Jung began what he called *analytical psychology.*

The Life of Jung

Jung was raised in a small village in northern Switzerland near the famous Rhine Falls. By his own account, his childhood was lonely, isolated, and unhappy (Jung, 1961). His father was a clergyman who had apparently lost his faith and was often moody and irritable. His mother suffered from emotional disorders and her behavior was erratic, changing in an instant from that of a happy housewife to that of a witch-like demon who mumbled incoherently.

The marriage was an unhappy one. Jung learned at an early age not to trust or confide in his parents and, by extension, in the external world. As a result, he turned inward to the world of his dreams, visions, and fantasies—the world of his unconscious. Dreams and the unconscious, not the conscious world of reason, became his guides in childhood and for the rest of his life.

At crucial times in his life Jung resolved problems and made decisions on the basis of what his unconscious told him through his dreams. When he was ready to begin his university studies, the solution to the problem of what to major in was revealed to him in a dream in which he found himself unearthing bones of prehistoric animals. He interpreted this to mean that he should study nature and science. That dream of digging beneath the surface, plus a dream he had had at the age of three in which he was in an underground cavern, determined the direction of his future study of personality: the unconscious forces that lie beneath the mind's surface.

In 1900 Jung graduated with a medical degree from the University of Basel. He became attracted to psychiatry and his first professional appointment was at the psychiatric clinic at the University of Zurich, which was directed by Eugen Bleuler, a psychiatrist noted for his work on schizophrenia. In 1905 Jung was appointed lecturer in psychiatry at the university, but after several years he resigned to devote his efforts to research, writing, and private practice. He occasionally treated patients aboard his sailboat on Lake Zurich and was also proficient at yodeling.

Jung became interested in Freud's work in 1900 after reading *The Interpretation of Dreams*, which he described as a masterpiece. By 1906 the two men had begun to correspond, and a year later Jung went to Vienna to meet Freud. At their initial meeting they talked with great animation for 13 hours, an exciting beginning for their close but short-lived friendship. In 1909 Jung accompanied Freud to the United States for the Clark University commemorative ceremonies, at which they both delivered lectures.

It is important to note that unlike most of Freud's disciples, Jung had already established his professional reputation at the time he began his association with Freud. He was the best known of the early converts to psychoanalysis. As a result, he was perhaps less malleable, less suggestible, than younger persons who became Freud's early followers, many of whom were still students, unsure of their professional identities.

An early Freudian, Carl Jung (1875–1961) came to disagree with Freud over the issues of the unconscious mind and the importance of sex, and developed his analytical psychology.

Although he did become a disciple of Freud's, Jung was never—even at the beginning of the relationship—an uncritical one, although he did suppress his criticisms early in their affiliation. Later, while writing *The Psychology of the Unconscious* (1912), he was troubled because he realized that this public statement of his position, which was at variance with Freud's, would damage their relationship. For months he was unable to proceed with the book, so disturbed was he at Freud's possible reaction. Of course, he did publish, and the inevitable occurred.

In 1911, at Freud's insistence, and in spite of opposition from its Viennese members, Jung became the first president of the International Psychoanalytic Association. Freud believed that anti-Semitism might impede the psychoanalytic movement if a Jew headed the group. The Viennese members, almost all of whom were Jewish, distrusted and resented Jung, who was clearly Freud's favorite. They not only had seniority in the movement, but also believed Jung himself to be anti-Semitic.

Shortly after Jung was elected, his friendship with Freud showed signs of strain. Jung had begun to deemphasize the role of sex in his system and expressed a different concept of the libido in his 1912 book and in lectures at Fordham University. Friction grew, and in 1912 the two men agreed to terminate their personal correspondence. Relations were severed in 1914 when Jung resigned his presidency and withdrew from the association.

Beginning in 1913, when Jung was 38, he underwent a period of intense inner turmoil lasting three years, just as Freud had suffered at the same time of life. Believing that he was going insane, Jung was unable to carry on any intellectual work or even read a scientific book. (It is interesting, however, that he continued to treat his patients.) Jung resolved his emotional suffering in essentially the same way Freud had, by confronting his unconscious. Although he did not analyze his dreams systematically, as Freud had, he nonetheless listened to and followed the impulses of his unconscious as they were revealed in his dreams and fantasies. As with Freud, this emotional crisis of Jung's was a time of immense creativity, and it led to the formulation of his unusual approach to personality.

In line with his interest in the relevance of myths for the individual, Jung made a number of field expeditions to Africa and the southwestern United States in the 1920s to study the mental processes of preliterate peoples. In 1932 he was appointed professor at the Federal Polytechnical University in Zurich, a position he occupied until poor health forced him to resign in 1942. In 1944 a chair of medical psychology was founded for him at the University of Basel, but again illness prevented his keeping the position for more than a year. He remained active in research and writing for most of his 86 years, publishing an astonishing array of books. His many awards include honorary degrees from Harvard and Oxford universities.

Jung's System: Analytical Psychology

A major point of difference between the views of Jung and Freud concerns the nature of libido. Whereas Freud defined libido in predominantly sexual terms, Jung regarded it as a generalized life energy, of which sex was only one part. For Jung, this libidinal life energy expressed itself in growth and reproduction, as well as in other kinds of activity, depending on what was most important for an individual at a given time.

Jung's refusal to regard the basic life energy as exclusively sexual left him free to give different interpretations to behavior that Freud could define only in sexual terms. For instance, during the first three to five years of life (which Jung called the *presexual* phase), the Jungian view is that libidinal energy serves the functions of nutrition and growth, with none of the sexual overtones of Freud's conception of these early years. Jung rejected the Freudian Oedipus complex and explained the child's attachment to its mother in terms of a dependency need, with satisfactions and rivalries associated with the mother's food-providing function.[2] As the child matures and develops sexual functioning, Jung maintained, the nutritive functions become overlaid with sexual feelings. To Jung, libidinal energy took a heterosexual form only after puberty. Jung did not altogether deny the existence of sexual factors, but he reduced the role of sex to one of several drives that compose libido.

The second basic difference between Jung and Freud is in the direction of the forces that influence the human personality. Whereas Freud viewed people as victims of childhood events, Jung believed that we are shaped by our future goals, hopes, and aspirations as well as by our past. Our behavior is not fully determined by childhood experiences but is subject to change later in life.

A third difference between Jung and Freud is that Jung placed an even stronger emphasis on the unconscious. He tried to probe more deeply into the unconscious and added a new dimension to it, the inherited experiences of humans as a species and those of their animal ancestors (the "collective unconscious").

Jung used the term *psyche* to refer to the mind, which he said consisted of three levels: the conscious, the personal unconscious, and the collective unconscious. At the center of consciousness is the *ego*, which is generally akin to our conception of ourselves. *Consciousness* includes perceptions and memories and is the avenue of contact with reality that enables us to adapt to our environment.

Jung believed that too much attention had been paid to the conscious. He considered it to be second in importance to the *unconscious*. The conscious aspect of the psyche is like the visible portion of an island. A larger, unknown part exists beneath the small part that can be seen above the waterline, and Jung focused on this mysterious, hidden base.

He postulated two levels of the unconscious. Just beneath consciousness is the *personal unconscious*, which belongs to the individual. It consists of all the memories, impulses, wishes, faint perceptions, and numerous other experiences in an individual's life that have been suppressed or forgotten. Incidents from the personal unconscious can easily be recalled to conscious awareness, however, indicating that this level of unconsciousness is not very deep.

The experiences in the personal unconscious are grouped into *complexes*. These are patterns of emotions, memories, and wishes with common themes that are characterized by a preoccupation with some idea, such as power or inferiority. A person may be preoccupied with power, for example, and this will influence his or her behavior. A complex is essentially a smaller personality that forms within the total personality.

Below the personal unconscious is the third and deepest level of the psyche, the *collective unconscious*, which contains, unknown to the individual, the cumulative experiences of all previous generations, including our animal ancestors. The collective unconscious consists of universal evolutionary experiences and forms the basis of personality. It directs all present behavior and is therefore the most powerful force in the personality. It bears repeating that these evolutionary experiences are unconscious. We do not remember them or have images of them, as we do of the experiences that are

---

[2] Jung described his own mother as fat and unattractive, which may explain his rejection of Freud's notion that every boy has a sexual longing for his mother. Such a view did not reflect Jung's own childhood experiences.

found in the personal unconscious. Indeed, we are not at all aware of them. Jung believed that the universality of the collective unconscious could be accounted for by evolutionary theory, through the similarity of brain structure evident in all human races.

Viewed in terms of our island analogy, a number of small islands rising above the surface of the water represent the individual conscious awarenesses of a number of people. Land areas just beneath the water, which are exposed by the action of the tides, represent each individual's personal unconscious. The ocean floor, on which all the islands ultimately rest, is the collective unconscious.

Jung emphasized the powerful forces preserved in the collective unconscious because he believed that they contributed the most to psychic development. The inherited tendencies in the collective unconscious he termed *archetypes*, which are preexisting determinants of mental experience that dispose an individual to behave in a manner similar to that manifested by ancestors who confronted analogous situations.

Archetypes are experienced as emotions and other mental events and are typically associated with such significant human experiences as birth and death, with particular stages of life such as adolescence, and with reactions to extreme dangers. Jung's intensive investigation of the mythical and artistic products of various civilizations resulted in the discovery of symbols common to all, even in cultures so widely separated in time and place that there was no possibility of direct influence. In his patients' dreams Jung found what he considered to be definite traces of these same symbols.

Four of the many archetypes Jung described seemed to occur more often than others, to be laden with high levels of emotional significance, and to be traceable to ancient myths of diverse origins. These principal archetypes, which Jung viewed as separate personality systems, are the persona, the anima and animus, the shadow, and the self.

The *persona*, or outermost aspect of personality, conceals the true self. It is the mask we wear when we come into contact with others, and it presents us as we want to appear to society. Thus, the persona may not correspond to our true personality. The notion of persona appears to be similar to the sociological concept of role playing, in which persons act as they think others expect them to act.

The archetypes *anima* and *animus* reflect the notion that each sex exhibits both masculine and feminine tendencies. The anima refers to feminine characteristics in man; the animus denotes masculine characteristics in woman. As with the other archetypes, these arise from the primitive past of the species, in which men and women took on some of the behavioral and emotional tendencies of the other sex.

The *shadow* archetype (our darker self) is the inferior, animal-like part of the personality, our racial heritage from the lower forms of life. It contains all immoral, passionate, and objectionable desires and activities. Jung wrote that the shadow urges us to do those things that we ordinarily would not allow ourselves to do. Having performed such actions, we usually insist that something came over us. Jung claimed that the "something" is the primitive part of our nature. However, the shadow also has a positive side. It is the source of spontaneity, creativity, insight, and deep emotion, all necessary for full human development.

Jung considered the *self* to be the most important archetype in his system. Composed of all aspects of the unconscious, the self provides unity and stability to the entire structure of personality. As a representation of the whole person, the self attempts to achieve complete integration, and can be likened to a drive or urge toward self-realization or self-actualization. By *self-actualization*, Jung meant a harmony and fullness or completeness of every aspect of the personality, the fullest development of the self. He believed that this state could not occur until middle age. (Middle age was the time when Jung thought he had achieved such an integration of his self following the resolution of his neurotic crisis.) Jung suggested that the total unity and wholeness toward which we all strive was represented by the *mandala* or magic circle, a symbol that he found repeatedly in various cultures.

Jung is well known for his discussion of *introversion and extroversion*, which are defined in terms of the direction of libidinal energy. He regarded them as two *attitudes* or modes of reacting to specific situations and viewed them as part of consciousness. The extrovert directs the libido outside the self to external events, people, and situations. A person of this type is strongly influenced by forces in the environment and is sociable and self-confident in a wide range of situations. The libido of the introvert is directed inward. The introvert is more contemplative, introspective, and resistant to external influence, less confident in relations with other people and with the external world, and relatively unsociable and shy.

Jung believed that these opposing attitudes exist in every person to some degree but that one is usually more pronounced than the other. No one is a total extrovert or introvert. The dominant attitude at a given moment can be influenced by the situation. For example, a normally introverted person may become sociable and outgoing in a situation in which he or she is vitally interested.

According to Jung, personality differences are also manifested through the *functions*, which we use to orient ourselves to both the external objective world and the internal subjective world. Functions include thinking, feeling, sensing and intuiting. *Thinking* is a conceptual process that provides meaning and understanding; *feeling* is a subjective process of weighing and valuing. *Sensing* is the conscious perception of physical objects; *intuiting* involves perceiving in an unconscious manner.

Thinking and feeling are rational modes of responding because they involve reason and judgment. Sensing and intuiting are considered nonrational because they depend on the concrete and specific stimulus world and do not involve the use of reason. Within each pair only one mode can be dominant at a given time. This dominance of function can be combined with the dominance of extroversion or introversion to produce eight psychological types.

Jung developed the *word-association test* as a therapeutic and diagnostic tool to uncover personality complexes in his patients. He began his research on word association after a colleague who had been working in Germany brought back news of Wundt's association experiment (Von Franz, 1975). In Jung's word-association procedure, a list of words is read to a patient who responds to each word with the first word that comes to mind. Jung measured the time taken to respond to each word, as well as changes in breathing and in the electrical conductivity of the skin. The two physiological measures provided additional evidence of emotional reactions to specific words. If a particular word produced a long response time, irregularity in breathing, and a change in skin conductivity, Jung deduced the existence of an unconscious emotional problem connected with the stimulus word or with the reply. Jung also used the word-association test as a form of lie detector and twice identified persons who were guilty of theft.

Comment

Jung's work has had some influence on psychology and psychiatry but more on such fields as religion, history, art, and literature. Many historians, theologians, and writers have acknowledged him as a source of inspiration. For the most part, however, scientific psychology has ignored analytical psychology. Many of Jung's books were not translated into English until the 1960s, and his less than lucid writing style impedes understanding. His disdain for traditional scientific methods repels experimentally oriented psychologists, for whom Jung's writings, with their mysticism and religiosity, hold even less appeal than Freud's. The criticisms noted in Chapter 13 about Freud's supporting evidence are also applicable to Jung's work. He too relied on clinical observation and interpretation rather than on controlled laboratory investigation. Analytical psychology has received less searching criticism than Freudian psychoanalysis, probably because Freud's stature in the field has relegated Jung and others to second place in terms of professional attention.

Jung's views on psychological types, however, have stimulated considerable research. Of particular importance is the development of the Myers–Briggs Type Indicator, a personality test constructed in the 1920s by Katharine Briggs and Isabel Briggs Myers. It has since become the primary tool for conducting research on Jung's psychological types. Jung's work also inspired another popular personality test that measures the attitudes of introversion and extroversion. Called the Maudsley Personality Inventory, it was developed by Hans Eysenck, an English psychologist who was affiliated with the Maudsley Hospital in London.

Research using these tests has provided some degree of empirical support for Jung's formulations of the psychological types, particularly with regard to the attitudes of introversion and extroversion. Although not all of the research has been supportive, the fact that research has been conducted demonstrates that at least some of Jung's ideas are amenable to experimental test. As with Freud's work, however, the larger aspects of the theory—such as complexes, the collective unconscious, and the archetypes—have resisted attempts at scientific validation.

Jung has made other important contributions to psychology. The word-association test has become a standard projective technique and served to spur the development of the Rorschach Inkblot Test. The concept of self-actualization anticipated the work of Abraham Maslow (Chapter 15) and others who have since developed that theme. Jung's suggestion that middle age is a time of crucial personality change was embraced by Maslow and Erik Erikson and has been widely adopted by psychology. Despite these notable contributions, the bulk of Jung's work has not been accepted by psychology.

SOCIAL PSYCHOLOGICAL THEORIES IN PSYCHOANALYSIS: THE *ZEITGEIST* STRIKES AGAIN

Freud was influenced by the mechanistic and positivist outlook that pervaded nineteenth-century science. Toward the end of the nineteenth century new disciplines were offering ways of viewing human nature that went beyond the biological and physical frames of reference. Anthropology, sociology, and social psychology were finding evidence to support the proposition that human beings are the product of the social forces and institutions that make up their environment. This suggested that humans should be studied as social rather than strictly biological beings.

As anthropologists reported their studies of different cultures, it became clear that some of the neurotic symptoms and taboos hypothesized by Freud were not universal, as he had believed. For example, taboos against incest did not exist in all societies. Further, sociologists and social psychologists found that much human behavior stemmed from social conditioning instead of the attempt to satisfy biological needs.

Thus, the intellectual spirit of the times, the *Zeitgeist*, was calling for a revised conception of human nature, but Freud, to the dismay of some of his followers, continued to stress biological determinants of personality. Some younger theorists, less constrained by tradition, drifted away from orthodox Freudian psychoanalysis and began to reshape psychoanalytic theory along lines congruent with the orientation of the social sciences. Their view that personality is more a product of environment than of biology was compatible with American culture and thought and represented a more hopeful and optimistic image of human nature than Freud's position did. We shall discuss two of these socially oriented dissenters: Alfred Adler and Karen Horney.

ALFRED ADLER (1870–1937)

Adler is usually considered to be the first proponent of the social psychological brand of psychoanalysis because he broke with Freud in 1911. He developed a theory in which "social interest" plays a major role, and he is the only psychologist to have a string quartet named after him (Hall, 1970).

The Life of Adler

Adler was born to wealthy parents in a suburb of Vienna, Austria. His unhappy childhood was marked by sickness, jealousy of an older brother, and feelings of being small, unattractive, and rejected by his mother. Despite this unpromising beginning, he worked with great intensity as he grew older to become popular with his peers. As a result, he achieved a sense of acceptance and self-esteem with others that he had not found with his family (Orgler, 1965).

Initially, Adler was a poor student, so inept that a teacher told his father that the boy was unfit for any job except as a shoemaker's apprentice. But through persistence and dedication, Adler rose from the bottom to the top of his class. Both socially and academically, he worked hard to overcome his handicaps and inferiorities, thus becoming an example of his later theory of the necessity of compensating for one's weaknesses. The description of feelings of inferiority, which was to form a central part of his system, is a direct reflection of his own early experiences. Adler acknowledged this when he confessed, "Those who are familiar with my life work will clearly see the accord existing between the facts of my childhood and the views I expressed" (Bottome, 1939, p. 9).

At the age of four, while recovering from a near-fatal bout with pneumonia, Adler decided to become a physician. He received his medical degree from the University of Vienna in 1895. After specializing in ophthalmology and then practicing general medicine, he went into psychiatry. In 1902 he began meeting with Freud's weekly discussion group as one of its four charter members.

Alfred Adler (1870–1937), who broke with Freud in 1911, viewed human motivation as the drive for superiority and stressed the unity of personality and social factors in his individual psychology.

Over the next several years Adler developed a theory of personality that was different from Freud's in a number of ways. By 1911 he had become openly critical of Freud's emphasis on sexual factors. A year earlier Freud had named Adler president of the Viennese Analytic Society, apparently in an effort to reconcile the growing differences between them. The inevitable split was complete in 1911, when Adler resigned his presidency and officially broke with the Freudian position. The two men remained bitter toward each other. Adler later described Freud as a swindler and called psychoanalysis "filth" (Roazen, 1975, p. 210).

Adler served as a physician in the Austrian army during World War I and later organized child guidance clinics in the Vienna school system. During the 1920s his individual psychology attracted favorable attention throughout the world, and many followers came to study with him in Vienna. He lectured in several countries, and in 1926 came to the United States, where he received a warm welcome. He made several visits and in 1934 was appointed professor of medical psychology at the Long Island (New York) College of Medicine. In 1937, while on a strenuous lecture tour, he died in Aberdeen, Scotland.

Freud, replying to a friend who was greatly saddened by Adler's death, wrote, "I don't understand your sympathy for Adler. For a Jewish boy out of a Viennese suburb a death in Aberdeen is an unheard-of career in itself and a proof of how far he had got on. The world really rewarded him richly for his service in having contradicted psychoanalysis" (Scarf, 1971, p. 47).

Adler wrote numerous books and articles, many of them directed to the lay public. Adlerian theories continue to be propounded in the *American Journal of Individual Psychology* and by the American Society of Individual Psychology.

Adler's System: Individual Psychology

The theoretical positions of Adler and Freud differed sharply. Whereas Freud emphasized the past as an influence on behavior, Adler's orientation was toward the future. The division of personality into separate parts is an essential feature of Freudian theory. In contrast, the Adlerian approach stresses the unity of personality.

In another departure from Freud, Adler developed his system of individual psychology along social lines. He believed that human behavior is determined not by biological forces but by social forces. He suggested that we can understand personality only by investigating a person's social relationships and attitudes toward others. Adler proposed that this *social interest*, which can be defined as an innate potential to cooperate with others to achieve personal and societal goals, develops in infancy:

> The first social situation that confronts a child is its relation to its mother, from the very first day. By her educational skill the child's interest in another person is first awakened. If she understands how to train this interest in the direction of cooperation, all the congenital and acquired capacities of the child will converge in the direction of social sense. (Adler, 1930, p. 403)

Thus, social attitude and interest are developed through learning experiences. Like Freud, Adler recognized the importance of the early formative years of childhood, but his focus was on social rather than biological forces. He also minimized the role of sex in shaping personality.

Another point of difference between the theories of Freud and Adler concerns the importance of consciousness. Freud focused on unconscious determinants of behavior, but Adler emphasized the conscious. He considered humans to be conscious beings, aware of their motivations. To Freud, human behavior was determined by past experiences. Adler believed that we are more strongly influenced by what we think the future holds. Strivings for future goals or anticipations of future events can modify and influence our present behavior. For example, a person living in fear of eternal damnation after death will behave in accordance with this expectation.

Adler emphasized the essential unity and consistency of personality. He posited a dynamic driving force that channels the various resources of personality toward one overriding goal. This final goal, toward which we all strive, is *superiority*, or perfection, which includes more complete and perfect development, accomplishment, fulfillment, and realization of the self. In this view, sex is not the dominant drive but is one of a number of means to the end of superiority.

Adler saw this striving in every aspect of personality:

> It runs parallel to physical growth. It is an intrinsic necessity of life itself. . . . All our functions follow its direction; rightly or wrongly they strive for conquest, surety, increase. The impetus from minus to plus is never-ending. The urge from "below" to "above" never ceases. Whatever premises all our philosophers and psychologists dream of—self-preservation, pleasure principle, equalization—all these are but vague representations, attempts to express the great upward drive. (Adler, 1930, pp. 398–399)

This striving for superiority is innate, according to Adler, and is responsible for all progress, not only by the individual but throughout civilization. It carries person and society upward from one level of achievement to the next.

We noted that Adler did not agree with Freud that the primary basis of motivation is sex. He believed instead that a general feeling of *inferiority* is the determining force in behavior, as it apparently was in his own life. At first, Adler related this feeling of inferiority to defective parts of the body. The child with a hereditary organic weakness will attempt to *compensate* for the defect, overemphasizing the deficient function. For example, Demosthenes forcefully overcame his stuttering to become a great speaker; likewise, a child with a weak body may, through intensive exercise, come to excel as an athlete or dancer.

Adler later broadened this concept to include any physical, mental, or social handicap, whether real or imagined. He also believed that an infant's helplessness and smallness produce a general feeling of inferiority that is experienced by everyone; all children are totally dependent on their environment. The child, consciously aware of this inferiority, is at the same time driven by the innate striving for superiority. Thus, the child is goaded by the need to overcome inferiority and insecurity. Adler believed that this pushing and pulling process continues throughout life, impelling an individual toward greater accomplishments.

Feelings of inferiority function to the advantage of both the individual and society because they lead to continuous improvement. In childhood, however, feelings of inferiority that are met with excessive pampering or with rejection by the parents can bring about abnormally expressed compensatory behaviors. In addition, failure to compensate for feelings of inferiority leads to the development of an *inferiority complex*, which renders the person incapable of dealing with the problems of life.

According to Adler, our overriding goal—superiority—is universal, but there are a variety of behaviors by which people may reach this goal. We manifest our striving for superiority in different ways, and each of us develops a characteristic mode of responding, what Adler called a *style of life*.

> It appears that after the fourth or fifth year of life the style of life has been fashioned as a prototype, with its particular way of seizing upon life, its strategy for conquering it, its degree of ability to cooperate. (Adler, 1930, p. 403)

The style of life involves the behaviors by which we compensate for a real or imagined inferiority. In our example of the child with a weak body, his or her style of life involves all those activities, such as exercise or practice at sports, that will result in increased physical strength and stamina. This life style, formed in childhood, becomes fixed and difficult to change, and it provides the framework within which all later experiences are handled.

We can see that Adler emphasized the importance of the early years of life in the formation of personality much as Freud did. He differed from Freud in his belief that the individual consciously creates his or her own life style or self.

Adler also focused on the family as a factor in personality development. A child with a handicap may consider himself or herself a failure but through compensation and with the help of understanding parents can transform inferiorities into strengths. On the other hand, a child who is overly indulged by parents may become self-centered, have no social interest, and expect others to accede to his or her wishes. A neglected child may develop a style of life that involves seeking revenge against society. Both pampering and neglect undermine our confidence in our ability to cope with the demands of life.

Adler's concept of the *creative power of the self* is considered the pinnacle of his theory. He suggested that we have the capacity to determine our personality in accordance with our unique style of life. The creative power represents an active principle of human existence that may be likened to the older concept of soul. Certain abilities and experiences come to us through our heredity and environment, but it is the way we actively use and interpret these experiences that provides the basis for our attitude toward life.

The concept of the creative power of the self means that we are consciously involved in shaping our own personalities and destinies. Adler believed that people are capable of participating directly in determining their own fate, rather than having it passively determined for them by past experiences.

In examining the childhoods of his patients, Adler became interested in the relationship between personality and *birth order*. He believed that the oldest, middle, and youngest child, because of their position in the family, have different social experiences that result in different personalities. The oldest child, for example, receives a great deal of attention until dethroned by the birth of a second child. Then the first-born may become insecure and hostile, authoritarian and conservative, with a strong interest in maintaining order and authority. Adler suggested that criminals, neurotics, and perverts are often first-born children. (Freud was a first-born.)

Adler found the second child to be intensely ambitious, rebellious, and jealous, constantly trying to surpass the first-born. Adler, a second-born child, had such a competitive relationship with his older brother (whose name was Sigmund) all his life. Nevertheless, Adler considered the second-born to be better adjusted than either a first-born or a youngest child. The youngest child was believed to be spoiled and the most likely to have behavior problems as a child and as an adult.

Comment

Adler's theories were warmly received by many people who were dissatisfied with or disgusted by Freud's picture of human nature as dominated by sexual forces and determined by childhood experiences. It is, after all, more pleasant to consider ourselves consciously directing our own development. Adler presented a satisfying and optimistic image of human nature. His belief in the importance of social factors, to the relative exclusion of biological determinants, is usually considered a positive contribution. This attitude reinforced an already growing interest in the social sciences and the beginnings of a reorientation within psychoanalysis to render its principles more applicable to the diversity of human behavior.

Adler's system does not lack critics. Many claim that his theories are superficial, relying on commonsense observations from everyday life. Others consider his observations to be shrewd and insightful.

It is also argued that Adler was not a consistent or systematic theorist and that his position, like that of other theorists, leaves a number of questions unanswered. What, precisely, is this creative force by which we direct our behavior? What prevents people from becoming reconciled to their inferiority? What are the relative roles of heredity and environment in this process? In addition, the criticisms directed by more experimentally oriented psychologists at Freud and Jung also apply to Adler.

Adler's observations of his patients cannot be duplicated, nor were they conducted in controlled and systematic fashion. He did not attempt to verify the accuracy of his patients' reports, and, like Freud and Jung, he did not explain the procedures by which he analyzed the data and reached his conclusions.

Most of Adler's concepts have resisted attempts at experimental validation, although his ideas about birth order have been the subject of considerable research. These studies show that first-borns are high in the need for achievement and that they tend to be dependent on others and anxious in stressful situations (Breland, 1974; Schachter, 1963, 1964). The findings support Adler's view that first-borns are made anxious and fearful when they are dethroned by the arrival of a second child. Adler predicted that last-born children, if excessively pampered, may have difficulty as adults in coping with life's problems. This idea has received support from many studies showing that more last-borns than early-borns are likely to become alcoholics (Barry & Blane, 1977).

In general, Adler's influence on post-Freudian psychoanalysis has been substantial. His emphasis on social forces in personality can be seen in the work of Karen Horney. His focus on the unity of personality is reflected in the theory of Gordon Allport. His stress on the creative power of the individual to shape his or her own life influenced the work of Maslow, who wrote that "Adler becomes more correct year by year" (Maslow, 1970, p. 13). Adler's influence extends into the 1980s, to the work of social learning theorist Julian Rotter.

Some psychologists have suggested that Adler was far ahead of his time, that his emphases on cognitive and social variables are more compatible with trends in psychology today than they were with the psychology of his own day.

KAREN HORNEY (1885–1952)

Horney, an early feminist, was trained as a Freudian psychoanalyst in Berlin. She characterized her work as modifying and extending Freud's system rather than as being opposed to it.

The Life of Horney

Horney was born in Hamburg, Germany. Her father was a devout, morose ship captain many years older than her mother, a liberal and vivacious woman. Horney's childhood was far from idyllic. Her mother rejected her in favor of an older brother, and her father constantly belittled her appearance and intelligence, leaving her with strong feelings of worthlessness and hostility. This lack of love fostered what she later called "basic anxiety," and it provides another example of the influence of personal experiences on a theorist's view of personality (Rubins, 1978).

In spite of opposition from her father, Horney entered medical school at the University of Berlin and received her M.D. in 1913. From 1914 to 1918 she undertook orthodox psychoanalytic training at the Berlin Psychoanalytic Institute. She began private practice in 1919 and became a faculty member at the institute.

Over the next 15 years Horney wrote many journal articles, most of them concerned with problems of the feminine personality, demonstrating her disagreement with certain of Freud's concepts. In 1932 she came to the United States as associate director of the Chicago Institute for Psychoanalysis. She established a private practice and taught at the New York Psychoanalytic Institute but a growing disaffection for orthodox Freudian theories led her to break with this group. She founded the American Institute of Psychoanalysis and remained its head until her death.

Before discussing Horney's system, let us consider her points of disagreement with Freud. First, she thought of herself as a disciple of Freud's and accepted several of his basic principles. "Though retaining what I considered the fundamentals of Freud's teaching, I realized . . . that my search for a better understanding has led me in directions that were at variance with Freud" (Horney, 1945, p. 13). However, parts of her system are so greatly at variance with Freud's that it occasionally becomes difficult to recognize her ideas as falling within the Freudian framework.

Horney believed that some of Freud's basic assumptions were influenced by the spirit of the times in which he worked, and that by the 1930s and 1940s, when Horney set about formulating her system, times had changed dramatically. The intellectual and cultural mores differed, and attitudes about sexual conduct and the roles of the sexes had been revised. Obviously, Freud's theories were no longer consistent with the *Zeitgeist*.

Not only were the times in which Horney worked different from Freud's, but so was the place. Horney developed her theories in the United States, which had its own popular attitudes about sex. In addition, her American patients were unlike her previous European patients, and the differences could only be accounted for in terms of social influences, not universal biological factors as Freud claimed.

Thus, Horney did not agree with Freud that personality development depends on unchangeable biological forces. She denied the preeminent position of sexual factors, challenged the validity of the Oedipus theory, and discarded the concept of libido and the Freudian structure of personality. Opposed to Freud's belief that women are motivated by penis envy, Horney argued that men are motivated by womb envy, that they envy women for their ability to give birth. Horney believed that this womb envy and its accompanying resentment are manifested unconsciously in men through behaviors designed to disparage and belittle women, to maintain their inferior status. By denying women equal rights, minimizing their opportunities to contribute to society, and downgrading their efforts to achieve, men attempt to retain their alleged natural superiority. To Horney, the underlying reason for such masculine behavior is a sense of inferiority resulting from womb envy.

Freud and Horney also differed in their fundamental conceptions of human nature:

Although Karen Horney (1885–1952) shared Freud's emphasis on early childhood, she viewed basic anxiety arising from environment and culture as the major force motivating people to seek safety and security.

> Freud's pessimism as regards neuroses and their treatment arose from the depths of his disbelief in human goodness and human growth. Man, he postulated, is doomed to suffer or to destroy. . . . My own belief is that man has the capacity as well as the desire to develop his potentialities and become a decent human being . . . I believe that man can change and go on changing as long as he lives. (Horney, 1945, p. 19)

There are additional differences, but the important point is that Horney rejected much of Freud's system. She did accept, however, certain tenets, including the notion of unconscious motivation and the existence of emotional, nonrational motives.

Horney's System

The underlying concept in Horney's theory is *basic anxiety,* defined as "the feeling a child has of being isolated and helpless in a potentially hostile world" (Horney, 1945, p. 41). This basic anxiety can result from various parental actions toward the child, including an attitude of dominance, lack of protection, lack of love, and erratic behavior. Anything that disturbs the secure relationship between child and parents is capable of producing anxiety. Thus, basic anxiety is not innate. Rather, it results from environmental factors, from social causes.

In place of Freud's life and death instincts as major motivating forces, Horney considered the helpless infant to be seeking security in a hostile and threatening world. She claimed that the decisive driving power for human behavior is the need for safety, security, and freedom from fear.

Horney shared with Freud the belief that personality develops in early childhood, but she also thought that personality could change throughout life. Whereas Freud detailed psychosexual stages of development, Horney focused on the way the growing child is treated by the parents. She denied any such universal developmental phases as an oral stage or an Oedipus complex. She suggested that a child's possible development of anal or oral or phallic tendencies results from parental behaviors, and that nothing in a child's development is universal. Everything depends on cultural and social–environmental factors. Horney attempted to show how the developmental conflicts Freud ascribed to biological sources could be attributed instead to social forces.

Thus, Horney focused on the early childhood experiences involving the parents' interaction with the child, because parents can either satisfy or frustrate the child's need for safety and security. The environment provided for the child and the way the child reacts to it form the structure of personality.

As noted, basic anxiety arises from the parent–child relationship. When this socially or environmentally produced anxiety appears, the child develops a number of behavioral strategies to deal with the resulting feelings of insecurity and helplessness. The child structures his or her personality in response to the demands of the environment (the parents' attitudes and behavior).

If any of these behavioral strategies becomes a fixed part of the personality, it is called a *neurotic need,* a mode of defense against anxiety. Horney postulated 10 neurotic needs, including the needs for affection and approval, prestige, personal achievement, perfection, and self-sufficiency. She later grouped the neurotic needs in three directional categories: (1) movement toward people (the compliant type), as in the need for love; (2) movement away from people (the detached type), as in the need for self-sufficiency; and (3) movement against people (the aggressive type), as in the need for power.

Movement toward people involves acceptance of helplessness and an attempt to win the affection of others and be dependent on them. This is the only way in which the individual can feel secure with others. Movement away from people involves staying apart from others to avoid any situation of dependence. Movement against people involves hostility, rebellion, and aggression against others.

Horney believed that none of these needs is a realistic way to deal with anxiety. The needs themselves can give rise to basic conflicts because of their incompatibility. Once a person establishes a method of coping with anxiety, his or her behavior ceases to be flexible enough to permit alternative modes of expression. When a fixed behavior is inappropriate for a particular situation, the person is unable to change it to meet that situation's demands. These entrenched behaviors intensify the individual's difficulties because they come to permeate the entire personality, "as a malignant tumor pervades the whole organic tissue. They end by encompassing not only the person's relation to others but also his relation to himself and to life in general" (Horney, 1945, p. 46).

Horney also invoked the concept of the *idealized self-image*, which provides a false picture of the personality. This self-image is an imperfect and misleading mask that prevents neurotic persons from understanding and accepting their true selves. In donning the mask, neurotics deny the existence of inner conflicts. The self-image, which to neurotic persons is genuine, enables them to believe that they are far superior to the persons they actually are.

Horney believed that the basic conflicts of a neurotic person are neither innate nor inevitable, but arise from undesirable situations in childhood. They can be prevented if the child's home life is characterized by understanding, security, love, and warmth.

Comment

Horney's optimism about the possibility of avoiding neurotic conflicts was welcomed by many people as a relief from the pessimism of Freudian theory. Her contribution to psychology is noteworthy because she introduced a model of personality based on social factors, attributing little, if anything, to innate factors.

Horney's theory of personality may be weaker than Freud's in clarity, internal consistency, and level of formal development. Many psychologists believe, however, that it would have been easier to accept or reject Freudian theory than to attempt to reshape it, as Horney did. So radical is her departure from basic Freudian concepts that her system is frowned on by more orthodox psychoanalysts. Also, her evidence, like that of Jung, Adler, and Freud, is taken from clinical observations and thus is subject to the questions of scientific credibility noted earlier. Little research has been conducted on any aspect of Horney's theory, a fact some critics seize on as a major limitation of her work. However, some of the research we cited in Chapter 13 to refute Freud's notion that women have inadequately developed superegos and inferior conceptions of their bodies may be taken as support for some of Horney's views.

Although Horney had no loyal band of disciples or a journal in which to develop and disseminate her ideas, her work nevertheless has exerted considerable influence. Her ideas have drawn a large public following, increased in recent years by the changing role of women in American society.

CRITICISMS OF THE SOCIAL PSYCHOLOGICAL THEORIES

The social psychological theorists we have discussed—Alfred Adler and Karen Horney—have an obvious point of similarity in that both emphasize the role of social variables in personality development. Although they acknowledge varying degrees of intellectual debt to the work of Freud, each system constitutes a vigorous protest against the Freudian notion of the primacy of biological forces in the formation of personality.

These and other social psychological theorists see human behavior as determined not by biological forces but by the interpersonal relationships to which the individual is exposed, particularly in childhood.

Just as biological forces are minimized, so is the role of the libido and its manifestations, such as the Oedipus complex and the psychosexual stages of development. Anxiety and other expressions of abnormal behavior do not originate in instincts, libido, and sex, but instead develop from early social relationships. We are not doomed to anxiety, as in Freud's deterministic theory, because anxiety can be avoided by the proper childhood social experiences.

According to Freud, human behavior is universally determined. In contrast, the social psychological theorists consider behavior to be flexible and capable of being consciously and continuously changed by each person. Our social institutions too are flexible and open to change. Although the social psychological theorists recognize that social mores can be modified only gradually and with difficulty, they optimistically agree that people are capable of developing the kind of social system that is most appropriate for their needs.

Several points of criticism have been directed against the social psychological theorists. Their image of humans as rational, conscious, and socialized beings is often unconvincing in light of frequent instances of disappointing and irrational behavior. If we shape our society to suit our needs, how do we account for a society that permits or fosters violent and unjust behavior? We are left with the paradox of rational, perfectible, socialized beings who nevertheless have developed social systems that are inadequate for (often injurious to) our needs.

The social psychological theorists have also been accused of neglecting the social processes through which we are shaped, leaving unanswered the question of how we learn to be properly functioning members of society. They draw on the general concept of learning to explain personality formation but fail to explain the specific mechanisms of the learning process.

THE DESCENDANTS

We have seen that Freudian psychoanalytic theory is no longer the sole approach to the understanding of the human personality. Our mention of the changes introduced by the neo-Freudian loyalists and our discussion of the work of Jung, Adler, and Horney highlighted some of the alternative approaches developed during Freud's lifetime.

The area of personality theory and research has grown immensely since the time of Freud and has splintered into many conflicting views. Contemporary textbooks dealing with theories of personality typically discuss 15 or more fully developed theories. Although these approaches differ in their specifics and generalities, they have a common heritage. They all owe their origin and form, in some degree, to the founding efforts of Freud.

Thus, Freud served the same purpose on the psychoanalytic side of the history of psychology that Wundt served on the experimental side, as a source of either inspiration or opposition. Every structure, whether actual or theoretical, depends on the soundness of its foundation, and Freud, like Wundt, provided a solid and challenging base on which later theorists could build. As examples of the evolution in personality theory since the time of Freud we shall discuss the works of three descendants: Gordon Allport, Henry Murray, and Erik Erikson.

Gordon Allport (1897–1967)

Over the course of a long, productive career at Harvard University, Allport, more than any other individual, made the study of personality an academically respectable part of psychology. Never psychoanalyzed or in private practice himself, Allport took the study of personality out of the clinical setting and brought it into the university.

As a boy, Allport felt isolated and rejected by other children, but his home life was happy and filled with trust and affection. Unlike Freud and the immediate post-Freudians, Allport does not seem to have had childhood experiences that led directly to his adult view of personality. Perhaps that is why he approached the field from an intellectual and academic standpoint rather than from a more personal one through psychoanalysis.

Before he began his graduate studies, Allport met Sigmund Freud in Vienna, an event that may also have influenced his approach to personality. Ushered into the great man's office, young Allport could think of nothing to say. Freud sat still, looking at him, waiting for him to start the conversation. Finally, Allport blurted out an account of an incident that had occurred on the streetcar that morning involving a small boy with an obvious and extreme fear of dirt. When Allport finished the story, Freud stared in silence for a moment and then asked, "Was that little boy you?" Freud was expressing his belief that Allport was revealing his own inner conflicts and fears through his story (Allport, 1968, pp. 383–384). It has been suggested that Freud's question to Allport was insightful and much to the point. "Allport was indeed a person who was neat, meticulous, orderly and punctual—possessing many of the characteristics associated by Freud with the compulsive personality" (Pervin, 1984, p. 267).

Allport was shaken by Freud's question. He began to suspect that psychoanalysis focused too much on the unconscious to the neglect of conscious motives, and he went on to fashion a view of personality that was different from Freud's. Allport minimized the role of the unconscious in normal adults, arguing that they function in more rational and conscious terms. Only neurotics, Allport said, are influenced by the unconscious. He also disagreed with Freud over the role of childhood experiences and conflicts in adult life, insisting that we are influenced much more by present experiences and by our hopes for the future than by our past.

Another major difference is Allport's conviction that the only way to investigate personality is through the study of normal adults, not neurotics. Unlike Freud, he did not believe that there was a continuum between the normal and the neurotic. He argued that there were no similarities between normal and neurotic individuals and thus no basis for comparison. Allport also stressed the uniqueness of the individual personality. He did not believe that there were universal laws or themes that could be applied to everyone, as Freud had suggested.

To Allport, the core of any personality theory is its treatment of motivation. To explain motivation in the normal adult, he proposed the concept of *functional autonomy*, the idea

Gordon Allport (1897–1967) stressed the uniqueness of the individual personality, and made personality theory a major part of psychology.

that a motive is not functionally related to any childhood experience. Human motives are independent of the original circumstances in which they appeared. An analogy can be made with a tree, which is no longer functionally related to the seed from which it grew. The tree becomes self-determining just as the adult human being does. For example, when you begin your career, you will work very hard, motivated perhaps to attain the goals of money and security. Years later, when you are successful and financially secure, you may still work hard even though your original goals have been reached. Motivation, in Allport's view, cannot be traced to childhood, but can only be understood in terms of a person's present behavior and intentions (Allport, 1937, 1961).

Allport's term for the self is *proprium,* used in the sense of "appropriate." The self is what belongs to or is appropriate to each of us. It includes everything that is unique, that sets us apart from all others, and it is an important, conscious part of the personality. The proprium develops through seven stages from infancy to adolescence. These developmental stages are not psychosexual, nor do they involve Freudian conflicts around erogenous zones. Social relationships, particularly those with the mother, and not sexual conflicts, are crucial in the development of the proprium.

Allport's study of the traits of personality, which began with his doctoral dissertation, was the first ever conducted in the United States. He distinguished between *traits*, which are common to a number of people, such as members of a particular culture, and *personal dispositions,* which are the traits unique to each person. Both can be inferred from the observation of behavior over a period of time, looking for consistencies and regularities. Allport postulated three kinds of traits: *cardinal traits,* the ruling passions that dominate every aspect of life; *central traits,* the behavioral themes such as aggressiveness or sentimentality; and *secondary traits,* the behavior displayed less frequently and consistently than the other two kinds of traits.

Allport's theory has been more influential in psychology than the work of the traditional psychoanalysts. It has not stimulated a great deal of research because of the difficulty of translating some of his concepts into propositions sufficiently specific to study under laboratory conditions. Allport's own most notable research dealt with what he called *expressive behavior,* which includes facial expressions, vocal inflections, gestures, and mannerisms that tend to reveal, to trained observers, facets of personality.

Critics charge that Allport's exclusive focus on the individual makes it impossible to generalize from one person to another and to formulate laws of behavior. Nevertheless, Allport is considered to be a significant figure in the study of personality. His books are clear and his concepts easily understood. Allport developed a psychological test, the Study of Values, to assess the values an individual holds. The test has proven to be a successful assessment device for research, guidance, counseling, and personnel selection. Although it does not contribute to the empirical testing of Allport's theory, it is nonetheless a useful outgrowth of his theory. His definition and assessment of traits and his work in developing psychological tests with which to measure the human personality constitute major contributions to psychology.

Henry Murray (1893–   )

Whereas Allport's theory of personality was a complete rejection of Freud's, Murray's system of *personology* built on Freud's theory. Like Allport, Murray chose to study personality in a university setting rather than in a clinic. Although he underwent psychoanalysis, he did not practice it, preferring to investigate the human personality through the intensive study of normal individuals.

Murray's childhood was characterized by rejection from his mother, a high level of sensitivity to the sufferings of other people, and some Adlerian compensation for two defects—stuttering and ineptitude at sports. Murray noted that "an Adlerian factor was at work" in his participation in football and boxing to compensate for physical weakness (Murray, 1967, p. 302). After graduating from Columbia University medical school, he interned in surgery, conducted biochemical research, and earned a Ph.D. in biochemistry at Cambridge University, certainly one of the more circuitous routes to a career in psychology. After spending three apparently illuminating weeks with Carl Jung and an unforgettable evening with Freud and his daughter Anna, Murray began his work on personality at the Harvard Psychological Clinic.

It is not surprising, considering his training in medicine and biochemistry, that Murray chose to emphasize physiological functioning as it relates to personality. He stressed the concept of tension reduction, which he considered to be a primary law of human behavior, much as Freud did. Also in the Freudian vein, Murray noted the importance of the unconscious and the effect of childhood experiences on adult behavior. He incorporated Freud's notions of the id, ego, and superego in his system, albeit with some modifications.

Murray divided the personality into three structures: the id, the ego, and the superego (Murray, 1938). The *id* contains our innate, impulsive tendencies and provides the energy for the operation of the personality. This view is virtually identical to Freud's. In addition to primitive and lustful impulses, the id in Murray's system contains more socially desirable tendencies such as empathy, identification, and forms of love other than lust. Although parts of the id must be suppressed for normal development to occur, other parts must be allowed full expression. We can see here the influence of Jung's concept of the shadow archetype, which also contained desirable and undesirable qualities.

In Murray's system the *ego* assumes a much more active role in determining behavior than it does in Freud's theory. Murray believed that the ego is not merely the servant of the id but a consciously choosing organizer of all behavior. The ego acts to suppress the undesirable id impulses and facilitates the expression of the desirable ones.

Murray agreed with Freud that the *superego* represents the internalization of cultural values and that individuals evaluate their own behavior in terms of those internalized values. He differed with Freud about the forces that shape the superego and the period over which it is formed. Murray argued that the superego is formed not only by the teachings of one's parents, but also by one's peer group and by the literature and mythology of the society. The superego is not fixed by the age of five but continues to develop throughout life.

Motivation is central to Murray's theory of personality, and his classification of *needs* to explain motivation is his most important contribution. Needs involve a chemical force in the brain that organizes intellectual and perceptual functioning. Needs arouse tension levels in the organism, which can be reduced only by the satisfaction of the needs. Thus, needs activate behavior and direct it in whatever ways are necessary to bring about this satisfaction. Murray's research identified 20 needs including achievement, affiliation, aggression, autonomy, dominance, and rejection.

Like Freud, Murray believed that personality develops through a series of stages in childhood. Each stage is characterized by some condition that gives pleasure, and each leaves its imprint on personality in the form of a *complex*, a normal pattern of behavior that unconsciously directs all of the person's later development. The pleasurable conditions of childhood and their complexes bear some similarity to Freud's stages of psychosexual development:

> Claustral complex: the secure existence within the womb
> Oral complex: the sensuous enjoyment of sucking nourishment while being held
> Anal complex: the pleasure resulting from defecation
> Urethral complex: the pleasure accompanying urination
> Castration complex: genital pleasures

Murray's proposed needs have had considerable impact on the construction of psychological tests, especially the Thematic Apperception Test (TAT) he devised with Christiana Morgan. This is a projective technique widely used to study and assess many aspects of personality. Another popular test, the Edwards Personal Preference Schedule, measures 15 of the needs identified by Murray.

Murray's theory has generated considerable research on specific needs and on the techniques he developed to assess personality. Much of that research has supported his views, especially on the needs for affiliation and achievement. There has been no scientific support for such other aspects of his theory as the three divisions of personality or the stages of personality development.

Murray has exerted an impressive influence on the study of personality. Of particular importance is his list of needs, which has proven to be of great value not only for research but also for clinical diagnosis and personnel selection. Work on these aspects of his theory continues today.

Erik Erikson (1902–   )

Erikson was trained in orthodox psychoanalysis by Anna Freud. He developed a popular approach to personality that retains much of Freudian psychoanalysis while extending it in several ways, first, by elaborating on the stages of development and arguing that personality continues to grow throughout life, and, second, by recognizing the impact of culture, history, and society on personality.

Erikson is well known for his concept of the *identity crisis*, an idea that may have arisen from personal crises of identity he experienced in his early years. "No doubt," he wrote, "my best friends will insist that I needed to name this crisis and to see it in everybody else in order to really come to terms with it in myself" (Erikson, 1975, pp. 25–26).

The first such crisis for Erikson involved his name. For many years he believed his last name was Homburger, which was the name of his stepfather whom Erikson thought was his natural father. A second crisis of identity occurred at school in Germany. Erikson considered himself to be German, but his classmates rejected him because he was also Jewish. At the same time, his Jewish classmates rejected him because of his blond, Aryan appearance.

The third crisis occurred after his graduation from high school. He withdrew from society for several years and wandered throughout Europe seeking an identity. Finally, at the age of 25, he reached Vienna and took a job teaching in a small school that had been established for the children of Freud's patients and friends. Erikson received training in psychoanalysis, married, and succeeded in finding both a personal and a professional identity. He had no formal education beyond high school but went on to teach at Harvard and to become one of the most influential psychoanalysts of modern times.

Erikson's theory of personality takes a developmental or life-span approach in that it focuses on personality growth over the life of the individual. The central theme in the development of personality is the search for an *ego identity*. Erikson divided the human life span into eight *stages of psychosocial development*, each of which involves a conflict that must be resolved.

The conflicts arise as the environment makes new demands on the individual. Erikson called these confrontations with the environment *crises*. In each stage of growth the person is faced with a choice between two ways of coping with the environment, an

adaptive way or a maladaptive way. Only when each crisis is resolved, which involves a change in the personality, does the person have sufficient strength to deal with the next stage of development.

Erikson's first four stages of development are similar to Freud's oral, anal, phallic, and latency periods, although Erikson stresses social rather than biological and sexual factors. The last four stages are unique to Erikson's system. They carry the individual from adolescence through old age, levels of development ignored by Freud. Erikson's eight stages of growth, the approximate years in which each occurs, and the opposing ways of adapting are as follows:

(1) Oral–sensory, birth to 1 year — Trust–Mistrust
(2) Muscular–anal, 1–3 years — Autonomy–Doubt, shame
(3) Locomotor–genital, 3–5 years — Initiative–Guilt
(4) Latency, 6–11 years — Industry–Inferiority
(5) Adolescence, 12–18 years — Identity–Role confusion
(6) Young adulthood, 19–35 years — Intimacy–Isolation
(7) Adulthood, 35–55 years — Generativity–Stagnation
(8) Maturity, 55+ years — Ego integrity–Despair

The question of one's basic ego identity must be resolved during adolescence. This is a time of consolidation, in which the person must form a self-image that makes sense and provides both a continuity with the past and an orientation toward the future.

Erikson believes that the shaping and acceptance of one's identity is a difficult and anxiety-filled task, in which the adolescent must experiment with different roles and ideologies to determine the best fit. Those who achieve a strong sense of identity are equipped to face the problems of adulthood. Those who fail to achieve an identity are said to be experiencing an identity crisis. They may drop out of the normal life sequence—education, job, marriage—as Erikson himself did for a time, and seek a negative identity in criminal activity, drug addiction, or other socially unacceptable behavior.

One controversial aspect of Erikson's work is his agreement with Freud that personality differences between the sexes are biologically based, originating in the possession or lack of a penis. Erikson based his conclusion on research with children, particularly a study in which boys and girls ages 10–12 constructed various scenes with toy figures and wooden blocks (Erikson, 1968). The scenes built by the girls were low, static structures into which animals and male figures tried to force their way. The boys' creations were action oriented and featured tall, towering structures. Erikson interpreted these play constructions to mean that girls and boys were symbolically expressing their genitals. He suggested that genital differences lead to personality differences but conceded that personality differences could also result from sex-role training in which boys are taught to be more aggressive than girls.

Erikson's work has been highly influential in psychoanalysis as well as in education and social work. His books are popular with professionals and with the public, and his photograph has appeared on the covers of *Newsweek* and the *New York Times Magazine*, an unusual sign of recognition for a psychologist.

Considerable research has been conducted on Erikson's concept of ego identity. Adolescents who developed a strong, positive ego identity were found to have coped with the crises of the earlier developmental stages in an adaptive way. Adolescents who developed a weak ego identity had resolved the earlier stages in a maladaptive way (Waterman, Buebel, & Waterman, 1970). These findings are in line with Erikson's predictions. In general, although there is a great deal of research support for the notion of ego identity, the experimental evidence for the earlier stages of development is less impressive.

Critics of Erikson's theory charge that it is more applicable to boys than to girls and that more attention is paid to infancy and childhood than to adult life, despite the claim to be a life-span theory. However, many psychologists and psychiatrists have found that Erikson's proposed stages of psychosocial development offer a useful framework for analyzing the developmental histories of their patients. The field of life-span developmental psychology owes much of its impetus to Erikson's emphasis on the continuing evolution of personality throughout life.

COMMENT

We have described something of the diversity that characterizes developments in the psychoanalytic tradition during and after Freud's lifetime. Some of the contemporary positions bear little resemblance to Freud's views, and may be labeled "psychoanalytic" only by default to distinguish them from the behavioral–experimental tradition in psychology. Although they owe their origin to Freud, in that they grew out of opposition to his views, they may share with orthodox psychoanalysis only a broad interest in understanding the human personality. A theorist such as Allport, who diverged so far from Freudian views, might more appropriately be classified as a humanistic psychologist. Other positions, such as those of Murray and Erikson, bear a clearer similarity to Freud's work. These viewpoints are certainly Freudian in their particulars, although they differ from Freudian psychoanalysis on both major and minor points.

There is considerably more divisiveness and fragmentation within the psychoanalytic tradition than within the behaviorist tradition in psychology. Despite the changes introduced by neobehaviorists and neo-neobehaviorists, all agree with founder John B. Watson that *behavior* in some form should be a focus of study. In contrast, not all, or even most, of Freud's heirs agree that the focus of their study should be unconscious or biological forces, or that the motivators of human conduct are sex and aggression.

Today there are many more subschools of psychoanalysis than of behaviorism. This greater plurality of views may be seen as the field's major strength and vitality, or its major weakness and failing, but at present these developments are too recent to judge. They are still history in the making.

SUGGESTED READINGS

Jung

Brome, V. (1978). *Jung*. New York: Atheneum.
Hannah, B. (1976). *Jung: His life and work*. New York: G. P. Putnam's Sons.

Jung, C. G. (1961). *Memories, dreams, reflections.* New York: Random House. (Jung's autobiography).

McGuire, W. (Ed.). (1974). *The Freud/Jung letters: The correspondence between Sigmund Freud and C. G. Jung.* Princeton, NJ: Princeton University Press.

McGuire, W., & Hull, R. F. C. (Eds.). (1977). *C. G. Jung speaking: Interviews and encounters.* Princeton, NJ: Princeton University Press.

Storr, A. (1973). *C. G. Jung.* New York: Viking Press.

Von Franz, M. (1975). *C. G. Jung: His myth in our time.* Boston: Little, Brown.

Adler

Adler, A. (1930). Individual psychology. In C. Murchison (Ed.), *Psychologies of 1930* (pp. 305–405). Worcester, MA: Clark University Press.

Adler, A. (1939). *Social interest.* New York: G. P. Putnam's Sons.

Ansbacher, H. L. (1981). *Alfred Adler revisited.* New York: Praeger.

Ansbacher, H. L., & Ansbacher, R. (Eds.). (1956). *The individual psychology of Alfred Adler.* New York: Basic Books.

Dreikurs, R. (1952–1953). Adler's contribution to medicine, psychology, education. *American Journal of Individual Psychology, 10,* 83–86.

Orgler, H. (1965). *Alfred Adler: The man and his work.* New York: G. P. Putnam's Sons.

Sperber, M. (1974). *Masks of loneliness: Alfred Adler in perspective.* New York: Macmillan.

Horney

Horney, K. (1937). *The neurotic personality of our time.* New York: W. W. Norton.

Horney, K. (1942). *Self-analysis.* New York: W. W. Norton.

Horney, K. (1967). *Feminine psychology.* New York: W. W. Norton.

Horney, K. (1980). *The adolescent diaries of Karen Horney.* New York: Basic Books.

Martin, A. R. (1975). Karen Horney's theory in today's world. *American Journal of Psychoanalysis, 35,* 297–302.

Rubins, J. L. (1978). *Karen Horney: Gentle rebel of psychoanalysis.* New York: Dial Press.

Wolman, B. (1954). Psychoanalysis without libido: An analysis of Karen Horney's contribution to psychoanalytic theory. *American Journal of Psychotherapy, 8,* 21–31.

Freudian Descendants

Allport, G. (1955). *Becoming: Basic considerations for a psychology of personality.* New Haven, CT: Yale University Press.

Allport, G. (1967). Autobiography. In E. G. Boring & G. Lindzey (Eds.), *A history of psychology in autobiography* (vol. 5, pp. 1–25). New York: Appleton-Century-Crofts.

Erikson, E. H. (1968). *Identity: Youth and crisis.* New York: W. W. Norton.

Maddi, S. R., & Costa, P. T. (1972). *Humanism in personology: Allport, Maslow, and Murray.* Chicago: Aldine-Atherton.

Murray, H. A. (1938). *Explorations in personality.* New York: Oxford University Press.

Murray, H. A. (1967). Autobiography. In E. G. Boring & G. Lindzey (Eds.), *A history of psychology in autobiography* (vol. 5, pp. 283–310). New York: Appleton-Century-Crofts.

Roazen, P. (1976). *Erik H. Erikson: The power and limits of a vision.* New York: Free Press.

15

Beyond the Schools of Thought: More Recent Developments

SCHOOLS OF THOUGHT IN PSYCHOLOGY

Throughout this book we have described how the major schools of thought in psychology came into being, prospered for a time, and then—with the exception of psychoanalysis—became part of the mainstream of contemporary American psychology or contributed to it. We have also seen that each movement grew strong and vital through its opposition to another system. When there was no longer any need for protest, when the new school had vanquished its opposition, that school died as a movement and became an established position, at least for a time.

Each of the schools of thought was successful. Each made substantial contributions to psychological thought. Each, therefore, was a fruitful protest and accomplished its mission. This is true even for structuralism, although it left little direct imprint on the modern psychological scene. There are no longer structuralists of the Titchenerian variety in psychology, nor have there been for decades. Yet structuralism was an enormous success because it helped in the enterprise begun by Wundt, the establishment of an independent science of psychology that was finally free of philosophy. That structuralism failed to remain the dominant position in psychology for more than a short time does not detract from its revolutionary achievement as the first school of thought of a new science and a source of opposition for the schools that came later.

Consider the success of functionalism, which also has not lasted as a separate school of thought. As an attitude or point of view, which was all it hoped to be, functionalism has permeated contemporary American psychological thought. To the extent that American psychology today is as much profession as science and is applying its findings to virtually every aspect of life, the functional, utilitarian viewpoint has won a great many converts. Whether this applied/professional orientation will be to the ultimate benefit of psychology is being debated, but there is no argument about the source of that orientation. It derived from the functional psychologists of the early years of the twentieth century.

What of Gestalt psychology? It, too, on a more modest scale, accomplished its mission. Its opposition to elementism, its support of a molar approach, and its continuing

351

interest in consciousness have influenced psychologists in the areas of clinical psychology, learning, perception, social psychology, and thinking. Unlike structuralism and functionalism, Gestalt psychology maintains the character of a separate school of thought. There are psychologists today who define their research and professional identity along Gestalt lines. Although the Gestalt school did not transform psychology the way its founders hoped it would, it still had a considerable impact and must, for this reason, be defined as a successful movement.

As noteworthy as the accomplishments of structuralism, functionalism, and Gestalt psychology have been, they take second place to the phenomenal influence of behaviorism and psychoanalysis. Not only have the effects of these two movements been pronounced, but their continuing identity as separate schools of thought is also important. Large numbers of psychologists, particularly in the United States, have no difficulty describing themselves as belonging to either the behaviorist or the psychoanalytic tradition. Although there has been some rapprochement between these two positions in recent years, in general they remain apart as major forces in psychology today.

We discussed how both schools splintered into various positions since the days of their founders, Watson and Freud. There is today no single form of behaviorism or of psychoanalysis that has won allegiance from all members of either school (although Skinner did enjoy prominence in behaviorism for many years). The emergence of sub-schools has divided both viewpoints into competing factions, each with its own map of the true path. Despite the internal diversity of the schools, however, behaviorists and psychoanalysts stand firmly against each other in their definitions of and approaches to psychology. Skinnerian behaviorists still have much more in common with socio-behaviorist followers of Bandura, for example, than they do with Jungian or Adlerian psychoanalysts.

The vitality of these two major schools of thought is found in the fact that they are still evolving. As we have seen, Skinnerian psychology was not the last stage in the development of behaviorism any more than Adlerian psychology was the final stage of psychoanalysis.

In this chapter we consider four developments that have characterized American psychology in the last half of the twentieth century. Two of these developments are practical and advance psychology as a profession. The other two are theoretical and advance psychology's scientific evolution while also contributing to the application of psychology to real-world concerns. On the professional side we discuss the growth of applied psychology in the United States and the role of women in psychology. On the theoretical side we deal with two movements that have helped to reshape and redefine the field. These are humanistic or third force psychology and cognitive psychology, both of which served to return the study of consciousness to psychology. We discuss their nature and status and trace their relationship to the major schools of thought.

THE GROWTH OF APPLIED PSYCHOLOGY

As we saw in previous chapters, psychology began to be applied to problems in the real world early in the twentieth century, under the influence of functionalism and of Watson's highly popular behaviorism. The discipline was no longer restricted to the laboratory world of pure science where Wundt and, later, Titchener had tried valiantly to keep it.

Although the applied movement in psychology dates its beginnings to the years 1900–1917, before World War I, its progress during that time was slow. Suddenly, with America's entry into the war in 1917, applied psychologists were called upon to deal with many immediate and practical problems. Psychology was thrust into the public arena where both lay persons and psychologists themselves realized that psychological knowledge and methods could be used to improve human welfare in many aspects of life. G. Stanley Hall wrote that the war "has given applied psychology a tremendous impulse. This will, on the whole, do good, for psychology . . . [We] must not try to be too pure" (Hall, 1919, p. 48). Some psychology journals, such as the *Journal of Experimental Psychology*, ceased publication during the war years, but the *Journal of Applied Psychology* thrived.

In the aftermath of the war, particularly in the 1920s, psychology became a "national mania" (Dennis, 1984, p. 23). People throughout the United States came to believe that psychologists were capable of curing everything from marital disharmony and job dissatisfaction to the problem of how best to sell deodorant.

World War II provided another pressing set of problems for psychologists to solve and served to broaden the influence of the field. In the years since the end of that war in 1945, psychology as a whole has experienced the most dramatic period of growth in its history. Within the field, the most significant growth has occurred in the applied areas. Indeed, applied psychology has outstripped the academic and research-oriented side of psychology that predominated for so many years. No longer was it true that the majority of psychologists belonged to college and university faculties.

In 1940, just before the United States entered World War II, 75 percent of all psychologists worked in academic settings. By 1962 the figure had fallen to 47 percent and by 1980 to 42 percent (Gilgen, 1982). One result has been a shift in power within the American Psychological Association. The applied psychologists are now in a commanding position.

We examine here the three areas of applied psychology that have the deepest historical roots: psychological testing, industrial/organizational psychology, and clinical psychology. Testing is covered first because much of the development of the other two areas derived from it.

The Psychological Testing Movement

In our discussions of the work of Francis Galton and James McKeen Cattell we referred to the origins of the mental testing movement. It was Cattell who coined the term "mental tests," but it remained for Alfred Binet, a French psychologist, to develop the first truly psychological test of mental ability.

Binet disagreed with the approach taken by Galton and Cattell, which used tests of sensory–motor processes to measure intelligence. He believed that assessing such cognitive functions as memory, attention, imagination, and comprehension would provide a better measurement of intelligence. His opportunity to prove his point came in response to a practical need. In 1904 the French Ministry of Public Instruction appointed a commission to study the learning abilities of children who were having difficulties in school. Binet and a psychiatrist, Théodore Simon, were appointed to the commission and together they investigated the kinds of intellectual tasks that most children could master at different ages.

From their delineation of these tasks they constructed the first test of intelligence. It consisted of 30 problems arranged in ascending order of difficulty and focused on three cognitive functions: judgment, comprehension, and reasoning. Three years later, in 1908, the test was revised and expanded and the concept of *mental age* was introduced. This was described as the age at which children of average ability could perform certain tasks. For example, if a four-year-old child passed all the tests that the sample of average five-year-olds had passed, that child was assigned a mental age of five. A third revision of the test was prepared in 1911, but with Simon's death the development of the test and of intelligence testing in general shifted to the United States.

The test was introduced in the United States by Henry Goddard, a former student of Hall's and a psychologist at a school for mentally retarded children in Vineland, New Jersey. Goddard called his translation of the test the Binet–Simon Measuring Scale for Intelligence.

In 1916 Lewis M. Terman developed a version of the test that has since become a standard. He named it the Stanford–Binet, after the university with which he was affiliated, and adopted the concept of the *intelligence quotient* (IQ). The IQ measure, defined as the ratio between mental age and chronological age, had originally been proposed by William Stern, a German psychologist. The Stanford–Binet has undergone several revisions and continues to be widely used.

On the day that World War I was declared, Titchener's Society of Experimental Psychologists was meeting at Harvard. Robert Yerkes, the president of the American Psychological Association was in attendance. Yerkes urged the psychologists present to discuss how psychology could aid in the war effort. Titchener demurred, explaining that he was a British subject. It has been suggested that the real reason Titchener declined to involve himself in war work was his intense dislike of applying psychology to practical problems. He may have feared that efforts to help win the war would cause "psychologists to trade a science for a technology" (O'Donnell, 1979, p. 289).

The army was faced with the problem of assessing the intelligence of great numbers of people so as to screen and classify them. One limitation of the Stanford–Binet is that it is an individual test of intelligence, and a highly trained person is required to administer it. Such a test cannot be used for any large-scale testing program where many persons must be tested in a short span of time. For that purpose, a group test that is simpler to administer is desired. Yerkes, given a commission as a major, assembled a staff of 40 psychologists to develop a group intelligence test. They examined a number of tests, none of which was in general use, and selected as a model one developed by Arthur S. Otis, who had been a student of Terman's. Otis had introduced the multiple-choice type of question. Based on Otis's test, the Yerkes group prepared the Army Alpha and the Army Beta tests. The Beta was a version for use with non-English-speaking and illiterate persons. Instead of relying on oral or written directions, instructions were given by demonstration or pantomime.

The establishment of the testing program proceeded slowly and the order to initiate testing was not given until three months before the end of the war. More than one million men were tested, however, but the results were no longer needed by the military. Although the tests had little impact on the war effort, they had a major impact on

Alfred Binet (1857–1911) developed the first truly psychological test of mental ability, which has since evolved into the Stanford–Binet.

psychology. The testing program provided a great deal of publicity, recognition, and status for psychology. Millions of people came to view the field as one that could make contributions far beyond the experimental laboratory. The tests themselves became the prototypes for the many tests that were devised later.

It was not only group intelligence testing that was spurred by the war but also group personality testing. Prior to that time only limited attempts had been made to measure personality. For example, in the closing years of the nineteenth century, Emil Kraepelin, a German psychiatrist, had used what he called a "free association test," in which patients responded to stimulus words with the first word that came to mind. The technique had been originated by Francis Galton and, in 1910, Carl Jung had developed a similar device, the "word association test," to measure complexes in his patients. Both of these were individual tests.

During World War I, the army wanted to determine which of its recruits were highly neurotic. Robert Woodworth constructed the Personal Data Sheet, a self-report inventory on which respondents indicated the neurotic symptoms that applied to them. Like the Army Alpha and Army Beta, the Personal Data Sheet saw little actual use during the war years, but it too served as a prototype for the development of group personality tests for use with civilians in peacetime.

Applied psychology won its own victory in the war, the victory that came with recognition and acceptance by the public. Soon, thousands of job candidates, school children, and college applicants found themselves facing batteries of tests, the results of which could determine the course of their lives.

An epidemic of testing swept the United States, but in the haste to answer the call of businesses and educational institutions it was inevitable that poorly designed and inadequately researched tests would appear, leading to disappointing results. As a consequence, many companies abandoned the use of psychological tests during the mid-1920s. "The testing boom of the 1920s, based on the indiscriminate use of tests, may have done as much to retard as to advance the progress of psychological testing" (Anastasi, 1982, p. 12). In time, better tests were developed that enabled industry to select better people for jobs, and better jobs for people, and today personnel selection and placement testing have become essential parts of the employment process.

Testing also became part of an important social controversy in the 1920s. The results obtained from the testing of army recruits during the war were released in 1921 and they were shocking. The data showed that the mental age of the draftees—and, by extension, of the white population as a whole—was 13! Previous estimates had placed it at 16. The results also indicated that almost half of all white Americans were categorized as either morons or as feeble-minded. Goddard, Yerkes, and others believed, based on the test results, that blacks had a lower level of measured intelligence than whites, as did immigrants from Mediterranean countries such as Italy and Latin countries such as Mexico. Only Northern European immigrants had IQs as high as white Americans.

These findings raised many questions. How could a democratic form of government survive if the populace was so stupid? Should groups with low IQs be allowed to vote? Should the government refuse entry to immigrants from low-IQ countries? How could the notion that all people were created equal continue to be meaningful?

Sober and responsible psychologists responded by charging that the tests themselves were at fault and in time the controversy faded, only to be revived in the 1970s with allegations of innate differences between whites and blacks based on their performance on intelligence tests. Since that time, psychologists have worked to develop tests that are freer of cultural and educational bias and that more accurately assess human abilities. There remains a great practical need for tests, and testing for selection, counseling, and diagnostic purposes continues to represent a major segment of applied psychology.

Industrial/Organizational Psychology

Psychology applied to the world of work can be traced back to 1895. In that year, Harlow Gale, a psychologist at the University of Minnesota, conducted research on the effectiveness of advertisements. Credit for fathering industrial psychology, however, is usually given to Walter Dill Scott, a student of Wundt's, who published *The Psychology of Advertising* in 1908. This was the first book to deal with psychology and some aspect of business. Scott also directed his attention to problems of personnel selection and ways to increase worker efficiency. In 1916 he became the first professor of applied psychology with his appointment at the Carnegie Institute of Technology in Pittsburgh, Pennsylvania.

Scott volunteered his services to the United States Army during World War I and developed a rating scale for selecting captains, based on scales he had developed for rating business leaders. By the end of the war Scott had evaluated the job qualifications of three million soldiers, and his work provided another highly publicized example of the practical worth of psychology.

After the war, business, industry, and government vied for the services of psychologists to revamp their personnel procedures and to introduce psychological tests as selection devices. In 1919 Scott formed his own company (called, imaginatively, the Scott Company), which provided consulting services to more than 40 corporations in selection and in techniques for increasing efficiency. Two years later James McKeen Cattell established the Psychological Corporation, a consulting firm to promote the application of psychology to the business world.

A second book dealing with industrial psychology had appeared in 1913. *Psychology and Industrial Efficiency*, written by Hugo Münsterberg, the German psychologist brought to Harvard by William James, was concerned with employee selection, the design of the work environment, and the application of psychology to the problem of how to increase sales. At the outbreak of World War I, Münsterberg was ostracized because of his outspoken support of the German cause. When he died in 1916, psychology lost one of its most important figures.

The primary focus of industrial psychology during the 1920s was the proper selection and placement of job applicants, matching the right individual with the right job. The scope of the field broadened considerably in 1927 with the start of the most famous series of studies ever conducted in industrial psychology. Called the Hawthorne studies, because they were undertaken at the Hawthorne, Illinois, plant of the Western Electric Company, this research took the field beyond selection and placement to the more complex problems of human relations, motivation, and morale.

The research began as a straightforward investigation of the effects of the physical work environment on worker efficiency (Roethlisberger & Dickson, 1939). The results were astounding to the psychologists and the plant managers. It was found that the social and psychological conditions of the work environment were much more important than the physical conditions under which the work was performed. The Hawthorne studies opened up new areas of exploration into such factors as the quality and nature of leadership, the informal groups that workers formed among themselves, the workers' attitudes toward their jobs, communications between labor and management, and a host of other social-psychological forces capable of influencing, even determining, employee efficiency, motivation, and job satisfaction.

World War II brought more than 2000 psychologists directly into the war effort. As in World War I, their major contribution was the testing, screening, and classifying of millions of recruits, although far more sophisticated tests had by then been devised. The increasingly complex weapons of war required more complex human skills for their operation, and the need to identify persons who possessed the ability to learn these skills resulted in the refinement of selection and training procedures.

Hugo Münsterberg
(1863–1916) was
influential in promoting
both industrial and
clinical psychology.

These weapons systems also spawned a new specialty within industrial psychology called engineering psychology (also known as human engineering, human factors engineering, and ergonomics). Working closely with engineers, engineering psychologists supply information about human capabilities and limitations for operating complex equipment such as high-speed aircraft. Their input affects the design of the equipment to make it more compatible with the people who have to use it. Engineering psychologists today work not only on military hardware but also on the design of consumer products such as computer keyboards, office furniture, and automobile dashboard displays.

Since the 1950s business leaders have become more aware of the influence of motivation, leadership, and other psychological factors on job performance. These aspects of the work environment have assumed greater importance along with the recognition of the impact of the entire social-psychological climate in which work takes place. Psychologists today study the nature of different types of organizations, their patterns and styles of communication, and the formal and informal social structures they produce to determine the effects on employee behavior. So significant is this emphasis on organizational variables that in 1970 the Division of Industrial Psychology of the American Psychological Association became the Division of Industrial and Organizational Psychology (now the Society for Industrial and Organizational Psychology).

Clinical Psychology

The field of clinical psychology, the application of psychology to the assessment and treatment of abnormal behavior, began fewer than 20 years after Wilhelm Wundt founded psychology as a science. It was begun by a former student of Wundt's, Lightner Witmer, who received his Ph.D. from Leipzig in 1892. Witmer, an American, replaced Cattell at the University of Pennsylvania when Cattell went to Columbia. In 1896 Witmer founded a psychological clinic at the University of Pennsylvania, the first such clinic in the United States. He also offered the first college course on the subject, coined the term "clinical psychology," and started the first journal, which he edited for 29 years (Garfield, 1985).

Two books provided an early impetus to the field. *A Mind That Found Itself* (1908), written by Clifford Beers, a former mental patient, became immensely popular and focused attention on the need to deal more humanely with the mentally ill. The book stimulated the growth of the mental hygiene movement. Hugo Münsterberg's *Psychotherapy* (1909), also widely read, detailed techniques for treating a variety of mental disorders ranging from drug addiction to phobias. The book promoted clinical psychology by showing specific ways disturbed persons could be helped.

The first child guidance clinic was established in 1909 by William Healey, a Chicago psychiatrist. Many more such clinics followed throughout the country. Their purpose was to treat childhood disorders early so they would not develop into more serious disturbances in adulthood. The clinics were the first to use the team approach in which all aspects of a patient's problems were dealt with by psychologists, psychiatrists, and social workers.

Also influential, of course, in the development of clinical psychology was the work of Sigmund Freud. His visit to Clark University in 1909 received widespread attention. As noted in Chapter 13, more than 200 books had been published on Freud by 1920 and the lay public had become fascinated by psychoanalysis. His work provided clinical psychologists with their first psychological techniques of therapy.

Despite these influences, clinical psychology advanced slowly. As late as 1940 it was still a minor part of psychology. There were few treatment facilities for disturbed adults and, consequently, few job opportunities for clinical psychologists. There were not even any educational programs specifically to train clinical psychologists, and their duties were limited, in general, to the administration of tests (Garfield, 1985).

The situation changed abruptly in 1941 with the entry of the United States into World War II. It was that event more than any other that made clinical psychology the large and dynamic applied specialty area it has since become. During the war the army established training programs for several hundred clinical psychologists who were needed to treat a variety of emotional disturbances among military personnel.

After the war the need for clinical psychologists was even greater. The Veterans Administration (VA), responsible for thousands of disabled veterans, funded graduate programs at several universities and paid students in return for their work at VA hospitals and clinics. Since then, clinical psychologists have found employment in mental health centers, schools, and industry, as well as in private practice. By 1980 clinical psychology had become the largest of all the applied areas of psychology with 35 percent of all Ph.D. students enrolled in the field (Stapp & Fulcher, 1982).

WOMEN IN THE HISTORY OF PSYCHOLOGY

More than 25 percent of the psychologists in the United States are women, yet we have only touched on the work of such notables as Margaret Floy Washburn, Mary Whiton Calkins, Mary Cover Jones, Bluma Zeigarnik, Anna Freud, and Karen Horney. There are sound historical reasons why, as Florence Denmark put it, "women have been unrecognized, undervalued, and invisible in [psychology's] recorded history" (Denmark, 1980, p. 1057). One reason is that women faced restrictions, discrimination, and inequities in graduate schools for many years. Recall the example of Washburn who, because she was a woman, could not be admitted to Columbia University. "Prior to the early 1890s, very few graduate programs in any field were open to women, and none of the institutions granting doctoral degrees in psychology admitted women as degree candidates" (Furumoto & Scarborough, 1986).

A major cause of these restrictions and another form of discrimination women faced was society's belief in the intellectual superiority of men. Even if women were provided with opportunities equal to those for men, so proponents of this view believed, their innate intellectual deficits would prevent them from being equally productive. Many prominent psychologists agreed with this view including Hall, Thorndike, Cattell, and Freud. Even today this belief has not completely disappeared.

Another reason why the contributions of women to psychology have been underrecognized lies in the nature of the areas to which they have been largely restricted. Consider universities, which, until recently, were the major employers of psychologists. In many fields it was difficult for women to be hired as faculty members until such discrimination was declared unlawful. Even so, women continue to face indirect forms of discrimination in hiring, promotion, and tenure decisions at some colleges and universities.

Because they were effectively locked out of university jobs for so long, women found employment in certain of the applied fields, notably, the helping professions, clinical and counseling psychology, child guidance, and educational psychology. Jobs in these nonacademic settings, unlike college teaching, usually do not provide the time or the

Leta Stetter Hollingworth (1886–1939) refuted widely accepted notions of female inferiority and suggested that women were constrained more by social than biological factors.

financial support for conducting research and for writing articles and books, the primary vehicles for establishing professional visibility. Thus, in these settings, one's contributions are rarely known beyond the walls of the institution in which one works.

Even women in colleges and universities who were able to publish faced another obstacle that deprived them of recognition as *women* psychologists. The method of documentation, the way in which authors' names are listed in professional publications, can make it impossible to determine the authors' sex. When only a last name and the initial of the first name are given, readers may tend to assume that the author is a man. Thus, the recognition of the contributions to psychology made by women as a group is likely to be less than it should be.

Further, "we will probably never know how much work was done by women but credited to men: how many footnotes of appreciation should rightfully have been co-authorship, how many times junior authorship should have been senior authorship, or how many times it was the male coauthor who should have received the footnote" ([Maxine] Bernstein & [Nancy] Russo, 1974, p. 131).

Historians of psychology have begun to correct such injustices. There has developed a greater sensitivity to and recognition of the work of women psychologists. Where women have been given opportunities equal to those of men, they have made major contributions to the field.

In addition to advancing psychology as a science and profession, women psychologists have contributed to the growing body of literature on the psychology of women. Although that topic is beyond the scope of this book, the pioneering efforts of Leta Stetter Hollingworth (1886–1939) should be mentioned.

When Hollingworth received her Ph.D. from Columbia in 1916, she had already published significant work on the psychology of women. She conducted extensive empirical research on what was called the variability hypothesis, the idea that in terms of both physical and intellectual abilities, women were a more homogeneous group than men. Because men showed greater variation and thus were more likely to exhibit above-average and superior abilities, they would obviously benefit from diverse educational and career opportunities. Women, being more alike and more clustered in the average range of abilities, need only be educated for domestic duties.

Hollingworth's data refuted the variability hypothesis and other notions of female inferiority. She also found that the female menstrual cycle was not related to any performance decrements in perceptual and motor skills or intellectual abilities. Her work challenged the idea that women could find satisfaction only through motherhood and that the desire to achieve in other fields was somehow abnormal. She suggested that social attitudes rather than biological characteristics kept women from contributing more as members of society (Benjamin, 1975; Shields, 1975). Thus, Hollingworth, who advanced these ideas in the period from 1913 into the 1930s, must be recognized as a precursor to contemporary thinking on the psychology of women.

HUMANISTIC PSYCHOLOGY: THE THIRD FORCE

In the early 1960s a movement developed in American psychology known as *humanistic psychology*, or the third force. It was not intended to be a revised or adapted form of a current school of thought as was the case with some of the neo-Freudian and neo-Skinnerian positions. Instead, as the term "third force" implies, humanistic psychology wanted to replace behaviorism and psychoanalysis, the two major forces in psychology.

Although humanistic psychology is a relatively recent development in the history of psychology, its presence cannot be ignored because it already has its own history. It is approximately three decades old, a significant period of time in a discipline that itself is only a little more than 100 years old. We shall examine the historical antecedents and contemporary nature of humanistic psychology and discuss the work of two proponents, Abraham Maslow and Carl Rogers.

Historical Antecedents of Humanistic Psychology

The basic themes of humanistic psychology, like those of all movements, had been recognized and called for in earlier times. The essential points were an emphasis on conscious experience; a belief in the wholeness of human nature and conduct; a focus on free will, spontaneity, and the creative power of the individual; and the study of all that is relevant to the human condition. These ideas can be found, at least in part, in the works of earlier psychologists.

Consider Franz Brentano (Chapter 4), an opponent of Wundt and a precursor of Gestalt psychology. Brentano criticized the natural science, mechanistic, reductionist approach to psychology and proposed that psychology study consciousness as an active, molar quality rather than as a passive, molecular content. Oswald Külpe demonstrated that not all conscious experience could be reduced to elementary form or be explained in terms of responses to stimuli. William James argued against the mechanistic approach to psychology and urged a focus on consciousness and the whole individual.

The Gestalt psychologists believed that psychology should take a molar approach to consciousness, and in the face of the primacy of behaviorism, they continued to insist that conscious experience was a legitimate and profitable area of study for psychology. Another view is that there is such a strong similarity between humanistic psychology and Gestalt psychology that there is no reason to give the newer movement a new name. The label "Gestalt" is adequate to describe the themes encompassed by humanistic psychology (Wertheimer, 1978).

There are several antecedents of the humanistic position in psychoanalysis. Adler, Horney, Erikson, and Allport opposed Freud's view that personality is determined by biological forces and past events. They also disagreed with Freud's notion that people are ruled by unconscious forces. These dissenters from orthodox psychoanalysis believed us to be primarily conscious beings who possess spontaneity and free will, and who are influenced by the present and future at least as much as by the past. They credited personality with the creative power to shape itself.

As with other movements in modern psychology, the *Zeitgeist* seems to be largely responsible for turning antecedents into an actual movement. Humanistic psychology appeared to be reflecting the unrest and disaffection voiced by young people in the 1960s against the mechanistic and materialistic aspects of contemporary Western culture. Humanistic psychologists implied that behaviorism, if not antihuman, was ahuman, and they resisted the conception of human beings as animals who functioned in a deterministic fashion in response to the environment or to childhood experiences.

Many social critics noted that Western (particularly American) culture had dehumanized, depersonalized, and deindividualized human beings to the extent that people were regarded as infinitesimal parts of an immense societal machine. It was suggested that people were no longer viewed as humans but as personnel, data, or averages. As individuals, we were seen to have a diminished sense of personal identity and a lessened ability to shape our own lives. Society, through the giant bureaucracies, molded our destinies to a greater and greater extent. We were growing increasingly estranged from society and from ourselves, regimented, controlled, computerized, manipulated, alienated, numbered, and helpless. We seemed to possess all the qualities that were ideal for the behaviorist view of humans functioning smoothly as well-ordered machines.

Voices of protest were raised against the dehumanizing forces of modern society, warning us against the dangers of an overly objective and numbered society. This *Zeitgeist* of social criticism was reflected in the humanistic psychologists' plea for the study of people as human beings rather than as machines.

The Nature of Humanistic Psychology

We have said that every new movement has used its older opponent, the establishment, as a base against which to push to gain its own momentum. In practical terms, the new viewpoint needs to state clearly, articulately, and loudly the weaknesses and failings of the current view. Humanistic psychology had two targets, the established forces of (1) behaviorism and (2) psychoanalysis. Before we discuss what the humanistic psychologists stand for, let us examine what they were against.

Humanistic psychologists believed that behaviorism was a narrow, artificial, and relatively sterile approach to the understanding of human nature. The emphasis on overt behavior was dehumanizing, reducing us "to a larger white rat or a slower computer" (Bugental, 1967, p. vii). The image provided by the stimulus–response orientation presented at best an incomplete picture of human nature and at worst an inaccurate one. Behaviorism did not come to grips with uniquely human characteristics, those subjective conscious qualities and capacities that set people apart from laboratory animals. A psychology based on discrete conditioned responses makes of the individual a mechanized organism that responds deterministically to the stimuli presented. The humanistic psychologists argued that we are much more than robots and that we cannot be objectified, quantified, and reduced to stimulus–response units. We are not empty organisms.

The humanistic psychologists believed that the vast amounts of research on overt behavior have added little to our understanding of human nature. "We are offered beautifully executed, precise, elegant experiments which, in at least half the cases, have nothing to do with enduring human problems" (Maslow, 1965, p. 21). Others suggested that behaviorist–experimental psychology was becoming less relevant because it continued to emulate the Galilean model of physics, which, as we shall see, had been rendered obsolete. Thus, humanistic psychologists opposed the behaviorist approach, with its mechanistic, reductionist, elementist, and simplistic tendencies.

The proponents of humanistic psychology were also against the deterministic tendencies of the Freudian approach to psychology and its minimization of the role of consciousness. The Freudians were criticized for studying only disturbed individuals: neurotics and psychotics. If psychology focused only on mental illness, how could we learn anything about our positive qualities and characteristics? By disregarding such attributes as joy, satisfaction, contentment, ecstasy, kindness, and generosity and concentrating on the dark side of the human personality, psychology ignored distinctly human strengths and virtues.

Thus it was in response to the narrow, ahuman, and sterile psychology promoted by both behaviorism and psychoanalysis that the humanistic psychologists advanced their alternative, the third force in psychology. Humanistic psychology hoped to be a fresh orientation, a new framework or attitude toward psychology, rather than a new school of thought. Its protagonists, like the founders of functionalism, did not wish to begin a new school but rather to reshape the prevailing forces in psychology and to build upon them. The study of overt behavior and the mentally ill are vital to an understanding of human nature, but in themselves they are insufficient to define psychology completely. J. F. T. Bugental, the first president of the American Association for Humanistic Psychology, founded in 1962, described the movement in this way:

> Humanistic psychology has as its ultimate goal the preparation of a complete description of what it means to be alive as a human being. . . . Such a complete description would necessarily include an inventory of man's native endowment; his potentialities of feeling, thought, and action; his growth, evolution, and decline; his interaction with various environing conditions . . . the range and variety of experience possible to him; and his meaningful place in the universe. (1967, p. 7)

All aspects of uniquely human experience come under the purview of the humanistic psychologist: love, hate, fear, hope, happiness, humor, affection, responsibility, and the meaning of life. These aspects of human existence are not treated in many modern textbooks of psychology because they are not amenable to operational definition, quantification, and laboratory manipulation.

In a paper published to advance the new movement (Bugental, 1967), Bugental noted six fundamental points that distinguish humanistic psychology from behaviorism.

1. An adequate understanding of human nature cannot be based exclusively or even largely on research findings from animals. A psychology based on animal data excludes human processes and experiences.

2. Research problems in psychology must be meaningful in terms of human existence and not selected solely on the basis of their suitability for laboratory investigation and quantification. Many topics not amenable to experimental treatment have been ignored.

3. Attention should be focused on subjective internal experiences instead of the elements of overt behavior. It is not necessary to discard overt behavior as a subject of study, but it should not be the only subject of investigation.

4. The continuing and mutual influence of the so-called pure psychology and applied psychology should be recognized. The attempt to divorce them is detrimental to both.

5. Psychology should be concerned with the individual case instead of the average performance of groups. The emphasis on groups ignores the atypical, the exceptional case, the person who deviates from the average.

6. Psychology should seek that which may enrich human experience.

If these attempts to define goals and techniques seem vague, then they adequately represent the nature of humanistic psychology. It is easier to describe what humanistic psychologists are against than what they are for or how they hope to achieve their goals. This is a significant criticism of the movement. The term "humanistic psychology" has come to have many meanings and "it is highly unlikely that an explicit definition of it could be written that would satisfy even a small fraction of the people who call themselves 'humanistic psychologists'" (Wertheimer, 1978, p. 743).

In part, this imprecision may mirror the relative youth of the movement and the fact that it lacks a single leader or founder who can speak authoritatively for the position, as Watson and Freud did for their schools of thought. It may also reflect the looser structure forced upon the movement by the elusive subject matter with which it is grappling.

Humanistic Psychotherapies

Humanistic psychology, unlike the early psychoanalytic positions, focused more on psychologically healthy persons than on neurotics and psychotics. As a result, their approach to therapy is different. This aspect of humanistic psychology, called growth therapy or the human potential movement, proliferated in the 1960s and 1970s. Millions of people enrolled in encounter groups, T-groups, sensitivity sessions, and the like in schools, businesses, churches, prisons, and private centers throughout the country. These groups have declined in popularity in the 1980s.

Deriving in part from the work of Lewin (see Chapter 12), growth therapies are used with people of normal or average mental health to help them raise their levels of consciousness, relate better to themselves and to others, and release hidden potentials for creativity and development. They were designed to enhance psychological health and self-actualization, to enable people to become all they are capable of becoming.

Unfortunately, the human potential movement attracted more than its share of quacks, well-intentioned but untrained practitioners, and self-styled gurus or messiahs who did more harm than good. Evidence indicates that not only were some people not helped by encounter groups, but they may actually have been hurt. Studies of the aftereffects of participation in encounter groups revealed psychological casualty rates ranging from less than 1 percent to almost 50 percent (Hartley, Robach, & Abramowitz, 1976).

Encounter groups represented to many people what humanistic psychology was all about. Humanistic psychology is much more than sensitivity sessions, however. It is a serious study of human nature and conduct, perhaps best expressed in the work of Abraham Maslow and Carl Rogers.

Abraham Maslow (1908–1970)

Maslow has been called the spiritual father of humanistic psychology and probably did more than anyone else to spark the movement and confer on it an academic respectability. Wanting to understand the highest potentials human beings are capable of reaching, Maslow studied a small sample of the psychologically healthiest people he could find to determine how they differed from those of average or normal mental health. Out of that study he developed a theory of personality that focuses on the motivation to grow, develop, and actualize the self, to fulfill our human potentials and capabilities.

Initially, Maslow was an ardent behaviorist, convinced that the mechanistic, natural science approach provided answers to all the world's problems. A series of personal experiences—ranging from the birth of his first child to the start of World War II—plus an exposure to other approaches to the understanding of human nature (philosophy, Freudian psychoanalysis, and Gestalt psychology), persuaded him that behaviorism was too limited to be relevant to enduring human problems. Maslow was also influenced by his contact with some of the European psychologists who fled Nazi Germany and settled in the United States, namely, Alfred Adler, Karen Horney, and Max Wertheimer. His feelings of awe toward Wertheimer and toward the American anthropologist Ruth Benedict led to his first study of psychologically healthy, self-actualizing persons. They were his models of the best of human nature.

Abraham Maslow (1908–1970), the spiritual father of humanistic psychology, emphasized each person's capacity for self-actualization.

Working primarily at Brandeis University from 1951 to 1969, Maslow developed and refined his theory in a series of lucid and provocative books. He supported the sensitivity group movement and the Esalen Institute in California and became one of the most widely known psychologists of the 1960s. He was elected president of the American Psychological Association in 1967.

In Maslow's view, each person possesses an innate tendency to become *self-actualizing* (Maslow, 1970). This highest level of human existence involves the supreme development and use of all our qualities and capacities, the realization of all our potential. To become self-actualizing, it is necessary to satisfy the needs that stand lower in the *hierarchy of needs*. These needs are innate, and each must be satisfied in turn before the next need in the hierarchy emerges to motivate us. The needs in the hierarchy, in the order in which they must be satisfied, are (1) the physiological needs for food, water, air, sleep, and sex; (2) the safety needs for security, stability, order, protection, and freedom from fear and anxiety; (3) the belonging and love needs; (4) the needs for esteem from others and from oneself; and (5) the need for self-actualization.

The bulk of Maslow's research focused on the characteristics of persons who have satisfied the need for self-actualization, who are considered to be psychologically healthy. Maslow referred to them as the "growing tip" of humanity, and they include fewer than 1 percent of the population, in his view. They are free of neuroses and psychoses, almost always middle-aged or older, and models of maturation.

Maslow found that self-actualizing persons share the following characteristics: an objective perception of reality; a full acceptance of their own natures; a commitment and dedication to some kind of work; simplicity and naturalness in their behavior; a need for autonomy, privacy, and independence; mystical or peak experiences (moments of intense ecstasy, wonder, awe, and delight); empathy with and affection for all humanity; a resistance to conformity; a democratic character structure; an attitude of creativeness; and a high degree of social interest (a concept borrowed from Adler).

Maslow offered an optimistic and flattering image of human nature, a view of psychological health and fulfillment that is seen as a welcome antidote to the sickness, prejudice, and hostility that we may witness or exhibit in our daily lives. Many people found it reassuring to believe that at least some of us are capable of reaching a state of perfection.

Maslow's research method and data have been criticized on the grounds that his sample of two dozen people is too small to allow for generalization, his subjects were selected according to his own subjective criteria of psychological health, and his terms were defined ambiguously and inconsistently.

The self-actualization theory has limited empirical laboratory support. Indeed, most research has failed to support the theory. It is being applied in industry today where many executives believe that the need for self-actualization is a useful motivating force and a potential source of job satisfaction. Despite its popularity with business leaders, however, a review of the evidence shows that the theory has a low degree of scientific validity and limited applicability to the world of work (Miner, 1984).

Carl Rogers (1902–   )

Rogers is known for a popular approach to psychotherapy called client-centered or person-centered therapy. On the basis of data derived from his therapy, Rogers developed a theory of personality that focuses on a single overriding motivation that is similar to Maslow's concept of self-actualization. Rogers proposed that each person possesses an innate tendency to actualize all of the abilities and potentials of the self.

Unlike Maslow, however, Rogers's views were not formulated from the study of healthy people but from the treatment of disturbed individuals through person-centered therapy. The name of his therapy suggests something of his view of the human personality. By placing the responsibility for change on the client rather than on the therapist (as is the case in traditional psychoanalysis), Rogers assumes that people can consciously and rationally change their thoughts and behaviors from undesirable to desirable ones. He does not believe that people are controlled by unconscious forces or by childhood experiences. Personality is shaped by the present and by how we consciously perceive it.

Rogers's idea that personality can be examined and understood only in terms of our subjective experiences may reflect an incident in his own life. When he was 22 and attending a Christian student conference in China, he began to question his parents' fundamentalist religious beliefs and to develop a more liberal philosophy of life (Rogers, 1967). He became convinced that people must depend on their own experience and that they can consciously improve themselves, concepts that were to become cornerstones of his personality theory. Over the course of an active career, Rogers has developed his theory of personality and approach to psychotherapy, expressing them through a number of popular articles, papers, and books.

Rogers believes that the major motivating force in personality is the actualization of the self (Rogers, 1961). Although this urge toward self-actualization is innate, it can be helped or hindered by childhood experiences and learning. Rogers emphasizes the importance of the mother–child relationship as it affects the child's growing sense of self. If the mother satisfies the infant's need for love, which Rogers calls *positive regard*, then the infant will tend to become a healthy personality.

When the mother makes her love for the child conditional on proper behavior (*conditional positive regard*), then the child will internalize the mother's attitude and develop *conditions of worth*. In this situation, the child feels a sense of self only under certain conditions, and comes to avoid those behaviors that bring disapproval from the mother. As a result, the self is not allowed to develop fully because all of its aspects cannot be expressed.

Thus, the primary requisite for the development of psychological health is the receipt of *unconditional positive regard* in infancy, when the mother demonstrates her full love and acceptance of the child regardless of the child's behavior. In this case, the child will not develop conditions of worth and therefore will not have to repress any aspects of the emerging self. Only in this way can a state of self-actualization be reached.

To achieve self-actualization is to reach the highest level of psychological health, a process Rogers calls *fully functioning*. It is a level of supreme development that is equal, in principle but not in content, to Maslow's state of self-actualization. The theories differ on the characteristics of psychologically healthy or fully functioning persons.

To Rogers, fully functioning persons are characterized by an openness to all experience, a tendency to live fully in every moment of existence, an ability to be guided by trust in their own instincts about a situation rather than by reason or by the opinions of others, a sense of freedom in thought and action, and a high degree of creativity (Rogers, 1961).

In terms of general popularity and influence in psychology, Rogers's person-centered approach to psychotherapy has had more of an impact than his theory of personality. Nevertheless, the theory has been well received, particularly its emphasis on the importance of the self. Criticism has been directed at the lack of specificity in stating the nature of the innate potentiality to actualization, and at the emphasis on subjective, conscious experiences to the exclusion of possible unconscious influences.

Rogers's theory and therapy have generated an enormous amount of supportive research and have been widely used in the clinical setting. As a method of treatment, person-centered therapy is as popular as Freudian psychoanalysis. Rogers has also been influential in the human potential movement, which his views support. His work, like that of Maslow, was a major part of the growing movement to humanize psychology.

The Status of Humanistic Psychology

Humanistic psychology displayed early in its development the same characteristics we have seen in other revolutionary movements. Its members were vocal in pointing out the weaknesses of the older positions. Behaviorism and psychoanalysis were both well-developed bases against which to push. Many humanistic psychologists were filled with zeal and a sense of righteousness to do battle with the evils of the establishment. The movement became formalized by the establishment of the *Journal of Humanistic Psychology* in 1961, the American Association for Humanistic Psychology in 1962, and the Division of Humanistic Psychology of the American Psychological Association in 1971.

Thus, the characteristics of an establishment, with the distinguishing traits of a formal school of thought, were in evidence. Humanistic psychologists offered their own definition of psychology, distinct from the definitions offered by the two major forces in contemporary psychology, and their own subject matter, methods, journals, associations, meetings, and terminology. Above all, they possessed what every other school of thought boasted in its early days, a passionate conviction that their path was the best one for psychology to follow.

Despite all these symbols and characteristics of a school of thought, humanistic psychology did not actually become a school. That was the judgment of humanistic psychologists themselves, expressed when they met in 1985 to discuss the nature of the field nearly three decades after it began. "Humanistic psychology was a great experiment," one said, "but it is basically a failed experiment in that there is no humanistic school of thought in psychology, no theory that would be recognized as a philosophy of science" (Cunningham, 1985, p. 18).

Carl Rogers agreed. "Humanistic psychology has not had a significant impact on mainstream psychology," he said. "We are perceived as having relatively little importance" (Cunningham, 1985, p. 16). Rogers told his supporters that if they wanted evidence to prove his statement they had only to examine any introductory psychology textbook. There they would find the same topics that characterized psychology a quarter of a century ago, with little mention of the whole person.

What has been the impact of humanistic psychology? Why did it not, like earlier movements, become part of the mainstream of psychological thought? One reason is that most humanistic psychologists are in private clinical practice rather than universities. Consequently, they have not conducted as much research as academic psychologists, or published as many papers, or, more important, trained new generations of graduate students to carry on their tradition.

Another reason has to do with the timing of their protest. In their peak years, the 1960s and the early 1970s, humanistic psychologists may have been arguing against positions that were no longer as dominant as they once had been. The humanistic psychologists opposed Freudian psychoanalysis and Skinnerian behaviorism at a time when both schools had been tempered or weakened by divisiveness within their own ranks. Both were already changing in the direction the humanistic psychologists were urging. By the 1960s, for example, psychoanalysis was characterized by many different points of view, some incorporating the idea of persons consciously and freely choosing to shape their own lives. These positions were far removed from orthodox Freudian psychoanalysis, which Maslow and others were so vocally attacking.

Behaviorism was also changing in the 1960s as theorists introduced various ideas about cognitive factors. This development took behaviorism far beyond the position of Skinner, which the humanistic psychologists were criticizing. Like the Gestalt psychologists when they first came to the United States, the humanistic psychologists in the 1960s were protesting against movements that were no longer dominant in their original forms.

Although humanistic psychology has not transformed psychology as a whole, it has contributed to the shift away from Freud among the psychoanalysts. It reinforced the growing recognition of consciousness and helped to foster methods of therapy that emphasize self-actualization and fulfillment, personal responsibility and freedom of choice, and the consideration of the person in the total context of his or her family, work, and social environments. The humanistic movement may also have helped to reinforce the developing recognition of consciousness on the part of academic psychologists because it was contemporaneous with the cognitive movement.

The Association for Humanistic Psychology has some 5000 members, not all of whom are psychologists, and the movement is still calling for a psychology that focuses on expanding and enriching all human experience.

THE COGNITIVE MOVEMENT IN PSYCHOLOGY

"Psychology," John B. Watson wrote in his behaviorist manifesto of 1913, "must discard all reference to consciousness." This was a strong and highly successful appeal. The many psychologists who followed Watson eliminated from psychology the mind, conscious processes, and mentalistic terms. The result was that "psychology, having first bargained away its soul and then gone out of its mind, seems now, as it faces an untimely end, to have lost all consciousness" (Burt, 1962, p. 229).

Words like "will," "feeling," "image," "mind," and "consciousness" were effectively banned from psychology. They became taboo, never to be uttered by behaviorists except in tones of derision. And so Skinner could talk about the empty organism and build an influential system of psychology that never attempted to investigate what might be going on inside that organism. For decades introductory textbooks in psychology did not contain any reference to the mind or to consciousness. Psychology had indeed lost consciousness, forever, it appeared.

Suddenly—or so it seemed, although it had been building gradually for some time— there was ample and visible evidence that psychology was prepared to regain consciousness. The taboo words were being uttered aloud in the forums from which they had been so vehemently excluded for so long. In 1979, in the *American Psychologist*, the official journal of the American Psychological Association, there appeared an article entitled "Behaviorism and the Mind: A (Limited) Call for a Return to Introspection" (Lieberman, 1979). Not only did the author use the word "mind," but he also mentioned in the title that suspect technique of introspection. A few months earlier the same journal contained an article with a one-word title—"Consciousness"—blatantly and openly displayed. "After decades of deliberate neglect," the author wrote, "consciousness is again coming under scientific scrutiny, with discussions of the topic appearing at entirely respectable locations in psychology's literature" (Natsoulas, 1978, p. 906).

In his presidential address to the American Psychological Association in 1976, Wilbert J. McKeachie told the assembled audience that our conception of psychology is changing and that the change involves a return to consciousness. As a result, McKeachie said, psychology's image of human nature is becoming "*human* rather than mechanical" (McKeachie, 1976, p. 831).

When an officer of the American Psychological Association and a prestigious journal discuss consciousness so openly and optimistically, we might suspect that a new movement, another revolution in psychology, is under way. And when introductory textbooks in psychology now define the field as "the science that studies behavior and mental processes" (Hilgard, Atkinson, & Atkinson, 1975, p. 12), and "the science that systematically studies and attempts to explain observable behavior and its relationship to the unseen mental processes that go on inside the organism" (Kagan & Havemann, 1972, p. 9), we realize how far contemporary psychology has moved beyond the desires of Watson and Skinner.

Like all movements in psychology, the cognitive revolution did not spring up overnight. It formally began around 1960, but early, though weak, signs first appeared in the 1930s. One of the earliest proponents was E. R. Guthrie (see Chapter 11), who for most of his career was an ardent behaviorist. Toward the end of his life he came to deplore the mechanistic model of psychology and argued that stimuli cannot always be reduced to physical terms. Nor, he said, can overt responses always be reduced to physical "movement in space." We must describe the stimuli with which psychology deals in perceptual or cognitive terms so that they will "have meaning for the responding organism" (Guthrie, 1959, p. 17). Psychologists cannot deal with "meaning" solely in strict behaviorist terms, because it is a mentalistic or conscious process.

E. C. Tolman (Chapter 11), with his purposive behaviorism (a molar approach) is another precursor to the cognitive movement. His form of behaviorism made ample recognition of the importance of cognitive variables. His emphasis on intervening variables as a way of operationally defining internal, unobservable states; his use of cognitive maps; and his attribution of purpose to animals all helped to contribute to the decline of the stimulus–response approach to behaviorism and the rise of interest in cognitive factors.

A positivist philosopher, Rudolf Carnap, called, in 1956, for a return to introspection, noting that "a person's awareness of his own state of imagining, feeling, etc., must be recognized as a kind of observation, in principle not different from external observation, and therefore as a legitimate source of knowledge" (Koch, 1964, p. 22). Even P. W. Bridgman (1959), the physicist who gave psychology the notion of operational definitions that is so compatible with behaviorism (see Chapter 11), later renounced behaviorism and insisted that introspective reports from the individual subject be invoked to make meaningful operational analyses.

To some psychologists, Gestalt psychology is a precursor of the cognitive movement. "Present-day cognitive psychology—with its emphasis on organization, structure, relationships, the active role of the subject, and the important part played by perception in learning and memory—reflects the influence of its Gestalt antecedents" (Hearst, 1979, p. 32). It can be argued that Gestalt psychology certainly helped to keep alive at least a peripheral interest in consciousness during the years when the behaviorist position was dominant.

Psychologist Jerome Bruner was active in fomenting the cognitive revolution in the 1950s and 1960s. In 1956 he and two colleagues published *A Study of Thinking*, which helped to persuade psychologists that the higher mental processes, the conscious processes, could be studied experimentally (Bruner, Goodnow, & Austin, 1956).

In 1960 Bruner and George Miller started the Center for Cognitive Studies at Harvard. In addition to fostering research on cognitive variables, the center helped to revive interest in the work of the Swiss developmental psychologist Jean Piaget (1896–1980). Piaget had described the development of the child not in psychosexual or psychosocial stages but in terms of cognitive stages of growth. His emphasis on cognition, once relatively ignored by American psychologists, was welcomed by proponents of the cognitive movement.

By the early 1970s cognitive psychology had attracted so many followers that its own journals had become necessary. Within a decade, six new journals were started: *Cognitive Psychology* (1970), *Cognition* (1971), *Memory and Cognition* (1973), *Journal of Mental Imagery* (1977), *Cognitive Therapy and Research* (1977), and *Cognitive Science* (1977).

As with all historical events, looking at the cognitive movement in retrospect yields the impression of an orderly and rapid transition—indeed, a revolution—that shook the foundations of the psychological world in a few short years. At the time, of course, such was not apparent. The progression of history is only clear after the event.

The Influence of the *Zeitgeist*

When we find such a dramatic change in the evolution of a science, it is instructive to look for antecedent changes in the *Zeitgeist* in which the science functions. As we have seen, a science, like a living species, changes in response to new demands and conditions in its environment.

What was the *Zeitgeist* that led to the cognitive revolution, that dictated a tempering of behaviorism by the readmission of consciousness? We may look to the *Zeitgeist* in physics, a role model for psychology, which has influenced the field since its beginnings as a science. Around the beginning of the twentieth century a new viewpoint developed in physics as the result of the work of Albert Einstein, Neils Bohr, Werner Heisenberg, and others. The approach resulted in the rejection of the Galilean–Newtonian mechanistic model of the universe. It was from that model that psychology drew its mechanistic, reductionist, lawful, and predictable view of human nature expounded by psychologists from Wundt to Skinner. As a result of the new work in physics, the classical Galilean world of total objectivity and the complete separation of the external world from the observer was discarded. There was a new model with important implications for psychology.

Physicists came to recognize that we cannot observe the course of nature without disturbing it. The artificial gap between the observer and the observed—the inner world and the outer world, the world of conscious experience and the world of matter posited in the work of Descartes and in Locke's primary and secondary qualities—was thus bridged. The focus of scientific investigation shifted from an independent and objectively knowable universe to our observation of the universe. Modern scientists, no longer detached from the focus of their observation, became instead participant–observers.

The ideal of a totally objective reality was seen as unattainable. Today, physics is characterized by the belief that what we call objective knowledge is actually subjective in that it is dependent on the observer. All knowledge, therefore, is "personal knowledge" (Polanyi, 1958). It is a position that sounds suspiciously like what Berkeley proposed some 200 years ago; that all knowledge is subjective because it is dependent on the person perceiving it (see Chapter 2).

Another writer described the situation in the following terms. Our picture of the world, "far from being a genuine photographic reproduction of an independent reality 'out there,' [is] rather more on the order of a painting: a subjective creation of the mind which can convey a likeness but can never produce a replica" (Matson, 1964, p. 137).

Physicists' rejection of an objective, machinelike subject matter and their recognition of subjectivity restored the vital role of conscious experience in obtaining knowledge of the world. The revolution in physics was an effective argument for the acceptance of consciousness as a legitimate part of the subject matter of psychology.

Scientific psychology successfully resisted the model of the new physics for about a half-century, clinging to an outdated model of science by considering itself to be an objective science of behavior. But psychology has since responded to the *Zeitgeist* and has modified its form.

The Role of the Computer

Clocks and automata served in the seventeenth century as metaphors for the mechanical view of the universe and by extension for the mind as well (see Chapter 2). Those machines were readily available and easily understood models for the way in which the mind was said to operate. Today the mechanical model of the universe and the behaviorist form of psychology that derived from it have been superseded by other points of view—the new look in physics and the cognitive movement in psychology.

It is apparent that the clock is no longer a useful example for the twentieth-century view of the mind. A new metaphor is needed and a twentieth-century machine has emerged to serve as a model: the computer. Today the computer is used increasingly as an explanation for cognitive phenomena. Indeed, the advance of computer technology has been a major source of influence on the development of cognitive psychology.

Computer programs, which are essentially sets of instructions for dealing with symbols, can be said to operate similarly to the human mind. Both the computer and the mind receive and digest large amounts of information (stimuli) from the environment. They process this information, manipulating, storing, and retrieving it, and acting on it in various ways. Thus, computer programming is the pattern for the cognitive view of human information processing, problem solving, and reasoning.

It is the program and not the computer itself—the software, not the hardware—that serves us as the metaphor for the operation of the human mind. In the same way, cognitive psychologists are interested in the sequence of symbol manipulation that underlies thought rather than in the physiological correlates of thought. Again, the software not the hardware. The goal of the cognitive psychologist is to discover that "library of programs the human has stored away in memory—programs that enabled the person to understand and produce sentences, to commit certain experiences and rules to memory, and to solve novel problems" (Howard, 1983, p. 11).

This information-processing view of the human mind can be said to underlie cognitive psychology. In its 100-year history, psychology has moved from clocks to computers as models for its subject matter. But it is significant that in both the older and the newer views the metaphors remain machines. We are left to wonder about the prescience of La Mettrie who announced in the eighteenth century that man was a machine. Perhaps the expression "the more things change, the more they remain the same," contains a lesson about history for those who try to learn from it.

The Nature of Cognitive Psychology

We saw in Chapter 11 how the cognitive revolution in the form of Bandura's socio-behavioristic approach has tempered the nature of American behaviorism. It is not only in behaviorist psychology, however, that the cognitive revolution has had an impact. Cognitive factors have influenced many other areas of the field: attribution theory in social psychology; the information-processing approach to decision making and problem solving, learning, memory, and perception; motivation and emotion; and personality. In these areas, as well as in applied areas such as clinical, community, industrial and organizational, and school psychology, there is an increasing emphasis on cognitive factors. "The various subspecialties of psychology are once again approaching psychology with concepts that offer hope not only of communication and integration of psychology, but also of understanding the whole person as a cognitive, conative, affective, biological, and social individual" (McKeachie, 1976, p. 819).

Cognitive psychology differs from behaviorism on several points. First, cognitive psychologists focus on the process of knowing, not simply responding to stimuli. The emphasis clearly is on mental processes and events, not on stimulus–response connections; on the mind rather than on behavior. This does not mean that cognitive psychologists ignore behavior. What it does mean is that behavioral responses are not the sole object of research. Responses are used as sources for inference about the mental processes that accompany them.

Second, cognitive psychologists are interested in the mind's structuring or organizing of experience. The Gestalt psychologists as well as Piaget argued that the tendency to organize conscious experience (sensations and perceptions) into meaningful wholes and patterns is innate. Thus, the mind gives form and coherence to mental experience, and it is this process of organizing that is the subject matter of cognitive psychology. The British empiricists and associationists and their twentieth-century derivatives (the Skinnerian behaviorists) hold that the mind possesses no such inherent organizational ability.

Third, in the cognitive view the individual is actively and creatively organizing the stimuli received from the environment. We are capable of participating in the acquisition and use of knowledge, deliberately attending to some aspects of experience and choosing to commit others to memory. People are not passive responders to external forces or blank slates on which sensory experience will write. You will recognize the latter idea as the dominant behaviorist position in psychology derived from the empiricists and associationists.

As we noted, few areas of psychology today have escaped the cognitive onslaught. Psychologists working in the areas of perception, memory, and learning have reinterpreted these processes in terms of information processing. Cognitive explanations of behavior can be found, for example, in Festinger's theory of cognitive dissonance (Festinger, 1957), Witkin's perception-based cognitive styles of personality (Witkin, 1978), and research on sleep and dreams.

Experimental studies identifying rapid eye movement (REM) sleep as the stage at which most dreaming occurs provide an excellent example of how to combine objective physiological data with subjective conscious data. Remembered dreams are conscious products. Their demonstrated relationship to the underlying physiological processes makes such subjective data more acceptable to psychology today. These consciously recalled experiences would not have been allowed within the strict behaviorist framework.

Psychologists are now studying the effects of drugs on behavior in terms of changes both in physiological responses and in reported conscious experiences, that is, what the person does under the influence of the drug and what the person says he or she feels. These data were inadmissible to the behaviorists. Even such nonconscious processes as biofeedback, in which persons learn to control such physiological functions as heart rate, muscle tension, and body temperature, may rely more on cognitive processes than was previously supposed. Therapists using biofeedback are paying more attention to the role of their patients' plans, goals, and expectations in bringing about the physiological changes.

As conscious mental processes have returned to psychology they have fostered an increasing interest in unconscious mental processes. Recall that the unconscious had also been banned from experimental psychology by the behaviorists. Current research on selective attention, subliminal perception, and visual phenomena involving perceptual processing strongly suggests that the first stage of cognition in response to stimulation is unconscious (Shevrin & Dickman, 1980).

Consciousness is once again being attributed to animals as well as to humans. A recent book entitled *Animal Thinking* infers evidence of animal consciousness from observations of animal behavior, particularly behavior that shows adaptability to changing environmental circumstances and challenges (Griffin, 1984). The work focuses on the ability of animals to think about specific objects and events, even when those objects and events are not present, and then to initiate some action. Other work on animal cognition has investigated problems of memory, demonstrating that such cognitive processes as coding, organization, and symbolization exist in animal memory as they do in humans (Roitblat, Bever, & Terrace, 1984).

When we add to this cognitive influence in experimental psychology the emphasis on consciousness in humanistic psychology and in much of psychoanalysis since the time of Freud, we can see that consciousness has reclaimed the central position in psychology that it had 100 years ago. It has made a vigorous and substantial comeback.

Comment

The cognitive revolution has obviously been a success. Jerome Bruner described the movement as "a revolution whose limits we still cannot fathom" (Bruner, 1983, p. 274). Its influence has extended over most fields of psychology and has moved beyond the United States to encompass psychological thought in Western Europe and the Soviet Union.

No revolution, however successful, is without its critics. Most Skinnerian behaviorists oppose the cognitive movement, but even those who support it have pointed out weaknesses and limitations. They argue that the field has not yet come of age, that there are few concepts on which the majority of cognitive psychologists agree or even consider important, and that there is considerable confusion about terminology and definitions (White, 1985).

Others charge that the progress of cognitive psychology is more illusory than real because many psychologists have simply adopted the word "cognitive" without making any fundamental changes in the way they approach their research problems. Skinner noted that it has become "fashionable to insert the word 'cognitive' wherever possible" (Skinner, 1983, p. 194). George Miller, a leader of the cognitive movement, agrees.

> What seems to have happened is that many experimental psychologists who were studying human learning, perception, or thinking began to call themselves cognitive psychologists without changing in any obvious way what they had always been thinking and doing—as if they suddenly discovered they had been speaking cognitive psychology all their lives. So our victory may have been more modest than the written record would have led you to believe. (Miller, cited in Bruner, 1983, p. 126)

It is too early to judge the ultimate impact of cognitive psychology. It is not yet finished; it is not yet history. Cognitive psychology is still very much history in the making and certainly lays a legitimate claim to dominating the psychology of the 1980s. It enjoys many of the trappings and characteristics of a school of thought. Although we do not speak of "cognitivism" the way we do of "functionalism" or "behaviorism," cognitive psychology appears—through its journals, jargon, conviction, and zeal—on the threshold of becoming formalized as a school. That, after all, is the natural progression of revolutions and movements when they become successful.

If the history of psychology as portrayed in these chapters tells us anything at all, it is that when a movement becomes formalized into a school, it gains a momentum that can be stopped only by its own success in overthrowing the established position. When that happens, as we have seen, the unobstructed arteries of the once vigorous and youthful movement begin to harden. Flexibility turns to rigidity, revolutionary passion to protection of position, and eyes and minds close to new ideas. In short, a new establishment is born. And so it is in the progress of any science, an evolutionary building to ever-higher levels of development. There is no culmination but only continuing growth, as newer species evolve from older ones in the never-ending process of adapting to a continually changing environment.

SUGGESTED READINGS

Psychological Testing

Cassel, R. N. (1968). Eleven great tests that have made major contributions to measurement theory. *Psychology: A Journal of Human Behavior, 5,* 17–22.

Cronbach, L. J. (1975). Five decades of public controversy over mental testing. *American Psychologist, 30,* 1–14.

Doyle, K. O. (1974). Theory and practice of ability testing in ancient Greece. *Journal of the History of the Behavioral Sciences, 10*, 202–212.

DuBois, P. H. (1970). *A history of psychological testing.* Boston: Allyn and Bacon.

Levine, M. (1976). The academic achievement test: Its historical content and social functions. *American Psychologist, 31*, 228–238.

Samelson, F. (1977). World War I intelligence testing and the development of psychology. *Journal of the History of the Behavioral Sciences, 13*, 274–282.

Wolf, T. H. (1964). Alfred Binet: A time of crisis. *American Psychologist, 10*, 762–771.

Yerkes, R. M. (March, 1923). Testing the human mind. *Atlantic Monthly,* pp. 358–370.

Industrial/Organizational Psychology

Kappauf, W. E. (1947). History of psychological studies of the design and operation of equipment. *American Psychologist, 2*, 83–86.

Kavruck, S. (1956). Thirty-three years of test research: A short history of test development in the U.S. Civil Service Commission. *American Psychologist, 11*, 329–334.,

Kuna, D. P. (1976). The concept of suggestion in the early history of advertising psychology. *Journal of the History of the Behavioral Sciences, 12*, 347–353.

Lynch, E. C. (1968). *Walter Dill Scott: Pioneer in personnel management.* Austin: Bureau of Business Research, University of Texas.

McCollom, I. N. (1968). Industrial psychology around the world: I. America and Western Europe. *International Review of Applied Psychology, 17*, 3–16.

Moskowitz, M. J. (1977). Hugo Münsterberg: A study in the history of applied psychology. *American Psychologist, 32*, 824–842.

Münsterberg, M. (1922). *Hugo Münsterberg: His life and work.* New York: Appleton-Century-Crofts.

Clinical Psychology

Hersch, C. (1969). From mental health to social action: Clinical psychology in historical perspective. *American Psychologist, 24*, 909–916.

Levine, M., & Wishner, J. (1977). The case records of the psychological clinic at the University of Pennsylvania (1896–1961). *Journal of the History of the Behavioral Sciences, 13*, 59–66.

Nawas, M. M. (1972). Landmarks in the history of clinical psychology from its early beginnings through 1971. *Journal of Psychology, 82*, 91–110.

Riesman, J. M. (1976). *A history of clinical psychology* (2nd ed.). New York: Irvington Publishers.

Seeman, J. (1968). The psychological center: A historical note. *American Psychologist, 23*, 522–523. (About the work of Lightner Witmer).

Sexton, V. S. (1965). Clinical psychology: An historical survey. *Genetic Psychology Monographs, 72*, 401–434.

Shakow, D. (1978). Clinical psychology seen some fifty years later. *American Psychologist, 33*, 148–158.

Watson, R. I. (1953). A brief history of clinical psychology. *Psychological Bulletin, 50*, 321–346.

Watson, R. I. (1962). The experimental tradition and clinical psychology. In A. J. Bachrach (Ed.), *Experimental foundations of clinical psychology* (pp. 3–25). New York: Basic Books.

Women in the History of Psychology

Bernstein, M. D., & Russo, N. F. (1974). The history of psychology revisited: Or, up with our foremothers. *American Psychologist, 29*, 130–134.

Denmark, F. (1980). Psyche: From rocking the cradle to rocking the boat. *American Psychologist, 35*, 1057–1065.

Furumoto, L. (1979). Mary Whiton Calkins (1863–1930): Fourteenth president of the American Psychological Association. *Journal of the History of the Behavioral Sciences, 15*, 346–356.

Goodman, E. S. (1980). Margaret F. Washburn (1871–1939): First woman Ph.D. in psychology. *Psychology of Women Quarterly, 5*, 69–80.

Logan, D. D. (1980). Mary Cover Jones: Feminine as asset. *Psychology of Women Quarterly, 5*, 103–115.

O'Connell, A. N., & Russo, N. F. (Eds.). (1983). *Models of achievement: Reflections of eminent women in psychology.* New York: Columbia University Press.

Rossiter, M. W. (1982). *Women scientists in America: Struggles and strategies to 1940.* Baltimore: Johns Hopkins University Press.

Russo, N. F., & O'Connell, A. N. (1980). Models from our past: Psychology's foremothers. *Psychology of Women Quarterly, 5*, 11–54.

Shields, S. A. (1975). Ms. Pilgrim's progress: The contribution of Leta Stetter Hollingworth to the psychology of women. *American Psychologist, 30*, 852–857.

Washburn, M. F. (1932). Some recollections. In C. Murchison (Ed.), *A history of psychology in autobiography* (vol. 2, pp. 333–358). Worcester, MA: Clark University Press.

Humanistic Psychology

Bugental, J. F. T. (1964). The third force in psychology. *Journal of Humanistic Psychology, 4*, 19–26.

Child, I. L. (1973). *Humanistic psychology and the research tradition: Their several virtues.* New York: Wiley.

Goble, F. G. (1970). *The third force: The psychology of Abraham Maslow.* New York: Grossman. ·

Maslow, A. H. (1968). *Toward a psychology of being* (2nd ed.). New York: Van Nostrand Reinhold.

Maslow, A. H. (1971). *The farther reaches of human nature.* New York: Viking Press.

Misiak, H., & Sexton, V. S. (1973). *Phenomenological, existential, and humanistic psychologies: A historical survey.* New York: Grune and Stratton.

Rogers, C. R. (1961). *On becoming a person.* Boston: Houghton Mifflin.

Severin, F. T. (Ed.). (1973). *Discovering man in psychology: A humanistic approach.* New York: McGraw-Hill.

Smith, M. B. (1978). Humanism and behaviorism in psychology: Theory and practice. *Journal of Humanistic Psychology, 18*, 27–36.

Wertheimer, M. (1978). Humanistic psychology and the humane but tough-minded psychologist. *American Psychologist, 33*, 739–745.

The Cognitive Movement

Bruner, J. (1983). *In search of mind: Essays in autobiography.* New York: Harper & Row.

Burghardt, G. M. (1985). Animal awareness: Current perceptions and historical perspective. *American Psychologist, 40*, 905–919. (Relates the work of Romanes and Morgan to contemporary cognitive animal psychology).

Dember, W. N. (1974). Motivation and the cognitive revolution. *American Psychologist, 29*, 161–168.

Hilgard, E. (1980). Consciousness in contemporary psychology. *Annual Review of Psychology, 31*, 1–26.

Lieberman, D. A. (1979). Behaviorism and the mind: A (limited) call for a return to introspection. *American Psychologist, 34*, 319–333.

McKeachie, W. J. (1976). Psychology in America's bicentennial year. *American Psychologist, 31*, 819–833.

Natsoulas, T. (1978). Consciousness. *American Psychologist, 33*, 906–914.

Pagels, H. R. (1981). *The cosmic code: Quantum physics as the language of nature.* New York: Simon and Schuster.

Segal, E. M., & Lachman, R. (1972). Complex behavior or higher mental process: Is there a paradigm shift? *American Psychologist, 27*, 46–55.

Turkle, S. (1984). *The second self: Computers and the human spirit.* New York: Simon and Schuster.

References

Adler, A. (1930). Individual psychology. In C. Murchison (Ed.), *Psychologies of 1930* (pp. 395–405). Worcester, MA: Clark University Press.

Allen, G. W. (1967). *William James*. New York: Viking Press.

Allport, G. W. (1937). *Personality: A psychological interpretation*. New York: Holt.

Allport, G. W. (1968). *The person in psychology*. Boston: Beacon Press.

Anastasi, A. (1982). *Psychological testing* (5th ed.). New York: Macmillan.

Anderson, R. J. (1980). Wundt's prominence and popularity in his later years. *Psychological Research, 42*, 87–101.

Angell, J. R. (1904). *Psychology*. New York: Holt.

Angell, J. R. (1907). The province of functional psychology. *Psychological Review, 14*, 61–91.

Atkinson, J. W. (1981). Studying personality in the context of an advanced motivational psychology. *American Psychologist, 36*, 117–128.

Averill, L. A. (1982). Recollections of Clark's G. Stanley Hall. *Journal of the History of the Behavioral Sciences, 18*, 341–346.

Baldwin, B. T. (Ed.). (1980). In memory of Wilhelm Wundt. In W. G. Bringmann & R. D. Tweney (Eds.), *Wundt studies: A centennial collection* (pp. 280–308). Toronto: C. J. Hogrefe.

Bandura, A. (1977). *Social learning theory*. Englewood Cliffs, NJ: Prentice-Hall.

Bandura, A. (1982). Self-efficacy mechanism in human agency. *American Psychologist, 37*, 122–147.

Barber, B. (1961). Resistance by scientists to scientific discovery. *Science, 134*, 596–602.

Barry, H., & Blane, H. T. (1977). Birth order of alcoholics. *Journal of Individual Psychology, 62*, 62–79.

Becker, E. (1973). *The denial of death*. New York: Free Press.

Beers, C. (1908). *A mind that found itself*. London: Longmans, Green.

Bekhterev, V. M. (1932). *General principles of human reflexology*. New York: International Publishers.

Ben-David, J., & Collins, R. (1966). Social factors in the origin of a new science: The case of psychology. *American Sociological Review, 31*, 451–465.

Benjamin, L. T. (1975). The pioneering work of Leta Hollingworth in the psychology of women. *Nebraska History, 56*, 493–505.

Benjamin, L. T. (1986). Why don't they understand us? A history of psychology's public image. *American Psychologist, 41*, in press.

Berkeley, G. (1957). An essay towards a new theory of vision. In M. W. Calkins (Ed.), *Berkeley: Essay, principles, dialogues* (pp. 1–98). New York: Chas. Scribner's Sons. (Original work published 1709).

Berkeley, G. (1957). A treatise concerning the principles of human knowledge. In M. W. Calkins (Ed.), *Berkeley: Essay, principles, dialogues* (pp. 99–216). New York: Chas. Scribner's Sons. (Original work published 1710).

Berman, L. (1927). *The religion called behaviorism.* New York: Boni & Liveright.

Bernstein, M. D., & Russo, N. F. (1974). The history of psychology revisited: Or, up with our foremothers. *American Psychologist, 29*, 130–134.

Bettelheim, B. (1982). *Freud and man's soul.* New York: Alfred A. Knopf.

Binet, A. (1971). *The psychic life of micro-organisms.* West Orange, NJ: A. Saifer. (Original work published 1889).

Bjork, D. W. (1983). *The compromised scientist: William James in the development of American psychology.* New York: Columbia University Press.

Blumenthal, A. L. (1975). A reappraisal of Wilhelm Wundt. *American Psychologist, 30*, 1081–1088.

Blumenthal, A. L. (1977). Wilhelm Wundt and early American psychology: A clash of two cultures. *Annals of the New York Academy of Sciences, 291*, 13–20.

Blumenthal, A. L. (1979). Wilhelm Wundt: The founding father we never knew [Book review]. *Contemporary Psychology, 24*, 547–550.

Blumenthal, A. L. (1980). Wilhelm Wundt: Problems of interpretation. In W. G. Bringmann & R. D. Tweney (Eds.), *Wundt studies: A centennial collection* (pp. 435–445). Toronto: C. J. Hogrefe.

Boakes, R. (1984). *From Darwin to behaviourism: Psychology and the minds of animals.* Cambridge, England: Cambridge University Press.

Boas, M. (1961). *The scientific renaissance: 1450–1630.* London: Collins.

Boorstin, D. J. (1983). *The discoverers.* New York: Random House.

Boring, E. G. (1929). *A history of experimental psychology.* New York: Appleton.

Boring, E. G. (1950). *A history of experimental psychology* (2nd ed.). New York: Appleton-Century-Crofts.

Boring, E. G. (1963). *History, psychology, and science: Selected papers.* New York: Wiley.

Boring, E. G. (1967). Titchener's experimentalists. *Journal of the History of the Behavioral Sciences, 3*, 315–325.

Bottome, P. (1939). *Alfred Adler: A biography.* New York: G. P. Putnam's Sons.

Brentano, F. (1874). *Psychology from an empirical standpoint.* Leipzig: Duncker & Humblot.

Breuer, J., & Freud, S. (1895). Studies on hysteria. Leipzig and Vienna: Franz Deuticke. (In *Standard edition*, vol. 2).

Bridgman, P. W. (1927). *The logic of modern physics.* New York: Macmillan.

Bridgman, P. W. (1954). Remarks on the present state of operationism. *Scientific Monthly, 79*, 224–226.

Bridgman, P. W. (1959). *The way things are.* Cambridge, MA: Harvard University Press.

Bringmann, W. G., & Tweney, R. D. (Eds.). (1980). *Wundt studies: A centennial collection.* Toronto: C. J. Hogrefe.

Bringmann, W. G., Balance, W., & Evans, R. (1975). Wilhelm Wundt 1832–1920: A brief biographical sketch. *Journal of the History of the Behavioral Sciences, 11*, 287–297.

Bringmann, W. G., Bringmann, N. J., & Ungerer, G. A. (1980). The establishment of Wundt's laboratory: An archival and documentary study. In W. G. Bringmann & R. D. Tweney (Eds.), *Wundt studies: A centennial collection* (pp. 123–157). Toronto: C. J. Hogrefe.

Broad, W., & Wade, N. (1982). *Betrayers of the truth: Fraud and deceit in the halls of science.* New York: Simon & Schuster.

Brown, J. A. C. (1963). *Freud and the post-Freudians.* London: Cassell.

Brožek, J. (1980). The echoes of Wundt's work in the United States, 1887–1977: A quantitative citation analysis. *Psychological Research, 42,* 103–107.

Bruner, J. S. (1982, May). Psychology has been responding to the so-called post-industrial revolution. *Psychology Today,* pp. 42–43.

Bruner, J. S. (1983). *In search of mind: Essays in autobiography.* New York: Harper & Row.

Bruner, J. S., Goodnow, J. J., & Austin, G. A. (1956). *A study of thinking.* New York: Wiley.

Buckley, K. W. (1982). The selling of a psychologist: John Broadus Watson and the application of behavioral techniques to advertising. *Journal of the History of the Behavioral Sciences, 18,* 207–221.

Bugental, J. (1967). *Challenges of humanistic psychology.* New York: McGraw-Hill.

Burnham, J. (1968). On the origins of behaviorism. *Journal of the History of the Behavioral Sciences, 4,* 143–151.

Burt, C. (1962). The concept of consciousness. *British Journal of Psychology, 53,* 229–242.

Carr, H. A. (1925). *Psychology.* New York: Longmans, Green.

Carr, H. A. (1930). Functionalism. In C. Murchison (Ed.), *Psychologies of 1930* (pp. 59–78). Worcester, MA: Clark University Press.

Cattell, J. McK. (1890). Mental tests and measurements. *Mind, 15,* 373–381.

Cattell, J. McK. (1896). Address of the president before the American Psychological Association, 1895. *Psychological Review, 3,* 134–148.

Cattell, J. McK. (1904). The conceptions and methods of psychology. *Popular Science Monthly, 66,* 176–186.

Cattell, J. McK. (1928). Early psychological laboratories. *Science, 67,* 543–548.

Cofer, C., & Appley, M. (1964). *Motivation: Theory and research.* New York: Wiley.

Comte, A. (1896). *The positive philosophy of Comte.* London: Bell. (Original work published 1830).

Cunningham, S. (1985, May). Humanists celebrate gains, goals. *APA Monitor,* pp. 16, 18.

Cuny, H. (1965). *Ivan Pavlov: The man and his theories.* New York: Paul S. Eriksson.

Dallenbach, K. (1967). Autobiography. In E. B. Boring & G. Lindzey (Eds.), *A history of psychology in autobiography* (vol. 5, pp. 57–93). New York: Appleton-Century-Crofts.

Danziger, K. (1980a). The history of introspection reconsidered. *Journal of the History of the Behavioral Sciences, 16,* 241–262.

Danziger, K. (1980b). Wundt's psychological experiment in the light of his philosophy of science. *Psychological Research, 42,* 109–122.

Darwin, C. (1859). *On the origin of species by means of natural selection.* London: J. Murray.

Darwin, C. (1871). *The descent of man.* London: J. Murray.

Darwin, C. (1872). *The expression of the emotions in man and animals.* London: J. Murray.

Darwin, C. (1877). A biographical sketch of an infant. *Mind, 2,* 285–294.

Darwin, F. (Ed.). (1892). *Charles Darwin, His life told in an autobiographical chapter and in a selected series of his published letters.* New York: Appleton.

Denmark, F. L. (1980). Psyche: From rocking the cradle to rocking the boat. *American Psychologist, 35*, 1057–1065.

Dennis, P. M. (1984). The Edison questionnaire. *Journal of the History of the Behavioral Sciences, 20*, 23–37.

Descartes, R. (1912). *A discourse on method*. London: Dent. (Original work published 1637).

Dewey, J. (1886). *Psychology*. New York: Harper.

Dewey, J. (1896). The reflex arc concept in psychology. *Psychological Review, 3*, 357–370.

Dewey, J. (1900). Psychology and social practice. *Psychological Review, 7*, 105–124.

Diamond, S. (1977). Francis Galton and American psychology. *Annals of the New York Academy of Sciences, 291*, 47–55.

Diamond, S. (1980). A plea for historical accuracy [Letter to the editor]. *Contemporary Psychology, 25*, 84–85.

Drinka, G. F. (1984). *The birth of neurosis: Myth, malady, and the Victorians*. New York: Simon & Schuster.

Ebbinghaus, H. (1885). *On memory*. Leipzig: Duncker & Humblot.

Ebbinghaus, H. (1902). *The principles of psychology*. Leipzig: Veit.

Ebbinghaus, H. (1908). *A summary of psychology*. Leipzig: Veit.

Egan, D. E. (1983). Retrospective reports reveal differences in people's reasoning. *Bell System Technical Journal, 62*, 1675–1697.

Ellenberger, H. F. (1970). *The discovery of the unconscious: The history and evolution of dynamic psychiatry*. New York: Basic Books.

Ellenberger, H. F. (1972). The story of "Anna O": A critical review with new data. *Journal of the History of the Behavioral Sciences, 8*, 267–279.

Erikson, E. H. (1968). *Identity: Youth and crisis*. New York: Norton.

Erikson, E. H. (1975). *Life history and the historical moment*. New York: Norton.

Evans, R. B. (1972). E. B. Titchener and his lost system. *Journal of the History of the Behavioral Sciences, 8*, 168–180.

Evans, R. B., & Scott, F. J. D. (1978). The 1913 International Congress of Psychology: The American congress that wasn't. *American Psychologist, 33*, 711–723.

Evans, R. I. (1968). *B. F. Skinner: The man and his ideas*. New York: Dutton.

Fancher, R. E. (1984, January). The examined life: Competitive examinations in the thought of Francis Galton. *History of Psychology Newsletter*, pp. 13–20.

Fechner, G. (1966). *Elements of psychophysics*. New York: Holt, Rinehart and Winston. (Original work published 1860).

Fernald, D. (1984). *The Hans legacy: A story of science*. Hillsdale, NJ: Erlbaum.

Ferster, C. B., & Skinner, B. F. (1957). *Schedules of reinforcement*. New York: Appleton-Century-Crofts.

Festinger, L. A. (1957). *A theory of cognitive dissonance*. Stanford, CA: Stanford University Press.

Fine, R. (1985). Anna Freud (1895–1982) [Obituary]. *American Psychologist, 40*, 230–232.

Fisher, S., & Greenberg, R. P. (1977). *The scientific credibility of Freud's theories and therapy*. New York: Basic Books.

Flugel, J., & West, D. (1964). *A hundred years of psychology*. New York: Basic Books.

Freud, A. (1936). *The ego and the mechanisms of defense*. London: Hogarth Press.

Freud, A. (Ed.). (1945–   ). *The psychoanalytic study of the child* (annual vols.). New York: International Universities Press.

Freud, S. (1895). On the origins of psycho-analysis. In J. Strachey (Ed. & Trans.), *The standard edition of the complete psychological works of Sigmund Freud* (vol. 1). London: Hogarth Press.

Freud, S. (1896). Heredity and the aetiology of the neuroses. In *Standard edition* (vol. 3, pp. 142–156). London: Hogarth Press.

Freud, S. (1900). The interpretation of dreams. In *Standard edition* (vols. 4, 5). London: Hogarth Press.

Freud, S. (1901). The psychopathology of everyday life. In *Standard edition* (vol. 6). London: Hogarth Press.

Freud, S. (1905a). Fragment of an analysis of a case of hysteria. In *Standard edition* (vol. 7, pp. 3–122). London: Hogarth Press.

Freud, S. (1905b). Three essays on the theory of sexuality. In *Standard edition* (vol. 7, pp. 125–243). London: Hogarth Press.

Freud, S. (1910). Five lectures on psycho-analysis. In *Standard edition* (vol. 11, pp. 3–55). London: Hogarth Press.

Freud, S. (1914). On the history of the psycho-analytic movement. In *Standard edition* (vol. 14, pp. 3–66). London: Hogarth Press.

Freud, S. (1920). Beyond the pleasure principle. In *Standard edition* (vol. 18, pp. 3–64). London: Hogarth Press.

Freud, S. (1933). New introductory lectures on psycho-analysis. In *Standard edition* (vol. 22, pp. 3–182). London: Hogarth Press.

Freud, S. (1940). An outline of psycho-analysis. In *Standard edition* (vol. 23, pp. 141–207). London: Hogarth Press.

Freud, S. (1941). Findings, ideas, problems. In *Standard edition* (vol. 23, pp. 299–300). London: Hogarth Press.

Freud, S. (1954). *The origins of psychoanalysis: Letters to Wilhelm Fliess, drafts and notes: 1887–1902*. New York: Basic Books.

Furumoto, L., & Scarborough, E. (1986). Placing women in the history of psychology: The first American women psychologists. *American Psychologist, 41*, 35–42.

Galton, F. (1869). *Hereditary genius*. London: Macmillan.

Galton, F. (1874). *English men of science: Their nature and nurture*. London: Macmillan.

Galton, F. (1889). *Natural inheritance*. London: Macmillan.

Gantt, W. H. (1941). Introduction. In I. P. Pavlov, *Lectures on conditioned reflexes*. New York: International Publishers.

Gantt, W. H. (1979, February). [Interview with Professor Emeritus W. Horsley Gantt]. *Johns Hopkins Magazine*, pp. 26–32.

Garfield, S. L. (1985). Clinical psychology. In E. M. Altmaier & M. E. Meyer (Eds.), *Applied specialties in psychology* (pp. 19–44). New York: Random House.

Gay, P. (1983). *The bourgeois experience: Victoria to Freud: Vol. 1. Education of the senses*. New York: Oxford University Press.

Geldard, F. A. (1980). Clark and the psychology of the "schools." *Journal of the History of the Behavioral Sciences, 16*, 225–227.

Gengerelli, J. A. (1976). Graduate school reminiscences: Hull and Koffka. *American Psychologist, 31*, 685–688.

Gholson, B., & Barker, P. (1985). Kuhn, Lakatos, and Laudan: Applications in the history of physics and psychology. *American Psychologist, 40*, 755–769.

Gilgen, A. R. (1982). *American psychology since World War II: A profile of the discipline*. Westport, CT: Greenwood Press.

Gould, S. J. (1976). Darwin and the captain. *Natural History, 85*(1), 32–34.

Gould, S. J. (1986). Knight takes Bishop? *Natural History, 95*(5), 18–33.

Green, M., & Rieber, R. W. (1980). The assimilation of psychoanalysis in America. In R. W. Rieber & K. Salzinger (Eds.), *Psychology: Theoretical-historical perspectives* (pp. 263–304). New York: Academic Press.

Griffin, D. R. (1984). *Animal thinking*. Cambridge, MA: Harvard University Press.

Gruber, C. (1972). Academic freedom at Columbia University, 1917–1918: The case of James McKeen Cattell. *American Association of University Professors Bulletin, 58*(3), 297–305.

Guthrie, E. R. (1935). *The psychology of learning*. New York: Harper.

Guthrie, E. R. (1959). Association by contiguity. In S. Koch (Ed.), *Psychology: A study of a science* (vol. 2, pp. 158–195). New York: McGraw-Hill.

Hall, E. (1970, February). Alfred Adler, a sketch. *Psychology Today*, pp. 45, 67.

Hall, G. S. (1904). *Adolescence*. New York: Appleton.

Hall, G. S. (1917). *Jesus, the Christ, in the light of psychology*. Garden City, NY: Doubleday.

Hall, G. S. (1919). Some possible effects of the war on American psychology. *Psychological Bulletin, 16*, 48–49.

Hall, G. S. (1920). *Recreations of a psychologist*. New York: Appleton.

Hall, G. S. (1922). *Senescence*. New York: Appleton.

Hall, G. S. (1923). *The life and confessions of a psychologist*. New York: Appleton.

Harlow, H. F. (1969). William James and instinct theory. In R. B. MacLeod (Ed.), *William James: Unfinished business* (pp. 21–30). Washington, DC: American Psychological Association.

Harris, B. (1979). Whatever happened to little Albert? *American Psychologist, 34*, 151–160.

Harrison, R. (1963). Functionalism and its historical significance. *Genetic Psychology Monographs, 68*, 387–423.

Hartley, D. (1749). *Observations on man, his frame, his duty, and his expectations*. London: Leake and Frederick.

Hartley, D., Robach, H. B., & Abramowitz, S. I. (1976). Deterioration effects in encounter groups. *American Psychologist, 31*, 247–255.

Hartmann, H. (1964). *Essays on ego psychology*. New York: International Universities Press.

Hearst, E. (Ed.). (1979). *The first century of experimental psychology*. Hillsdale, NJ: Erlbaum.

Heidbreder, E. (1933). *Seven psychologies*. New York: Appleton.

Helmholtz, H. (1856–1866). *Physiological optics*. Leipzig: Voss.

Helmholtz, H. (1954). *On the sensation of tone*. New York: Dover. (Original work published 1863).

Henle, M. (1974). E. B. Titchener and the case of the missing element. *Journal of the History of the Behavioral Sciences, 10*, 227–237.

Henle, M. (1977). The influence of Gestalt psychology in America. *Annals of the New York Academy of Sciences, 270*, 14–20.

Henle, M. (1978a). Gestalt psychology and gestalt therapy. *Journal of the History of the Behavioral Sciences, 14*, 23–32.

Henle, M. (1978b). One man against the Nazis: Wolfgang Köhler. *American Psychologist, 33*, 939–944.

Henle, M. (1984). Robert M. Ogden and Gestalt psychology in America. *Journal of the History of the Behavioral Sciences, 20*, 9–19.

Herrnstein, R. J. (1973). Introduction to John B. Watson's *Comparative psychology*. In M. Henle, J. Jaynes, & J. J. Sullivan (Eds.), *Historical conceptions of psychology* (pp. 98–115). New York: Springer.

Herrnstein, R. J. (1977). The evolution of behaviorism. *American Psychologist, 32*, 593–603.

Herrnstein, R. J., & Boring, E. G. (Eds.). (1965). *A source book in the history of psychology.* Cambridge, MA: Harvard University Press.

Hilgard, E. (1956). *Theories of learning* (2nd ed.). New York: Appleton-Century-Crofts.

Hilgard, E., Atkinson, R., & Atkinson, R. (1975). *Introduction to psychology* (6th ed.). New York: Harcourt Brace Jovanovich.

Hobbs, N. (1980). Sidney Leavitt Pressey (1888–1979) [Obituary]. *American Psychologist, 35*, 669–671.

Hochberg, J. (1979). Sensation and perception. In E. Hearst (Ed.), *The first century of experimental psychology* (pp. 89–142). Hillsdale, NJ: Erlbaum.

Hollender, M. H. (1980). The case of Anna O.: A reformulation. *American Journal of Psychiatry, 137*, 797–800.

Holt, E. B. (1915). *The Freudian wish and its place in ethics.* New York: Holt.

Horney, K. (1945). *Our inner conflicts.* New York: Norton.

Howard, D. V. (1983). *Cognitive psychology: Memory, language and thought.* New York: Macmillan.

Hull, C. L. (1933). *Hypnosis and suggestibility.* New York: Appleton.

Hull, C. L. (1943). *Principles of behavior.* New York: Appleton.

Hull, C. L. (1951). *Essentials of behavior.* New Haven, CT: Yale University Press.

Hull, C. L. (1952). *A behavior system.* New Haven, CT: Yale University Press.

Hull, C. L., Hovland, C. L., Ross, R. T., Hall, M., Perkins, D. T., & Fitch, F. G. (1940). *Mathematico-deductive theory of rote learning: A study in scientific methodology.* New Haven, CT: Yale University Press.

Hume, D. (1739). *A treatise of human nature.* London: Noon.

Jahoda, M. (1963). Some notes on the influence of psycho-analytic ideas on American psychology. *Human Relations, 16*, 111–129.

James, H. (Ed.). (1920). *The letters of William James.* Boston: Atlantic Monthly.

James. W. (1890). *The principles of psychology.* New York: Holt.

James, W. (1899). *Talks to teachers.* New York: Holt.

James, W. (1902). *The varieties of religious experience.* New York: Longmans, Green.

James, W. (1907). *Pragmatism.* New York: Longmans, Green.

Jaynes, J. (1970). The problem of animate motion in the seventeenth century. *Journal of the History of Ideas, 31*, 219–234.

Johnson, R.C., McClearn, G. E., Yuen, S., Nagoshi, C. T., Ahern, F. M., & Cole, R. E. (1985). Galton's data a century later. *American Psychologist, 40*, 875–892.

Jonçich, G. (1968). *The sane positivist: A biography of Edward L. Thorndike.* Middletown, CT: Wesleyan University Press.

Jones, E. (1953, 1955, 1957). *The life and work of Sigmund Freud* (3 vols.). New York: Basic Books.

Jones, G. V. (1980). Lloyd Morgan at Bristol [Letter to the editor]. *Contemporary Psychology, 25*, 277.

Jones, M. C. (1924). A laboratory study of fear: The case of Peter. *Pedagogical Seminary, 31*, 308–315.

Jones, M. C. (1974). Albert, Peter, and John B. Watson. *American Psychologist, 29*, 581–583.

Jung, C. G. (1912). *The psychology of the unconscious.* Leipzig: Franz Deuticke.

Jung, C. G. (1961). *Memories, dreams, reflections.* New York: Random House.

Kagan, J., & Havemann, E. (1972). *Psychology: An introduction* (2nd ed.). New York: Harcourt Brace Jovanovich.

Kimble, G. A. (1984). Psychology's two cultures. *American Psychologist, 39*, 833–839.

Kirsch, I. (1976). The impetus to scientific psychology: A recurrent pattern. *Journal of the History of the Behavioral Sciences, 12*, 120–129.

Koch, S. (1964). Psychology and emerging conceptions of knowledge as unitary. In T. Wann (Ed.), *Behaviorism and phenomenology* (pp. 1–41). Chicago: University of Chicago Press.

Koelsch, W. A. (1970). Freud discovers America. *Virginia Quarterly Review, 46*, 115–132.

Koffka, K. (1921). *The growth of the mind.* New York: Harcourt.

Koffka, K. (1922). Perception: An introduction to Gestalt-theorie. *Psychological Bulletin, 19*, 531–585.

Koffka, K. (1935). *Principles of Gestalt psychology.* New York: Harcourt.

Köhler, W. (1917, 1927). *The mentality of apes.* Berlin: Royal Academy of Sciences; New York: Harcourt Brace.

Köhler, W. (1920). *Static and stationary physical Gestalts.* Braunschweig: Vieweg.

Köhler, W. (1929). *Gestalt psychology.* New York: Liveright.

Köhler, W. (1938). *The place of value in a world of facts.* New York: Liveright.

Köhler, W. (1940). *Dynamics in psychology.* New York: Liveright.

Köhler, W. (1947). *Gestalt psychology: An introduction to new concepts in modern psychology.* New York: Liveright.

Köhler, W. (1959). Gestalt psychology today. *American Psychologist, 14*, 727–734.

Köhler, W. (1969). Gestalt psychology. In D. Krantz (Ed.), *Schools of psychology* (pp. 69–85). New York: Appleton-Century-Crofts.

Köhler, W., & Wallach, H. (1944). Figural after-effects. *Proceedings of the American Philosophical Society, 88*, 269–357.

Kuhn, T. S. (1970). *The structure of scientific revolutions* (2nd ed.). Chicago: University of Chicago Press.

Külpe, O. (1893). *Outline of psychology.* Leipzig: Engelmann.

Lakatos, I. (1978). *The methodology of scientific research programs.* Cambridge, England: Cambridge University Press.

Landes, D. S. (1983). *Revolution in time: Clocks and the making of the modern world.* Cambridge, MA: Harvard University Press.

Larson, C. (1979, May). Highlights of Dr. John B. Watson's career in advertising. *The Industrial-Organizational Psychologist*, pp. 3–5.

Larson, C., & Sullivan, J. J. (1965). Watson's relation to Titchener. *Journal of the History of the Behavioral Sciences, 1*, 338–354.

Lashley, K. (1929). *Brain mechanisms and intelligence.* Chicago: University of Chicago Press.

Laudan, L. (1977). *Progress and its problems.* Berkeley, CA: University of California Press.

Laudan, L. (1981). *Science and hypothesis.* Boston: Reidel.

Leahey, T. H. (1981). The mistaken mirror: On Wundt's and Titchener's psychologies. *Journal of the History of the Behavioral Sciences, 17*, 273–282.

Lewin, K. (1936). *Principles of topological psychology.* New York: McGraw-Hill.

Lewin, K. (1939). Field theory and experiment in social psychology: Concept and methods. *American Journal of Sociology, 44*, 868–896.

Lewin, K., Lippitt, R., & White, R. (1939). Patterns of aggressive behavior in experimentally created social climates. *Journal of Social Psychology, 10*, 271–299.

Leys, R. (1984). Meyer, Watson, and the dangers of behaviorism. *Journal of the History of the Behavioral Sciences, 20*, 128–149.

Lieberman, D. A. (1979). Behaviorism and the mind: A (limited) call for a return to introspection. *American Psychologist, 34*, 319–333.

Locke, J. (1959). *An essay concerning human understanding.* New York: Dover. (Original work published 1690).

Logan, D. D. (1980). Mary Cover Jones: Feminine as asset. *Psychology of Women Quarterly, 5*, 103–115.

Lowry, R. (1982). *The evolution of psychological theory: A critical history of concepts and presuppositions* (2nd ed.). Hawthorne, NY: Aldine.

McDougall, W. (1908). *Introduction to social psychology.* London: Methuen.

McDougall, W. (1912). *Psychology: The study of behavior.* London: Oxford University Press.

McGuire, W. (Ed.). (1974). *The Freud/Jung letters.* Princeton, NJ: Princeton University Press.

Mach, E. (1914). *The analysis of sensations.* Chicago: Open Court. (Original work published 1885).

McKeachie, W. J. (1976). Psychology in America's bicentennial year. *American Psychologist, 31*, 819–833.

Mackenzie, B. (1976). Darwinism and positivism as methodological influences on the development of psychology. *Journal of the History of the Behavioral Sciences, 12*, 330–337.

Mackenzie, B. (1977). *Behaviourism and the limits of scientific method.* Atlantic Highlands, NJ: Humanities Press.

McKinney, F. (1978). Functionalism at Chicago: Memories of a graduate student: 1929–1931. *Journal of the History of the Behavioral Sciences, 14*, 142–148.

MacLeod, R. B. (1959). Review of *Cumulative record* by B. F. Skinner. *Science, 130*, 34–35.

MacLeod, R. B. (Ed.). (1969). *William James: Unfinished business.* Washington, DC: American Psychological Association.

Malcolm, J. (1984). *In the Freud archives.* New York: Alfred A. Knopf.

Malthus, T. (1914). *Essay on the principle of population.* New York: Dutton. (Original work published 1789).

Marx, M., & Hillix, W. A. (1979). *Systems and theories in psychology* (3rd ed.). New York: McGraw-Hill.

Maslow, A. H. (1965). A philosophy of psychology: The need for a mature science of human nature. In F. T. Severin (Ed.), *Humanistic viewpoints in psychology* (pp. 17–33). New York: McGraw-Hill.

Maslow, A. H. (1970). *Motivation and personality* (2nd ed.). New York: Harper & Row.

Masson, J. M. (1984). *The assault on truth: Freud's suppression of the seduction theory.* New York: Farrar Straus Giroux.

Masson, J. M. (Ed.). (1985). *The complete letters of Sigmund Freud to Wilhelm Fliess, 1887–1904.* Cambridge, MA: Harvard University Press.

Matson, F. W. (1964). *The broken image.* New York: George Braziller.

Maurice, K., & Mayr, O. (Eds.). (1980). *The clockwork universe: German clocks and automata 1550–1650.* New York: Neale Watson.

May, R. (1967). *Psychology and the human dilemma.* Princeton, NJ: D. Van Nostrand.

May, W. W. (1978). A psychologist of many hats: A tribute to Mark Arthur May. *American Psychologist, 33*, 653–663.

Merton, R. (1957). Priorities in scientific discovery. *American Sociological Review, 22*, 635–659.

Meyer, M. (1911). *The fundamental laws of human behavior.* Boston: R. G. Badger.

Mill, J. (1829). *Analysis of the phenomena of the human mind*. London: Baldwin & Cradock.

Miller, G. (1962). *Psychology: The science of mental life*. New York: Harper & Row.

Miller, G., & Buckhout, R. (1973). *Psychology: The science of mental life* (2nd ed.). New York: Harper & Row.

Miner, J. B. (1984). The validity and usefulness of theories in an emerging organizational science. *Academy of Management Review, 9*, 296–306.

Mueller, C. G., & Schoenfeld, W. N. (1954). Edwin R. Guthrie. In W. Estes, et al. (Eds.), *Modern learning theory* (pp. 345–379). New York: Appleton-Century-Crofts.

Münsterberg, H. (1909). *Psychotherapy*. New York: Moffat Yard.

Münsterberg, H. (1913). *Psychology and industrial efficiency*. Boston: Houghton Mifflin.

Murray, H. A. (1938). *Explorations in personality*. New York: Oxford University Press.

Murray, H. A. (1967). Autobiography. In E. G. Boring & G. Lindzey (Eds.), *A history of psychology in autobiography* (vol. 5, pp. 283–310). New York: Appleton-Century-Crofts.

Natsoulas, T. (1978). Consciousness. *American Psychologist, 33*, 904–916.

O'Donnell, J. M. (1979). The crisis of experimentalism in the 1920s: E. G. Boring and his uses of history. *American Psychologist, 34*, 289–295.

Orgler, H. (1965). *Alfred Adler: The man and his work*. New York: G. P. Putnam's Sons.

Pauly, P. J. (1979, December). Psychology at Hopkins: Its rise and fall and rise and fall and. . . . *Johns Hopkins Magazine*, pp. 36–41.

Pavlov, I. P. (1955). *Selected works*. Moscow: Foreign Languages Publishing House.

Pervin, L. (1984). *Personality: Theory and research* (4th ed.). New York: Wiley.

Pickering, G. (1974). *Creative malady*. New York: Oxford University Press.

Pillsbury, W. (1911). *Essentials of psychology*. New York: Macmillan.

Planck, M. (1949). *Scientific autobiography*. New York: Philosophical Library.

Polanyi, M. (1958). *Personal knowledge*. Chicago: University of Chicago Press.

Raphelson, A. C. (1982). The history course as the capstone of the psychology curriculum. *Journal of the History of the Behavioral Sciences, 18*, 279–285.

Remley, N. R. (1980). J. B. Watson and J. J. B. Morgan: The original drive theory of motivation. *Bulletin of the Psychonomic Society, 16*, 314–316.

Rice, B. (1968, March 17). Skinner agrees he is the most important influence in psychology. *New York Times Magazine*, pp. 27ff.

Richards, R. J. (1980). Wundt's early theories of unconscious inference and cognitive evolution in their relation to Darwinian biopsychology. In W. G. Bringmann & R. D. Tweney (Eds.), *Wundt studies: A centennial collection* (pp. 42–70). Toronto: C. J. Hogrefe.

Richards, R. J. (1983). Why Darwin delayed, or interesting problems and models in the history of science. *Journal of the History of the Behavioral Sciences, 19*, 45–53.

Roazen, P. (1975). *Freud and his followers*. New York: Alfred A. Knopf.

Roback, A. A. (1952). *History of American psychology*. New York: Library Publishers.

Robinson, D. N. (1981). *An intellectual history of psychology* (rev. ed.). New York: Macmillan.

Roethlisberger, F. J., & Dickson, W. J. (1939). *Management and the worker: An account of a research program conducted by the Western Electric Company, Chicago*. Cambridge, MA: Harvard University Press.

Rogers, C. R. (1961). *On becoming a person*. Boston: Houghton Mifflin.

Rogers, C. R. (1967). Autobiography. In E. G. Boring & G. Lindzey (Eds.), *A history of psychology in autobiography* (vol. 5, pp. 341–384). New York: Appleton-Century-Crofts.

Roitblat, H. L., Bever, T. G., & Terrace, H. S. (Eds.). (1984). *Animal cognition*. Hillsdale, NJ: Erlbaum.

Romanes, G. J. (1883). *Animal intelligence*. London: Routledge & Kegan Paul.

Romm, S. (1984). *The unwelcome intruder: Freud's struggle with cancer*. New York: Praeger.

Rosenthal, R. (Ed.). (1965). *Clever Hans: The horse of Mr. Von Osten*. New York: Holt, Rinehart and Winston.

Ross, D. (1972). *Granville Stanley Hall: The psychologist as prophet*. Chicago: University of Chicago Press.

Rubins, J. L. (1978). *Karen Horney: Gentle rebel of psychoanalysis*. New York: Dial Press.

Ruckmick, C. A. (1913). The use of the term "function" in English textbooks of psychology. *American Journal of Psychology, 24*, 99–123.

Samelson, F. (1980a). Early behaviorism, Part 3: The stalemate of the twenties. Paper presented at the meeting of the International Society for the History of the Behavioral and Social Sciences (Cheiron), June 19–21, 1980, at Bowdoin College, Brunswick, Maine.

Samelson, F. (1980b). J. B. Watson's little Albert, Cyril Burt's twins, and the need for a critical science. *American Psychologist, 35*, 619–625.

Samelson, F. (1981). Struggle for scientific authority: The reception of Watson's behaviorism, 1913–1920. *Journal of the History of the Behavioral Sciences, 17*, 399–425.

Sarton, G. (1936). *The study of the history of science*. New York: Dover.

Scarf, M. (1971, February 28). The man who gave us "inferiority complex," "compensation," "aggressive drive" and "style of life." *New York Times Magazine*, pp. 10ff.

Schachter, S. (1963). Birth order, eminence, and higher education. *American Sociological Review, 28*, 757–767.

Schachter, S. (1964). Birth order and sociometric choice. *Journal of Abnormal and Social Psychology, 68*, 453–456.

Schur, M. (1972). *Freud: Living and dying*. New York: International Universities Press.

Scott, W. D. (1908). *The psychology of advertising*. New York: Arno Press.

Seaman, J. D. (1984). On phi-phenomena. *Journal of the History of the Behavioral Sciences, 20*, 3–8.

Shakow, D. (1930). Hermann Ebbinghaus. *American Journal of Psychology, 42*, 505–518.

Shakow, D. (1969). Psychoanalysis. In D. Krantz (Ed.), *Schools of psychology* (pp. 87–122). New York: Appleton-Century-Crofts.

Shevrin, H., & Dickman, S. (1980). The psychological unconscious: A necessary assumption for all psychological theory? *American Psychologist, 35*, 421–434.

Shields, S. (1975). Ms. Pilgrim's progress: The contributions of Leta Stetter Hollingworth to the psychology of women. *American Psychologist, 30*, 852–857.

Skinner, B. F. (1938). *The behavior of organisms*. New York: Appleton.

Skinner, B. F. (1948). *Walden Two*. New York: Macmillan.

Skinner, B. F. (1953). *Science and human behavior*. New York: Macmillan.

Skinner, B. F. (1956). A case history of scientific method. *American Psychologist, 11*, 221–233.

Skinner, B. F. (1957). *Verbal behavior*. New York: Appleton.

Skinner, B. F. (1959). John B. Watson, behaviorist. *Science, 129*, 197–198.

Skinner, B. F. (1963). Behaviorism at fifty. *Science, 140*, 951–958.

Skinner, B. F. (1967). Autobiography. In E. G. Boring & G. Lindzey (Eds.), *A history of psychology in autobiography* (vol. 5, pp. 387–413). New York: Appleton-Century-Crofts.

Skinner, B. F. (1968). *The technology of teaching.* New York: Appleton-Century-Crofts.

Skinner, B. F. (1969). *Contingencies of reinforcement.* New York: Appleton-Century-Crofts.

Skinner, B. F. (1971). *Beyond freedom and dignity.* New York: Alfred A. Knopf.

Skinner, B. F. (1976). *Particulars of my life.* New York: Alfred A. Knopf.

Skinner, B. F. (1979). *The shaping of a behaviorist.* New York: Alfred A. Knopf.

Skinner, B. F. (1983). *A matter of consequences.* New York: Alfred A. Knopf.

Sokal, M. M. (1971). The unpublished autobiography of James McKeen Cattell. *American Psychologist, 26,* 626–635.

Sokal, M. M. (1981a). *An education in psychology: James McKeen Cattell's journal and letters from Germany and England, 1880–1888.* Cambridge, MA: MIT Press.

Sokal, M. M. (1981b). The origins of the Psychological Corporation. *Journal of the History of the Behavioral Sciences, 17,* 54–67.

Sokal, M. M. (1984). The Gestalt psychologists in behaviorist America. *American Historical Review, 89,* 1240–1263.

Spencer, H. (1855). *The principles of psychology.* London: Smith and Elder.

Stapp, J., & Fulcher, R. (1982). The employment of 1979 and 1980 doctoral recipients. *American Psychologist, 37,* 1159–1185.

Stumpf, C. (1883). *Psychology of tone.* Leipzig: Hirzel.

Sulloway, F. J. (1979). *Freud: Biologist of the mind.* New York: Basic Books.

Thorndike, E. L. (1905). *The elements of psychology.* New York: A. G. Seiler.

Thorndike, E. L. (1931). *Human learning.* New York: Appleton.

Titchener, E. B. (1896). *An outline of psychology.* New York: Macmillan.

Titchener, E. B. (1898a). The postulates of a structural psychology. *Philosophical Review, 7,* 449–465.

Titchener, E. B. (1898b). *Primer of psychology.* New York: Macmillan.

Titchener, E. B. (1901). *Experimental psychology.* New York: Macmillan.

Titchener, E. B. (1909). *A text-book of psychology.* New York: Macmillan.

Titchener, E. B. (1912a). Prolegomena to a study of introspection. *American Journal of Psychology, 23,* 427–448.

Titchener, E. B. (1912b). The schema of introspection. *American Journal of Psychology, 23,* 485–508.

Titchener, E. B. (1921). Wilhelm Wundt. *American Journal of Psychology, 32,* 161–178.

Tolman, E. C. (1932). *Purposive behavior in animals and men.* New York: Appleton.

Tolman, E. C. (1945). A stimulus-expectancy need-cathexis psychology. *Science, 101,* 160–166.

Tolman, E. C. (1952). Autobiography. In E. G. Boring, H. S. Langfeld, H. Werner, & R. Yerkes (Eds.), *A history of psychology in autobiography* (vol. 4, pp. 323–339). Worcester, MA: Clark University Press.

Traxel, W. (1985, April). Hermann Ebbinghaus: In memoriam. *History of Psychology Newsletter,* pp. 37–41.

Turner, F. J. (1947). *The significance of the frontier in American history.* New York: Holt.

Turner, M. (1967). *Philosophy and the science of behavior.* New York: Appleton-Century-Crofts.

Tyler, L. (1981). More stately mansions: Psychology extends its boundaries. *Annual Review of Psychology, 32,* 1–20.

Von Franz, M. (1975). *C. G. Jung: His myth in our time.* Boston: Little, Brown.

Von Hartmann, E. (1869). *Philosophy of the unconscious.* Berlin: Carl Duncker.

Washburn, M. F. (1908). *The animal mind: A text-book of comparative psychology.* New York: Macmillan.

Washburn, M. F. (1932). Autobiography. In C. Murchison (Ed.), *A history of psychology in autobiography* (vol. 2, pp. 333–358). Worcester, MA: Clark University Press.

Waterman, C. K., Buebel, M. E., & Waterman, A. S. (1970). Relationship between resolution of the identity crisis and outcomes of previous psychosocial crises. *Proceedings of the Annual Convention of the APA, 5,* 467–468.

Watson, J. B. (1908). Review of Pfungst's *Das Pferd des Herrn Von Osten. Journal of Comparative Neurology and Psychology, 18,* 329–331.

Watson, J. B. (1913). Psychology as the behaviorist views it. *Psychological Review, 20,* 158–177.

Watson, J. B. (1914). *Behavior: An introduction to comparative psychology.* New York: Holt.

Watson, J. B. (1919). *Psychology from the standpoint of a behaviorist.* Philadelphia: Lippincott.

Watson, J. B. (1925). *Behaviorism.* New York: Norton.

Watson, J. B. (1928). *Psychological care of the infant and child.* New York: Norton.

Watson, J. B. (1929). Behaviorism. *Encyclopedia Britannica* (vol. 3, pp. 327–329).

Watson, J. B. (1930). *Behaviorism* (rev. ed.). New York: Norton.

Watson, J. B. (1936). Autobiography. In C. Murchison (Ed.), *A history of psychology in autobiography* (vol. 3, pp. 271–281). Worcester, MA: Clark University Press.

Watson, J. B., & McDougall, W. (1929). *The battle of behaviorism.* New York: Norton.

Watson, J. B., & Morgan, J. J. B. (1917). Emotional reactions and psychological experimentation. *American Journal of Psychology, 28,* 163–174.

Watson, J. B., & Rayner, R. (1920). Conditioned emotional reactions. *Journal of Experimental Psychology, 3,* 1–14.

Watson, R. I. (1978). *The great psychologists* (4th ed.). Philadelphia: Lippincott.

Weiss, A. P. (1925). *A theoretical basis of human behavior.* Columbus, OH: Adams.

Wertheimer, M. (1912). Experimental studies of the perception of movement. *Zeitschrift für Psychologie, 61,* 161–265.

Wertheimer, M. (1938). Gestalt theory. In W. D. Ellis (Ed.), *A source book of Gestalt psychology* (pp. 1–11). London: Routledge & Kegan Paul.

Wertheimer, M. (1945). *Productive thinking.* New York: Harper.

Wertheimer, M. (1978). Humanistic psychology and the humane but tough-minded psychologist. *American Psychologist, 33,* 739–745.

Wertheimer, M. (1979). *A brief history of psychology* (2nd ed.). New York: Holt, Rinehart and Winston.

White, A. D. (1965). *A history of the warfare of science with theology in Christendom* (rev. & abr.). New York: Free Press. (Original work published 1896).

White, M. J. (1985). On the status of cognitive psychology. *American Psychologist, 40,* 117–119.

Windholz, G. (1983). Pavlov's position toward American behaviorism. *Journal of the History of the Behavioral Sciences, 19,* 394–407.

Windholz, G., & Lamal, P. A. (1985). Köhler's insight revisited. *Teaching of Psychology, 12,* 165–167.

Witkin, H. A. (1978). *Cognitive styles in personal and cultural adaptation.* Worcester, MA: Clark University Press.

Wittels, F. (1924). *Sigmund Freud.* New York: Dodd, Mead.

Woodworth, R. S. (1918). *Dynamic psychology.* New York: Columbia University Press.

Woodworth, R. S. (1921). *Psychology.* New York: Holt.

Woodworth, R. S. (1930). Dynamic psychology. In C. Murchison (Ed.), *Psychologies of 1930* (pp. 327–336). Worcester, MA: Clark University Press.

Woodworth, R. S. (1938). *Experimental psychology.* New York: Holt.

Woodworth, R. S. (1943). The adolescence of American psychology. *Psychological Review, 50,* 10–32.

Woodworth, R. S. (1948). *Contemporary schools of psychology* (2nd ed.). New York: Ronald Press.

Woodworth, R. S. (1958). *Dynamics of behavior.* New York: Holt.

Wundt, W. (1858). *Contributions to the theory of sensory perception.* Leipzig: Winter.

Wundt, W. (1863). *Lectures on the minds of men and animals.* Leipzig: Voss.

Wundt, W. (1873–1874). *Principles of physiological psychology.* Leipzig: Engelmann.

Wundt, W. (1888). Zur Erinnerung an Gustav Theodor Fechner. *Philosophische Studien, 4,* 471–478.

Wundt, W. (1896). *Outline of psychology.* Leipzig: Engelmann.

Wundt, W. (1900). *Folk psychology.* Leipzig: Engelmann.

Zeigarnik, B. (1938). On finished and unfinished tasks. In W. D. Ellis (Ed.), *A source book of Gestalt psychology* (pp. 300–314). London: Routledge & Kegan Paul. (Original work published 1927).

Index

A

Abramowitz, S. I., 366
Acoustics, 44, 46, 77–78
Act psychology (Brentano), 76–77
Adaptation, biological. *See* Evolutionary theory
Adler, A., 303, 323, 332–337, 341, 342, 345, 352, 363, 366, 368
Agassiz, L., 132
Aggression (Freud), 309
Albert study of conditioned fear (Watson), 214, 217
Aldini, G., 41
Allen, G. W., 132, 134, 135
Allport, G., 279, 337, 343–345, 349, 363
American Psychological Association (APA), founding of, 3, 143
Analytical psychology (Jung), 325–331
Anastasi, A., 356
Anderson, R. J., 58
Anecdotal method (animal research), 124
Angell, J. R., 79, 135, 145, 155–160, 167, 173, 176, 193, 196, 197, 199
Anima/animus archetypes (Jung), 329
Animal consciousness, 114, 123–125, 175–177, 182, 376
Animal learning, 181–184, 187–191, 226, 231–234, 246–249
Animal psychology, 114, 123–125, 139, 171, 175–192, 210, 226, 239, 275–277, 285, 376

Animal reflexes, 40–42
Anna O. case, 298–299, 301, 306
Anxiety, 311, 340
Apparent movement phenomenon, 262, 278
Apperception, 67, 68, 290
Appley, M., 241
Applied psychology, 108, 150–152, 192, 352–360
Archetypes (Jung), 329
Aristotle, 1, 21, 22, 29, 72, 296
Army Alpha/Army Beta tests, 354, 356
Associated reflexes (Bekhterev), 191–192
Association (learning), 67–69, 71–75, 81–82, 121, 181–184, 188, 190, 259–262
Associationists. *See* British empiricists and associationists
Associations, verbal, 68–69, 121, 330, 331, 355
Associative memory (Loeb), 176
Astronomy, 39, 42, 68
Atkinson, J. W., 10
Atkinson, R., 372
Atomism, 210, 261, 262
Attention span research, 68
Audition, 44, 46, 77–78
Austin, G. A., 373
Averill, L. A., 144

B

Bacon, R., 24
Balance, W., 59
Baldwin, B. T., 58, 62
Baldwin, J. M., 149, 197
Bandura, A., 254–255, 352, 375
Barber, B., 316

Barker, P., 13
Barry, H., 337
Basic anxiety (Horney), 340
Becker, E., 309
Beers, C., 359
Behaviorism, 173–193
    evaluation and current status, 219–223, 253–255, 352
    founding of, 173–175, 195, 207–208
    methods and subject matter, 208–216
    neobehaviorism, 228–253
    original source material, 201–207
    Watsonian, 195–223
Behavior-modification techniques, 251–252
Bekhterev, V. M., 191–192, 209
Ben-David, J., 55
Benedict, R., 264, 366
Benedikt, M., 295
Benjamin, L. T., 88, 218, 219, 362
Bentham, J., 295
Berkeley, G., 29, 32–34, 39, 374
Berman, L., 217
Bernstein, M. D., 361
Bessel, F. W., 39, 42, 68
Bettelheim, B., 8, 309
Bever, T. G., 376
Binet, A., 151, 175, 295, 353–355
Biological influences on behavior (Hull), 238–241
Biological influences on personality (Freud), 294–295, 318
Biosocial influences on behavior (Weiss), 225
Birth order (Adler), 336
Bjork, D. W., 135, 151

Blane, H. T., 337
Bleuler, E., 325
Blumenthal, A. L., 58, 61, 66, 128, 152
Boakes, R., 40, 41, 128, 145, 175, 180
Bohr, N., 373
Boorstin, D. J., 17, 18
Boring, E. G., 12, 22, 55, 59, 63, 73, 87, 89, 102, 136, 151, 222, 228, 292, 320, 321
Bottome, P., 332
Boyle, R., 18
Braid, J., 293
Brain extirpation method, 41, 226
Brain functioning, early work on, 40–42
Breland, H. M., 337
Brentano, F., 75–77, 83, 260, 363
Breuer, J., 298–301, 306
Bridgman, P. W., 227–228, 318, 372
Briggs, K., 331
Bringmann, N. J., 2, 62
Bringmann, W. G., 2, 59, 62, 70
British empiricists and associationists, 21, 28–37, 42, 54, 64, 67, 71, 72, 85, 91, 210, 228, 251, 259, 295, 375
Broad, W., 11
Broca, P., 41
Brown, J. A. C., 323
Brožek, J., 63
Brücke, E., 295, 297, 298, 315
Bruner, J., 254, 373, 376, 377
Buckhout, R., 62, 134
Buckley, K. W., 199
Buebel, M. E., 349
Bugental, J. F. T., 364, 365
Bühler, K., 82
Bunsen, R., 61
Burnham, J., 192
Burt, C., 210, 371

C

Calkins, M. W., 135, 207, 360
Carnap, R., 372

Carr, H. A., 159–167, 170–171
    original source material, 161–167
Cartwright, D., 284
Case history approach, 308, 317, 331, 337, 341
Catharsis, 296, 299, 300
Cattell, J. McK., 3, 62, 68, 85, 119, 143, 146–152, 154, 167, 168, 180, 192, 197, 198, 303, 353, 357, 359, 360
Charcot, J. M., 293, 294, 300
Chicago, University of, functionalist school, 155–161
Child guidance clinics, 359
Child study movement, 145
Childhood experiences and behavior (Watson), 200, 217
Childhood experiences and personality (Freud), 294, 301–302
Clark University commemorative ceremonies (1909), 144, 303, 304, 320, 325, 359
Clever Hans, 178–179
Client-centered therapy (Rogers), 368–369
Clinical psychology, 359–360
Clocks and the mechanistic viewpoint, 17–22
Cocaine, Freud's use of, 297–298
Cofer, C., 241
Cognitive maps (Tolman), 233
Cognitive psychology, 371–377
    and behaviorism, 253–255
Collective unconscious (Jung), 328–329
Collins, R., 55
Color vision research (Helmholtz), 46
Columbia University, functionalist school, 146–151, 167–170
Comparative psychology, 114, 123–125, 139, 171, 175–192, 210, 226, 239, 277, 285, 376

Compensation (Adler), 335
Complexes, 328, 330, 346–347
Computers and the cognitive viewpoint, 374–375
Comte, A., 28, 103, 174–175
Conarium, 27
Conditioned fears, 214–215
Conditioning, 187–191, 208–210, 238, 241, 246–247
Connectionism (Thorndike), 181–184
Conscience (Freud), 310
Consciousness, 107–108, 114, 136–138, 192–193, 224, 309, 328, 362–364
    in animals, 114, 123–125, 175–177, 182, 376
    in cognitive psychology, 253–255, 371
    elements of, 64–69, 76–77, 80–81, 89–90, 92–94
Contiguity theories of learning, 36, 37, 235
Cordes, C., 251
Correlational method, 119
Creative synthesis (Wundt), 67
Cultural psychology (Wundt), 63
Cunningham, S., 370
Cuny, H., 188

D

Dallenbach, K., 88
Danziger, K., 65, 66
Darwin, C., 70, 108–115, 117, 123, 125, 128, 129, 131, 139, 151, 154, 178, 182, 184, 289, 294–295
Darwin, E., 109
Darwin, F., 110, 175
Death instinct (Freud), 309
Defense mechanisms (Freud), 311
Delezenne, C., 53
Denmark, F., 360
Dennis, P. M., 353
Depth perception (Berkeley), 33–34
Derived ideas (Descartes), 27

Descartes, R., 18, 21–29, 36, 41, 114, 123, 174, 290, 373
Determining tendency (mental set), 82
Determinism, 19, 221–222, 251, 315–316, 318
Developmental psychology (Hall), 145–146
Dewey, J., 140, 143, 147, 155–157, 168, 196
Diamond, S., 64, 148
Dickman, H., 376
Dickson, W. J., 357
Dollard, J., 242
Donaldson, H. H., 176
Donders, F. C., 68
Dream analysis (Freud), 302–303, 306–307
Drinka, G. F., 293
Drives, 169–170, 240–241
Du Bois-Reymond, E., 295, 315
Dunlap, K., 193
Dynamic psychology (Woodworth), 168–170

E

Ebbinghaus, H., 1, 7, 71–74, 79, 83, 104
Edwards Personal Preference Schedule, 347
Egan, D. E., 105
Ego, 310, 323–324, 328, 346
Ego identity (Erikson), 347–349
Einstein, A., 11, 278, 373
Electrical stimulation (brain research), 41
Elementism and Gestalt psychology, 259–261
Elements of consciousness. *See* Consciousness
Elements of Psychophysics (Fechner), 54, 55, 61, 72, 108, 290
Ellenberger, H., 9, 51, 296, 299
Emotions, 66–68, 79, 93, 114, 123, 139–140, 213–215
Empiricism, 21. *See also* British empiricists and associationists
Encounter groups, 284, 366

Engineering psychology, 358–359
English empiricists. *See* British empiricists and associationists
Environmentalism (Watson), 212–213, 217
Eponymy, 12
Erikson, E., 331, 343, 347–349, 363
Eugenics (Galton), 117–118, 149
Evans, R. B., 59, 94, 197
Evans, R. I., 246
Evolutionary theory, 107–115, 125, 128–131, 156, 239, 294–295. *See also* Darwin, C.
Experimental method, early applications of, 42–54
Expressive behavior (Allport), 345
Extirpation method, 41, 226
Extroversion (Jung), 330, 331
Eysenck, H. J., 331

F

Fancher, R., 117
Fear, conditioned, 214–215
Fechner, G., 7, 42, 44, 49–55, 61, 65, 72, 77, 108, 114, 115, 288–290
Feminine psychology (Horney), 318, 337–341
Fernald, D., 178
Ferster, C. B., 249
Festinger, L., 284, 376
Field theory (Lewin), 280–284
Fine, R., 324
Fisher, S., 319
Fitzroy, R., 113
Flourens, P., 40, 41
Flugel, J., 122, 277
Folk psychology (Wundt), 63
Forgetting, 71–75
Founding of schools of thought
  Watson, 173–175, 195, 207–208
  Wundt, 54–55, 58, 61, 69–70
Frame of reference (Hull), 238–239

Free association, 300, 302, 305
Freeman, L., 298
French, J. P., 284
Freud, A., 305, 324, 345, 347, 360
Freud, S., 7–9, 51, 75, 82, 109, 144, 217, 288–321, 352, 359, 360, 362–366, 369, 371, 376
  and the neo-Freudians, 323–349
  original source material, 312–315
Freudian slip, 303
Friedline, C., 88, 91–92
Fritsch, G., 41
Fulcher, R., 360
Functional autonomy of motives (Allport), 343–344
Functionalism, 107–125, 128–152, 154–172
  at Chicago, 155–161
  at Columbia, 146–151, 167–170
  definition and subject matter, 154–159, 161, 170–171
  evaluation and current status, 170–172, 351
  founding, 154–155
  influence on behaviorism, 192–193
  methods, 114–115, 139, 161, 171
  original source material, 161–167
Furumoto, L., 360

G

Gale, H., 356
Galilean–Newtonian mechanism, 13, 17–18, 31, 32, 36, 54, 91, 251, 261, 364, 373
Galton, F., 68, 70, 108, 109, 115–122, 145, 148–152, 154, 243, 353, 355
Galvani, L., 41
Gantt, W. H., 186, 187
Garfield, S. L., 359, 360
Gay, P., 295, 302

Geldard, F. A., 94, 267
Gengerelli, J., 222
German universities and
    experimental psychology,
    42–44
Gestalt, definition, 268
Gestalt psychology, 27, 67, 105,
    137, 161, 230, 232–233,
    257–286, 371
  and cognitive psychology, 372,
    375
  evaluation and current status,
    284–286, 351–352
  and humanistic psychology,
    363, 366
  original source material,
    269–273
Gestalt therapy (Perls), 257
Gholson, B., 13
Gilgen, A. R., 353
Goddard, H., 354, 356
Goldstein, K., 263
Goodnow, J. J., 373
Gottsched, J. C., 19
Gould, S. J., 113
Green, M., 320
Greenberg, R. P., 319
Griffin, D. R., 376
Group dynamics (Lewin), 284
Growth therapies, 366
Gruber, C., 149
Gruhle, H., 263
Guthrie, E. R., 228, 229,
    234–236, 241, 372

H

Habit (James), 140
Habit strength (Hull), 241
Hall, E., 332
Hall, G. S., 3, 85, 141–147, 149,
    152, 154, 159, 303, 353,
    354, 360
Hall, M., 40, 41
Harlow, H., 212
Harris, B., 214
Harrison, R., 155
Hartley, David, 29, 35–36, 41
Hartley, Deanna, 366
Hartmann, H., 323
Harvey, W., 26

Havemann, E., 372
Hawthorne studies, 357
Healey, W., 359
Hearst, E., 372
Hedonism, 295
Heidbreder, E., 14, 52, 83, 136,
    139, 155, 268, 320
Heisenberg, W., 373
Helmholtz, H., 28, 42, 44–46,
    49, 61, 68, 77, 115, 295,
    315
Henle, M., 94, 257, 267, 279,
    280
Henri, V., 151
Henslow, J. S., 110
Herbart, J. F., 52, 290
Herrnstein, R., 22, 200, 253
Hierarchy of needs (Maslow),
    367–368
Hilgard, E. R., 242, 372
Hillix, W. A., 65
Historical research and theory,
    6–12
History of psychology, reasons
    for study of, 3–6
Hitzig, E., 41
Hobbs, N., 250
Hochberg, J., 284
Hollender, M. H., 299
Hollingworth, L. S., 361, 362
Holt, E. B., 224–225, 229
Hooker, J., 110, 112, 113
Horney, K., 318, 323, 332,
    334–342, 360, 363, 366
Hovland, C., 242
Howard, D., 374
Hull, C. L., 222, 225, 228, 229,
    234, 236–244, 247
Human potential movement, 366
Humanistic psychology,
    362–371
Humanistic psychotherapies,
    366
Hume, D., 29, 34–35
Husserl, E., 77
Huxley, T. H., 113
Hypnosis, 238, 293–294, 299,
    300
Hypothetico-deductive method
    (Hull), 240
Hysteria, 293, 299, 300

I

Id, 310, 346
Ideas, 27–31, 34–37
Identity crisis (Erikson),
    347–349
Imageless thought, 81
Individual differences, 115–122,
    150–151
Individual psychology (Adler),
    332–337
Industrial/organizational
    psychology, 356–359
Inferiority feelings (Adler), 335
Information-processing model,
    374–375
Inhibited ideas (Herbart), 290
Innate ideas (Descartes), 27, 29
Insight (Köhler), 277, 285
Instincts
  Freud, 309
  Watson, 211–213
Intelligence quotient (IQ), 354
Intelligence tests, 151, 353–356
International Congress of
    Psychology (1929), 279,
    282
Intervening variables (Tolman),
    231–232
Introspection, 65–69, 74–75,
    77–82, 90–92, 139, 161,
    207–209, 221, 371–372
  criticisms of, 103–105
Introspection-by-analogy
    (animal research), 124
Introversion (Jung), 330, 331
Isomorphism, 278–279

J

Jaensch, E. R., 261
Jahoda, M., 316
James, H., 70, 132
James, W., 70, 85, 122,
    131–141, 146, 151, 152,
    154, 155, 157, 168, 180,
    190, 214, 260, 303, 357,
    363
James–Lange theory of emotion,
    140
Janet, P., 293, 294
Jastrow, J., 152, 218
Jaynes, J., 25, 26

Johnson, R. C., 120
Jonçich, G., 152, 180, 183, 184
Jones, E., 9, 290, 301, 303, 305, 306, 308
Jones, G. V., 125
Jones, M. C., 198, 214–215, 360
Journals, founding of, 2–3, 5, 61, 73–74, 143, 149, 152, 177, 246, 253, 263, 353, 370, 373
Jung, C., 121, 144, 302, 303, 323, 325–331, 337, 341, 342, 345, 346, 352, 355
Just noticeable difference, 48–49, 52

K

Kagan, J., 372
Kant, I., 54, 103, 259–260
Katz, D., 261
Kelley, H. H., 284
Kepler, J., 18
Kimble, G. A., 14
Kinkade, K., 251
Kirsch, I., 40
Koch, S., 229, 372
Koelsch, W. A., 145
Koffka, K., 229, 262–265, 279, 280
Köhler, W., 257, 261–268, 274–281, 285
König, A., 73
Kraepelin, E., 355
Krafft-Ebing, R., 294, 301
Kuhn, T., 13
Külpe, O., 65, 79–82, 85, 87, 90, 103, 263, 363

L

Laboratories, founding of, 61, 62, 67–69, 73, 77, 79–82, 86, 90–93, 119–120, 134, 135, 143–144, 152, 189
Ladd, G. T., 168
Lakatos, I., 13
Lamal, P., 285
Lamarck, C., 109, 113
La Mettrie, J., 21, 375
Landes, D. S., 18
Lange, C., 140

Langfeld, H., 279
Larson, C., 199, 200, 219
Lashley, K., 212, 226–227
Latent learning (Tolman), 233
Laudan, L., 13
Law of acquisition (Skinner), 247
Law of effect (Thorndike), 179, 183–184
Law of equipotentiality (Lashley), 226
Law of exercise (Thorndike), 183
Law of mass action (Lashley), 226
Law of parsimony (Morgan), 125
Law of reinforcement (Pavlov), 179–180
Leacock, S., 218–219
Leahey, T. H., 58
Learned drives (Hull), 240–241
Learning, 181–184, 187–189, 213, 226, 231–236, 241–242, 246–249. *See also* Association
   Gestalt approach, 274–278
Leibnitz, G. W., 290, 291
Leipzig laboratory, 61, 62, 65, 67–70, 74, 77, 79
Lewin, K., 280–284, 366
Leys, R., 197
Libido (Freud), 309
Lieberman, D. A., 105, 371
Life instincts (Freud), 309
Life space (Lewin), 282–283
Likert, R., 284
Lippitt, R., 284
Locke, J., 29–32, 34, 36, 39, 373
Loeb, J., 175–176, 182, 188, 196
Logan, D. D., 214
Lowry, R., 25, 31, 243
Ludwig, C., 295, 315
Lyell, C., 109, 110, 112

M

McDougall, W., 3, 174, 193, 208, 219–222
McGuire, W., 325
Mach, E., 260
McKeachie, W., 372, 375
Mackenzie, B., 114, 124, 171, 176, 182, 208, 232

McKinney, F., 154
MacLeod, R., 134, 244
Malcolm, J., 302
Malleus maleficarum, 292
Malthus, T., 112
Marbe, K., 81
Marx, M., 65
Maskelyne, N., 39
Maslow, A. H., 264, 331, 337, 362, 364, 366–369
Masson, J. M., 298, 301–302
Materialism, 28
Matson, F., 374
Maudsley, H., 103
Maudsley Personality Inventory, 331
Maurice, K., 18, 19, 26
May, R., 5
May, W. W., 156
Mayr, O., 18, 19, 26
Maze learning, 176, 233
Mechanism, 17–22, 24–28, 31, 37, 42, 91, 174–175, 210, 239, 245–246, 251, 295, 315–316, 374–375
Memory, 71–75
Mendel, G., 10
Mental acts (Brentano), 76–77
Mental elements. *See* Consciousness, elements of
Mental hygiene movement, 359
Mental illness, early therapy for, 292–294
Mental imagery, 34, 81, 121
Mental inheritance (Galton), 117–118
Mental tests, 119–121, 150–151, 353
Mentalism (Berkeley), 33
Mentality of Apes (Köhler), 266, 275–277
Merton, R., 112
Mesmer, F. A., 293
Mesmerism, 293
Meyer, M., 193
Mill, J., 29, 36–37, 67, 91
Miller, G., 62, 134, 185, 258, 373, 377
Miller, N., 242
Mind–body interaction (Descartes), 24–28

Miner, J. B., 368
Modeling (Bandura), 254
Monadology (Leibnitz), 290
Morgan, C., 346
Morgan, C. Lloyd, 124–125,
    175, 180, 182, 192
Morgan, J. J. B., 170
Morgulis, S., 177
Motivation, 82, 224–225, 241,
    343–344
Motivology (Woodworth), 169
Mowrer, H., 242
Mueller, C. G., 236
Müller, G. E., 74–75, 261
Müller, J., 40, 42, 61, 295
Münsterberg, H., 135, 152,
    357–359
Murray, H. A., 343, 345–347,
    349
Myers, I. B., 331
Myers–Briggs Type Indicator,
    331

N

Natsoulas, T., 371
Naturalistic theory of history,
    9–12
Nazi regime and European
    psychology, 267, 279, 282,
    305, 366
Need reduction theory of
    learning (Hull), 241–242
Needs (Murray), 346–347
Needs hierarchy theory
    (Maslow), 367–368
Neobehaviorists, 228–253
Neo-Freudians, 323–349
Neurophysiology, early work in,
    40–42, 45–46
Neurotic needs (Horney),
    340–341
Neurypnology (Braid), 293
Newton, I., 17, 36, 251. See also
    Galilean–Newtonian
    mechanism
Nonsense syllables
    (Ebbinghaus), 72–73

O

Objective methods (Watson),
    208–210

Observational learning
    (Bandura), 254
O'Donnell, J. M., 354
Oedipal theory (Freud), 296,
    302, 312, 314, 319, 338
Ogden, R., 279
On the Origin of Species (Darwin),
    108, 109, 112, 117, 123, 131
One-trial learning (Guthrie), 235
Operant behavior (Skinner),
    246–247, 252
Operationism, 227–228
Order of birth (Adler), 336
Orgler, H., 332
Orth, J., 81
Otis, A. S., 354

P

Paradigms in psychology, 13
Pauly, P. J., 199
Pavlov, I. P., 177, 179, 184–191,
    209, 213, 235, 238, 241,
    244, 247, 257, 279
Pearson, K., 119
Peirce, C. S., 139
Penis envy (Freud), 338
Perception, Gestalt approach to,
    264, 267–268, 273–274
Peripheral theory of thinking
    (Watson), 216
Perls, F., 257
Person-centered therapy
    (Rogers), 368–369
Persona (Jung), 329
Personal Data Sheet, 356
Personal unconscious (Jung),
    328–329
Personalistic theory of history,
    9–12
Personality development,
    309–312, 327–330,
    334–336, 340–341,
    343–349, 366–369
Personality tests, 331, 345–347,
    355–356
Personality traits (Allport), 345
Personnel psychology, 357
Personology (Murray), 345–347
Pervin, L. A., 343
Petites perceptions (Leibnitz), 290
Pfungst, O., 178–179

Phenomenology, 77–78,
    260–261, 285–286
Phi phenomenon (Wertheimer),
    262
Philosophy, influence on
    psychology, 17–37
Physics, influence on psychology,
    13, 17–18, 65, 208, 225,
    227–228, 239, 261, 266,
    279, 315–316, 373–374
Physiology, influence on
    psychology, 2, 26, 39–55,
    64
Piaget, J., 373, 375
Pickering, G., 110
Pillsbury, W., 193, 203
Planck, M., 14, 261, 266
Plateau, J., 262
Plato, 1, 24, 290
Pleasure principle (Freud), 295,
    310
Polanyi, M., 374
Popularization of psychology,
    152, 199–200, 216–219
Positive reinforcement. See
    Reinforcement
Positivism, 28, 37
Pragmatism, 139
Pressey, S., 250
Primary drives (Hull), 240–241
Primary qualities, 31–32
Principles of Physiological
    Psychology (Wundt), 55, 61,
    63, 108, 142
Principles of Psychology (James),
    134–140, 155, 180
Productive thinking
    (Wertheimer), 277–278
Progressive education movement
    (Dewey), 155, 156
Proprium (Allport), 344
Pseudo-problems (Bridgman),
    227, 318
Psyche (Jung), 328
Psychiatry, nineteenth-century,
    292–294
Psychoanalysis, 288–321
    evaluation and current status,
    317–321, 352
    neoanalytic developments,
    323–349

original source material,
312–315
and psychology, 316–317
Psychoanalytic therapy, 305–308
Psychological clinics, 359–360
Psychological Corporation, 150,
357
Psychological testing movement,
353–356
Psychophysical methods, 49,
51–54, 65, 68, 114
Psychosexual stages of
development (Freud),
311–315
Psychosocial stages of
development (Erikson),
347–349
Purposive behaviorism (Tolman),
229–231, 372
Puzzle boxes (Thorndike),
182–183

Q
Questionnaire method, 121, 145
Quetelet, A., 118

R
Raphelson, A. C., 4
Rayner, R., 198–200, 214
Reaction time experiments, 46,
68
Reagents (human subjects), 91,
210
Reality principle (Freud), 310
Reductionism, 19
Reflexes, 26, 40–42, 156,
191–192, 226
Reinforcement, 241, 246–249,
251–252, 254
Remley, N. R., 170
Renouvier, C., 134
Repression (Freud), 306, 311
Resistances (Freud), 305–306
Respondent behavior, 246–247.
See also Conditioning
Rice, B., 250, 252
Richards, R. J., 111, 123, 125
Rieber, R. W., 320
Roazen, P., 302, 333
Robach, H. B., 366
Roback, A., 86

Robinson, D. N., 2, 28, 64
Roethlisberger, F. J., 357
Rogers, C. R., 362, 366,
368–370
Roitblat, H. L., 376
Romanes, G. J., 123–125, 175,
176, 182, 192, 209, 294
Romm, S., 304
Rorschach Inkblot Test, 331
Rosenthal, R., 178
Ross, D., 141, 145
Rotter, J. B., 337
Rowe, F. B., 92
Rubin, E., 261
Rubins, J. L., 338
Ruckmick, C. A., 170
Rush, B., 292–293
Russo, N. F., 361

S
Samelson, F., 198, 208, 214
Sarton, G., 174
Scarborough, E., 360
Scarf, M., 334
Schachter, S., 284, 337
Schedules of reinforcement
(Skinner), 248–249
Schlosberg, H., 168
Schoenfeld, W. N., 236
Schools of thought,
characteristics of, 12–15,
351–352
Schopenhauer, A., 306
Schumann, F., 75
Schur, M., 305
Scopes, J. T., 113
Scott, F. J. D., 197
Scott, W. D., 356–357
Seaman, D. J., 262
Sears, R., 242
Secondary drives (Hull),
240–241
Secondary qualities, 31–32
Seduction theory (Freud),
301–302
Self actualization, 330, 331,
367–369
Self archetype (Jung), 329–330
Sensitivity training, 284, 366
Sex research, 7, 92, 145, 198

Sexual influences on personality,
294, 301–303, 309,
311–315
Shadow archetype (Jung), 329,
346
Shakow, D., 72, 316
Sheehan, M., 168
Sherrington, C. S., 168
Shevrin, H., 376
Shields, S., 362
Sign gestalts (Tolman), 232–233
Simon, T., 151, 354
Skinner, B. F., 8–9, 13, 179, 200,
217–219, 222, 228, 229,
234, 243–254, 257, 352,
362, 371–373, 375, 377
Skinner box, 246–249
Small, W. S., 176
Socrates, 65
Social action research (Lewin),
284
Social Darwinism, 130
Social interest (Adler), 334
Social learning (Bandura),
254–255, 375
Social psychological theories of
psychoanalysis, 331–342
Sokal, M., 147–149, 217, 267,
279
Spence, K., 242
Spencer, H., 128–131
Stanford–Binet Intelligence
Scale, 354
Stapp, J., 360
Statistical methods, 118–119
Stern, W., 354
Stimulus error (Titchener), 89,
93
Stimulus–response (S–R)
connections, 168, 182,
187–191, 209–215, 238,
241, 246–247
Structuralism, 85–106
definition, 94, 154–155
evaluation and current status,
102–106, 351
original source material,
94–102
Study of Values, 345
Stumpf, C., 75, 77–79, 83, 178,
264, 267

Sullivan, J. J., 199
Sulloway, F. J., 294, 296, 299, 301, 316
Superego, 310, 346
Synthetic philosophy (Spencer), 128–131
Systematic experimental introspection (Külpe), 79–82, 90

T

Terman, L. M., 354
Terrace, H. S., 376
Tests. *See* Intelligence tests, Mental tests, Personality tests
Thematic Apperception Test (TAT), 346
Third force psychology. *See* Humanistic psychology
Thorndike, E. L., 135, 145, 151, 167, 176, 177, 179–184, 188, 213, 235, 236, 241, 247, 252, 257, 274, 277, 360
Thought, 81–82, 215–216
Threshold measurement, 48–49, 52
Titchener, E. B., 58–59, 64, 65, 72, 74, 83, 85–105, 107, 108, 115, 128, 131, 135, 145, 151, 152, 154–155, 170, 171, 173, 176, 192, 193, 199, 202, 210, 222, 229, 257, 280, 285, 288, 303, 351, 353, 354
original source material, 94–102
Titchener experimentalists, 88–89, 354
Tolman, E. C., 225, 228–234, 241, 279, 280, 372
Tones (acoustical), 44, 46, 77–78
Training (T) groups, 284, 366
Traits of personality (Allport), 345
Transference (Freud), 306
Traxel, W., 72

Trial-and-error learning (Thorndike), 183, 277
Tridimensional theory of feelings (Wundt), 66–68, 93
Tropism theory of animal behavior (Loeb), 175–176
Turner, F. J., 130
Turner, M., 103, 228
Tweney, R. D., 70
Two-point threshold (Weber), 48
Tyler, L., 13

U

Unconscious processes, 289–292, 309–310, 328–329
Ungerer, G. A., 2, 62
Utilitarianism (Bentham), 295

V

Verbal associations, 68–69, 121, 330, 331, 355
Verbal behavior (Skinner), 249–250
Verbal report (Watson), 208
Verbal thinking (Watson), 216
Veterans Administration, 360
Vicarious reinforcement, 254
Vierordt, K., 53
Vision (Helmholtz), 44, 46
Visual perception, Gestalt principles of, 273–274
Volkmann, A. W., 53
Voluntarism (Wundt), 64
Von Ehrenfels, C., 75, 260, 263, 270
Von Franz, M., 330
Von Hartmann, E., 291
Von Osten, W., 178–179

W

Wade, N., 11
Walden Two (Skinner), 243, 250–251
Wallace, A. R., 10, 111–112
Wallach, H., 267
Washburn, M. F., 89, 176–177, 208, 214, 360

Waterman, A. S., 349
Waterman, C. K., 349
Watson, J. B., 7, 87, 159, 170, 173–177, 179, 184, 192, 193, 195–226, 228–231, 234, 239, 242, 244, 250, 251, 253, 257, 261, 274, 288, 349, 352, 365, 371, 372
original source material, 201–207
Watson–McDougall debates, 219–222
Watson, Robert, 54, 122, 207
Watson, Rosalie, 198–200, 214
Watt, H., 81–82
Weber, E., 42, 46–49, 52–54, 77, 115, 206
Weiss, A. P., 225
Wertheimer, Max, 260–264, 268–275, 277–278, 280, 281, 288, 366
original source material, 269–273
Wertheimer, Michael, 5, 6, 257, 264, 363, 365
West, D., 122, 277
White, A. D., 24, 113
White, M. J., 377
White, R., 284
Whytt, R., 10
Wiggam, A., 218
Wilberforce, S., 113
Windholz, G., 190, 285
Witkin, H., 376
Witmer, L., 359
Wittels, F., 316
Wolff, C., 19
Womb envy (Horney), 338
Women in the history of psychology, 360–362
Woodworth, R. S., 135, 151, 167–170, 190, 193, 231, 356
Word association test, 121, 330, 331, 355
World Wars I and II, impact on applied psychology, 353–360

Wundt, W., 2, 12–13, 28, 42, 44, 54–55, 58–83, 85, 86, 90, 93, 101, 103, 104, 107, 108, 114, 115, 121–123, 125, 128, 131, 134–138, 142–144, 146, 148, 149, 151, 152, 154, 157, 161, 171, 173, 190–192, 195, 208, 210, 222, 228, 257, 258, 260, 262, 267, 280, 285, 288, 292, 316, 323, 330, 342, 343, 351, 353, 356, 359, 363, 373

Wundtian experimental psychology, 54–70
evaluation, 69–70
and Titchener's structural psychology, 58–59
Würzburg laboratory (Külpe), 75, 79–82, 93

Y

Yerkes, R., 176, 177, 206, 226, 354, 356
Young, T., 46
Young–Helmholtz theory of color vision, 46

Z

Zander, A., 284
Zeigarnik, B., 283, 360
Zeigarnik effect, 283
Zeitgeist, 10–13, 17–21, 42–44, 54–55, 109, 128–130, 136, 151–152, 188, 192–193, 219, 257, 261, 264, 279–280, 291, 295–296, 320, 331–332, 338, 363, 373–374